TERROR
ON TAPE

ON TAPE

A COMPLETE GUIDE TO OVER 2,000 HORROR MOVIES ON VIDEO

JAMES O'NEILL

BILLBOARD BOOKS
An imprint of Watson-Guptill Publications/New York

First published in 1994 by Billboard Books,
an imprint of Watson-Guptill Publications,
a division of BPI Communications, Inc.,
1515 Broadway, New York, NY 10036

Library of Congress Cataloging-in-Publication Data
O'Neill, James, 1956–
        Terror on tape: a complete guide to over 2,000 horror movies on
video / James O' Neill.
        ISBN 0-8230-7612-1
        1. Horror films—Catalogs.   2. Video recordings—Catalogs.
I. Title.
PN1995.9.H6054   1994
791.43'616—dc20   94-25496
                                                         CIP

Manufactured in the United States of America

First printing, 1994

1 2 3 4 5 6 7 8 9 / 99 98 97 96 95 94

This book is dedicated with warmth and affection
to my two good friends Mike Magauran
and James Taylor (no, not the singer).

INTRODUCTION

From *The Cabinet of Dr. Caligari* to *The Silence of the Lambs,* horror films have always been and always will be with us. Making up one of the most popular yet misunderstood genres of film, they rarely win awards, are treated like the stepchildren of the industry by studio executives, and are bashed regularly by the critical establishment. But still they endure while other, more "respectable" genres, like westerns and musicals, fall by the wayside.

The video revolution, beginning in the late '70s, has been a double-edged sword for movie horror. Although it's made available many titles not often seen (everything from Tod Browning's *Freaks* to Herschell Gordon Lewis's *Blood Feast),* it's also become the dumping ground for all manner of direct-to-video dreck, as anyone who's ever suffered through *The Devil's Gift* or *Zombie Lake* can solemnly attest.

Intended as a convenient reference for those looking for a decent night's rental or a sound purchase (however, try to avoid those cheaply priced LP- or ELP-recorded "bargain" tapes), *Terror on Tape* includes titles released on video through 1994. Although most of the films included in this volume are currently available for purchase, some of the older titles have been withdrawn from general release but are still available for rental at many video stores. In addition to a plot summary and review, each of the listings specifies the current distributor, year of original release, Motion Picture Association of America rating (where applicable), running time, director, cast, and a half- to four-star rating (the outlined star symbolizes a half star; refer to the charts on page ix for an explanation of the MPAA and star ratings that are used). If the film is also known by another title (many, many movies are retitled for video, some more than once), this is mentioned in the synopsis, and the listings are cross-referenced for all English-language variant titles. Also included are sidebar articles on one hundred artists (actors, directors, writers, and other creative collaborators) specializing in the horror genre. Each sidebar appears near the review of an important film on which the sidebar subject worked.

As for the reviews themselves, well—one person's fave is another's bow-wow. Besides, I've always found that the smartest critics were the ones who agreed with me, so if you find yourself concurring with my critiques, congratulations on having such discerning taste. If not, well, as someone once said, "It's only a movie, only a movie, only a movie...."

STAR RATINGS

★★★★   Excellent

★★★☆   Very Good

★★★   Good

★★☆   Average

★★   Fair

★☆   Poor

★   Very Poor

☆   The Worst

MOTION PICTURE ASSOCIATION OF AMERICA (MPAA) RATINGS

G   General Audiences
All ages may be admitted for viewing.

PG   Parental Guidance Suggested
All ages may be admitted but parental guidance is suggested.

PG-13   Parental Guidance Suggested; Parents of Children Strongly Cautioned
All ages may be admitted but parental guidance is suggested,
especially for children under 13.

R   Restricted
Admission is restricted to persons over a specified age (usually 17)
unless accompanied by a parent or guardian.

NC-17   No One Under 17 Admitted
Admission is restricted to persons over 17 years of age.

X   No One Under 18 Admitted
Admission is restricted to persons over 18 years of age.

Where MPAA ratings were not applicable, the following designations were used:

NR   Not Rated
Films that were made prior to the establishment of the MPAA (in 1968),
as well as many made-for-TV movies.

UR   Unrated
Films released without an MPAA rating, including many European-made films and
re-releases containing additional or restored scenes of graphic violence or sex.

TERROR

ON TAPE

ABBOTT AND COSTELLO MEET DR. JEKYLL AND MR. HYDE

★★☆ MCA/Universal Home Video, 1953, NR, 76 min. Dir: Charles Lamont. Cast: Bud Abbott, Lou Costello, Boris Karloff, Craig Stevens, Helen Westcott, John Dierkes, Reginald Denny, Edwin Parker.

Entertaining attempt to recapture the fun of *A&C Meet Frankenstein* with Bud and Lou as unlikely London bobbies on the trail of a murderer who turns out to be the eminent Dr. Jekyll (Karloff) while in the monstrous form of Mr. Hyde (mostly played by stuntman Parker). Bland direction making unimaginative use of familiar Universal back lot settings but Karloff is excellent and there are plenty of belly laughs.

ABBOTT AND COSTELLO MEET FRANKENSTEIN

★★★★ MCA/Universal Home Video, 1948, NR, 82 min. Dir: Charles T. Barton. Cast: Bud Abbott, Lou Costello, Bela Lugosi, Lon Chaney, Jr., Lenore Aubert, Glenn Strange, Jane Randolph, Frank Ferguson, Charles Bradstreet, voice of Vincent Price.

Easily A&C's best film and the best horror-comedy ever made. The boys are Florida baggage clerks who get mixed-up in Dracula's (Lugosi) plan to transplant a weak, easy-to-control brain into the head of the Frankenstein monster (Strange)—guess whose? Fortunately for our heroes, werewolf Larry Talbot (Chaney) arrives to help. Much better than most of Universal Pictures' other, "straight" horror films of the '40s, with handsome production values and playful performing from Bela and Lon. Look for the scene where Chaney subs for an injured Strange in the Frankenstein monster get-up. Best line: "What we need today is young blood—and brains!" Released in England as *Abbott and Costello Meet the Ghosts*.

ABBOTT AND COSTELLO MEET THE GHOSTS

See: *Abbott and Costello Meet Frankenstein.*

ABBOTT AND COSTELLO MEET THE INVISIBLE MAN

★★★ MCA/Universal Home Video, 1951, NR, 82 min. Dir: Charles Lamont. Cast: Bud Abbott, Lou Costello, Arthur Franz, Nancy Guild, Adele Jergens, Sheldon Leonard, William Frawley, Gavin Muir.

One of the team's funniest horror spoofs with the guys as recent detective school grads who try to help invisible prize fighter Franz (who's taken Claude Rains' old formula to hide from the cops) prove himself innocent of murder. Good FX and a great supporting cast pepper this fun entry.

ABBOTT AND COSTELLO MEET THE KILLER

See: *Abbott and Costello Meet the Killer, Boris Karloff.*

ABBOTT AND COSTELLO MEET THE KILLER, BORIS KARLOFF

★★ Goodtimes Home Video, 1949, NR, 84 min. Dir: Charles T. Barton. Cast: Bud Abbott, Lou Costello, Boris Karloff, Lenore Aubert, Gar Moore, Donna Martell, Alan Mowbray, James Flavin.

Dull murder-mystery take-off with maybe the most misleading title in screen history—it's giving away nothing at this late date to report that Karloff does *not* play the killer! Boy, talk about your false advertising. Some unexpected black comedy involving the disposal of pesky corpses in the best tradition of *The Trouble with Harry* and an exciting climax set in a bottomless cavern but Boris has little to do as a phony swami from Brooklyn. Aka *Abbott and Costello Meet the Killer.*

BUD ABBOTT AND LOU COSTELLO
(1895–1973)   (1905–1959)

This fast-talking '40s comedy team ranked among the top Hollywood stars of the Second World War years and saved a rapidly plummeting post-war career by matching "wits" with Universal Studios' stable of popular monsters. Low-brow and funny, the boys were never really appreciated by critics in their day, but many of their films hold up far better than many of the more "prestigious" comedies of the period.

Hold That Ghost ('41); Abbott and Costello meet Frankenstein ('48); Abbott and Costello Meet the Killer, Boris Karloff ('49); Abbott and Costello Meet the Invisible Man ('51); Abbott and Costello Meet Dr. Jekyll and Mr. Hyde ('53); Abbott and Costello Meet the Mummy ('55); The Thirty-Foot Bride of Candy Rock (Costello alone, '59).

Vincent Price and Virginia North get intimate in The Abominable Dr. Phibes *(1971).*

ABBOTT AND COSTELLO MEET THE MUMMY

★★☆ MCA/Universal Home Video, 1955, NR, 79 min. Dir: Charles Lamont. Cast: Bud Abbott, Lou Costello, Marie Windsor, Michael Ansara, Dan Seymour, Richard Deacon, Kurt Katch, Mel Welles, Peggy King, Edwin Parker.

The last of A&C's *"meet"* movies, this is fun but rarely scales the heights of some of their earlier work. Bud and Lou are in Egypt where Costello swallows an amulet engraved with a map showing the way to a tomb containing a fabulous treasure and the living mummy Klaris (Parker). Some good bits ("The shovel *is* my pick!") and Windsor makes for a very fetching villainess but the mummy make-up is awful.

ABOMINABLE DR. PHIBES, THE

★★★☆ Orion, 1971, PG, 94 min. Dir: Robert Fuest. Cast: Vincent Price, Joseph Cotten, Terry-Thomas, Hugh Griffith, Virginia North, Peter

Jeffrey, Aubrey Woods, Susan Travers, Sean Bury, Caroline Munro.

One of Price's best, this casts him in the tailor-made role of Dr. Anton Phibes, a horribly disfigured musical genius and religious scholar who avenges the operating table death of his beautiful wife (Munro) by murdering the doctors he holds responsible in grisly methods inspired by the Old Testament plagues. Campy good fun, this sports a rich ambiance of 1920s art deco elegance and a cleverly inventive script perfectly suited to Price's arch, tongue-in-cheek screen image. Sequel: *Dr. Phibes Rises Again!*

ABOMINATION, THE

☆ Donna Michele Video, 1985, R, 88 min. Dir: Max Raven. Cast: Van Connery, Victoria Chaney, Gaye Bottoms, Suzy Meyer.

Mother-fixated nerd boy Connery is possessed by a 3,000-year-old monstrosity sending him on an eyeball-gouging, chainsaw-wielding rampage. The title sez all in this low-grade backyard yawner.

ABSOLUTION

★★★ Avid Entertainment, 1979, R, 105 min. Dir: Anthony Page. Cast: Richard Burton, Domonic Guard, Dai Bradley, Billy Connolly, Andrew Keir, Willoughby Gray.

Anthony Shaffer wrote this intriguing psycho-thriller about a repressed gay priest (Burton, in one of his last great performances) who lusts for a student (Guard) who confesses to him that he is a murderer. But is this just a bad practical joke? Held up for release for five years, this chiller is worthy of rediscovery.

ABSURD

See: *Monster Hunter.*

ADDAMS FAMILY, THE

★★★ WorldVision Home Video, 1964-66, NR, 50 min. per tape. Dirs: Sidney Lanfield, Jean Yarbrough, Arthur Hiller, others. Cast: John Astin, Carolyn Jones, Jackie Coogan, Ted Cassidy, Blossum Rock, Lisa Loring, Ken Weatherwax, Felix Silla.

One of the great weird TV sitcoms of the '60s, this is based on the darkly comic cartoons of Charles Addams. Unlike "The Munsters," these aren't monsters who want to be regular suburbanites but off-the-wall humans who revel in their own strangeness. Astin and Jones are great as Gomez and Morticia, the most amorous married couple on '60s TV, and they're ably supported by Coogan as the electrifying Uncle Fester, Cassidy as the zombie-like butler Lurch, and Silla as four-foot mumbling hairball, Cousin Itt.

ADDAMS FAMILY, THE

★★☆ Paramount Home Video, 1991, PG-13, 99 min. Dir: Barry Sonnenfeld. Cast: Anjelica Huston, Raul Julia, Christopher Lloyd, Christina Ricci, Dan Hedaya, Elizabeth Wilson, Judith Malina, Carel Struycken, Jimmy Workman, Dana Ivey.

That creepy, kooky, mysterious, and spooky family is back in this lavish reincarnation of the popular TV show. The casting is perfect—Ricci *is* Wednesday—and there are impressive settings and great FX to bring the walking hand "Thing" to life but this is more of a series of vignettes than a real movie. The school play scene probably spills more blood than in any Paramount release since the first *Friday the 13th.*

ADDAMS FAMILY VALUES

★★☆ Paramount Home Video, 1993, PG-13, 94 min. Dir: Barry Sonnenfeld. Cast: Anjelica Huston, Raul Julia, Christopher Lloyd, Christina Ricci, Joan Cusack, Carol Kane, Carel Struycken, Jimmy Workman, Dana Ivey, David Krumholtz.

Morticia and Gomez have a baby (the aptly named Pubert), Wednesday gets a boyfriend at summer camp (no, not Jason), and Uncle Fester marries nanny-from-hell Cusack in this harmless, fun sequel. The best moments are provided by Cusack (really lettin' 'er rip) and, natch, Ricci, who even manages to top her performance in the original.

ADRIFT

★★ WorldVision Home Video, 1993, NR, 92 min. Dir: Christian Duguay. Cast: Kate Jackson, Bruce Greenwood, Kenneth Welsh, Kelly Rowan.

"In the style of *Dead Calm,*" i.e., a predictable TV movie rip-off, this time with *two* psychos terrorizing a wealthy couple on their yacht. Jackson, who got her start on *Dark Shadows,* is always welcome in any horror film—only next time get a better vehicle, huh, Kate?

AFRAID OF THE DARK

★★☆ Columbia/TriStar Home Video, 1991, R, 91 min. Dir: Mark Peploe. Cast: James Fox, Fanny Ardant, Ben Keyworth, Clare Holman, Paul McGann, Robert Stephens.

A young boy (Keyworth) is slowly going blind and fantasizes about his mother and older sister being blind themselves and a mad slasher with a fixation on sightless women. This British psycho chiller is well-directed and has one startling twist halfway through, but its jarring switches in tone and unsympathetic central figure make it difficult to navigate.

AFTER MIDNIGHT

★★ CBS/Fox Video, 1989, R, 93 min. Dirs: Ken and Jim Wheat. Cast: Jillian McWherter, Marg Helgenberger, Ramy Zada, Marc McClure, Pamela Segall, Nadine van de Velde, Judie Aronson, Billy Ray Sharkey.

Indifferent anthology about a college psych prof (Zada) who holds a private seminar exploring the ramifications of fear resulting in the telling of three horror tales. A couple encounter a mad killer—or do they?—in a "haunted" house; teen girls are savaged by a pack of wild junkyard dogs; and a female phone operator with a broken leg is menaced by a psycho crank caller. The usual chills.

AGAINST ALL ODDS

★★ Republic Home Video, 1968, PG, 81 min. Dir: Jess [Jesus] Franco. Cast: Christopher Lee, Richard Greene, Shirley Eaton, Maria Rohm, Tsai Chin, Howard Marion Crawford.

No, this isn't the steamy Rachel Ward starrer. Actually, it's the cheesy fourth entry in Lee's *Fu Manchu* series originally titled *The Blood of Fu Manchu*. This time the arch-fiend is in Brazil where he infects ten beauties with a deadly poison they transmit to anyone they kiss. The girls are then sent out to give Fu's most hated enemies a fatal smooch. Not the worst of its series but still pretty mediocre and seems to have been cut from a spicier Europrint. Aka *Kiss and Kill*, *Kiss of Death*, and *Fu Manchu's Kiss of Death*.

ALCHEMIST, THE
★ Edde Entertainment, 1981, R, 84 min.
Dir: James Amante [Charles Band]. Cast: Robert Ginty, Robert Glaudini, Lucinda Dooling, John Sanderford, Viola Kate Stimpson.

Lifeless Empire Pictures cheapie about an ageless glassblower (Ginty) suffering the bestial curse of an evil alchemist (Glaudini) whom he must fight for the soul of his reincarnated wife (Dooling). Shelved until 1985, this clunker is enlivened briefly by some icky make-ups and colorful opticals but is otherwise a badly acted and directed waste of 84 minutes of your precious time.

ALFRED HITCHCOCK PRESENTS
★★★ MCA/Universal Home Video, 1955-59, NR, 75 min. Dir: Alfred Hitchcock. Cast: Barbara Bel Geddes, John Williams, Tom Ewell, Allan Lane, Kenneth Haigh, Harold J. Stone, Hilda Plowright, Reginald Gardiner.

A trio of Hitch-directed episodes from his well-remembered mystery/horror/suspense program. The best is Roald Dahl's *Lamb to the Slaughter*, with Bel Geddes as a brazen husband killer; the weakest is *The Case of Mr. Pelham* (remade as the feature *The Man Who Haunted Himself*), with Ewell taunted by a high-living doppelganger. It's all perfectly capped by the droll *Banquo's Chair*, with Williams as a British police inspector who turns to the supernatural to solve a murder.

ALIAS JOHN PRESTON
★★ Sinister Cinema, 1956, NR, 66 min.
Dir: David MacDonald. Cast: Christopher Lee, Betta St. John, Alexander Knox, Sandra Dorne.

Lee is good in an early starring role as a man who seeks psychiatric help for his dangerous split personality. Fair Brit suspenser with *Jekyll and Hyde* overtones.

ALICE, SWEET ALICE
★★★ Goodtimes Home Video, 1977, R, 107 min.
Dir: Alfred Sole. Cast: Paula Sheppard, Linda Miller,

Niles McMaster, Brooke Shields, Rudolph Willrich, Mildred Clinton, Alphonse DeNoble, Lillian Roth.

Brooke debuts in a small but pivotal role in this strong, anti-Catholic slasher set in early 1960s New Jersey. When young Karen (Shields) is strangled and immolated at her first Holy Communion, suspicion falls on her jealous, disturbed older sister, Alice (Sheppard), who likes to lurk around in a rain slicker and plastic doll mask. But, is she the killer? Originally titled *Communion* and reissued in a cut version called *Holy Terror*, this impressive first film from Sole (who's done nothing notable since) makes good use of its restricted budget and features startling plot twists and bizarre murders recalling the early Dario Argento.

ALIEN
★★★ Fox Video, 1979, R, 116 min.
Dir: Ridley Scott. Cast: Sigourney Weaver, Tom Skerritt, Veronica Cartwright, John Hurt, Yaphet Kotto, Harry Dean Stanton, Ian Holm.

An intergalactic oil freighter picks up a distress signal from a windswept alien planet where something inside a weird, leathery egg secreted in the bowels of a derelict spacecraft spells doom for the crew, as it mutates through several violent, horrid stages of development. This uniquely directed, photographed, and designed combination of sci-fi hardware and horror movie scare tactics is one of the scariest and most influential (if itself overly influenced by the likes of *It! The Terror From Beyond Space*, *Planet of the Vampires*, and *Queen of Blood*) films of the '70s. The film is marred only by its basically unsympathetic characters and muddled motivations—both alien and otherwise. Followed by *Aliens* and *Alien 3*.

ALIEN CONTAMINATION
★★ Cannon Home Video, 1980, R, 88 min.
Dir: Lewis Coates [Luigi Cozzi]. Cast: Ian McCulloch, Louise Marleau, Marino Masé, Sigfried Rauch, Gisela Hahn, Carlo de Mejo.

Junky but fun Italian-made bogus *Alien* sequel/rip-off about extraterrestrial eggs brought to Earth that cause people to explode whenever they get egg slime on themselves. Ultra-gory hooey with a phony-looking monster making a token appearance at the climax. Aka *Contamination* and *Toxic Spawn*.

ALIEN DEAD, THE
☆ Academy Entertainment, 1980, R, 71 min.
Dir: Fred Olen Ray. Cast: Buster Crabbe, Linda Lewis, Ray Roberts, Mike Bonavia.

Flesh-eating zombies played by guys in crappy makeup terrorize Florida swamp dwellers in this bargain basement Ray effort, his first, shot in 16mm. Everybody's favorite Flash Gordon (Crabbe) is on hand as the bone-headed sheriff, and there's a totally gratuitous skinny-dipping scene and ample opportunity for anyone who watches this to doze off. Aka *It Fell From the Sky*.

ALIEN PREDATOR

★★ Video Treasures, 1984, R, 90 min. Dir: Deran Sarafian. Cast: Dennis Christopher, Lynn-Holly Johnson, Martin Hewitt, Luis Prendes, J.O. Bosso.

Student tourists in Spain (the star trio, all of whom have seen better days) encounter some very nasty little critters that were spawned by microbes that attached themselves to Skylab when it fell to Earth in 1979. Shot under the title *Origins Unknown* and then briefly known as *The Falling*, this film sat on the shelf for three years before being outfitted with a new moniker recalling both *Alien* and *Predator* and going the direct-to-video route. The likable leads and some unexpectedly gory bits of action enliven a pretty much run-of-the-mill outing.

ALIEN PREY

★ Continental Video, 1977, R, 85 min. Dir: Norman J. Warren. Cast: Barry Stokes, Glory Annen, Sally Faulkner, Sandy Chimney.

A cannibalistic alien, who looks like a cut-rate werewolf, takes on the identity of a man it murders and then spends the weekend with a lesbian couple it both seduces and devours. This bloody low-budget Brit exploiter is made offensive by a dark misogynistic streak and by a very stereotypical presentation of the lesbians. Aka *Prey*.

ALIENS

★★★☆ Fox Video, 1986, R, 137 min. Dir: James Cameron. Cast: Sigourney Weaver, Michael Biehn, Lance Henricksen, Carrie Henn, Paul Reiser, Bill Paxton, Jenette Goldstein, William Hope.

Powerhouse sequel to *Alien* picking up some 57 years later with Weaver rescued from suspended animation and then charged with the deaths of her crew mates and the destruction of their ship. To clear herself, Sig must lead a squadron of marines back to the now settled alien planet where colonists have been slaughtered by a whole horde of toothy monsters—still slimy after all these years. Less a horror film than a futuristic, feminist war movie, there are still plenty of shocks, terrific pacing (despite a two hour-plus running time), and a

---

LANCE HENRIKSEN
(1944–)

Though this lean character actor started out as a sort of low-budget Roy Scheider, he very quickly established himself as one of modern horror's top and most talented actors. His best and best-known work may be as the gentle android Bishop in 1986's *Aliens*.

Mansion of the Doomed ('76), *Damien—Omen II* ('78), *The Visitor* ('79), *Piranha II: The Spawning* ('82), *Nightmares* ('83), *Aliens* ('86), *Near Dark* ('87), *Pumpkinhead* ('88), *The Horror Show* ('89), *The Pit and the Pendulum* ('91), *Alien 3* ('92), *Jennifer 8* ('92), *Man's Best Friend* ('93).

---

nice undercurrent of humor, making this a superior sequel. Weaver is excellent and was, in fact, nominated for a best actress Oscar for her performance.

ALIEN TERROR

★ MPI Home Video, 1968, PG, 90 min. Dirs: Enrique Vergara and Jack Hill. Cast: Boris Karloff, Christa Linder, Enrique Guzman, Maura Monti, Yerye Beirute, Sergio Kleiner.

Karloff's next-to-last feature, this was one of four awful low-budget U.S.-Mexican co-productions the great actor filmed a few months before his death in 1969. Scientist Boris accidentally contacts invisible aliens who possess brutal sex-murderer Beirute, leading to a string of pointless killings. Originally titled *Invasion Siniestra*: *Sinister Invasion*, this sat unreleased until 1974 and should have stayed that way.

ALIEN 3

★★☆ Fox Video, 1992, R, 114 min. Dir: David Fincher. Cast: Sigourney Weaver, Charles Dance, Charles S. Dutton, Lance Henriksen, Brian Glover, Paul McGann.

Downbeat third—and final?—entry in the series, with Weaver crashing on an all male prison planet where she battles a familiarly fanged monster one last time. Poorly directed by Fincher but good acting from a shaven-headed Weaver, Dance, and Dutton and a striking ending make this worth a watch. Henriksen, though, is wasted.

ALISON'S BIRTHDAY

★★ VidAmerica, 1979, PG, 95 min. Dir: Ian Coughlan. Cast: Joanne Samuel, Lou Brown, Bunney Brooke, John Bluthal, Maggie McCrae, Martin Vaughn.

Routine occult thriller made in Australia for a slight change of accent. A ouija board predicts danger for pretty Alison (Samuel) on her nineteenth birthday, a prediction brought to life by a sinister Druid cult seeking to reincarnate an ancient deity. Of limited interest thanks to the fresh appeal of Samuel (Mel Gibson's doomed wife in *Mad Max*), but ultimately undistinguished fare.

ALL-AMERICAN MURDER
★★ Prism Entertainment, 1991, R, 92 min. Dir: Anson Williams. Cast: Christopher Walken, Charlie Schlatter, Josie Bissett, Joanna Cassidy, Amy Davis, Mitchell Anderson, Richard Kind, Woody Watson.

When reformed arsonist college boy Schlatter's new girlfriend, Bissett, is gruesomely immolated he's the prime suspect, natch. Less likely events crop up when tough cop Walken gives Charlie twenty-four hours to catch the killer himself. Yes, it's *Happy Days'* own Potsie who directed this OK thriller that dresses up its contrived story line with some surprisingly gory murders and an imitation Pino Donaggio musical score.

ALLEY OF NIGHTMARES
See: *She Freak.*

ALLIGATOR
★★★ Lightning Video, 1980, R, 91 min. Dir: Lewis Teague. Cast: Robert Forster, Robin Riker, Henry Silva, Dean Jagger, Jack Carter, Michael Gazzo, Sue Lyon, Angel Tompkins, Perry Lang, Bart Braverman.

Witty monster movie send-up scripted by John Sayles. A little girl buys a pet alligator called Ramone, which her gator-hatin' dad flushes down the john. Twelve years later, a steady diet of radioactive lab dogs secretly dumped into the city's sewers has transformed Ramone into a 36-foot man-eater—his first victim is a sewer worker named Ed Norton! Lots of goofy dialogue and situations (like a vendor selling alligator memorabilia after one of Ramone's attacks) are well played off some real scares, and there's a terrific cast with Silva an especial hoot as a Great White Hunter hired to dispose of the pesky critter.

ALLIGATOR II: THE MUTATION
★★ New Line Home Video, 1991, R, 92 min. Dir: Jon Hess. Cast: Joseph Bologna, Dee Wallace Stone, Steve Railsback, Richard Lynch, Woody Brown, Holly Gagnier, Bill Dailey, Brock Peters.

Straight-faced follow-up to the tongue-in-cheek original with cops Bologna and Brown hunting another big gator that's after human hamburger at a lakeside real estate develop-ment. A sharp cast and some good action notwithstanding, this is sluggishly directed and has a monster that changes size more often than Oprah.

ALL MONSTERS ATTACK
See: *Godzilla's Revenge.*

ALL THAT MONEY CAN BUY
See: *The Devil and Daniel Webster.*

ALMOST HUMAN
See: *Shock Waves.*

ALONE IN THE DARK
★★☆ New Line Home Video, 1982, R, 93 min. Dir: Jack Sholder. Cast: Jack Palance, Donald Pleasence, Martin Landau, Dwight Schultz, Deborah Hedwall, Erland Van Lidth de Jeude, Lee Taylor-Allan, Carol Levy.

Amusingly self-effacing slasher about four fruitcakes who escape from a New Jersey mental hospital during a power outage. Later, they turn up at the home of their hated new psychiatrist to terrorize the doc and his oblivious family. Unexpectedly lighthearted with some hilariously over-the-top performances (Pleasence, sending-up his *Halloween* role, and Landau are at their most unrestrained) and a smattering of gory Tom Savini FX.

ALTERED STATES
★★★ Warner Home Video, 1980, R, 102 min. Dir: Ken Russell. Cast: William Hurt, Blair Brown, Charles Haid, Bob Balaban, Thaao Penghlis, Drew Barrymore.

DICK SMITH
(1922–)

One of the great makeup men of the movies, Smith is the father of the modern Latex makeup effect. Beginning in early '60s television, Dick eventually graduated to major '70s features like *The Exorcist* and the *Godfather* films, ultimately winning Oscars for his work in 1984's *Amadeus* and 1992's *Death Becomes Her*.

The Strange Case of Dr. Jekyll and Mr. Hyde ('68), *House of Dark Shadows* ('70), *The Exorcist* ('73), *The Stepford Wives* ('75), *Burnt Offerings* ('76), *The Sentinel* ('77), *Exorcist II: The Heretic* ('77), *The Fury* ('78), *Altered States* ('80), *Scanners* ('81), *The Fan* ('81), *Ghost Story* ('81), *Spasms* ('83), *The Hunger* (83), *Poltergeist III* ('88), *Tales From the Darkside: The Movie* ('90), *Death Becomes Her* ('92).

This wacked-out version of the Paddy Chayefsky novel (he requested his screenplay credit be supplanted with the fictitious "Sidney Aaron") plays like a remake of the '50s chiller *Monster on the Campus* on LSD. College prof Hurt (in his film debut) experiments with an isolation tank and mind-expanding drugs to trace the origin of man through racial memory, eventually transforming into a prehistoric ape-man and later into even more bizarre manifestations. Dick Smith's incredible make-up and Russell's flashy visuals help redeem cold performances and an over-reliance on verbose, pseudo-scientific dialogue. Look for *Night Court's* John Larroquette.

ALUCARDA
See: *Sisters of Satan.*

AMAZING COLOSSAL MAN, THE
★★★ Columbia/TriStar Home Video, 1957, NR, 79 min. Dir: Bert I. Gordon. Cast: Glenn Langan, Cathy Downs, William Hudson, Larry Thor, James Seay, Russ Bender.

Surprisingly engrossing '50s monsterama with Langan excellent as an army colonel exposed to a plutonium blast that alters his cell structure; he doubles in size every day until he becomes a rampaging 60-foot giant who attacks Las Vegas. One of schlockmeister Gordon's best, this has all his usual tatty effects but also some unexpected insight into the emotions of its "monster" and those who care about him. Later ripped off by the comedy *Honey, I Blew Up the Kid*. Sequel: *War of the Colossal Beast.*

AMAZING MR. H, THE
See: *They Saved Hitler's Brain!*

AMAZING MR. X, THE
★★☆ Sinister Cinema, 1948, NR, 79 min. Dir: Bernard Vorhaus. Cast: Turhan Bey, Lynn Bari, Richard Carlson, Cathy O'Donnell, Donald Curtis, Virginia Gregg.

Phony psychic Bey teams with supposedly dead husband Curtis to bilk his wealthy "widow" (Bari) of her fortune. This road company *Nightmare Alley* has a good cast and some effective direction but is terminally predictable. Aka *The Spiritualist.*

AMAZING STORIES
★★ MCA/Universal Home Video, 1985-87, NR, 90 min. per tape. Dirs: Steven Spielberg, Martin Scorsese, Robert Zemeckis, Tim Burton, Paul Bartel, others. Cast: Kevin Costner, Danny DeVito, John Lithgow, Christopher Lloyd, Sam Waterston, Carrie Fisher, Charlie Sheen, Sondra Locke, Lea Thompson,

---

BERT I. GORDON
(1922–)

Mr. B.I.G. specialized in popular but kinda dumb '50s monster flicks for which he, along with wife Flora, also created the not-so-special effects. Never able to break out of the low-budget stakes, Gordon's films can be fun as long as you don't take them too seriously. His best efforts are undoubtably the well-acted *The Amazing Colossal Man* and the sub-Sinbad *The Magic Sword.*

King Dinosaur ('55), *The Cyclops* ('57), *Beginning of the End* ('57), *The Amazing Colossal Man* ('57), *Earth vs. the Spider* ('58), *War of the Colossal Beast* ('58), *Attack of the Puppet People* ('58), *Tormented* ('60), *The Magic Sword* ('62), *Village of the Giants* ('65), *Picture Mommy Dead* ('66), *Necromancy* ('72), *Food of the Gods* ('76), *Empire of the Ants* ('77), *The Coming* ('81), *Satan's Princess* ('90).

Patrick Swayze, Gregory Hines, Rhea Perlman, Andrew McCarthy, Helen Shaver.

Spielberg's mostly misfired fantasy-horror series often showcased top talent, but the sum of the parts rarely equaled a very memorable whole. Perhaps the best segments were *The Doll*, an eerie love story with an Emmy-winning Lithgow at his best; Scorsese's genuinely scary *Mirror, Mirror;* and Burton's amusing animated *Family Dog.*

AMBULANCE, THE
★★☆ Columbia/TriStar Home Video, 1990, R, 95 min. Dir: Larry Cohen. Cast: Eric Roberts, Megan Gallagher, James Earl Jones, Red Buttons, Eric Braedon, Janine Turner, Laureen Landon, Stan Lee.

Typically quirky Cohen thriller about a mystery ambulance whisking accident victims off the streets of New York City; said victims are never seen again, at least in one piece. Not up to some of Larry's other horrors—the basic premise is too muddled—but there is some good acting, especially Buttons—Buttons!—as a sleazy tabloid reporter.

AMERICAN GOTHIC
★★ Vidmark Entertainment, 1987, R, 85 min. Dir: John Hough. Cast: Rod Steiger, Yvonne De Carlo, Michael J. Pollard, Sarah Torgov, Fiona Hutchinson, Mark Lindsay Chapman.

Offbeat chiller about a planeload of obnoxious yuppies stranded on a northwestern island

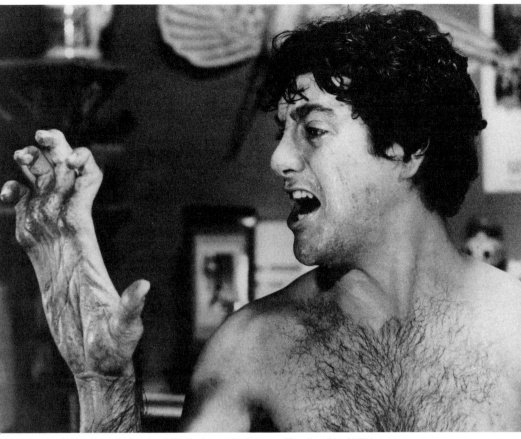

David Naughton lends a hand in An American Werewolf in London *(1981).*

with a family of homicidally regressive retardos led by fundamentalists Steiger and De Carlo. An exceptional cast and some nice, sick touches, but this fumbles the ball where it counts, especially in a needlessly rushed ending. Pollard is his usual ingratiatingly weird self.

AMERICAN WEREWOLF IN LONDON, AN
★★★ Vestron Video, 1981, R, 97 min. Dir: John Landis. Cast: David Naughton, Jenny Agutter, Griffin Dunne, John Woodvine, Brian Glover, Lila Kaye.

An affecting sense of humor permeates this high-spirited diffusion of classic horror film lore and modern comedy from the director of *Animal House.* A pair of New York University students traveling on the foggy English moors are attacked by a werewolf. One boy (Dunne) dies but returns to warn the survivor (Naughton) that, come the next full moon he, too, will become a wolf man. Rick Baker's

Oscar-winning makeup FX are a marvel to behold although Dunne steals it as a walking corpse with a sense of humor.

AMITYVILLE: A NEW GENERATION
★★ Republic Home Video, 1993, R, 92 min. Dir: John Murlowski. Cast: Ross Partridge, Lala Sloatman, Julia Nickson-Soul, David Naughton, Terry O'Quinn, Richard Roundtree, Barbara Howard, Robert Rusler.

An antique mirror from the old Amityville digs brings out the worst in a bunch of pretentious New York conceptual artists. Things get especially bizarre for one photographer (Partridge) who turns out to be the son of the original Amityville mass murderer. Yet another vaguely related sequel; it's well directed but the story fizzles out well before the lame (and obvious) conclusion. The supporting cast has a lot more verve than the bland leads. Aka *Amityville 1993: The Image of Evil.*

RICK BAKER
(1952–)

An Oscar-winning makeup man, Baker started his career inventing creatures for *Famous Monsters of Filmland* magazine before graduating to Dick Smith protégé and eventual makeup superstardom. One of the pioneers in the wave of '70s cable-controlled monster FX, he won the first Oscar for makeup for *An American Werewolf in London*.

Octaman ('71), *The Thing With Two Heads* ('72), *Schlock* ('73), *The Exorcist* ('73), *Track of the Moon Beast* ('73), *It's Alive!* ('74), *Squirm* ('76), *King Kong* ('76), *The Incredible Melting Man* ('77), *The Fury* ('78), *It Lives Again!* ('78), *The Howling* ('81), *The Funhouse* ('81), *An American Werewolf in London* ('81), *Videodrome* ('83), *Gremlins 2: The New Batch* ('90), *Wolf* ('94).

AMITYVILLE CURSE, THE
★☆ Starmaker Home Video, 1990, R, 91 min.
Dir: Tom Berry. Cast: Kim Coates, Dawna Wightman, Jan Rubes, Cassandra Gava, Helen Hughes, David Stein.

This in-name-only follow-up to the previous *Amityville* outings concerns yet another haunted house in the dreaded Long Island burg: the former home of murdered priest Rubes, bought by an annoying bunch of yuppie-something types who get knocked off none-too-quickly for yours truly. Super-dull, this has more yawns than yikes.

AMITYVILLE HORROR, THE
★★☆ Goodtimes Home Video, 1979, R, 114 min.
Dir: Stuart Rosenberg. Cast: James Brolin, Margot Kidder, Rod Steiger, Murray Hamilton, Don Stroud, John Larch, Michael Sacks, Helen Shaver.

Moderately effective but overly episodic screen treatment of the allegedly true story of George and Kathy Lutz, whose Long Island

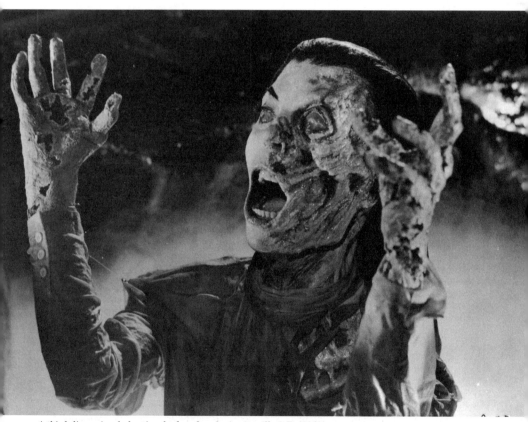

A third-dimensional ghostie asks for a hug in Amityville 3-D *(1983).*

dream home turned out to be a haunted house of horrors built on an ancient Indian burial ground and once the sight of a grisly mass murder. There are some tense scenes and Kidder is sympathetic, but this is undone by the excessive hamming of Brolin and Steiger and an incredibly anticlimactic ending. Followed by a "prequel" and five unrelated "sequels."

AMITYVILLE II: THE POSSESSION
★★★ Nelson Home Entertainment, 1982, R, 104 min. Dir: Damiano Damiani. Cast: James Olson, Burt Young, Rutanya Alda, Jack Magner, Diane Franklin, Andrew Prine.

I'm probably going out on a limb here (and sawing it off) by saying that this is the best of the *Amityvilles*. Actually a prequel to the original, this deals with a blue-collar dysfunctional family moving into the Long Island horror house, where the teen son (Magner) is possessed and kills off his entire family with a shotgun. Laughably anxiety-ridden acting but there are some good makeup FX and flamboyant camera work guaranteed to give you whiplash.

AMITYVILLE 3-D
★★☆ Video Treasures, 1983, PG, 93 min. Dir: Richard Fleischer. Cast: Tony Roberts, Tess Harper, Candy Clark, Robert Joy, Lori Loughlin, Meg Ryan.

This third entry in the series totally refuses to take itself seriously. Doubting Thomas reporter Roberts moves into the Amityville house in order to disprove its haunted history and, naturally, falls victim to its supernatural influence. Brimming with cartoony FX and gimmicky 3-D sequences (the tape is *not,* however, in 3-D), this has a pleasing funhouse feel not attempted by its more serious forerunners and is all the better for it. A young Ryan makes one of her earliest screen appearances as a teen who fantasizes about having sex with a ghost. TV title: *Amityville: The Demon.*

AMITYVILLE 4: THE EVIL ESCAPES
★★ Starmaker Home Video, 1989, R, 95 min. Dir: Sandor Stern. Cast: Patty Duke, Jane Wyatt, Norman Lloyd, Fredric Lehne, Brandy Gold, Geri Betzler, Aron Eisenberg, Robert Alan Browne.

Wyatt's sister buys a possessed lava lamp at an Amityville yard sale and sends it to sis in California, where it takes over the household appliances—a chainsaw comes to life, the pet budgie turns up in the toaster oven, the garbage disposal chops off a young electrician's hand—in an attempt to capture the soul of Jane's young granddaughter. After an atmospheric opening replete with the requisite thunderstorm, swarming flies, and blood-oozing walls, this TV sequel (inexplicably rated R on tape) quickly degenerates into the usual clichés. Aka *Amityville: The Evil Escapes.*

AMITYVILLE 1992: IT'S ABOUT TIME
★★ Republic Home Video, 1992, R, 95 min. Dir: Tony Randel. Cast: Stephen Macht, Shawn Weatherly, Megan Ward, Damon Martin, Nita Talbot, Dick Miller.

Actually, it's about time they stopped making these annoying video follow-ups to previous horror hits. A cursed clock from you-know-where takes over the California tract house (which looks like it was decorated by the Mother of Whispers from *Suspiria*) of architect Macht and his family. This owes more to *Poltergeist* than to any of the other *Amityvilles,* with ideas pinched freely from *The Omen, They Came From Within,* and *The Blob* and cameos by Talbot and Miller. Originally announced as *Amityville 5* until somebody realized that there already *was* a fifth *Amityville* movie!

AMITYVILLE 1993: THE IMAGE OF EVIL
See: *Amityville: A New Generation.*

AMITYVILLE: THE DEMON
See: *Amityville 3-D.*

AMITYVILLE: THE EVIL ESCAPES
See: *Amityville 4: The Evil Escapes.*

AMOK
See: *Schizo.*

AMONG THE LIVING DEAD
See: *A Virgin Among the Living Dead.*

AMSTERDAMNED
★★☆ Vestron Video, 1988, R, 112 min. Dir: Dick Maas. Cast: Huub Stapel, Monique Van De Ven, Serge Henri Valcke, Hidde Maas, Wim Zomer, Tatum Daglett.

A disfigured psycho-skin diver is terrorizing the canals of Amsterdam in this overlong but good-looking mixture of police thriller and slasher flick from the director of *The Lift.* The dubbing stinks, but try to ignore that for the strong imagery—like a hooker's gory corpse splattering the roof of a glass-topped tourist boat—and a great speedboat chase to rival anything in any James Bond film.

ANATOMY OF A PSYCHO
★★ Something Weird Video, 1961, NR, 75 min. Dir: Brooke L. Peters [Boris Petroff]. Cast: Ronnie Burns, Pamela Lincoln, Darrell Howe, Judy Howard, Russ Bender, Don Devlin.

Only vaguely a horror film, this JD exploiter was made to cash in on Hitchcock's you-know-what. Howe is the titular teen out to avenge his brother's execution. Burns (the son of George and Gracie) is the innocent forced to take the rap for Darrell's crimes. Sometimes effective in its sleaziness but spoiled by a really unbelievable ending.

AND COMES THE DAWN...
BUT COLORED RED!
See: *Web of the Spider.*

—AND NOW THE SCREAMING STARTS!
★★☆ Prism Entertainment, 1973, R, 84 min. Dir: Roy Ward Baker. Cast: Peter Cushing, Stephanie Beacham, Ian Ogilvy, Herbert Lom, Patrick Magee, Guy Rolfe, Rosalie Crutchley, Geoffrey Whitehead.

Virgin bride Beacham is cursed by a disfigured ghost and a living severed hand when she moves into husband Ogilvy's ancestral manor. A good cast and excellent art direction help this somewhat muddled Brit programmer. Originally 87 minutes, this video edition is taken from a heavily edited TV print. Aka *Fengriffen* and *Bride of Fengriffen.*

AND SOON THE DARKNESS
★★☆ HBO Video, 1970, PG, 100 min. Dir: Robert Fuest. Cast: Pamela Franklin, Michele Dotrice, Sandor Elés, John Nettleton, Clare Kelly.

Efficient, if slow, Brian Clemens–penned lady-in-distresser about a pair of English student nurses on a bicycle tour of northern France who encounter a brutal rapist-murderer. Embellished with a remarkable claustrophobic feel despite being mostly set on a bright country road and with a strong lead performance by Franklin—the Jamie Lee Curtis of the early '70s.

AND THEN THERE WERE NONE
★★★★ Video Communications, 1945, NR, 97 min. Dir: René Clair. Cast: Barry Fitzgerald, Walter Huston, Louis Hayward, June Duprez, Roland Young, Judith Anderson, C. Aubrey Smith, Richard Haydn, Mischa Auer, Queenie Leonard.

The first and best screen version of Agatha Christie's classic murder puzzle about 10 people lured to an isolated mansion on an island where they're killed one by one by a mysterious maniac as just punishment for their past crimes. Both eerie *and* funny, with a wonderfully Hitchcockian sense of black humor and a morgueful of delightful actor-victims. Remade three different times as *Ten Little Indians.*

Geoffrey Whitehead returns from the grave for some acne cream in —And Now the Screaming Starts! *(1973).*

AND THEN THERE WERE NONE
See: *Ten Little Indians* (1975).

. . . AND YOU'LL LIVE IN TERROR!
See: *Seven Doors of Death.*

ANDY WARHOL'S DRACULA
★★★ Triboro Entertainment, 1974, X, 103 min. Dir: Paul Morrissey. Cast: Udo Kier, Joe Dallesandro, Vittorio De Sica, Maxime McKendry, Arno Juerging, Stefania Casini.

Kier, the sickliest-looking Dracula you've ever seen, travels to Catholic Italy in search of the blood of "whergins" (his pronunciation), only to graphically vomit up the red stuff provided by the sleek necks of nobleman De Sica's "pure" daughters. Full of hilariously stilted dialogue ("That Count Dracula is no good for anyone and he never was!"), nudity, sex, and outrageous gore, including an ax-wielding climax you've got to see to disbelieve. Originally called *Blood for Dracula* and reissued as *Young Dracula,* you can usually find it in the "Adults Only" section of your local video store, though there's no hardcore action. An edited 93-minute R-rated version is also available. Look for a cameo by Roman Polanski during the pub sequence.

ANDY WARHOL'S FRANKENSTEIN

★★☆ Triboro Entertainment, 1973, X, 95 min. Dir: Paul Morrissey. Cast: Udo Kier, Monique Van Vooran, Joe Dallesandro, Arno Juerging, Srdjan Zelenovic, Dalila Di Lazzaro.

Icky, gore-dripping, 3-D "version" of the oft-told tale with the Baron (Kier, looking like Basil Rathbone's degenerate son) now a necrophile married to his own sister and trying to create a "master race" while having sex with corpses and endlessly lecturing his bumbling assistant. Funny almost in spite of itself, with priceless acting and dialogue ("Why did you wake me? You know I have insomnia!") and amazingly tasteless scenes of heads, entrails, and other body parts flying off the screen—in the original 3-D version, anyway. Also titled *Flesh for Frankenstein, Frankenstein 3-D,* and *The Frankenstein Experiment,* for followers of Warhol's film odyssey and gorehounds everywhere this is one not to be missed. Everyone else will just have to learn to live with it. Both this and Warhol's *Dracula* were supervised (though not actually directed, as some sources claim) by Italian horror vet Antonio Margheriti.

ANGEL FOR SATAN, AN

★★☆ Sinister Cinema, 1966, NR, 82 min. Dir: Camillo Mastrocinque. Cast: Barbara Steele, Anthony Steffen, Ursula Davis, Aldo Berti.

Steele is a beautiful tourist at a mountain village where she's possessed by a vengeful spirit formerly housed in a statue found at the bottom of a lake. One of Barbara's more obscure Euro-horrors, she's in good form as the whip-wielding heroine, but this is available from Sinister currently only in unsubtitled Italian. A dubbed version used to turn up on TV from time to time.

ANGEL HEART

★★☆ International Video Entertainment, 1987, UR, 113 min. Dir: Alan Parker. Cast: Mickey Rourke, Robert De Niro, Lisa Bonet, Charlotte Rampling, Stoker Fontrlieu, Kathleen Wilhoite.

Intriguing mix of film noire melodrama and satanic horror with Rourke in good form as '50's private dick, Harry Angel, whose search for a long-missing big band singer involves him with New Orleans voodoo and murder. Superstar De Niro contributes a chilling cameo as the mysterious Louis Cypher (get it?), but too much of the plotting is pretty obvious and the twist ending owes a lot to *The Haunted Strangler.* Based on William Hjortsberg's novel "Falling Angel," this unrated video differs from the R-rated theatrical cut only in the inclusion of a few seconds of Mickey's blood-spattered bare ass during a love scene with Cosby kid Bonet.

ANGEL OF VENGEANCE
See: *Ms. 45.*

ANGUISH

★★ Key Video, 1987, R, 85 min. Dir: Bigas Luna. Cast: Zelda Rubinstein, Michael Lerner, Talia Paul, Clara Pastor, Angel Jove, Isabel Garcia Loria.

Transparent *Demons* cash-in with a similar theme: a horror movie called *The Mommy,* about a mother-dominated eyeball-stabber, is watched one too many times by a loony in ugly running shoes who goes on a killing spree in the theater. The first 20 minutes concerning the movie-within-the-movie (featuring Rubinstein and Lerner) are fairly stylish, but once the true nature of the plot is revealed, you lose interest fast, everything finally petering out in a confusing "shocker" ending.

ANTHROPOPHAGUS
See: *The Grim Reaper.*

ANTHROPOPHAGUS 2
See: *Monster Hunter.*

ANTHROPOPHAGUS BEAST, THE
See: *The Grim Reaper.*

ANTICHRIST, THE
See: *The Tempter.*

ANTS!

★★☆ Star Classics, 1977, NR, 91 min. Dir: Robert Sheerer. Cast: Robert Foxworth, Lynda Day George, Myrna Loy, Suzanne Somers, Bernie Casey, Anita Gillette, Brian Dennehy, Steve Franken.

Poisonous ants have a people picnic in this fun tele-movie. Construction work near a lakefront hotel unearths the creepy-crawlers, which lay waste to the staff and guests. Not as scary as *The Naked Jungle* nor as imaginative as *Phase IV* but a pleasant time-killer also known as *It Happened at Lakewood Manor* and *Panic at Lakewood Manor.* Fans of *Three's Company* take special note: this is probably the only chance you'll ever have to see Suzanne Somers devoured alive by ants.

APARTMENT ZERO

★★★ Academy Entertainment, 1988, R, 116 min. Dir: Martin Donovan. Cast: Colin Firth, Hart Bochner, Dora Bryan, Liz Smith, Fabrizio Bentivoglio, Mirella D'Angelo.

In this odd psychological thriller Firth is a fastidious, lonely film buff who runs a revival house in Buenos Aires. When he takes in handsome, sexually ambiguous stranger Bochner as a roommate, Firth's repressed homosexuality and dangerous fantasies come to the fore. Not for all tastes but definitely worth working with; often recalling Paul Verhoeven's *The 4th Man.* Video prints, though, are missing several key moments underlying the blatant sexual tension between the two "heroes."

A*P*E

☆ Paragon Home Video, 1976, PG, 87 min. Dir: Paul Leder. Cast: Joanna De Varona, Rod Arrants, Alex Nicol, Lee Nak Hoon, Woo Hion Jong.

The *Plan Nine From Outer Space* of *King Kong* rip-offs, this Korean cheapie, released theatrically in 3-D, has a guy in a raggy monkey suit as the giant ape that battles armies (he gives them the finger), beats up big rubber sharks, and tramples towns in search of his lady love, De Varona. Totally terrible but only occasionally amusingly so; my favorite scene has dozens of confused extras dashing about in vague panic as an off-screen announcer calmly proclaims: "Please proceed in an orderly fashion. Do not take valuables, they will only slow you down." Aka *Attack of the Horny Gorilla.*

APE, THE

★★ Sinister Cinema, 1940, NR, 62 min. Dir: William Nigh. Cast: Boris Karloff, Maris Wrixon, Gene O'Donnell, Gertrude Hoffman, Henry Hall, Dorothy Vaughn.

Not a highlight of Karloff's career; he finished out his Monogram contract with this Curt Siodmak–scripted monkey business about a small-town doctor who kills a gorilla that's escaped from a circus and dons its skin to murder locals for the spinal fluid he needs to cure the paralysis of pretty neighbor girl, Wrixon. Boris manages to maintain his dignity throughout, but this is still one of his silliest features. Aka *Gorilla.*

APE MAN, THE

★★ Sinister Cinema, 1943, NR, 63 min. Dir: William Beaudine. Cast: Bela Lugosi, Louise

Currie, Wallace Ford, Minerva Urecal, Henry Hall, Emil Van Horn.

Awesomely ridiculous Lugosi Monogram flick reducing the Hungarian horror great to the humiliating role of a part-ape, part-man scientist who can only remain human in appearance by injecting himself with human spinal fluid—do I suspect a trend here? Scenes of poor Bela sleeping in a gorilla cage or fretting over his preposterous situation are more sad than funny though, as ever, Lugosi manages to add his distinctive touch to even drek like this. Shown in England as *Lock Your Doors,* the surprise ending, appropriately enough, makes a joke of the entire film.

APOLOGY

★★ HBO Video, 1986, NR, 98 min. Dir: Robert Bierman. Cast: Lesley Ann Warren, Peter Weller, John Glover, Harvey Fierstein.

Fair cable thriller with Lesley Ann Warren as a conceptual artist whose latest work, a telephone confessional gimmick, attracts a mad killer who commits brutal murders just to have something to confess. Typically fine work from Lesley Ann, but still awfully routine stuff.

APPOINTMENT, THE

★★☆ Sony Video, 1980, NR, 90 min. Dir: Lindsey C. Vickers. Cast: Edward Woodward, Jane Merrow, Samantha Weysen, John Judd, Ken Julian.

A pre-"Equalizer" Woodward is good in this interesting British chiller about a neglective father placed under a curse by his young daughter. Slow but involving supernatural suspense tale is better than it sounds.

APPOINTMENT WITH FEAR

★ International Video Entertainment, 1987, R, 90 min. Dir: Alan Smithee [Ramzi Thomas]. Cast: Michele Little, Michael Wyle, Kerry Remsen, Debisue Voorhees, Douglas Rowe, Garrick Dowhen.

Dowhen is possessed by some ancient Egyptian tree god or some such nonsense, kills his wife, and then stalks the teen babysitter caring for his baby son. Rock-bottom slasher with little to offer beyond the odd laugh or two.

APPRENTICE TO MURDER

★★ Starmaker Home Video, 1987, PG-13, 92 min. Dir: R. L. Thomas. Cast: Donald Sutherland, Chad Lowe, Mia Sara, Rutanya Alda, Eddie Jones, Knut Husebo.

In 1927 Pennsylvania a teenage factory worker becomes the assistant to a local faith healer whose supernatural abilities lead them into battle against a black magician. Filmed in Scandinavia, this Amish *Svengali* has good acting and photography but is more coming-of-age drama than horror movie.

APRIL FOOL, THE
See: *Killer Party.*

APRIL FOOL'S DAY
See: *Slaughter High.*

APRIL FOOL'S DAY
★★☆ Paramount Home Video, 1986, R, 88 min. Dir: Fred Walton. Cast: Deborah Foreman, Amy Steel, Clayton Rohner, Deborah Goodrich, Thomas F. Wilson, Griffin O'Neal.

Slick but routine slasher-mystery. Pretty little rich girl Muffy (Foreman) invites college pals to her family's remote island mansion for an April Fool's Day party. The usual gags and pranks eventually escalate into murder—or is it? The rich ambiance and pleasant young actors help make up for Danilo Bach's overly manipulative screenplay.

ARACHNOPHOBIA
★★☆ Hollywood Pictures Home Video, 1990, PG-13, 103 min. Dir: Frank Marshall. Cast: Jeff Daniels, Julian Sands, Harley Jane Kozak, John Goodman, Henry Jones, Peter Jason, Stuart Pankin, Mark L. Taylor.

If this lavish B movie is *ever* remembered in the future, it will undoubtedly be for the invention of the advertising buzz word "Thrill-omedy," surely the most ridiculous length *anyone* has ever gone to disguise the fact that they've made a horror film. Otherwise this killer-spider opus has its moments but falls flat for trying to be too many things for too many audiences. The low-budget *Kingdom of the Spiders* handled a similar theme much better and much more cheaply.

ARE YOU DYING, YOUNG MAN?
See: *The Beast in the Cellar.*

ARE YOU IN THE HOUSE ALONE?
★★ Goodtimes Home Video, 1978, NR, 96 min. Dir: Walter Grauman. Cast: Kathleen Beller, Blythe Danner, Tony Bill, Dennis Quaid, Robin Mattson, Scott Colomby.

An initially suspenseful but ultimately frustrating mix of stalker movie and "Afterschool Special" with Beller in a familiar role as a shy high school girl plagued by a phantom secret admirer who eventually assaults her. A good cast works hard but TV censorship spoils the overall effect.

ARIZONA RIPPER
See: *Terror at London Bridge.*

ARMY
See: *Severed Ties.*

ARMY OF DARKNESS
★★☆ MCA/Universal Home Video, 1992, R, 80 min. Dir: Sam Raimi. Cast: Bruce Campbell, Embeth Davidtz, Marcus Gilbert, Richard Grove, Ian Abercrombie, Patricia Tallman, Ted Raimi, Bridget Fonda.

Take *Evil Dead II,* extract most of the horror, and cross it with a Three Stooges version of *A Connecticut Yankee in King Arthur's Court,* and it comes out like this: Raimi's most ambitious but frustrating feature to date. Luckless hero Ash (Campbell, looking more like a live-action cartoon than ever) is magically transported back to the 14th century, where he saves a castle full of "primitive screwheads" from an army of Ray Harryhausenesque skeletal warriors led by his own evil alter ego. Truckloads of not-so-subtle homages are paid to everything from *The Day the Earth Stood Still* to *The Manster.* A breathless pace and Campbell's patented form of deadpan comic line reading help make this fun; a sell-out-for-mass-audience-appeal (which it didn't get anyway) only makes you wish Sam had gone the straight horror road. Don't sneeze or you'll miss Fonda's contribution entirely. Aka *Evil Dead III,* the European print runs 95 minutes and has a different, more satisfying downbeat ending.

ARNOLD
★★☆ Prism Entertainment, 1973, PG, 94 min. Dir: Georg Fenady. Cast: Stella Stevens, Roddy McDowall, Elsa Lanchester, Farley Granger, Shani Wallis, Victor Buono, Patric Knowles, John McGiver, Bernard Fox, Jamie Farr.

A horror-comedy obviously inspired by the *Dr. Phibes* movies. Stevens is a delight as the bubbly golddigger who marries a corpse called Arnold at his funeral and will inherit his fortune if she remains always faithful to him. Meanwhile various friends and relatives begin dying in bizarre "accidents"—seemingly rigged by Arnold himself. Certainly uneven, but the cast is game and there are some amusing twists.

AROUSERS, THE
★★☆ New World Home Video, 1970, R, 84 min. Dir: Curtis Hanson. Cast: Tab Hunter, Cheri Latimer, Linda Leider, Nadyne Turney, Isabel Jewell, Roberta Collins.

Often jokingly referred to as a high point in Hunter's career, this is actually a fairly taut

Is that really Corporal Klinger (Jamie Farr) under that Hindu outfit in Arnold *(1973)?*

psycho-thriller with Tab as a sexually repressed high school gym coach whose impotence leads to the strangulation of several young girls. Some effective scenes and offbeat touches of dark humor make this less unsavory than it might seem. Aka *The Sweet Kill* and *A Kiss From Eddie*. Look for Angus Scrimm—billed here as Rory Guy—in a small role.

ARRIVAL, THE
★★ Prism Entertainment, 1990, R, 103 min. Dir: David Schmoeller. Cast: Joseph Culp, Robin Frates, John Saxon, Robert Sampson, Michael J. Pollard.

Sampson is an old man hit by a meteor fragment who develops a hankering for blood, starts to grow younger (eventually turning into handsome Culp, son of Robert), and is hunted by FBI guy Saxon while stalking his former nurse (Frates). Standard low-budget sci-fi/horror from the director of *Tourist Trap*

and the original *Puppetmaster,* both of which are much better.

ARSENIC AND OLD LACE
★★★☆ MGM/UA Home Video, 1944, NR, 118 min. Dir: Frank Capra. Cast: Cary Grant, Priscilla Lane, Raymond Massey, Peter Lorre, Jack Carson, Josephine Hull, Jean Adair, Edward Everett Horton, John Alexander, James Gleason.

Hilarious adaptation of the Joseph Kesselring play about a New York theater critic (an energetic Grant at his double-taking best) who discovers that his maiden aunts have been poisoning the gentlemen callers at their Brooklyn home with arsenic-laced elderberry wine and burying the bodies in the basement. One of the best ever movie versions of a Broadway play, this boasts a fine comic cast in top form and misses only in the casting of Massey in the role of Grant's homicidal maniac brother made famous on stage by Boris Karloff.

ART OF DYING, THE

★★☆ Imperial Entertainment, 1991, R, 90 min. Dir: Wings Hauser. Cast: Wings Hauser, Kathleen Kinmont, Sarah Douglas, Michael J. Pollard, Gary Werntz.

Wings directs himself as a detective on the trail of a maniac (Werntz) who kills his victims in reenactments of famous murder scenes from films like *Psycho* and *The Texas Chainsaw Massacre*. A well-made, imaginative exploiter with a good cast.

ASPHYX, THE

★★☆ Interglobal Video, 1972, PG, 99 min. Dir: Peter Newbrook. Cast: Robert Stephens, Robert Powell, Jane Lapotaire, Fiona Walker, Ralph Arliss, Alex Scott.

Grim period chiller about a Victorian scientist whose experiments with the "asphyx," or spirit of death, render him immortal but bring death to just about everyone else around him. Talky but compelling, with a strong cast and interesting plot twists. Aka *Spirit of the Dead.*

ASSAULT

★★ Embassy Home Entertainment, 1970, PG, 89 min. Dir: Sidney Hayers. Cast: Suzy Kendall, Frank Finlay, Freddie Jones, Lesley-Anne Down, James Laurenson, Tony Beckley.

Routine mystery-horror about a series of rape-murders committed in a girls school with Kendall as sexy art teacher who suspects supernatural forces. This has a good cast of British actors—including Down in her debut—but is rather listlessly directed—its best sequence, in fact, comes during the opening credits! Aka *In the Devil's Garden, Tower of Terror,* and *The Creepers.*

ASSIGNMENT ISTANBUL

See: *The Castle of Fu Manchu.*

ASSIGNMENT TERROR

See: *Dracula vs. Frankenstein* (1969).

ASTOUNDING SHE MONSTER, THE

★ Sinister Cinema, 1958, NR, 60 min. Dir: Ronnie Ashcroft. Cast: Robert Clarke, Marilyn Harvey, Kenne Duncan, Jeanne Tatum, Ewing Brown, Shirley Kilpatrick.

Kilpatrick is a *Frederick's of Hollywood*–proportioned female alien with Brooke Shields eyebrows and a lethal touch who terrorizes a couple of Z movie actors in a cardboard cabin set in this dimestore sci-fi/horror epic that's so numbingly bad it's almost hypnotic. For the most rabid Robert Clarke fans only.

ASTRAL FACTOR, THE

See: *The Invisible Strangler.*

ASTRO ZOMBIES, THE

★ Wizard Video, 1968, PG, 83 min. Dir: Ted V. Mikels. Cast: John Carradine, Wendell Corey, Joan Patrick, Tom Pace, Tura Satana, Rafael Campos.

Wayne Rogers (of "M*A*S*H" fame) co-produced and co-wrote this incredibly shoddy, but quite funny, no-budget wonder about a mad doctor (Carradine, who rarely seemed more out of it) creating skull-faced zombies from various human organs, then sending his machete-wielding monsters out to collect more spare parts. An irrepressible blend of ludicrous plotting, inane dialogue, and fabulously bad performing, with standout contributions from Corey—in his final role—as an order-barking FBI chief and Santana and Campos as evil foreign agents of the Boris and Natasha school of espionage. Also out in a cut version called *Space Zombies.*

ASYLUM

★★★ Prism Entertainment, 1972, PG, 88 min. Dir: Roy Ward Baker. Cast: Peter Cushing, Britt Ekland, Herbert Lom, Barbara Parkins, Charottle Rampling, Patrick Magee, Richard Todd, Robert Powell, Sylvia Syms, Barry Morse.

Psychiatrist Powell interviews four inmates at a remote country asylum in order to ascertain which of them is the former head of the institution. The patients' various case histories

---

HERBERT LOM
(1917–)

This commanding-looking Czech actor (born Herbert Charles Angelo Kuchacevich ze Schluderpacheru, whew!) with the melodious basso voice has been a character actor in Britain since the late '30s. He became a second-string horror guy in the '60s and a popular comic actor in the '70s, thanks to his recurring role in the *Pink Panther* series. Lom spoofed his horror image hilariously in *The Pink Panther Strikes Again!* in '76.

The Dark Tower ('43), *Mysterious Island* ('61), *The Phantom of the Opera* ('62), *Mark of the Devil* ('70), *Dorian Gray* ('70), *Murders in the Rue Morgue* ('71), *Asylum* ('72), *—And Now the Screaming Starts!* ('73), *Ten Little Indians* ('75), *The Dead Zone* ('83), *Ten Little Indians* ('89), *The Masque of the Red Death* ('90), *The Devil's Daughter* ('91).

concern everything from a living dismembered corpse to a magical suit to a schizophrenic murderess to killer voodoo dolls. This solid collection of Robert Bloch short stories is his best Amicus anthology, with sharp direction, a fine cast (including Lom at his charmingly intense best), and a genuinely shocking surprise ending. Reissued as *House of Crazies.*

ASYLUM EROTICA
See: *Slaughter Hotel.*

ASYLUM OF SATAN
★ Academy Entertainment, 1971, PG, 78 min. Dir: William Girdler. Cast: Charles Kissinger, Carla Borelli, Nick Jolley, Sherry Stein.

Girdler's first film was this barrel-scraper about a pretty singer (Borelli) held prisoner in a private psychiatric clinic run by a ageless devil worshipper. Highlighted by a scene where an old lady in a wheelchair is attacked by a horde of Crackerjack prize rubber insects; you know you're in trouble when the hero looks like "Meathead" from *All in the Family,* the devil is played by someone in horn-topped *Planet of the Apes* makeup, and the musical score sounds like out-takes from *Mannix.*

ATOM-AGE VAMPIRE
★★ Sinister Cinema, 1960, NR, 87 min. Dir: Richard McNamara [Anton Giulio Majano]. Cast: Alberto Lupo, Susanne Loret, Sergio Fantoni, Franca Parisi.

There are no vampires, atomic or otherwise, in this anemic continental horror inspired by *The Horror Chamber of Dr. Faustus.* A scientist (Lupo) restores the lost beauty of a disfigured dancer (Loret), though, predictably, the cure doesn't last, forcing Lupo to kill women for their faces—all the while transforming into a crusty-faced monster for no discernable reason. Some nice visuals help distract from the very inept dubbing. Aka *Seddock, L'Ereda de Satana; Seddock, Heir of Satan;* and *Seddock, Son of Satan.*

ATOMIC BRAIN, THE
See: *Monstrosity.*

ATTACK OF THE BEAST CREATURES
☆ WesternWorld Video, 1983, R, 83 min. Dir: Michael Stanley. Cast: Julia Rust, Robert Nolfi, Lisa Pak.

Filmed as *Hell Island,* this virtually unknown Connecticut-shot oddity may well be the *Plan Nine* of a new generation. In the 1920s a boatload of amateur actors is shipwrecked on an uncharted island with acid-laced water streams and living doll inhabitants who bear more than a passing resemblance to the Zuni

fetish warrior in *Trilogy of Terror.* Awful, but also bizarrely fascinating, with loads of laughs but some pretty gruesome moments as well.

ATTACK OF THE BLIND DEAD
See: *Return of the Evil Dead.*

ATTACK OF THE CRAB MONSTERS
★★★ Sinister Cinema, 1957, NR, 64 min. Dir: Roger Corman. Cast: Richard Garland, Pamela Duncan, Russell Johnson, Leslie Bradley, Mel Welles, Ed Nelson.

An irresistibly cheap '50s classic about scientists investigating atomic activity on a Pacific atoll and falling victim to huge mutant crabs with the ability to absorb the minds of their victims. Genuinely suspenseful in places, with Corman achieving an air of menace not even negated by the fact that the crab monsters are just about the stupidest creatures ever to scuddle across the screen on visible sneakers—one of the sneaker wearers is rumored to be Jack Nicholson!

ATTACK OF THE 50-FOOT WOMAN
★★☆ Fox Video, 1958, NR, 66 min. Dir: Nathan Hertz [Nathan Juran]. Cast: Allison Hayes, William Hudson, Yvette Vickers, Roy Gordon.

Legendary '50s idiocy beautifully marrying soap opera silliness with some of the tattiest special effects on record, everything draped about the shoulders of titanic Hayes in her most famous role. As bitchy, neglected heiress Nancy Archer, Allison is transformed into a sheet-swarthed giant through contact with a huge bald alien and uses her newfound size and strength to avenge herself on her two-timing hubby, Harry (Hudson). Not really a good movie, but think of it as an early cinematic feminist manifesto with crummy FX and you'll do just fine.

ATTACK OF THE 50-FOOT WOMAN
★★ HBO Video, 1993, NR, 89 min. Dir: Christopher Guest. Cast: Daryl Hannah, Daniel Baldwin, William Windom, Paul Benedict, Hilary Shepard.

This made-for-cable remake is a more intentional comedy than was the original but, despite the improved FX work, really isn't superior. Hannah is the manipulated heiress who gets back at her controlling father and husband once she gains skyscraper height, but this time the feminist subtext is more prominent and more heavy-handed, making this much less fun than the unpretentious original.

ATTACK OF THE GIANT LEECHES
★★☆ Sinister Cinema, 1958, NR, 62 min. Dir: Bernard L. Kowalski. Cast: Ken Clarke, Yvette

---

ALLISON HAYES
(1930–1977)

Hayes was a statuesque '50s leading lady and model whose beauty and talent graced many a B epic of the period. A good actress, she was rarely given material worthy of her abilities, with her most (in)famous role being the lead in the legendary *Attack of the 50-Foot Woman*.

The Undead ('57), *Zombies of Mora Tau* ('57), *The Unearthly* ('57), *The Disembodied* ('57), *Attack of the 50-Foot Woman* ('58), *The Hypnotic Eye* ('60), *The Crawling Hand* ('63).

Vickers, Jan Shepard, Michael Emmet, Bruno Ve Sota, Gene Roth.

Man-sized leeches spawned by atomic radiation menace the poor-white-trash dwellers of a Florida swamp, occasionally dragging some poor boob into their underwater cave to drain him of blood. Though the monster suits are so lousy you can actually see the actors' air tanks underneath, this grungy American international flick provides a minor kick thanks to solid acting (especially Vickers in her best role as Ve Sota's sex kitten wife) and some surprisingly grisly moments. Aka *The Giant Leeches* and *Demons of the Swamp*.

ATTACK OF THE HORNY GORILLA
See: *A*P*E*.

ATTACK OF THE KILLER TOMATOES
★★ Media Home Entertainment, 1978, PG, 86 min.
Dir: John De Bello. Cast: David Miller, Sharon Tyler, Jack Riley, George Wilson, Eric Christmas.

One of those "It's so dumb, it's fun" cheap comedies, this one spoofs 1950s monster epics with the tomatoes of the world growing large and deadly, jumping out of glasses of V-8, chasing people down city streets, and even inundating a pretty swimmer á la *Jaws*. Sometimes recaptures the shoddy look and feel of the old films, although many of them are much funnier—though they usually don't mean to be. Sequels: *Return of the Killer Tomatoes, Killer Tomatoes Strike Back!* and *Killer Tomatoes Eat France!*

ATTACK OF THE MAYAN MUMMY
☆ Sinister Cinema, 1963, NR, 77 min.
Dirs: Jerry Warren and Rafael Portillo. Cast: Richard Webb, Nina Knight, John Burton, Steve Conte, Bruno Ve Sota, Emma Roland, Ramon Gay, Rosita Arenas.

Listen up, as this gets kinda complicated. Schlockmeister Warren took a nice, harmless little Mexican monster movie called *The Aztec Mummy* and then, seven years after its production, "Americanized" it by adding boring new footage of people sitting around and talking out the plot (saves on dubbing) after the fact—the original Mexican cast isn't even credited! The Aztecs are now the Mayans—what's in a culture?—but everything else is the usual curses and tombs and reincarnation—at least, as far as you can make out. For more Warren reedited Mexi-monster madness, see *Creature of the Walking Dead, Curse of the Stone Hand,* and *Face of the Screaming Werewolf*.

ATTACK OF THE MONSTERS
See: *Gamera vs. Guiron*.

ATTACK OF THE SWAMP CREATURE
☆ Thrillervideo, 1972, PG, 92 min.
Dir: Don Barton. Cast: Marshall Grauer, Sanna Ringhaver, Paul Galloway, Wade Popwell.

A dumpy, middle-aged scientist with all the charisma of Elmer Fudd transforms himself into an amphibious catfish monster in this mundane '50s throwback. Better known as both *Zaat* and *Blood Waters of Dr. Z* (and presented here with pseudonymous credits), this is the worst filmed-in-Florida horror movie ever—and with competition like *Island Claws,* that's saying a real mouthful.

ATTIC, THE
★★☆ Unicorn Home Video, 1980, PG, 92 min.
Dir: George Edwards. Cast: Carrie Snodgress, Ray Milland, Rosemary Murphy, Ruth Cox, Marjorie Eaton, Patrick Brennan.

Fragile Snodgress is excellent as a spinster caring for venom-spitting crippled dad Milland. She discovers not only that is he faking his paralysis but that he murdered her long-missing fiance, whose withered corpse she finds in the attic. Curtis Harrington associate Edwards directed this semi-sequel to Harrington's *The Killing Kind* (with Snodgress in the Luana Anders role) with a nice eye for detail. It's sometimes unintentionally funny, but has a faded elegance perfectly suited to its tragic characters and their wasted lives.

AUDREY ROSE
★★☆ MGM/UA Home Video, 1977, PG, 113 min.
Dir: Robert Wise. Cast: Marsha Mason, Anthony Hopkins, John Beck, Susan Swift, Norman Lloyd, John Hillerman, Robert Walden, Philip Sterling.

Somber variation on the usual '70s possession shocker done in the style of a Val Lewton thriller. Weird Hopkins tries to convince Manhattanites Mason and Beck that their troubled daughter is the reincarnation of his own dead child, Audrey Rose. Mason comes to accept this but Beck's bone-headed stubbornness leads to tragedy. Wise's commanding use of wide-screen framing suffers on the tube, and the acting, apart from the always terrific Hopkins, tends to be overwrought, but the film does hold one's interest, though it almost loses it during the ridiculously drawn-out courtroom climax.

AUNTIE LEE'S MEAT PIES

★☆ Columbia/Tristar Home Video, 1990, R, 100 min. Dir: Joseph F. Robertson. Cast: Karen Black, Pat Morita, Pat Paulsen, Huntz Hall, Michael Berryman, Teri Weigel, Kristine Rose, Ava Fabian.

Robertson, producer of classic drek like *The Slime People* and *The Crawling Hand,* directs this mostly worthless Sweeney Todd knockoff with a touch or two of *Arsenic and Old Lace.* Black runs a boarding house where guests end up as ingredients of her popular pot pies. The talented comic cast is given very little to work with.

AUTOPSY

★★ Prism Entertainment, 1974, R, 95 min. Dir: Armando Crispino. Cast: Mimsy Farmer, Barry Primus, Ray Lovelock, Gaby Wagner, Angela Goodwin.

Grisly murder mystery about a med student (Farmer) doing a thesis on suicide who discovers that a wave of suicides currently sweeping Rome—and blamed on sun-spot activity—are actually murders. This undistinguished Argento clone has a moody Ennio Morricone score and some pretty graphic sequences (involving a real autopsy that later turned up in *Faces of Death II* and a dream scene where corpses come to life to have sex on an embalming table) cut from some prints, but is otherwise pretty missable. Aka *Macchie Solari: Sun Spots.*

AVENGER, THE

★★☆ Sinister Cinema, 1960, NR, 90 min. Dir: Karl Anton. Cast: Heinz Drache, Ingrid van Bergen, Klaus Kinski, Rainer Brandt, Ina Duscha, Maria Litto.

Originally titled *Der Raecher: The Headhunter,* this is the first of a lengthy series of German Edgar Wallace mystery-horror films—or *krimis,* as they were called in their country of origin—shot throughout the '60s and early '70s. This one involves the making of a mystery movie disrupted by a psycho head-chopper

with a fatal fixation on the film's leading lady (van Bergen) and has a good role for Kinski, in his first of many krimi appearances, as an egotistical screenwriter who loses his head. Not bad, with atmosphere and plot devices that obviously influenced other filmmakers like Bava and Argento.

AVENGING CONSCIENCE, THE

★★☆ Sinister Cinema, 1914, NR, 78 min. Dir: D. W. Griffith. Cast: Henry B. Walthall, Blanche Sweet, Mae Marsh, Robert Harron, Ralph Lewis, Spottiswoode Aiken.

One of the earliest film adaptations of an Edgar Allan Poe story, this silent variation on "The Tell-Tale Heart" has Walthall as an obsessed young man who murders crotchety old uncle Aiken when the latter refuses to allow him to marry Sweet, his "Annabel Lee." Eventually guilt over the crime drives Walthall mad. With striking editing and photography, this is visually arresting but a bit of a strain for the modern viewer.

AVENGING SPIRIT

See: *Dominique is Dead.*

AWAKENING, THE

★★ Warner Home Video, 1980, R, 102 min. Dir: Mike Newell. Cast: Charlton Heston, Stephanie Zimbalist, Susannah York, Jill Townsend, Patrick Drury, Bruce Myers.

Dreary big-budget remake of the crackerjack Hammer quickie *Blood From the Mummy's Tomb* with a stoic Heston (from that period when all the big stars were doing horror films) miscast as a British archeologist whose teen daughter (Zimbalist) is possessed by the evil spirit of an ancient Egyptian queen. This borrows a lot from *The Exorcist* and *The Omen* (and little from its source novel, Bram Stoker's *The Jewel of Seven Stars*) and has lots of scriptural loose ends but *is* graced by Jack Cardiff's beautifully rich photography and a fine score by Claude Bolling.

AWFUL DR. ORLOF, THE

★★☆ Sinister Cinema, 1962, NR, 86 min. Dir: Jess [Jesus] Franco. Cast: Howard Vernon, Perla Cristal, Conrado San Martin, Diana Lorys, Riccardo Valle, Maria Silva.

Franco's first big hit was this OK Spanish rip-off of *The Horror Chamber of Dr. Faustus* with Vernon as a surgeon searching for the proper face to restore the lost looks of his disfigured daughter. Well-photographed and Vernon is good. This was the first of an entire series of Orlof(f) Euro-thrillers. Aka *Gritos en la Noche:*

Cries in the Night; first sequel: *Dr. Orloff's Monster.*

AXE, THE
See: *The California Axe Massacre.*

AZTEC MUMMY, THE
See: *Attack of the Mayan Mummy.*

AZTEC MUMMY VS. THE HUMAN ROBOT, THE
See: *The Robot vs. the Aztec Mummy.*

BABY, THE
★★☆ WesternWorld Video, 1972, R, 86 min. Dir: Ted Post. Cast: Ruth Roman, Anjanette Comer, Marianna Hill, Suzanne Zenor, David Manzy, Michael Pataki.

Well-acted weirdness about a social worker (Comer) who becomes obsessed with the case of Baby (Manzy), the teen son of man-hater Roman, who keeps the kid in diapers and mentally undeveloped beyond the infant stage. Sometimes funny, sometimes oddly touching, and with good acting, but the silly surprise ending will make your jaw hit the floor.

BABYSITTER, THE
★★☆ HBO Video, 1980, NR, 96 min. Dir: Peter Medak. Cast: Patty Duke, William Shatner, Stephanie Zimbalist, John Houseman, Quinn Cummings, David Wallace.

Decent psychological chiller about a teenaged housekeeper (Zimbalist) who preys upon the weaknesses of her employers and turns dangerously psychotic when they attempt to break free of her domination. A commanding performance from Zimbalist and some eerie moods keep this tele-movie humming.

BAD BLOOD
See: *A Woman Obsessed.*

BAD CHANNELS
★ Paramount Home Video, 1992, R, 86 min. Dir: Ted Nicolaou. Cast: Martha Quinn, Paul Hipp,

Charlie Spradling, Aaron Lustig, Ian Patrick Williams, Melissa Behr.

One of the absolute worst movies to come from Charles Band's Full Moon stables, this has an alien monster (whose head looks like a mass of melted black vinyl) taking over a small-town radio station and shrinkin' good-lookin' babes to imprison in glass tubes. Why? I don't know and I don't care, either. A real dud with a few snatches of Blue Oyster Cult on the soundtrack and some of the cheesiest FX you've ever seen. Sort-of sequel: *Dollman vs. Demonic Toys.*

BAD DREAMS
★★ CBS/Fox Video, 1988, R, 84 min. Dir: Andrew Flemyng. Cast: Jennifer Rubin, Bruce Abbott, Richard Lynch, Harris Yulin, Dean Cameron, Elizabeth Dailey, Susan Ruttan, Louis Giambalvo, Susan Barnes, Sy Richardson.

Derivative *Nightmare on Elm Street* rip (stealing most of its ideas from *Nightmare 3*) about a '70s hippy (Rubin) who awakens from a 15-year coma to be stalked by the ghost—or is it?—of her dead commune leader (Lynch). Gory and with a good cast, but the twist ending gives new meaning to the word Huh?

BAD RONALD
★★☆ International Video Entertainment, 1974, NR, 74 min. Dir: Buzz Kulik. Cast: Scott Jacoby, Kim Hunter, Dabney Coleman, Pippa Scott, Cindy Eilbacher, Lisa Eilbacher, Cindy Fisher, John Larch, Aneta Corseaut, Linda Watkins.

Peculiar TV movie with Jacoby as a crazy teen hidden away in a secret room by mom Hunter after he accidentally kills a neighbor girl. After Hunter dies, the house is sold and a new family moves in, not realizing that there's a psycho lurking behind the walls. About as credulity-stretching as you can get, but sympathetic playing and several offbeat elements keep your interest up.

BAD SEED, THE
★★★ Warner Home Video, 1956, NR, 129 min. Dir: Mervyn LeRoy. Cast: Nancy Kelly, Patty McCormack, Eileen Heckart, Henry Jones, Evelyn Varden, William Hopper, Paul Fix, Jesse White.

Still pretty potent "Hollywoodized" version of Maxwell Anderson's play, from William March's novel, about an amoral eight-year-old (McCormack) who commits calculated, cold-blooded murder for personal gain and the terrified mother (Kelly) who discovers her daughter's secret. Kelly and Heckart (the latter in an Oscar-winning turn) overdo but Patty is perfection as the evil little Rhoda (calmly playing "Clair de lune" on the piano while one victim burns to death). The tacked-on shock ending, added to appease the censors, actually works quite well. Remade for television in 1985.

BAD TASTE

★★☆ Magnum Home Entertainment, 1987, UR, 87 min. Dir: Peter Jackson. Cast: Mike Minett, Terry Potter, Pete O'Herne, Craig Smith, Doug Wren, Peter Jackson.

At last, a movie that lives up to its title! Cannibalistic aliens (who drink each other's vomit and look about as extraterrestrial as the residents of Hooterville) invade New Zealand and are battled by a trio of dimwitted government agents with the combined IQ of a block of wood. Virtually plotless, this good-natured gore comedy has gallons of blood, loads of loose limbs, and more bullet hits than in the entire Steven Seagal filmography. Too bad the heavy accents and lack of interesting characters make this energetically directed movie, a sort-of splatter *The Adventures of Buckaroo Banzai,* such a trial to sit through. Jackson's *Dead Alive* is much more like it.

BAFFLED!

★★ Avid Entertainment, 1972, NR, 91 min. Dir: Philip Leacock. Cast: Leonard Nimoy, Susan Hampshire, Vera Miles, Rachel Roberts, Valerie Taylor, Jewel Blanch, Angharad Rees, Ray Brooks.

Contrived TV movie with Nimoy as a race driver with ESP who uses his ability to help the young daughter of a film star menaced by a mystery stalker at a British seaside resort. Looking like an extended episode of the old Gary Collins series *The Sixth Sense,* this has a strong cast and a good surprise ending but is dully directed.

BANANA MONSTER, THE

★★★ WesternWorld Video, 1972, PG, 80 min. Dir: John Landis. Cast: John Landis, Eliza Garrett, Saul Kahn, Eric Allison, E.G. Hardy, Charles Villiers.

Originally called *Schlock,* Landis' first film is a funny spoof of the Joan Crawford classic *Trog* about a prehistoric ape man terrorizing a California tract home community. Landis himself wears Rick Baker's Schlockthropus suit, and some of his reactions to his various encounters with modern civilization are priceless. Aka *The Banana Murders,* this has many inspired bits of lunacy (though, like *Airplane,* it eventually gets to be a bit much), with spoofs of everything from *King Kong* and *Frankenstein* to *2001* and *Elvira Madigan,* not to mention the omnipresent Forrest J. Ackerman cameo.

BANANA MURDERS, THE
See: *The Banana Monster.*

BANKER, THE

★★ Virgin Vision, 1989, R, 95 min. Dir: William Webb. Cast: Robert Forster, Duncan Regehr, Shanna Reed, Richard Roundtree, Jeff Conaway, Leif Garrett.

Cop Forster investigates a series of hooker murders in which the victims are run through with a crossbow bolt and eventually traces them to Wall Street businessman Regehr. The image of a Brooks Brothers–suited psycho and an above-average exploitation cast help this by-the-book thriller.

BARN OF THE NAKED DEAD
See: *Terror Circus.*

BARON BLOOD

★★☆ HBO Video, 1972, PG, 90 min. Dir: Mario Bava. Cast: Joseph Cotten, Elke Sommer, Antonio Cantafora, Massimo Girotti, Rada Rassimov, Alan Collins.

Atmosphere-laced Italian chiller about an evil, disfigured Austrian nobleman accidentally resurrected during the restoration of his castle. Bava's overuse of his zoom lens is self-defeating, but his dense milieu of swirling mists and colored lighting is typically inspired. Aka *The Torture Chamber of Baron Blood,* the slightly longer European print has more explicit violence and a different musical score and is available on the Redemption video label.

BARON OF TERROR, THE
See: *The Brainiac.*

BARRACUDA

★ VidAmerica, 1978, PG, 90 min. Dir: Harry Kerwin. Cast: Wayne David Crawford, Jason Evers, Roberta Leighton, Bert Freed, Cliff Emmich.

Fishermen fall prey to a killer barracuda transformed by toxic radiation in this dull *Jaws* clone designed for your less discriminating drive-in patrons. Aka *The Lucifer Project,* this is about as much fun as being locked in the trunk on $2-a-carload night.

BASIC INSTINCT

★★★ LIVE Home Video, 1992, UR, 127 min. Dir: Paul Verhoeven. Cast: Michael Douglas, Sharon Stone, George Dzundza, Jeanne Tripplehorn, Leilani Sarelle, Dorothy Malone.

After the brutal sex-slaying of a wealthy ex-rock star, Frisco cop Douglas becomes involved with the chief suspect: amoral, bisexual, cool-as-an-ice-pick mystery author Stone.

This *very* politically incorrect thriller is too convoluted as a mystery (owing a lot of uncredited influence from Argento's *Unsane*) but has plenty of bravura scenes of graphic sex and violence (one elevator slashing is lifted directly from DePalma's *Dressed to Kill*) and a marvelously sexy/creepy turn from Stone in what may amount to a definitive role. With an atmospheric Pino Donaggio–inspired score by Jerry Goldsmith and a scene with Ashley Laurence in *Hellraiser* playing on TV, the unrated version differs from the R theatrical cut only in about a half minute's worth of nudity—including a brief frontal of Mike.

BASKET CASE

★★★ Video Treasures, 1982, UR, 90 min. Dir: Frank Henenlotter. Cast: Kevin Van Hentenryck, Terri Susan Smith, Beverly Bonner, Robert Vogel, Diana Browne, Lloyd Pace.

This crude charmer tells the tale of Duane Bradley (Van Hentenryck), a handsome young lad who brings his deformed former Siamese twin brother, Belial, to NYC in a wicker laundry basket to seek revenge on the doctors who separated them and left poor Belial for dead. Extremely gory (try to avoid the 83-minute R-rated cut) but also very funny, with authentically sleazy 42nd Street atmosphere and lots of oddly likable characters.

BASKET CASE 2

★★☆ Shapiro-Glickenhaus Entertainment, 1990, R, 89 min. Dir: Frank Henenlotter. Cast: Kevin Van Hentenryck, Annie Ross, Heather Rattray, Kathryn Meisle, Ted Sorel, Jason Evers.

Those fabulous Bradley boys are back in this fun if less-than-necessary sequel. Duane and Belial—the former looking surprisingly chipper for a guy who was castrated, slashed, and tossed out an upstairs window at the end of the last outing—take up with Long Island freak-lover Granny Ruth (well-limned by Ross) and eventually take an appropriate revenge on the heartless tabloid reporters out to exploit them. Even more of a comedy than its predecessor, this runs out of steam about a reel before the climax but still gets the job done. The final twist is deliciously ironic.

BASKET CASE 3: THE PROGENY

★★ MCA/Universal Home Video, 1991, R, 90 min. Dir: Frank Henenlotter. Cast: Kevin Van Hentenryck, Annie Ross, Gil Roper, Tina Louise Hilbert, Dan Biggers, Jim O'Doherty.

Belial and his equally twisted lady friend Eve birth a beastly brood in this sometimes broadly funny third entry in the series. Not as strongly scripted as parts one and two and often needlessly mean-spirited, but made watchable by some good bits (like Ross singing "Personality" backed by an all-freak band and a side-splitting parody of "Geraldo") and a wonderfully ingratiating performance from Van Hentenryck.

BAT, THE

★★★ Sinister Cinema, 1926, NR, 103 min. Dir: Roland West. Cast: Louise Fazenda, Jack Pickford, Emily Fitzroy, Eddie Gribben, Robert McKim, Sojin.

The first and best version of Mary Roberts Rhinehart's popular thunderstorm mystery play, this beautifully cinematic silent about a hooded fiend searching an old estate for a hidden treasure is corny but imaginative, with clever photography and set design. Remade in 1930 as *The Bat Whispers* and again under the original title in 1959.

BAT, THE

★★ Goodtimes Home Video, 1959, NR, 80 min. Dir: Crane Wilbur. Cast: Vincent Price, Agnes Moorehead, Gavin Gordon, John Sutton, Lenita Lane, Elaine Edwards, Darla Hood, John Bryant.

Bland remake with Moorehead as a mystery author who rents for the summer an old mansion haunted by a black-masked and clawed figure known as "The Bat," who's after some stolen bank funds. Price is wasted in the sort of red-herring role Bela Lugosi used to play in the '40s, while former "Little Rascals" star Hood is seen as one of the maniac's victims.

BAT PEOPLE, THE

★☆ HBO Video, 1974, PG, 95 min. Dir: Jerry Jameson. Cast: Stewart Moss, Marianne McAndrew, Michael Pataki, Paul Carr, Arthur Space, Pat Delaney.

Patently awful American International chiller with Moss as a young scientist bitten on his honeymoon by a rabid bat, thereafter periodically transforming into a killer bat-thing. Prettily photographed, but it's hard to imagine a duller monster movie than this, with Stan Winston's effective bat-creature design barely glimpsed. Filmed as *It Lives By Night*, even exploitation vet Pataki (as a lecherous sheriff) can't save it.

BAT WHISPERS, THE

★★☆ Sinister Cinema, 1930, NR, 90 min. Dir: Roland West. Cast: Chester Morris, Una Merkel, Grayce Hampton, Maude Eburne, Gustav von Seyffertitz, Hugh Huntley.

Enjoyable sound remake of the original version of *The Bat,* from the same director, with yet another black-shrouded stalker on the loose. The acting and pacing are typical of an early talkie, stilted and slow, but there are some truly spectacular camera moves and lots of old-fashioned spooky movie atmosphere.

BAY COVEN
See: *Eye of the Demon.*

BAY OF BLOOD
★★★ Gorgon Video, 1971, R, 84 min.
Dir: Mario Bava. Cast: Claudine Auger, Luigi Pistilli, Claudio Volonté, Laura Betti, Anna Maria Rosati, Chris Avram, Brigitte Skay, Isa Miranda.

Bava single-handedly invented the "Body Count" subgenre with this stylish, graphically gory whodunit, better known as *Twitch of the Death Nerve.* When wheelchair-ridden Countess Federica (Miranda) is garrotted by her conniving husband, this sets off a string of gruesome homicides as various interested parties vie for her valuable bayside estate. Fans of the *Friday the 13th* series will be amazed at how much those movies (not to mention *Halloween, Dressed to Kill,* and scores of others) stole from this seminal slasher. From machetes to the face, to beheading by ax, to a couple lanced by a mariner's spear, to some of the costuming (including inspirations for Betsy Palmer's sweater in *Friday* and Angie Dickinson's white-on-white outfit in *Dressed*), this bad-boy has everything. Add to this Mario's trademark zooming, swirling camerawork, a lush Stelvio Cipriani score, and Skay in the shortest miniskirt known to civilized man, and you've got a full evening's entertainment and then some. Aka *Antefatteo: Before the Fact, The Ecology of Crime, Carnage, Bloodbath,* and *The Last House on the Left, Part II* (!!).

BEACH GIRLS AND THE MONSTER, THE
★ Sinister Cinema, 1964, NR, 70 min. Dir: Jon Hall. Cast: Jon Hall, Sue Casey, Walter Edmiston, Arnold Lessing, Elaine Du Pont, Read Morgan.

Forties star Hall made an ill-advised comeback directing himself in this laugh-riot tale of the terrible consequences of adolescent sloth. Big Jon is a scientist who despises the rockin' teens who hang with his son near Hall's beachfront Malibu home and takes the obvious action: he dresses up in a seaweed suit and big rubber fish head and begins doing them all in. Not that this is gonna put a stop to these kids' fun; they even have a nighttime hootenanny on the very spot where one beach bunny—named Bunny, no less—bought it. Needless to say, this pisses our hero off no end. With plenty of surfing scenes (some of them in color), a swingin' Frank Sinatra, Jr., score, and a monster that looks like an escapee

from *Sesame Street,* this is one turkey you don't have to wait until Thanksgiving to enjoy. Shown on TV as *Monster From the Surf,* and aka *Surf Terror.*

BEAKS—THE MOVIE
★ Imperial Entertainment, 1987, R, 87 min.
Dir: René Cardona, Jr. Cast: Christopher Atkins, Michelle Johnson, Sonia Infanté, Salvador Pineda, Carol Connery, Gabriele Tinti.

As opposed to what—*Beaks—The Nose*? A real bird-brained Hitchcock rip-off with flocks of feathered fiends attacking people all over the globe (well, okay, in Spanish-speaking countries all over the globe), the catastrophe investigated by pouty TV reporter Johnson and her terminally grinning cameraman Atkins. Filmed as *Birds of Prey,* this is a really lame attempt to make pigeons look scary, with a couple of gory insert shots of eyes being gouged out but mostly just ludicrous slow-motion scenes of people running, screaming, and being pecked.

BEAST, THE
See: *Equinox.*

BEAST FROM HAUNTED CAVE, THE
★★☆ Sinister Cinema, 1959, NR, 64 min.
Dir: Monte Hellman. Cast: Sheila Carol, Michael Forest, Frank Wolff, Richard Sinatra, Wally Campo, Chris Robinson.

What starts out as a gangster-heist picture ingeniously flips around into a spooky monster pic about a huge, cobwebby spider-thing preying on those who trespass near its Colorado cave. Good performing and some really creepy moments make this one of the better Filmgroup horrors. Future *General Hospital* star Robinson plays the beast in a suit of his own design.

BEAST FROM 20,000 FATHOMS, THE
★★★ Warner Home Video, 1953, NR, 80 min.
Dir: Eugene Lourie. Cast: Paul Christian, Paula Raymond, Cecil Kellaway, Kenneth Tobey, Donald Woods, Lee Van Cleef.

Archtypical '50s monster-on-the-loose tale (based on "The Foghorn" by Ray Bradbury) about a prehistoric "Rhedosaurus" awakened from its arctic ice tomb by atomic testing. Eventually the beast heads for New York, where it terrorizes Wall Street and dies in the midst of a blazing Coney Island rollercoaster. Superb Ray Harryhausen special effects belie this film's low ($120,000) cost. Kellaway is amusing as an impish paleontologist eaten by the monster. The obvious inspiration for

Godzilla, King of the Monsters, this was more-or-less remade by Lourie as both *The Giant Behemoth* and *Gorgo.*

BEAST IN THE CELLAR, THE

★★ Cannon Home Video, 1971, R, 87 min. Dir: James Kelly. Cast: Beryl Reid, Flora Robson, Tessa Wyatt, John Hamill, T.P. McKenna, Dafydd Harvard.

The performances of venerable British character actresses Reid and Robson slightly elevate this otherwise mundane movie about a series of murders at an army base traced to a mysterious bricked-up room in the ladies' basement. Choppy and perplexing (due in part from pre-release cutting from 101 minutes), though when these actresses have the screen to themselves there are moments to treasure. Aka *Are You Dying, Young Man?* and *Young Man, I Think You're Dying!*

BEAST MUST DIE, THE

★★☆ JTC Video, 1974, PG, 93 min. Dir: Paul Annett. Cast: Calvin Lockhart, Peter Cushing, Marlene Clark, Charles Gray, Anton Diffring, Ciaran Madden.

Enjoyable Amicus adaptation of the James Blish story "There Shall Be No Darkness" about a big-game hunter (Lockhart) who invites a select group of jet-setters to his remote estate in the hope that one of them is

---

RAY HARRYHAUSEN
(1922–)

The modern master of stop-motion animation effects, Ray was inspired to his career by a boyhood viewing of *King Kong.* He would eventually work with *Kong* FX man Willis O'Brien in *Mighty Joe Young* and create an imaginative body of work of his own from the '50s through the '80s. Although today's computer-generated FX have easily surpassed Harryhausen's hands-on approach, they usually lack his spark of human personality and charm.

Mighty Joe Young ('49), *The Beast From 20,000 Fathoms* ('53), *It Came From Beneath the Sea* ('55), *The Animal World* ('56), *Earth vs. the Flying Saucers* ('56), *Twenty Million Miles to Earth* ('57), *The 7th Voyage of Sinbad* ('58), *The Three Worlds of Gulliver* ('60), *Mysterious Island* ('61), *Jason and the Argonauts* ('63), *The First Men in the Moon* ('64), *One Million Years B.C.* ('67), *The Valley of Gwangi* ('69), *The Golden Voyage of Sinbad* ('74), *Sinbad and the Eye*

---

the only prey he's never faced—a werewolf. Bland direction and lots of ugly mid-'70s fashions but the cast is in grand form and there's even a "Guess the Werewolf Break" à la *Homicidal's* infamous "Fright Break." Aka *Black Werewolf.*

BEAST OF MOROCCO

★★ Sinister Cinema, 1966, NR, 86 min. Dir: Frederic Goode. Cast: William Sylvester, Diane Clare, Aliza Gur, Edward Underdown, Terence de Marney.

Sylvester is excellent in this fatalistic low-budget British chiller about a widower in Casablanca who falls under the spell of a gorgeous vampire princess whose tomb has recently been excavated. Slow and suffering from an anemic supporting cast (apart from de Marney as a lascivious vampire slave who rots in the sunlight) but there are some good parts, including an imaginative credit sequence. British title: *The Hand of Night.*

BEAST OF THE YELLOW NIGHT

★★☆ Edde Entertainment, 1971, PG, 87 min. Dir: Eddie Romero. Cast: John Ashley, Mary Wilcox, Leopoldo Salcedo, Eddie Garcia, Vic Diaz.

One of Romero's better pictures, this has the ubiquitous Ashley as a WWII army deserter who sells his soul to the devil (Diaz) for immortality. Ashley's soul then passes from body to body until he genuinely falls in love with his latest host's wife (Wilcox). His punishment for these reawakened emotions is to transform nightly into a crusty-faced monster that rampages through Manila. No classic but much more watchable than most Filipino horror junk, with plot elements predating Warren Beatty's *Heaven Can Wait* and a lot of gore for a PG-rated movie.

BEAST OF YUCCA FLATS, THE

☆ Sinister Cinema, 1960, NR, 60 min. Dir: Coleman Francis. Cast: Tor Johnson, Douglas Mellor, Barbara Francis, Tony Cardoza.

Tor's last starring role casts him as a Soviet scientist mutated into a "monster" by an atomic blast in this infamous Z movie. Like *The Creeping Terror,* this features little dialogue and lots of ponderous narration and is only worth seeing for completists who'll sit through *anything.*

BEAST WITH FIVE FINGERS, THE

★★★ MGM/UA Home Video, 1946, NR, 88 min. Dir: Robert Florey. Cast: Peter Lorre, Robert Alda, Andrea King, Victor Francen, J. Carrol Naish, Charles Dingle.

An Italian villa in the early 20th century is terrorized by the living dismembered hand of a famous concert pianist—or so it seems. The last straight Hollywood horror film produced during the 1940's, this moody gothic piece is easily Florey's best work, with outstanding FX and photography, a manic Lorre at his most eye-bulging, and a pleasantly nonstereotypical supporting cast. Based on William Fryer Harvey's story "The Beast," this is let down only by a dumb ending that actually spoofs the entire picture—much like that of *The Ape Man*, not a movie you want as inspiration. Luis Buñuel allegedly helped with the crawling hand sequences, which may account for their creepy effectiveness.

BEAST WITHIN, THE

★★☆ MGM/UA Home Video, 1982, R, 98 min. Dir: Philippe Mora. Cast: Ronny Cox, Bibi Besch, Paul Clemens, Don Gordon, Kitty Moffatt, R. G. Armstrong, L. Q. Jones, Luke Askew.

Tom Holland scripted this '50s-type monster movie, from Edward Levy's novel about a woman (Besch) raped by some half-human thing while passing through a small southern town on her honeymoon. Seventeen years later her son (Clemens) returns to town and goes on a killing spree while turning into some weird insectoid monster. Fun to watch, this makes little sense but is enlivened considerably by its hammy acting, rubber-balloon makeup FX by Tom Burman, and unacknowledged similarities to the Hammer Films' classic *The Curse of the Werewolf.*

BEDLAM

★★★ Turner Home Entertainment, 1946, NR, 79 min. Dir: Mark Robson. Cast: Boris Karloff, Anna Lee, Richard Fraser, Billy House, Glenn Vernon, Ian Wolfe, Jason Robards, Sr., Elizabeth Russell.

The last of the Val Lewton psychological horror films, this is a rich, if somewhat pretentious, period drama about a willful young actress (Lee) falsely committed to the infamous asylum of Our Lady of Bethlehem, commonly called Bedlam, by its cruel superintendent (Karloff), the latter ending up bricked up alive behind a wall by the vengeful inmates. Complex performances and good period detail help make up for the general lack of hard horror, with Karloff in one of his best roles as the purringly evil asylum master.

BEDROOM WINDOW, THE

★★☆ Video Treasures, 1987, R, 113 min. Dir: Curtis Hanson. Cast: Steve Guttenberg, Elizabeth McGovern, Isabelle Huppert, Paul Shenar, Wallace Shawn, Carl Lumbly, Frederick Coffin, Brad Greenquist.

Modestly entertaining Hitchcockian horror about an ad exec (Guttenberg) whose affair with his boss' beautiful wife (Huppert) is complicated when she witnesses a near-murder from his bedroom window. Soon both they and the would-be victim (McGovern) are stalked by the psychotic attacker. Very slickly done, with director Hanson managing to recall assorted Hitchcock techniques without openly aping them and good work from the ladies.

BEES, THE

★ Warner Home Video, 1978, PG, 86 min. Dir: Alfredo Zacharias. Cast: John Saxon, Angel Tompkins, John Carradine, Claudio Brook, Alicia Encinias.

Laughable rip-off of *The Swarm* about a cloud of killer bees descending on the States from South America, with scientists Saxon, Tompkins, and Carradine (wadda team!!) finally destroying them by turning them gay! Don't worry, I didn't get it either. A mind-numbing crap classic from the maker of *Demonoid*.

BEETLEJUICE

★★★ Warner Home Video, 1988, PG, 92 min. Dir: Tim Burton. Cast: Michael Keaton, Geena Davis, Alec Baldwin, Winona Ryder, Jeffrey Jones, Catherine O'Hara, Sylvia Sidney, Glenn Shadix, Dick Cavett, Robert Goulet.

Frantic horror comedy about a likable young couple (Davis and Baldwin) who are killed in a freak auto accident and return to haunt their quaint New England home. When an obnoxious nouveau riche family moves in, the inexperienced ghosts turn to the ghoulish "bio-exorcist" Betelgeuse (Keaton) for help. A nonstop barrage of outrageous characters and bizarre sight gags, with Keaton a howl; octogenarian actress Sidney stealing scenes as a sardonic caseworker from Hell; and Oscar-winning makeup FX by Bob Short, Ve Neill, and Steve Laporte. Still Burton's best film; followed by a cartoon series.

BEFORE DAWN

★★ Turner Home Entertainment, 1933, NR, 60 min. Dir: Irving Pichel. Cast: Warner Oland, Stuart Erwin, Dorothy Wilson, Dudley Digges, Frank Reicher, Jane Darwell.

Character actor Pichel (*Dracula's Daughter*) directed this minor '30s old-dark-house chiller based on a story by Edgar Wallace. A series of murders in a gloomy old mansion lead to a supposed haunting and are solved by a girl with psychic abilities. The usual stuff with a good cast of familiar faces.

John Saxon and Angel Tompkins get bugged in The Bees *(1978).*

BEFORE I HANG

★★☆ RCA/Columbia Home Video, 1940, NR, 62 min. Dir: Nick Grindé. Cast: Boris Karloff, Evelyn Keyes, Bruce Bennett, Edward Van Sloan, Ben Taggert, Pedro de Cordoba.

Routine Karloff mad doctor opus about a scientist's experiments with a youth serum derived from a killer's blood. One injection and Boris becomes both a younger man *and* a homicidal maniac. OK B-level thrills with the usual solid casting and budget atmospherics.

BEFORE THE FACT

See: *Bay of Blood.*

BEGUILED, THE

★★★ MCA/Universal Home Video, 1971, R, 109 min. Dir: Don Siegel. Cast: Clint Eastwood, Geraldine Page, Elizabeth Hartman, Jo Ann Harris, Darlene Carr, Melody Thomas, Mae Mercer, Pamelyn Ferdin.

Stylish, offbeat Eastwood vehicle set during the last days of the Civil War. Clint is a wounded northern soldier cared for by a group of lonely, repressed females at a southern girls school. When Eastwood begins manipulating his nursemaids for his own selfish ends, he unknowingly sets the stage for his own destruction. A failure in its day, this richly appointed chiller is like the horrific flip side of *Gone With the Wind*'s honeydewed gentility.

BEHIND THE WALL

See: *The Cold Room.*

BEING, THE

★★☆ HBO Video, 1980, R, 82 min. Dir: Jackie Kong. Cast: Martin Landau, José Ferrer, Dorothy Malone, Ruth Buzzi, Marianne Gordon-Rogers, Rexx Coltrane [William Osco].

Bargain basement bogusity about a lost little boy transformed by nuclear waste into a one-eyed, toothy, slime- spitting monster that chows down on the residents of a small Idaho township. Filmed as *Easter Sunday*, this sounds totally irredeemable, but it's actually fast-paced, funny, and kinda fun, with a cast of familiar faces and a nice line in self-deprecating humor. The monster, though, glimpsed only from the waist up, looks like he's riding around in a shopping cart. Coltraine/Osco was the producer and the director's husband at the time.

BELA LUGOSI MEETS A BROOKLYN GORILLA
★ Admit One Video, 1952, NR, 75 min.
Dir: William Beaudine. Cast: Bela Lugosi, Duke Mitchell, Sammy Petrillo, Charlita, Muriel Landers.

The fading horror cycle, drug addiction, and poor money management finally brought poor Bela to this: starring in a fifth-rate horror comedy opposite a second-rate pair of Martin and Lewis imitators in an old-hat plot about a mad doctor trying to turn a man into an ape. Aka *The Monster Meets the Gorilla* and *The Boys From Brooklyn,* this unfunny spoof is enough to make you cry.

BELA LUGOSI: THE FORGOTTEN KING
★★☆ MPI Home Video, 1987, NR, 55 min.
Dir: Dave Stuckey. Cast: Forrest J. Akerman.

Forry hosts this often overly reverential but otherwise entertaining documentary on Bela's life and times. The usual clips and trailers but with some nice insights into what made the Hungarian horror king tick ("I make a living"). Aka *Lugosi: The Forgotten King* and originally made for PBS!

BELIEVERS, THE
★★☆ CBS/Fox Video, 1987, R, 113 min.
Dir: John Schlesinger. Cast: Martin Sheen, Helen Shaver, Robert Loggia, Harley Cross, Jimmy Smits, Harris Yulin, Elizabeth Wilson, Lee Richardson, Richard Masur, Carla Pinza.

Sheen is a NYC police psychologist who gets mixed up in a series of brutal child murders that turn out to be ritual sacrifices held by a cult of wealthy Santoria worshipers. This mildly diverting combo of *The Exorcist* and *The Possession of Joel Delaney* starts off fine and boasts a couple of really creepy moments—like a horde of spiders bursting from a zit on a possessed Shaver's face—but it soon stumbles into contrivance, with seemingly everyone Sheen knows having some sort of involvement with the cult. Typically fine work from Loggia.

BELL FROM HELL, A
★★☆ Unicorn Home Video, 1973, PG, 97 min.
Dir: Claudio Guerin Hill. Cast: Viveca Lindfors, Renaud Verley, Aflredo Mayo, Maribel Martin, Nuria Gemino, Christine Betzner.

Confusing Spanish psychological thriller about a recently institutionalized young heir with a penchant for macabre practical jokes whose death is plotted by his wheelchair-bound aunt and three beautiful cousins. Not really successful but kept interesting by the offbeat direction of Hill, who, incidentally, fell to his death on the last day of shooting from the bell tower that plays an important part in the film's action.

BELLS
See: *Murder By Phone.*

BE MY VALENTINE, OR ELSE!
See: *Hospital Massacre.*

BEN
★☆ Prism Entertainment, 1972, PG, 93 min.
Dir: Phil Karlson. Cast: Lee H. Montgomery, Joseph Campanella, Meredith Baxter, Rosemary Murphy, Arthur O'Connell, Kaz Garaz, Paul Carr, Kenneth Tobey.

This mostly worthless sequel to *Willard* tries unsuccessfully to wring a few more chills out of a limited formula. Ben and his rat pack befriend a sickly—not to mention sickening—little boy (Montgomery) who lives down the street from *Willard,* the dopey kid not realizing that his new playmates are terrorizing the community. Scenes of Lee H. playing with and—oh, God!—*singing* to Ben are maudlin enough to kill off a roomful of diabetics, and the film totally wastes the vivaciousness of Baxter in her movie debut. "Ben's Theme" was an early solo hit for Michael Jackson; "Beat It!" would have been more appropriate.

BENEATH THE DARKNESS
See: *Humanoids From the Deep.*

BERSERK!
★★☆ Columbia/TriStar Home Video, 1967, NR, 96 min. Dir: Jim O'Connolly. Cast: Joan Crawford, Ty Hardin, Diana Dors, Michael Gough, Judy Geeson, Robert Hardy, Geoffrey Keen, George Claydon.

A leggy Crawford (still looking great in tights at 63!) presides over this gory Herman Cohen product about a gloved killer murdering the performers at Joan's British circus. Gough gets a spike in the head, Dors is sawed in half, Hardin falls onto a bed of bayonets, and the murderer turns out to be . . . well, you only have to see *Strait-Jacket* to figure that one out. My favorite part, though, is Phyllis Allen's Intelligent Poodles. Aka *Circus of Blood.*

BERSERKER
★☆ Starmaker Home Video, 1987, R, 85 min.
Dir: Jef Richard. Cast: Joseph Alan Johnson, Valerie

Sheldon, Greg Dawson, Beth Toussaint, Rodney Montague, George "Buck" Flower.

A quartet of attractive but unsympathetic college types goes camping at a remote spot being terrorized by a berserker, a legendary Nordic werebear used in times past by invading Viking hordes as a sort-of psychotic advance guard. Just what this bearboy is doing in this low-grade *Friday the 13th* clone is one of this film's many unanswered questions. A funny *On Golden Pond* shtick and the welcome presence of Flower, the Gabby Hayes of low-budget horror, provide the sole distractions. Aka *Berserker: The Nordic Curse*.

BEST OF SEX AND VIOLENCE, THE
★★ Wizard Video, 1981, R, 90 min. Dir: Ken Dixon. Cast: John Carradine, David Carradine, Keith Carradine.

Early trailer compilation still being stocked on some video shelves. John and his boys tie together gory bits from a couple of dozen horror-exploitation and soft-core flicks, including *Zombie, The Boogey Man,* and some of the other usual suspects. Not the best of its kind but maybe worth a look for you more undescriminating gorehounds.

BEVERLY HILLS BODYSNATCHERS
★ Shapiro-Glickenhaus Entertainment, 1988, R, 85 min. Dir: Jon Mostow. Cast: Vic Tayback, Frank Gorshin, Rodney Eastman, Brooke Bundey, Warren Seikeo, Art Metrano.

Only those who just *have* to see Vic's final performance will want to suffer though this laughless horror comedy about a mortician (Tayback) and a mad scientist (Gorshin) who team up to find a way to revive the dead, financing their experiments with money borrowed from the local godfather (Metrano). Ultra-lame filmmaking from that era in Hollywood when every comedy had to have the words Beverly Hills in the title.

BEVERLY HILLS VAMP
★★ Vidmark Entertainment, 1988, R, 88 min. Dir: Fred Olen Ray. Cast: Eddie Deezen, Britt Ekland, Tim Conway, Jr., Tom Shell, Brigette Burdine, Robert Quarry, Pat McCormick, Jay Richardson, Michelle Bauer, Jillian Kessner.

Well, at least this is better than *Beverly Hills Bodysnatchers*. One of Ray's more accomplished quickies, this silly comedy has veteran geek Deezen discovering that sultry madam Ekland and her bordello babes are actually a band of vampires. Will anyone listen to him? Would you? And where's "Hard Copy" when you need them? Modest laughs beefed up by a terrific cast of budget thespians.

BEWARE! THE BLOB
See: *Son of Blob.*

BEYOND, THE
See: *7 Doors of Death.*

BEYOND DARKNESS
★ Imperial Entertainment, 1991, R, 94 min. Dir: Clyde Anderson [Carlos Aured]. Cast: Gene LeBrock, Barbara Bingham, David Brandon, Michael Stephenson, Theresa F. Walker, Stephen Brown.

Awful shot-in-the-U.S.-by-Italians (and a Spanish director) *Exorcist/Poltergeist/Amityville* yawner about a family of bad actors—Dad's a minister—who move into a Louisiana country house already inhabited by a bunch of black-veiled old hags and a blinding white light in the attic everyone keeps stupidly referring to as "The Darkness." This annoying hairball of a movie is set to stock musical themes from the same producers' *Witchery,* and just when you think it can't get any worse, it always goes that extra mile.

BEYOND DREAM'S DOOR
★★ Panorama Video, 1989, R, 86 min. Dir: Jay Woelfel. Cast: Nick Balsadare, Susan Pinsky, Rick Kesler, Darby Vasbiner.

Muddled but semi-interesting little vid flick with Baldasare as a college student whose recurrent nightmares turn out to be populated by the victims of a demonic serial killer. This started life as an Ohio State University student project and, although occasionally strained, may be worth a look.

BEYOND EVIL
★★ Video Treasures, 1980, R, 94 min. Dir: Herb Freed. Cast: John Saxon, Lynda Day George, Michael Dante, David Opatoshu, Mario Milano, Janice Lynde.

Standard possession flick about an attractive middle-aged honeymoon couple (Saxon and Day George) whose Caribbean holiday is disrupted when the bride is taken over by the spirit of a vengeful, man-hating witch. Pleasant enough, with cartoony special FX, but you've seen it all before.

BEYOND THE DOOR
★☆ Video Treasures, 1974, R, 94 min. Dir: Oliver Hellman [Ovidio Assonitis]. Cast: Juliet Mills, Richard Johnson, Gabriele Lavia, Barbara Fiorini, David Colin, Jr.

Popular but dumb *Exorcist* clone about a pregnant San Francisco housewife (Mills) who is possessed by the devil, thanks to a satanic pact made by a former lover (Johnson). Shot in some phony-baloney process called "Possess-O-Sound," it gives you all the usual cuss words, vomit, and spinning heads—only twice as loud. Juliet (of *Nanny and the Professor* fame and sis to Hayley) is lovely, but this U.S.-Italian co-production—originally titled *Chi Sei?: Who Are You?* and retitled *Devil Within Her* in England—is still a clunker.

BEYOND THE DOOR II
★★☆ Video Treasures, 1977, R, 92 min.
Dir: Mario Bava. Cast: Daria Nicolodi, John Steiner, David Colin, Jr., Ivan Rassimov.

Totally unrelated to the "original," this pseudo-sequel is actually closer to a cross between *Repulsion* and *The Omen* than *The Exorcist.* Nicolodi is first-rate as a woman whose second marriage, and later sanity, are destroyed by her creepy young son who may—or may not—be possessed by the spirit of his murdered dad. Originally known as *Shock*, this last directorial effort from the great Bava, with assistance from son Lamberto, is sabotaged by poor editing and a weak script, but is full of his trademark rich imagery.

BEYOND THE DOOR III
★★ RCA/Columbia Home Video, 1989, R, 93 min.
Dir: Jeff Kwitney. Cast: Bo Svenson, Mary Kohnert, Victoria Zinny, Savina Gersak, William Geiger, Alex Vitalé.

Beverly (Kohnert) is a shy, virginal college student with a birthmarked belly supposedly marking her as the devil's bride. During a class trip to Yugoslavia a miscast Svenson leads a number of satanists in attacks on Bev and her boring friends aboard a speeding train. Another "What's any of this got to do with parts one and two?" "sequel" mixing devil and disaster movie clichés into a sleek but stupid brew. Good locations and a pretty score; awful acting and heavily trimmed gore scenes.

BEYOND THE FOG
See: *Tower of Evil.*

BEYOND THE GATE
See: *Human Experiments.*

BEYOND THE LIVING
See: *Hospital of Terror.*

BEYOND THE LIVING DEAD
★★ Unicorn Home Video, 1972, R, 89 min.
Dir: John Davidson [José Luis Merino]. Cast: Paul Naschy, Stan Cooper, Dianik Zurakowska, Gerard Tichy, Maria Pia Conté, Charles Quincey.

Routine Naschy nonsense; this time it's his contribution to the post–*Night of the Living Dead* zombie cycle. A 19th-century scientist (Tichy) creates an army of the living dead while Paul hangs around on the sidelines as a red herring ghoul who likes to photograph corpses. Pretty dull until the gory ending kicks in. Aka *La Orgia de los Muertos: Orgy of the Dead, Bracula—The Terror of the Living Dead, Return of the Zombies, House of Terror,* and *The Hanging Woman.*

BIG DUEL IN THE NORTH SEA
See: *Godzilla vs. the Sea Monster.*

BIGFOOT
★☆ Norstar Video, 1970, PG, 84 min.
Dir: Robert F. Slatzer. Cast: Joi Lansing, John Carradine, Chris Mitchum, Lindsay Crosby, James Craig, Judy Jordan, John Mitchum, Doodles Weaver.

Platinum-tressed parachutist Lansing is kidnapped by a tribe of ape-like monsters living in the northwest woods and it's up to a band of beer-guzzling bikers and country cracker Carradine—who's out to exploit the monsters à la *King Kong* and even repeats Robert Armstrong's famous closing line—to rescue her. Though this got the drop on several other bigfoot pics by a couple of years, this lunkhead of a movie has little to recommend it, apart from featuring lots of relatives of the stars.

BIGGEST FIGHT ON EARTH, THE
See: *Ghidrah, the Three-Headed Monster.*

BIG MAN ON CAMPUS
★★☆ Vestron Video, 1989, PG-13, 105 min.
Dir: Jeremy Paul Kagan. Cast: Allan Katz, Corey Parker, Melora Hardin, Tom Skerritt, Jessica Harper, Cindy Williams.

Surprisingly likable teen comic updating of *The Hunchback of Notre Dame* with Katz as the hunched bellringer at a college where prof Skerritt instructs student Parker to "civilize" our modern Quasimodo for extra credit. Boy, talk about grading on a curve! Modestly amusing with a pro cast and witty script penned by Katz.

BIKINI ISLAND
★☆ Prism Entertainment, 1991, R, 85 min.
Dir: Anthony Markes. Cast: Holly Floria, Alicia Anne, Jackson Robinson, Shannon Stiles, Cyndi Pass.

Hot babes gathered at a tropical island for a *Sports Illustrated*–like cheesecake photo session are murdered by a mystery maniac in this predictably low-brow outing. This badly acted time-waster has more cleavage than cleavers.

BILLY THE KID VS. DRACULA

★★ Embassy Home Entertainment, 1965, NR, 73 min. Dir: William Beaudine. Cast: John Carradine, Chuck Courtney, Melinda Plowman, Virginia Christine, Olive Carey, Roy Barcroft.

A kiddie matinee classic with Carradine at his hammiest. The Count arrives in the American West, where he places a pretty young rancher (Plowman) under his spell, not counting on her boyfriend (Courtney) being the newly reformed Billy the Kid. You can't get much cornier than this with great bat-on-a-string special effects and juicy lines like "Oh God, the vampire test!"

BIOHAZARD

★☆ Cinema Group, 1984, R, 78 min. Dir: Fred Olen Ray. Cast: Aldo Ray, Angelique Pettyjohn, Carroll Borland, David Pearson, Richard Hench, William Fair, Loren Crabtree, Christopher Ray.

Typical zero-budget Ray flick blending *E.T.* and *Alien* into this tacky tale of a vicious pint-sized monster (played by the director's young son) rampaging through L.A. Token veterans Ray, Pettyjohn, and Borland look more amused than terrified—especially Aldo, who keeps flubbing his lines. Filmed for about 200 bucks and partly remade as *Deep Space,* this is a slight improvement on Fred's earlier works *The Alien Dead* and *Scalps,* but then, what wouldn't be?

BIOHAZARD

See: *Warning Sign.*

BIRDS, THE

★★★☆ MCA/Universal Home Video, 1963, PG-13, 119 min. Dir: Alfred Hitchcock. Cast: Tippi Hedren, Rod Taylor, Jessica Tandy, Suzanne Pleshette, Veronica Cartwright, Ethel Griffies, Charles McGraw, Ruth McDevitt.

Hitchcock's last classic, this features a debuting Hedren as Melanie Daniels, a headstrong heiress whose arrival in the sleepy California fishing village of Bodega Bay sets off a string of seemingly unrelated bird attacks on both herself and the local populace. Despite stiff acting, contrived situations, and often flat dialogue, the master of suspense manages to ride above it all, thanks to his unerring attention to detail in both picture and sound composition, giving this adaptation of the Daphne Du Maurier story an air of reality unique in the nature-runs-amok subgenre. The then-state-of-the-art FX still hold up quite well too. As for the cameo, look for Hitch and his terriers outside the pet shop.

BIRDS II: LAND'S END, THE

★★ MCA/Universal Home Video, 1994, NR, 83 min. Dir: Rick Rosenthal. Cast: Brad Johnson, Chelsea Field, Tippi Hedren, Jan Rubes, Stephanie Milford, Megan Gallacher.

This belated sequel relocates the action on the East Coast, where more unexplained bird attacks bedevil the folks of a small vacation island. Although Hedren reappears, she plays a different character; everything else, though, is pretty much the same, making this made-for-cable follow-up watchable but eminently forgettable.

BIRDS OF PREY

See: *Beaks—The Movie.*

BIRD WITH THE CRYSTAL PLUMAGE, THE

★★★ Republic Home Video, 1970, PG, 96 min. Dir: Dario Argento. Cast: Tony Musante, Suzy Kendall, Eva Renzi, Enrico Maria Salerno, Mario Adorf, Reggie Nalder.

Argento's first film, this sharply plotted suspenser, derived from the Frederic Brown novel *Screaming Mimi,* has Musante as an American writer adrift in Rome who witnesses a near-murder in an art gallery and then finds both his girlfriend (Kendall) and himself stalked by a maniac whose psychosis is triggered by a macabre painting. A surprise international hit, this crisp cosmopolitan chiller, trimmed slightly for a PG rating, is the perfect starting place for those unacquainted with the Italian maestro's oeuvre. Aka *The Gallery Murders* and *Phantom of Terror.*

BITE, THE

See: *Curse II: The Bite.*

BLACK ABBOT, THE

★★★ Sinister Cinema, 1961, NR, 95 min. Dir: Franz Gottlieb. Cast: Joachim Fuchsberger, Eva Scholtz, Dieter Borsche, Grit Bottcher, Eddi Arent, Klaus Kinski.

A murderous hooded "Abbot" is prowling the grounds of an old English estate and after the heirs to a vast fortune in this well-done German Edgar Wallace flick. Probably the best of Gottlieb's several krimi, with dank atmospherics and a solid cast.

BLACK CAT, THE

★★★☆ MCA/Universal Home Video, 1934, NR, 65 min. Dir: Edgar G. Ulmer. Cast: Boris Karloff, Bela Lugosi, David Manners, Jacqueline Wells, Lucille Lund, Egon Brecher, Harry Cording, John Carradine.

The first and best of Karloff and Lugosi's seven screen teamings, this *very* loose adapta-

Bela Lugosi and Boris Karloff play chess to decide who gets top billing in The Black Cat *(1934).*

tion of the Edgar Allan Poe story features Boris as an evil architect/devil worshipper and Bela (in a rare heroic performance—well, sort of) as an obsessed, cat-hating psychiatrist out to avenge his wife's death. Stylish direction from low-budget luminary Ulmer and handsome art deco settings hardly date this at all, despite the corny antics of innocent honeymoon couple Manners and Wells. Aka *The Vanishing Body* and *House of Doom;* remade as *The Kiss of the Vampire.*

BLACK CAT, THE

★★ Rhino Home Video, 1981, R, 92 min. Dir: Lucio Fulci. Cast: Mimsy Farmer, Patrick Magee, David Warbeck, Dagmar Lassander, Al Cliver, Daniela Doria.

Fulci's homage to Roger Corman's Poe films, this muddled mystery concerns a series of murders in a small English village, apparently committed by the title feline. Not as gory as some of Lucio's other work and only vaguely related to Poe (though it does use the original story's twist ending), this is still offbeat enough to sustain your interest and is notable for containing Magee's last screen appearance.

BLACK CHRISTMAS

★★★☆ Warner Home Video, 1974, R, 98 min. Dir: Bob Clark. Cast: Olivia Hussey, Keir Dullea, Margot Kidder, John Saxon, Andrea Martin, Marian Waldman, Art Hindle, Lynne Griffin.

Supremely scary Canadian shocker predating *Halloween* in its mixture of traditional holiday atmosphere with a psychotic killer's activities. A sorority house's attic is invaded by an unseen madman who makes obscene phone calls from the house mother's private line and begins murdering the few remaining residents over Christmas break. This packs more suspense and shocks than a dozen of the post-*Halloween* slashers combined, with a topnotch cast and a creepy open ending director Clark (*Murder by Decree, Porky's*) later regretted. Once pulled from an NBC showing for being too frightening, this is aka *Silent Night, Evil Night* and *Stranger in the House.*

BLACK DRAGONS

★☆ Sinister Cinema, 1942, NR, 64 min.
Dir: William Nigh. Cast: Bela Lugosi, Joan Barclay, Clayton Moore, George Pembroke, Robert Fraser, Kenneth Harlan.

This dire Monogram quickie is one of Bela's worst, casting him as a renegade plastic surgeon who transforms Japanese spies into the likenesses of prominent American businessmen. When the Nippon government double-crosses Lugosi, he seeks a murderous revenge. No wonder hero Moore later donned a mask as TV's "The Lone Ranger." Also out in a computer-colorized version.

BLACKENSTEIN

★ Media Home Entertainment, 1972, R, 86 min.
Dir: William A. Levy. Cast: John Hart, Ivory Stone, Roosevelt Jackson, Andrea King, Joe DeSue, Liz Renay.

The bottom of the blaxploitation horror barrel is scraped with this crap about a modern descendant of Baron you-know-who turning a paraplegic Vietnam vet into a limb-tearing monster with jutting brow and Afro flat-top. Too pathetic to be funny, with the veteran actors on hand utterly wasted and a grating musical score apparently composed by the makers of Excedrin. Aka *Black Frankenstein*.

BLACK FRANKENSTEIN

See: *Blackenstein*.

BLACK MAGIC

See: *Meeting at Midnight*.

BLACK MAGIC

★★☆ Sinister Cinema, 1949, NR, 102 min.
Dirs: Gregory Ratoff and Orson Welles. Cast: Orson Welles, Akim Tamiroff, Nancy Guild, Raymond Burr, Frank Latimore, Valentina Cortesa, Margot Grahame, Berry Kroeger.

Welles, whose co-direction is uncredited, adds his florid touch to this pokey period melodrama (with horror touches) about the legendary 18th-century hypnotist Cagliostro. An excellent cast and imaginative photography make this worth checking out.

BLACK MAGIC MANSION

See: *Cthulhu Mansion*.

BLACK MAGIC WOMAN

★★ Vidmark Entertainment, 1990, R, 91 min.
Dir: Deryn Warren. Cast: Mark Hamill, Amanda Wyss, Apollonia Kotero, Victor Rivers, Abidah Viera, Larry Hankin.

A voodoo *Fatal Attraction* with Hamill as a smug yuppie art gallery owner who falls into an affair with sexy Apollonia. When he dumps her for old girlfriend Wyss, Appie puts a curse on Hamill, resulting in a physical/mental degeneration. Glossy but dull, this uselessly tries to drum up sympathy for characters you care very little about and has an twist ending stolen from *Burn, Witch, Burn.*

BLACKOUT

★★★ HBO Video, 1985, NR, 98 min.
Dir: Douglas Hickox. Cast: Richard Widmark, Kathleen Quinlan, Keith Carradine, Michael Beck, Gerald Hiken, Paul Drake.

Suspenseful made-for-cable slasher-type thriller about an amnesia victim (Carradine) stalked by an obsessed ex-cop (Widmark) who suspects him of being a maniac who butchered his entire family years earlier and vanished without a trace. A taut combination of elements from the Hammer film *Hysteria* and the yet-to-be-filmed *The Stepfather*, its ending may be a bit predictable but it still has considerable impact, and Widmark is excellent.

BLACKOUT

★☆ Magnum Home Entertainment, 1988, R, 90 min.
Dir: Doug Adams. Cast: Carol Lynley, Gail O'Grady, Joanna Miles, Michael Keys Hall, Joseph Gian, Deena Freeman.

Poor suspense film, with O'Grady returning to her childhood house of horrors after receiving a cryptic letter from her long- missing dad and quickly locking horns with her hostile mom (Lynley) while digging up family skeletons. The uncanny resemblance between Lynley and O'Grady makes this watchable for a while, but this Joseph Stefano–scripted flick's supposedly shocking revelations are obvious and much of the dialogue is downright awful.

BLACK PIT OF DR. M, THE

★★☆ Sinister Cinema, 1958, NR, 71 min.
Dir: Fernando Mendez. Cast: Gaston Santos, Rafael Bertrand, Mapita Cortes, Carlos Ancira.

Really weird Mexican horror about scientists who make a pact that if one of them dies he will return to inform the other about the afterlife. Both die but one (Santos) possesses a disfigured corpse to avenge his death. None of this makes any sense, but it's all beautifully directed by south-of-the-border horror specialist Mendez. Originally titled *Misterios de Ultratumba: Mysteries From Beyond the Grave.* Sinister's print is in unsubtitled Spanish only.

BLACK RAINBOW

★★★ CBS/Fox Video, 1989, R, 103 min.
Dir: Mike Hodges. Cast: Rosanna Arquette, Jason

Robards, Tom Hulce, Mark Joy, Ron Rosenthal, Linda Pierce.

Strikingly directed thriller about a pretty Bible-belt medium (Arquette) who begins seeing deaths before they occur—including an organized crime hit that now makes her a potential target. Though it has trouble blending its disparate story points, strong acting from Arquette and Robards (as her alcoholic father) and sharp atmospherics from Hodges (who also scripted) keep this critically acclaimed chiller always offbeat and interesting.

BLACK ROOM, THE

★★★ Goodtimes Home Video, 1935, NR, 67 min. Dir: Roy William Neill. Cast: Boris Karloff, Marian Marsh, Robert Allen, Katherine De Mille, Thurston Hall, Edward Van Sloan.

One of Karloff's best casts him as twin brothers in early 19th-century Austria suffering a family curse predicting that the younger brother will someday murder the elder one. Boris is at his best here, investing each sibling with fascinating little personal ticks and character traits, while director Neill gives this low-cost period piece a nice gloss. Everything's topped with an exciting, wonderfully ironic ending.

BLACK ROOM, THE

★★☆ Vestron Video, 1983, R, 87 min. Dirs: Elly Kenner and Norman Thaddeus Vane. Cast: Stephen Knight, Cassandra Gaviola, Jim Stathis, Clara Perryman, Linnea Quigley.

Brother and sister vampires Knight and Gaviola rent rooms to kinky couples they spy on and eventually drain of vital fluids—oh, and blood too. Static-looking but with a well-thought-out script and interesting characters—including Linnea in a small role.

BLACK ROSES

★ Imperial Entertainment, 1988, R, 83 min. Dir: John Fasano. Cast: John Martin, Julie Adams, Ken Swofford, Sal Viviano, Karen Planden, Carmine Appici.

Crappy direct-to-video mess about a satanic heavy-metal band who turn a high schoolful of head-bangers into a bunch of low-rent zombies. A dumb, reactionary cheapie shot in upstate New York with a few effective make-up scenes but nothing else. The garish, puff-plastic video box should be warning enough.

BLACK SABBATH

★★★☆ HBO Video, 1964, NR, 95 min. Dir: Mario Bava. Cast: Boris Karloff, Mark Damon, Michele Mercier, Jacqueline Pierreux, Susy Anderson, Lidia Alfonsi.

WILLIS H. O'BRIEN
(1886–1962)

The pioneer of stop-motion animation special effects, "Obie," as he was affectionately known, became interested in movie FX while working as a cartoonist for a San Francisco newspaper. His first effort, 1915's *The Dinosaur and the Missing Link,* was released by the Edison company. His best-known effort was, of course, *King Kong,* and he won an Oscar in 1950 for his work on *Mighty Joe Young.* O'Brien's ability to breathe life and personality into his miniature creations remains unsurpassed.

The Dinosaur and the Missing Link ('15), *The Ghost of Slumber Mountain* ('19), *The Lost World* ('25), *King Kong* ('33), *Son of Kong* ('33), *Mighty Joe Young* ('49), *The Animal World* ('56), *The Black Scorpion* ('57), *The Giant Behemoth* ('59), *The Lost World* ('60).

This excellent anthology of short chillers is one of Bava's best. Karloff hosts this trilogy, which contains a very scary Chekhov ghost story about a medium's ambulatory corpse, a so-so tale of telephone calls from beyond the grave, and a Tolstoy mini-epic of a Russian peasant family overcome by vampirism. Bava's imaginative, artistic use of color and lighting are case-book examples of how to get every ounce of atmosphere out of even the most meager of materials, while Karloff, so amusing in the connecting segments, is genuinely chilling in his only vampire role. Aka *I Tre Volti Della Paura: The Three Faces of Fear.* Euro-prints are longer, with the stories in a different order, a different musical score, and a lesbian subplot in the second tale.

BLACK SCORPION, THE

★★★ Warner Home Video, 1957, NR, 87 min. Dir: Edward Ludwig. Cast: Richard Denning, Mara Corday, Carlos Rivas, Mario Navarro.

Good Willis O'Brien FX highlight this creepy big-bug flick about volcanic activity in Mexico unleashing a horde of huge prehistoric scorpions on the countryside. Basically a remake of *Them!* with a nastier edge (and a lower budget); the best scene has the scorpions derailing a train and feasting on the terrified passengers.

BLACK SUNDAY

★★★★ Sinister Cinema, 1960, NR, 83 min. Dir: Mario Bava. Cast: Barbara Steele, John

Richardson, Ivo Garrani, Andrea Checchi, Arturo Dominici, Enrico Olivieri.

Executed witch Steele—who had a spiked golden mask hammered onto her face—is accidentally revived from her grave as a vampire and seeks revenge on the descendants of her enemies while attempting to possess a lookalike princess (also Steele). The *best* Italian horror film, this hauntingly photographed monochrome classic—filmed as *La Maschera del Demonio: Mask of the Demon* and shown in Britain as *Revenge of the Vampire*—established cinematographer Bava as one of the great horror film stylists and made a cult star of extraordinary Brit actress Steele. Originally released in the States by American International, the video version features different dubbed voices and the original Italian musical track.

BLACK TORMENT, THE
See: *Estate of Insanity.*

BLACK VAMPIRE
See: *Blood Couple.*

BLACK WEREWOLF
See: *The Beast Must Die.*

BLACULA
★★★ Orion Home Video, 1972, PG, 92 min.
Dir: William Crain. Cast: William Marshall, Vonetta McGee, Denise Nicholas, Thalmus Rasulala, Charles Macauley, Gordon Pinsent, Ketty Lester, Elisha Cook.

Though dated by its costumes and jive-talkin' dialogue, this remains the best of the early '70s blaxploitation horror films. Marshall is magnificent as African Prince Mamuwalde, cursed by Dracula and unearthed in modern L.A., where he puts the bite on a pair of gay antique dealers, a lady cabbie, and a night club photographer while romancing a young woman (the beautiful McGee) he takes for the reincarnation of his late wife. Sometimes looks like a cross between *Count Yorga, Vampire* and an episode of *Good Times*, but strong acting and some effective shock sequences make it a kick to watch. Sequel: *Scream, Blacula, Scream.*

BLADE IN THE DARK, A
★★ Vestron Video, 1983, R, 96 min.
Dir: Lamberto Bava. Cast: Andrea Occhipini, Anny Papaas, Fabiola Toledo, Michele Sovai, Valeria Cavalli, Stanko Molnar.

A composer (Occhipini) rents a lonely villa for the solitude needed to score a slasher film, only to find himself enmeshed in the activities of a knife-wielding, woman-hating, transvestite psychopath. The younger Bava manages to embellish a slight story line with some nice touches, though in the end this remains little more than your standard slasher shenanigans with an ironic twist ending stolen from *Blow Out.* Aka *La Casa con la Scala nel Buio: House of the Dark Staircase.*

BLADE OF THE RIPPER
See: *Next!*

BLADES
★ Media Home Entertainment, 1988, R, 98 min.
Dir: Thomas Rondinella. Cast: Robert North, Jeremy Whelan, Victoria Scott, Holly Stevenson, Roy Towner.

Pathetically unfunny spoof combining *Jaws* with *Caddyshack*—now there's a natural for ya!—in this tale of a killer lawn mower slicing up victims at a posh country club's golf course. Way too long considering its slight premise, with no laughs, minimal bloodshed, and a bland cast headed by a guy who looks like Treat Williams' untalented brother.

BLIND DATE
★☆ Vestron Video, 1984, R, 100 min.
Dir: Nico Mastorakis. Cast: Joseph Bottoms, Kirstie Alley, Keir Dullea, Lana Clarkson, James Daughton, Marina Sirtis.

Not to be confused with the bad Bruce Willis comedy of the same name, this concerns blind Bottoms' attempt to catch a scalpel-wielding

---

MARIO BAVA
(1914–1980)

A gifted Italian cinematographer and director, Bava defined the look and feel of Italian horror in the 1960s. An enormously talented filmmaker who, like so many horror film craftsmen, was never properly appreciated in his lifetime, he has had a vast influence on the work of Dario Agento, Brian De Palma, John Carpenter, and others.

The Devil's Commandment (photographer, '56), *Caltiki, the Immortal Monster* (photographer, '59), *Black Sunday* ('60), *Hercules in the Haunted World* ('61), *The Evil Eye* ('62), *What!* ('63), *Black Sabbath* ('64), *Blood and Black Lace* ('65), *Planet of the Vampires* ('65), *Dr. Goldfoot and the Girl Bombs* ('66), *Kill, Baby, Kill* ('67), *Hatchet for the Honeymoon* ('69), *Five Dolls for an August Moon* ('70), *Twitch of the Death Nerve* ('71), *Baron Blood* ('72), *The House of Exorcism* ('75), *Beyond the Door II* ('77), *Inferno* (special effects, '80).

slasher in Athens through the use of a brain implant that literally lets him "see" through sonic signals. A contrived premise coupled with a bored cast and a record number of shower scenes add up to yet another disappointing stalker movie. Nice Greek locations, though.

BLIND DEAD, THE
See: *Tombs of the Blind Dead.*

BLIND FEAR
★☆ Academy Entertainment, 1989, R, 87 min. Dir: Tom Berry. Cast: Shelley Hack, Jan Rubes, Jack Langedijk, Kim Coates, Heidi von Palleske, Geza Kovacs.

Dull suspense yarn about a blind switchboard operator (Hack) menaced at a closed-down hotel by a trio of psychopathic robbers. Mechanical in the extreme, with hollow echoes of *Wait Until Dark* and *See No Evil;* even a good twist at the end can't help much. Aka *The Long Dark Night.*

BLIND MAN'S BLUFF
See: *Cauldron of Blood.*

BLIND TERROR
See: *See No Evil.*

BLOB, THE
★★☆ Goodtimes Home Video, 1958, NR, 82 min. Dir: Irwin S. Yeaworth, Jr. Cast: Steve McQueen, Aneta Corseaut, Earl Rowe, Olin Howlin, Stephen Chase, John Burton.

An enjoyable '50s almost-classic with rebellious teens, misunderstanding parents, hostile cops, drag races, midnight horror shows, and a monster like no other: a mass of intergalactic jello that grows and grows as it absorbs every living thing in sight. McQueen is good as the oldest rebel teen hero on record, and the effects work quite well for such an inexpensive production, shot in fabulous Downingtown, PA. Followed by *Son of Blob* and the 1988 remake.

BLOB, THE
★★★ RCA/Columbia Home Video, 1988, R, 92 min. Dir: Chuck Russell. Cast: Kevin Dillon, Shawnee Smith, Donovan Leitch, Candy Clark, Jeffrey DeMunn, Joe Seneca, Ricky Paull Goldin, Michael Kenworthy.

Excellent remake that actually improves on the original, thanks to a more pronounced sense of humor and eye-popping FX. It's the same story about a small town inundated by a mass of man-eating ooze but with a couple of new twists: the blob is now a manmade ultimate weapon gone wrong, and the Steve McQueen character (Leitch) is killed off halfway through, with pretty cheerleader Smith becoming the film's true hero! An underserved box-office flop, this *demands* video rediscovery.

BLOOD AND BLACK LACE
★★★☆ Sinister Cinema, 1964, NR, 87 min. Dir: Mario Bava. Cast: Cameron Mitchell, Eva Bartok, Thomas Reiner, Mary Arden, Ariana Gorini, Claude Dantes, Alan Collins, Harriet White Medin.

Bava's seminal stalker movie about a stable of glamorous fashion models haunted by a masked maniac after the inflammatory diary of his first victim. Bava's neon-colored atmosphere paved the way for the lush cosmopolitan thrillers of Dario Argento and has violence which, though not overly gory, is still pretty strong stuff: one girl is severely burned against a red hot heater while another is smashed in the face with a spiked glove that would give Freddy Krueger pause. Only the poor dubbing (all the males, including star Mitchell, are voiced by the familiar tones of Paul Frees) detracts from the overall effect. Aka *Sei Donne Per L'Assassino: Six Women for the Murderer* and *Fashion House of Death.*

BLOOD AND LACE
★★☆ HBO Video, 1971, PG, 87 min. Dir: Philip Gilbert. Cast: Gloria Grahame, Melody Patterson, Vic Tayback, Milton Selzer, Len Lesser, Dennis Christopher.

One of the sickest PG-rated flicks ever, this has Grahame running a small town orphanage where runaways are killed and quick frozen as part of a plan to bilk the state child welfare service and tough-talkin' heroine Patterson ("F-Troop"'s Wrangler Jane, who is supposed to be 17 but looks about 30) being haunted by a claw-hammer-wielding creep in a horror mask. A typically winning turn from Gloria makes this sleazy '70s sicko worth a look.

BLOOD AND ROSES
★★★ Paramount/Gateway Home Video, 1961, NR, 73 min. Dir: Roger Vadim. Cast: Mel Ferrer, Elsa Martinelli, Annette Vadim, Marc Allegret.

Vadim's beautifully directed but slow French-Italian version of J. Sheridan LeFanu's *Carmilla,* with wife number two Annette (she came after Brigitte Bardot but before Jane Fonda) as a modern girl possessed by her bisexual vampire ancestress Millarca Karnstein. Haunting autumnal landscapes, beautiful women, and an intuitive use of color—and often the lack thereof—help make up for some simply awful dubbing and continuity problems. Best scene: Vadim kissing a drop of blood from the lips of gorgeous Martinelli. Original title: *Et Mourir de Plaisir: And Die of Pleasure.*

BLOODBATH
See: *Bay Of Blood.*

BLOODBATH AT THE HOUSE OF DEATH
★★ Video Treasures, 1984, R, 88 min.
Dir: Ray Cameron. Cast: Vincent Price, Kenny Everett, Pamela Stephenson, Gareth Hunt, Sheila Steafel, Madeline Smith.

Minor Brit horror comedy about a bumbling team of parapsychologists investigating an old gothic mansion well known for its violent history. Sporadically funny, with Price in good form in an extended cameo as the dreaded "Sinister Man."

BLOOD BEACH
★★ Media Home Entertainment, 1981, R, 89 min.
Dir: Jeffrey Bloom. Cast: John Saxon, Marianna Hill, David Huffman, Burt Young, Otis Young, Stefan Gierash.

Mediocre handling blunts the edge of this potentially fun '50s-style monster flick about California sunbathers pulled down into the sands of a popular beach by a hungry critter revealed at the end, for a split second, to be a cross between a huge clam and a Venus fly-trap. A would-be rapist's castration by the horny beastie provides one of the high spots; Saxon's amusingly grouchy performance is another.

BLOOD BEAST FROM OUTER SPACE
See: *Night Caller from Outer Space.*

BLOOD BEAST TERROR, THE
★☆ Monterey Home Video, 1968, NR, 87 min.
Dir: Vernon Sewell. Cast: Peter Cushing, Robert Flemyng, Wanda Ventham, Vanessa Howard, David Griffin, Roy Hudd.

Crummy rip-off of the Hammer film *The Reptile* with Flemyng (in a role intended for Basil Rathbone, who died shortly before the start of filming) as an entomologist whose "daughter" (Ventham) is actually an oversized death's-head moth in human form. Cushing, who calls this his worst horror film, is the Van Helsing–like police inspector on the blood-drinking monster's trail. Original title: *The Vampire Beast Craves Blood.*

BLOOD BRIDES
See: *Hatchet for the Honeymoon.*

BLOOD CASTLE
★☆ Wizard Video, 1971, R, 90 min.
Dir: José L. Merino. Cast: Jeffrey Chase, Jennifer Hartly, Agostina Belli, Ronald Grey.

An Italian film originally titled *Ivanna,* this was picked up by New World Pictures and retitled *Scream of the Demon Lover,* concerning a series of gore murders committed by a hideously burned mad baron. An undistinguished mix of soft-core sex and blood. Aka *Killers of the Castle of Blood* and now under this unimaginative moniker.

BLOOD CEREMONY
See: *The Legend of Blood Castle.*

BLOOD COUPLE
★★★ Video Gems, 1973, R, 78 min.
Dir: Bill Gunn. Cast: Duane Jones, Marlene Clark, Bill Gunn, Sam Waymon, Leonard Jackson, Mabel King.

A badly butchered version of a beautifully crafted blaxploitation vampire film originally known as *Ganja and Hess.* An earnest young doctor (Jones, from the original *Night of the Living Dead*) is stabbed with an ancient African dagger and transforms into a vampire, claiming his assistant's wife (Clark, who's very good) as a victim before committing suicide by standing in the shadow of a cross. Derivative of *Blacula* to a certain extent but also offbeat enough to stand on its own merits. Aka *Double Possession* (for a post-*Exorcist* reissue), *Black Vampire,* and *Blackout: A Moment of Fear.*

BLOOD CREATURE
See: *Terror Is a Man.*

BLOOD CULT
★ United Home Video, 1985, UR, 89 min.
Dir: Christopher Lewis. Cast: Julie Andelman, Charles Ellis, Josef Hardt, James Vance, Fred Graves, Bennie Lee McGowan.

Black-gloved maniac chops up various vacuous coeds at a small midwestern college as part of a ritual for a cult of hooded dog worshippers. The first made-for-video horror movie, this shot-in-Tulsa cheapo is flatly directed and poorly acted—the heroine looks like Linda Blair, the hero like Bud Cort!—and has lots of second-rate gore effects. Followed by *Revenge.*

BLOOD DEMON, THE
See: *The Torture Chamber of Dr. Sadism.*

BLOOD DINER
★★☆ Lightning Home Video, 1987, UR, 88 min.
Dir: Jackie Kong. Cast: Rick Burks, Carl Crew, Lisa

Guggenheim, Drew Godderis, Lanetta La France, Roger Dauer.

Kong's tribute to H. G. Lewis' *Blood Feast,* this sometimes quite funny spoof features Burks and Crew as a couple of inept, diner-owning brothers out to reincarnate an ancient Egyptian goddess by committing a series of gruesome dismemberment murders, all under the guidance of the disembodied brain of their late Uncle Anwar (Godderis). A mild diversion for splatter fans with surprisingly lush-looking production values. Godderis is a real piss as abusive ol' Uncle Anwar.

BLOODEATERS
See: *Toxic Zombies.*

BLOOD EVIL
See: *Demons of the Mind.*

BLOOD FEAST
★★☆ Sleaziest Video, 1963, NR, 67 min. Dir: Herschell Gordon Lewis. Cast: Connie Mason, Thomas Wood, Mal Arnold, Scott H. Hall, Lyn Bolton, Toni Calvert.

The original splatter film, this is a laugh riot of gore-drenched inanity about a Miami caterer (Arnold) who butchers a number of young women—removing a leg, brain, and tongue—in an attempt to reanimate an Egyptian love goddess and serves the leftovers at various social functions. Technically inept and featuring ludicrous acting (especially that of Mason, "*Playboy*'s favorite Playmate"), this slash-happy bloodbath is sick fun, thanks to its ridiculously over-the-top gore effects—the tongue torn from a girl's mouth looks long enough to have come out of a giraffe!—and goofy dialogue ("Call the Fremonts, fast," shouts a panicky hero, "and for Pete's sake, don't let them eat anything!").

BLOOD FEAST
See: *Night of a Thousand Cats.*

BLOOD FIEND
See: *Theatre of Death.*

BLOOD FOR DRACULA
See: *Andy Warhol's Dracula.*

BLOOD FRENZY
★☆ Hollywood Family Entertainment, 1987, R, 90 min. Dir: Hal Freeman. Cast: Wendy MacDonald, Lisa Loring, Tony Montero, Hank Garrett.

Totally boring, cliché-ridden stalker movie about a lady shrink and her therapy group sliced-n-diced by your usual psycho killer while on a desert retreat. Yawn. More or less remade by the same production team (in a different climate) as the even worse *Iced.*

BLOOD HOOK
★ Prism Entertainment, 1987, R, 93 min. Dir: James Mallon. Cast: Mark Jacobs, Lisa Todd, Patrick Danz, Sara Hauser.

Another trite slasher (with comic overtones) about vacationers in Wisconsin menaced by a maniac wielding a deadly king-sized fish hook. Just one more reason not to vacation in Wisconsin, I guess.

BLOOD ISLAND
★★☆ Academy Entertainment, 1967, NR, 99 min. Dir: David Greene. Cast: Gig Young, Carol Lynley, Oliver Reed, Flora Robson, Ann Bell, Rick Jones.

Actually, this is that late show staple *The Shuttered Room* with Young and Lynley as May-September newlyweds who visit the old mill house Carol has recently inherited and discover it to be "haunted" by a deadly presence. Based on a novel by H. P. Lovecraft and August Derleth (though Lovecraft did none of the actual writing), this is slow and weirdly directed but has excellent acting, especially Robson as Lynley's witch-like aunt, and some creepy scenes to recommend it.

BLOOD LEGACY
★★☆ Video Gems, 1971, R, 85 min. Dir: Carl Monson. Cast: John Carradine, Faith Domergue, John Russell, Jeff Morrow, Merry Anders, Richard Davalos, Brooke Mills, Buck Kartalian.

The veteran cast members ham it up in this gory multiple murder piece about the family of a dead millionaire (Carradine) fighting over his fortune and dying via beheading, shooting, poisoning, electrocution, bee stings, and piranha bites. This semi-remake of *The Curse of the Living Corpse* (note the similar decapitated-head-on-a-platter gag) is tacky fun, but beware edited prints with all the murders cut out. Aka *Legacy of Blood.*

BLOOD LINK
★★☆ Embassy Home Entertainment, 1983, R, 98 min. Dir: Alberto De Martino. Cast: Michael Moriarty, Penelope Milford, Cameron Mitchell, Geraldine Fitzgerald, Virginia McKenna, Martha Smith.

Moriarty is unusually subdued (so to speak) in this German-shot psychic thriller about a doctor haunted by visions of the misogynistic murders being committed by his former Siamese twin brother. Similar to the later *Dead Ringers,* with an obsessive Ennio Morricone score, a bevy of beauteous babes who undress at the drop of a hat, and Mitchell in top fighting form as an over-the-hill pug.

BLOODLUST

★★ Sinister Cinema, 1959, NR, 68 min.
Dir: Ralph Brooke. Cast: Wilton Graff, Lilyan Chauvin, Robert Reed, June Kenney, Walter Brooke, Gene Perrson, Joan Lora, Troy Patterson.

Cheapie knock-off of *The Most Dangerous Game* with Graff overacting as the mad hunter after shipwrecked teens (including future "Brady Bunch" dad Reed) on his misty island. Deadly slow, this picks up a bit in the second half, but the interior jungle settings give it the look of a bad '50s TV show.

BLOODLUST: SUBSPECIES III

★★ Paramount, 1993, R, 82 min.
Dir: Ted Nicolaou. Cast: Anders Hove, Denice Duff, Melanie Shatner, Kevin Blair, Ion Haiduc, Michael Dellafemina.

Heroine Michelle (Duff) begins "life" as a vampire as her sister, Rebecca (Shatner), makes one last attempt to save her in this third and weakest in the series—filmed back-to-back with part II. The story is paper-thin, but there are some good bits and a spectacular end—or is it?—for demon vampire Radu (Hove).

BLOOD MOON

See: *The Werewolf vs. the Vampire Woman.*

BLOODMOON

★★ LIVE Home Video, 1989, R, 101 min.
Dir: Alec Mills. Cast: Leon Lissek, Christine Amor, Ian Williams, Helen Thomson.

A well-produced but routine girls school stalker movie about a shadowy killer garrotting victims at a private Aussie Catholic academy. Nondescript cast and overfamiliar situations.

BLOOD OF DRACULA

★★☆ RCA/Columbia Home Video, 1957, NR, 69 min. Dir: Herbert L. Strock. Cast: Sandra Harrison, Louise Lewis, Gail Ganley, Jerry Blaine, Heather Ames, Malcolm Atterbury.

Dracula has nothing to do with this fun American International teen horror about a moody girls school student (Harrision) transformed into a tight-sweatered, marble-faced vampire by the hypnotic amulet of feminist chemistry teacher Lewis. Dankly atmospheric and even a bit creepy in places but fast-forward through Blaine's awful "Puppy Love" number. Aka *Blood of the Demon* and *Blood Is My Heritage.*

BLOOD OF DRACULA'S CASTLE

★ Interglobal Video, 1967, PG, 84 min.
Dir: Al Adamson. Cast: John Carradine, Paula Raymond, Alex D'Arcy, Robert Dix, Gene O'Shane, Barbara Bishop, Vicki Volante, Ray Young.

Crud of Dracula's Castle is more like it. Another bargain basement Adamson paean to ineptitude, this doesn't even have Carradine in his expected role as Dracula but as a moon-worshipping butler called George. The Count is played by Egyptian ham-actor D'Arcy who, along with Countess Raymond (in a role intended for Jayne Mansfield) drink the blood of kidnapped mini-skirted chicks chained up in the basement of their desert digs. Dix is also on hand as a sadistic werewolf in footage added from the TV version. Not even as much cheesy fun as *Dracula vs. Frankenstein.* Aka *Dracula's Castle.*

BLOOD OF FRANKENSTEIN, THE

See: *Dracula vs. Frankenstein* (1971).

BLOOD OF FU MANCHU, THE

See: *Against All Odds.*

BLOOD OF GHASTLY HORROR, THE

★ VidAmerica, 1971, R, 87 min.
Dir: Al Adamson. Cast: John Carradine, Regina Carrol, Tommy Kirk, Kent Taylor, Roy Morton, Rich Smedley.

Originally shot in 1965 as *Psycho-A-Go-Go,* new scenes were added in '69 and again in '71 for this current incarnation. Carradine is a mad doc who turns a Vietnam vet into a crazed zombie, Carrol is his busty daughter, and former Disney star Kirk is a detective who receives a severed head in the mail. Compelling viewing, to state the obvious. Aka *The Fiend With the Synthetic Brain, The Man With the Synthetic Brain,* and *The Fiend With the Atomic Brain.*

BLOOD OF NOSTRADAMUS, THE

★ Sinister Cinema, 1960, NR, 98 min.
Dir: Federico Curiel. Cast: German Robles, Julio Aleman, Domingo Soler, Aurora Alvarado, Mander.

The last, longest, and worst of the *Nostradamus* series finds the vampire avenging himself on his enemy Professor Duran by attempting to vampirize his lovely daughter Anna, only to be staked through the heart and fall over a cliff. There's absolutely no logical reason to put yourself through this Mexican monstrosity—so don't.

BLOOD OF THE DEMON

See: *Blood of Dracula.*

LINDA HAYDEN
(1951–)

This blonde Brit sex bomb specializes in teen teasers and tramps. Though Linda started out as the usual innocent Hammer Films ingenue, she quickly carved a niche for herself in British horror as a sort of satanic Lolita, although her uninhibitedness didn't take her career as far as it should have.

Taste the Blood of Dracula ('70), *The Blood on Satan's Claw* ('71), *Night Watch* ('73), *Madhouse* ('74), *The House on Straw Hill* ('75), *The Boys From Brazil* ('78), *Black Carrion* ('84).

BLOOD OF THE MAN DEVIL
See: *House of the Black Death.*

BLOOD OF THE UNDEAD
See: *Schizo.*

BLOOD OF THE VAMPIRE
★★ MPI Home Video, 1958, NR, 85 min.
Dir: Henry Cass. Cast: Donald Wolfit, Barbara Shelley, Vincent Ball, Victor Maddern, William Devlin, Andrew Faulds.

This blatant imitation of Hammer's *The Curse of Frankenstein* and *Horror of Dracula* (scripted by Jimmy Sangster) opens with a mad scientist-cum-vampire (Wolfit) getting a stake through the heart. Sometime later he's revived by a heart transplant (there's a novel twist) and sets up shop in a prison where he experiments in the creation of a blood substitute needed to cure his condition. Wolfit (made up to look like Bela Lugosi) hams outrageously and hero Ball looks like an effeminate Errol Flynn, but the beauty of Brit horror queen Shelley more than compensates. Video quality is very shoddy; you might do better taping this off your local TV station's Monster Chiller Horror Theatre.

BLOOD ON HIS LIPS
See: *The Hideous Sun Demon.*

BLOOD ON SATAN'S CLAW, THE
★★★ MGM/UA Home Video, 1971, R, 93 min.
Dir: Piers Haggard. Cast: Linda Hayden, Patrick Wymark, Barry Andrews, Michele Dotrice, James Hayter, Wendy Padbury, Tamara Ustinov, Simon Williams.

Atmospheric British horror set in early 19th-century Cornwall where an innocent plowboy (Andrews) unearths the remains of Satan himself. Soon a teenage cult headed by the extraodinarily sexy Hayden begins a series of sacrifices to bring the devil back to life. This mood piece (originally intended as an anthology, with the three segments ultimately edited into one story line) is almost in the category of *The Conqueror Worm,* thanks to strong performances, hard-edged violence, and convincing period detail. Aka *Satan's Skin* and *Satan's Claw.*

BLOOD ORGY
See: *The Gore-Gore Girls.*

BLOOD ORGY OF THE SHE DEVILS
★ WesternWorld Video, 1973, PG, 73 min.
Dir: Ted V. Mikels. Cast: Lila Zaborin, Tom Pace, William Bagdad, Leslie McRae.

Don't let the classy title fool you into watching this lifeless tripe about witch Zaborin and her female cult operating out of a California mansion, from the director of *The Astro- Zombies* and *The Corpse Grinders.* Only for those who find watching a test pattern too much of an intellectual strain. Aka *Female Plasma Suckers.*

BLOOD RAGE
★☆ Prism Entertainment, 1984, R, 82 min.
Dir: John W. Grissmer. Cast: Louise Lasser, Mark Soper, Marianne Kanter, Julie Gordon, Jayne Bentzen, William Fuller.

Unimaginative slasher about an evil twin who frames his innocent brother for a brutal slaying at the drive-in (where Ted Raimi is selling condoms in the bathroom). Years later the good bro excapes from prison on Thanksgiving, inspiring the bad bro to do a little more carving than is necessary. Lasser, as the boys' long-suffering mom, is fun but it's otherwise a waste. Filmed as *Complex* and released to theatres and cable as *Nightmare at Shadow Woods.*

BLOOD RELATIONS
★★☆ Orion Home Video, 1988, R, 85 min.
Dir: Graeme Campbell. Cast: Jan Rubes, Lydie Denier, Kevin Hicks, Ray Walston, Lynne Adams, Stephen Saylor.

This starts out as a dull gothic thriller with Hicks as an obnoxious rich guy using French girlfriend Denier in a plot to gain control of the family fortune. Then it becomes a Bela Lugosi Monogram flick with Rubes as a mad surgeon still in love with his late wife, everything finally ending in a twist so outrageously sick you wonder if it belongs to the same movie. This is peopled with far too many annoying characters, but is worth it for Rubes' expansive performance, Denier's frequent nude scenes, and that hard-to-shake conclusion.

BLOOD RITES
See: *The Ghastly Ones.*

BLOOD SALVAGE
★★ Magnum Home Entertainment, 1989, R, 98 min. Dir: Tucker Johnson. Cast: Danny Nelson, Lori Birdsong, John Saxon, Ray Walston, Christian Hesler, Ralph Pruitt Vaughn, Laura White, Evander Holyfield.

The Texas Chainsaw Massacre meets *Coma* when a trio of hillbilly religious zealots run a backwoods auto graveyard *and* a successful black market organ service, kidnapping motorists (including Saxon and his unsympathetic family) and cutting them up for their best parts. Slick and competently acted but more distasteful than scary, with obnoxious characters (even the wheelchair-bound teen heroine is an unlikable bitch) and forced attempts at black humor—though the Elvis cameo provides a grin.

BLOOD SEEKERS, THE
See: *Dracula vs. Frankenstein* (1971).

BLOOD SIMPLE
★★★ MCA/Universal Home Video, 1984, R, 98 min. Dir: Joel Coen. Cast: John Getz, Frances McDormand, Dan Hedaya, M. Emmet Walsh, Samm Art Williams, Deborah Neumann.

Stylized mixture of *Diabolique* and *The Postman Always Rings Twice* about lovers (Getz and McDormand) whose passion is complicated by her slovenly husband (Hedaya), who remains a thorn in their side even after he's been murdered. A bit *too* studied in spots but with great work from Hedaya and Walsh (the latter as a sleazy private eye) and a corker of a gory shock ending.

BLOOD SISTERS
See: *Sisters.*

BLOOD SISTERS
★ Sony Video, 1986, R, 86 min. Dir: Roberta Findlay. Cast: Amy Brentano, Shannon McMahon, Dan Erickson, Maria Machart, Elisabeth Rose, Ruth Collins.

Dull campus slasher, a poor combination of *The House on Sorority Row* and *The Nesting,* about a bunch of babes on a scavenger hunt in a haunted old bordello stalked by a cross-dressing killer. Grainy photography, ragged editing, and awful acting in one of the most lifeless films of its kind—hardly anything happens for the first 60 minutes! Filmed as *Slash.*

BLOOD SONG
★ Video Communications, 1981, R, 90 min. Dir: Alan J. Levi. Cast: Frankie Avalon, Donna Wilkes, Richard Jaeckel, Antoinette Bower, Dane Clark, Lenny Montana.

This shaggy gore story is so old it has fleas. After an opening `50s flashback, the main plot deals with a flute-playing psycho played by Avalon—I guess Troy Donahue was unavailable—who terrorizes lame high schooler Wilkes (whose leg brace is used less for character development than to make it harder for her to run away from the maniac), who has a psychic link with the killer since receiving a blood transfusion from him—I know, I know! Pretty awful stuff not even redeemed by that "Love Boat"–style cast and some unintended laughs.

BLOOD-SPATTERED BRIDE, THE
★★ Gorgon Video, 1972, R, 83 min. Dir: Vicente Aranda. Cast: Maribel Martin, Alexandra Bastedo, Simon Andreu, Dean Selmier.

Artsy but dumb rip-off of Hammer's *The Vampire Lovers* about a lesbian undead (Bastedo) who seduces a young bride away from her new husband on their honeymoon. Badly edited—the original 102-minute Spanish version is called *La Novia Ensangrentada: The Bloody Fiancee*—but helped by some beautiful images and offbeat, though often senseless, touches.

BLOODSPELL
★☆ Forum Home Video, 1988, R, 87 min. Dir: Derwyn Warren. Cast: Anthony Jenkins, Aarin Teich, Alexandra Kennedy, Theodora Louise, John Reno, Edward Dloughy.

Vapid video nonsense about a halfway house for wayward teens terrorized by a resident possessed by the evil spirit of his occultist dad. Imagine a cross between *Friday the 13th Part V* and a post-*Exorcist* '70s occult pic—a *bad* cross—and you get the picture. Very poor.

BLOOD SPLASH
See: *Nightmare* (1981).

BLOODSTONE: SUBSPECIES II
★★☆ Paramount Home Video, 1993, R, 87 min. Dir: Ted Nicolaou. Cast: Anders Hove, Denice Duff, Melanie Shatner, Kevin Blair, Michael Denish, Ion Haiduc.

Superior sequel with Radu (Hove) revived by his diminutive undead minions and then taking off for Bucharest in pursuit of half-vampire heroine Michele (Duff, replacing Laura Tate). His object: to retrieve from her an ancient artifact called the Bloodstone. Beautifully directed, with strong visuals and performances, but since this was shot back-to-back with part III, it fails to come up with a satisfying ending.

BLOODSUCKERS
★★☆ Media Home Entertainment, 1970, R, 80 min. Dir: Robert Hartford-Davis. Cast: Peter Cushing, Patrick Macnee, ALexander Davion, Patrick Mower, Madeline Hinde, Johnny Sekka, Imogen Hassel, Edward Woodward.

Convoluted adaptation of Simon Raven's novel *Doctors Wear Scarlet*, in which vampirism is treated as a sexual dysfunction rather than a supernatural curse. While studying in Greece, a young Oxford don falls under the spell of a female vampire. Back in England he begins to show vampiric designs toward his uptight fiancee. Well photographed and still mildly intriguing but full of silly psychedelic touches and suffering from choppy continuity. Cushing and Macnee are wasted in small roles. Aka *Doctors Wear Scarlet* and *Incense for the Damned*.

BLOOD SUCKERS, THE
See: *Gallery of Horrors.*

BLOODSUCKING FREAKS
☆ Media Home Entertainment, 1978, R, 88 min. Dir: Joel M. Reed. Cast: Seamus O'Brien, Niles Mc Master, Viji Krem, Louis De Jesus, Alan Dellay, Dan Fauci.

The Great Sardu is a New York white slaver who uses the women he kidnaps as part of his gruesome SoHo stage act, which involves the dismemberment and murder of his female "assistants." Filmed as *The Incredible Torture Show* and reissued in '81 with this more infamous moniker, this tries hard to be funny but isn't, with an outlook so nihilistic and misogynistic—all the women, apart from the heroine, are raped, sodomized, and sliced up while frontally nude—it's often hard to watch. Picketed by women's groups in the early '80s, this is one of the few horror films truly deserving of such condemnation. Of course, this will be taken as recommendation for some, but honestly, proceed at your own risk.

BLOODSUCKING NAZI ZOMBIES
See: *Oasis of the Zombies.*

BLOODSUCKING PHARAOHS IN PITTSBURGH
★☆ Paramount Home Video, 1990, R, 89 min. Dir: Dean Tschetter. Cast: Jake Dengel, Joe Sharkey, Susan Fletcher, Jane Esther Hamilton, Beverly Penberthy, Shawn Elliott.

Lunkheaded splatter parody with a series of gross hooker murders committed *Blood Feast*–style by a fez-topped Egyptian psycho killer. Add to this a dumbbell cop team with all the appeal of pond scum, *Airplane*-type gags that fall distressingly flat, severely edited Tom Savini makeup FX (note the frequent jumps in the music track), and an overall vile sexism supposedly balanced out by making the maniac (played by former porn star Hamilton aka Veronica Hart) a woman. Makes *Hollywood Chainsaw Hookers* look like *The Texas Chainsaw Massacre.*

BLOODTHIRSTY BUTCHERS
★ Midnight Video, 1970, R, 79 min. Dir: Andy Milligan. Cast: John Miranda, Annabelle Wood, Berwick Kaler, Jane Helay, Michael Cox, Linda Driver.

Inept version of the Sweeney Todd legend with the dreaded "Demon Barber of Fleet Street" slashing throats and dismembering bodies, with the remains turning up in the meat pies sold by neighbor lady Mrs. Lovett. Probably the best known of Staten Island auteur Milligan's 16mm wonders, this has amateurish acting, shaky photography, and horrible sound but also flying meat cleavers, severed mannequin hands and heads covered in ketchup, and a rubber breast in a pie. With some footage shot on location in England, obviously, this is only for Andy fans.

BLOOD TIDE
★ Continental Video, 1981, R, 82 min. Dir: Richard Jeffries. Cast: James Earl Jones, José Ferrer, Lila Kedrova, Mary Louise Weller, Martin Kove, Deborah Shelton.

Awful sea-monster saga shot in Greece, with Jones as a fortune hunter who uses the purity of the lovely Shelton to lure a legendary sea monster—who looks about as scary as Captain Kangaroo's Mr. Moose—from its underwater hideout. This *Alien-Jaws* rip-off is a real embarrassment for the veteran stars it exploits. Aka *Demon Lake.*

BLOOD VOYAGE
★ Monterey Home Video, 1976, R, 78 min. Dir: Frank Mitchell. Cast: Jonathan Lippe, Laurie Rose, Midori, Mara Modair, John Hart, Gene Tyburn.

Junky sea-going slasher saga about a series of brutal murders committed on millionare Hart's yacht. Is moody Vietnam vet Lippe responsible? There are episodes of "Laverene and Shirley" with more suspense.

BLOOD WILL HAVE BLOOD
See: *Demons of the Mind.*

ANDY MILLIGAN
(1929–1991)

The king of Staten Island trash terror, Milligan made films that were nothing if not ambitious—period chillers done on a budget that wouldn't pay for a nice living room set but are often so torturously inept in the acting, directing, and writing departments as to be almost impossible to sit through. Still, his movies have an individuality that makes them instantly recognizable. After a decade of inactivity he made a genre comeback with several direct-to-video flicks in the mid-'80s.

The Ghastly Ones ('69), *Bloodthirsty Butchers* ('70), *Torture Dungeon* ('70), *The Body Beneath* ('71), *Guru, the Mad Monk* ('71), *The Rats Are Coming! The Werewolves Are Here!* ('72), *The Man With Two Heads* ('72), *Blood* ('74), *Carnage* ('83), *The Weirdo* ('88), *Monstrosity* ('89), *Surgikill* ('90).

BLOODY BIRD

See: *Stage Fright* (1987).

BLOODY BIRTHDAY

★☆ Starmaker Home Video, 1980, R, 84 min.
Dir: Ed Hunt. Cast: Susan Strasberg, José Ferrer, Lori Lethin, Julie Brown, Joe Penny, Elizabeth Hoy, K. C. Martel, Billy Jacoby, Andy Freeman, Michael Dudikoff.

A surprisingly good cast appears in this monumentally stupid slasher rip-off of *The Bad Seed*, with three evil kids going on a violent rampage on their common 10th birthday. Parents, teachers, classmates, and the usual horny teens fall victim until our plucky babysitting heroine (Lethin) takes a hand. Crude but not especially bloody, this was shelved until 1986 before being unleashed on an unsuspecting world.

BLOODY MOON

★★☆ TransWorld Entertainment, 1981, R, 84 min.
Dir: Jess (Jesus) Franco. Cast: Olivia Pascal, Christoph Moosbrugger, Nadja Gerganoff, Alexander Waechter.

A series of gruesome murders at a continental language school—blood at Berlitz?—coincides with the release from an asylum of a brutal sex murderer. Too derivative of various American slasher films to have the same sort of sick impact as some of Franco's other, more personal features, this is nonetheless distinguished by some extremely sadistic killings, including a chainsaw disembowelment, a knife through the breast, and an especially brutal beheading via buzzsaw.

BLOODY NEW YEAR

★★ Academy Entertainment, 1987, R, 87 min.
Dir: Norman J. Warren. Cast: Suzy Aitchinson, Nikki Brooks, Colin Heywood, Mark Powley, Catherine Roman, Julian Ronnie.

Three teen couples are shipwrecked on an island where time stands still and zombies and various other horrors roam. Confusing Brit shocker with a few neat FX (a girl pulled into a mirror, a man jumping out of an old movie to attack the guy watching it), but too disjointed and badly acted to create much interest. Aka *Timewarp Terror*.

BLOODY PIT OF HORROR, THE

★★☆ Sinister Cinema, 1965, NR, 72 min.
Dir: Max Hunter [Massimo Pupillo]. Cast: Mickey Hargitay, Walter Brandi, Luisa Baratto, Alfredo Rizzo, Mo-Thai, Femi Benussi.

Former Mr. Universe *and* Mr. Jayne Mansfield Hargitay has a field day in this gory Italian cheapie about a repressed homosexual actor possessed by the spirit of the dreaded "Crimson Executioner," who tortures and murders a bevy of cover girls and photographers staying at the executioner's old castle for a publicity shoot. Similar to *Baron Blood* (but without the ambiance), this is supposedly based on the writings of the Marquis de Sade (who most certainly would be writing for the movies today were he alive) and packs lots of tacky entertainment value. Aka *Il Boia Scarlatto: The Scarlet Executioner, The Crimson Executioner, The Red Hangman, The Scarlet Hangman,* and *Virgins for the Hangman.*

BLOODY POM-POMS

See: *Cheerleader Camp.*

BLOODY VAMPIRE, THE

★★☆ Sinister Cinema, 1961, NR, 98 min.
Dir: Miguel Morayta. Cast: Carlos Agosti, Begona Palacios, Erna Martha Bauman, Antonio Raxell, Bertha Moss, Raoul Farell.

A vampire named Count Frankenhausen (Agosti) is terrorizing a small Mexican hamlet, forcing a Van Helsing type named Count Cagliostro (Ferell) to use his daughter, posing as a maid at the Frankenhausen estate, as bait. This English-dubbed version has been considerably hacked down from the Mexican original—running 110 minutes—resulting in some confusion, but it is distinguished by good atmosphere (especially scenes of Frankenhausen sweeping down dank corridors with his cape billowing behind him) and an unexpectedly downbeat ending. Sequel: *Invasion of the Vampires.*

JOHN CARRADINE
(1906–1988)

Has anyone ever been in more movies than this man, the undisputed king of the cameos? Once a highly respected Shakespearean actor and popular character man for John Ford, Long John had a difficult time shaking his image as a popular Z horror villain, a situation not helped much by his insistence on appearing in small roles in seemingly every other cheap horror opus released in the 20 years before his death. Never one to shirk when there was hamming to be done, he added a distinctive touch to every role.

The Invisible Man ('33), *The Black Cat* ('34), *Bride of Frankenstein* ('35), *The Hound of the Baskervilles* ('39), *Whispering Ghosts* ('42), *Captive Wild Woman* ('43), *Revenge of the Zombies* ('43), *The Mummy's Ghost* ('44), *Voodoo Man* ('44), *The Invisible Man's Revenge* ('44), *Return of the Ape Man* ('44), *Bluebeard* ('44), *House of Frankenstein* ('44), *House of Dracula* ('45), *Face of Marble* ('46), *Half Human* ('55), *The Black Sleep* ('56), *The Unearthly* ('57), *Invisible Invaders* ('59), *Invasion of the Animal People* ('60), *Curse of the Stone Hand* ('64), *House of the Black Death* ('65), *Billy the Kid vs. Dracula* ('66), *Munster Go Home!* ('66), *Dr. Terror's Gallery of Horrors* ('67), *Hillbillys in a Haunted House* ('67), *Autopsy of a Ghost* ('67), *Mrs. Death* ('68), *The Devil's Pact* ('68), *Vampire Girls* ('68), *The Astro Zombies* ('68), *Daughter of the Mind* ('69), *Blood of the Iron Maiden* ('69), *Bigfoot* ('70), *Crowhaven Farm* ('70), *Horror of the Blood Monsters* ('70), *Blood of Ghastly Horror* ('71), *Legacy of Blood* ('71), *Silent Night, Bloody Night* ('72), *The Night Strangler* ('73), *The Cat Creature* ('73), *Terror in the Wax Museum* ('73), *The House of Seven Corpses* ('73), *Hex* ('73), *Mary, Mary, Bloody Mary* ('75), *Death at Love House* ('76), *Shock Waves* ('76), *The Sentinel* ('77), *Crash!* ('77), *The White Buffalo* ('77), *Satan's Cheerleaders* ('77), *Vampire Hookers* ('78), *Monster* ('78), *The Bees* ('78), *Nocturna* ('79), *The Boogey Man* ('80), *Satan's Mistress* ('80), *Dr. Dracula* ('80), *Frankenstein Island* ('81), *The Monster Club* ('81), *The Howling* ('81), *The Nesting* ('81), *The Scarecrow* ('82), *House of the Long Shadows* ('83), *Evils of the Night* ('83), *The Tomb* ('85), *Revenge* ('86), *Monster in the Closet* ('86), *Evil Spawn* ('87), *Buried Alive* ('88).

BLOW OUT

★★☆ Goodtimes Home Video, 1981, R, 107 min. Dir: Brian De Palma. Cast: John Travolta, Nancy Allen, John Lithgow, Dennis Franz, Peter Boyden, Curt May.

Travolta is a Philadelphia-based horror film sound effects man who accidentally records audio evidence of a political assassination and finds both himself and another witness (Allen) stalked by psychotic hit man Lithgow. Probably De Palma's least effective thriller, this plays too much like a combined remake of *Blow-Up* and *The Conversation* with slasher movie trimmings. Stunningly photographed and with an amusing film-within-a-film opening, but the twist ending is needlessly cruel and hurtful.

BLUEBEARD

★★★ Sinister Cinema, 1944, NR, 71 min. Dir: Edgar G. Ulmer. Cast: John Carradine, Jean Parker, Nils Asther, Ludwig Stossel, Teala Loring, Iris Adrian.

Probably poverty-row film company PRC's best horror movie, this stylish, ultra-low-budget treatment of a familiar theme was obviously made to cash in on the success of the same year's Jack the Ripper flick *The Lodger*. Carradine is excellent in one of his most complex roles as an artist-puppeteer driven to strangle his models, while Parker is equally fine as the sister of one of his victims who almost falls victim herself. Ulmer does wonders with cheap sets and lighting to create the atmosphere of 19th-century Paris and there's a nice use of classical music to create mood.

BLUEBEARD

★★ USA Video, 1972, R, 117 min. Dir: Edward Dmytryk. Cast: Richard Burton, Raquel Welch, Joey Heatherton, Virna Lisi, Marilu Tolo, Agostina Belli, Karin Schubert, Sybil Danning.

Dopey *Dr. Phibes* clone with a miscast Burton as wife-murdering Baron von Sepper, whose latest spouse (the leggy Heatherton) discovers the frozen corpses of her predecessors whose deaths Burton then recounts at boring length. Lots of female skin and creative deaths: beheading, impaling, drowning, suffocation, and even "falconating," but mostly on the dull side. Welch (as a motormouthed ex-nun) and Lisi (as a horrible songstress with a simply endless repertoire) steal what there is of the film to take.

BLUE EYES OF THE BROKEN DOLL

See: *House of Psychotic Women*.

BLUE HOLOCAUST

See: *Buried Alive* (1979).

BLUE MAN, THE
See: *Eternal Evil.*

BLUE MONKEY
★★ RCA/Columbia Home Video, 1987, R, 96 min. Dir: William Fruet. Cast: Steve Railsback, Gwynyth Walsh, Susan Anspach, John Vernon, Joe Flaherty, Robin Duke, Don Lake, Helen Hughes.

A sometimes fun throwback to all those '50s big bug flicks, with a Canadian hospital menaced by a huge, murderous cootie monster. Despite the opportunities of playing it for comedy, the earnest cast (save "SCTV" regulars Flaherty and Duke) plays it amazingly straight. Aka *Green Monkey* and *The Insect.*

BLUE STEEL
★★☆ MGM/UA Home Video, 1990, R, 102 min. Dir: Kathryn Bigelow. Cast: Jamie Lee Curtis, Ron Silver, Clancy Brown, Louise Fletcher, Elizabeth Pena, Philip Bosco.

A glossy updating of JLC's early '80s slashers with Jamie as a rookie cop romanced by slick psycho Silver, whose obsession with violence darkly mirrors her own. Overstates its case, featuring far too many credulity-stretching moments—including a protracted ending right out of *Halloween*—but very well acted and directed with gusto by Bigelow (*Near Dark*).

BLUE SUNSHINE
★★★ Vestron Video, 1977, R, 94 min. Dir: Jeff Lieberman. Cast: Zalman King, Deborah Winters, Mark Goddard, Robert Walden, Charles Siebert, Ann Cooper, Stefan Gierash, Alice Ghostley.

A well-handled mix of horror, black comedy, and social satire about the decade-delayed reactions a group of former hippies have to a batch of mutant LSD called "Blue Sunshine," which transforms them into homicidal maniacs. Full of marvelous touches (the former longhairs go bald with their insanity) and deft performances from a super cast, this is another winner from the underrated Lieberman.

BLUE VELVET
★★★ Lorimar Home Video, 1986, R, 120 min. Dir: David Lynch. Cast: Kyle MacLachlan, Isabella Rossellini, Dennis Hopper, Laura Dern, Hope Lange, Dean Stockwell, Brad Dourif, Jack Nance.

A callow small-town college student (MacLachlan) finds a severed human ear behind his parents' home and is thereafter thrust into a living nightmare involving a local night club chanteuse (Rossellini) and a psychopathic drug dealer (Hopper). A fascinating, though often hard to watch, examination of the creepiness lurking behind the apple pie sweetness of America's heartland, with good turns from Hopper (excellent in his comeback performance), Dern, and Stockwell. The obvious inspiration for Lynch's later TV series "Twin Peaks."

BODIES SHOW SIGNS OF CARNAL VIOLENCE, THE
See: *Torso.*

BODY BAGS
★★☆ Republic Home Video, 1993, R, 94 min. Dirs: John Carpenter, Tobe Hooper, and Larry Sulkis. Cast: Stacey Keach, Mark Hamill, David Warner, Twiggy, David Naughton, Sheena Easton, Robert Carradine, Deborah Harry, Alex Datcher, John Agar, George "Buck" Flower, John Carpenter.

Made-for-cable anthology with good directors and casts making the most of routine material. Carpenter is a ghoulish morgue attendant who introduces tales about a female cashier terrorized by a psycho at an all-night gas station, a guy (Keach) whose obsession with his hair loss leads to a hair-raising discovery, and a baseball pitcher (Hamill) whose personality is dangerously altered after an eye transplant. The middle tale is best, with a knockout performance from Keach and a very funny one from Warner. The first story has pleasant echoes of *Halloween,* and the last one has a great *X—The Man with the X-Ray Eyes*–inspired ending, but they are, overall, less satisfying. Look for cameos by Hopper, Wes Craven, Roger Corman, and Tom Arnold.

BODY BENEATH, THE
★ WesternWorld Video, 1971, R, 85 min. Dir: Andy Milligan. Cast: Gavin Reed, Jackie Skarvellis, Susan Clark, Colin Gordon.

Dracula, Milligan style. Another low-rent junkster from the king of Staten Island cinema, this one concerning a stuffy British family falling victim to a suave vampire Count. Your geeky cousin could make a more professional-looking movie with his camcorder and a couple of high school friends.

BODY DOUBLE
★★★ Goodtimes Home Video, 1984, R, 114 min. Dir: Brian De Palma. Cast: Craig Wasson, Melanie Griffith, Gregg Henry, Deborah Shelton, Dennis Franz, Guy Boyd.

Wasson is an unemployed actor, fired from a schlocky vampire pic, who falls in love with beautiful neighbor Shelton, whom he spies on with a telescope while house-sitting in the Hollywood hills. When she is brutally murdered with a power drill, the grief-stricken actor soon comes to suspect that he's been set up. One of De Palma's most enjoyable thrillers, this is marred by an often absurd plot and a weak performance from Wasson, but is enhanced by sleek photography, a breathless Pino Donaggio score, and some spirited scene-stealing from Griffith as the kooky porn star

---

BORIS KARLOFF
(1887–1969)

Born William Henry Pratt, Karloff remains the best-known horror movie star in the world. After a decade of undistinguished work in both silent and sound films, he was cast as the monster in James Whale's *Frankenstein,* which made him a star and one of the most popular character actors in Hollywood history. Always grateful for his horror fame, Karloff appeared both in and out of the genre in a variety of roles for more than 30 years, playing everything from mad doctors to Indian chiefs and narrating the Dr. Seuss holiday classic, "How the Grinch Stole Christmas."

The Unholy Night ('29), *The Mad Genius* ('31), *Frankenstein* ('31), *The Old Dark House* ('32), *The Mask of Fu Manchu* ('32), *The Mummy* ('32), *The Ghoul* ('33), *The Black Cat* ('34), *The Bride of Frankenstein* ('35), *The Black Room* ('35), *The Raven* ('35), *The Invisible Ray* ('36), *The Man Who Lived Again* ('36), *The Walking Dead* ('36), *Charlie Chan at the Opera* ('37), *Son of Frankenstein* ('39), *Tower of London* ('39), *The Man They Could Not Hang* ('39), *Black Friday* ('40), *Before I Hang* ('40), *The Ape* ('40), *You'll Find Out* ('40), *The Man With Nine Lives* ('40), *The Devil Commands* ('41), *The Boogie Man Will Get You* ('42), *The Climax* ('44), *House of Frankenstein* ('44), *The Body Snatcher* ('45), *Isle of the Dead* ('45), *Bedlam* ('46), *Abbott and Costello Meet the Killer, Boris Karloff* ('49), *The Strange Door* ('51), *The Black Castle* ('52), *Abbott and Costello Meet Dr. Jekyll and Mr. Hyde* ('53), *Voodoo Island* ('57), *The Haunted Strangler* ('58), *Frankenstein 1970* ('58), *Corridors of Blood* ('58), *The Raven* ('63), *The Terror* ('63), *The Comedy of Terrors* ('64), *Black Sabbath* ('64), *Die, Monster, Die!* ('65), *The Ghost in the Invisible Bikini* ('66), *Mad Monster Party* ('67), *The Sorcerers* ('67), *Targets* ('68), *Cauldron of Blood* ('68), *The Crimson Cult* ('68), *The Snake People* ('68), *The Incredible Invasion* ('68), *The Fear Chamber* ('68), *House of Evil* ('68).

---

who unknowingly holds the key to the mystery. Look for Barbara Crampton and Brinke Stevens in small roles.

BODY PARTS
★★ Paramount Home Video, 1991, R, 88 min. Dir: Eric Red. Cast: Jeff Fahey, Brad Dourif, Kim Delaney, Lindsay Duncan, Zakes Mokae, Peter Murnik.

When his right arm is severed in a freak auto accident, psychologist Fahey gets a new limb from radical transplant specialist Duncan. Predictably, though, the new addition turns out to have come from a mad killer and begins developing a murderous agenda all its own. Good acting (especially Dourif) saves this ridiculously contrived distillation of Maurice Renard's *The Hands of Orlac* and Pierre Boileau-Thomas Narcejac's *Choice Cuts,* which really flies off into the stratosphere during an especially absurd climax.

BODY SNATCHER, THE
★★★★ Turner Home Entertainment, 1945, NR, 78 min. Dir: Robert Wise. Cast: Boris Karloff, Bela Lugosi, Henry Daniell, Edith Atwater, Russell Wade, Rita Corday, Sharyn Moffett, Donna Lee, Robert Clarke, Mary Gordon.

The very best of the Val Lewton B horror series, this is a literate and beautifully enacted adaptation of the Robert Louis Stevenson story of grave robbing and medical ethics in 19th-century Edinburgh. Karloff is outstanding in the title role and Lugosi has a nice character part, but this film really belongs to Daniell, a cold-hearted medical man working for the good of a humanity he can't even relate to, let alone help. A great film with a truly scary ending.

BODY SNATCHERS:
THE INVASION CONTINUES
★★★ Warner Home Video, 1993, R, 87 min. Dir: Abel Ferrara. Cast: Gabrielle Anwar, Billy Wirth, Meg Tilly, R. Lee Ermey, Christine Elise, Forest Whitaker, Terry Kinney, Reilly Murphy.

Long shelved, this underrated sequel-remake to the '78 *Invasion of the Body Snatchers* from rough-n-tumble action director Ferrara relocates the story at a southern military base, where pretty Anwar begins to notice something odd about everyone around her—her dad and new stepmom included. This underplays special effects in favor of action and character development and, despite a few concessions to modern audiences—the teen leads, precocious little kid, lots of gunplay—remains remarkably true to the spirit of the original, including a creepily downbeat ending. Tilly has one of her best roles as Anwar's pod-possessed stepmother.

BOG
★ Video Treasures, 1978, PG, 85 min. Dir: Don Keeslar. Cast: Gloria De Haven, Aldo Ray, Marshall Thompson, Leo Gordon.

Fifties-type low-rent monster movie about a clawed, fish-headed creature that rises from the depths of a boggy lake to mutilate fishermen and find a human mate. A goreless bore with a cast of old-timers (De Haven in *two* roles) just going through the motions.

BONEYARD, THE
★★☆ Prism Entertainment, 1990, R, 98 min. Dir: James Cummins. Cast: Ed Nelson, Phyllis Diller, Norman Fell, Deborah Rose, Jim Eustermann, Denise Young.

Oddball living dead flick about little kid zombies terrorizing a very strange bunch of heroes—including 300-pound psychic heroine Rose—trapped in an old mortuary. The *Return of the Living Dead*–inspired plot makes almost no sense, but a good cast (with Diller first-rate in a serious character role), creepy makeup, and some really wild touches (like a huge mutant poodle-monster) make it worthwhile.

BOOGEY MAN, THE
★★☆ Magnum Home Entertainment, 1980, R, 81 min. Dir: Ulli Lommel. Cast: Suzanna Love, John Carradine, Ron James, Nicholas Love, Raymond Boyden, Felicite Morgan.

In 1960 a little girl and her older brother murder their mother's sadistic lover. Twenty years later a shard of mirror possessed by the lover's ghost sets off a rash of creative deaths at the farm where the siblings now reside. Colorful mix of elements from *Halloween, The Exorcist,* and *The Amityville Horror,* directed with style and imagination by Swedish art filmmaker Lommel.

BOOGEY MAN II
★ Gemstone Video, 1983, R, 79 min. Dir: Bruce Starr. Cast: Suzanna Love, Shannah Hall, Ulli Lommel, Shoto von Douglas, Bob Rosenfarb, Rhonda Aldrich.

Tacky sequel padded with much footage from part I (with original *Boogey Man* director Lommel virtually playing himself). Heroine Love visits friends in Hollywood who are convinced that her past experiences with the supernatural would make one helluva horror movie. Guess what happens when a certain piece of broken mirror turns up? One of the

worst follow-ups ever, with lots of ludicrous gore (including death by electric toothbrush, already done in Lommel's *Olivia*) and stock footage of John Carradine.

BOOK OF THE DEAD
See: *The Evil Dead.*

BORROWER, THE
★★☆ Cannon Home Video, 1989, R, 91 min. Dir: John McNaughton. Cast: Rae Dawn Chong, Don Gordon, Tom Towles, Antonio Fargas, Madchen Amick, Larry Pennell.

An insectoid alien criminal is punished by his fellow creatures by being given human form and banished to Earth. The trouble is, however, his heads have a nasty habit of exploding—Why? Who knows?—forcing him to murder various individuals for replacement noggins. Though the premise is often downright stupid, this second effort from *Henry* helmer McNaughton has a good cast, a couple of interesting twists (the ending is borrowed from *The Crawling Hand*), and a wry sense of humor. The Kevin Yagher–supervised makeup FX, however, leave a lot to be desired, with the alien's body size and skin color inexplicably changing with each new head.

BOWERY AT MIDNIGHT
★★☆ Sinister Cinema, 1942, NR, 63 min. Dir: Wallace Fox. Cast: Bela Lugosi, Wanda McKay, John Archer, Dave O'Brien, Tom Neal, Vince Barnett.

Not another entry in the long-running *Bowery Boys* series but a fun and fairly complex Lugosi Monogram vehicle. Bela is cast as a college professor (whose pet student's thesis is called "Final Thoughts Before Death!") who is also a murderous underworld kingpin on the side (everyone should have a hobby). The supernatural is also worked in with a subplot about Bela's various victims rising up as vengeful zombies into whose clammy clutches our Hungarian godfather stumbles at climax time. Much better than you'd think.

BOXING HELENA
★★☆ Orion, 1993, R, 105 min. Dir: Jennifer Lynch. Cast: Julian Sands, Sherilyn Fenn, Bill Paxton, Kurtwood Smith, Art Garfunkel, Nicolete Scorsese.

This is Lynch's controversial directorial debut in a film about a crazed surgeon (Sands) whose obsession with beautiful but cold Helena (Fenn) leads to his cutting off her limbs and keeping her in a box. Little more than just another retelling of *The Collector,* with Frankensteinian overtones, this has good acting from a talented cast struggling with impossible roles, solid direction from the promising Ms. Lynch, and a *Dead of Night*–inspired final twist.

BOYS FROM BRAZIL, THE

★★☆ Avid Entertainment, 1978, R, 123 min. Dir: Franklin J. Schaffner. Cast: Gregory Peck, Laurence Olivier, James Mason, Lilli Palmer, Uta Hagen, Steve Guttenberg, Anne Meara, John Dehner, Michael Gough, Linda Hayden.

An overlong but delightfully tasteless adaptation of Ira Levin's novel about the plan of Dr. Josef Mengele (Peck, cast against type and playing with gusto) to reincarnate Adolf Hitler through cloning. Ludicrous but fun, with notable contributions from Olivier (trying out his mittle-European shtick for the first of several consecutive performances), Hagen, and the always sexy Hayden.

BOYS FROM BROOKLYN, THE

See: *Bela Lugosi Meets a Brooklyn Gorilla*.

BRACULA—THE TERROR OF THE LIVING DEAD

See: *Beyond the Living Dead*.

BRAIN, THE

★★★ Monterey Home Video, 1963, NR, 83 min. Dir: Freddie Francis. Cast: Peter Van Eyck, Anne Heywood, Bernard Lee, Ellen Schwiers, Cecil Parker, Maxine Audley, Miles Malleson, Jack MacGowran.

Moody British–West German remake of *Donovan's Brain*. Van Eyck is the scientist controlled by the disembodied brain of a dead financier, on which he's experimenting, driven to search out and punish the man's killer. Stark settings and contrasting lighting often give this the look of an old German Expressionist film, and there's a fine cast to help you wade through a melodramatic midsection. A good solo directorial debut for cinematographer Francis. Aka *Vengeance* and *Over My Dead Body*.

BRAIN, THE

See: *Brain of Blood*.

BRAIN, THE

★★ International Video Entertainment, 1988, R, 91 min. Dir: Edward Hunt. Cast: Tom Breznahan, Cyndy Preston, David Gale, George Buza, Brett Pearson, Christina Kossack.

Silly Canadian shocker about a madman (Gale) who, aided by a huge floating brain with a face and spinal cord tail, is using a TV self-help program to brainwash an entire town into doing his bidding. This dumb combo of *Invasion of the Body Snatchers* and *The Brain*

From Planet Arous gets a lot of mileage out of Gale's typically enthusiastic histrionics, but a dull supporting cast and goofy special effects make it one of our less intelligent brain movies.

BRAIN DAMAGE

See: *Brain of Blood*.

BRAIN DAMAGE

★★☆ Paramount Home Video, 1987, R, 83 min. Dir: Frank Henenlotter. Cast: Rick Herbst, Jennifer Lowry, Gordon MacDonald, Theo Barnes, Lucille Saint-Peter, voice of John Zacherle.

Henenlotter, the auteur of the *Basket Case* movies, wrote and directed this monster drug parable. Brian (Herbst) is a nice, good-looking boy who becomes the host for "Elmer," a slimy parasite that eats human brains and secretes a strange blue liquid that gives poor Brian a perpetual high and forces him to find more and more brains for the voracious critter. Elmer (whose lines are spoken by Zacherle) is a personable enough little monster and there are some inspired bits of sick humor, but this gory black comedy is weakened by too many unsympathetic characters (especially the females) and heavy MPAA cuts. Look for *Basket Case* stars Kevin Van Hentenryck and Beverly Bonner in cameos.

BRAIN DEAD

★★☆ MGM/UA Home Video, 1989, R, 84 min. Dir: Adam Simon. Cast: Bill Pullman, Bill Paxton, Bud Cort, George Kennedy, Patricia Charbonneau, Nicholas Pryor.

Based on a 25-year-old screenplay by the late fantasist Charles Beaumont, this metaphysical shocker concerns a neurologist (Pullman) who begins sharing the delusions of a paranoid mental patient (Cort) who murdered his family but claims that another man was responsible. Confusing at times but extremely well acted (Paxton is at his best as Pullman's smarmy best friend), with a hallucination vs. reality structure strongly similar to the later *Jacob's Ladder*.

BRAIN DEAD

See: *Dead Alive*.

BRAIN EATERS, THE

★★☆ Columbia/TriStar Home Video, 1958, NR, 60 min. Dir: Bruno Ve Sota. Cast: Ed Nelson, Joanna Lee, Alan Frost, Jack Hill, Jody Fair, Leonard Nimoy.

Awkward but quite creepy AIP '50s schlock horror about creatures from the bowels of the

JOHN AGAR
(1921–)

The '50s monster hunter par excellence, this Chicago-born actor may be best known to the world at large as the first husband of Shirley Temple, but to the horror fan he is the ultimate monster-flick leading man. His enthusiasm and good spirits have elevated many a Z thriller.

Revenger of the Creature ('55), *Tarantula* ('55), *The Mole People* ('56), *Daughter of Dr. Jekyll* ('57), *The Brain from Planet Arous* ('58), *Attack of the Puppet People* ('58), *Invisible Invaders* ('59), *The Hand of Death* ('61), *Journey to the 7th Planet* ('62), *Curse of the Swamp Creature* ('66), *Zontar, the Thing from Venus* ('66), *Night Fright* ('66), *King Kong* ('76), *Fear* ('89), *Nightbreed* ('90), *The Perfect Bride* ('91), *Body Bags* ('93).

earth (they look like fuzzy bedroom slippers with antenna) attaching themselves to the necks of several small-town civic leaders as prelude to an all-out invasion. A fast and cheap adaptation of Robert Heinlein's "The Puppet Masters," with an unrecognizable Nimoy in a small role at the end.

BRAIN FROM PLANET AROUS, THE
★★☆ Rhino Home Video, 1958, NR, 70 min. Dir: Nathan Hertz [Nathan Juran]. Cast: John Agar, Joyce Meadows, Robert Fuller, Thomas B. Henry.

The best brain from outer space movie ever, with Agar in top form as a scientist who becomes possessed by an evil alien brain-creature with eyes—a brain with eyes? Hey, it could happen!—for John's girl (Meadows). Can a recently arrived good brain from outer space put a stop to all this cranial carnage? One of those "It's so dumb it's fun" cheapies with an especially funny-intense performance from Agar.

BRAINIAC, THE
★★★ Sinister Cinema, 1961, NR, 77 min. Dir: Chano Ureta. Cast: Abel Salazar, Rosa Maria Gallardo, Ruben Rojo, Carmen Montejo, German Robles, Ariadne Welter.

One of the wildest of the Mexican horror films, with Salazar as an executed sorcerer who returns 300 years after his death to seek revenge on the descendants of his enemies by sucking their brains out with a foot-long forked tongue while in the form of a hideous horny-toad monster with an inflatable head!

I'm not making this up. About as off-the-wall as any movie ever made; it hardly ever makes any sense, but it's never dull. So what's not to like? Aka *El Baron del Terror: The Baron of Terror*.

BRAIN OF BLOOD
★☆ Magnum Home Entertainment, 1971, R, 88 min. Dir: Al Adamson. Cast: Grant Williams, Kent Taylor, Regina Carrol, Reed Hadley, Vicki Volante, Angelo Rossitto, John Bloom, Zandor Vorkov.

Just what the world needs, an Al Adamson version of an Eddie Romero movie! Surgeon Williams (of *The Incredible Shrinking Man* fame) is forced to transplant the brain of a Middle Eastern despot (whose body is preserved in Reynolds Wrap) into the skull of hulking monster Bloom by mad scientist Taylor, so that the latter can gain control of the dictator's oil-rich country. Also along for the ride are busty Carrol as a bottle-blonde double agent and dwarf star Rossitto as a sadistic dungeon master who ends up stabbed with a hypodermic syringe by captive Volante. Don't say you weren't warned. Aka *The Brain, Brain Damage, The Undying Brain,* and *The Creature's Revenge*.

BRAIN SNATCHER, THE
See: *The Man Who Changed His Mind*.

BRAIN THAT WOULDN'T DIE, THE
★★★ Rhino Home Video, 1960, NR, 81 min. Dir: Joseph Green. Cast: Jason Evers, Virginia Leith, Adele Lamont, Leslie Daniel, Lola Mason, Eddie Carmel.

A tacky, tasteless, ludicrous piece of trash—in other words, a must-see! Dr. Evers takes the decapitated head of girlfriend Leith (beheaded by his fast driving) to his private lab, where he hooks it up to some tatty life-support device. The doc then starts cruising for the proper stripper or bikini model onto which he can attach his honey's unattached noggin, little realizing that Virgie's begun a psychic communication with the deformed monster (who looks like Baldar Conehead's ugly brother) that Evers conveniently keeps locked in the closet. So when our horny medico comes home with slightly scarred, but stacked, model (Lamont), Virginia orders the monster to rescue the girl, a pesky Bunsen burner is overturned and . . . guess what happens? Originally distributed by Warner in a heavily cut edition, this early gore epic is now available from Rhino in all its clunky glory. A Martin Scorsese favorite.

BRAINWAVES
★★ Embassy Home Entertainment, 1982, R, 81 min. Dir: Ulli Lommel. Cast: Suzanna Love, Keir Dullea, Tony Curtis, Vera Miles, Percy Rodrigues, Eve Brent Ashe.

Vicki Volante realizes that she's left her Halloween decorations up a tad too long in Brain of Blood *(1971).*

Fair mix of sci-fi and stalker horror with Love as an accident victim whose damaged brain is stimulated back to normalcy by the brain-waves of a murdered young woman. Trouble arises when Suzanne begins having flashbacks of the other girl's murder and soon finds the killer on *her* trail. Polished looking and well acted but too leisurely to build much suspense.

BRAM STOKER'S COUNT DRACULA
See: *Count Dracula*.

BRAM STOKER'S DRACULA
See: *Dracula* (1974).

BRAM STOKER'S DRACULA
★★★ Columbia/TriStar Home Video, 1992, R, 127 min. Dir: Francis Ford Coppola. Cast: Gary Oldman, Anthony Hopkins, Winona Ryder, Keanu Reeves, Richard E. Grant, Bill Campbell, Cary Elwes, Sadie Frost, Tom Waits, Jay Robinson.

Coppola's first horror film since *Dementia 13,* this grandiose, Oscar-winning remake of the Stoker novel isn't as letter-perfect-to-the-book as its advance publicity claimed and isn't even the best adaptation but *is* one of the best-looking, most lavish, and imaginatively directed horror films to come out of Hollywood in quite a while. Oldman is first-rate as the Count, who this time travels to Victorian England to seek out the reincarnation of his long-lost wife (an idea pinched from the Dan Curtis TV version of nearly two decades earlier), vamping the vixenish Frost and the sexually repressed Ryder, and finding a nemesis in Hopkins' wonderfully flamboyant Van Helsing. This often looks like the most expensive Roger Corman movie ever made, with flashy sets, costumes, special effects, and camera work, as well as deft homages to Draculas past. Oldman casts a shadow like Max Schreck, talks like Bela Lugosi, and wears Christopher Lee red contacts and fangs. Not the genre classic it wants to be, but still a notable achievement.

BREEDERS

★★ Vestron Video, 1985, R, 77 min. Dir: Tim Kincaid. Cast: Teresa Farley, Lance Lewman, Frances Raines, Amy Brentano.

Gruesome no-budgeter about monster rape and the grisly aftermath—sort of like *Humanoids From the Deep,* but in *bad* taste. An outer space invader impregnates a number of Manhattan lovelies in order to father an invasion by proxy. Unfortunately non-virgins (not a hard-to-come-by commodity in NYC) give birth to grotesque Ed French–designed mutants. A couple of chuckles, loads of female skin, and another *Carrie*-esque nightmare finale for the *very* undiscriminating.

BRIDE, THE

★★☆ Goodtimes Home Video, 1985, R, 118 min. Dir: Franc Goddam. Cast: Sting, Jennifer Beals, Clancy Brown, David Rappaport, Geraldine Page, Anthony Higgins, Veruschka, Quentin Crisp.

This elaborate sequel-remake-homage to *Bride of Frankenstein* starts out great, with a meticulous color recreation of the atmosphere of the classic horror films of the '30s. Things then go downhill fast as this turns into a kind of horrific Jill Clayburgh movie, with the Baron's female creation (a miscast Beals) becoming a liberated unmarried woman. Fortunately, a delightful subplot about the Monster's (Brown) friendship with circus dwarf Rappaport has genuine charm and carries this uneven, overlong movie along in high style.

BRIDE AND THE BEAST, THE

★★ Admit One Video 1958, NR, 78 min. Dir: Adrian Weiss. Cast: Charlotte Austin, Lance Fuller, Johnny Roth, Steve Calvert, William Justine, Jeanne Gerson.

Ed Wood scripted this awesomely inept jungle horror about a baby-faced big-game hunter (Fuller) whose new bride (Austin) discovers that she is a reincarnated gorilla! Later, on African safari, Char abandons Lance for the hairy embrace of the nearest guy in an ape suit. With lots of angora sweaters, moth-eaten monkey costumes, and jungle movie stock footage, this oddly downbeat '50s programmer proves that *Plan Nine* was no fluke. Aka *Queen of the Gorillas.*

BRIDE OF FENGRIFFEN

See: —*And Now the Screaming Starts!*

BRIDE OF FRANKENSTEIN

★★★★ MCA/Universal Home Video, 1935, NR, 75 min. Dir: James Whale. Cast: Boris Karloff, Colin Clive, Valerie Hobson, Elsa Lanchester, Ernest Thesiger, Una O'Connor, O. P. Heggie, E. E. Clive, Gavin Gordon, Douglas Walton, Dwight Frye, John Carradine.

Surviving the mill fire that supposedly destroyed him at the end of the original *Frankenstein,* the monster (Karloff) is taught to speak by a blind hermit (Heggie) and, after falling under the bad influence of sinister Dr. Pretorious (Thesiger), demands of its creator (Clive) the construction of a mate. This masterpiece is the apex of Hollywood's '30s horror cycle and one of the few sequels to top its predecessor. With Whale's trademark black humor given free reign, Lanchester coyly cast as both authoress Mary Shelley and the frizzy-haired bride, a grand Franz Waxman musical score, and Karloff in one of his most brilliant performances—the Monster laughs, loves, and cries. Remade as *The Bride.*

BRIDE OF RE-ANIMATOR

★★☆ LIVE Home Video, 1990, UR, 96 min. Dir: Brian Yuzna. Cast: Jeffrey Combs, Bruce Abbott, David Gale, Fabiana Udenio, Claude Earl Jones, Kathleen Kinmont.

So-so sequel to the modern classic, with Combs (whose reappearance after his death at the end of the original is never explained) teaming up again with Abbott to create a female being à la *Frankenstein.* Not as adept at mixing dark comedy and ultra-gore as was the first but still brimming with mind-blowing FX

JAMES WHALE
(1889–1957)

Whale was a flamboyant British director in Hollywood who was undoubtably the most talented director specializing in horror in the 1930s. His inventive use of the camera and sardonic wit made his films far fresher than most others from the same period. However, Whale's outspokenness and well-known homosexual lifestyle made him fall quickly out of favor in the ultra-conservative Hollywood of the late '30s and early '40s. He died under mysterious circumstances, drowned in his swimming pool, and his death remains one of Hollywood's great unsolved mysteries.

Frankenstein ('31), *The Old Dark House* ('32), *The Invisible Man* ('33), *Bride of Frankenstein* ('35).

Colin Clive gives away the blushing Elsa Lanchester in Bride of Frankenstein *(1935).*

work and bubbling-just-below-the-surface homosexual tension between Combs and Abbott; the always sardonic Gale, though, is wasted as a flying severed head. Also available in a slightly shorter R-rated version.

BRIDE OF THE ATOM

See: *Bride of the Monster.*

BRIDE OF THE GORILLA

★☆ Sinister Cinema, 1951, NR, 65 min.
Dir: Curt Siodmak. Cast: Barbara Payton, Raymond Burr, Lon Chaney, Jr., Tom Conway, Paul Cavanagh, Woody Strode.

Laugher set in an indoor African jungle where the nasty actions of a brooding Burr curse him with nightly transformations into a rampaging ape—well, maybe. This dopey Z flick wastes a good cast in embarrassing roles and has a rushed, confusing ending that doesn't even properly explain the ultimate fate of the film's heroine (Payton).

BRIDE OF THE MONSTER

★★ Sinister Cinema, 1955, NR, 69 min.
Dir: Edward D. Wood, Jr. Cast: Bela Lugosi, Tor Johnson, Tony McCoy, Loretta King, Harvey B. Dunn, George Becwar.

A withered Lugosi (just before he had himself committed to a state institution for drug dependency) stars as a mad scientist attempting to create a race of supermen in an old house in the woods. So far, though, all he's managed to come up with are big, bald Johnson and an inert rubber octopus. One of the cheapest, funniest horrors ever made, with a photo enlarger and some kitchen appliances standing in for Bela's mad lab equipment, a supporting cast with all the talent of finger puppets, and some of the best bad dialogue you've ever heard. Aka *Bride of the Atom;* sequel: *Night of the Ghouls.*

BRIDES OF BLOOD

See: *Brides of the Beast.*

BRIDES OF BLOOD ISLAND

See: *Brides of the Beast.*

BRIDES OF DRACULA

★★★☆ MCA/Universal Home Video, 1960, NR, 85 min. Dir: Terence Fisher. Cast: Peter Cushing, Martita Hunt, Yvonne Monlaur, David Peel, Freda Jackson, Andree Melly, Mona Washbourne, Miles Malleson, Michael Ripper, Marie Devereaux.

Fisher's beautifully mounted sequel to *Horror of Dracula* (but without Dracula) details the further exploits of the Count's destroyer, Dr. Van Helsing (Cushing). Here he battles the foppish Baron Meinster (Peel), who's rampaging through a girls school after being innocently released from his silver chains by a young French teacher (Monlaur) visiting his mother's chateau. A sumptuous production rich in color and detail, this has top-flight acting from a super cast and boldly touches on elements of incest, lesbianism, homosexuality, and other theretofore unexplored sexual aspects of the vampire condition.

Yvonne Monlaur thinks twice about her engagement to David Peel in Brides of Dracula *(1960).*

DAVID CRONENBERG
(1943–)

Canadian director Cronenberg's gruesome films mix sex, violence, and various bodily functions; he created the self-described "venereal horror" subgenre. He is a strong visual stylist; not all of whose films work, but each shows a remarkable personal vision unmistakably Cronenbergian.

They Came From Within ('76), *Rabid* ('77), *The Brood* ('79), *Scanners* ('81), *Videodrome* ('83), *The Dead Zone* ('83), *The Fly* ('86), *Dead Ringers* ('88), *Nightbreed* (actor, '90), *Naked Lunch* ('91).

BRIDES OF THE BEAST

★☆ Regal Home Video, 1968, R, 94 min. Dirs: Gerardo de Leon and Eddie Romero. Cast: John Ashley, Kent Taylor, Beverly Hills, Mario Montenegro, Eva Darren, Oscar Keesee.

The first in a trio of soft-core sex and gore opuses set on the conveniently radiation-beset environs of Blood Island, where plantation owner Montenegro mutates nightly into a horny Desi Arnaz–accented monster that looks like a cross between the Michelin tire man and a pickle and likes to rape and mutilate naked native women. Thanks to a stilted cast headed by former AIP star Ashley, B-movie stalwart Taylor, and has-been-who-never-was Hills, this Filipino favorite is good for a couple of laughs and was successful enough on the drive-in circuit to inspire a pair of sequels: *The Mad Doctor of Blood Island* and *Beast of Blood*. Aka *Brides of Blood*, *Brides of Blood Island*, *Grave Desires*, and *The Island of Living Horror*.

BRIDGE ACROSS TIME

See: *Terror at London Bridge*.

BRIGHTON STRANGLER, THE

★★☆ Turner Home Entertainment, 1945, NR, 67 min. Dir: Max Nosseck. Cast: John Loder, June Duprez, Michael St. Angel, Miles Mander, Rose Hobart, Gilbert Emery.

Solid '40s psycho chiller with Loder as an actor who receives a head injury in the London Blitz and begins acting out his stage role as the crazed "Brighton Strangler" in real life. A cast of familiar character actors and a tense script make this an enjoyable small-scale thriller.

BRIMSTONE & TREACLE

★★ MGM/UA Home Video, 1982, R, 85 min. Dir: Richard Loncraine. Cast: Sting, Denholm Elliott, Joan Plowright, Suzanna Hamilton.

Sting made his big screen bow in this offbeat but not really successful thriller (adapted from a British TV play) about a middle-aged couple with a pretty, catatonic daughter who are visited by a strange young man who may either be their daughter's concerned boyfriend, a madman, or the devil himself. Good work from Elliott and Plowright but this (with lots of Police tunes on the soundtrack) is mainly for fans of der Stingle.

BROOD, THE

★★★☆ Embassy Home Entertainment, 1979, R, 91 min. Dir: David Cronenberg. Cast: Oliver Reed, Samantha Eggar, Art Hindle, Cindy Hinds, Henry Beckman, Susan Hogan, Nuala Fitzgerald, Robert Silverman.

One of Cronenberg's best, this plays like an horrific variation on *Kramer vs. Kramer*. Eggar is an abusive mom being treated by pop psychologist Reed, whose experimental technique—called psychoplasmics—gives Sam the ability to personify her rage in the form of deformed, child-like clones she births from an external womb and sends out on murderous missions against her parents, her husband's suspected lover, and others. A deeply disturbing film that uses its grotesque violence to tell a story rather than to shock for its own sake, with Reed and Eggar (who makes her character surprisingly sympathetic, all things considered) giving perhaps their best performances ever.

RONDO HATTON
(1894–1946)

Famous as the only Universal monster character not to need any special makeup, Rondo was a Florida-based reporter who developed the disfiguring disease acromegaly and fell into Hollywood bit parts thanks to his distorted look. Cast by Universal as the dreaded Hoxton Creeper in the Sherlock Holmes thriller *The Pearl of Death*, Hatton was boosted to minor horror sensation in several quickies completed virtually back-to-back in the months before his disease finally took his life.

The Hunchback of Notre Dame (bit, '39), *The Pearl of Death* ('44), *Jungle Captive* ('45), *The Spider Woman Strikes Back!* ('46), *House of Horrors* ('46), *The Brute Man* ('46).

BROTHERHOOD OF SATAN, THE

★★★ Goodtimes Home Video, 1971, PG, 92 min.
Dir: Bernard McEveety. Cast: Strother Martin, Ahna
Capri, L.Q. Jones, Charles Bateman, Charles
Robinson, Alvy Moore.

Eerie low-budgeter about a small California
town under the spell of a cult of aging
satanists out to reincarnate themselves in the
bodies of young children. One of the better
early '70s *Rosemary's Baby* spin-offs, with able
acting from the great Martin as the coven's
leader and a creepily ambiguous ending.

BRUTE MAN, THE

★★ Sony Video, 1946, NR, 58 min. Dir: Jean
Yarbrough. Cast: Rondo Hatton, Jane Adams, Tom
Neal, Jan Wiley, Donald McBride, Peter Whitney.

One of Universal's last low-budget horrors of
the '40s, this was considered so bad, even for
them, they gave it to PRC to distribute! Sure
it's no *House of Horrors,* but as a swan song for
Hatton's Creeper it isn't *that* bad. Rondo's
back snapping spines but this time he gets to
romance blind piano teach Adams (sort of)
and we get the alleged back story of how he
was once a handsome college jock disfigured
in a lab explosion. You've probably seen
worse 58-minute movies.

BUCKET OF BLOOD, A

★★★ Rhino Home Video, 1959, NR, 65 min.
Dir: Roger Corman. Cast: Dick Miller, Barboura
Morris, Antony Carbone, Julian Burton, Judy Bamber,
Ed Nelson, Burt Convy, Bruno Ve Sota.

Zestful Corman quickie spoofing the 1950s
beatnik movement as well as *House of Wax*–
type horror films. Miller is terrific in his signa-
ture role of Walter Paisley, a schnook of a busboy who commits murders and covers his victims in clay in order to pass them off as "sculp-
tures" he uses to impress the artistic types who
hang out in the coffee shop where he works. It
runs out of steam before it reaches its climax,
but is a nice precursor to Corman's even
cheaper classic, *The Little Shop of Horrors,* with
great work from Miller, Morris, and Burton.

BUFFY, THE VAMPIRE SLAYER

★★☆ Fox Video, 1992, PG-13, 85 min. Dir: Fran
Rubel Kuzui. Cast: Kristy Swanson, Luke Perry,
Donald Sutherland, Rutger Hauer, Paul Ruebens,
Candy Clark, David Arquette, Mark De Carlo.

Here's the sitch: Like, Buff's a cheerleader who
discovers her heritage as an ace vampire
hunter just as a pack of bloodsuckers move
into the Valley. No way! Way! As dumb as it
sounds, this spoof ain't half bad, with Swanson perfectly cast as the vacuous val turned

butt-kicking distaff teen Van Helsing. Perry, of
"90210," is also quite likable as the grunge guy
whose neck all the—conspicuously male—
vampires have a hankerin' for, but both
Sutherland and, especially, Hauer are wasted.

BUG

★★ Paramount Home Video, 1975, PG, 99 min.
Dir: Jeannot Szwarc. Cast: Bradford Dillman, Joanna
Miles, Richard Gilliland, Jamie Smith Jackson, Patty
McCormack, Alan Fudge, Jesse Vint, Brendan Dillon.

William Castle produced and co-wrote this
gleefully icky version of Thomas Page's *The
Hephaestus Plague.* Considering this was shot
for a PG they got away with *a lot* as incendiary
foot-long cockroaches chew on people and set
them on fire in a small desert community.
Miles and McCormack (the former *Bad Seed*)
are among those bugged by the hungry roaches, while Dillman is at his most wigged-out as
an obsessed science teacher who accidentally
helps the bugs along the evolutionary scale.
Castle's last film.

'BURBS, THE

★★ MCA/Universal Home Video, 1989, PG-13,
101 min. Dir: Joe Dante. Cast: Tom Hanks, Carrie
Fisher, Bruce Dern, Rick Ducommun, Corey Feldman,

"Now, where'd I put those Roach Motels?"
wonders Patty McCormack in Bug *(1975).*

Wendy Schaal, Henry Gibson, Brother Theodore, Gale Gordon, Dick Miller.

Slight horror-comedy about a suburbanite (Hanks) who comes to suspect that the new neighbors who've moved into the creepy old house next door are a family of psychopaths. A talented cast and the usual Dante in-jokes help you through the uneven, basically one-joke story line, which peters out about 20 minutes before its limp wrap-up.

BURIAL GROUND
★★ Vestron Video, 1980, UR, 85 min.
Dir: Andrea Bianchi. Cast: Karin Weil, Gian Luigi Chirezzi, Maria Angela Giordano, Simone Mattioli, Antonella Antinori, Peter Bark.

A particularly zesty band of walking stiffs raised by Etruscan black magic (or something) lays into a band of particularly badly dubbed dumbbells in this unrelentingly stupid second cousin to Lucio Fulci's *Zombie*. It's the sort of movie in which couples stop to have sex in an overgrown cemetery and a woman (Giordano) rather unwisely offers an ample breast for her newly zombied son to suckle. Gorehounds should give this a minor thumbs-up, but everyone else will want to give this grim Italian puppy a wide berth. Aka *La Notte del Terrore: Night of Terror*, *Zombie Horror*, and *Zombie 3*.

BURIED ALIVE
★★ Thrillervideo, 1979, UR, 85 min. Dir: Joe D'Amato [Aristide Massacesi]. Cast: Kieran Canter, Cinzia Monreale, Franca Stoppa, Anna Cardini.

One of the sickest Italian gore movies ever, this tells the touching tale of sentimental necrophile Canter, who exhumes, stuffs, and loves his late girlfriend while brutally murdering anyone who intrudes on his affair. Originally titled *Buio Omega: Blue Holocaust*, this features infamous evisceration, heart munching, and cremation sequences and is recommended for only the strongest of stomachs.

BURIED ALIVE
★★ RCA/Columbia Home Video, 1988, R, 95 min. Dir: Gerard Kirkoine. Cast: Robert Vaughn, Donald Pleasence, John Carradine, Karen Witter, Ginger Lynn Allen, Bill Butler.

Convoluted South Africa–shot "adaptation" of Poe's "The Premature Burial" set at a school for wayward girls where some fiend in a Ronald Reagan mask (!!!) is bricking up babes behind the cellar walls. Occasionally stylish and helped by a few over-the-top moments (like a scalping via electric egg beater) but mostly a mess, with heavy-duty hamming from Vaughn, a bewigged Pleasence, and a briefly viewed Carradine in his last role.

BURIED ALIVE
★★ MCA/Universal Home Video, 1990, PG-13, 96 min. Dir: Frank Darabout. Cast: Tim Matheson, Jennifer Jason Leigh, William Atherton, Hoyt Axton.

Routine suspense film with Matheson as a cuckold who rises from the grave for revenge after being buried alive by unfaithful spouse Leigh. Matheson comes off like a poor man's Bruce Willis, and too many of the twists are far too obvious. The shock ending is effective, though. Aka *Til Death Do Us Part*.

BURKE AND HARE
See: *The Horrors of Burke and Hare*.

BURNING, THE
See: *Don't Go In the House*.

BURNING, THE
★★ HBO Video, 1981, R, 90 min. Dir: Tony Maylam. Cast: Brian Matthews, Leah Ayres, Brian Backer, Larry Joshua, Ned Eisenberg, Jason Alexander, Fisher Stevens, Carolyn Houlihan, Holly Hunter, Lou David.

By-the-numbers *Friday the 13th* clone about an upstate New York summer camp haunted by a fire-disfigured killer called Cropsy (David). Among those he stalks with his extra-large hedge shears are Alexander ("Seinfeld") and

Oliver Reed searches for his weed whacker in Burnt Offerings *(1976).*

Oscar-winner Hunter. Most of Tom Savini's gruesome FX had to be cut for an R but there *is* an intense score by Yes keyboardist Rick Wakeman.

BURNIN' LOVE
See: *Love at Stake.*

BURNT OFFERINGS
★★☆ MGM/UA Home Video, 1976, PG, 116 min.
Dir: Dan Curtis. Cast: Karen Black, Oliver Reed, Bette Davis, Lee H. Montgomery, Burgess Meredith, Eileen Heckart, Dub Taylor, Anthony James.

Slick haunted house thriller about a family who rent a suspiciously inexpensive country mansion as a summer home and falls victim to its evil influences, the house restoring itself by feeding off their life force. Good acting (though Davis is wasted) and production values but slow pacing and a typically '70s downbeat atmosphere make this rough going for all but the most patient of viewers.

BURN, WITCH, BURN
See: *Mark of the Devil.*

BUTCHER, BAKER, NIGHTMARE MAKER
See: *Night Warning.*

CABINET OF DR. CALIGARI, THE
★★★★ Goodtimes Home Video, 1919, NR, 69 min.
Dir: Robert Wiene. Cast: Werner Krauss, Conrad Veidt, Lil Dagover, Friedrich Feher, Hans Heinz Von Twardowski, Rudolf Klein-Rogge.

Generally regarded as the original horror film, this highly influential psychological chiller tells of sideshow magician Dr. Caligari (Krauss), who exhibits a zombie-like somnambulist (Veidt) whom he also uses as a hypnotized weapon for murder. In the end, though, everything turns out to be the ravings of an asylum inmate. With its stylized painted flat sets and exaggerated makeup and acting technique, *Caligari* single-handedly established the Expressionistic school of German filmmaking and created many standard horror plot devices—the mad doctor, the zombie, the abducted heroine carried off over the rooftops, the shock-twist ending—still in use. Remade in 1962 as *The Cabinet of Caligari*.

CAGE, THE
See: *My Sister, My Love*.

CAGED VAMPIRES
See: *Dungeon of Terror*.

CAGED VIRGINS
See: *Dungeon of Terror*.

CAGE OF DOOM
See: *Terror From the Year 5000*.

CALIFORNIA AXE MASSACRE, THE
★ Wizard Video, 1974, R, 66 min. Dir: Frederick R. Friedel. Cast: Leslie Lee, Jack Canon, Ray Green, Frederick R. Friedel.

Crummy *Last House on the Left* rip about a trio of sadistic crooks who hide out in the farmhouse of a pretty psycho (Lee) who seeks a hatchet-wielding revenge when they kill her grandfather. Cheesy gore job shot in North Carolina as *Lisa, Lisa* and released to theatres in 1977 as *The Axe* on a twin bill with the equally depressing *The Child*.

CALLER, THE
★★☆ TransWorld Entertainment, 1987, R, 98 min. Dir: Arthur Allan Seidelman. Cast: Malcolm McDowall, Madolyn Smith.

Widow Smith is stalked at her remote mountain cabin by mysterious McDowall, who may or may not want to kill her. This well-acted two-character melodrama with horror and sci-fi overtones may frustrate some viewers with its oblique dialogue and plot twists, but it's worth working with.

CALTIKI, THE IMMORTAL MONSTER
★★ Sinister Cinema, 1959, NR, 76 min. Dir: Robert Hampton [Riccardo Freda]. Cast: John Merivale, Didi Sullivan, Gerard Herter, Daniela Rocca.

Passable Italian spin-off of *The Blob* and *The Creeping Unknown*, about archaeologists in Mexico who discover an ancient Mayan temple guarded by a mass of pulsating, flesh-eating matter that, when touched, turns one of the group (Herter) into a madman. Visually imaginative, thanks to the photography of Mario Bava (billed here as John Foam) but this is otherwise routine, with silly special effects. Aka *The Immortal Monster*.

CAMERON'S CLOSET
★★ Sony Video, 1988, R, 87 min. Dir: Armand Mastroianni. Cast: Cotter Smith, Mel Harris, Scott Curtis, Tab Hunter, Leigh McCloskey, Chuck McCann, Kim Lankford, Gary Hudson.

Any movie that begins with the full-frontal decapitation of Tab Hunter can't be all bad, right? Well, this isn't *too* bad. Little Cameron (Curtis) sure has his hands full trying to handle Dad's recent beheading *and* Mom's obnoxious new live-in boyfriend. Wouldn't you know it, then, that a murderous demon would move into his bedroom closet—which is roughly the size of an average Manhattan apartment. The cast is better than their material—adapted by Gary *The Howling* Brandner from his novel—which is full of silly inconsistencies; equally silly is Carlo Rambaldi's plastic closet creature.

CAMPFIRE TALE
See: *Madman*.

CAMPSITE MASSACRE
See: *The Final Terror*.

CANDLE FOR THE DEVIL, A
See: *Nightmare Hotel*.

CANDYMAN
★★★★ Columbia/TriStar Home Video, 1992, R, 98 min. Dir: Bernard Rose. Cast: Virginia Madsen, Tony Todd, Xander Berkeley, Kasi Lemmons, Vanessa Williams, DeJuan Guy, Michael Culkin, Carolyn Lowery.

This superlative adaptation of Clive Barker's short story "The Forbidden" is one of the best, most intense horror films of the past 10 years. Madsen is a graduate student at the University of Chicago whose thesis on urban legends leads to her accidentally summoning up the "Candyman," a hook-handed killer with a velvet voice who frames our heroine for several gruesome murders. Madsen is excellent as the luckless student and Todd brilliant as the seductive, destructive Candyman, while Rose beautifully captures the despair and sadness of the ghetto environment in which much of the action takes place. This is one of the few recent genre films to actually have the courage of its convictions and end on a wonderfully scary, downbeat note, this is by far the finest horror film achievement yet of the '90s.

CANNIBAL APOCALYPSE
See: *Invasion of the Flesh Hunters*.

CANNIBAL FEROX
See: *Make Them Die Slowly*.

CANNIBAL HOLOCAUST
★★★ Mogul Video, 1978, R, 95 min.
Dir: Ruggero Deodato. Cast: Francesca Ciardi, Luca Barbareschi, Robert Kerman, Percy Perkamin.

One of the first and most infamous Italian cannibal horror films, this tells of an unlikable group of filmmakers in South America making a documentary on native life. When the natives prove too docile for the exploitation filmmakers' liking, they prod them into violence—with horrible consequences. One of the most disturbing films of its subgenre, this lacks the grim humor of other, safer cannibal gut-munchers. Its near-brilliance, in fact, lies in its unrelenting ability to get under your skin and stay with you for days. Not really a good movie in the traditional sense, but most definitely an unforgettable one. Note in passing: most extant prints are missing the celebrated "piranha bait" scene.

CANNIBAL ORGY, OR THE MADDEST STORY EVER TOLD
See: *Spider Baby*.

CANNIBAL VIRUS
See: *Night of the Zombies*.

CAPE FEAR
★★★ MCA/Universal Home Video, 1962, NR, 105 min. Dir: J. Lee Thompson. Cast: Gregory Peck, Robert Mitchum, Polly Bergen, Martin Balsam, Telly Savalas, Lori Martin.

Heavy influences from *Psycho*—including casting Balsam as a detective and a Bernard Herrman score—dominate this slick shocker about a lawyer (Peck) whose family is menaced by psychotic ex-con Mitchum (virtually reprising his *Night of the Hunter* role), whom Peck once sent up the river. Well-done nail-biter with able acting and direction.

CAPE FEAR
★★★☆ MCA/Universal Home Video, 1991, R, 128 min. Dir: Martin Scorsese. Cast: Robert DeNiro, Nick Nolte, Jessica Lange, Juliette Lewis, Joe Don Baker, Robert Mitchum, Gregory Peck, Martin Balsam, Illeana Douglas, Fred Dalton Thompson.

This elaborate remake has Nolte (who's very good) as the put-upon lawyer, but really pulls out all the stops in its casting of DeNiro as the vengeful ex-con. He's genuinely terrifying, whether biting off the cheek of Douglas or cozying up to Nolte's pretty teen daughter (Lewis). Though this runs too long and typically overdoes it in a *Friday the 13th*–derived climax, this is the best of the big-budget '90s thrillers, with beautiful photography by Fred-die Francis, a powerful re-scoring of the original Bernard Herrmann music (by Elmer Bernstein), and amusing cameos from Mitchum, Peck, and Balsam.

CAPTAIN KRONOS, VAMPIRE HUNTER
★★★ Paramount/Gateway Home Video, 1973, R, 91 min. Dir: Brian Clemens. Cast: Horst Janson, Caroline Munro, John Cater, Shane Briant, John Carson, Ian Hendry, Lois Dane, Wanda Ventham.

Underrated Hammer vampire adventure. The captain (Janson) is a swashbuckling swordsman out to eradicate the plague of vampirism from the world, in this case battling a monster that drains youth, not blood, from its victims. Haunting visuals (like flowers wilting as the vampire passes), a good sense of humor, and a fine cast (including Munro in her best role) distinguish this from the rest of the herd. Aka *Kronos*.

CAR, THE
★★ MCA/Universal Home Video, 1977, PG, 95 min. Dir: Elliot Silverstein. Cast: James Brolin, Kathleen Lloyd, Ronny Cox, John Marley, R. G. Armstrong, John Rubinstein, Kim Richards, Kyle Richards.

There are laughs aplenty in this lemon, which unsuccessfully attempted to combine elements of *Duel*, *The Exorcist*, and *Jaws*. A driverless black sedan speeds around a tiny desert

---

CAROLINE MUNRO
(1948–)

A statuesque Brit scream queen, Munro exudes a sweet personality and honest sex appeal that have sparked many a horror and fantasy film. She made her horror debut as Vincent Price's well-preserved dead wife in *The Abominable Dr. Phibes*. Her best roles are the fiery gypsy heroine of *Captain Kronos—Vampire Hunter* and the bewitching slave girl in *The Golden Voyage of Sinbad*. Although she has been a cult figure for more than 20 years, major stardom has always eluded her. More's the pity.

The Abominable Dr. Phibes ('71), *Dr. Phibes Rises Again!* ('72), *Dracula A.D. 1972* ('72), *Captain Kronos—Vampire Hunter* ('73), *The Golden Voyage of Sinbad* ('74), *The Devil Within Her* ('75), *At the Earth's Core* ('76), *Maniac* ('81), *The Last Horror Film* ('82), *Don't Open Till Christmas* ('84), *Slaughter High* ('86), *Howl of the Devil* ('87), *Faceless* ('88), *The Black Cat* ('91).

community, running down various towns-folk—including the movie's only two likable characters—while sheriff Brolin (during his John Agar wannabe period) tries to stop it. About as scary as a rerun of *My Mother, the Car* (well, maybe not *that* scary) but there's a good cast and effective desert locales, often making this resemble a color version of a '50s Jack Arnold flick.

CARMILLA

★★ Cannon Home Video, 1989, NR, 52 min. Dir: Gabrielle Beaumont. Cast: Meg Tilly, Ione Skye, Roddy McDowall, Roy Dotrice.

Mild tele-version of the J. Sheridan Le Fanu classic, reset, for no apparent reason, in the post–Civil War South. Lonely Skye befriends haunting, homeless Tilly, who turns out to be a lesbian vampire. This *Nightmare Classics* episode is pretty bland apart from a striking scene where Meg hangs upside down from a tree to feast bat-like on Ione's neck and the unexpected gory demise of vampire hunter McDowall.

CARNAGE

See: *Bay of Blood*.

CARNAGE

★ Media Home Entertainment, 1983, R, 91 min. Dir: Andy Milligan. Cast: Leslie Den Dooven, Michael Chiodo, John Garitt, Dean Veeder.

Milligan made a needless comeback with this minimalistic haunted house hokum about a young couple who buy a murder-laden mansion. A sort-of *Amityville Horror* on five bucks a day, with amateur-hour acting and gore FX. Aka *Hell House*.

CARNIVAL OF BLOOD

★☆ United American Video, 1970, R, 80 min. Dir: Leonard Kirtman. Cast: Burt Young, Judith Resnick, Earle Edgerton, Martin Barolsky, Kaly Mills, Gloria Spivak.

Dull gore film shot on Coney Island with a pre-*Rocky* Young as the geeky main suspect in a series of mutilation murders along the boardwalk: one girl comes out of the funhouse decapitated, another is stabbed through the eye, and so on. Bloody enough but not much fun, though Spivak is hilarious as an obnoxious fat blonde. Aka *Death Rides the Carousel*.

CARNIVAL OF SOULS

★★★★ Magnum Home Entertainment, 1962, NR, 84 min. Dir: Herk Harvey. Cast: Candace Hilligoss, Sidney Berger, Frances Feist, Stanley Leavitt, Art Ellison, Herk Harvey.

Classic eerie mood piece shot on a box-lunch budget in Salt Lake City and Lawrence, Kansas. Hilligoss survives a car crash into a Kansas river and immediately leaves town for a church organist job in Salt Lake. Already aloof, she finds it increasingly difficult to relate to others and soon finds herself stalked by a mysterious pale-faced man (director Harvey) while continually drawn to a crumbling lakeside pavilion. A haunting diamond-in-the-rough lost in the shuffle of early '60s quickies—it was originally co-billed with *The Devil's Messenger*—yikes! Thanks to late-night TV and now video, this is finally finding an increasingly growing audience to appreciate its creepy monochromic charms. Aka *Corridors of Evil*.

CARNOSAUR

★★☆ New Horizons Home Video, 1993, R, 83 min. Dir: Adam Simon. Cast: Diane Ladd, Raphael Sbarge, Jennifer Runyon, Clint Howard.

Mad geneticist Ladd (doing an on-target Louise Fletcher imitation) develops a virus designed to wipe out most of the world's female population as they give birth to a new breed of superintelligent dinosaur, which she believes should inherit the earth. This downbeat Roger Corman quickie is as violent and visceral as *Jurassic Park* should have been, with good budget FX and lots of gore. The climax looks like test footage for an H. G. Lewis remake of *Dinosaurus*. Unfortunately, this switches gears once too often and tends to spread its canvas amongst far too many uninteresting characters.

CARPATHIAN EAGLE, THE

★★ Thrillervideo, 1980, NR, 50 min. Dir: Francis Megahy. Cast: Suzanne Danielle, Anthony Valentine, Sian Phillips, Pierce Brosnan.

Undistinguished episode of the *Hammer House of Horror* TV series, with leggy Danielle as a reporter investigating a series of murders in which the victims' hearts have been clawed out. It has its moments but the steamier elements have been rather ham-fistedly edited out, dulling this entry's edge.

CARPENTER, THE

★★ Republic Home Video, 1987, UR, 87 min. Dir: David Wellington. Cast: Wings Hauser, Lynne Adams, Pierce Lenior, Barbara-Ann Jones.

Ghost meets *The Toolbox Murders* in this silly gore job with Hauser as the deceased handyman who falls in love with Adams (the unhappily married new owner of his old house) and begins hacking her enemies apart with whatever tool is handy. Splashy but stupid; any film where Wings gives a restrained performance (if you can imagine such a thing) hardly seems worth the effort. Also out in an edited R version.

CARRIE
★★★☆ MGM/UA Home Video, 1976, R, 97 min.
Dir: Brian De Palma. Cast: Sissy Spacek, Piper Laurie, John Travolta, Amy Irving, William Katt, Nancy Allen, Betty Buckley, P.J. Soles.

Spacek shines in her first Oscar-nominated role as Carrie, the scapegoat of Bates High, tormented by her peers and her religious fanatic mom (Laurie), who discovers her formidable telekinetic abilities just as some of her fellow students plot to alter her destiny forever at the senior prom. This first and best screen version of a Stephen King best-seller is a treat for anyone who hated high school. It's got an excellent cast, flashy direction, and a powerful final jolt that still grabs you despite years of imitation.

CARRY ON SCREAMING
★★ Sinister Cinema, 1966, NR, 97 min.
Dir: Gerald Thomas. Cast: Kenneth Williams, Harry H. Corbett, Fenella Fielding, Charles Hawtry, Joan Sims, Jim Dale, Angela Douglas, Jon Pertwee.

This obligatory horror spoof from Britain's "Carry On" gang is sort of like a cockney version of The Bowery Boys Meet the Monsters with low-budget versions of Frankenstein's monster and the mummy, and with Fielding in good, slinky form as a Morticia Addams lookalike vampire called Valeria. A few laughs.

THE CASE OF THE MISSING BRIDES
See: The Corpse Vanishes.

CASSANDRA
★★ Virgin Vision, 1987, R, 90 min.
Dir: Colin Eggleston. Cast: Tessa Humphries, Shane Briant, Briony Behets, Kit Taylor, Lee James, Susan Barling.

Slow Australian thriller about a famous fashion photog's daughter (Humphries) with psychic powers who sees murders from the point-of-view of the killer committing them. A well-photographed but uninvolving mix of Eyes of Laura Mars and Carrie, with one-time Hammer leading man Briant looking remarkably youthful and fit as the heroine's dad.

CAST A DEADLY SPELL
★★☆ HBO Video, 1991, NR, 92 min.
Dir: Martin Campbell. Cast: Fred Ward, David Warner, Julianne Moore, Clancy Brown, Alexandra Powers, Charles Hallahan.

STEPHEN KING
(1948–)

Written by the most widely read author in the world today, King's often overlong but always readable horror novels and stories are so visual they easily lend themselves to cinematic adaptation. Too bad so many of the adapters have been so inept. Brian De Palma's Carrie, the only King film to improve on the original novel, and David Cronenberg's atypical The Dead Zone remain the best of the King films so far, with King's own directorial debut, Maximum Overdrive, still the worst.

Carrie ('76), Salem's Lot ('79), The Shining ('80), Creepshow (original screenplay, '82), Cujo ('83), The Dead Zone ('83), Christine ('83), Children of the Corn ('84), Firestarter ('84), Cat's Eye ('85), Silver Bullet (original novella, Cycle of the Werewolf, '85), Maximum Overdrive (original story, "Trucks"; also director, '86), Creepshow 2 (original stories, '87), Return to Salem's Lot (original characters, '87), Pet Sematary ('89), Tales From the Darkside: The Movie (original story, "Cat From Hell," '90), Graveyard Shift ('90), It ('90), Misery ('90), Sometimes They Come Back ('91), The Lawnmower Man ('92), Sleepwalkers (original screenplay, '92), Pet Sematary Two (original characters, '92), The Dark Half ('93), Children of the Corn II: The Final Sacrifice (original characters, '93), The Tommyknockers ('93), Needful Things ('93), The Stand ('94).

A clever concept—Mickey Spillane meets H. P. Lovecraft—succumbs to a bad case of the cutes with too much Who Framed Roger Rabbit? for its own good. Ward is good as private eye Howard Phillips Lovecraft in 1948 Hollywood, who comes up against supernatural terror when an eccentric millionaire (Warner) hires him to find the celebrated witchcraft bible, The Necromonicon. Mildly watchable with Gremlins-like FX.

CASTLE IN THE DESERT
★★★ Key Video, 1942, NR, 62 min.
Dir: Harry Lachman. Cast: Sidney Toler, Sen Yung, Richard Derr, Lenita Lane, Douglass Dumbrille, Henry Daniell, Milton Parsons, Ethel Griffies.

Good Charlie Chan horror-mystery about a series of poisonings at a Death Valley castle owned by a descendant of the infamous Lucretia Borgia. Slick production values and a great supporting cast in this last of the Chans made at 20th Century-Fox.

CASTLE OF BLOOD

★★★ Sinister Cinema, 1964, NR, 82 min. Dir: Anthony M. Dawson [Antonio Margheriti]. Cast: Barbara Steele, Georges Riviere, Margarete Robsahm, Montgomery Glenn, Henry Kruger, Umberto Raho.

Above-average Steele vehicle based on the unpublished Poe tale "Danse Macabre" about a reporter (Riviere) who accepts a wager to spend the night in an eerie castle haunted by bloodsucking ghosts doomed one night each year to relive their violent deaths. Barbara is shown to good advantage as the dreamy Elisabeth (a lesbian scene involving her with Robsahm was cut from English-dubbed prints) and there's a wholly unexpected shock-twist ending. Aka *Danse Macabre, Terror, The Long Night of Terror, Dimensions in Death, Coffin of Terror,* and *Castle of Terror;* remade as *Web of the Spider.*

CASTLE OF BLOODY LUST, THE

See: *Castle of the Creeping Flesh.*

CASTLE OF DOOM

See: *Vampyr.*

CASTLE OF EVIL

★★☆ Republic Home Video, 1967, NR, 80 min. Dir: Francis D. Lyon. Cast: Scott Brady, Virginia Mayo, David Brian, Lisa Gaye, Hugh Marlowe, Shelley Morrison.

Six people are summoned to the tropical island castle of a disfigured electronics genius for the reading of his will. Upon their arrival they are stalked by a homicidal robot cast in its creator's image. Solid low-budgeter that makes up for its lack of production dough with a charismatic cast (Mayo is at her best as aging good-time-girl Sable) and some clever twists on the usual reading-of-the-will-in-the-creepy-old-mansion plot.

CASTLE OF FREAKS

See: *Frankenstein's Castle of Freaks.*

CASTLE OF FU MANCHU, THE

★ American Video, 1968, PG, 86 min. Dir: Jess [Jesus] Franco. Cast: Christopher Lee, Richard Greene, Maria Perschy, Rosalba Neri, Tsai Chin, Howard Marion Crawford.

Cut-and-paste final entry in Lee's Fu series, involving everything from a formula to freeze the world's water to the first—and probably last, too—in-cave heart transplant. A depress-

ing exercise in tacky futility (also out as *Assignment Istanbul*), this features stock sinking ocean liner shots from the classic *A Night to Remember* and some lab footage from *The Brides of Fu Manchu.*

CASTLE OF TERROR

See: *The Virgin of Nuremberg.*

CASTLE OF TERROR

See: *Castle of Blood.*

CASTLE OF THE CREEPING FLESH

★☆ Magnum Home Entertainment, 1967, NR, 80 min. Dir: Percy G. Parker [Adrian Hoven]. Cast: Howard Vernon, Elvira Berndorff, Claudia Butenuth, Janine Reynaud.

A sleeper in the worst sense, this deadly dull German flick features Euro-junk movie superstar Vernon as a count who suffers a family curse and commits murder in order to supply his dying daughter with a new heart. Sounds a lot more interesting than it is, with a real cheater of a title. Aka *Im Schloss der Bluten Begierde: The Castle of Bloody Lust.*

CASTLE OF THE LIVING DEAD

★★☆ Sinister Cinema, 1964, NR, 89 min. Dirs: Luciano Ricci and Michael Reeves. Cast: Christopher Lee, Gaia Germani, Philippe Leroy, Jacques Stanislawski, Alan Collins, Donald Sutherland.

Lee is Count Drago, a creepy guy who laughs out loud at hangings and wears too much mascara. When he invites a troupe of actors to perform at his castle, little do they realize that he's really planning to add them to his private collection of petrified humans and animals. Rich atmosphere (much of it provided by Reeves) and an amusing Sutherland screen debut (he plays both a boobish army officer *and* an old witch!) make this a standout in the hefty roster of interchangeable '60s continental horror films.

CASTLE OF THE WALKING DEAD

See: *The Torture Chamber of Dr. Sadism.*

CATACOMBS

See: *Curse IV: The Ultimate Sacrifice.*

CAT AND THE CANARY, THE

★★★☆ Sinister Cinema, 1927, NR, 70 min. Dir: Paul Leni. Cast: Laura La Plante, Creighton Hale, Forrest Stanley, Tully Marshall, Gertrude Astor, Arthur Edmund Carewe, Flora Finch, Martha Mattox.

The granddaddy of all those creaky reading-of-the-will-in-the-old-dark-house mystery thrillers first presented on the Broadway stage

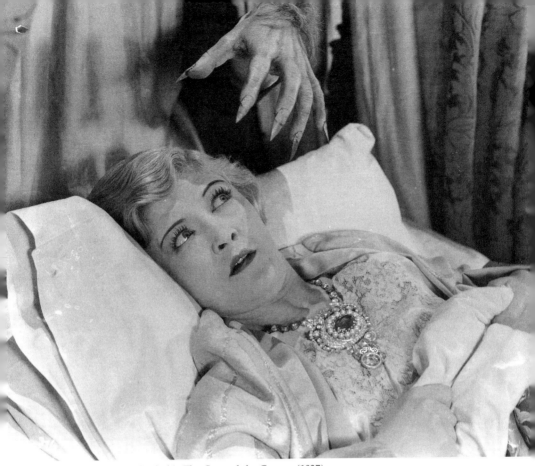

Laura La Plante gets clutched in The Cat and the Canary *(1927).*

in 1922. La Plante is an heiress who must spend the night in an eerie old mansion in order to collect her inheritance, a condition complicated by greedy relatives and an escaped maniac known as the Cat. The film is heavily burdened with often disruptive comic relief but is visually stunning, with wonderful scenes of billowing draperies, clutching claws, and wide-eyed, corridor-roaming heroines. Remade in 1930 (as *The Cat Creeps*) and again in 1939 and 1978, this is the best of the plethora of silent old-house chillers.

CAT AND THE CANARY, THE

★★★ RCA/Columbia Home Video, 1978, PG, 91 min. Dir: Radley Metzger. Cast: Carol Lynley, Michael Callan, Honor Blackman, Daniel Massey, Olivia Hussey, Peter McEnery, Wendy Hiller, Wilfrid Hyde-White.

Enjoyable remake with Lynley ideally cast as the put-upon heiress battling money-hungry relatives and the hideous maniac the Cat in a remote, stormbound mansion. Spirited acting from the veteran cast (including the delightful Hyde-White in a clever cameo) and sharp direction from premier porno purveyor Metzler keep this constantly on the mark.

CAROL LYNLEY
(1942–)

Lovely blonde Carol, born Carol Jones, has long been popular in both film and TV. Classy and talented, she's graced a number of genre roles with her cool beauty, most notably as the distraught single mom in *Bunny Lake Is Missing* and the terrorized heroine of the '78 version of *The Cat and the Canary.*

Shock Treatment ('64), *Bunny Lake Is Missing* ('65), *The Shuttered Room* ('67), *The Maltese Bippy* ('69), *The Night Stalker* ('72), *Son of Blob* ('72), *If It's a Man, Hang Up!* ('75), *The Cat and the Canary* ('78), *In Possession* ('84), *Dark Tower* ('87), *Blackout* ('89), *Howling VI: The Freaks* ('91), *Spirits* ('91).

CAT GIRL

★★☆ Columbia/TriStar Home Video, 1957, NR, 69 min. Dir: Alfred Shaughnessy. Cast: Barbara Shelley, Robert Ayres, Kay Callard, Ernest Milton, Lilly Kann, Paddy Webster.

Slight Brit variation on *Cat People* with Shelley splendid as a girl suffering from a hereditary curse that transfers her soul into the body of a murderous leopard. Solid minor chiller with appropriately dank photography, this has many interesting twists, though it slips into familiar contrivance as it nears conclusion.

CATHY'S CURSE

★ Continental Video, 1976, R, 86 min. Dir: Eddy Matalon. Cast: Alan Scarfe, Beverly Murray, Randi Allen, Roy Withan, Mary Morter, Dorothy Davis.

More *Exorcist* excess: A little girl is possessed by the spirit of her dead aunt, formerly imprisoned in an old rag doll, and goes through all the usual manifestations. Next to *Exorcism*, this Canadian film is the dullest possession pic ever, with lots of scenes of people crying or shouting at each other while you wait for something more interesting to happen. It never does. Aka *Cauchemars: Nightmares*.

CAT O' NINE TAILS

★★☆ JTC Video, 1971, PG, 90 min. Dir: Dario Argento. Cast: James Franciscus, Karl Malden, Catherine Spaak, Cinzia De Carolio, Aldo Reggiani, Rada Rassimov.

Blind Malden teams with reporter Franciscus to catch a killer driven by a chromosome imbalance to slash up the staff of a Roman research hospital. One of Argento's weaker thrillers, this has a couple of bravura sequences but is the edited-for-TV version and is missing over 20 minutes of sex and violence.

CAT PEOPLE

★★★☆ Turner Home Entertainment, 1942, NR, 72 min. Dir: Jacques Tourneur. Cast: Simone Simon, Kent Smith, Tom Conway, Jane Randolph, Jack Holt, Alan Napier, Elizabeth Russell, Teresa Harris.

This celebrated first film in the Val Lewton psychological horror series tells of Irena (Simon), a beautiful Serbian dress designer who also happens to be one of the cat people—shape-shifters who transform into black panthers when aroused by passion or violence. She is unable to consummate her marriage to the dull Oliver (Smith), who then turns to ex-girlfriend Randolph, which brings out Irena's feline fury. A remarkably adult film for its time; some of the acting and dialogue may seem stiff and artificial, but it's all

beautifully shot on sets left over from Orson Welles' *The Magnificent Ambersons* and highlighted by those famous scare scenes (the walk through the park and the attack at the swimming pool) that still pack a punch. This is far superior to the 1982 remake; sequel, *Curse of the Cat People*.

CAT PEOPLE

★★☆ MCA/Universal Home Video, 1982, R, 118 min. Dir: Paul Schrader. Cast: Nastassja Kinski, Malcolm McDowall, John Heard, Annette O'Toole, Ruby Dee, Ed Begley, Jr., Scott Paulin, John Larroquette, Lynn Lowry, Berry Berenson.

Kinski is incredibly sexy as Irena, an orphan who visits brother McDowall in New Orleans and is told by him that they are the last of the cat people, who transform into black panthers post coitus. The only way to prevent this is to mate with one of their own kind. Is incest best? This horny remake is marred by a disjointed screenplay (scenes from the original are interpolated with little regard for narrative cohesion) and heavy-handed eroticism (a little less nudity and a little more tease would have helped here; Kinski *clothed* is enough to drive you up the wall). Nevertheless, it sustains marginal interest through sumptuous visual design, strong acting (from the women most especially), and well-done (though barely glimpsed) Tom Burman makeup FX.

CAT'S EYE

★★☆ MGM/UA Home Video, 1985, PG-13, 94 min. Dir: Lewis Teague. Cast: Drew Barrymore, James Woods, Robert Hays, Candy Clark, Alan King, Kenneth McMillan, James Naughton, Mary D'Arcy.

Trio of Stephen King stories bridged by the travels of a wayward cat. First and best segment is a hilarious dark comedy with Woods joining a sadistic smoke-enders clinic; second, and weakest, has Hays as a tennis pro who accepts a dangerous wager from his lover's mobster husband. The last segment features Barrymore as a little girl terrorized by a troll living in her bedroom wall. It's fun but insubstantial, with good Carlo Rambaldi FX in the *Trilogy of Terror*–inspired final episode. Aka *Stephen King's Cat's Eye*.

CAULDRON OF BLOOD

★★ Republic Home Video, 1967, PG, 100 min. Dir: Edward Mann [Santos Alcocer]. Cast: Boris Karloff, Jean-Pierre Aumont, Viveca Lindfors, Rosenda Monteros, Jacqui Speed, Milo Queseda.

In one of his last features, not released until after his death, Karloff plays a wheelchair-bound blind sculptor who unknowingly uses human skeletons as armatures for his work? Why? Well, it all has something to do with his drug-addicted wife (Lindfors) and her involvement in a white slavery ring, though just *what* that involvement is no one bothers to explain. Good photography and Boris' scant scenes distinguish an otherwise very minor Spanish melodrama. Aka *El Coleccionista de Cadaveres: The Corpse Collector* and *Blind Man's Bluff.*

CAVE MAN
See: *One Million B.C.*

CAVEMAN
★★☆ CBS/Fox Video, 1981, PG, 91 min. Dir: Carl Gottlieb. Cast: Ringo Starr, Barbara Bach, Dennis Quaid, Shelly Long, Jack Gilford, John Matusak.

Pleasant comic spoof of the Raquel Welch classic *One Million Years B.C.* with Ringo as a bumbling cave guy and amusing stop-motion dinosaurs by Dave Allen. Better than its reputation suggests.

CELIA, CHILD OF TERROR
★★★ Trylon Video, 1988, PG, 98 min. Dir: Ann Turner. Cast: Rebecca Smart, Nicholas Eadie, Victoria Longley, Mary-Anne Fahey.

Low-key Aussie psycho-drama about an imaginative nine-year-old called Celia (Smart) whose dark dreams about monsters, voodoo dolls, and her recently deceased grandmother eventually lead to murder. Set in the late '50s, this involves topical events (the Red Scare, the wild rabbit infestation of Australia) and the terror-of-childhood themes of movies like *Curse of the Cat People* and *The Reflecting Skin,* resulting in an exceptionally well-acted (most especially by young Smart) and written (by director Turner) little gem of psychological horror.

CELLAR, THE
★ Southgate Entertainment, 1989, PG-13, 85 min. Dirs: Kevin S. Tenney and John Woodward. Cast: Patrick Kilpatrick, Suzanne Savoy, Chris Miller, Ford Rainey.

Annoying low-budget kiddie thriller (started by Woodward, finished by Tenney) about an estranged family who move into a western ranch house with a cavernous basement that harbors a monstrous Indian demon-creature. It's choppy and confusing, with Kevin Costner-wannabe Kilpatrick's performance as the boneheaded dad particularly irritating.

CELLAR DWELLER
★★ Starmaker Video, 1987, R, 78 min. Dir: John Carl Buechler. Cast: Debrah Mulrooney,

Brian Robbins, Yvonne De Carlo, Vince Edwards, Pamela Bellwood, Jeffrey Combs.

An ancient supernatural tome brings the monstrous lead character from cartoonist Mulrooney's comic strip to life. The creature then preys on her fellow students at the Throckmorton School of the Arts. A fun but trivial comic shocker with a game cast and some imaginative touches undermined by routine splashes of gore and nudity and a rather rubbery-looking monster.

CEMETERY GIRLS
See: *Invasion of the Bee Girls.*

CEMETERY HIGH
★ Unicorn Home Video, 1988, R, 80 min. Dir: Gorman Bechard. Cast: Debi Thibeault, Karen Nielsen, Lisa Schmidt, Ruth Collins.

Cemetery Low would be more to the point. A laughless slasher spoof about a quartet of high school rape victims who seek a gory revenge on the male scum of their school. Filmed as *Hack 'em High,* this has all the comic spark of a three-car pile-up.

CENTERFOLD GIRLS
★★ Media Home Entertainment, 1974, R, 91 min. Dir: John Peyser. Cast: Andrew Prine, Tiffany Bolling, Aldo Ray, Francine York, Ray Danton, Jeremy Slate, Jennifer Ashley, Mike Mazurki, Dan Seymour, Jaime Lyn Bauer.

A good exploitation cast sparks this otherwise routine maniac movie about a sexually repressed religious zealot (Prine) stalking and killing the models who've posed for a skin rag's annual calendar. Though it lacks the gore that this same storyline would've been drenched in a decade later, this is mildly diverting, thanks to Prine's welcome histrionics—he's always *very* funny when taking these sort of silly characters seriously.

CHAINSAW DEVIL
See: *Pieces.*

CHAIR, THE
★☆ Imperial Entertainment, 1987, R, 90 min. Dir: Waldemar Korzeniowsky. Cast: James Coco, Trini Alvarado, Stephen Geoffreys, Paul Benedict, John Bentley, Gary McCleary.

Prison warden Benedict is possessed by the vengeful spirit of an earlier prison official fried in the electric chair by the revolting inmates decades before. The weakest of a half-dozen "Horror in the Big House" shockers shot in 1987-88, this has an interesting cast (including Coco in his last role) wasted on threadbare material.

CHAMBER OF HORRORS
★★☆ Sinister Cinema, 1940, NR, 79 min.
Dir: Norman Lee. Cast: Leslie Banks, Lilli Palmer, Romilly Lunge, Gina Malo, David Horne, Cathleen Nesbitt.

No, it's not the one with the "Fear Flasher" and the "Horror Horn" but a rather sedate Edgar Wallace old-house chiller from England with heiress Palmer menaced by consummate sadist Banks (more or less recreating his Count Zaroff role from *The Most Dangerous Game*). Crudely photographed but well acted and amusing. Aka *The Door With Seven Locks* and remade under that title.

CHANGELING, THE
★★★ Vestron Video, 1980, R, 107 min.
Dir: Peter Medak. Cast: George C. Scott, Trish Van Devere, Melvyn Douglas, Jean Marsh, John Colicos, Barry Morse, Madeline Thornton-Sherwood, Frances Hyland.

Low-key ghost movie with Scott at his best as a composer who rents a huge old Seattle mansion haunted by the spirit of a crippled child out to avenge his murder. Though overlong, this exudes a genuinely chilly air of supernatural fascination that's well sustained throughout despite innumerable plot contrivances and lapses in logic.

CHARLIE BOY
★★ Thrillervideo, 1980, NR, 50 min.
Dir: Robert Young. Cast: Leigh Lawson, Angela Bruce, Marius Goring, Frances Cuka.

Undistinguished "Hammer House of Horror" mini-chiller about a group of people in a photograph, all of them doomed to die thanks to the curse of an African fetish doll nicknamed "Charlie Boy." The plotting is obvious and the performances are rather hokey, but there are a few creepy scenes and a fair share of laughs.

CHARLIE CHAN AT THE OPERA
★★★ Key Video, 1936, NR, 66 min.
Dir: H. Bruce Humberstone. Cast: Warner Oland, Boris Karloff, Charlotte Henry, Keye Luke, Margaret Irving, William Demerest.

In one of the best of the Chans, Karloff guest stars as a mad baritone–mental hospital escapee who becomes the main suspect when the diva, his one-time lover, is slain. This is good fun, with a well-thought-out plot and surprisingly effective comic relief—the usual stumbling-block in these things. One bright line from the harried stage manager: "This show goes on even if Frankenstein walks in!" He does.

CHARLIE CHAN AT THE WAX MUSEUM
★★★ Key Video, 1940, NR, 63 min.
Dir: Lynn Shores. Cast: Sidney Toler, Sen Yung, Marguerite Chapman, C. Henry Gordon, Marc Lawrence, Joan Valerie.

This is an atmospheric entry in the series with Charlie taking part in a radio crime show broadcast from an eerie wax museum where a murderer strikes. There are lots of horror touches, and the killer's identity proves a genuine surprise.

CHARLIE CHAN'S SECRET
★★☆ Key Video, 1936, NR, 71 min.
Dir: Gordon Wiles. Cast: Warner Oland, Rosina Lawrence, Henrietta Crosman, Charles Quigley, Astrid Allwyn, Arthur Edmund Carewe.

Charlie investigates a murder committed during a seance. There's a routine plot (virtually reprised in *Meeting at Midnight*) and a dull supporting cast (apart from spritely dowager Crosman) but the pic is aided immeasurably by Rudolph Maté's pale gray photography and Oland's as-usual winning ways.

CHEERLEADER CAMP
★☆ Prism Entertainment, 1987, R, 88 min.
Dir: John Quinn. Cast: Betsy Russell, Leif Garrett, Lucinda Dickey, Travis McKenna, Vickie Benson, George "Buck" Flower.

The bimbo cheerleaders at Camp Hurrah are being stalked and murdered by a maniac who might be the nightmare-plagued heroine but (if you've seen even a couple of these things) probably isn't. Dull retreat of every slasher cliché you ever saw, with flatulent comic relief and a good cast wasted. I liked the original title, *Bloody Pom-Poms,* much better.

CHILD, THE
★★ Magnum Home Entertainment, 1976, R, 83 min.
Dir: Robert Voskanian. Cast: Laurel Barnett, Richard Hanners, Rosalie Cole, Frank Janson, Ruth Ballan.

Cheap gore job with Cole as a young girl who avenges her mom's murder by raising the dead from a local cemetery. Static and slow, with all the usual eye-gouging and skull-smashing but also a few stray wisps of atmosphere and a personable heroine (Barnett) with the lyrically unlikely name of Alicianne Del Mar. Aka *Zombie Child* and *Kill and Go Hide.*

CHILD OF DARKNESS, CHILD OF LIGHT
★★ Paramount Home Video, 1991, R, 85 min.
Dir: Marina Sargenti. Cast: Brad Davis, Sela Ward, Sydney Penny, Kristen Dattilo, Anthony John Dennison, Viveca Lindfors, Paxton Whitehead, Claudette Nevins.

Moderate made-for-cable adaptation of James Patterson's *Virgin*, with a pair of parochial schoolgirls' supposed virgin pregnancies attracting the attention of the Catholic church. Are the spawn of God and Satan about to be reborn? A good cast helps this needlessly complicated *Rosemary's Baby–Omen* spin-off.

CHILDREN, THE
★ Rhino Home Video, 1980, R, 89 min.
Dir: Max Kalmanowicz. Cast: Martin Shaker, Gale Garnett, Gil Rogers, Tracy Griswold, Joy Glaccum, Michelle Le Mothe.

This is an awful exploitation shocker about a busload of school kids transformed by a radioactive cloud into a pack of mini-zombies who can kill with a touch. Often unintentionally funny, with inept direction and acting, the only real interest comes from listening to composer Harry Manfredini try out a few familiar themes later reused to better effect in the *Friday the 13th* series.

CHILDREN OF THE CORN
★☆ Video Treasures, 1984, R, 93 min.
Dir: Fritz Kiersch. Cast: Peter Horton, Linda Hamilton, R. G. Armstrong, Courtney Gaines, John Franklin, Robby Kiger.

Chintzy adaptation of one of Stephen King's scariest stories. Dumbbell couple Horton and Hamilton (who doubtlessly look upon this as a career highlight) stumble into a creepy little Nebraska town where the children have murdered all the adults and worship some hokey corn god called "He Who Walks Behind the Rows." He who rents this tacky goofball gets what he deserves. A surprise hit, this is followed by *two*, count 'em, sequels!

CHILDREN OF THE CORN II: THE FINAL SACRIFICE
★★ Paramount Home Video, 1993, R, 94 min.
Dir: David F. Price. Cast: Terence Knox, Paul Scherrer, Rosalind Allen, Ryan Bollman, Christie Clark, Ned Romero.

Tabloid reporter Knox and his obnoxious teen son Scherrer descend on the town of Gatlin to do an exposé on its kid cult murders and guess what? Effeminite local boy Bollman is possessed by an evil force in a cornfield and nasty sacrifices start again. This is a (very slight) improvement on part I, with good photography and decent FX, but, as before, doesn't add up to much more than tasteless scenes of bratty kids offing dopey adults. And the final explanation for all this mayhem is really lame. Followed by *Children of the Corn III: Urban Nightmare*.

CHILDREN OF THE DAMNED
★★★ MGM/UA Home Video, 1963, NR, 89 min.
Dir: Anton M. Leader. Cast: Ian Hendry, Alan Badel, Barbara Ferris, Alfred Burke, Sheila Allen, Clive Powell.

Superior sequel to *Village of the Damned*. Six strange children from various nations share similar supernatural powers and band together in London to plot the elimination of the inferior human race. Complex characters (the two heroes live together in what is an obvious, though never stressed, homosexual relationship), a thoughtful script, and glistening monochrome photography help make this one of the most underrated horror movies of the '60s.

CHILDREN OF THE FULL MOON
★★ Thrillervideo, 1980, NR, 50 min.
Dir: Tom Clegg. Cast: Diana Dors, Celia Gregory, Christopher Cazanove, Robert Urquhart.

A good cast tries to salvage this rather ponderous tale of a young couple who fall prey to a forest-dwelling family of werewolves. It's another underwhelming episode of the "Hammer House of Horror" vid series.

CHILDREN OF THE NIGHT
See: *Daughters of Darkness*.

CHILDREN OF THE NIGHT
★★☆ Paramount Home Video, 1991, R, 91 min.
Dir: Tony Randel. Cast: Karen Black, Peter DeLuise, Ami Dolenz, Garrett Morris, Evan MacKenzie, Maya McLaughlin, Josette De Carlo, David Sawyer.

A small midwestern town is overrun by vampires led by evil reverend Sawyer in this not bad *Salem's Lot*–like video chiller from Fangora Films. There are some unusually clever touches (like the undead scarfing up bloody leeches), and Black is very good but wasted in a small role as a sexy vampire mom.

CHILDREN SHOULDN'T PLAY WITH DEAD THINGS
★★★ VCL Video, 1972, PG, 85 min.
Dir: Benjamin [Bob] Clark. Cast: Alan Ormsby, Anya Ormsby, Valerie Mamches, Jane Daly, Jeffrey Gillen, Paul Cronin.

A funny semi-spoof of *Night of the Living Dead*, this one's about a troupe of hedonistic young actors who ferry themselves to a small cemetery island where they play foolish practical jokes and get eaten when the dead rise in response to a supposedly phony supernatural ritual. Bear with a talky and sometimes heavy-handed first half and you should enjoy the surprisingly gory and downbeat conclusion.

The imaginative makeups were created by screenwriter-star Mr. Ormsby.

CHILD'S PLAY

★★★ MGM/UA Home Video, 1988, R, 87 min. Dir: Tom Holland. Cast: Catherine Hicks, Chris Sarandon, Alex Vincent, Brad Dourif, Dinah Manoff, Jack Colvin.

A Chicago single mom (Hicks) gives her young son a "Good Guy" doll called Chucky as a birthday present, which little Andy (Vincent) quickly discovers harbors the soul of voodoo-practicing mass murderer Charles Lee Ray (Dourif). A tremendous hit, this combines elements from several old *Twilight Zone* episodes with the atmosphere of the TV movie classic *Trilogy of Terror*. In spite of such derivativeness, it's a lot of fun, with clever FX and the cast treating it all with a mock seriousness that becomes quite funny. Unfortunately, like too many modern horror films, this fails to come up with a decent ending.

CHILD'S PLAY 2

★★☆ MCA/Universal Home Video, 1990, R, 84 min. Dir: John Lafia. Cast: Alex Vincent, Jenny Agutter, Gerrit Graham, Christine Elise, Grace Zabriskie, Peter Haskell, Beth Grant, voice of Brad Dourif.

To the surprise of no one, Chucky returns to stalk young Andy again while making new, improved wisecracks in the voice of Dourif. This OK sequel has more elaborate FX work and is often quite amusing but suffers from too many logic loopholes (i.e., supposedly

Christine Elise gets chummy with Chucky in Child's Play 2 *(1990).*

taking place shortly after the events in the original, kid actor Vincent is obviously several years older) and has a mean streak that allows for the offing of several likable characters.

CHILD'S PLAY 3

★★ MCA/Universal Home Video, 1991, R, 89 min. Dir: Jack Bender. Cast: Justin Whalen, Perrey Reeves, Jeremy Sylvers, Andrew Robinson, Peter Haskell, voice of Brad Dourif.

Years after his last rampage, a reactivated Chucky heads for the tough military academy where the now-16-year-old Andy (Whalen) is in residence. This needless third installment is pretty much a rerun of all that's gone before, but still, Wil Wheaton lookalike Whalen gives a good performance and there's a reasonably tense climax set in an amusement park funhouse.

CHILLER

★★ Fame Entertainment, 1985, NR, 91 min. Dir: Wes Craven. Cast: Michael Beck, Beatrice Straight, Paul Sorvino, Laura Johnson, Jill Schoelen, Dick O'Neill.

BRAD DOURIF
(1950–)

Intense young actor Dourif received an Oscar nomination for his screen debut in 1975's *One Flew Over the Cuckoo's Nest* but *really* entered the big time as Charles Lee Ray, the evil spirit inhabiting Chucky, the devil doll in the *Child's Play* movies. A fine performer who usually manages to steal every picture he's in, Dourif in the past few years has become a welcome fixture in the horror genre.

Eyes of Laura Mars ('78), *I, Desire* ('82), *Blue Velvet* ('86), *Sonny Boy* ('87), *Child's Play* ('88), *The Exorcist III* ('90), *Spontaneous Combustion* ('90), *Grim Prairie Tales* ('90), *Child's Play 2* (voice only, '90), *Graveyard Shift* ('90), *Child's Play 3* (voice only, '91), *Body Parts* ('91), *Critters 4* ('92), *Trauma* ('93).

Fair Craven tele-flick with Beck emerging from cryogenic suspension as a soulless personification of evil. Straight is his terrified mom, who takes it upon herself to destroy this hell spawn. There's some creepy atmosphere and good acting but it's all too slow to build the needed suspense.

CHILLERS

★★☆ Raedon Entertainment, 1988, R, 86 min. Dir: Daniel Boyd. Cast: Jesse Emery, Marjorie Fitzsimmons, Laurie Pennington, Jim Wolfe, David Wohl, Gary Brown, Thom Deventhal, Kimberly Harbour.

Enjoyable direct-to-video anthology with five people in a remote bus depot relating to each other their worst nightmares, which involve a haunted swimming pool, a werewolf boy scout leader, a vampire TV newsman, a guy with the ability to raise the dead, and a coed possessed by an ancient Aztec deity. This is surprisingly slick-looking for a film shot in West Virginia on a $250,000 budget; it has good gore and a talented cast of unknowns. The melancholy vampire tale is best.

CHILLING, THE

★☆ Hemdale Home Video, 1989, R, 95 min. Dirs: Deland Nuse and Jack A. Sunseri. Cast: Linda Blair, Dan Haggerty, Troy Donahue, Ron Vincent.

A cheapo zombie flick, this has a horde of cryogenically frozen corpses returning to life as murdering cannibals. Amateurish and dull, with half-hearted attempts at humor. La Blair is wasted.

CHOPPER CHICKS IN ZOMBIE TOWN

★★☆ New Line Home Video, 1991, R, 84 min. Dir: Dan Hoskins. Cast: Jamie Rose, Vicki Frederick, Don Calfa, Martha Quinn, Ed Gale.

A sporadically amusing spoof (with a great title) that has a band of tough motorcycle babes hitting a small desert town just as a pack of zombies—raised by local mortician Calfa in a nod to *Dead & Buried* and *Return of the Living Dead*—burst from their mine-shaft prison. Much of the humor is forced, but the scene where a busload of blind teenagers arm themselves with Uzis to battle the walking dead hits just the right note of lunacy.

CHOPPING MALL

★★☆ Lightning Video, 1986, R, 76 min. Dir: Jim Wynorski. Cast: Kelli Maroney, Tony O'Dell, John Terlesky, Russell Todd, Barbara Crampton, Paul Bartel, Mary Woronov, Dick Miller, Gerrit Graham, Mel Welles.

A sometimes effective slasher variant that has a group of your typical movie post-adoles-cents terrorized by a shopping mall's haywire robot security guards. Splashy FX—including a memorable exploding noggin for *Re-Animator* co-star Crampton—and a terrific supporting cast help a lot. Aka *Killbots*.

CHOSEN, THE

See: *Holocaust 2000.*

CHRISTINE

★★☆ RCA/Columbia Home Video, 1983, R, 110 min. Dir: John Carpenter. Cast: Keith Gordon, Alexandra Paul, John Stockwell, Harry Dean Stanton, Robert Prosky, Christine Belford, Roberts Blossom, Stu Charno.

Christine, a haunted '57 Plymouth Fury, takes over the life of its geeky teen owner (Gordon), transforming him into a sleek, seductive murderer. A not-bad adaptation of Stephen King's semi-satirical novel (a sort-of horror version of TV's *Happy Days*) with a solid cast, good FX, and a nice streak of dark humor. A tighter running time might've made this a classic.

CHRISTMAS EVIL

★★ Saturn Home Video, 1980, R, 95 min. Dir: Lewis Jackson. Cast: Brandon Maggart, Jeffrey De Munn, Diane Hull, Joe Jamrog, Scott McKay, Peter Friedman.

Maggart is first-rate as Harry, a capering psycho who loves Christmas and dresses up as Kris Kringle to murderously strike out at those who corrupt the holiday spirit. One of the oddest post-*Halloween* slashers, this one has precious little gore and plays its story more for black comedy than straight horror but is too long and meandering to be very effective. Maggart's captivating performance is the sole reason to seek it out. Aka *Santa, You Better Watch Out,* and *Terror in Toyland.*

C.H.U.D.

★★☆ Video Treasures, 1984, R, 87 min. Dir: Douglas Cheek. Cast: John Heard, Daniel Stern, Kim Greist, Christopher Curry, George Martin, John Goodman.

This is a fun '50s-type monster movie about toxic waste dumped in New York's sewer system, turning derelicts and street people into clawed, glow-eyed mutants: cannibalistic, humanoid, underground dwellers—get it? It's marred by ragged editing, but an appealing cast in offbeat roles and good makeups by John Caglione, Jr., make this a pleasant surprise.

C.H.U.D. II: BUD THE C.H.U.D.

★☆ Vestron Video, 1988, R, 85 min. Dir: David Irving. Cast: Brian Robbins, Tricia Leigh

Fisher, Bill Calvert, Gerrit Graham, Robert Vaughn, Bianca Jagger, Larry Linville, June Lockhart, Norman Fell, Rich Hall.

Crappy comic sequel about a couple of high school hoseheads who steal a frozen corpse from a government science lab (a popular teen prank, I'm sure) and end up accidentally resurrecting the last of the C.H.U.D.s (Graham). A gifted physical comedian, Graham is really quite funny but not much else in this labored farce is. Pretty Fisher is the daughter of Eddie Fisher and Connie Stevens.

CHURCH, THE
★★★ Southgate Entertainment, 1989, NR, 102 min. Dir: Michele Sovai. Cast: Barbara Cupisti, Tomas Arana, Hugh Quarshie, Asia Argento, Feodor Chaliapin, Antonella Vitalé, John Morgan, John Richardson.

Originally conceived as *Demon Cathedral,* this ostensive third installment in producer Dario Argento's *Demons* series jettisons most connections to the other movies and instead emerges as an imaginative mix of *The Omen, Rosemary's Baby,* and *The Name of the Rose.* Restoration of an old Hungarian church accidentally triggers an ancient curse, which traps a diverse group of visitors and clergy within the church's ancient walls. Brooding art direction and imaginative visual touches make this involving Italian shocker the best Big Boot bloodbath since Sovai's impressive debut feature, *Stage Fright.* It's also available in an edited R-rated form.

CIRCUS OF BLOOD
See: *Berserk!*

ANTON DIFFRING
(1918–1990)

This cold-looking German actor with steely blue eyes became a minor Brit horror star thanks to back-to-back terror hits, *The Man Who Could Cheat Death* and *Circus of Horrors.* A specialist at evil doctors and crazed Nazis, Diffring was at his best in *Circus* as the surgeon turned on by female disfigurement.

The Man Who Could Cheat Death ('59), *Circus of Horrors* ('60), *The Iguana With the Tongue of Fire* ('70), *Mark of the Devil Part II* ('73), *Seven Deaths in the Cat's Eye* ('73), *The Beast Must Die* ('74), *Kiss Me and Die* ('74), *Sherlock Holmes and the Masks of Death* ('84), *Faceless* ('88).

CIRCUS OF FEAR
★★ Saturn Home Video, 1966, NR, 89 min. Dir: John [Llewellyn] Moxey. Cast: Christopher Lee, Suzy Kendall, Leo Genn, Klaus Kinski, Margaret Lee, Heinz Drache, Anthony Newlands, Cecil Parker, Eddi Arent, Skip Martin.

OK Edgar Wallace mystery-horror flick about murder at a circus' winter quarters as various folk search for hidden bank loot. There's an impressive cast, but Lee goes through more than half the movie with a black hood over his head! Aka *Das Ratsel Des Silbernen Dreiecks: The Puzzle of the Silver Triangles, Psycho-Circus* (a shortened version still playing on some local TV channels), and *The Man Without a Face.*

CIRCUS OF HORRORS
★★★ Republic Home Video, 1960, NR, 87 min. Dir: Sidney Hayers. Cast: Anton Diffring, Erika Remberg, Yvonne Monlaur, Donald Pleasence, Jane Hylton, Kenneth Griffith, Vanda Hudson, Yvonne Romain.

In this sharp British shocker, the incomparable Diffring stars as a sadistic plastic surgeon hiding out in a continental circus after a botched operation. He staffs the place with facially altered thieves, murderers, and prostitutes and offs them in gory, crowd-pleasing "accidents" when they attempt to leave his employ. The fine supporting cast includes Remberg as a saucy aerialist, Monlaur as Diffring's sweet adopted niece, a toupeed Pleasence as the circus' ill-fated original owner, and Romain as an acid-scarred babe in a tight satin dress and spectacular push-up bra. Memorable "Look for a Star" theme song too.

CITY OF THE DEAD
See: *Horror Hotel.*

CITY OF THE LIVING DEAD
See: *The Gates of Hell.*

CITY OF THE WALKING DEAD
★ Cinema Group, 1980, UR, 88 min. Dir: Umberto Lenzi. Cast: Hugo Stiglitz, Laura Trotter, Mel Ferrer, Maria Rosaria Omaggio.

Originally called *Incubo Salla Citta Contaminata: Nightmare in a Contaminated City,* this is yet another lousy fill-in-the-blanks Spanish-Italian zombie epic in which, once again, we're reminded that "Ya gotta shoot them in the head!" Somebody get me a gun! Loads of cut-rate gore and Ferrer strictly along for the ride. Funniest scene: the zombies attacking an "American Bandstand"–style TV dance show. Aka *Nightmare City* and *Invasion of the Zombies.*

CLAIRVOYANT, THE
See: *The Evil Mind.*

CLAIRVOYANT, THE
See: *The Killing Hour.*

CLASS OF NUKE 'EM HIGH, THE
★★ Video Treasures, 1986, R, 81 min. Dirs: Richard W. Haines and Samuel Weil. Cast: Janelle Brady, Gilbert Brenton, Robert Prichard, R. L. Ryan.

Kids at Tromaville High fall prey to toxic reefer and a mutant monster living in the school's basement. Troma's first attempt at cashing in on the success of *The Toxic Avenger* isn't as good but still packs enough loopy comedy and unrestrained splatter for a fair evening's entertainment.

CLASS OF NUKE 'EM HIGH PART II: SUBHUMANOID MELTDOWN, THE
★☆ Media Home Entertainment, 1991, R, 95 min. Dir: Eric Louzil. Cast: Brick Bronsky, Lisa Gaye, Leesa Rowland, Michael Kurtz.

Bronsky uses his position as ace reporter on Troma High's school paper to investigate an evil plan to turn the students into mutant monsters. This needless, smart-assed sequel is bad even by Troma standards, with wretched acting and dialogue. One redeeming feature: Tromie, the nuclear squirrel.

CLASS REUNION MASSACRE
★ Cinema Group, 1978, R, 84 min. Dir: Constantine S. Gochis. Cast: T. G. Finkbinder, Jeannetta Arnette, Damien Knight, Gyr Patterson, Nick Carter, Nikki Barthen.

Released theatrically as *The Redeemer* and *The Redeemer—Son of Satan,* this ham-fisted combo of *The Omen* and *Ten Little Indians* concerns six "sinners" (who number among them an effeminate gay, a tough lesbian, and other undesirables) lured to a bogus high school reunion by a masked satanic figure who begins doing away with them in various violent ways. Trite moralizing meets low-budget gore in this unwatchable drivel.

CLONUS HORROR, THE
See: *Parts: The Clonus Horror.*

CLOWNHOUSE
★★ RCA/Columbia Home Video, 1988, R, 82 min. Dir: Victor Salva. Cast: Nathan Forest Winters, Brian McHugh, Sam Rockwell, Viletta Stillman.

Young Casey (Winters), who has a fear of clowns, is laughed at by his cruel eldest brother (Rockwell) but indulged by his understanding middle brother (McHugh). When three

psychos escape from an asylum and don clown costumes and makeup, Casey's fears seem to be coming true. This deliberately slow low-budgeter sometimes recalls the atmosphere of *Phantasm* (with a touch of *Killer Klowns from Outer Space*) but is too draggy until it just slams to a halt in a too-abrupt conclusion.

CLUB, THE
See: *Invitation to Hell.*

CLUB DEAD
See: *Terror at Red Wolf Inn.*

CODE NAME: TRIXIE
See: *The Crazies.*

COFFIN OF TERROR
See: *Castle of Blood.*

COLD ROOM, THE
★★ Media Home Entertainment, 1983, NR, 95 min. Dir: James Dearden. Cast: George Segal, Amanda Pays, Renee Soutendijk, Warren Clarke, Anthony Higgins, Ursula Howells.

A slow psycho thriller, this is a sort-of *Vertigo* meets *The Diary of Anne Frank* with Pays as a frustrated schoolgirl who visits East Berlin with journalist dad Segal and discovers that she is the reincarnation of a German girl who hid a young Jew from the Nazis during World War II. The acting is good but the pace is slow in this made-for-cable adaptation of a novel by Jeffrey Caine. Aka *Behind the Wall.*

COLLECTOR, THE
★★☆ RCA/Columbia Home Video, 1965, NR, 119 min. Dir: William Wyler. Cast: Terence Stamp, Samantha Eggar, Mona Washbourne, Maurice Dallimore.

A well-directed but cold and uninvolving adaptation of John Fowles' novel about a deranged butterfly collector (Stamp) who kidnaps a beautiful art student (Eggar) and holds her prisoner at a remote country house. Eggar is excellent and always sympathetic as the doomed heroine and there is a fair amount of legitimate suspense in the first half, but Stamp is woefully miscast as the crazed "hero" and the film's overall lack of feeling is fairly distasteful.

COLOR ME BLOOD RED
★☆ Continental Video, 1965, NR, 79 min. Dir: Herschell Gordon Lewis. Cast: Don Joseph, Candi Conder, Elyn Warner, Scott H. Hall, Patricia Lee.

An egotistical, obnoxious artist (Joseph) paints

abstract portraits of beautiful women and then murders his models, using their blood to bring his pictures to "life." A poor semi-remake of Lewis' seminal *Blood Feast* with a dull plot and bad acting beefed up by a couple of strikingly gross moments, like Joseph rubbing a model's bloody face against a canvas or milking a trussed-up girl's torn-out large intestine. Remade as *Playgirl Killer*.

COMA

★★★ MGM/UA Home Video, 1978, R, 113 min. Dir: Michael Crichton. Cast: Genevieve Bujold, Michael Douglas, Richard Widmark, Elizabeth Ashley, Rip Torn, Lois Chiles, Tom Selleck, Ed Harris.

This is an effectively plotted medical chiller based on the book by Robin Cook. Bujold is an intern at Boston Memorial Hospital who discovers that certain patients are being placed in comas and later chopped up as part of a black market organ operation. Strong acting and tense direction make this the best of the "Horror in a Hospital" subgenre, which also includes *Halloween II, Visiting Hours,* and *Hospital Massacre.* There's also an eerie score by Jerry Goldsmith.

COMEBACK, THE

★★ Lorimar Home Video, 1978, R, 100 min. Dir: Pete Walker. Cast: Jack Jones, Pamela Stephenson, David Doyle, Sheila Keith, Bill Owen, Richard Johnson, Holly Palance, Peter Turner.

A convoluted psycho-shocker, this has Jones as a '60s pop singer whose attempted comeback in England is disrupted by an ax-wielding fiend in a witch mask. There are a couple of gory killings and a good cast (plus one really unbelievable twist at the end), but this is mostly for Jack Jones fans—whom I somehow doubt catch many splatter films. Aka *The Day the Screaming Stopped!*

COMEDY OF TERRORS, THE

★★★ HBO Video, 1964, NR, 82min. Dir: Jacques Tourneur. Cast: Vincent Price, Peter Lorre, Boris Karloff, Basil Rathbone, Joyce Jameson, Joe E. Brown.

Price and Lorre are bumbling 19th-century undertakers who decide to improve business by murdering landlord Rathbone and then staging an elaborate funeral. The trouble is, Basil doesn't die that easily. Though clearly slapped together in a hurry to take advantage of the success of *The Raven,* this farce has a funny script by Richard Matheson and gets a lot of mileage out of its once-in-a-lifetime cast, with Lorre in especially winning form. Aka *The Graveside Story.*

COMMITTED

★★☆ Media Home Entertainment, 1990, R, 88 min. Dir: William A. Levey. Cast: Jennifer O'Neill, Robert Forster, Ron Palillo, William Windom, Sydney Lassick, Richard Alan.

Another one of those wrongly-incarcerated-heroine-in-a-madhouse-of-horrors melodramas, with O'Neill as the girl in peril. Railroaded into committing herself by evil doctor Windom, Jennifer is nearly electrocuted, almost raped by slobbering inmate Lassick, and finally escapes in a fairly clever twist ending. It's well acted, but the canned music makes your teeth hurt.

COMMUNION

See: *Alice, Sweet Alice.*

COMPANY OF WOLVES, THE

★★☆ Vestron Video, 1984, R, 95 min. Dir: Neil Jordan. Cast: Angela Lansbury, David Warner, Sarah Patterson, Micha Bergese, Georgia Stowe, Terence Stamp.

This retelling of "Little Red Riding Hood" in the form of a post-*Howling* werewolf movie is

---

RICHARD MATHESON
(1926–)

This successful novelist wrote his first screenplay when he adapted his book *The Shrinking Man* for Jack Arnold's sci-fi classic *The Incredible Shrinking Man* in '57. In the '60s Matheson wrote the scripts for several of Roger Corman's Poe flicks and for TV shows like *The Twilight Zone* and *Star Trek.* In the '70s he concentrated on made-for-TV movies, including several for Dan Curtis.

House of Usher ('60), *The Pit and the Pendulum* ('61), *Tales of Terror* ('62), *Burn, Witch, Burn* (co-screenplay, '62), *The Last Man on Earth* (writing as "Logan Swanson," from his novel *I Am Legend,* '64), *The Comedy of Terrors* ('64), *Die! Die! My Darling!* ('65), *The Devil's Bride* ('68), *DeSade* ('69), *The Omega Man* (based on his novel *I Am Legend,* '71), *Duel* ('71), *The Night Stalker* ('72), *The Night Strangler* ('73), *The Legend of Hell House* (based on his novel *Hell House,* '73), *Dying Room Only* ('73), *Dracula* ('74), *Scream of the Wolf* ('74), *The Stranger Within* ('74), *Trilogy of Terror* (co-screenplay, '75), *Dead of Night* ('77), *The Strange Possession of Mrs. Oliver* ('77), *Twilight Zone, the Movie* (co-screenplay, '83), *Jaws 3-D* (co-screenplay, '83) beautiful looking but difficult to follow. Pretty teenager Patterson is warned by her granny (the delightful Lansbury) about strange men whose eyebrows meet and often turn into monsters. Well-designed makeup FX by Christopher Tucker and handsome Anton Furst sets make this a visual feast, even if the plotting (with stories within stories and a *Carrie*-inspired final shock) leaves much to be desired.

COMPUTER KILLERS, THE

See: *Horror Hospital.*

CONFESSIONAL, THE

★★★ Prism Entertainment, 1975, R, 104 min. Dir: Pete Walker. Cast: Anthony Sharp, Susan Penhaligon, Stephanie Beacham, Norman Eshley, Sheila Keith, Mervyn Johns.

Probably Brit horror director Walker's most disturbing film, this has Sharp as a deranged, sex-obsessed priest who blackmails parishioners by taping their confessions and bumps off his victims with ecclesiastical weapons like a rosary, incense burner, and poisoned host. Catholics, view this well-acted sicko at your own risk. Aka *House of Mortal Sin.*

CONQUEROR WORM, THE

★★★☆ HBO Video, 1968, PG, 87 min. Dir: Michael Reeves. Cast: Vincent Price, Ian Ogilvy, Hilary Dwyer, Rupert Davies, Robert Russell, Patrick Wymark, Nicky Henson, Wilfrid Brambell.

Originally titled *Witchfinder General,* this is Reeves' masterpiece and, sadly, his last film. Price is brilliantly restrained as professional witch-finder Matthew Hopkins, who terrorized Puritan England at the time of Oliver Cromwell, executing suspected witches for a price. Splendidly evocative photography and an intelligent script that perfectly contrasts the lush green countryside with the grisly violence of Hopkins' reign make this one of the finest horror films of the '60s. Be warned, though; the video prints are missing Paul Ferris' beautiful original score due to copyright problems.

CORPSE, THE

See: *Crucible of Horror.*

CORPSE GRINDERS, THE

★ WesternWorld Video, 1971, PG, 72 min. Dir: Ted V. Mikels. Cast: Sean Kenney, Monika Kelly, Sanford Mitchell, J. Byron Foster, Warren Ball, Vince Barbi.

A cat food manufacturer's product becomes the most popular on the market after a dead body is accidentally added to the recipe. To keep up with the demand, a pair of murderous body snatchers are pressed into service, while the country's most contented kitties develop an uncontrollable hunger for human flesh. Probably the best known of Mikels' cheapie trash horrors, this has bad acting aplenty and unintentionally hilarious scenes of people being pushed into the cardboard "grinding machine" with raw hamburger coming out the other end.

CORPSE VANISHES, THE

★★☆ Goodtimes Home Video, 1942, NR, 63 min. Dir: Wallace Fox. Cast: Bela Lugosi, Luana Walters, Tristram Coffin, Elizabeth Russell, Minerva Urecal, Angelo Rossitto.

In one of his most entertaining Monogram epics, Lugosi is a botanist who kidnaps virgin brides (a more common commodity in the '40s, I guess) with the whiff of a drugged orchid and drains their glandular fluids to restore the youthful bloom to aged wife Russell. Sense isn't one of this flick's strong suits, but Bela is in peak form, the plot moves at a good pace, and there's even some snappy black comic dialogue: "If the bride folds up this time there won't be any snatching!" Aka *The Case of the Missing Brides.*

CORRIDORS OF BLOOD

★★☆ MPI Home Video, 1958, NR, 85 min. Dir: Robert Day. Cast: Boris Karloff, Betta St. John, Francis Matthews, Christopher Lee, Finlay Currie, Adrienne Corri, Francis DeWolff, Nigel Green.

Despite the lurid title, this is actually a fairly sober variation of *The Body Snatcher* in which Karloff discovers of an early form of anesthesia, becomes hooked on the drug, and gets mixed up with a band of murderous drug-dealing grave robbers. The exceptional cast includes Lee in one of his last pre-stardom minor roles. Aka *The Doctor of Seven Dials.*

CORRIDORS OF EVIL

See: *Carnival of Souls.*

COSMIC MONSTERS, THE

★☆ Rhino Home Video, 1958, NR, 75 min. Dir: Gilbert Gunn. Cast: Forrest Tucker, Gaby Andre, Martin Benson, Alec Mango.

A Brit big-bug movie that's pretty boring as these things go. Tucker is an American scientist working on a project in England that accidentally punches a hole in the ionosphere and magnifies insects a thousandfold. It has stodgy acting and transparent special effects. Aka *The Strange World of Planet X.*

COUNT DRACULA

★★ Republic Home Video, 1970, PG, 88 min.
Dir: Jess [Jesus] Franco. Cast: Christopher Lee, Herbert Lom, Klaus Kinski, Maria Rohm, Soledad Miranda, Paul Muller.

Promoted at the time of its making as the first "definitive" version of Bram Stoker's *Dracula*, this deviates from the text almost immediately and is hampered by cheap production values and Franco's ham-fisted direction. On the plus side are Lee's excellent performance as the Count (who grows progressively younger, as in the novel), good support from Lom and Kinski, and rich color photography. Aka *Bram Stoker's Count Dracula*.

COUNT DRACULA
AND HIS VAMPIRE BRIDE

See: *The Satanic Rites of Dracula.*

COUNT DRACULA'S GREAT LOVE

See: *Dracula's Great Love.*

COUNT YORGA, VAMPIRE

★★★☆ HBO Video, 1970, PG, 90 min.
Dir: Bob Kelljan. Cast: Robert Quarry, Roger Perry, Michael Murphy, Donna Anders, Michael Macready, Judith Lang, Edward Walsh, voice of George Macready.

In one of the best vampire movies of the early '70s, Quarry is excellent as the sardonic Bulgarian vampire in L.A. preying on a group of college students. It's funny and scary in about equal proportions, with slick, though inexpensive, production values (costing only $125,000, it grossed millions); some minor bloodshed and sensuality; and a jolting, if predictable, surprise ending. Sequel: *The Return of Count Yorga.*

Robert Quarry steps out for a bite in Count Yorga, Vampire *(1970).*

ROBERT QUARRY
(1928–)

A short-lived horror sensation in the early '70s, thanks to his role as *Count Yorga, Vampire*, Quarry (who made his screen bow with a bit part in Hitchcock's *Shadow of a Doubt*) brought a marvelous sense of sardonic humor to his horror roles. His career was cut short by injuries suffered in a mid-'70s car crash, but he's made a welcome return to the genre in recent years.

Count Yorga, Vampire ('70), *The Return of Count Yorga* ('71), *The Death Master* ('72), *Dr. Phibes Rises Again!* ('72), *Madhouse* ('74), *Sugar Hill* ('74), *Beverly Hills Vamp* ('88), *Sexbomb* ('89), *Evil Spirits* ('91), *Spirits* ('91), *Haunting Fear* ('91), *Teenage Exorcist* ('92).

COVER-UP
See: *Frightmare II.*

CRADLE WILL FALL, THE
★★ Lorimar Home Video, 1983, NR, 96 min.
Dir: John Llewellyn Moxey. Cast: Lauren Hutton, James Farentino, Ben Murphy, Charita Bauer, Joe Ponazecki, Peter Simon.

Lushly atmospheric but dull TV adaptation of Mary Higgins Clark's suspenser about an evil gynecologist (Farentino) conducting age retardation experiments on his patients and killing the failures. Hutton is the D.A. who suspects the truth. The acting and photography are good but this still isn't much.

CRATER LAKE MONSTER, THE
★☆ VCL Video, 1977, PG, 85 min.
Dir: William R. Stromberg. Cast: Richard Cardella, Glen Roberts, Mark Siegel, Kacey Cobb, Bob Hyman, Richard Garrison.

A fiery meteorite hatches a dinosaur egg secreted at the bottom of a mountain lake and unleashes a man-eating monster on the countryside. Terrific stop-motion FX but amateurish acting and direction and moronic comedy relief make this a real chore to sit through. This is for patient animation fans only.

CRAVING, THE
★★ Vestron Video, 1980, R, 92 min.
Dir: Jacinto Molina. Cast: Paul Naschy, Silvia Aguilar, Azucena Hernandez, Julia Saly, Beatriz Elorietta, Pilar Alcon.

A loose remake of Naschy's *The Werewolf vs.* the Vampire Woman with three female students reviving and falling victim to the evil Countess Elisabeth Bathory (Aguilar) and her werewolf manservant (guess who?). Originally titled *El Returno del Hombre Lobo: The Return of the Wolf Man* and directed by Naschy under his real name, this comeback picture was a flop in Paul's native Spain. It's not much different from his earlier efforts, although the werewolf makeup is slightly more elaborate and the dubbed dialogue is sprinkled with lots of hilariously gratuitous cursing.

CRAWLING EYE, THE
★★★ Media Home Entertainment, 1958, NR, 83 min. Dir: Quentin Lawrence. Cast: Forrest Tucker, Laurence Payne, Janet Munro, Jennifer Jayne, Warren Mitchell, Frederick Schiller.

Taut British programmer about huge alien monsters that resemble large eyeballs and live in a radioactive fogbank above a remote Alpine village, decapitating anyone who happens their way. Highly suspenseful, this lets down only near the end, thanks to some sadly inadequate special effects. Aka *The Trollenberg Terror.*

CRAWLING HAND, THE
★ Rhino Home Video, 1963, NR, 88 min.
Dir: Herbert L. Strock. Cast: Peter Breck, Kent Taylor, Rod Lauren, Sirry Steffen, Allison Hayes, Richard Arlen, Alan Hale, Arline Judge.

This is one crummy sci-fi/horror updating of *The Beast With Five Fingers*, about the radioactive severed hand and arm of a dead astronaut possessing a bad Frankie Avalon clone (Lauren), strangling his landlady (Judge), terrorizing his girlfriend ("Sex Iceberg" Steffen), and fighting a pack of hungry junkyard cats. The movie has stilted acting (*50-Foot Woman* Hayes is utterly wasted as a NASA secretary), a few bursts of early gore, two riffs from the rock classic "The Bird is the Word," and production values that make AIP look like MGM.

CRAWLSPACE
★★ Lightning Video, 1986, R, 80 min.
Dir: David Schmoeller. Cast: Klaus Kinski, Talia Balsam, Barbara Whinnery, Carol Francis.

Kinski at his craziest as a neo-Nazi madman who conducts cruel behavioralist experiments on the female boarders in his old rooming house, spying on them from the title place. This provides minor psycho thrills, with Klaus in fine form ("You've got to have a sense of humor," he reminds us as he merrily lances the boils on his hand) and a typically persuasive Pino Donaggio score.

CRAZE

★★☆ Simitar Video, 1974, R, 96 min.
Dir: Freddie Francis. Cast: Jack Palance, Diana Dors, Trevor Howard, Edith Evans, Hugh Griffith, Julie Ege, Suzy Kendall, Martin Potter, Michael Jayston, David Warbeck, Percy Herbert, Kathleen Byron.

This moderate Herman Cohen–produced mix of *Frenzy* and *Rosemary's Baby* has an out-of-control Palance as a London antique dealer who murders women as blood sacrifices to an African demon god called Chuku. Talented actors like Evans and Griffith are wasted in meaningless supporting parts, while Francis directs with far less than his usual acumen and an overabundance of shaky zooms into mangled corpses and Chuku's bug-eyed puss. Aka *The Infernal Idol* and *Demon Master.*

CRAZED VAMPIRES

See: *Dungeon of Terror.*

CRAZIES, THE

★★☆ Vista Video, 1973, R, 103 min.
Dir: George A. Romero. Cast: Lane Carroll, W.G. McMillan, Harold Wayne Jones, Lloyd Hollier, Lynn Lowry, Richard Liberty.

An accidental chemical spill into the water supply of a small Pennsylvania town turns the citizens into homicidal maniacs, forcing the authorities to call in the army. In Romero's malevolent comedy of errors, everything that can possibly go wrong does. This is an interesting treatment of Vietnam analogy as horror film, although it's often too unfocused and downbeat for its own good. It's well edited, though, with the idea of the military becoming just as big a threat as the "crazies" well brought off. Aka *Code Name: Trixie;* partly remade as *Impulse* (1984).

CRAZY FAT ETHEL II

★ Video Treasures, 1987, R, 60 min.
Dir: Nick Philips. Cast: Patricia Alden, Michael Flood, Jane Lambert, Robert Copple.

In this sorry sequel to the equally inane *Criminally Insane* from the same director and cast, the amazin' Alden returns as Ethel, just as hungry and homicidal as ever, turning a halfway house for rehabilitated maniacs into a slaughter house for dead rehabilitated maniacs. Really bad but also oddly compelling, thanks mostly to the demented presence of star Alden, this is not likely to turn up as the ABC Sunday Night Movie anytime soon. Aka *Death Nurse.*

CREATED TO KILL

See: *Embryo.*

CREATURE

★★★ Media Home Entertainment, 1985, R, 94 min.
Dir: William Malone. Cast: Stan Ivar, Wendy Schaal, Klaus Kinski, Diane Salinger, Lyman Ward, Annette McCarthy.

This is a likable *Alien* hybrid about a rescue mission sent to Saturn's moon Titan to search for a missing archeological team. There they encounter survivor Kinski and an alien crocodile monster with the talents of mind control and raising the dead. Good production design similar to that of *Planet of the Vampires* and pleasant actors (especially Schaal) make this a nice discovery. Aka *The Titan Find.*

CREATURE FROM BLACK LAKE

See: *Terror in the Swamp.*

CREATURE FROM THE BLACK LAGOON

★★★☆ MCA/Universal Home Video, 1954, NR, 79 min. Dir: Jack Arnold. Cast: Richard Carlson, Julie Adams, Richard Denning, Antonio Moreno, Nestor Paiva, Whit Bissell, Ben Chapman, Ricou Browning.

In this classic '50s monster-movie about an expedition up the Amazon that encounters a vicious half-man, half-fish "Gill-Man," the creature (played on land by Chapman and in the water by Browning) is captured but escapes. Taking a liking to heroine Adams, he carries her off to his misty cave. The film is full of powerful scares and steamy eroticism—the famous swimming scene was obviously the inspiration for the opening sequence in *Jaws.* Originally released in 3-D, this film's great success led to the sequels *Revenge of the Creature* and *The Creature Walks Among Us* and an entire school of monster-from-the-deep B movies.

CREATURE FROM THE HAUNTED SEA

★★☆ Sinister Cinema, 1960, NR, 72 min.
Dir: Roger Corman. Cast: Antony Carbone, Betsy Jones-Moreland, Edward Wain [Robert Towne], Beach Dickerson, Robert Bean, Sonia Noemi Gonzalez.

Another amusing Corman quickie in the same vein as *The Little Shop of Horrors.* Gangsters helping Cuban loyalists escape the revolution with the national treasury decide to kill the Cubans and steal the money themselves, blaming the deaths on a fictional sea monster. Soon, though, a *real* monster turns up and begins bumping off *everyone* until only it is left to claim the loot. Often resembling a cross between *Creature From the Black Lagoon* and *Beat the Devil,* this doesn't sparkle as brightly as *Little Shop* but is still fun. Best line: "Oh, Mary-Belle, I love you so much I could split!"

Julie Adams smells something fishy in Creature From the Black Lagoon *(1970).*

CREATURE OF DESTRUCTION

★ Sinister Cinema, 1967, NR, 80 min.
Dir: Larry Buchanan. Cast: Les Tremayne, Pat
Delaney, Aron Kincaid, Neil Fletcher, Annabelle
McAdams, Suzanne Ray.

This impoverished remake of *The She Creature*
features Tremayne as the top-hatted, opera-
cloaked hypnotist who regresses beautiful
assistant Delaney back to her first incarnation
as a prehistoric sea monster to commit the
murders he's "predicated" will occur at an
exclusive mountain resort. Tremayne tries to
give this an air of credibility but it's a no-go,
thanks to the rubbery, pop-eyed, zipper-
backed creature and lantern-jawed AIP
regular Kincaid's even funnier casting as a
psychologist.

CREATURE OF THE WALKING DEAD

★☆ Goodtimes Home Video, 1964, NR, 70 min.
Dirs: Jerry Warren and Frederic Corte [Fernando
Cortes]. Cast: Rock Madison, Ann Wells, Willard
Gross, George Todd, Katherine Victor, Bruno Ve Sota,
Fernando Casanova, Sonia Furio.

A young doctor (Casanova) revives his long-
dead lookalike scientist grandfather using the
latter's mad lab equipment. Granddad then
begins kidnapping young girls in order to
drain them of their vitality to stay young and
healthy. Another Warren Americanized Mexican monster-movie with the atmospheric original footage coming from a 1960 feature called
La Marca del Muerto: The Mark of Death, while
the pedestrian new material features Madison
as an investigating detective and Victor as a
helpful psychic.

CREATURES FROM BEYOND THE GRAVE

See: *From Beyond the Grave.*

CREATURES FROM THE PREHISTORIC PLANET

See: *Horror of the Blood Monsters.*

CREATURE'S REVENGE, THE

See: *Brain of Blood.*

CREATURES THE WORLD FORGOT

★★ RCA/Columbia Home Video, 1971, PG, 95 min.
Dir: Don Chaffey. Cast: Julie Ege, Tony Bonner,
Brian O'Shaughnessy, Robert John, Marcia Fox,
Rosalie Crutchley.

Hammer's last prehistoric horror film has no
dinosaurs and precious little excitement as
well, instead concentrating on sex and sadism
(some of it cut to get a PG rating), with Nor-
wegian sex bomb Ege the put-upon cave babe

PETER CUSHING
(1913–1994)

Hammer superstar Cushing started his
acting career with a brief sojourn to Hollywood in the late '30s where, coincidentally, he would make his debut in
Frankenstein director James Whale's 1939
The Man in the Iron Mask. Cushing found
his first major success, however, in British
TV plays in the '50s. After the phenome-
nal success of Hammer's *The Curse of
Frankenstein* in '57, in which he played
Baron Frankenstein for the first of six
times, Peter fast became a major genre
star and, with Christopher Lee, created
one of the most popular movie acting
teams of all time. One of the finest character actors ever to grace the screen, Cushing was without peer at bringing dignity,
class, and even a sense of fun to even the
least worthwhile horror films.

The Curse of Frankenstein ('57), *The Abom-
inable Snowman of the Himalayas* ('57),
Horror of Dracula ('58), *The Revenge of
Frankenstein* ('58), *The Hound of the
Baskervilles* ('59), *The Mummy* ('59), *Mania*
('60), *Brides of Dracula* ('60), *Night Crea-
tures* ('62), *The Evil of Frankenstein* ('64),
The Gorgon ('64), *Dr. Terror's House of Hor-
rors* ('65), *She* ('65), *The Skull* ('65), *Island of
Terror* ('66), *Frankenstein Created Woman*
('67), *The Mummy's Shroud* (narrator, '67),
Torture Garden ('68), *The Blood Beast Terror*
('68), *Corruption* ('68), *Frankenstein Must
Be Destroyed!* ('69), *Scream and Scream
Again!* ('70), *Bloodsuckers* ('70), *The Vam-
pire Lovers* ('70), *The House That Dripped
Blood* ('71), *I, Monster* ('71), *Twins of Evil*
('72), *Tales From the Crypt* ('72), *Horror
Express* ('72), *Fear in the Night* ('72), *Asy-
lum* ('72), *Dr. Phibes Rises Again!* ('72),
Dracula A.D. 1972 ('72), *Nothing But the
Night* ('72), *The Creeping Flesh* ('73), *—And
Now the Screaming Starts!* ('73), *Franken-
stein and the Monster From Hell* ('73), *The
Satanic Rites of Dracula* ('73), *From Beyond
the Grave* ('74), *Madhouse* ('74), *The Beast
Must Die* ('74), *Legend of the 7 Golden Vam-
pires* ('74), *Tendre Dracula* ('74), *The Ghoul*
('75), *Legend of the Werewolf* ('75), *Shock
Waves* ('75), *Land of the Minotaur* ('76), *The
Uncanny* ('77), *House of the Long Shadows*
('83), *Sherlock Holmes and the Masks of
Death* ('84).

Peter Cushing gets a big hand in The Creeping Flesh *(1973)*.

this time. It's beautifully photographed but a real snooze.

CREATURE WALKS AMONG US, THE

★★☆ MCA/Universal Home Video, 1956, NR, 78 min. Dir: John Sherwood. Cast: Jeff Morrow, Rex Reason, Leigh Snowden, Gregg Palmer, James Rawley, Maurice Manson, Don Megowan, Ricou Browning.

The third and last installment in the *Creature* series finds the Gill-Man "humanized" by psychotic scientist Morrow and eventually going on a rampage when he is framed for murder. Talky but well acted, this has some unexpected plot twists and shocking bursts of violence in the final third. Megowan plays the creature on land, while Browning is the monster in its original form.

CREEPER, THE

★★ International Video Entertainment, 1948, NR, 63 min. Dir: Jean Yarbrough. Cast: Onslow Stevens, Eduardo Cianelli, June Vincent, Ralph Morgan, Janis Wilson, John Baragrey.

A scientist (Stevens) commits murders with a clawed cat's paw he sprouts after taking a mysterious serum. Like *The Brute Man,* this is another Universal B-minus chiller sold off to another company (in this case 20th Century-

Fox) when the bottom dropped out of the post-war horror market. It borrows everything from *The Wolf Man* and *Cat People* except their entertainment value and seriously wastes an exceptional cast.

CREEPERS, THE

See: *Assault.*

CREEPERS

★★★ Video Treasures, 1984, R, 83 min. Dir: Dario Argento. Cast: Jennifer Connelly, Donald Pleasence, Daria Nicolodi, Patrick Bauchau, Dalila Di Lazzaro, Fiore Argento.

Originally called *Phenomena,* this is one of Argento's silliest, but more underrated, works. Connelly is the attractive new student at the Richard Wagner Academy, a Swiss boarding school terrorized by a violent killer, and uses her psychic bond with insects to track the maniac down. Derivative of *Poltergeist, The Funhouse, Friday the 13th,* and much of the director's earlier work, the film makes little sense but is buoyed by an audacious sense of the absurd—especially in its concluding scenes.

CREEPING FLESH, THE

★★★ RCA/Columbia Home Video, 1972, PG, 92 min. Dir: Freddie Francis. Cast: Peter Cushing,

Christopher Lee, Lorna Heilbron, George Benson, Kenneth J. Warren, Michael Ripper.

In this handsome gothic chiller, Cushing is outstanding as a Victorian scientist experimenting with a weird skeleton from New Guinea that sprouts flesh when touched by water and which he hopes to prove is the remains of an ancient personification of evil. Lee also impresses as Cushing's half-brother and scientific rival, as does Heilbron as Peter's mad daughter, although the subplot involving her possible cure through an injection of the skeleton's blood is shoehorned rather uncomfortably into the main action.

CREEPING TERROR, THE
☆ United Home Video, 1963, NR, 75 min.
Dir: Art J. Nelson. Cast: Vic Savage [Art J. Nelson], Shannon O'Neil, William Thourlby, John Carison.

Here's one for the books: a cheapo monster-movie filmed in Lake Tahoe, Nevada, where the soundtrack was lost and only partly restored. Most of the film is silent, with voice-over narration. The plot, what there is of it, involves an alien creature (which looks like a cross between a soggy bath mat and an asparagus tip) chowing down on various extras while a couple of nitwits ineptly try to stop it. Hilarity rules as hapless victims push themselves into the monster's maw to simulate alien chewing and several human feet are clearly visible beneath the beastie at any given time. Aka *Dangerous Charter*.

CREEPOZOIDS
★☆ Urban Classics, 1987, R, 72 min.
Dir: David De Coteau. Cast: Linnea Quigley, Richard Hawkins, Ken Abraham, Kim McKamy, Michael Aranda, Joi Wilson.

Here's another bargain-basement *Alien* knock-off set in the near future where five army deserters—three male, two female—wander around an abandoned factory and do battle with giant rats, a mutant baby, and a tusked, Giger-esque creature covered in shellac. This "everything but the kitchen sink" exploiter is noteworthy for Linnea alone.

CREEPSHOW
★★★ Warner Home Video, 1982, R, 120 min.
Dir: George A. Romero. Cast: Hal Holbrook, Adrienne Barbeau, Leslie Nielsen, Fritz Weaver, Carrie Nye, E. G. Marshall, Viveca Lindfors, Ed Harris, Ted Danson, Gaylen Ross, Tom Atkins, Stephen King.

In this fun King-scripted tribute to the E. C. horror comics of the '50s, *Creepshow*, a gory horror comic book comes to life to dramatize five stories. A murdered patriarch returns from the grave to claim his Father's Day cake; meteor juice turns a dimwitted farmer into a human plant; a cuckold drowns his unfaithful wife and her lover, who rise up as water-logged zombies; a hen-pecked college professor uses the voracious contents of an old crate to end his unhappy marriage; and a persnickety billionaire's pristine penthouse is invaded by billions of cockroaches during a New York blackout. Romero's stylish, color-saturated direction and the gung-ho performances are better than King's often obvious stories. This film's popularity led to a brief resurgence of multi-story horror pics—*Twilight Zone, the Movie; Nightmares; The Offspring*; and the inevitable *Creepshow 2*.

CREEPSHOW 2
★★ Starmaker Home Video, 1987, R, 89 min.
Dir: Michael Gornick. Cast: Lois Chiles, George Kennedy, Dorothy Lamour, Tom Savini, Tom Wright, Daniel Beer, Jeremy Green, Page Hannah, David Holbrook, Stephen King.

This lifeless sequel to the '82 horror hit presents three tales of boredom rather than terror, linked by some especially awful animation. A wooden Indian statue comes to life to avenge the murders of Kennedy and Lamour; four teens are trapped on a raft on a mountain lake inhabited by a man-eating blob that looks like a soggy Hefty bag; and Chiles (who's great) is a hit-and-run driver tormented by the living corpse of the hitchhiker she ran down. Only the final segment and some good makeup FX in the blob story make this styleless follow-up worth sitting through.

CRIES IN THE NIGHT
See: *Funeral Home.*

CRIME OF DR. CRESPI, THE
★★☆ Sinister Cinema, 1935, NR, 63 min.
Dir: John H. Auer. Cast: Erich von Stroheim, Dwight Frye, Paul Guilfolye, Harriet Russell, Geraldine Kay, John Bohn.

In this forgotten '30s cheapie chiller, von Stroheim (chewing the scenery) plays a pompous surgeon who injects the new husband of his former sweetie with a death-semblance serum and arranges for him to be buried alive. Supposedly based on Poe's "The Premature Burial," this also has ace mad lab assistant Frye in a straight role as one of von Stroheim's fellow medicos. Surprisingly grim for its time.

CRIMES AT THE DARK HOUSE
★★☆ Sinister Cinema, 1940, NR, 69 min.
Dir: George King. Cast: Tod Slaughter, Sylvia Marriott, Hilary Eaves, Geoffrey Wardell, Hay Petrie.

This loose adaptation of Wilkie Collins' "The Woman in White" (treated here more as horror than mystery melodrama) has Slaughter at his hambone best as the sinister duke who marries into a wealthy family and then arranges to drive his new bride insane. It's static but enjoyable and has hilariously grandiose dialogue.

CRIMES OF STEPHEN HAWKE, THE
★★ Sinister Cinema, 1936, NR, 65 min. Dir: George King. Cast: Tod Slaughter, Marjorie Taylor, Eric Portman, D. J. Williams, Ben Soutten.

Another Slaughter extravaganza, this has the Todster essaying the title role of a kindly money-lender by day, a vicious strangler known as the "Spine-Breaker" by night. More low-brow hijinks from the uncrowned king of overacting. Aka *Strangler's Morgue.*

CRIMES OF THE BODY SNATCHERS
See: *The Greed of William Hart.*

CRIMES OF THE WAX MUSEUM
See: *Nightmare in Wax.*

CRIMINALLY INSANE
★ WesternWorld Video, 1974, R, 60 min. Dir: Nick Philips. Cast: Priscilla Alden, Michael Flood, Jane Lambert, Robert Copple.

Alden is unforgettable as Ethel, an enormously overweight misanthrope who murders anyone who comes between her and the most important thing in her life—food. This film's grainy slice-of-life atmosphere sometimes makes it look like *Henry: Portrait of a Serial Killer* (if that film had starred Cass Elliott), but Philips' overall lack of talent and home-movie-style production values soon take their toll. This one's for only the most desperately curious. Sequel: *Crazy Fat Ethel II.*

CRIMSON ALTAR, THE
See: *Curse of the Crimson Cult.*

CRIMSON CULT, THE
See: *Curse of the Crimson Altar.*

CRIMSON EXECUTIONER, THE
See: *The Bloody Pit of Horror.*

CRITTERS
★★☆ RCA/Columbia Home Video, 1986, PG-13, 86 min. Dir: Stephen Herek. Cast: Dee Wallace-Stone, Billy Green Bush, M. Emmet Walsh, Scott Grimes, Nadine Van Der Velde, Don Opper, Terrence Mann, Billy Zane.

In this silly *Gremlins* derivation, farmer Brown and his family find their pleasant little Kansas spread invaded by furry mini-monsters from space sought by a team of alien bounty hunters. It evokes a nice '50s B-movie feel, with corny dialogue and goofy character behavior to spare and clever special effects by the Chiodo Brothers.

CRITTERS 2: THE MAIN COURSE
★★ RCA/Columbia Home Video, 1988, PG-13, 85 min. Dir: Mick Garris. Cast: Scott Grimes, Liane Curtis, Don Opper, Barry Corbin, Terrence Mann, Sam Anderson, Herta Ware, Eddie Deezen.

In this well-made but needless sequel, teenager Grimes returns to his old hometown to visit Grandma Ware for Easter just as another critter invasion begins. More violent than its predecessor, it's also less amusing (though it tries hard to be funny), with the critters this time about as scary as furry bowling balls.

CRITTERS 3
★★ New Line Home Video, 1991, PG-13, 84 min. Dir: Kristine Peterson. Cast: Aimee Brooks, John Calvin, Leonard DiCaprio, Katherine Cortez, Geoffrey Blake, Diana Bellamy, Don Opper, Terrence Mann.

This direct-to-video third entry is actually a monster movie variation on *Die Hard* with the critters this time seeking victims in a big-city apartment building. The David Schow script has some clever moments, but the low budget shows and the ending is nothing more than an annoying setup for part 4—shot back-to-back with this one.

CRITTERS 4
★★ New Line Home Video, 1992, PG-13, 95 min. Dir: Rupert Harvey. Cast: Don Opper, Brad Dourif, Angela Bassett, Paul Whitthorne, Anders Hove, Eric DaRae, Terrence Mann, voice of Martine Beswicke.

The series moves into *Alien* territory as the critters invade a futuristic space station looking for new victims. There's a great cast but the critters have even less to do here than they did in part 3. And is it always necessary to put a cute little kid in these things?

CROCODILE
★ HBO Video, 1979, R, 95 min. Dir: Sompote Sands. Cast: Nat Puvanai, Tany Tim, Angela Wells, Kirk Warren.

A Korean-made *Jaws* rip-off set in Thailand, where a gigantic guess-what is terrorizing villagers, livestock, and tourists—not necessarily in that order. Genre vet Herman Cohen was executive producer on this drek, which looks for all the world like a bad *Alligator* cash-in, except that this was made first. It also has plastic special effects.

CRUCIBLE OF HORROR

★★★ MGM/UA Home Video, 1971, PG, 90 min. Dir: Viktors Ritelis. Cast: Michael Gough, Yvonne Mitchell, Sharon Gurney, Simon Gough, Olaf Pooley, David Butler.

Gough is an unbelievable tyrant of a husband and father who is murdered by long-suffering wife Mitchell and daughter Gurney, only to seemingly return from the grave for revenge. Talky but well-acted *Diabolique* variant with haunting photography and music and some actual suspense. Unfortunately, a choppy, unconvincing ending hurts. Probably Gough's finest hour. Aka *The Corpse* and *Velvet House.*

CRUCIBLE OF TERROR

★★ Goodtimes Home Video, 1971, PG, 85 min. Dir: Ted Hooker. Cast: Mike Raven, Mary Maude, James Bolam, Ronald Lacey, Melissa Stribling, Beth Morris, Judy Matheson, Me Me Lay.

This is an uneasy blending of the usual crazed-artist-covering-his-models-with-bronze-and-passing-them-off-as-statues nonsense with a possession subplot. Raven is typically hammy as a Cornish artist whose seaside household is menaced by a killer who turns out to be wearing a haunted kimono (I swear!) belonging to a beautiful Asian model Raven has murdered. It's dumb but has some stray bits of atmosphere and moodiness. Available

---

MICHAEL GOUGH
(1917–)

The Lionel Atwill of the '60s, this incisive British character actor rode the crest of the English horror boom in the late '50s through the early '70s with supporting performances in Hammer films and leads in various Herman Cohen flicks. Now best known for playing Alfred, the butler in Tim Burton's *Batman* movies, Gough's haughty demeanor was best displayed in *Horrors of the Black Museum* and *The Phantom of the Opera.*

The House in the Woods ('57), *Horror of Dracula* ('58), *Horrors of the Black Museum* ('59), *Konga* ('61), *No Place Like Homicide* ('61), *The Phantom of the Opera* ('62), *Black Zoo* ('63), *Dr. Terror's House of Horrors* ('65), *The Skull* ('65), *Berserk!* ('68), *The Crimson Cult* ('68), *Trog* ('70), *Crucible of Horror* ('71), *The Legend of Hell House* ('73), *Horror Hospital* ('73), *Satan's Slave* ('76), *The Boys From Brazil* ('78), *Venom* ('82), *The Serpent and the Rainbow* ('88).

---

on many labels but always in a heavily cut version missing much violence and nudity from the original Brit print.

CRUCIFER OF BLOOD

★★☆ Turner Home Entertainment, 1991, NR, 131 min. Dir: Fraser C. Heston. Cast: Charlton Heston, Richard Johnson, Susanna Harker, John Castle, Clive Wood, James Fox.

If you can accept the casting of Heston as Sherlock Holmes (he really isn't bad), then you may enjoy this loose adaptation of Conan Doyle's "The Sign of the Four," previously done as a play by Paul Giovanni, with Holmes investigating the bloody murders committed by a mysterious cult. It's surprisingly gory for a cable movie, with nice period atmosphere and a fun Dr. Watson in Johnson.

CRUISE INTO TERROR

★☆ Prism Entertainment, 1978, NR, 96 min. Dir: Bruce Kessler. Cast: Hugh O'Brian, Stella Stevens, Frank Converse, Christopher George, Lynda Day George, Ray Milland, John Forsythe, Lee Meriwether, Dirk Benedict, Hilary Thompson, Jo Ann Harris, Marshall Thompson.

An odd assortment of vacationers on a cruise off the Mexican coast discover an underwater Egyptian tomb containing a child-sized sarcophagus, itself containing the remains of the anti-Christ! A real laugh-riot of outrageously contrived plotting and heavy-duty overacting (Forsythe and Meriwether take the cake as a bible-thumping minister and his repressed wife), this strikingly bent tele-movie looks like a bad Halloween episode of *The Love Boat.* Aka *Voyage Into Evil.*

CRUSH, THE

★☆ Warner Home Video, 1993, R, 89 min. Dir: Alan Shapiro. Cast: Alicia Silverstone, Cary Elwes, Jennifer Rubin, Kurtwood Smith, Gwynyth Walsh, Amber Benson.

Elwes, the sort of doofus who dresses with his bathroom door half open just so we can sneak a peek at his ass, is the unaccountable obsession of 14-year-old Silverstone, who makes Lolita look like Rebecca of Sunnybrook Farm. This cliché-driven psycho flick keeps promising to be a hoot but is played too straight-faced for that, with absurdly illogical plot twists and a ridiculous *Strangers on a Train–*derived climax.

CRY OF THE BANSHEE

★★☆ HBO Video, 1970, PG, 87 min. Dir: Gordon Hessler. Cast: Vincent Price, Elisabeth Bergner, Essy Persson, Hugh Griffith, Hilary Dwyer,

Patrick Mower, Sally Geeson, Robert Hutton, Carl Rigg, Quinn O'Hara.

When 16th-century Irish magistrate Price fatally breaks up witch Bergner's coven, she places a curse upon his family involving a murderous demon called a sidhee, embodied in handsome stable boy Mower. A fairly neat combination of Price's earlier hits *The Masque of the Red Death* and *The Conqueror Worm,* this starts to get out of hand as it races toward its confusing conclusion. Advertised as based on the works of Poe, it isn't.

CRY OF THE WEREWOLF
★★ Goodtimes Home Video, 1944, NR, 63 min. Dir: Henry Levin. Cast: Nina Foch, Stephen Crane, Osa Massen, Barton MacLane, Blanche Yurka, Fritz Leiber, John Abbott, Milton Parsons.

Columbia imitates Val Lewton by way of Universal with this minor entry that presents Foch as a fiery gypsy princess who's also a bloodthirsty werewolf. The transformations occur mostly off-screen (à la *Cat People*) and the "werewolf" is really just a big dog, but a colorful supporting cast and eerie moods in a museum devoted to the macabre make this passable B-movie stuff. Aka *Daughter of the Werewolf.*

CRYPT OF THE LIVING DEAD
★☆ MPI Home Video, 1972, R, 83 min. Dir: Ray Danton. Cast: Andrew Prine, Mark Damon, Patty Sheppard, Teresa Gimpera, Frank Brana, Ihsan Genik.

A low-cost vampire tale (appropriately shot in Turkey) telling of beauteous Hannah (Gimpera), the undead wife of crusader Louis VII, who is revived in modern times by an especially crazed-looking Damon. With so many side issues to wallow through—romantic interludes, several murders, and a totally incongruous "Wild Man" running amok—poor Hannah, sporting a paste tiara making her look like the hometown beauty queen, is given short shrift indeed, spending most of her time in her tomb before being set on fire and staked. Some days it just doesn't pay to get out of bed. Aka *Hannah, Queen of the Vampires; Young Hannah, Queen of the Vampires;* and *Vampire Woman.*

CTHULHU MANSION
★★ Republic Home Video, 1991, R, 92 min. Dir: Juan Piquer Simon. Cast: Frank Finlay, Marcia Layton, Brad Fisher, Melanie Shatner, Paul Birchard, Frank Brana.

What's Lovecraft got to do with it? Not much, actually, as that wonderful character actor Fin-

lay (as Chandu the magician), his daughter, and some drug-dealing punks are trapped in the title abode by murderous demonic forces. Strictly low-rent. Aka *Black Magic Manson.*

CUJO
★★★ Warner Home Video, 1983, R, 91 min. Dir: Lewis Teague. Cast: Dee Wallace, Danny Pintauro, Daniel Hugh-Kelly, Christopher Stone, Ed Lauter, Mills Watson.

A stark, effective adaptation of the Stephen King novel about a young mother (Wallace) and her little son (Pintauro) trapped in their disabled Pinto by Cujo, a rabid Saint Bernard. Jan De Bont's photography is splendidly effective (particularly his 360-degree spin inside the car) and the acting (especially Wallace) is first-rate, making this one of the best of the King movies.

CULT OF THE COBRA
★★☆ MCA/Universal, 1955, NR, 80 min. Dir: Francis D. Lyon. Cast: Faith Domergue, Marshall Thompson, Richard Long, Kathleen Hughes, Jack Kelly, David Janssen, William Reynolds, James Dobson.

In this serpentine reworking of *Cat People,* Domergue has a definitive role as Lisa Moya, a foreign beauty with the ability to transform into a deadly cobra, going after six American G.I.s who witness a secret snake-cult ceremony. This is sometimes unintentionally funny but has imaginative direction and a good '50s cast, including a young Janssen as the most likable of the doomed soldiers.

CULT OF THE DAMNED
★☆ MPI Home Video, 1968, PG, 90 min. Dirs: Juan Ibanez and Jack Hill. Cast: Boris Karloff, Julissa Santanon, Carlos East, Ralph Bertrand.

This jumbled mixture of devil worshippers, zombies, LSD, and police investigations has Karloff strictly along for marquee value in his few scenes as an occult expert. The first of Boris' four Mexican fiascos, this isn't as bad as some of the others but that's faint praise. Aka *La Muerte Viviente: The Living Dead; The Snake People;* and *Isle of the Snake People.*

CURSE, THE
★★☆ Video Treasures, 1987, R, 85 min. Dir: David Keith. Cast: Wil Wheaton, Claude Akins, John Schneider, Cooper Huckabee, Amy Wheaton, Malcolm Danare, Hope North, Kathleen Jordan Gregory.

Actor Keith made his directorial bow with this rather dull but well-acted version of H. P. Lovecraft's "The Color Out of Space." A meteor falls on the farm of religious zealot Akins and contaminates the food supply, turning livestock and residents into hideous mutants. It tries its best, but schlocky makeup and special effects keep it strictly second-rate. The same story was previously filmed as *Die, Monster, Die!* Aka *The Farm* and followed by three bogus sequels.

CURSE II: THE BITE

★★ TransWorld Entertainment, 1989, UR, 97 min.
Dir: Fred Goodwin [Federico Prosperi]. Cast: Jill Schoelen, J. Eddie Peck, Bo Svenson, Jamie Farr, Al Fann, Sydney Lassick.

With nothing to do with the original *Curse,* this plays, instead, like a junior-league remake of *Sssssss.* After Peck is bitten by a mutated snake out in the desert, his arm transforms into a weird snake-creature while his entire body eventually becomes an incubator for serpents of all sorts. Some truly knock-your-socks-off Screaming Mad George FX (including a woman's jaw torn off and a heart pulled out through a throat), but unsympathetic characters and slack pacing fail to measure up. Aka *The Bite* and also out in an R-rated version.

CURSE III: BLOOD SACRIFICE

★★ RCA/Columbia Home Video, 1991, R, 91 min.
Dir: Sean Barton. Cast: Christopher Lee, Jenilee Harrison, Henry Celé, Andre Jacobs.

American bride Harrison breaks up a South African voodoo ceremony and is cursed by a witch doctor; subsequently her entire family is wiped out by a machete-wielding monster. Well, there's some breathtakingly beautiful location photography but you can catch a National Geographic special for *that.* Otherwise, this wastes Lee as a red herring doctor and has a Chris Walas–designed creature that's about as scary as Kermit the Frog on steroids. And what's *any* of this got to do with *The Curse* and *Curse II*? Aka *Panga.*

CURSE IV: THE ULTIMATE SACRIFICE

★★ Columbia/TriStar Home Video, 1988, R, 84 min.
Dir: David Schmoeller. Cast: Timothy Van Patten, Laura Shaeffer, Jeremy West, Ian Abercrombie, Feodor Chaliapin, Mapi Galan.

You may be wondering how a part IV could have been made *before* parts II and III but there *is* an explanation. Actually, this is a forgotten Empire flick called *Catacombs,* about demonic possession at an Italian monastery, outfitted with a phony new title to give it some video shelf life. Although this has one truly amazing scene where Christ comes to life on the cross, pulls out the nails holding him there, and stabs an awestruck priest to death

with one of them, the ultimate sacrifice is just sitting through this dull sub-*Exorcist* to the end.

CURSE OF DARK SHADOWS

See: *Night of Dark Shadows.*

CURSE OF FRANKENSTEIN, THE

★★★ Warner Home Video, 1957, NR, 83 min.
Dir: Terence Fisher. Cast: Peter Cushing, Christopher Lee, Hazel Court, Robert Urquhart, Valerie Gaunt, Melvyn Hayes.

The first in Hammer Films' long-running series of *Frankenstein* movies, this recounts the experiments of young Baron Frankenstein (Cushing), who creates a pasty-faced monster (Lee) from various corpses. A '50s classic whose success sparked a revival in gothic horror after nearly a decade of sci-fi monsters, this has an awkward flashback structure but crisp direction and excellent acting from Cushing and Lee. It was remade as *The Horror of Frankenstein* and followed by five sequels, beginning with *The Revenge of Frankenstein.*

CURSE OF KING TUT'S TOMB, THE

★★ RCA/Columbia Home Video, 1980, NR, 92 min.
Dir: Philip Leacock. Cast: Robin Ellis, Eva Marie Saint, Raymond Burr, Harry Andrews, Wendy Hiller, Tom Baker, Barbara Murray, voice of Paul Scofield.

A big-name cast adds some needed class to this TV movie based on the supposedly bizarre circumstances surrounding the opening of the tomb of King Tutankhamen. It's really little more than a jumble of warmed-over "Kharis the mummy" clichés set to outtakes from the score from *Moses the Lawgiver.* A turbaned Burr is 400 pounds of pure ham in a role tailor-made for George Zucco.

CURSE OF NOSTRADAMUS, THE

★☆ Sinister Cinema, 1960, NR, 78 min.
Dir: Federico Curiel. Cast: German Robles, Julio Aleman, Domingo Soler, Aurora Alvarado, Mander.

In 1960, Robles starred in a 12-chapter Mexican serial concerning the adventures of a vampiric descendant of the prophet Nostradamus. Later they were recut into four cheap features sold directly to American TV and this was the first. Nostradamus promises to murder 13 prominent citizens unless his arch-nemesis Professor Duran gets off his caped back. Naturally, the prof refuses to cooperate and the vampire is apparently destroyed in a cave-in. We should be so lucky! Laughable pseudo-chills with Mander hilarious as Robles' rat-petting henchguy Leo. Sequels: *The Monster Demolisher, Genie of Darkness,* and *The Blood of Nostradamus.*

CURSE OF THE AZTEC MUMMY
★★ Sinister Cinema, 1957, NR, 85 min.
Dir: Rafael Portillo. Cast: Ramon Gay, Rosita Arenas, Crox Alvarado, Luis Aceves.

In this first sequel to *The Aztec Mummy*— "Americanized" as *Attack of the Mayan Mummy*—an evil scientist known as "The Bat" attempts to hypnotize pretty heroine Arenas into revealing the whereabouts of the Aztec mummy and his treasure. This is far from being a good movie but marked by the sort of sweet naiveté and silly dubbing one always finds so reassuring in these Mexi-monster flicks. Followed by *The Robot vs. the Aztec Mummy.*

CURSE OF THE BLACK WIDOW
★★ Prism Entertainment, 1977, NR, 96 min.
Dir: Dan Curtis. Cast: Anthony Franciosa, Donna Mills, Patty Duke, Vic Morrow, June Allyson, Roz Kelly, Max Gail, June Lockhart, Sid Caesar, Jeff Corey.

Unintentionally a howl, this made-for-TV homage to the horror flicks of the '50s has Franciosa as a private detective after a female killer who leaves her dismembered male victims enmeshed in a silken web. Of course, she turns out to be a schizo plain Jane who was bitten as a baby by a horde of black widow spiders and can now mutate herself into a huge, murderous arachnid at will. It happens all the time. It's fun for a while with some offbeat casting and interesting minor characters, but Curtis was clearly directing by-the-numbers by this time in his '70s TV horror career. It's notable mostly for the sight of Lockhart in a fright wig, Duke talking with a Bela Lugosi accent, and Mills manhandled by a big puppet spider. Aka *Love Trap.*

CURSE OF THE BLOOD-GHOULS
See: *Slaughter of the Vampires.*

CURSE OF THE CAT PEOPLE
★★★ Turner Home Entertainment, 1944, NR, 70 min. Dirs: Robert Wise and Gunther Von Fritsch. Cast: Simone Simon, Kent Smith, Jane Randolph, Ann Carter, Elizabeth Russell, Julia Dean, Eve March, Sir Lancelot.

Unconventional sequel to the 1942 hit with Simon returning as a friendly ghost who becomes the imaginary playmate of the lonely young daughter of the dead cat-woman's husband and his second wife. Good acting and a delicate atmosphere make this the most unusual film in the Val Lewton canon, not so much a horror film (despite a token dark old house) as a gentle fantasy.

CURSE OF THE CRIMSON ALTAR, THE
★★☆ HBO Video, 1968, PG, 88 min.
Dir: Vernon Sewell. Cast: Boris Karloff, Christopher Lee, Barbara Steele, Mark Eden, Virginia Wetherell, Michael Gough, Rupert Davies, Rosemarie Reede.

Originally released in the U.S. as *The Crimson Cult*, this was Karloff's last legit feature (discounting his four Mexican atrocities) and his only film with both Lee and Steele (though they share no scenes). When his brother disappears in a small English village, Eden investigates and uncovers a devil cult headed by green-faced reincarnated witch Steele. Ostensibly based on Lovecraft's "Dreams in the Witch House" and sharing some plot similarities to the superior *Horror Hotel*, this has a few moments. The video has the more complete European version (with some brief nudity) but also has an awful new electronic score and features Gough in his worst-ever role as Lee's retard manservant.

CURSE OF THE CRYING WOMAN
★★☆ Sinister Cinema, 1961, NR, 74 min.
Dir: Rafael Baledon. Cast: Abel Salazar, Rosita Arenas, Rita Macedo, Carlos Lopez Montezuma.

Routine Mexican horror pic based on an actual south-of-the-boarder legend, with Arenas inheriting from her late aunt an old mansion inhabited by a disfigured caretaker and the title spook. Dank atmosphere, dumb dubbing, familiar thrills.

CURSE OF THE DEAD
See: *Kill, Baby, Kill!*

CURSE OF THE DEMON
★★★★ Goodtimes Home Video, 1958, NR, 95 min.
Dir: Jacques Tourneur. Cast: Dana Andrews, Peggy Cummins, Niall MacGinnis, Maurice Denham, Athene Seyler, Liam Redmond.

Andrews is a psychologist who steadfastly refuses to believe in the supernatural but finds his skepticism tested to the max when he's marked for death by a powerful black magician and fated to die at the hands of a hideous demon. Supposedly the victim of producer interference, with the title monster made visible at the beginning and end of the film against director Tourneur's wishes, this still emerges as the finest horror film produced during the 1950s, with a wealth of rich plot detail. It's based on the story "Casting the Runes" by Montague R. James and boasts excellent performances—particularly MacGinnis as the urbane sorcerer. First released in the U.S. on a twin bill with Hammer's *The Revenge of Frankenstein* in a cut version, but thankfully

Here's the producer-approved creature from hell from Curse of the Demon *(1958).*

it is the full, original British print that has been issued on video. A must-see; aka *Night of the Demon.*

CURSE OF THE DEVIL
★★☆ United American Video, 1973, R, 80 min.
Dir: Charles [Carlos] Aured. Cast: Paul Naschy, Fabiola Falcon, Maria Silva, Marita Olivares, Antonio Vidal Molina, Ana Fara.

In his seventh outing as werewolf Waldemar Daninsky, Naschy is cursed by the activities of an Inquisitor ancestor and becomes the wolf man when marked on the chest by the fangs of a wolf's skull. Aka *El Retorno de la Walpurgis: The Return of Walpurgis*, this Spanish-Mexican co-production is fun, thanks to Paul's as always boundless enthusiasm for the monster genre. Favorite come-on line: "I come here a virgin; I'm not leaving the same way!"

CURSE OF THE DOLL PEOPLE
★★★ Sinister Cinema, 1960, NR, 83 min.
Dir: Benito Alazrahi. Cast: Elvira Quintana, Ramon Gay, Roberto E. Rivera, Jorge Mondragon, Nora Veryan, Luis Aragon.

Bad editing and the usual goofy dubbing notwithstanding, this really creepy voodoo thriller is one of the best of the Mexican horrors. A group of men who steal some Haitian artifacts are stalked by child-sized voodoo dolls (midgets in dark suits and spooky masks) bent on their destruction. Aka *Los Munecos Infernales: Devil Doll Men.*

CURSE OF THE FULL MOON
See: *The Rats are Coming! The Werewolves are Here!*

CURSE OF THE LIVING CORPSE, THE
★★★ Prism Entertainment, 1964, NR, 84 min.
Dir: Del Tenney. Cast: Roy Scheider, Helen Waren, Robert Milli, Margot Hartman, Candace Hilligoss, Linda Donovan.

Grand Guginol on 10 bucks a day, this Stamford, Connecticut–lensed gothic cheapie is Tenney's best film. When tyranical millionaire Rufus Sinclair is seemingly buried alive by his less-than-loving family, soon everyone is stalked by a black-caped figure who kills them via their worst dread come true: drowning, burning, decapitation, suffocation, etc. This offers surprising bursts of gore and semi-nudity, Scheider in his film debut, and shapely maid Donovan's head served on a breakfast tray.

CURSE OF THE LIVING DEAD
See: *Kill, Baby, Kill!*

CURSE OF THE STONE HAND
★ Sinister Cinema, 1964, NR, 72 min.
Dirs: Carl Schleipper, Carlos Hugo Christensen, and Jerry Warren. Cast: John Carradine, Katherine Victor, Lloyd Nelson, Sheila Bon, Charles Torres, Ernest Walch, Barbara Wells, voice of Bruno Ve Sota.

JACQUES TOURNEUR
(1904–1977)

Born in Paris, the son of leading French director Maurice Tourneur, Jacques was one of the guiding forces behind the Val Lewton psychological horror films of the '40s. He was a master of mood and suggestive horror whose best work was the '50s classic *Curse of the Demon.*

Cat People ('42), *I Walked With a Zombie* ('43), *The Leopard Man* ('43), *Curse of the Demon* ('58), *The Comedy of Terrors* ('64), *War-Gods of the Deep* ('65).

Ve Sota desperately tries to add some coherence to this awful combination of a 1946 Chilean adaptation of R. L. Stevenson's "The Suicide Club" with an obscure 1959 Mexican horror film. The results are pure fool's gold and the definitive Warren cut-and-paste job. The two tales presented involve a bridegroom forced to pay for gambling debts with his life and an artist who steals away his brother's fiancee while under the influence of an evil stone hand—I think. Certain Expressionistic scenes in the first segment have atmosphere, but the second's a riot, with the usual spliced-in American footage featuring Carradine and Victor and a totally pointless "surprise" ending. This is best viewed while not completely conscious.

CURSE OF THE SWAMP CREATURE
★ Sinister Cinema, 1966, NR, 78 min. Dir: Larry Buchanan. Cast: John Agar, Francine York, Shirley McLine, Jeff Alexander, Cal Dugan, Bill McGhee.

We don't need this junky backwoods remake of *Voodoo Woman* with Alexander as a rude mad scientist who mistreats his sexy wife (York) and turns jungle dwellers into big, bald Tor Johnson lookalikes with plastic fangs and Ping Pong–ball eyes. This is a mind-numbing experience with Agar as a sports shirt-clad, chain-smoking hero; a South American jungle that looks like someone's backyard; and a swimming poolful of alligator stock footage.

CURSE OF THE WEREWOLF, THE
★★★☆ MCA/Universal Home Video, 1961, NR, 90 min. Dir: Terence Fisher. Cast: Clifford Evans,

Oliver Reed wolfs-out in The Curse of the Werewolf *(1961).*

Oliver Reed, Yvonne Romain, Catherine Fellar, Anthony Dawson, Richard Wordsworth, Hira Talfrey, Michael Ripper.

OLIVER REED
(1938–)

This brooding Brit bully boy made his debut as a Hammer leading man before going on to international success as a mainstream actor. He still makes the occasional horror appearance and brings to all his roles his peculiarly effective mix of whispery menace and beefy presence.

The Two Faces of Dr. Jekyll ('60), *The Curse of the Werewolf* ('61), *These Are the Damned* ('61), *Night Creatures* ('62), *Paranoic* ('63), *The Shuttered Room* ('67), *The Devils* ('71), *Ten Little Indians* ('75), *Burnt Offerings* ('76), *The Brood* ('79), *Dr. Heckyl and Mr. Hype* ('80), *Venom* ('82), *Spasms* ('83), *The House of Usher* ('89), *The Pit and the Pendulum* ('91), *Severed Ties* ('92).

One of Hammer Films' best movies chronicles the short, tragic life of werewolf Leon (Reed), the son of a mute serving girl raped by an animalistic beggar, who was born on Christmas day and grows into a monster who menaces a small Spanish village. A loose adaptation of Guy Endore's *The Werewolf of Paris* in a different locale, this is deliberately paced and places an accent on character and incident, with the handsome, brooding Reed excellent in his first starring role and excellent Roy Ashton make-up not revealed until the last 10 minutes.

CURTAINS
★★☆ Vestron Video, 1983, R, 88 min. Dir: Jonathan Stryker [Richard Ciupka]. Cast: Samantha Eggar, John Vernon, Linda Thorson, Lynne Griffin, Anne Ditchburn, Lesleh Donaldson.

Actresses up for the lead in director Vernon's new film, *Audra,* are literally dying for the part as a psycho in an old-hag mask begins eliminating them one by one. Hampered by production difficulties and a confusing storyline, this still manages to rise above the average, thanks to a talented cast and some eerie, oddball touches. Eggar is excellent as an aging latter-day Joan Crawford and chief suspect in the killings. Good score by Paul Zaza.

CUTTING CLASS
★★ Republic Home Video, 1989, R, 87 min. Dir: Rospo Pallenberg. Cast: Jill Schoelen, Donovan Leitch, Brad Pitt, Roddy McDowall, Martin Mull, Brenda Lynn Klemm.

Routine high school body count pic. When students and teachers start getting offed, all evidence points to former mental patient Brian (hunky Leitch in a crappy haircut), though heroine Paula (Schoelen) has her doubts—what with the bizarre behavior of boyfriend Pitt and principal McDowall. About all that distinguishes this interchangeable flick from dozens of others is its eclectic cast and off-the-wall sense of humor. Otherwise, it's business as usual.

CYCLOPS, THE
★★ Thrillervideo, 1957, NR, 75 min. Dir: Bert I. Gordon. Cast: James Craig, Gloria Talbott, Lon Chaney, Jr., Tom Drake, Vincent Padula, Dean Parkin.

Talbott, searching for her missing pilot fiance, leads an expedition to a Mexican valley where radiation has transformed animals and birds into giants and Gloria's missing honey into a disfigured one-eyed monster. Though the one-eyed makeup design is kinda effective, the other effects are anything but special and the script's pretentious parallels to Homer's *The Odyssey* are about as effective as a Saturday morning cartoon version of *Paradise Lost*.

DADDY'S DEADLY DARLING
★ Paragon Video, 1972, R, 83 min. Dir: Marc Lawrence. Cast: Toni Lawrence, Marc Lawrence, Jesse Vint, Katherine Ross, Walter Barnes, Jim Antonio.

Dopey psycho-thriller cum *Willard* rip-off about a young murderess who teams up with a psychotic cafe owner for a series of killings, with the bodies fed to a pen of pigs the latter

keeps behind his establishment. Pretty pathetic, with cheap attempts at humor. Aka *Pigs* and *The Love Exorcist*.

DADDY'S GONE A-HUNTING
★★★ Warner Home Video, 1969, PG, 108 min. Dir: Mark Robson. Cast: Carol White, Scott Hylands, Paul Burke, Mala Powers, Barry Cahill, Andrea King.

Pretty good psycho thrills with White as a British bird in San Francisco who discovers that photographer boyfriend Hylands is dangerously psychotic. Pregnant with his child, Carol has an abortion and flees; years later our now happily married heroine finds her new baby menaced by a vengeful Scott. Scripted by Lorenzo Semple, Jr., and Larry Cohen, originally as a Hitchcock project, this has good work from White and Hylands and a suspenseful rooftop finale.

DAMIEN—OMEN II
★★★ Fox Video, 1978, R, 107 min. Dir: Don Taylor. Cast: William Holden, Lee Grant, Jonathan Scott-Taylor, Lew Ayres, Sylvia Sidney, Robert Foxworth, Elizabeth Shepherd, Lance Henricksen, Leo McKern, Ian Hendry.

In this good sequel the young anti-Christ (Scott-Taylor) is now 13 and living with relatives Holden and Grant while attending a Chicago military academy. Predictably, whenever anyone catches on to Damien's true identity, they meet a ghastly end, the best being Shepherd's encounter with a bloodthirsty raven and Ayres drowning under an icy lake. Good score by Jerry Goldsmith; look for Meshach Taylor of "Designing Women" as the young doctor cut in half by an elevator cable.

DANCE MACABRE
★☆ Columbia/TriStar Home Video, 1991, R, 96 min. Dir: Greydon Clark. Cast: Robert Englund, Michelle Zeitlen, Marianna Moen, Julene Renee, Nina Goldman, Irina Davidoff.

A bad rip-off of *Suspiria* from the director of *Satan's Cheerleaders*. Zeitlen is an irritating U.S. ballet student at a Russian dance academy being stalked by a mystery killer; is it head teach Englund? This is sleek but very silly, with a script borrowing elements from both an unfilmed sequel to Englund's *Phantom of the Opera* remake to be called *Terror of Manhattan* and co-executive producer Harry Alan Towers' unrealized slasher version of Poe's *The Raven*. Good for a couple of laughs (with Bob in a ridiculous dual role) but that's about it; did communism really fall just so the Russians could get involved in exploitation filmmaking? Aka *Dance With Death*.

Elizabeth Shepherd encounters an extra from The Birds *in* Damien–Omen II *(1978).*

DANCE OF DEATH

★ MPI Home Video, 1968, PG, 83 min.
Dirs: Juan Ibanez and Jack Hill. Cast: Boris Karloff, Julissa Santanon, Angel Espinoza, Andres Garcia, Manuel Alvarado, Beatrice Baz.

This is noteworthy as Karloff's final film but that's all. Boris is a crazy inventor whose heirs gather at his old mansion, where they're murdered by his mannequin-like robots. This laughable Mexican loser is a sad finale to a great career. Aka *Macabre Serenade* and *House of Evil*.

DANCE OF THE DAMNED

★★☆ Virgin Vision, 1989, R, 83 min.
Dir: Katt Shea Rubin. Cast: Starr Andreeff, Cyril O'Reilly, Deborah Ann Nassar, Maria Ford.

Self-destructive stripper Andreeff meets sexy, broody vampire O'Reilly and they begin a bizarre, death-tinged dialogue lasting from midnight until dawn. This talky contribution to the late '80s cycle of vampire flicks hasn't much excitement but is thoughtful and well acted enough to maintain interest. Remade as *To Sleep With a Vampire*.

DANCE OF THE VAMPIRES

See: *The Fearless Vampire Killers or Pardon Me, But Your Teeth Are in My Neck.*

DANCE WITH DEATH

See: *Dance Macabre.*

DANGEROUS CHARTER

See: *The Creeping Terror.*

DANSE MACABRE

See: *Castle of Blood.*

DARK, THE

★★ Media Home Entertainment, 1979, R, 92 min.
Dir: John "Bud" Cardos. Cast: William Devane, Cathy Lee Crosby, Richard Jaeckel, Keenan Wynn, Vivian Blaine, Biff Elliot, Jacqueline Hyde, Casey Kasem, Philip Michael Thomas, John Bloom.

Originally to be directed by Tobe Hooper, this started life as a *Night Stalker*–style chiller about a TV reporter (Crosby) investigating a series of decapitations committed by a walking corpse; post-production tampering altered it into a confusing, poorly edited alien invasion tale about a murderous creature from space with death-ray eyes. There's a great cast, though, and enough residual tension to make it watchable if you're in an especially expansive mood.

DARK AGE

★★★ Charter Entertainment, 1987, R, 90 min. Dir: Arch Nicholson. Cast: John Jarratt, Nikki Coghill, Max Phipps, Burnam Burnam, David Gulpilil, Ray Meagher.

Surprisingly well directed and suspenseful, this Aussie *Jaws* copy concerns a 25-foot man-eating crocodile rampaging through the outback and hunted by stalwart Jarratt and a pair of aborigines whose tribe worships the croc as a god. No Hollywood film would ever show a cute little baby being swallowed whole by the monster, and it's that sort of nastiness that makes the difference in this gritty, well-done creature feature—though a last minute attempt at making the crocodile into some sort of tragic figure proves, as if there were ever any doubt, that it's hard to work up much empathy for a reptile.

DARK EYES OF LONDON, THE

See: *The Human Monster.*

DARK FORCES

★★☆ Media Home Entertainment, 1980, PG, 96 min. Dir: Simon Wincer. Cast: Robert Powell, David Hemmings, Broderick Crawford, Carmen Duncan, Mark Spain, Alyson Best.

This Rasputin in modern dress concerns an enigmatic magician–faith healer (Powell) who worms his way into the household of an important politician by curing his son's leukemia. Starts out strong but soon succumbs to a plethora of the usual post-Halloween clichés. Aka *Harlequin* and *The Minister's Magician.*

DARK HALF, THE

★★★ Orion Home Video, 1992, R, 121 min. Dir: George A. Romero. Cast: Timothy Hutton, Amy Madigan, Michael Rooker, Julie Harris, Robert Joy, Rutanya Alda, Royal Dano, Chelsea Field.

One of the best recent Stephen King movies, this has Hutton as a respected author who actually makes most of his money through a series of violent thrillers he publishes under a pen name. When Hutton decides to give up the thrillers and "kill" his alter ego, this violent pseudonym erupts into life to begin a series of gory murders—or does he? Excellent acting, solid direction and scripting by Romero, and exceptional special effects make the difference in this finely crafted, if much delayed, shocker.

DARKMAN

★★★ MCA/Universal Home Video, 1990, R, 96 min. Dir: Sam Raimi. Cast: Liam Neeson, Frances McDormand, Larry Drake, Colin Friels, Nelson Mashita, Jenny Agutter.

A cross between *Batman* and *The Phantom of the Opera* with a touch of James Bond, this exhilaratingly directed horror-fantasy-adventure features Neeson as a scientist whose face has been horribly disfigured and who seeks revenge upon the gangster (Drake) responsible. In addition, he tries to rekindle his romance with a girlfriend (McDormand) who believes he is dead by donning a life-like mask of artificial skin he can mold into any likeness. Lots of fun, with fine makeup by Tony Gardner and a nice blending of action, laughs, and chills. Funny cameo by Bruce Campbell at the very end.

DARK NIGHT OF THE SCARECROW

★★★ Key Video, 1981, NR, 91 min. Dir: Frank DeFelitta. Cast: Charles Durning, Robert F. Lyons, Claude Earl Jones, Lane Smith, Tonya Crowe, Larry Drake, Jocelyn Brando, Jacqueline Scott.

Four redneck vigilantes kill a retarded man (Drake) hiding in a scarecrow costume when they mistakenly believe he has murdered a young neighbor girl. Afterward a mysterious scarecrow figure begins stalking and killing the men one by one in grisly ways. This TV chiller has a nice eerie mood and effective backwoods atmosphere, not to mention an above-average cast and murders that are surprisingly gruesome for network TV. Recommended.

DARK OF THE NIGHT

★★★ Lightning Video, 1984, R, 88 min. Dir: Gaylene Preston. Cast: Heather Bolton, David Letch, Margaret Umbers, Suzanne Lee, Gary Stalker, Danny Mulheron.

Similar in theme to the old Donna Mills tele-chiller *One Deadly Owner*, this New Zealand–made thriller is like a low-key feminist remake of *Christine*. Bolton buys a suspiciously cheap used Jaguar for a cross-country trip, only to find that it's haunted by the spirit of its brutally murdered previous owner who was slain by a psychopathic hitchhiker. Guess who our girl gives a lift? Not as contrived as it sounds, with squarish Bolton a very un-Hollywood-like leading lady and much suspense. Aka *Mr. Wrong.*

DARK PLACES

★★ Embassy Home Entertainment, 1973, PG, 85 min. Dir: Don Sharp. Cast: Christopher Lee, Joan

Collins, Herbert Lom, Robert Hardy, Jane Birkin, Jean Marsh.

Lackluster Brit thriller with Hardy as a former asylum inmate who inherits an old mansion and after moving in is possessed by the ghost of the previous owner—or is he just going mad again? Hardy hams it up while top-billed Lee, Collins, and Lom are given little to do. Lots of flashbacks.

DARK SECRET OF HARVEST HOME, THE

★★ MCA/Universal Home Video, 1978, NR, 119 min. Dir: Leo Penn. Cast: Bette Davis, David Ackroyd, Joanna Miles, Rosanna Arquette, Michael O'Keefe, René Auberjonois, Norman Lloyd, voice of Donald Pleasence.

Heavily edited movie version of the elephantine TV adaptation of Tom Tryon's *Harvest Home,* about a New England community run by an ancient matriarchy of black magic and worship of the gods of nature, where each year a male sacrifice is held to ensure a good corn crop. Corn is the dominating element of this malarkey, with ideas pinched from *The Wicker Man* and *The Stepford Wives* and Davis in a set of false teeth that make her look like a cross between Baby Jane Hudson and Alvin the Chipmunk.

DARK SHADOWS

★★★☆ MPI Home Video, 1966–71, NR, 105 min. per tape. Dirs: Dan Curtis, Henry Kaplan, Lela Swift, John Sedwick, Sean Dhu Sullivan. Cast: Jonathan Frid, Joan Bennett, David Selby, Grayson Hall, Alexandra Moltke, Kathryn Leigh Scott, Lara Parker, John Karlen, Nancy Barrett, Louis Edmonds, David Henesy, Joel Crothers, Thayer David, Jerry Lacy, Roger Davis, Kate Jackson.

The popular gothic soap about vampire Barnabas Collins (Frid) and his and the cursed Collins family's continuing involvement with various ghosts, witches, warlocks, werewolves, zombies, phoenixes, you name it. Just as enjoyable for its numerous technical gaffes (it was shot live-on-tape with all its bloopers intact) as for its dimestore atmospherics, this was a big enough hit to inspire a couple of theatrical spin-offs (*House of Dark Shadows* and *Night of Dark Shadows*) and a short-lived prime-time revival in 1991.

DARK SHADOWS

★★★ MPI Home Video, 1991, NR, 50 min. per tape. Dirs: Dan Curtis, Armand Mastroianni, Paul Lynch, Rob Bowman, Mark Sobel. Cast: Ben Cross, Jean Simmons, Barbara Steele, Roy Thinnes, Joanna Going, Barbara Blackburn, Lysette Anthony, Ely Pouget, Michael T. Weiss, Jim Fyfe.

This lavish remake of the classic series suffered from an overabundance of rehashed set-ups and situations but was distinguished by lush production trappings and on-target casting. Cross is a darker, more brooding Barnabas, and Anthony adds a sex-kittenish touch to wicked witch Angelique, so if you can overlook the familiar plots, this should be fun for fans—though it was abruptly canceled at a most awkward moment in its storyline, giving it a sadly unfinished feel.

DARK SIDE OF THE MOON, THE

★★☆ Vidmark Entertainment, 1989, R, 91 min. Dir: D. J. Webster. Cast: Will Bledsoe, Wendy MacDonald, Joe Turkel, Robert Sampson, Alan Blumenfeld, John Diehl.

A flawed but interesting mix of *Alien* and *Prince of Darkness* about a futuristic space mission that discovers a 1990s space shuttle circling the moon and containing a satanically possessed corpse that begins taking over the crew members. There are some fair FX and a couple of clever twists, but a slow pace makes it seem longer than it is. Aka *Something Is Out There.*

DARK TOWER

★☆ Video Treasures, 1987, R, 91 min. Dir: Ken Barnett [Freddie Francis]. Cast: Michael Moriarty, Jenny Agutter, Carol Lynley, Kevin McCarthy, Theodore Bikel, Ann Lockhart.

Silly haunted high-rise saga about a series of bizarre happenings plaguing a recently completed Barcelona office tower. Insurance investigator Moriarty, aided by psychic researcher Bikel and medium McCarthy, discovers that there is a malevolent spirit at work. With its hokey FX and tedious wasting of a talented cast, no wonder veteran Brit director Francis is hiding behind a pseudonym.

DAUGHTER OF DR. JEKYLL, THE

★★ Key Video, 1957, NR, 70 min. Dir: Edgar G. Ulmer. Cast: Gloria Talbott, John Agar, Arthur Shields, John Dierkes, Martha Wentworth, Mollie McCard.

Sometimes admired, though by whom I don't know, this zero-budgeted period chiller has Glo as an English heiress (with an aggressively American accent) who discovers that she's the offspring of you-know-who and chief suspect in a series of murders the locals blame on a werewolf. Has a certain amount of atmosphere (but check out the breakfast scene where you can see '50s cars speeding along the street right outside the window), with Ulmer making the best of limited materials.

Nevertheless, even at only 70 minutes this is *very* slow going.

DAUGHTER OF HORROR

★★ Sinister Cinema, 1954, NR, 55 min.
Dir: John Parker. Cast: Adrienne Barnett, Bruno VeSota, Ben Roseman, Richard Barron, Ed Hinkle, voice of Ed McMahon.

Barnett is a young girl picked up by a rich lecher she murders and mutilates—she cuts off his hand—when he makes a pass. Later guilt over her crime drives her mad. This bizarre no-budgeter is interestingly directed; it has no dialogue but is ponderously narrated by a pre–Johnny Carson McMahon. Aka *Dementia,* this is probably best known as the midnight horror show playing when the monster attacks the movie theatre in the original version of *The Blob.*

DAUGHTER OF THE WEREWOLF

See: *Cry of the Werewolf.*

DAUGHTERS OF DARKNESS

★★★ Cinema Group, 1971, R, 87 min.
Dir: Harry Kumel. Cast: Delphine Seyrig, Danielle Ouimet, John Karlen, Andrea Rau.

A beautifully atmospheric but slow version of the Elisabeth Bathory legend with Seyrig as the silky vampire who seduces a kinky honeymoon couple (former Miss Canada Ouimet and "Dark Shadows" star Karlen) who are staying at an almost deserted Ostend hotel. Gorgeous color photography and some jarring violence in this Belgian vampire flick. Aka *La Rouge aux Lévres: The Red Lips, The Promise of Red Lips,* and *Children of the Night.*

DAUGHTERS OF SATAN

★☆ Wood Knapp Video, 1972, PG, 92 min.
Dir: Hollingsworth Morse. Cast: Tom Selleck, Barra Grant, Tani Phelps Gutherie, Paraluman, Vic Salayan, Vic Diaz.

Boredom reigns supreme in this Filipino gabfest with Selleck in his first starring role as an art collector whose latest acquisition is a painting of three witches who look an awful lot like his wife and her two new friends. Guess what happens? For those who like to see popular actors in pre-stardom roles making jerks of themselves, also check out Bruce Dern in *The Incredible 2-Headed Transplant,* Bo Derek in *Orca,* Harrison Ford in *The Possessed,* and Kevin Costner in *Shadows Run Black.*

DAWN OF THE DEAD

★★★☆ HBO Video, 1979, UR, 127 min.
Dir: George A. Romero. Cast: Gaylen Ross, Ken Foree, David Emge, Scott H. Reininger, Tom Savini, George A. Romero.

Another zombie bites the big one in Dawn of the Dead *(1979).*

This terrific sequel to *Night of the Living Dead,* though shot a decade later, picks up shortly after its conclusion with the zombies taking over the world. Four people escape Philadelphia in a helicopter and hole up in a vast western Pennsylvania shopping mall. After it's cleared of the living dead, the mall becomes the perfect hideaway; that is, until a heavily armed motorcycle gang shows up, leading to a battle royal for rulership of this commercial kingdom. Breathtaking action matched with an intelligent script and performances make this as thought-provoking as it is stomach-turning—Tom Savini's trend-setting gore FX still have considerable impact—and one of the best horror films of the '70s, as well as one of Romero's finest hours. Aka *Zombie* and *Zombies;* sequel: *Day of the Dead.*

DAWN OF THE MUMMY
★★☆ HBO Video, 1981, UR, 88 min.
Dir: Frank Agrama. Cast: Brenda King, Barry Sattels, George Peck, Ellene Faison, John Salvo, Joan Levy.

A group of fashion models and photographers on an Egyptian location shoot foolishly disturb the rest of an evil pharaoh called Seferaman, who rises up with his cannibalistic minions to seek a violent revenge. Although this puppy must set some sort of record for stupid character behavior and has plot holes big enough to pilot Cleopatra's barge through, slick photography and some boffo gore FX make it fun to watch. Agrama also directed the seldom seen *Queen Kong.*

DAY AFTER HALLOWEEN, THE
★★ Catalina Video, 1979, R, 92 min.
Dir: Simon Wincer. Cast: Chantal Contouri, Sigrid Thornton, Robert Bruning, Hugh Keays-Byrne.

One of the great bogus titles of all time; people were actually tricked into believing that this dull Australian thriller—original title: *Snapshot*—was actually a sequel to the John Carpenter classic. Barnum was right. Anyway, this features the lovely Contouri of *Thirst* and has something to do with a model menaced by a scissors-wielding psycho. Originally billed with the likewise non-Carpenter *Beyond the Fog.*

DAY OF THE ANIMALS
★★☆ Media Home Entertainment, 1977, PG, 98 min. Dir: William Girdler. Cast: Christopher George, Lynda Day George, Leslie Nielsen, Ruth Roman, Richard Jaeckel, Michael Ansara, Paul Mantee, Jon Cedar, Susan Backlinie, Andrew Stevens.

A depleted ozone layer causes all manner of wildlife to go mad and attack backpackers in the High Sierra in this not-bad rip of *Jaws* and *The Birds* from the director of *Grizzly.* The great exploitation cast includes Nielsen in one of his colorful pre—*Naked Gun* villain roles. Aka *Something Is Out There.*

DAY OF THE DEAD
★★★ Media Home Entertainment, 1985, UR, 100 min. Dir: George A. Romero. Cast: Lori Cardille, Terry Alexander, Joe Pilano, Richard Liberty, Howard Sherman, Jarlah Conroy, John Amplas, Gary Klar.

Though it's doubtful that this is Romero's last word on the living dead, this supposed final entry in the series, although not up to either *Night of the Living Dead* or *Dawn of the Dead,* is a first-rate shocker full of interesting concepts and strong performances. The ghouls are slowly becoming the dominant species: they outnumber humans 40,000 to one. A small band of scientists hidden in an abandoned Florida missile silo are trying to find a way to control the flesh-hungry monsters, but hotheaded military types are more interested in blowing them away. Will mankind survive? Talky, but with some effective innovations in the standard formula, the best being the introduction of Bub (Sherman), the "sympathetic" zombie; this is much better than many have

---

TOM SAVINI
(1948–)

Savini is a Pittsburgh-based makeup man specializing in graphically gory FX. Thanks to his ultra-realistic work in films like *Dawn of the Dead* and *Friday the 13th,* Tom rode the crest of the splatter wave of the late '70s and early '80s. He's since turned his talents to less gruesome FX, eventually trying his hand at direction with the 1990 remake of *Night of the Living Dead.*

Deathdream ('73), *Deranged* ('74), *Martin* (also actor, '77), *Dawn of the Dead* (also actor, '79), *Effects* (actor, '80), *Friday the 13th* ('80), *Maniac* (also actor, '81), *The Burning* ('81), *Eyes of a Stranger* ('81), *The Prowler* ('81), *Alone in the Dark* ('82), *Midnight* ('82), *Creepshow* (also actor, '82), *Till Death Do Us Scare* ('83), *Friday the 13th—The Final Chapter* ('84), *Day of the Dead* ('85), *Creepshow 2* (also actor, 87), *Monkey Shines: An Experiment in Fear* ('88), *Two Evil Eyes* (also actor, '90), *Bloodsucking Pharaohs in Pittsburgh* ('90), *Night of the Living Dead* (director, '90), *Trauma* ('93), *Necronomicon* ('94).

claimed, with literally gut-wrenching Tom Savini FX and a nightmare-framing device borrowed from *Dressed to Kill.*

DAY OF THE TRIFFIDS, THE

★★☆ Goodtimes Home Video, 1963, 93 min. Dirs: Steve Sekley, Freddie Francis. Cast: Howard Keel, Nicole Maurey, Kieron Moore, Janette Scott, Mervyn Johns, Janina Faye.

Not-bad adaptation of the John Wyndham novel about a worldwide outbreak of blindness following a spectacular meteor shower; the meteors also bringing to earth a plague of mobile man-killing plants called triffids. Though shot on a restricted budget, the film tries for an expansive, big-budget feel (Ron Goodwin's grandiose Bernard Herrmann-esque score helps a lot) with variable effects work and a strong cast. An uncredited Francis directed the scenes of Moore and Scott at the lighthouse.

DAY OF THE WOMAN

See: *I Spit On Your Grave.*

DAY THE SCREAMING STOPPED, THE

See: *The Comeback.*

DEAD AGAIN

★★☆ Paramount Home Video, 1991, R, 107 min. Dir: Kenneth Branagh. Cast: Kenneth Branagh, Emma Thompson, Andy Garcia, Robin Williams, Derek Jacobi, Hanna Schygulla, Wayne Knight, Campbell Scott.

Private eye Branagh tries to help amnesia victim Thompson, only to discover that they are the reincarnations of a famous movie director and his murdered actress wife. This slick mainstream thriller is entertaining and involving, if a trifle contrived, with an able cast—Williams is unbilled as a parapsychologist working as a supermarket butcher!—and homages to Hitchcock, DePalma, and Argento.

DEAD ALIVE

★★★☆ Vidmark Entertainment, 1992, UR, 97 min. Dir: Peter Jackson. Cast: Timothy Balme, Diana Peñalver, Elizabeth Moody, Ian Watkin, Stuart Devenie, Brenda Kendall.

Ya gotta love this *very* moist New Zealand zombie flick with Balme as a nerdy nice guy whose overly possessive mum (Moody) is bitten by a Sumatran rat monkey and transformed into a very active zombie whose victims begin filling up the cellar. This *could* put a damper on our hero's budding relationship with the pretty Paquita (Peñalver) but *does* aid in evil Uncle Watkin's plan to take over the family fortune. Very much in the style of Jack-

son's debut feature *Bad Taste,* this is far superior, with a hilarious script, athletic direction, a likable cast, and the most on-screen splatter since the original *Evil Dead.* Aka *Braindead;* try to avoid the heavily edited 85-minute R version.

DEAD & BURIED

★★★ Vestron Video, 1981, R, 93 min. Dir: Gary Sherman. Cast: James Farentino, Melody Anderson, Jack Albertson, Lisa Blount, Dennis Redfield, Nancy Locke Hauser, Christopher Allport, Robert Englund, Michael Pataki, Barry Corbin.

A series of gruesome murders committed in the sleepy little New England town of Potter's Bluff baffle sheriff Farentino, even more so when the mutilated victims return to life. Offbeat zombie tale (scripted by Dan O'Bannon) with a flavorful atmosphere, strong cast (Albertson is great in his final role as a jovial mortician), and a mournful Joe Renzetti score. Ignored during its initial release, this comes highly recommended.

DEAD CALM

★★☆ Warner Home Video, 1989, R, 95 min. Dir: Phillip Noyce. Cast: Sam Neill, Nicole Kidman, Billy Zane, Rod Mullinar.

Somewhat overrated suspense-horror about an Australian couple who take a cruise to recover from the death of their toddler son and encounter the sole survivor of a disaster at sea who turns out to be a dangerous psychotic. Builds a little too slowly and oversells its dubious gimmick of psycho as handsome boy-next-door rather than hockey-masked hulk or twitchy cross-dressing mama's boy, but the photography is attractive, the editing sharp, and Kidman impresses in a star-making role as the endangered wife. Like that other "High Class" shocker *Fatal Attraction,* this, too, falls back on that most unfortunate of modern horror film clichés: the shock-twist ending.

DEAD DON'T DIE, THE

★★☆ WorldVision Home Video, 1975, NR, 73 min. Dir: Curtis Harrington. Cast: George Hamilton, Ray Milland, Linda Cristal, Joan Blondell, Ralph Meeker, Reggie Nalder, Milton Parsons, Yvette Vickers.

In Depression-era Chicago, seaman Hamilton investigates the murder his brother was wrongly executed for and discovers a plot by zombie-master Milland to take over the city with the living dead. Robert Bloch scripted this pulpy tribute to old-time B movies. The supporting cast is impeccable and Harrington directs with his usual nostalgic assurance, but this isn't quite as successful as the same team's other tele-chiller *The Cat Creature*. Best scene: zombie girl Cristal melting like a wax doll.

DEAD EYES OF LONDON, THE

★★☆ Sinister Cinema, 1961, NR, 100 min. Dir: Albert Vohrer. Cast: Karin Baal, Joachim Fuchsberger, Dieter Borsche, Eddi Arent, Klaus Kinski, Adi Berber.

Inspector Fuchsberger investigates a series of killings committed by a blind monster (Tor Johnson lookalike Berber) as part of an insurance scam. Solid remake of Lugosi's *The Human Monster* with an appealing cast and inventive direction making this one of the better German Edgar Wallace adaptations.

DEAD HEAT

★☆ Starmaker Home Video, 1988, R, 84 min. Dir: Mark Goldblatt. Cast: Treat Williams, Joe Piscopo, Lindsay Frost, Darren McGavin, Vincent Price, Clare Kirkconnell, Keye Luke, Robert Picardo.

Mostly awful "comic" mixture of *Dead & Buried* and *Lethal Weapon* about a couple of L.A. detectives (Williams and Piscopo) who stumble upon a rejuvenation plot among the Beverly Hills elite involving resurrected corpses; the cops themselves soon join the ranks of the living dead. McGavin and Price (in a small role) are good and Steve Johnson contributes some imaginative makeup FX, but the plot is absurd and Piscopo's constant mugging is a real turn-off.

DEAD KIDS

See: *Strange Behavior*.

DEADLINE

★★★ Paragon Video, 1980, R, 89 min. Dir: Mario Azzopardi. Cast: Stephen Young, Sharon Masters, Jeannie Elias, Cindy Hinds, Phillip Leonard, Todd Woodcroft.

Genuinely disturbing oddity about a Stephen King-like horror author (Young) whose fictional horror spills over into real life when his deranged kids begin acting out scenes from his books and movies. Difficult but worth the effort, this features startling enactments of Young's stories—everything from moppets who burn granny alive to cannibal nuns to a guy dismembered by a really nasty-looking piece of farm machinery—though the unpleasant characters may put you off at first.

DEADLY BLESSING

★★★ Embassy Home Video, 1981, R, 102 min. Dir: Wes Craven. Cast: Maren Jensen, Ernest Borgnine, Lois Nettleton, Sharon Stone, Susan Buckner, Lisa Hartman, Jeff East, Doug Barr, Colleen Riley, Michael Berryman.

One of Craven's most underrated films, this concerns sexy farm widow Jensen, who is threatened by both her strictly religious Hittite in-laws (led by a stern Borgnine) *and* a mysterious psycho killer who (in a ridiculously overplotted but busy finale) turns out to be a love-crazed hermaphrodite neighbor (Hartman) guarded by her/his overprotective mom (the always winning Nettleton doing a Betsy Palmer shtick). This won't ever win any awards for logic but *does* have some truly haunting visual touches, a lush *Omen-esque* score by James Horner, bodacious babes aplenty, and a ludicrous shock ending you have to see to appreciate.

DEADLY DREAMS

★★ Virgin Vision, 1987, R, 79 min. Dir: Kristine Peterson. Cast: Mitchell Anderson, Juliette Cummins, Xander Berkley, Beach Dickerson.

In this routinely plotted psychological thriller, Anderson is haunted by the long-ago murder of his parents and is slowly being driven out of his mind by girlfriend Cummins and brother Berkley. Tries for some surreal touches, but a bland cast and obvious twists make it less than compelling viewing.

DEADLY EYES

★★ Warner Home Video, 1982, R, 87 min. Dir: Robert Clouse. Cast: Sam Groom, Sara Botsford, Scatman Crothers, Lisa Langlois, Cec Linder, Lesleh Donaldson.

Silly but amiable giant rat saga derived from James Herbert's *The Rats* about mutant rodents spawned by toxic waste that are terrorizing the Toronto subway system. The rats are more cute than scary (played by dachshunds in rat suits, that's *exactly* what they look like—listen closely and you can even hear some of them barking!), but there are surprisingly glossy production values and a good cast. Aka *The Rats* and *Night Eyes.*

DEADLY FRIEND

★★ Warner Home Video, 1986, R, 90 min. Dir: Wes Craven. Cast: Matthew Laborteaux, Kristy Swanson, Anne Twomey, Michael Sharrett, Anne Ramsey, Richard Marcus.

Laborteaux is a teen computer genius and first-year med student (just your average Joe) who revives brain-dead girlfriend Swanson with a computer chip, unknowingly creating a murderous female Frankenstein. Not one of Craven's better efforts, this adaptation of the Diana Henstell novel *Friend* has a sincere cast but often looks like a mutant episode of TV's "Charles in Charge," with absurdity piled upon absurdity and one of the dumbest "shock" endings ever. Only Ramsey (whose head is splattered by a basketball in the movie's funniest, grossest scene) makes this worth a look.

DEADLY GAMES

★★ Monterey Home Video, 1980, R, 94 min. Dir: Scott Mansfield. Cast: Sam Groom, Steve Railsback, Jo Ann Harris, June Lockhart, Dick Butkis, Colleen Camp.

A black-gloved and masked psycho is preying on the women of a small midwestern town. The culprit couldn't be weird Vietnam vet and old movie bluff Railsback, could it? Nah! Assembly-line slasher uplifted slightly by some insightful characterizations and good direction. A dumb, inconclusive ending does it the most harm. Not to be confused with the Sally Kirkland starrer *Fatal Games.* Aka *The Eliminator* and *Who Fell Asleep?*

DEADLY MANTIS, THE

★★☆ MCA/Universal Home Video, 1957, NR, 78 min. Dir: Nathan Juran. Cast: Craig Stevens, William Hopper, Alix Talton, Donald Randolph, Florenz Ames, Pat Conway.

Familiar-looking '50s monster flick with a giant prehistoric preying mantis thawed from arctic ice and heading for New York and Washington, D.C. Borrows from *The Beast From 20,000 Fathoms, The Thing, Tarantula,* and *Them!,* and the effects are sometimes skimpy but the cast and a suspenseful first third make this enjoyable.

DEADLY SANCTUARY

★★ Monterey Home Video, 1968, R, 92 min. Dir: Jess [Jesus] Franco. Cast: Jack Palance, Klaus Kinski, Romina Power, Maria Rohm, Mercedes McCambridge, Akim Tamiroff, Sylva Koscina, Rosalba Neri.

Hilarious adaptation of a story by the Marquis de Sade (played here by Kinski) about wayward sisters Power and Rohm, whose "coming of age" involves them with everyone from sado-masochistic minister Palance to lesbian psycho McCambridge. Rampant ham galore in another important cinematic statement from the prolific (to put it mildly) Mr. Franco. Aka *Justine, or The Misfortunes of Virtue.*

DEADLY SPAWN, THE

See: *Return of the Aliens: The Deadly Spawn.*

DEADLY TREASURE OF THE PIRANHA

See: *Killer Fish.*

DEAD MEN WALK

★★ Sinister Cinema, 1943, NR, 67 min. Dir: Sam Newfield. Cast: George Zucco, Mary Carlisle, Nedrick Young, Dwight Frye, Fern Emmett, Robert Strange.

It's Zucco times two in this cheesy PRC vampire epic. George plays both a kindly country doctor and his evil undead twin who has unhealthy designs on niece Carlisle. Typical grade-C filler made notable by Frye's final performance as Zucco the vampire's slovenly hunchbacked manservant and the usual Zucco élan.

DEAD OF NIGHT

★★★★ Republic Home Video, 1945, NR, 103 min. Dirs: Alberto Cavalcanti, Charles Crichton, Basil Dearden, Robert Hamer. Cast: Michael Redgrave, Mervyn Johns, Googie Withers, Sally Ann Howes, Basil Radford, Naunton Wayne, Roland Culver, Judy Kelly, Frederick Valk, Antony Baird, Ralph Michael, Miles Malleson.

Classic horror anthology with Johns visiting a country house that he claims to have dreamt of, including its occupants, many times before. This sets off a string of eerie tales involving a phantom hearse; the ghost of a murdered child; a haunted mirror; a ghost on a golf course; and a ventriloquist convinced that his dummy is actually alive. Undoubtedly the best horror omnibus ever, with each story (apart from the comic golfing segment) building in intensity until the shattering final episode (with brilliant acting from Redgrave as the ventriloquist); everything is topped off by a fantastic twist ending that in subsequent years became a cliché. Originally released in the U.S. in a cut version but restored for video, this British classic comes highly recommended.

DEAD OF NIGHT

★★☆ Thrillervideo, 1977, NR, 74 min. Dir: Dan Curtis. Cast: Joan Hackett, Patrick Macnee, Anjanette Comer, Horst Buchholz, Lee H. Montgomery, Ed Begley, Jr., Christina Hart, Elisha Cook.

A follow-up of sorts to Curtis' popular *Trilogy of Terror* with Richard Matheson scripting a trio of tales based on stories by himself and Jack Finney. A restored antique car takes its driver into the past; a doctor's beautiful wife falls prey to a vampire; and a woman uses black magic to summon her drowned son back from the dead—this last segment clearly inspired by the "Prey" segment from *Trilogy.* An adequate anthology with a fine cast in good form. The vampire tale is best.

DEAD OF WINTER
★★★ Fox Video, 1987, R, 100 min.
Dir: Arthur Penn. Cast: Mary Steenburgen, Roddy
McDowall, Jan Rubes, William Russ, Mark Malone.

Steenburgen is terrific as a sweet New York
actress hired to replace the departing lead in a
horror film but actually set up to impersonate
a murder victim who had been blackmailing
her wealthy sister. Inspired by the '40s B melodrama *My Name is Julia Ross* and featuring
visual nods to *Vertigo* and *Suspicion,* this old-
fashioned chiller benefits from solid performing from Steenburgen in a well-calculated
triple role and McDowall as a mincing assistant villain in the grand tradition of Peter
Lorre and Dwight Frye.

DEAD ON: RELENTLESS II
★★ SVS/Triumph Home Video, 1992, R, 93 min.
Dir: Mark Sevi. Cast: Ray Sharkey, Leo Rossi, Meg
Foster, Miles O'Keeffe, Marc Poppel, Dale Dye.

Formula follow-up finds cop Rossi now
teamed with FBI agent Sharkey (coming on
like an effete, more articulate Bruce Willis)
and on the trail of Soviet serial killer O'Keeffe,
who garrots and disembowels his victims. A
hard-to-swallow plot and the utter wasting of
the glorious Foster doom this sequel to mediocrity. Aka *Relentless II: Dead On.*

DEAD PEOPLE
See: *Messiah of Evil.*

DEAD PIT
★★★ Imperial Entertainment, 1989, R, 98 min.
Dir: Brett Leonard. Cast: Cheryl Lawson, Jeremy
Slate, Danny Gochnauer, Steffen Gregory Foster,
Geha Getz, Joan Bechtel.

Enthusiastic, inventive zombie tale about an
amnesiac beauty (Lawson) who is placed in a
private institution where an earthquake
unleashes the long-dormant zombie slaves of
mad Dr. Ramzi (Gochnauer). Well crafted on a
budget, with solid acting, good direction, and
a disarming sense of dark humor. Don't let the
gaudy, gimmicky video box with the flashing-
eyed zombie put you off.

DEAD RINGER
★★ Warner Home Video, 1964, NR, 115 min.
Dir: Paul Henreid. Cast: Bette Davis, Karl Malden,
Peter Lawford, Philip Carey, Jean Hagen, George
Macready, Estelle Winwood, Cyril Delevanti.

Bette Davis plays twin sisters in one of her
lesser post–*Baby Jane* shockers directed by her
old *Now, Voyager* co-star Henreid. The poor
sister murders and impersonates the rich one,
but this scheme becomes complicated when it
turns out that the wealthy Davis killed her
husband for his money. Overlong and often
laughably melodramatic, but fans of the great
star should enjoy it.

DEAD RINGERS
★★★ Media Home Entertainment, 1988, R, 115 min.
Dir: David Cronenberg. Cast: Jeremy Irons,
Genevieve Bujold, Heidi von Palliske, Barbara
Gordon, Shirley Douglas, Stephen Lack.

Identical twin doctors with a strong psychic
bond find their lives destroyed when one of
them falls in love. Disturbing psychological
thriller based on the novel *Twins* by Bari
Wood and Jack Geasland, with Irons unforgettably effective in the lead roles—it *really* does
seem like two actors in the parts! One of Cronenberg's creepiest films, but without the
usual gross effects he's famous for, this once
again proves him a genre director of real force
and power, maybe the most original since
Hitchcock.

DEAD RISE FROM THE GRAVE, THE
See: *Horror Rises From the Tomb.*

DEAD SPACE
★☆ RCA/Columbia Home Video, 1990, R, 72 min.
Dir: Fred Gallo. Cast: Marc Singer, Laura Tate,
Judith Chapman, Bryan Cranston.

By-the-numbers remake of *Forbidden World*
with a haggard-looking Singer as the space
jockey trapped with scientists at a research
station terrorized by a bug-like "metamorphic
mutant." Sharply photographed but the original clearly has the edge with its far grosser FX
(from that more splattery era of the early '80s)
and outrageous dialogue and situations (like
the unforgettable vomiting monster climax).

DEAD THAT WALK, THE
See: *The Zombies of Mora Tau.*

DEADTIME STORIES
★☆ Cinema Group, 1985, R, 82 min.
Dir: Jeffrey Delman. Cast: Scott Valentine, Nicole
Picard, Cathryn de Prume, Matt Mitler, Melissa Leo,
Kathy Fleig, Michael Mesmer, Brian De Persera.

Dumb trilogy of fairy tale–inspired comic horror stories. A bored babysitting uncle tells his
obnoxious little nephew three bedtime stories:
two witches attempt to resurrect their dead
sister; Little Red Riding Hood meets a drug-
addicted werewolf; and a telekinetic, homicidal Goldilocks encounters a murderous family
named Baer. Filmed as *Freaky Fairy Tales* and
unreleased for several years, this was finally
put out to take advantage of Valentine's

"Family Ties" success (he has a brief nude scene) and is fairly heavy-handed and unfunny, with only some good Ed French makeups worth a nod.

DEAD ZONE, THE

★★★☆ Paramount Home Video, 1983, R, 103 min. Dir: David Cronenberg. Cast: Christopher Walken, Brooke Adams, Martin Sheen, Tom Skerritt, Herbert Lom, Colleen Dewhurst, Anthony Zerbe, Nicholas Campbell.

Walken is unforgettably sad and affecting as Johnny Smith, a gentle New England school-teacher who awakens from a five-year coma with psychic abilities. When he foresees a glad-handing local politician (Sheen) someday becoming president and starting World War III, Johnny is driven by this knowledge to become a political assassin. Unlike other films in the Cronenberg canon, this Stephen King adaptation isn't frightening because of violence or gory special effects; it's frightening because of its tragic inevitability. We know Walken is doomed and are drawn along with him because he makes us *care* about his plight, giving this an emotional edge few other '80s horror films possess. The snowy Norman Rockwell landscapes and sadly elegant music are also quite effective at establishing the melancholy mood.

DEAN R. KOONTZ'S SERVANTS OF TWILIGHT

See: *Servants of Twilight.*

DEAN R. KOONTZ'S WHISPERS

See: *Whispers.*

DEAR, DEAD DELILAH

★★☆ Embassy Home Entertainment, 1972, R, 97 min. Dir: John Farris. Cast: Agnes Moorehead, Will Geer, Michael Ansara, Dennis Patrick, Patricia Carmichael, Robert Gentry, Anne Meacham, Elizabeth Eis.

A wealthy southern family who behave like rejects from a Tennessee Williams play search their dilapidated Nashville plantation for a buried $600,000 and wind up being hacked to death by an ax-wielding maniac. A sometimes funny pastiche of *Hush, Hush . . . Sweet Charlotte, Strait-jacket,* and *Dementia 13,* with hammy acting, indifferent writing and direction from novelist Farris (*The Fury*), and lots of blood.

DEATH AND THE GREEN SLIME

See: *The Green Slime.*

DEATH AT LOVE HOUSE

★★☆ Prism Entertainment, 1976, NR, 74 min.

Dir: E. W. Swackhamer. Cast: Robert Wagner, Kate Jackson, Sylvia Sidney, Bill Macy, Joan Blondell, Dorothy Lamour, John Carradine, Marianna Hill.

This is a nostalgia-laced TV film about a husband-and-wife writing team doing a book on a Jean Harlow-like '30s glamour queen. They believe that the actress' hostile ghost continues to haunt her Hollywood mansion. Fairly sumptuous-looking and with a couple of fairly inspired moments (like faded star Lamour doing a TV coffee commercial) but mostly just run-of-the-TV-mill stuff. The sight of a virile Wagner being fondled in bed by a disfigured old lady *must* be some sort of television first, though.

DEATH BECOMES HER

★★ MCA/Universal Home Video, 1992, PG-13, 103 min. Dir: Robert Zemeckis. Cast: Meryl Streep, Goldie Hawn, Bruce Willis, Isabella Rosellini, Ian Ogilvy, Michelle Johnson, Nancy Fish, Fabio.

Well-cast but sluggish horror comedy with Streep an aging movie queen who takes a magical potion to restore her youth and render her immortal. Trouble starts when Meryl's brow-beaten husband (Willis) murders her; she still lives but as a nearly indestructible zombie. Streep and Hawn (as a vengeful nemesis) are great and Willis is effectively cast against type; there are some excellent sight gags and creative makeup FX by Dick Smith (including a head-twisting *Exorcist* homage) that won an Oscar; but despite some funny moments this falls flat too much of the time to really work.

DEATHBED

See: *Terminal Choice.*

DEATH BITE

See: *Spasms.*

DEATH CORPS

See: *Shock Waves.*

DEATH CRUISE

★★ Video Treasures, 1974, NR, 72 min. Dir: Ralph Senesky. Cast: Michael Constantine, Kate Jackson, Edward Albert, Polly Bergen, Tom Bosley, Celeste Holm, Richard Long, Cesare Danova.

Three couples win a cruise from some mysterious benefactor and are stalked and murdered by an unknown maniac whose identity is investigated by ship's doctor Constantine. A poor man's *Ten Little Indians* set at sea, this TV movie has a good cast but really stretches credulity a bit thin—especially in the "surprise" climax.

DEATH CURSE OF TARTU
★★☆ Active Video, 1966, NR, 87 min.
Dir: William Grefe. Cast: Fred Pinero, Babbette Sherrill, Bill Marcos, Mayra Christine, Frank Weed, Doug Hobart.

Minor but imaginative shot-in-Florida flick about a group of explorers who transgress on an Indian burial ground in the Everglades and incite the wrath of Tartu, a mummified, shape-shifting medicine man. Poor acting, but bleak locations and effective makeup make it a passable time-killer.

DEATH DORM
See: *The Dorm That Dripped Blood.*

DEATHDREAM
★★★ MPI Home Video, 1972, PG, 89 min.
Dir: Bob Clark. Cast: John Marley, Lynn Carlin, Richard Backus, Anya Ormsby, Henderson Forsythe, Jane Daly.

This very effective low-budgeter is "The Monkey's Paw" updated to the Vietnam era. MIA son Backus comes home from the war a sullen zombie who sits sadly in his room as he begins to decay; murders an old girlfriend at a drive-in showing of *The Deathmaster;* and is finally driven to the local cemetery for burial by despondent mom Carlin. Static production values mar an otherwise solid little number with early makeup work by Tom Savini. Aka *Night Walk, Dead of Night,* and *The Night Andy Came Home.*

DEATH DREAMS
★★ New Line Home Video, 1991, NR, 94 min.
Dir: Martin Donovan. Cast: Christopher Reeve, Marg Helgenberger, Fionnula Flanagan, George Dickerson, Cec Verrell, Taylor Frye.

After her young daughter is drowned, Helgenberger is repeatedly assaulted by disturbing visions of the child's specter, leading to a grim discovery about seemingly perfect second husband Reeve. A cross between *Don't Look Now* and *Audrey Rose,* this made-for-cable flick is another one of those cautionary tales in which smug, pampered rich folk suffer mightily—much to our delight. Slick but oh so routine.

DEATH DRIVE
See: *Fer-De-Lance.*

DEATH HOUSE
See: *Silent Night, Bloody Night.*

DEATH IN THE FULL MOON
See: *Werewolf in a Girl's Dormitory.*

DEATHMASK
★★ Prism Entertainment, 1983, NR, 103 min.
Dir: Richard Friedman. Cast: Farley Granger, Lee Bryant, Ruth Warrick, John McCurry, Arch Johnson, Danny Aiello.

Coroner Granger, obsessed with the drowning of his daughter, investigates the similar death of a young boy, eventually contacting a psychic for help. The cast is first-rate and the storyline holds promise, but uneven direction and production dress often make this resemble a Jack Klugman-less episode of "Quincy."

DEATHMOON
★☆ Prism Entertainment, 1978, NR, 96 min.
Dir: Bruce Kessler. Cast: Robert Foxworth, Barbara Trentham, France Nuyen, Joe Penny, Dolph Sweet, Debralee Scott, Charles Haid, Albert Harris.

A dumb werewolf-in-Hawaii TV movie with Foxworth as a burned-out ad exec who suffers a hairy curse when he visits the islands for a little R-and-R. Everybody bounces around in as little clothing as possible, and the transformations and makeup are right out of a '40s second feature.

DEATH SHIP
★★ Embassy Home Entertainment, 1980, R, 91 min.
Dir: Alvin Rakoff. Cast: George Kennedy, Richard Crenna, Sally Anne Howes, Nick Manusco, Kate Reid, Victoria Burgoyne.

This weird-n-wacky combination of *The Shining* and *The Poseidon Adventure* features a rusted old Nazi torture vessel that goes around sinking luxury liners and then picking up the survivors to kill them and live off their life force. The above-average cast act with extreme distaste and there's a record number of rotting corpses on hand, but not even enough unintended laughs to make it camp. Really bizarre.

DEATH SPA
★★ MPI Home Video, 1987, UR, 89 min.
Dir: Michael Fischa. Cast: William Bumiller, Brenda Bakke, Merritt Butrick, Rosalind Cash, Ken Foree, Alexa Hamilton, Robert Upton, Shari Shattruck.

Shattruck is a sexy ghost who possesses gay brother Butrick and haunts hubby Bumiller's popular health spa where various aerobics airheads are killed off via hot steam, flying ceramic tiles, and death-dealing Nautilus machines. This gore flick has a spirited cast but is hopelessly stupid and illogical; far more guts than brains are on display. Also out in a slightly cut R version.

DEATH TRAP
See: *Eaten Alive.*

DEATHTRAP

★★★ Warner Home Video, 1982, PG, 116 min.
Dir: Sidney Lumet. Cast: Michael Caine, Christopher Reeve, Dyan Cannon, Irene Worth, Henry Jones, Joe Silver.

Entertaining film version of Ira Levin's hit tongue-in-cheek suspense play about a once-popular thriller writer (Caine) who plots the murder of an unknown author (Reeve) in order to steal his brilliant new play. But things aren't quite as they seem. A combination of elements from *Diabolique* and *Sleuth*, the twists and surprises aren't as fresh as they probably once seemed, but it's still lots of fun, with a nimble Caine and a bubbly Cannon in fine form.

DEATH VALLEY

★★ MCA/Universal Home Video, 1982, R, 88 min.
Dir: Dick Richards. Cast: Paul LeMat, Catherine Hicks, Peter Billingsley, Stephen McHattie, Edward Herrmann, Wilford Brimley.

Billingsley (*A Christmas Story*) is a young kid who witnesses a brutal murder while on vacation in the Arizona desert; naturally no one believes him, giving the killer free reign to slash and hack anew. Mechanical stalker movie with a little boy lead rather than the usual teenage girl but everything else the same. A talented cast is given little to do.

DEATH WARMED OVER

See: *Death Warmed Up.*

DEATH WARMED UP

★★☆ Vestron Video, 1984, R, 83 min.
Dir: David Blyth. Cast: Michael Hurst, Margaret Umbers, William Upjohn, Norelle Scott, David Letch, Gary Day.

Inventive New Zealand splatter about an island-dwelling mad doctor (Day) whose stronghold, teeming with the brain-damaged results of his botched experiments, is invaded by the young hero (Hurst), who was conditioned by the doc to murder his own parents—Dad being Day's scientific rival. Heavy accents hamper the performances, but lively direction and lots of splat make it a good watch. Aka *Death Warmed Over.*

DEATH WEEKEND

★★★ Vestron Video, 1976, R, 89 min. Dir: William Fruet. Cast: Brenda Vaccaro, Don Stroud, Chuck Shamata, Richard Ayres, Kyle Edwards, Don Gransberry.

Originally called *The House by the Lake*, this *Last House on the Left* cash-in is actually better, with an improved cast and more suspense. Vaccaro and Shambata's adulterous weekend at a country cottage is disrupted by a quartet of vicious goons led by Stroud. Stroud is harrowing and the husky-voiced Vaccaro has never been better in this underrated thriller.

DEATH WHEELERS, THE

See: *Psychomania.*

DECOY FOR TERROR

See: *Playgirl Killer.*

DEEP RED

See: *Deep Red: The Hatchet Murders.*

DEEP RED: THE HATCHET MURDERS

★★★☆ HBO Video, 1975, R, 100 min.
Dir: Dario Argento. Cast: David Hemmings, Daria Nicolodi, Gabriele Lavia, Clara Calamai, Macha Meril, Giuliana Calandra.

Jazz pianist Hemmings witnesses the brutal murder of a psychic neighbor (who earlier foresaw her own death) and becomes obsessed with catching the mystery killer—and in so doing brings death to just about everyone around him. One of Argento's best, most accomplished films, this benefits from its strong use of color, jagged editing technique, and pulse-pounding score but rarely makes sense—though the longer Italian version is more coherent. Pay close attention to the first post-murder scene where you actually catch a glimpse of the murderer's face. Aka *Profundo Rosso: Deep Red, Dripping Deep Red,* and *The Hatchet Murders.*

DEEP SIX, THE

See: *Deepstar Six.*

DEEP SPACE

★★ TransWorld Entertainment, 1987, R, 90 min.
Dir: Fred Olen Ray. Cast: Charles Napier, Ann Turkel, Bo Svenson, Ron Glass, Julie Newmar, James Booth, Norman Burton, Anthony Eisley, Peter Palmer, Elisabeth Brooks.

Routine *Alien* derivation from schlock king Ray. A crashed experimental satellite unleashes a hungry monster with familiar-looking dental work hunted by L.A. cops Napier and Turkel. This partial reworking of Ray's *Biohazard* is very low-budget but has an all-pro cast whose tongue-in-cheek approach to the material is disarming rather than annoying. The title, by the way, has no meaning whatsoever.

DEEPSTAR SIX

★★ Avid Entertainment, 1989, R, 98 min.
Dir: Sean S. Cunningham. Cast: Greg Evigan, Nancy Everhard, Cindy Pickett, Taurean Blacque, Miguel Ferrer, Nia Peeples, Marius Weyers, Matt McCoy.

Run-of-the-mill potboiler about a team of government workers constructing a deep-sea missile silo who find themselves battling what looks like a reject from *Godzilla vs. the Sea Monster*. The first of several interchangeable undersea horror films released in '89, this is well made but mechanical in the extreme, right down to the predictable shock ending Cunningham actually rips from his original *Friday the 13th* hit. Aka *The Deep Six*.

DEF BY TEMPTATION

★★☆ Shapiro-Glickenhaus Entertainment, 1990, R, 91 min. Dir: James Bond III. Cast: James Bond III, Kadeem Hardison, Cynthia Bond, Melba Moore, Bill Nunn, Freddie Jackson.

An earnest divinity student (Bond III) visits wicked ol' NYC and nearly falls victim to Temptation (Bond), a satanic embodiment of forbidden lust. A sort-of Spike Lee version of *Night Angel,* this updated version of a '70s blaxploitation horror film is overly arty and pretentious but *does* have good performances and some interesting, if clumsily handled, ideas as compensation.

DEJA VU

★★ MGM/UA Home Video, 1984, R, 94 min. Dir: Anthony Richmond. Cast: Jaclyn Smith, Nigel Terry, Shelley Winters, Claire Bloom.

Dull horror-mystery with Terry as a screenwriter who comes to fear that the subject of his latest script—a '20s ballerina who allegedly committed suicide—is possessing his actress wife (Smith) and driving her to a similar fate. Transparent *Vertigo* rip-off with only an exquisitely photographed Smith and a lush Pino Donaggio score to hold your interest.

DELICATESSEN

★★★ Paramount Home Video, 1991, R, 95 min. Dirs: Jean-Pierre Jeunet and Marc Caro. Cast: Marie-Laure Dougnac, Dominique Pinon, Karin Viard, Jean Claude Dreyfus, Ticky Holgado, Anne Marie Pisani.

Some critics think this French black comedy is the best movie about cannibalism ever made. I won't go that far, but this strikingly original film about a post-apocalyptic butcher who provides human hamburger for his hungry neighbors in a meatless futuristic world is clever, gross, and very entertaining.

DELIVER US FROM EVIL

See: *Night Angel.*

DELUSION

★★ Embassy Home Entertainment, 1981, R, 83 min. Dir: Alan Beattie. Cast: Joseph Cotten, Patricia Pearcy, David Hayward, John Dukakis, Simone Griffith, Leon Charles.

Released to theatres as *The House Where Death Lives,* this minor psycho thriller earns a few points for not aping either *Psycho* or *Halloween* but is otherwise too tedious to work up much excitement over. A young nurse (Pearcy) cares for a wheelchair-bound millionaire (Cotten) whose household is being stalked by a killer. Positively languid.

DEMENTED

★ Media Home Entertainment, 1980, R, 88 min. Dir: Arthur Jeffreys. Cast: Sallee Elyse, Bruce Gilchrist, Deborah Altar, Kathryn Clayton, Bryan Charles, Chip Matthews.

Recovering from being gang-raped, doctor's wife Linda (Elyse) becomes unhinged when a trio of neighborhood teens play a practical joke on her and hacks them to pieces. This bottom-of-the-barrel *I Spit on Your Grave* clone is both boring and sleazy, a bad combination.

DEMENTIA

See: *Daughter of Horror.*

DEMENTIA 13

★★★ Goodtimes Home Video, 1963, NR, 74 min. Dir: Francis [Ford] Coppola. Cast: William Campbell, Luana Anders, Bart Patton, Mary Mitchell, Patrick Magee, Ethne Dunn.

Although not really Coppola's first film (as often documented), this is his first notable one, a Roger Corman–produced psycho flick shot in Ireland to cash in on the success of *Homicidal.* Anders has her best role as a greedy daughter-in-law who covers up her husband's death in order to remain in his wealthy mother's will; pretends a psychic connection with the woman's drowned daughter; and later is murdered by a shadowy figure clutching a large ax. Despite some rough edges and continuity flaws, this remains a creepy and atmospheric mini-classic of the '60s. Aka *The Haunted and the Hunted.*

DEMON

See: *God Told Me To.*

DEMON, THE

★☆ VidAmerica, 1981, R, 93 min. Dir: Percival Rubens. Cast: Cameron Mitchell, Jennifer Holmes, Craig Gardner, Zoli Markey.

South Africa–lensed sleeping pill about a series of murders committed by a maniac with a steel claw glove and investigated by psychic Mitchell. A few flashes of imagination but mostly dross.

DEMON BARBER OF FLEET STREET, THE

★★☆ Rhino Home Video, 1936, NR, 66 min.
Dir: George King. Cast: Todd Slaughter, Stella Rho, Bruce Seton, Eve Lister, John Singer, D.J. Williams.

Slaughter's nearly the whole show in this loose adaptation of the George Dibden-Pitt play (also the basis for the celebrated Stephen Sondheim musical) about the murderous barber who slashes his customers' throats ("Let me polish you off!" he gleefully exclaims) for their money and then turns the bodies over to a neighbor lady who makes them into meat pies—only hinted at here. This low-budget Brit flick is good, cheesy fun. Aka *Sweeney Todd, The Demon Barber of Fleet Street;* remade as *Bloodthirsty Butchers.*

DEMON CATHEDRAL

See: *The Church.*

DEMON LOVER, THE

See: *The Devil Master.*

DEMON MASTER, THE

See: *Craze.*

DEMON OF PARADISE

★☆ Warner Home Video, 1987, R, 83 min.
Dir: Cirio H. Santiago. Cast: Kathryn Witt, William Steis, Laura Banks, Fred Bailey.

A prehistoric monster terrorizes a Hawaiian resort, and pretty scientist Witt tries to stop it. A disguised remake of Santiago's awful *Up From the Depths,* this has attractive locations but weak acting and a laughable zipper-backed creature.

DEMONIC TOYS

★ Paramount Home Video, 1991, R, 83 min.
Dir: Peter Manoogian. Cast: Tracy Scoggins, Bentley Mitchum, Michael Russo, Jeff Weston.

Possessed playthings terrorize female cop Scoggins and several others in an old toy factory in this tenth-rate *Child's Play* meets a feminist *Die Hard.* Subpar FX and an annoying demon kid given to making unfunny wisecracks sink this Charles Band flick like a stone. Sequel: *Dollman vs. the Demonic Toys.*

DEMON IN MY VIEW, A

★★ Vidmark Entertainment, 1991, R, 99 min.
Dir: Petra Hafftner. Cast: Anthony Perkins, Uwe Bohm, Sophie Ward, Stratford Johns, Brian Bovell, Deborah Lacey.

The peerless Perkins (in his penultimate role) stars as an obsessively neat, psychotic bachelor—a cross between Felix Unger and Norman Bates—who loves a female mannequin that reminds him of Mom and who strangles women, putting the blame on another boarder in his rooming house with a similar name. Everything about this programmer adaptation of a Ruth Rendell novel, apart from Perkins' performance, is unadventurous and dull, with a supposedly ironic ending that falls very flat. A clear case of too much characterization and not enough carnage.

DEMONOID

★ Video Treasures, 1979, R, 80 min.
Dir: Alfredo Zacharias. Cast: Samantha Eggar, Stuart Whitman, Roy Cameron Jenson, Lew Saunders.

One of the shoddiest English-language horror films ever made; a hilarious mixture of *The Beast with Five Fingers* and *The Exorcist.* Archeologist Jenson is possessed by a living, dismembered hand found on a demonic altar in a Mexican cave and heads to Las Vegas to take up big-time gambling. Wife Eggar tries to help but Jenson is killed and then *his* severed mitt seeks someone to possess. Utterly senseless but extremely funny, with bad performances (especially Whitman as a priest with the only American-Irish-Spanish accent on record) and hack special effects. Aka *Macabra* and *Demonoid, Messenger of Death.*

DEMONOID, MESSENGER OF DEATH

See: *Demonoid.*

DEMON PLANET, THE

See: *Planet of the Vampires.*

DEMONS

★★★ Starmaker Home Video, 1985, UR, 88 min.
Dir: Lamberto Bava. Cast: Natasha Hovey, Urbano Barberini, Paola Cozzi, Karl Zinny, Fiore Argento, Nicoletta Elmi, Bobby Rhodes, Michele Soavi.

Dario Argento produced and co-wrote this stylish but only partly successful mix of *The Evil Dead* and *The Purple Rose of Cairo.* People are randomly selected to attend a special midnight screening of a horror film at a huge art deco Berlin theatre called the Metropol. When a hooker in the audience scratches her face on a prop mask from the film on display in the lobby, she becomes possessed and is transformed into a clawed demon that attacks and infects most of the rest of the audience. Clever and gripping for its first two-thirds, this loses it in a succession of increasingly annoying false climaxes. Followed by *Demons 2* and *The Church.*

DEMONS 2: THE NIGHTMARE RETURNS

★★☆ Imperial Entertainment, 1987, R, 89 min.
Dir: Lamberto Bava. Cast: David Knight, Nancy Brilli,

Supernatural possession leads to bad dribble problems in Demons *(1986).*

Coralina, Cataldi Tassoni, Virginia Bryant, Asia Argento, Bobby Rhodes.

Okay follow-up with the titular nasties emerging this time from a television set showing a documentary based on the events in the first *Demons* movie. They procede to infect the residents of a high-rise apartment building in scenes lifted from *They Came From Within*, *Videodrome*, and *Trilogy of Terror*. Trimmed slightly for an R rating, it still has gore to spare, lots of laughable dialogue, and one genuine scare when a demon spots a girl watching it on TV and comes leering out of the set after her.

DEMONS OF THE MIND
★★★ Thorn/EMI Home Video, 1972, R, 87 min. Dir: Peter Sykes. Cast: Brian Jones, Gillian Hills, Shane Briant, Robert Hardy, Patrick Magee, Michael Hordern, Yvonne Mitchell, Virginia Wetherell.

Offbeat Hammer psychological thriller in a gothic setting. Crazed baron Hardy keeps his grown children (Hills and Briant) locked away in the family castle because he believes them to be victims of inherited evil from their dead mother. Actually, though, it's Hardy who's the crazy one, willing Briant to escape from the castle and rape and murder several village girls. This has a nice atmosphere of green forests, cool gray castle corridors, and red rose

petals plus an excellent cast (though Hardy overdoes it), but its rushed, downbeat ending seems gratuitously violent. Aka *Blood Will Have Blood, Nightmare of Terror,* and *Blood Evil.*

DEMONS OF THE SWAMP
See: *Attack of the Giant Leeches.*

DEMONWARP
★ Vidmark Entertainment, 1987, R, 91 min. Dir: Emmett Alston. Cast: George Kennedy, David Michael O'Neill, Pamela Gilbert, Billy Jacoby, Colleen McDermott, Michelle Bauer.

Absurd tale of the backwoods search by a bunch of unsympathetic dolts for a bigfoot creature that, in a ludicrous ending, turns out to be the cover-up for the zombie-making activities of devil-worshipping alien cannibals. Really. This is a totally unworkable melee of guys in *Planet of the Apes* makeup chasing topless bimbos through the woods; cut-rate zombies in rubber masks; and a sci-fi climax (not to mention *Carrie* coda) that looks like a softcore "Dr. Who" episode.

DEMON WIND
★★ ☆ Prism Entertainment, 1989, R, 97 min. Dir: Charles Philip Moore. Cast: Eric Larson, Francine Lapensee, Bobby Johnson, Lynn Clark, Mark David Fritscher, Sherry Bendorf.

How's this for an original concept: a group of college students spend the weekend in the mountains and end up possessed and transformed into zombies by an ancient evil force. If this all sounds a little like the plot of *The Evil Dead*, well. . . . Actually, this has better acting, photography, and FX than you might expect so, as derivative rehashes go, it isn't bad.

DEMON WITCH CHILD
See: *The Possessed* (1974).

DERANGED
★★★ Moore Video, 1974, R, 82 min. Dirs: Jeff Gillen and Alan Ormsby. Cast: Roberts Blossom, Cosette Lee, Robert Warner, Marcia Diamond, Marion Waldman, Micki Moore, Pat Orr, Les Carlson.

Blossom's wonderfully capering performance as an Ed Gein–inspired maniac makes this grim little shocker into a minor classic. Ezra Cobb (Blossom) is a dedicated middle-aged mama's boy who fears sex, distrusts all women, and exhumes and stuffs Ma's body, occasionally murdering a passing female to keep her company. Since this lacks a strong central heroine figure (as in, say, *The Texas Chainsaw Massacre*) the audience ends up identifying, instead, with crazy ol' Ez; fortunately, Blossom makes him such a likable old cuss, in an admittedly demented sort of way, this doesn't come off as distasteful an idea as it sounds. Uneven direction and a silly use of narration and slow motion are compensated for by a harrowing mood and some early, and quite grisly, Tom Savini makeups.

DERANGED

★☆ Republic Home Video, 1987, R, 85 min. Dir: Chuck Vincent. Cast: Jane Hamilton, Paul Siederman, Jennifer Delora, Jamie Gillis.

Dull thriller with echoes of *Repulsion* and *Ms. 45* about a woman (Hamilton) who murders an intruder in her apartment and then goes slowly mad, killing anyone who visits her digs. A not bad performance from Hamilton (former porn queen Veronica Hart), but this cheap suspenser is otherwise easily forgotten.

DESTROYER

★★ Virgin Video, 1988, R, 94 min. Dir: Robert Kirk. Cast: Anthony Perkins, Deborah Foreman, Clayton Rohner, Lyle Alzado, Lannie Garrett, Tobias Anderson.

A low-budget movie company shooting an epic called *Big House Dolls* in an abandoned prison is terrorized by a muscle-bound, supposedly electrocuted psycho (Alzado). An interesting cast (Perkins is especially droll as the pretentious director) somewhat alleviates the routine scenario. Alzado's superhuman, Jason-like invulnerability is never explained, but his choice of weaponry (including an acetylene torch and a jackhammer) shows more originality than you'd expect. Aka *Shadow of Death.*

DEVIL AND DANIEL WEBSTER, THE

★★★☆ Embassy Home Entertainment, 1941, NR, 85 min. Dir: William Dieterle. Cast: Edward Arnold, Walter Huston, Simone Simon, James Craig, Anne Shirley, Jane Darwell, Gene Lockhart, John Qualen.

This excellent piece of horror-Americana is the Faustian tale of an innocent farmer (Craig) in 19th-century New England who sells his soul to the devil for a fortune in gold and seven years of good luck. Time passes and the once gentle and kind Craig becomes hard and cruel, leaving it up to garrulous politician Daniel Webster (Arnold) to bargain with Satan (Huston) for the young man's soul. Huston has the role of a lifetime as the devilish Mr. Scratch, while Arnold is enormously appealing as Webster and Simon is slyly sexy as Belle, the devil's handmaiden. Originally titled *All That Money Can Buy* and aka *Daniel and the Devil,* video and TV editions are taken from a heavi-

ly cut reissue version (the original ran 112 minutes); a more complete 105-minute print is available on laser disc.

DEVIL BAT, THE

★★★ Goodtimes Home Video, 1941, NR, 68 min. Dir: Jean Yarbrough. Cast: Bela Lugosi, Suzanne Kaaren, Dave O'Brien, Guy Usher, Donald Kerr, Yolande Mallott.

It's hard not to get a kick out of this grade-Z PRC opus about a chemist (Lugosi) who develops a breed of giant bat he attracts to his enemies with a special after-shave he advises users to rub "on the tender part of your neck." Loads of cheap fun, with cardboard sets and pathetic special effects; Bela seems to be having a ball and so should you. Aka *Killer Bats,* remade as *The Flying Serpent,* and followed by the totally bogus sequel *Devil Bat's Daughter.*

DEVIL BAT'S DAUGHTER

★☆ Sony Video, 1946, NR, 67 min. Dir: Frank Wisbar. Cast: Rosemary La Planche, John James, Michael Hale, Molly Lamont, Nolan Leary, Monica Mars.

One of the dumbest sequels of all time, this actually tries to prove that everything we saw Bela Lugosi so gleefully do in the original never really happened! La Planche is the titular offspring who visits Dad's old laboratory and begins having bad dreams about bats. When her psychiatrist's wife is murdered, naturally Rosemary (who, by the way, was a former Miss America) becomes the chief suspect. This attempted mix of psychological suspense and Z-level monster antics never adds up to much, despite some nice visual touches courtesy of director Wisbar.

DEVIL DOG: THE HOUND OF HELL

★★ Vestron Video, 1978, NR, 96 min. Dir: Curtis Harrington. Cast: Richard Crenna, Yvette Mimieux, Kim Richards, Ike Eisenmann, Victor Jory, Martine Beswick, R. G. Armstrong, Ken Kercheval.

No, it's not about a killer cupcake. Actually, this is TV's entry in the late '70s killer dog craze with a touch or two of *The Omen.* The dopey plot revolves around a suburban family who fall under the evil influence of the family pet: a German shepherd with glowing eyes who happens to be the embodiment of some South American goblin-dog-spirit. A good cast and director waste their time on a lousy script and punk special effects. Funny if you catch it in the right frame of mind; otherwise, forget it.

DEVIL DOLL, THE

★★★ MGM/UA Home Video, 1936, NR, 79 min. Dir: Tod Browning. Cast: Lionel Barrymore, Maureen

O'Sullivan, Frank Lawton, Rafaela Ottiano, Henry B. Walthall, Robert Greig, Grace Ford, Arthur Hohl.

Barrymore is a treat as a Devil's Island escapee who commandeers scientist Walthall's incredible shrinking machine and, disguised as an old lady dollmaker, uses miniature assassins to avenge himself on those who railroaded him to prison. Co-scripted by Erich von Stroheim, this has nicely ironic story line, a fine cast, good FX, and a minimum of hokey MGM sentimentality.

DEVIL DOLL
★★★☆ Gorgon Video, 1964, NR, 80 min.
Dir: Lindsay Shonteff. Cast: Bryant Halliday, William Sylvester, Yvonne Romain, Sandra Dorne, Alan Gifford, Francis de Wolff.

Terrific Brit B movie with Halliday as the Great Vorelli, popular stage hypnotist/ventriloquist with a living dummy named Hugo and a yen to capture the soul of the voluptuous Romain. Tense and eerie, with fine performances and sharp monochrome photography beautifully catching the slate-gray atmosphere of a pre-mod '60s London; everything capped by a wonderful twist ending. See it.

DEVIL DOLL MEN
See: *Curse of the Doll People.*

DEVILFISH
★☆ Vidmark Entertainment, 1984, R, 93 min.
Dir: John M. Old, Jr. [Lamberto Bava]. Cast: Michael Sopkiw, Iris Peynado, Valentine Monnier, Dagmar Lassander, William Berger, John Garko.

This Italian-made, Florida-lensed, *Jaws*-inspired fish story is just so much flotsam and jetsam. A prehistoric shark-squid creature munches on idiots while an evil scientist tries to cover up its activities for his own selfish purposes. Aka *Oceano Rosso: Red Ocean* and *Devouring Waves,* this is dull and ponderous, with little gore and no excitement.

DEVIL IN THE HOUSE
OF EXORCISM, THE
See: *The House of Exorcism.*

DEVIL MASTER, THE
★ Regal Video, 1976, R, 80 min.
Dir: Donald G. Jackson and Jerry Younkins. Cast: Gunnar Hansen, Christmas Robbins, Val Mayerik, Tom Hutton, Linda Conrad, Phil Foreman.

Originally titled *The Demon Lover,* this amateur night nonentity deals with a detective's investigation of a series of murders in which the killer is revealed as a huge horned demon and the victims are all members of a satanic cult.

Lots of in-jokes and blood and a guest appearance by *Texas Chainsaw Massacre*'s Hansen but ultimately still a waste of time. Aka *Master of Evil.*

DEVILS, THE
★★★ Warner Home Video, 1971, R, 109 min.
Dir: Ken Russell. Cast: Vanessa Redgrave, Oliver Reed, Gemma Jones, Dudley Sutton, Max Adrian, Michael Gothard.

Russell's mad mix of history, horror, and surrealism based on *The Devils of Loudon* by Aldous Huxley. In 1634 France, with the black death sweeping the continent, a wave of religious hysteria grips the people of Loudon, causing a repressed, hunchbacked nun (Redgrave) to lose her faith and begin lusting for a brawny priest (Reed), leading to accusations of heresy, witchcraft, and demonic possession. Originally released in an X-rated version but available now only in this cut R edition, this violent yet oddly beautiful film offers Redgrave in one of her most accomplished performances, a strangely sympathetic figure with her Quasimodo hump and impossible desire, while Reed makes for an imposing figure as the virile priest torn between God and the devil (characterized as carnal lust) and paying a horrible price for it. Not your usual exorcism movie.

DEVIL'S COMMANDMENT, THE
★★★ Sinister Cinema, 1956, NR, 71 min.
Dir: Robert Hampton [Riccardo Freda]. Cast: Gianna Maria Canale, Antoine Balpetre, Paul Muller, Wandissa Guida, Carlo D'Angelo, Dario Michaelis.

Canale stars as an aging countessa who is injected with a doctor's experimental youth serum derived from the blood of young girls; she turns younger but needs more and more serum to stay that way, becoming, in essence, a scientific vampire. The first film in the Italian horror renaissance and the obvious inspiration for much of the work of Mario Bava (who photographed) and Dario Argento, this is dated slightly by some silly additional footage shot in the U.S. (featuring Al Lewis!) but is still worth seeing for its atmosphere and mood. Bava also designed the special effects seen at the climax. Aka *I Vampiri: The Vampire* and *Lust of the Vampire.*

DEVIL'S DAUGHTER, THE
★★★☆ Republic Home Video, 1991, R, 116 min.
Dir: Michele Soavi. Cast: Kelly Curtis, Herbert Lom, Tomas Arana, Maria Angela Giordano, John Morghen.

Originally titled *The Sect,* this haunting blend of *Rosemary's Baby* and *The Wicker Man* is

Soavi's best film to date. Curtis (Jamie Lee's sister) is a schoolteacher chosen by Lom's cult, "The Faceless Ones," to become the mother of the apocalypse and give birth to the anti-Christ. Lots of startling camera moves and an always off-kilter script co-written by Dario Argento make this one of the most challenging Euro-shockers in years. Give the ending a chance, though.

DEVIL'S GIFT, THE

☆ Vestron Video, 1980, NR, 112 min.
Dir: Kenneth Berton. Cast: Bob Mendelsolin, Vicki Saputo, Steven Robertson.

Excruciating rip-off of the Stephen King story "The Monkey" about a toy monkey that spells disaster for an obnoxious little kid and his family. Few words can describe the awfulness of this direct-to-video challenge to your patience except one: BEWARE!

DEVIL'S MEN, THE

See: *Land of the Minotaur.*

DEVIL'S MESSENGER, THE

★ Sinister Cinema, 1959, NR, 72 min.
Dirs: Herbert L. Strock and Curt Siodmak. Cast: Lon Chaney, Jr., Karen Kadler, John Crawford, Michael Hinn, Gunnel Brostrom, Tammy Newmara.

Compiled from three episodes from an unsold Swedish TV series called "#13 Demon Street," this awesomely inept anthology casts a puffy Chaney as his satanic majesty, who uses seductive suicide Kadler to gather damned souls for him. The tales involve a photographer haunted in his pictures by a model he murdered; a scientist who falls in love with the frozen corpse of a beautiful girl; and that old chestnut about a man driven mad by a fortune teller's prediction that he will commit a murder. Murky and dull. Chaney looks like he may have been soused through most of it and probably was.

DEVIL'S NIGHTMARE, THE

★★☆ Monterey Home Video, 1972, R, 87 min.
Dir: Jean Brismée. Cast: Erika Blanc, Jean Servais, Daniel Emilfork, Jacques Monseau, Colette Emmanuelle, Shirley Corrigan.

Slightly above-average Belgian-Italian chiller about a group of tourists stranded at the castle of an old baron, where a demonic succubus in the guise of a beautiful woman (Blanc) does them in in various ways—decapitation, impalement, suffocation, snake bite—to punish them for their hedonistic ways: each victim symbolizes one of the seven deadly sins. A kinkily clad Erika is memorable as the she-demon. Aka *La Plus Longue Nuit du Diable: The Devil's Longest Night, Succubus, Vampire Playgirls, Castle of Death,* and *The Devil Walks at Midnight.*

DEVIL'S PARTNER, THE

★★☆ Sinister Cinema, 1958, NR, 61 min.
Dir: Charles Rondeau. Cast: Ed Nelson, Jean Allison, Edgar Buchanan, Richard Crane.

Minor but interesting '50s cheapie with Nelson as an aging satanist who reincarnates himself as a younger man (and passes himself off as his own nephew) in order to romance Allison while shape-shifting into different animals to do away with his enemies. Short and sweet, with good acting and lots of effective little touches.

DEVIL'S RAIN, THE

★★☆ Video Treasures, 1975, PG, 85 min.
Dir: Robert Fuest. Cast: Ernest Borgnine, Eddie Albert, Ida Lupino, William Shatner, Tom Skerritt, Joan Prather, Keenan Wynn, John Travolta.

Warlock Borgnine tries to claim a satanic "Book of Souls" from Lupino's family, transforming his victims into eyeless zombies whose souls are kept in a large glass container. When the container is smashed, it unleashes the "Devil's rain," which melts the coven into puddles of liquid wax. A surprisingly upscale cast play it all with amazingly straight faces and there are some good scenes, but this is notable mainly for its ridiculously protracted ending (which seems to go on forever), some effective makeups, and Travolta's film debut (don't blink, you might miss him).

DEVIL'S UNDEAD, THE

★★☆ Monterey Home Video, 1972, PG, 90 min.
Dir: Peter Sasdy. Cast: Christopher Lee, Peter Cushing, Diana Dors, Georgia Brown, Keith Barron, Gwyneth Strong.

The strange deaths of the aged trustees of a Scottish orphanage are investigated by police inspector Lee and pathologist Cushing, whose work leads them to uncover a bizarre soul-transplantation plot. Best known as *Nothing But the Night,* this confusing but interesting tale sees Chris and Peter in fine form and Dors pulling out all the stops as the psychopathic mom of one of the orphans. Aka *The Resurrection Syndicate.*

DEVIL'S WEDDING NIGHT, THE

★ Video Communications, 1973, R, 84 min.
Dir: Paolo Solvay. Cast: Mark Damon, Sarah Bay, Esmeralda Barros, Francesca Roma Davila.

Tacky Italian rip-off of Hammer Films' *Count-*

Joan Prather has a cross to bear—or is it the other way around?—in The Devil's Rain *(1975).*

ess Dracula and "Karnstein Trilogy" with the ever talentless Damon as twin brothers who get mixed up with Bay as Countess Dracula, who stays eternally young by bathing in the blood of virgins. Alternately silly and disgusting, with scenes of a nude Bay writhing about while stage blood is poured over her a guaranteed turn-off. Aka *Il Penilunio Delle Vergini: Full Moon of the Virgins*.

DEVIL TIMES FIVE

★★★ Video Treasures, 1973, R, 88 min.
Dir: Sean MacGregor. Cast: Gene Evans, Sorrell Booke, Shelley Morrison, Joan McCall, Taylor Lacher, Carolyn Steller, Leif Garrett, Dawn Lyn.

Really offbeat psycho-thriller about a group of strange children who turn up at the snowbound winter retreat of wealthy Evans (as "Papa Doc") and begin murdering him and his guests with axes, ropes, arrows, fire, and piranhas in the bath. This undeservedly neglected, one-of-a-kind movie is marred by slow pacing and some overblown performances but is still definitely worth checking out. Aka *People Toys* and *The Horrible House on the Hill*.

DEVIL WITHIN HER, THE

★★ Axon Video, 1975, R, 90 min.
Dir: Peter Sasdy. Cast: Joan Collins, Donald Pleasence, Ralph Bates, Eileen Atkins, Caroline Munro, John Steiner.

Routine *Rosemary's Baby/Exorcist/It's Alive!* rip-off about a former stripper (Collins) who gives birth to a murderous possessed baby thanks to the curse of a dwarf whose affections she once spurned. Occasionally tense and with a likable cast, but too much in the way of unintended humor spoils the intended effect. Aka *I Don't Want to Be Born*.

DEVONSVILLE TERROR, THE

★★ Embassy Home Entertainment, 1983, R, 82 min.
Dir: Ulli Lommel. Cast: Suzanna Love, Donald Pleasence, Robert Walker, Paul Willson, Mary Walden, Deanna Haas.

The *Raiders of the Lost Ark*–inspired climax is the best thing about this slow-moving witchcraft pic about three young modern women suspected by repressed New England villagers of being the reincarnation of a trio of witches executed some 300 years before; everything comes to a head in a noggin-exploding ending. Love, in a Jamie Lee Curtis hairdo, is okay as the troubled heroine but Pleasence is wasted yet again as a local doctor who spends most of his time pulling maggots out of little holes in his body!

DEVOURING WAVES

See: *Devilfish*.

DIABOLICAL DR. Z, THE

★★ Sinister Cinema, 1965, NR, 86 min.
Dir: Henri Baum [Jesus Franco]. Cast: Mabel Karr, Estella Blain, Fernando Montés, Howard Vernon.

Another of the pseudonymous Franko's sequels to his early hit *The Awful Dr. Orlof* with the doc (Vernon, as ever) getting bumped off early on by a heart attack and his daughter (Karr) using Dad's methods of mind control to turn a beautiful long-nailed feather dancer (Blain) into a seductive murder weapon directed at Orloff's enemies. Typical Franco tomfoolery with some interesting moments buried amidst a lot of baloney. Aka *Miss Muerte: Miss Death* and *In the Grip of the Maniac*.

DIABOLIQUE

★★★★ Goodtimes Home Video, 1955, NR, 107 min.
Dir: Henri-Georges Clouzet. Cast: Simone Signoret, Vera Clouzet, Paul Meurisse, Charles Vanel, Noel Roquevert, Therese Dorny.

Classic French chiller about the horrible headmaster (Meurisse) of a bleak boys school who is murdered by his long-suffering wife (Clouzet) and mistress (Signoret). The body is dumped into the school's disused swimming pool, but when the pool is later drained it is gone. Has the headmaster returned from the dead for revenge? The first foreign film to make a big splash at the U.S. box office, its dense atmosphere of stunted, pointless lives and whispered plots is beautifully captured by director Clouzet, who builds suspense masterfully right up to the shattering surprise ending—which will seem less of a surprise to anyone who's seen the countless suspense-horror films that have ripped this ending off. Aka *Les Diaboliques: The Fiends* and remade as *Games* (also with the magnificent Signoret) and the TV movies *Reflections of Murder* and *House of Secrets*.

DIAL: HELP!

★★ Prism Entertainment, 1988, R, 95 min.
Dir: Ruggero Deodato. Cast: Charlotte Lewis, Marcello Mondungno, Mattia Sbragia, Carola Stagnaro, Victor Cavallo, William Berger.

The luscious Lewis stars as Jenny, a moody fashion model who misdials a closed-down Lonelyhearts 976 service and thereafter finds herself menaced by ghostly emanations from phones of all kinds. Why? Don't ask me, as this Italian thriller never bothers to explain itself. Sumptuous photography from Renato Tafuri and lotsa Lewis in lingerie but otherwise a wrong number.

DIARY OF A MADMAN

★★★ MGM/UA Home Video, 1963, NR, 96 min.
Dir: Reginald Le Borg. Cast: Vincent Price, Nancy
Kovack, Chris Warfield, Elaine Devry, Ian Wolfe, Lewis
Martin, Stephen Roberts, voice of Joseph Ruskin.

Colorful adaptation of the Guy de Maupassant
story with Price as a 19th-century French magistrate possessed by an evil spirit called the
Horla (voiced by Ruskin). The low budget
shows but Kovack is excellent as the saucy
artist's model who falls victim to Vinnie,
there's a good score by Richard La Salle, and a
memorable decapitated-head-in-a-clay-bust
gag.

DIE BEAUTIFUL, MARIANNE!

See: *Die Screaming, Marianne!*

DIE! DIE! MY DARLING!

★★★ Goodtimes Home Video, 1965, NR, 96 min.
Dir: Silvio Narizzano. Cast: Tallulah Bankhead,
Stefanie Powers, Peter Vaughn, Yootha Joyce,
Donald Sutherland, Maurice Kaufman.

The dahling Tallulah tears up the screen in
this enjoyable Crazy Mama romp from Hammer Films. La Bankhead rightly revels in her
last role as Mrs. Trefoile, a stern religious
fanatic who imprisons her late son's ex-fiancee
(Powers) in an attempt to "cleanse" the sinful
girl (who does terrible things like wearing lipstick) so that she can be sacrificed to the son's
memory on an altar Mom keeps hidden in the
basement. A solid Richard Matheson adaptation of the book *Nightmare* by Anne Blaisdell,
with Stefanie in fine, early form, some good
laughs, and plenty of genuine suspense. Aka
Fanatic.

DIE, MONSTER, DIE!

★★☆ HBO Video, 1965, NR, 78 min.
Dir: Daniel Haller. Cast: Boris Karloff, Nick Adams,
Suzan Farmer, Freda Jackson, Terence de Marney,
Patrick Magee.

When scientist Adams visits girlfriend Farmer
at her secluded English estate, he discovers it
to be contaminated by radiation from a fallen
meteorite kept hidden in the cellar by her
father (Karloff). After Mom (Jackson) is transformed into a hideous mutant and dies, Dad
takes it upon himself to destroy the glowing
stone from space—with disasterous consequences. A decent adaptation of H. P. Lovecraft's "The Colour Out of Space" with good
work from Karloff and Jackson and eerie
moods provided by former Roger Corman
production designer Haller in his first turn
as director. Aka *Monster of Terror;* remade as
The Curse.

DIE SCREAMING, MARIANNE!

★☆ Magnum Entertainment, 1970, R, 90 min.
Dir: Pete Walker. Cast: Susan George, Barry Evans,
Christopher Sandford, Judy Huxtable, Leo Genn.

Go-go dancer George is terrorized at a remote
villa by villains after her inheritance. Z-z-z-z-z.
Boring girl-on-the-run thriller notable only as
Brit director Walker's first horror film and
Susan's first starring role. Aka *Die Beautiful,
Marianne!*

DIMENSIONS IN DEATH

See: *Castle of Blood.*

DINOSAURUS!

★★☆ Starmaker Home Video, 1960, NR, 83 min.
Dir: Irvin S. Yeaworth, Jr. Cast: Ward Ramsey, Kristina
Hansen, Paul Lukather, Alan Roberts, Fred Engelberg,
Gregg Martell.

Construction work on a Caribbean island
unearths a Tyrannosaurus, Brontosaurus, and
Neanderthal man restored to life by a lightning bolt. Kiddie-matinee-style monster movie
with a little kid hero, hissable bad guy, goofy
red-headed heroine carried away by the
Tyrannosaurus, and friendly caveman who
saves the day by throwing pies at the villains,
this is harmless fun (with uneven animation
effects by Tim Barr, Wah Chang, Marcel Del-
gado, and Gene Warren) from the makers of
The Blob.

DISCIPLE OF DEATH

★★ Unicorn, 1972, R, 82 min.
Dir: Tom Parkinson. Cast: Mike Raven, Ronald Lacey,
Stephen Bradley, Marguerite Hardiman, Virginia
Wetherell, Louise Jameson.

A drop of blood falling from the finger of the
heroine (Hardiman) during an engagement
pact onto the grave of a suicide revives the
occupant (Raven) as a bloodthirsty ghoul who
cuts out the hearts of young girls who then
become ghouls themselves. Good color and an
occasionally creepy scene (like a ghoulish
Wetherell tapping at a frosty window pane)
but done harm by cheesy makeup, a never
convincing period setting—some of the houses
have aluminum siding!—and the hammy
excesses of star Raven.

DISTORTIONS

★☆ Academy, 1986, R, 98 min. Dir: Armand
Mastroianni. Cast Olivia Hussey, Piper Laurie, Steve
Railsback, Edward Albert, Rita Gam, Terence Knox.

Well-cast but boring suspenser with Hussey
(in a real bad haircut) terrorized by various
weird goings-on while staying with her aunt
(Laurie) following the murder of her bisexual

husband (Albert). A really unexpected ending is about all this second-string suspenser has to offer other than the sight of Laurie made up to look like a latter-day Ann Sothern.

DISTURBED

★★★ LIVE, 1990, R, 91 min.
Dir: Charles Winkler. Cast: Malcolm McDowall, Pamela Gidley, Geoffrey Lewis, Priscilla Pointer, Clint Howard, Peter Murnick.

After psychiatrist McDowall accidentally murders patient Gidley, she seemingly returns from the dead for revenge—doesn't she? A stylish, funny combo of *Diabolique* and *One Flew Over the Cuckoo's Nest* with Malcolm pulling out all the stops. "You need professional help," says nurse Pointer. "I *am* professional help!" McDowall retorts.

DOCTOR AND THE DEVILS, THE

★★☆ Key, 1985, R, 92 min.
Dir: Freddie Francis. Cast: Timothy Dalton, Twiggy, Jonathan Pryce, Julian Sands, Stephen Rea, Phyllis Logan, Lewis Fiander, Beryl Reid.

Based on a 40-year-old screenplay by Dylan Thomas (perhaps written after seeing *The Body Snatcher* one too many times), this is yet another version of the Burke and Hare story. James Bond-to-be Dalton is the respected surgeon and Pryce and Rea are the slovenly graverobbers he employs to gather medical "specimens." There's a great cast and veteran director Francis creates a nice Hammer Films feel, but this is too draggy and pretentious for its own good.

DOCTOR BLOOD'S COFFIN

★★☆ Sinister Cinema, 1961, NR, 92 min.
Dir: Sidney J. Furie. Cast: Kieron Moore, Hazel Court, Ian Hunter, Kenneth J. Warren, Gerald C. Lawson, Fred Johnson.

Moore is a med school drop-out obsessed with the idea that he can restore life to the dead through heart transplants, conducting his experiments on the citizenry of a tiny Cornish village. Handsome but dull—much like its leading man—with sharp color photography and sincere performances. The walking corpse climax almost looks like it belongs to another picture entirely.

DOCTOR BUTCHER, M.D.

★★ Thrillervideo, 1979, UR, 81 min. Dir: Frank [Francisco] Martino. Cast: Ian McCulloch, Alexandria Delli Colli, Donald O'Brian, Sherry Buchanan.

The M.D. stands for Medical Deviate in this sanguinary saga about the mysterious Dr. Abrero (O'Brian), aka Dr. Butcher, who is creating zombies by placing living brains into the skulls of corpses and encouraging cannibalism among the locals who live near his island hideout. An enormously funny, though rather incomprehensible, mishmash of such surefire elements as flesh-eating, scalpings, eyeball-poppings, walking stiffs, lousy acting, and abrupt editing culled from both an Italian stomach-churner called *La Regina dei Cannibali: Queen of the Cannibals* and an unfinished New York gore flick called *Tales That'll Tear Your Heart Out!* that was released to surprising profits in 1981.

DOCTOR DEATH: SEEKER OF SOULS

★★ Prism, 1973, R, 89 min. Dir: Eddie Saeta. Cast: John Considine, Cheryl Miller, Barry Coe, Stewart Moss, Jo Morrow, Florence Marley, Leon Askin, Sivi Aberg, Moe Howard, Larry Vincent.

Considine does his Vincent Price imitation in this weak *Dr. Phibes* clone about an ageless madman who dabbles in soul transplantation. The campy supporting cast includes veteran eye-poker Moe in his final role.

DOCTOR GORE

★ United, 1972, R, 90 min.
Dir: J. G. "Pat" Patterson. Cast: J. G. Patterson, Jenny Driggers, Roy Mehaffey, Linda Faile.

H. G. Lewis–type gore comedy about a loony doc (Patterson) who murders women to get the parts needed to create the perfect woman. Surprisingly similar to the later *Frankenhooker*, this is played for broad laughs but really isn't all that funny. For gore completists only. Aka *Body Shop*.

DOCTOR OF DOOM

★★☆ Sinister Cinema, 1962, NR, 77 min.
Dir: René Cardona. Cast: Armando Silvestre, Lorna Velasquez, Elizabeth Campbell, Roberto Canedo, Chucho Salinas, Irma Rodriguez.

Wotta picture! A hooded mad doctor, known as the Mad Doctor, terrorizes Mexico City with his apeman Gomar and *lots* of henchmen, kidnapping young women to find the one into whom he can transplant Gomar's brain—what he needs is a girl with a lot of stamina. He finds her in the sister of popular wrestler Gloria Venus but quickly has his evil hands full when Gloria and her partner, the Golden Rubi, seek a muscular revenge. The first and best of a whole series of Mexican Wrestling Women horror flicks, this is fun as only a badly dubbed Mexican horror film can be. Aka *Las Luchadoras Contra El Medico Asesino: The Wrestling Women vs. the Murderous Doctor;* remade as *Night of the Bloody Apes*.

DOCTOR OF SEVEN DIALS, THE
See: *Corridors of Blood.*

DOCTORS WEAR SCARLET
See: *Bloodsuckers.*

DOCTOR X
★★★ MGM/UA, 1932, NR, 75 min. Dir: Michael
Curtiz. Cast: Lionel Atwill, Fay Wray, Lee Tracy,
Preston Foster, Arthur Edmund Carewe, Leila Bennett.

Fun early '30s Technicolor chiller about a
series of cannibalistic killings in New York
City traced to Atwill's medical school, where
he uses daughter Wray as bait to discover
which member of his staff is the gruesome
killer. Slightly better than the more popular
Mystery of the Wax Museum from the same
stars and director, this suffers from too much
corny comic relief but has some really creepy
scenes, including the famous "Synthetic Flesh"
sequence, as compensation.

DOGS
See: *Slaughter.*

DOLLMAN VS. DEMONIC TOYS
☆ Paramount, 1993, R, 64 min.
Dir: Charles Band. Cast: Tim Thomerson, Tracy
Scoggins, Melissa Behr, Phil Fondacaro.

It's bad enough when they make an unnecessary sequel to one Charles Band flick, but this
is an uncalled-for follow-up to no less than
three Full Moon losers: *Dollman, Demonic Toys,*
and *Bad Channels!* The mind boggles. Completely worthless, with Scoggins wasted (literally), offensive scenes of a foul-mouthed, sex-
starved baby doll fondling diminutive Behr,
and *lots* of flashback padding.

DOLLS
★★ Vestron, 1987, R, 77 min. Dir: Stuart Gordon.
Cast: Carrie Lorraine, Ian Patrick Williams, Carolyn
Purdey-Gordon, Guy Rolfe, Hilary Mason, Stephen Lee.

Disappointing entry from *Re-Animator* man
Gordon about travelers stranded by storm in a
dollmaker's shop where the dolls come murderously to life. Good FX notwithstanding,
this shows a real disdain toward women and
sports an obnoxiously sweet final moral about
the power of love—this coming after brutally
dispatching most of the cast in needlessly
gruesome ways! Watch *Trilogy of Terror* again
instead.

DOLLY DEAREST
★★☆ Vidmark, 1991, R, 93 min. Dir: Maria Lease.
Cast: Denise Crosby, Sam Bottoms, Rip Torn, Chris
Demertral, Candy Hutson, Lupe Ontiveros.

An evil force from an ancient Mexican tomb
invades a nearby doll factory and turns a
bunch of Barbies into a squadron of murdering distaff Chuckys. Not bad *Child's Play* rip
with scenes borrowed from *The Exorcist, The
Omen, Trilogy of Terror,* a few laughs, and
creepy doll FX. It gets a little goofy by the end
but it's still a fun ride.

DOMINIQUE
See: *Dominique Is Dead.*

DOMINIQUE IS DEAD
★★☆ Prism, 1979, PG, 95 min.
Dir: Michael Anderson. Cast: Cliff Robertson, Jean
Simmons, Jenny Agutter, Simon Ward, Ron Moody,
Judy Geeson, Flora Robson, David Tomlinson,
Michael Jayston, Jack Warner.

Originally called simply *Dominique,* this mild
Diabolique-inspired thriller (produced by former Amicus head Milton Subotsky) looks like
one of those minor '60s B&W Hammer suspense shockers. Simmons is the title character,
a crippled heiress driven to suicide by her
greedy hubby (Robertson), who is himself
haunted (or is he?) by her vengeful ghost.
Slow and obvious but helped enormously by
its professional cast and eerie atmosphere.
Aka *Avenging Spirit.*

DONOVAN'S BRAIN
★★★ MGM/UA, 1953, NR, 83 min.
Dir: Felix Feist. Cast: Lew Ayres, Nancy Davis, Gene
Evans, Steve Brodie, Lisa K. Howard, Tom Powers.

The best of the three screen versions (the others being *The Lady and the Monster* and *The
Brain*) of Curt Siodmak's novel about a
research scientist (Ayres) whose will is taken
over by the disembodied brain of an
unscrupulous financier on which he is experimenting. This evokes a marvelous mood of
both scientific and financial opportunism
(Ayers, who steals Donovan's brain for his
experiments, has *his* body stolen by the dead
man's powerful personality in a nice bit of
irony) and has first-rate acting from Ayres,
Evans, and future First Lady Davis (aka Mrs.
Ronald Reagan).

DON'T ANSWER THE PHONE
★ Media, 1980, R, 94 min. Dir: Robert Hammer.
Cast: James Westmoreland, Flo Gerrish, Nicholas
Worth, Ben Frank, Pamela Bryant, Denise Galik.

Filmed as *The Hollywood Strangler* and misleadingly advertised as another psycho vs.
babysitter opus in the vein of *When a Stranger
Calls,* this concerns the activities of a father-fix-
ated overweight Vietnam vet (Worth) who

CURT SIODMAK
(1902–)

A German-born screenwriter and novelist, Siodmak specialized in horror and fantastic themes. He was Universal Pictures' main horror scripter in the early '40s and created an entire mythos when he wrote *The Wolf Man,* whose invented werewolf legends are now taken as "fact." In the '50s he turned to directing. His most famous novel, *Donovan's Brain,* has been filmed three times.

The Invisible Man Returns (co-screenplay, '40), *Black Friday* (co-screenplay, '40), *The Ape* (co-screenplay, '40), *The Invisible Woman* (original story, '41), *The Wolf Man* ('41), *Invisible Agent* ('42), *Frankenstein Meets the Wolf Man* ('43), *I Walked With a Zombie* (co-screenplay , '43), *Son of Dracula* (original story, '43), *The Lady and the Monster* (from his novel *Donovan's Brain,* '44), *The Climax* (co-screenplay, '44), *House of Frankenstein* (original story, '44), *The Beast With Five Fingers* ('47), *Bride of the Gorilla* (also director, '51), *Donovan's Brain* (from his novel, '53), *Creature With the Atom Brain* ('55), *Curucu, Beast of the Amazon* (also director, '56), *The Devil's Messenger* (co-director, co-screenplay, '59), *The Brain* (from his novel *Donovan's Brain,* '63), *Sherlock Holmes and the Deadly Necklace* ('63), *Hauser's Memory,* (from his novel, '70).

stalks and strangles Hollywood honeys with a coin-filled stocking in order to prove his masculinity to his dead dad. Notable for Worth's lip-smacking, truly hilarious performance as the killer but otherwise too debasingly sexist to enjoy, with a hero (Westmoreland) almost as disturbing as the villain.

DON'T BE AFRAID OF THE DARK
★★★ USA, 1973, NR, 73 min.
Dir: John Newland. Cast: Kim Darby, Jim Hutton, Barbara Anderson, William Demerest, Pedro Armenariz, Jr., William Sylvester.

Better-than-usual TV horror with Darby and Hutton as a couple who inherit an old mansion from her grandmother inhabited by a trio of gruesome goblins living in a bricked-up fireplace. Creepy makeup and an eerie setting (with nice atmosphere provided by director Newland of "One Step Beyond" fame) make this a very watchable little shocker with a truly unexpected ending.

DON'T GO IN THE HOUSE
☆ Video Treasures, 1980, R, 83 min. Dir: Joseph Ellison. Cast: Dan Grimaldi, Robert Osth, Ruth Dardick, Johanna Brushay, O'Mara Leary, Gail Turner.

Nerdy Grimaldi, tortured with fire as a boy by sick mom Dardick, builds a special fire-proof room in his old mansion where he lures young women to a fiery demise. An offensive, leering movie that actually tries to get you to sympathize with its creepy killer and unappealing best buddy Osth (a macho jerk who cheats on his wife and is actually set up in the end as the hero!) while the female victims are all presented as bubble-brained bimbos and bitches. There *are* some good Tom Brumberger make-up FX, but they're not enough to make *anyone* sit through this trash. Aka *The Burning.*

DON'T GO IN THE WOODS
☆ Video Treasures, 1980, R, 82 min.
Dir: James Bryan. Cast: Jack McClelland, Mary Gail Artz, James P. Hayden, Angie Brown.

Total boredom as two unlikable couples run afoul of a limb-tearing "Wild Man" in a Utah forest. A bad combo of *The Texas Chainsaw Massacre* and *Friday the 13th,* this has plenty of gore but also plenty of scenes of people wandering aimlessly through the woods accompanied by a musical score that sounds like it's being played on a washing machine. Funniest scene: the hero accidentally impales some passing schnook in mistake for the killer and keeps yelling, "I'm sorry! I'm sorry!" as if he'd just stubbed the guy's toe or somethin'! Aka *Don't Go in the Woods Alone.*

DON'T GO IN THE WOODS ALONE
See: *Don't Go in the Woods.*

DON'T GO TO SLEEP
★★☆ Vidmark, 1982, NR, 96 min.
Dir: Richard Lang. Cast: Valerie Harper, Dennis Weaver, Ruth Gordon, Robert Webber, Robin Ignico, Oliver Robbins, Kristin Cumming, Claudette Nevins.

A little girl insists that her older sister keeps visiting her even though she was killed in a car wreck several months earlier. Then members of the family begin dying one by one. Surprisingly potent TV ghost story that pulls few punches and is often quite suspenseful—though it gets increasingly silly as it heads for its final jolt finale. The actors are all excellent.

DON'T LOOK IN THE BASEMENT
★☆ VidAmerica, 1972, R, 82 min. Dir: S. F. Brownrigg. Cast: Rosie Holotik, Anne McAdams, William Bill McGhee, Camilla Carr, Gene Ross, Jessie Lee Fulton.

A real bargain basement item about a new nurse (Holotik) at a psychiatric hospital where an inmate has quite literally taken over the asylum: a female patient masquerading as a doctor and killing folks in a variety of ways. A sort-of *One Slashed Over the Cuckoo's Nest* seen by millions of drive-in patrons thanks to saturation bookings throughout the '70s on the bottom half of innumerable double bills.

DON'T LOOK NOW

★★★☆ Paramount, 1973, R, 110 min.
Dir: Nicolas Roeg. Cast: Julie Christie, Donald Sutherland, Hilary Mason, Clelia Matania, Massimo Serato, Renato Scarpa.

Arty shocker based on the haunting Daphne Du Maurier story about a couple who travel to Venice following the tragic drowning of their young daughter and get caught up in a supernatural mystery involving a blind psychic and a phantom figure in a red plastic raincoat. Infamous at the time of its release for the nude love scene between Christie and Sutherland, this has lots of dreary off-season Venetian mood and a genuinely shocking ending.

DON'T OPEN TILL CHRISTMAS

★ Vestron, 1984, R, 86 min. Dir: Edmund Purdom. Cast: Edmund Purdom, Alan Lake, Belinda Mayne, Gerry Sundquist, Kelly Baker, Caroline Munro.

Tacky yuletide slasher from the makers of *Pieces*—so you know what to expect. A masked nutball, suffering the usual boyhood trauma, stalks and kills anyone he sees dressed as Santa in the London area, with various Clauses getting stabbed, shot, immolated, impaled, and even castrated. Purdom walks through the role of an investigating Scotland Yard man with a guilty secret (his direction is something of a guilty secret as well), while the curvaceous Caroline enlivens things briefly in a musical cameo as herself.

DOOM ASYLUM

★☆ Academy, 1987, UR, 77 min.
Dir: Richard Friedman. Cast: Patty Mullen, Michael Rogen, Ruth Collins, William Hay, Kristin Davis, Harrison White.

There are maybe three laughs maximum in this dopey gore comedy about a horribly disfigured palimony lawyer (I'm not kidding!) terrorizing a group of dunderheads stranded at a long-abandoned hospital and killing everyone but heroine Mullen with various embalming tools. Painfully awful dialogue and shoestring production values made somewhat bearable by some outrageous makeup and the pulchritude of *Penthouse* centerfold Patty.

DOOMWATCH

★★★ Embassy, 1972, PG, 92 min.
Dir: Peter Sasdy. Cast: Ian Bannen, Judy Geeson, George Sanders, Geoffrey Keen.

A solid Brit programmer adapted from a popular TV serial. Scientist Bannen visits a remote island off the coast of England, where radioactivity has transformed some of the locals into acromegalic monsters. A restrained approach to the acting, writing, direction, and makeup helps make this an intriguing minor gem.

DOORMAN, THE

See: *Too Scared to Scream.*

DOOR WITH SEVEN LOCKS, THE

See: *Chamber of Horrors.*

DOOR WITH SEVEN LOCKS, THE

★★☆ Sinister Cinema, 1962, NR, 96 min.
Dir: Alfred Vohrer. Cast: Heinz Drache, Sabina Sesselman, Eddi Arent, Werner Peters, Adi Berber, Klaus Kinski.

Entertaining remake of *Chamber of Horrors* with heiress Sesselman terrorized by weird goings-on at her late uncle's country mansion. One of the better West German Edgar Wallace adaptations, with clever direction and a nimble cast.

DOPPELGANGER: THE EVIL WITHIN

★★ Fox, 1992, R, 105 min.
Dir: Avi Nesher. Cast: Drew Barrymore, George Newborn, Leslie Hope, Dennis Christopher, Sally Kellerman, George Maharis, Dan Shor, Peter Dobson, Luana Anders, Jaid Barrymore.

Barrymore, who's quite appealing here, is either a schizo knife killer out to eliminate her entire family, or is being haunted by a ghostly double doing the murders in this sharp but confusingly structured movie. The main plot is dumb but not bad but this really gets out of hand in an awesomely ridiculous climax where Drew mutates into a pair of gooey mutants. Why? I couldn't tell you, and frankly, I don't think writer-director Nesher could either.

DORIAN GRAY

★☆ Republic, 1970, R, 92 min.
Dir: Massimo Dallamano. Cast: Helmut Berger, Herbert Lom, Richard Todd, Margaret Lee, Marie Liljedahl, Maria Rohm, Isa Miranda, Beryl Cunningham.

Sexed-up remake of Oscar Wilde's *The Picture of Dorian Gray* with Berger as the ageless aristocrat whose portrait ages and corrupts while he indulges in all sorts of decadent shenanigans.

Dumb in that the story seems to be taking place in little more than a year or two, making one wonder less why Dorian stays young and more why everyone else grows old so fast—bad drugs? There's lots of sex (both hetero and homo), nudity (both girl and boy), and only marginal entertainment value. Aka *The Secret of Dorian Gray*.

DORM THAT DRIPPED BLOOD, THE
★ Media, 1981, R, 85 min.
Dirs: Jeffrey Obrow and Stephen Carpenter. Cast: Laurie Lapinski, Stephen Saks, David Snow, Pamela Holland, Dennis Ely, Daphne Zuniga.

Five college students remain behind at their remote university during their winter break to close down an old dorm set for demolition and are stalked by a hooded killer whose modus operandi includes a machete, power drill, pressure cooker, and baseball bat. Dull, unimaginative addition to the slasher cycle, with Zuniga making an inauspicious film debut and a callous, obnoxious "twist" at the end. Aka *Pranks* and *Death Dorm*.

DOUBLE EXPOSURE
★★ Vestron, 1982, R, 94 min.
Dir: William Byron Hillman. Cast: Michael Callan, Joanna Pettet, James Stacy, Pamela Hensley, Cleavon Little, Seymour Cassel, David Young, Misty Rowe.

Photographer Callan keeps dreaming of the deaths of his beautiful models who, as if you didn't already know, start turning up dead in real life. Routine slice-and-dicer with a better-than-average cast but an ugly sexist edge and a surprise climax that owes more than a bit to *Doctor X*.

DWIGHT FRYE
(1899–1943)

This talented, neurotic-looking character actor was one of the great horror supporting performers of the '30s. Best known for his outstanding Renfield in *Dracula* and his bumbling hunchback in *Frankenstein*, he died in obscurity while doing factory war work.

Dracula ('31), *Frankenstein* ('31), *The Vampire Bat* ('33), *Strange Adventure* ('33), *The Invisible Man* ('33), *Bride of Frankenstein* ('35), *The Crime of Dr. Crespi* ('35), *The Ghost of Frankenstein* ('42), *Frankenstein Meets the Wolf Man* ('43), *Dead Men Walk* ('43).

DOUBLE POSSESSION
See: *Blood Couple*.

DRACULA
★★★☆ MCA/Universal, 1931, NR, 74 min.
Dir: Tod Browning. Cast: Bela Lugosi, Helen Chandler, David Manners, Edward Van Sloan, Dwight Frye, Frances Dade.

The original horror classic with Lugosi as the vampire Count who leaves his crumbling Transylvanian abode for the fresh warm blood of London. Little more than a photographed stage play in spots but always worth seeing for Bela's magical performance (his stiffness and unfamiliarity with the English language actually add to the aura of the role); fine support from Chandler, Van Sloan, and particularly Frye ("Rats! Rats!"); Karl Freund's misty photography; and plenty of classically quotable lines. Sequels: *Dracula's Daughter, Son of Dracula, House of Dracula*, etc. Remade more times than I have space to mention.

DRACULA
★★★ MCA/Universal, 1931, NR, 103 min.
Dir: George Melford. Cast: Carlos Villarias, Lupita Tovar, Pablo Alvarez Rubio, Barry Norton.

Filmed at night on the same sets as the Lugosi version, this Spanish-language adaptation is in some ways better, with more fluid direction and scenes of horror and sensuality only hinted at in the Browning movie. Unfortunately, this long-thought-lost and recently rediscovered curiosity runs too long and Villarias totally lacks the charisma of Bela Lugosi, proving once and for all who the movies' definitive Count Dracula *really* is.

DRACULA
See: *Horror of Dracula*.

DRACULA
★★☆ MPI, 1974, NR, 97 min.
Dir: Dan Curtis. Cast: Jack Palance, Simon Ward, Nigel Davenport, Fiona Lewis, Penelope Horner, Pamela Brown.

This Richard Matheson–scripted TV remake made great claims of returning to the spirit of the Bram Stoker novel when first broadcast but mainly emerges as a retread of familiar elements from Curtis' previous vampire pics *House of Dark Shadows* and *The Night Stalker*. Palance as a brooding Count and Lewis as a delicate Lucy are good, but the remainder of the cast is extremely colorless; Curtis' direction is perfunctory but Oswald Morris' lush photography and some well-chosen locations give it a lift. Aka *Bram Stoker's Dracula*.

Bela Lugosi and Helen Chandler neck in Dracula *(1931).*

DRACULA

★★ MCA/Universal, 1979, R, 109 min. Dir: John Badham. Cast: Frank Langella, Laurence Olivier, Donald Pleasence, Kate Nelligan, Trevor Eve, Jan Francis.

Vampires were big in '79, so Universal rushed out this lavish but stultifying big-budget version of the undead classic. Langella—who, like Lugosi, had played the part on Broadway—tries his best as a suavely romantic Dracula and Nelligan is a spirited Lucy, but Olivier is a laugh-riot as a ludicrously ineffectual Van Helsing (where's Peter Cushing when you really need him?) and the W. D. Richter screenplay is riddled with inconsistencies. A good score by John Williams, though.

DRACULA AGAINST FRANKENSTEIN

See: *The Screaming Dead.*

DRACULA AND SON

★☆ Goodtimes, 1975, PG, 78 min. Dir: Edouard Molinaro. Cast: Christopher Lee, Bernard Menez, Marie-Helene Breillat, Catherine Breillat.

There's no excuse for the poor handling this reportedly very funny French comedy (original title: *Dracula, Pere et Fils: Dracula, Father and Son*) received from its U.S. distributor. Hideously dubbed and cut down from 95 minutes, this features Lee (with another's voice) as the Count, who is kicked out of his castle by the communist government and travels to Paris, where he becomes a horror movie star. When his bumbling son (Menez, voiced to sound like Don Adams in "Get Smart") arrives on the scene, he falls for the actress Dad has targeted as his next victim. Tiresome.

DRACULA, FATHER AND SON

See: *Dracula and Son.*

VERONICA CARLSON
(1944–)

The blonde and buxom Veronica was one of Hammer Films' most lovely and talented leading ladies. After impressive performances in both *Dracula Has Risen From the Grave* and *Frankenstein Must Be Destroyed!* she made several other horror and comic films in both England and on the continent before attention to family cut short her career in the mid-1970s.

Dracula Has Risen From the Grave ('68), *Frankenstein Must Be Destroyed!* ('69), *The Horror of Frankenstein* ('70), *Old Dracula* ('74), *The Ghoul* ('75), *Freak Show* ('93).

MICHAEL RIPPER
(1913–)

A familiar face in dozens of Hammer and Amicus films in the '60s and '70s, this wonderful British character actor inhabits his roles, whether comic or sinister, with a true sense of reality. His best roles are the dedicated henchman in *Night Creatures* and the put-upon corporate toady in *The Mummy's Shroud.*

The Revenge of Frankenstein ('58), *The Ugly Duckling* ('59), *The Mummy* ('59), *Brides of Dracula* ('60), *The Curse of the Werewolf* ('61), *Night Creatures* ('61), *The Phantom of the Opera* ('62), *The Curse of the Mummy's Tomb* ('64), *Plague of the Zombies* ('66), *The Reptile* ('66), *The Deadly Bees* ('67), *The Mummy's Shroud* ('67), *Torture Garden* ('68), *Dracula Has Risen From the Grave* ('68), *The Lost Continent* ('68), *Taste the Blood of Dracula* ('70), *Girly* ('70), *Scars of Dracula* ('70), *The Creeping Flesh* ('73), *Legend of the Werewolf* ('75), *The Revenge of Billy the Kid* ('91).

DRACULA HAS RISEN FROM THE GRAVE

★★★ Warner, 1968, G, 92 min. Dir: Freddie Francis. Cast: Christopher Lee, Veronica Carlson, Rupert Davies, Barbara Ewing, Barry Andrews, Michael Ripper.

Solid entry in the Hammer series with Drac (Lee) revived from his icy tomb and fanging buxom Carlson, whose monsignor uncle (Davies) exorcised the Count's castle. Lots of religious symbolism, colorful lighting effects, and a memorable scene of Lee pulling a bloody five-foot wooden stake from his own heart.

DRACULA IS DEAD

See: *The Satanic Rites of Dracula.*

DRACULA IS DEAD·AND WELL AND LIVING IN LONDON

See: *The Satanic Rights of Dracula.*

DRACULA, PRISONER OF FRANKENSTEIN

See: *The Screaming Dead.*

DRACULA RISING

★★ New Horizons, 1993, R, 80 min. Dir: Fred Gallo. Cast: Christopher Atkins, Stacey Travis, Doug Wert, Zahari Vatahov.

Travis is an artist who is hired to restore an old painting of Vlad the Impaler and encoun-

116

"It's my teeth, isn't it?" Christopher Lee asks Veronica Carlson in Dracula Has Risen From the Grave *(1968).*

ters Dracula's son (Atkins) who sees in her the reincarnation of a lost love. Well directed, but the script is a jumble of half-cooked ideas and misplaced homages (to *Kiss of the Vampire, The Raven,* and even *The Silence of the Lambs*), and the casting of *Blue Lagoon* golden boy Atkins is questionable at best—there's even a flashback nude swimming scene as some sort of in-joke. Travis, however, is good and Wert amusing as a Lugosi-accented vampire-monk out to sabotage the Atkins-Travis romance out of homosexual jealousy.

DRACULA'S CASTLE

See: *Blood of Dracula's Castle.*

DRACULA'S DAUGHTER

★★★ MCA/Universal, 1936, NR, 71 min. Dir: Lambert Hillyer. Cast: Gloria Holden, Otto Kruger, Marguerite Churchill, Edward Van Sloan, Irving Pichel, Nan Grey, Gilbert Emery, Hedda Hopper.

Moody, underrated sequel to the Lugosi original with the vampire's gloomy daughter (the waxen-featured Holden) seeking a cure through London psychiatrist Kruger. When this fails she kidnaps his secretary (Churchill) in order to force Kruger into joining her in the world of the undead. Slow but atmospheric and very well acted, with the scene where Holden seduces model Grey (with its obvious lesbian subtext) the standout.

DRACULA'S DOG

★★ United, 1978, R, 88 min. Dir: Albert Band [Alfredo Antonini]. Cast: Michael Pataki, José Ferrer, Reggie Nalder, Jan Shutan, Arlene Martell.

Woof, woof! The Count's favorite pet is revived when a troop of communist soldiers break into the family vault. Then, aided by skull-faced Dracula manservant Nalder, our bloodsucking bowwow heads for California to find the last remaining member of the Dracula clan (Pataki). One of those dumb but fun movies efficiently directed and acted with gusto by a good sleaze movie cast. Aka *Zoltan, Hound of Dracula.*

DRACULA'S GREAT LOVE

★★☆ Sinister Cinema, 1972, R, 83 min. Dir: Javier Aquirre. Cast: Paul Naschy, Haydee Politoff, Rosanna Yanni, Mirta Miller, Ingrid Garbo, Vic Winner.

One of Naschy's most enjoyable efforts, this involves a group of young lovelies stranded at the remote castle of one Dr. Wendell Marlowe (Naschy), a guy in a black cape who's never seen in the daytime and turns out to be . . . well, you know. Though U.S. prints are rather choppy, this is worth seeing for such off-cen-

---

EDWARD VAN SLOAN
(1882–1964)

A Broadway and movie character actor, Van Sloan specialized in all-knowing professor roles in early horror films, most notably as Van Helsing in the original *Dracula,* a role he had earlier perfected on the stage. He was a fine actor whose distinctive voice and bearing brought class to the supporting ranks of many a '30s horror classic.

Dracula ('31), *Frankenstein* ('31), *Behind the Mask* ('32), *The Mummy* ('32), *The Black Room* ('35), *Dracula's Daughter* ('36), *Before I Hang* ('40), *The Monster and the Girl* ('41), *The Mask of Diijon* ('46).

---

ter touches as levitating vampire girls and a lovesick Count who commits suicide by stake. Aka *El Gran Amore del Conde Dracula: Count Dracula's Great Love, Dracula's Virgin Lovers, Vampire Playgirls,* and *Cemetery Girls.*

DRACULA'S LAST RITES

★ MGM/UA, 1980, R, 88 min. Dir: Dominic Paris. Cast: Patricia Lee Hammond, Michael David Lally, Victor Jorge, Gerald Fielding, Mimi Wendall.

Inept, zero-budget vampire fare shot in upstate New York. Lucard, the local mortician, is actually a vampire (and Dracula descendant) who destroys his victims to keep out the competition until one old dame manages to escape the stake and go on a fanged rampage of her own. Poor in every department, with plenty of vampire lore inconsistencies, terrible acting and direction, and the expected *Count Yorga*-esque twist ending. Aka *Last Rites.*

DRACULA'S VIRGIN LOVERS

See: *Dracula's Great Love.*

DRACULA'S WIDOW

★★ HBO, 1988, R, 86 min. Dir: Christopher Coppola. Cast: Sylvia Kristel, Lenny Von Dohlen, Rachel Jones, Josef Sommer, Marc Coppola, Stefan Schnabel.

Despite some stylish flourishes provided by first-time director Coppola (Francis Ford's nephew), this racks up as yet another tired post–*Fright Night* vamp flick. Former *Emmanuele* star Kristel seems haggard as Mrs. D, her coffin shipped to a Hollywood wax museum (though this was actually shot in North Carolina) where she makes the obnoxious young owner (Von Dohlen) her slave. Slick and amusing in spots but too lackluster overall to engender much interest.

DRACULA, THE BLOODLINE CONTINUES

★★ All Seasons, 1972, R, 91 min.
Dir: Leon Klimovsky. Cast: Tina Saenz, Tony Isbert, Helga Line, Cristina Suriani.

This odd Spanish flick (originally *La Saga de los Draculas: Saga of the Draculas*) is half vampire movie, half *Rosemary's Baby* rip-off. Saenz is the Count's pregnant granddaughter, who visits the family castle with unfaithful husband Isbert and is protected from all the vampish goings-on to ensure that her baby is born to carry on the Dracula legacy. This is of marginal interest but veers uneasily between black comedy and straight thrills.

DRACULA VS. FRANKENSTEIN

★★ United American, 1969, PG, 77 min.
Dir: Tulio Demicheli. Cast: Michael Rennie, Karin Dor, Craig Hill, Paul Naschy, Patty Sheppard, Peter Damon, Ella Gessler, Manuel de Blas.

Rennie (with a dubbed voice) is an alien scientist who revives various tatty Earth monsters—werewolf Waldemar Daninsky (Naschy), vampire Count de Meirhoff, the "Franksollen" monster (also Naschy), and the mummy Tao-Tet—as poor man's invasion force. Originally called *El Hombre Que Vino de Ummo: The Man Who Came from Ummo* and aka *Monsters of Terror,* this Spanish flick has been on TV for years as *Assignment Terror* and under any name is an enjoyably cheesy sci-fi variation on *House of Frankenstein.* Unfortunately, this video print is taken from the British theatrical version; it's dark and splicy and missing about nine minutes of footage. In addition, the title is *very* misleading in that the ersatz Dracula and Frankenstein never even encounter each other, let alone battle it out. It's hard to believe that the lovely Dor was in both this and Hitchcock's *Topaz* the same year.

DRACULA VS. FRANKENSTEIN

★★ VidAmerica, 1971, PG, 90 min. Dir: Al Adamson.
Cast: Lon Chaney, Jr., J. Carrol Naish, Russ Tamblyn, Regina Carrol, Anthony Eisley, Jim Davis, Zandor Vorkov, John Bloom, Angelo Rossitto, Greydon Clark, Anne Morrell, Forrest J. Ackerman.

I know this is a bit of a stretch, but this is probably Adamson's most entertaining film. I'm not saying it's *good,* just entertaining. The Count (Vorkov in an incredible non-performance) convinces the wheelchair-bound last descendant of Dr. Frankenstein (a feeble Naish) to revive a lumpy-faced Frankenstein's monster (Bloom) at the doc's secret laboratory beneath a Venice, California, House of Horrors amusement. The Dracula-Frankenstein footage was added at the last minute to a lousy gore movie called *The Blood Seekers,* shot almost two years earlier, which was probably pretty unwatchable without it. *With* these scenes we at least have a *fun* bad movie that was the final bow for both Naish and a cancer-ridden Chaney as "Groton, the Mad Zombie." Aka *The Blood of Frankenstein* and *The Revenge of Dracula.*

DR. BLACK AND MR. WHITE

See: *Dr. Black, Mr. Hyde.*

DR. BLACK, MR. HYDE

★★☆ United, 1976, R, 87 min. Dir: William Crain.
Cast: Bernie Casey, Rosalind Cash, Marie O'Henry, Milt Kogan, Stu Gilliam, Ji-Tu Cumbuka.

This blaxploitation variation on *Dr. Jekyll and Mr. Hyde* is surprisingly watchable, thanks to earnest acting from Casey and Cash. Dr. Henry Pride (Casey) tests his experimental serum for curing liver disease on himself and ends up turning into a homicidal white man—or more exactly, an obvious black man in homicidal white man makeup. Bear with its obvious lapses and you should have fun with this dated but dumbly enjoyable quickie. Aka *The Watts Monster.*

DR. CALIGARI

★★☆ SGE, 1988, R, 80 min. Dir: Stephen Sayadian.
Cast: Madeleine Reynal, Laura Albert, Fox Harris, Jennifer Balgobin, John Durban, David Parry.

Campy, bizarre, experimental sequel to the 1919 classic with Reynal as the granddaughter of you-know-who conducting experiments on her asylum patients with nympho Albert, her favorite subject. Full of freaky, surrealistic touches, this is worth seeing for its visual excesses alone, though its dark comedy and flat acting are somewhat less successful.

DR. CYCLOPS

★★☆ MCA/Universal, 1940, NR, 76 min.
Dir: Ernest B. Schoedsack. Cast: Albert Dekker, Janice Logan, Thomas Coley, Victor Killian, Charles Halton, Frank Yaconelli.

This early Technicolor mad-doctor movie never makes the best of its most interesting components. Bald, myopic Dekker is the jungle madman who uses his incredible shrinking machine to reduce five people to doll size. The tiny quintet, clad in colored handkerchiefs for both modesty *and* Technicolor effect, then attempt to regain their former stature while battling both the crazed Dekker and various jungle horrors—now magnified a thousand-fold. Dekker is good but everyone else is bland at best, and color (the video print is especially vibrant) adds little to the merely standard settings and special effects.

DREAMANIAC

★ Lightning, 1987, UR, 82 min.
Dir: David De Cocteau. Cast: Thomas Bern, Kim McKamy, Sylvia Summers, Lauren Peterson.

Another sorority house is terrorized by another brutal killer, in this case a deadly succubus from hell who crashes a party and offs a bunch of over-aged frat rats and sorority sluts who'll never be missed. Lots of unrated splat but with acting and direction barely up to the standard of Mom and Dad's vacation videos.

DREAM DEMON

★★☆ Warner, 1988, R, 89 min. Dir: Harley Cokliss. Cast: Kathleen Wilhoite, Jemma Redgrave, Timothy Spall, Jimmy Nail, Mark Greenstreet, Susan Fleetwood.

Brit bride-to-be Redgrave (Vanessa's daughter) keeps having bizarre dreams (like knocking off her groom's head at the wedding) soon after moving into an apartment house that turns out to be haunted. Wilhoite is a tough Yank babe whose muddled past is somehow tied up in the haunting. This fairly elegant *Elm Street* variant has some imaginative flourishes and good acting but gets too bogged down in the middle and is too obvious for its own good. The ending, as usual, goes on one scene too long to be effective.

DREAM LOVER

★★ MGM/UA, 1986, R, 104 min. Dir: Alan J. Pakula. Cast: Kristy McNichol, Ben Masters, Paul Shenar, Justin Deas, John McMartin, Gayle Hunnicutt.

McNichol, suffering from recurring nightmares after being assaulted in her New York apartment, visits dream research specialist Masters, whose radical treatment inadvertently transforms her into a potential murderess. Another failed attempt at a big-budget "class" chiller, this lumbering *Nightmare on Elm Street* for the thirtysomething crowd gets by on Kristy's considerable charm alone.

DREAM NO EVIL

★★ Active, 1971, PG, 84 min. Dir: John Hayes. Cast: Brooke Mills, Edmond O'Brien, Marc Lawrence, Michael Pataki, Arthur Franz, D. J. Anderson.

Creepy blending of *Elmer Gantry* with "The Monkey's Paw," with Mills as a girl who works for a traveling preacher and is so obsessed with the dead father (O'Brien) she never knew that she wills him back from the grave—maybe. Fair horror-character study along *Psycho* lines with good work from Mills and O'Brien (in his last film). Aka *Now I Lay Me Down to Die.*

DREAMSCAPE

★★☆ HBO, 1984, PG-13, 95 min. Dir: Joseph Ruben. Cast: Dennis Quaid, Kate Capshaw, Eddie Albert, Christopher Plummer, Max von Sydow, David Patrick Kelly, George Wendt, Cory Yothers.

Psychic Quaid, who has the ability to enter other people's dreams, is pressed into service by the U.S. government to save the president (Albert) from a similarly gifted villain (Kelly) out to assassinate the prez in his apocalyptic nightmares. Likable hybrid of horror, sci-fi, and political intrigue with a fun cast and terrific FX. Just don't think about it too much.

DRESSED FOR DEATH

See: *Straight On Till Morning.*

DRESSED TO KILL

★★★☆ Goodtimes, 1980, R, 105 min.
Dir: Brian De Palma. Cast: Michael Caine, Angie Dickinson, Nancy Allen, Keith Gordon, Dennis Franz, David Margulies.

In this loose remake of *Psycho*, Dickinson is a sexually frustrated New York matron brutally murdered in an elevator by a razor-wielding transsexual somehow involved with Angie's cooly detached psychiatrist Caine. De Palma pays tribute to Hitchcock, Bava, Argento, and even himself and creates here some of his best sequences aided by the hypnotic camerawork of Ralf Bode and lushly romantic music of Pino Donaggio. Caine, Dickinson, and Allen (playing a savvy Wall Street hooker who witnesses the murder) are great, and although most of the plotting is pretty obvious, De Palma's technique is never less than fascinating to watch.

BRIAN DE PALMA
(1940–)

The "modern Hitchcock" started his career making "with-it" semi-underground comedies in the late '60s before embarking on the horror trail with *Sisters*, his first critical and commercial success. For the next decade he concentrated on thrillers, creating a body of work that's the American equivalent of the Italian giallo films of the same period: sleek, glossy shockers that mask their lack of story content behind dollops of style.

Sisters ('73), *Phantom of the Paradise* ('74), *Obsession* ('76), *Carrie* ('76), *The Fury* ('78), *Dressed to Kill* ('80), *Blow-Out* ('81), *Body Double* ('84), *Raising Cain* ('92).

DR. GIGGLES

★☆ MCA/Universal, 1992, R, 94 min.
Dir: Manny Coto. Cast: Larry Drake, Holly Marie
Combs, Cliff De Young, Michelle Johnson, Glenn
Quinn, Nancy Fish.

Drake is a nut case who imagines himself a
doctor and escapes the asylum to terrorize his
old hometown with his handy bag of lethal
medical equipment. Can weak-hearted teen
heroine Combs stop him? Too familiar to be of
much interest, with the usual flip comic asides
and obnoxious teenage characters, but Combs
is pretty, Drake gives it the ol' college try, and
there is one standout scene involving a woman's corpse and a little boy in hiding.

DR. HACKENSTEIN

★☆ Forum, 1988, R, 88 min.
Dir: Richard Clark. Cast: David Muir, Stacey Tracis,
Catherine Davis Cox, Phyllis Diller, Anne Ramsey,
Logan Ramsey.

Glum *Re-Animator* rip about a daffy doc
searching for the right body onto which he can
attach the living decapitated noggin of his
sweetie—beheaded by a propeller during the
sinking of the *Lusitania*. A campy cast (including Ramsey in her last role) is wasted in this
silly trifle; the junk classic *The Brain That
Wouldn't Die* is much funnier and played its
similar storyline totally straight!

DR. HECKYL AND MR. HYPE

★★☆ Paragon, 1980, R, 98 min.
Dir: Charles B. Griffith. Cast: Oliver Reed, Sunny
Johnson, Maia Danziger, Virgil Frye, Mel Welles,
Jackie Coogan, Corinne Calvet, Dick Miller.

Reed is very funny in this off-the-wall *Dr.
Jekyll and Mr. Hyde* spoof (with apologies to
Robert Louis Stevenson) about a hideously
ugly podiatrist—he looks like Frederic
March's Mr. Hyde with a bad skin problem—
who overdoses on a miracle diet cure in a
botched suicide attempt and ends up transforming into a handsome lady killer—literally.
Strained at times but with moments approach-
ing the hilarity of writer-director Griffith's *Little Shop of Horrors* screenplay and the usual
effortless scene-stealing from Welles and
Miller.

DRIFTER, THE

★★ MGM/UA, 1989, R, 88 min.
Dir: Larry Brand. Cast: Kim Delaney, Miles O'Keeffe,
Timothy Bottoms, Al Shannon.

Delaney picks up hunky hitchhiker O'Keeffe
and after a one-night stand at a motel can't get
rid of him. But is it really he who subsequently terrorizes her? A minor-league *Fatal Attrac-*
tion–type thriller with a few effective twists
and characters who, if not entirely sympathetic, at least act like semi-believable human
beings, unlike in others of its ilk.

DRILLER KILLER, THE

★ Magnum, 1979, R, 88 min.
Dir: Abel Ferrara. Cast: Jimmy Laine [Abel Ferrara],
Carolyn Marz, Baybi Day, Harry Schultz, Rhodney
Montreal, Richard Howorth.

Cheapo Manhattan-shot vanity production
about a moody SoHo artist murdering street
people with a cordless Black & Decker.
Humorless and annoying, with minimalistic
production values and laughable attempts at
deep psychological meaning that would give
Dr. Joyce Brothers pause. Ferrara does far better in later films; this one is not even all that
gory.

DRIVE-IN MASSACRE

★ Magnum, 1976, R, 78 min.
Dir: Stuart Segall. Cast: Jake Barnes, Adam Lawrence,
Douglas Gudbye, Valdesta.

Early slasher effort about a madman on the
loose at a rural drive-in playing a spaghetti
western. Fairly short and certainly bloody
enough, but amateurish acting and direction
get on your nerves. Complete with dumb
twist ending that doubtlessly worked far
better in an actual drive-in theatre.

DR. JEKYLL AND MR. HYDE

★★★ Goodtimes, 1920, NR, 63 min.
Dir: John S. Robertson. Cast: John Barrymore, Martha
Mansfield, Nita Naldi, Brandon Hurst, Charles Lane,
Louis Wolheim.

The best and best known of about a dozen
silent versions of the Robert Louis Stevenson
classic with Barrymore distorting his famous
profile into the hideous, spider-like visage of
Mr. Hyde. A production of great historical
import, this is one of the oldest American-
made horror films still readily available for
viewing and was the first version of the story
to introduce the now standard subplot of two
women to mirror the different aspects of the
Jekyll/Hyde personality. Dated but worth seeing for Barrymore at the height of his thespic
powers.

DR. JEKYLL AND MR. HYDE

★★★ MGM/UA, 1931, NR, 95 min.
Dir: Rouben Mamoulian. Cast: Frederic March,
Miriam Hopkins, Rose Hobart, Holmes Herbert,
Halliwell Hobbes, Edgar Norton.

March won an Oscar for his double turn as the
handsome, boyish Jekyll and the bestial, ape-

like Hyde, in this case not an extension of Jekyll's evil nature but a personification of his primitive, impulsive side. Using his camera with flair and imagination, director Mamoulian draws us directly into the troubled mind of Jekyll to create a surprisingly three-dimensional character, though the scenes with fiancee Hobart are maudlin enough to induce vomiting. Heavily cut and then unseen for years, this video edition restores most of the missing footage but tends toward choppiness.

DR. JEKYLL AND MR. HYDE
★★★☆ MGM/UA, NR, 113 min.
Dir: Victor Fleming. Cast: Spencer Tracy, Ingrid Bergman, Lana Turner, Donald Crisp, Ian Hunter, Barton MacLane, C. Aubrey Smith, Sara Allgood.

My favorite version of the oft-told tale, this highlights psycho chills over more overt monster thrills and is all the better for it. Spence hated doing this but he's really real good, especially as the leering, husky-voiced Hyde, but this is really Ingrid's film all the way, as she turns what could have been just another pathetic victim role into a genuinely sad, tragic figure. Joseph Ruttenberg's luminous B&W photography is breathtaking, but avoid the hideous colorized version.

DR. JEKYLL AND MR. HYDE
★★☆ SVS, 1973, NR, 72 min.
Dir: David Winters. Cast: Kirk Douglas, Susan Hampshire, Michael Redgrave, Donald Pleasence, Susan George, Stanley Holloway.

Usually forgotten, this TV *musical* remake of the '41 version has Kirk and a vigorous British supporting cast attacking both songs (some of them quite good) and melodrama with equal élan. Hampered by unimaginative presentation but still a treat.

DR. JEKYLL AND SISTER HYDE
★★★ Republic, 1971, PG, 94 min. Dir: Roy Ward Baker. Cast: Ralph Bates, Martine Beswick, Gerald Sim, Lewis Fiander, Susan Broderick, Dorothy Alison.

Dr. Jekyll's (Bates) experiments in increasing human longevity result in his taking a formula derived from female hormones and transforming into seductive but sinister Sister Hyde (Beswick). Sounds dumb, but a taut Brian Clemens script, atmospheric Baker direction, and fine performances (Bates and Beswick really do resemble each other, adding to the effect) make this one of Hammer Films' most fun later efforts.

DR. JEKYLL AND THE WEREWOLF
See: *Dr. Jekyll and the Wolf Man.*

DR. JEKYLL AND THE WOLF MAN
★★☆ Sinister Cinema, 1971, R, 85 min.
Dir: Leon Klimovsky. Cast: Paul Naschy, Shirley Corrigan, Jack Taylor, Mirta Miller.

Another Naschy werewolf opus: Waldemar saves a young bride from the villains who killed her new husband, and she repays him by taking him to London to meet the grandson of the original Dr. Jekyll, in the hope that he can cure the werewolf condition. Instead, our hero ends up turning into some weird wolfman–Mr. Hyde hybrid. Contrived, to state the obvious, but with nudity and gore galore and a great transformation scene in a stalled elevator. Aka *Dr. Jekyll and the Werewolf.*

DR. JEKYLL'S DUNGEON OF DEATH
★ Wizard, 1978, R, 88 min. Dir: James Wood. Cast: James Mathers, John Kearney, Dawn Carver Kelly, Tom Nicholson.

This stupid movie is an insult to the good name of Dr. Jekyll—not to mention Mr. Hyde. Another grandson of the original doc sets up shop in '50s San Francisco where he develops a mind-control drug he uses to create kung-fu fightin' slaves. Boring in the extreme, this unworkable combo of R. L. Stevenson and Chuck Norris isn't even good for laughs.

DR. MANIAC
See: *The Man Who Lived Again.*

DROPS OF BLOOD
See: *Mill of the Stone Women.*

MARTINE BESWICK
(1941–)

The tigerish Martine first gained attention in the James Bond flicks *From Russia With Love* and *Thunderball* and was thereafter cast by Hammer Films as a second lead in their highly popular *One Million Years B.C.* The feisty Jamaica-born actress then took leading roles in *Prehistoric Women* and *Dr. Jekyll and Sister Hyde,* but her strength and aggressiveness made her difficult to cast, leading, sadly, to several years of acting inactivity.

One Million Years B.C. ('66), *Prehistoric Women* ('67), *The Penthouse* ('67), *Dr. Jekyll and Sister Hyde* ('72), *Seizure* ('74), *Devil Dog: The Hound of Hell* ('78), *The Offspring* ('87), *Evil Spirits* ('91), *Critters 4* (voice only, '92).

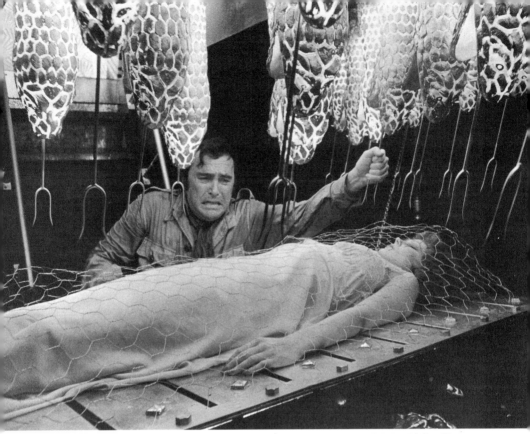

Robert Quarry rescues Fiona Lewis from a malfunctioning game of "Mousetrap" in Dr. Phibes Rises Again! *(1972).*

DR. ORLOFF'S MONSTER
★★ Sinister Cinema, 1964, NR, 88 min.
Dir: Jess [Jesus] Franco. Cast: Agnes Spaak, Hugo Blanco, Perla Cristal, Marcelo Arriota-Jauregui.

Fair sequel to Franco's *The Awful Dr. Orlof* with Arriota-Jauregui as the mad doc who transforms his brother (Blanco) into a "scientific zombie" after discovering that he is having an affair with Orloff's wife (Cristal). Spaak is Blanco's daughter, who comes for a visit and finds Papa acting a bit strange. Routine. Aka *El Secreto del Dr. Orloff: The Secret of Dr. Orloff.*

DR. PHIBES RISES AGAIN!
★★★ Orion, 1972, PG, 88 min. Dir: Robert Fuest. Cast: Vincent Price, Robert Quarry, Valli Kemp, Fiona Lewis, Peter Cushing, Beryl Reid, Terry-Thomas, Hugh Griffith, Peter Jeffrey, Caroline Munro.

Terrific sequel to *The Abominable Dr. Phibes* with Price at his tongue-in-cheek best. Phibes takes his well-preserved wife (Munro) to Egypt in order to revive her with a sail down the legendary River of Life. When he comes upon an archeological expedition (led by Quarry) with similar designs, Phibes goes to hilariously hideous lengths to stop them. Full of beautiful art deco atmosphere, clever killings, and inane, Noel Coward-ish dialogue, this is almost as much fun as its predecessor. Soundtrack note: about 30 seconds of Price and Kemp dancing to "Dancing in the Dark" and Vinnie warbling "Over the Rainbow" during the end credits have been excised due to copyright entanglements.

DR. STRANGE
★★☆ MCA/Universal, 1978, NR, 96 min.
Dir: Phil DeGuere. Cast: Peter Hooten, Jessica Walter, John Mills, Eddie Benton, Clyde Kusatu, Philip Sterling.

Hooten is Dr. Stephen Strange: a surgeon with supernatural abilities who is tutored by mentor Mills (in a delightful performance) to battle evil witch Walter (pulling out all the stops). Entertaining TV movie based on the Stan Lee comic-book character, with surprisingly elaborate set design and special effects and Hooten quite likable as the titular doc. Another unsold series pilot.

Peter Cushing deals death for Christopher Lee in Dr. Terror's House of Horrors *(1965).*

DR. TARR'S TORTURE DUNGEON

★★ Magnum, 1972, R, 88 min.
Dir: John L. [Jose Lopez] Moctezuma. Cast: Claudio Brook, Arturo Hansel, Ellen Sherman, Martin Lasalle.

Minor Mexican version of Poe's "The System of Dr. Tarr and Professor Feather" about a reporter (Hansel) who visits an asylum where one of the inmates (Brook) is passing himself off as a doctor and allowing the other patients to live out their most bizarre fantasies. You've seen worse. Aka *La Mansion de la Kocura: House of Madness.*

DR. TERROR'S HOUSE OF HORRORS

★★★ Republic, 1965, NR, 97 min.
Dir: Freddie Francis. Cast: Peter Cushing, Christopher Lee, Donald Sutherland, Roy Castle, Jennifer Jayne, Michael Gough, Ann Bell, Neil McCallum, Max Adrian, Ursula Howells, Bernard Lee, Katy Wild.

The first and one of the best anthologies from Britain's Amicus Productions, headlined by Cushing as tarot card-reading Dr. Schreck whose stacked deck spells doom for five train travelers. An architect runs afoul of a female werewolf; a family is menaced by a murderous vine; a jazz musician falls prey to a voodoo curse; an acidic art critic is terrorized by a crawling dismembered hand; and a doctor marries a beautiful vampiress. Francis' strong visual direction coupled with producer Milton Subotsky's derivative but fun script (the werewolf and hand segments are best) help make this an entertaining omnibus.

DUEL
★★★☆ MCA/Universal, 1971, PG, 88 min. Dir: Steven Spielberg. Cast: Dennis Weaver, Jacqueline Scott, Tim Herbert, Eddie Firestone, Lucille Benson, Lou Frizzell.

A salesman driving along a lonely stretch of California highway is menaced by a huge diesel truck driven by an apparent madman who's never seen and seems intent on killing him. It's amazing how much suspense Spielberg was able to wring out of such a simple premise, with the truck becoming one of the best movie "monsters" ever. Tight scripting by Richard Matheson, from his short story, and an excellent performance from Weaver help make this one of the best made-for-TV horror films. Originally broadcast at 73 minutes, 15 additional minutes (and the characters played by Scott and Frizzell) were added for foreign theatrical release and are included in the tape and TV syndication version.

DUEL OF THE SPACE MONSTERS
See: Frankenstein Meets the Space Monster.

DUNGEON OF HARROW
★ Sinister Cinema, 1962, NR, 74 min. Dir: Pat Boyett. Cast: Russ Harvey, Helen Hogan, William McNulty, Maurice Harris, Michele Boyett, Eunice Grey.

Claustrophobic Texas-shot rip-off of Roger Corman's Poe series about a pair of shipwreck survivors who stumble into the weird island household of the cruel Count DeSade. There's a stern nurse, huge black manservant, tongueless maid, and crazed, leperous countess kept locked in the dungeon. From its opening scene of a storm-tossed ship (simulated by shaking the camera while the actors stumble about) to its "ironic" twist ending, this cardboard curio is a wonder to behold—but behold it at a distance, please. Aka Dungeon of Horror.

DUNGEON OF HORROR
See: Dungeon of Harrow.

DUNGEON OF TERROR
★ Magnum, 1971, R, 95 min. Dir: Jean Rollin. Cast: Marie-Pierre Castel, Mireille Dargent, Philippe Gaste, Louise Dhour.

Two teen girls run away from an orphanage and end up in a castle dominated by a vampire count and his lesbian followers. The only one of French director Rollin's soft-core sex-horror films available on video, this is standard early '70s Euro-horror junk, arty and dumb and with an especially sexist outlook in its treatment of its female characters. Aka Requiem pour un Vampire: Requiem for a Vampire, Caged Virgins, Crazed Vampires, and Virgins and Vampires.

DUNWICH HORROR, THE
★★☆ Embassy, 1970, PG, 87 min. Dir: Daniel Haller. Cast: Sandra Dee, Dean Stockwell, Ed Begley, Sam Jaffe, Lloyd Bochner, Donna Baccala, Joanna Moore Jordan, Talia Shire.

Obviously made with the success of Rosemary's Baby in mind, this solid AIP adaptation of one of H. P. Lovecraft's best stories has a wild-eyed Stockwell (replacing Peter Fonda, who passed on this one for Easy Rider) using the Necromonicon and Dee's perenially virginal body to open a gateway to the dreaded "Old Ones." Fairly taut until a rather silly ending, with good acting from Dee and Begley and a memorable score by Les Baxter.

DUST DEVIL
★★★ Paramount, 1992, R, 87 min. Dir: Richard Stanley. Cast: Chelsea Field, Robert Burke, Zakes Mokae, Marianne Sagebrecht.

This serious South African horror movie was badly cut—from 125 minutes—for its negligible U.S. release, but even in this badly butchered state is worth noting. Field is a runaway housewife who keeps encountering demonic serial killer Burke. Visually imaginative, this actually gains from its heavy editing, which only enhances its disjointed, dream-like quality. A first-rate follow-up to Stanley's debut feature, Hardware.

DYING TRUTH
★★☆ Cornerstone, 1984, NR, 74 min. Dir: John Hough. Cast: David Carradine, Stephanie Beacham, Stephen Greif, Stephen Chase, Lesley Dunlop.

Carradine is a wrongly convicted murderer on his deathbed who wills himself back 10 years to the scene of the crime: a bleak seaside town where his married lover (Beacham) was pushed to her death over a cliff. Can he discover the true killer or, better yet, prevent his beloved's demise? Originally titled A Distant Scream, this Hammer tele-chiller is contrived but suspenseful, often playing like a macabre variation on Somewhere in Time.

EARTH VS. THE SPIDER
★★ RCA/Columbia, 1958, NR, 72 min.
Dir: Bert I. Gordon. Cast: Ed Kemmer, June Kenney, Gene Perrson, Sally Fraser, Gene Roth, Troy Patterson.

A small mountain community is menaced by a really big arachnid in this okay rip-off of Jack Arnold's *Tarantula*. Wobbly special effects share screen time with the most mature-looking bunch of high schoolers you've ever seen, a couple of good scares, and a cameo by the first issue of "Famous Monsters of Filmland." Aka *The Spider*.

EASTER SUNDAY
See: *The Being*.

EAST SIDE KIDS MEET BELA LUGOSI, THE
See: *Ghosts on the Loose*.

EATEN ALIVE
★★☆ Prism, 1976, R, 89 min.
Dir: Tobe Hooper. Cast: Neville Brand, Mel Ferrer, Stuart Whitman, Carolyn Jones, Marilyn Burns, William Finley, Crystin Sinclaire, Kyle Richards, Robert Englund, Roberta Collins.

The ever-loony Brand is the owner of a run-down old motel who feeds visitors to the pet crocodile he keeps penned in the swamp next door. Hooper's first post–*Texas Chainsaw Massacre* effort, this has lots of stylized lighting and a truly offbeat cast—everyone from Morticia Addams to Freddy Krueger—but has trouble mixing its good ol' boy humor with horror and lacks the pounding ferocity of *Chainsaw Massacre*. Filmed as *Death Trap* and aka *Starlight Slaughter, Horror Hotel Massacre,* and *Legend of the Bayou*.

EATING RAOUL
★★★ CBS/Fox, 1982, R, 83 min.
Dir: Paul Bartel. Cast: Paul Bartel, Mary Woronov, Robert Beltran, Buck Henry, Susan Saiger, Ed Begley, Jr., Hamilton Camp, Edie McClurg.

Uproarious black comedy about the Blands (Bartel and Woronov), a super-straight couple who decide to finance their dream restaurant (Chez Bland) by robbing and murdering the obnoxious swingers living in their apartment complex. When they run out of victims, they begin to advertise. Doesn't sustain itself all the way through but still is good, dirty fun with a marvelous cast.

EBIRAH, HORROR OF THE DEEP
See: *Godzilla vs. The Sea Monster*.

ECHOES
★★ VidAmerica, 1982, R, 89 min.
Dir: Arthur Alan Seidelman. Cast: Richard Alfieri, Nathalie Nell, Ruth Roman, Gale Sondergaard, Mercedes McCambridge, Mike Kellin.

Fair low-budget thriller about an artist (Alfieri) who begins having nightmares about his dead twin brother in which the twin kills him—but are they really dreams or perhaps something more? A strong supporting cast makes up for the colorless leads and unsure direction.

ECOLOGY OF CRIME, THE
See: *Bay of Blood*.

EDGE OF HELL, THE
See: *Rock 'n' Roll Nightmare*.

EDGE OF SANITY
★★ SVS, 1989, UR, 86 min. Dir: Gerard Kirkoine. Cast: Anthony Perkins, Glynis Barber, Sarah Maur-Thorp, David Lodge, Ben Cole, Jill Medford.

Perkins cuts a thick slice of ham in this bizarre *Dr. Jekyll and Mr. Hyde* variant shot in Budapest. The good doc performs the usual experiments, discovers what appears to be cocaine, and transforms into a demented-looking Moe Howard lookalike (and snazzy dresser) who begins slashing up prostitutes and becomes known as Jack the Ripper. Some stylish moments, good set design, and plenty of unintended laughs. Also out in a cut R version.

EDWARD SCISSORHANDS
★★★ CBS/Fox, 1990, PG, 98 min. Dir: Tim Burton. Cast: Johnny Depp, Winona Ryder, Dianne Weist, Anthony Michael Hall, Alan Arkin, Vincent Price.

Price is an aged inventor who creates Edward (Depp), a scarred, sad-looking young man clad in black leather with spiky hair and huge scissors for hands. When Price dies before he can replace Edward's hands with real ones, the lonely creation is taken in by a friendly Avon lady (Weist) whose daughter (Ryder) is at first repulsed by Edward but eventually comes to care for him. An odd, to put it mildly, modern fairy tale with touches of horror, social comment, and romance, this is another of Burton's patented weird takes on modern life, with touching performances from Depp, Weist, and the grandiloquent Price.

EEAGH!
★ Rhino, 1962, NR, 92 min.
Dir: Nicholas Merriwether [Arch Hall, Sr.].
Cast: Arch Hall Jr., Marilyn Manning, Richard Kiel, William Waters [Arch Hall, Sr.].

This micro-budgeted wonder richly deserves its reputation as a genuine laughingstock in the monster-on-the-loose genre. A tall cave man (Kiel in a shaggy wig and loin cloth) falls in love with a pretty, bubble-brained heiress who happens by his desert cave and carries her off, but she is rescued by her boyfriend and father. The monster then follows them home to Palm Springs, where he invades a pool party, terrifies several, and is tragically shot down by the police. Acted with cue-card precision by a god-awful cast (the singing hero, son of the producer-director, looks about 14 years old) and burdened with several endless musical numbers, this one has to be seen to be believed. And even then. . .

EERIE MIDNIGHT HORROR SHOW, THE
★ Continental, 1974, R, 86 min.
Dir: Mario Gariazzo. Cast: Stella Carnacina, Chris Avram, Lucretia Love, Luigi Pistilli.

Another junky Italian *Exorcist* spin-off, this time with Carnacina as a young artist possessed by an evil spirit previously imprisoned in a statue depicting one of the thieves crucified at Calvary. Features all the usual drek (highlighted by a scene where Stella imagines herself crucified). Aka *The Tormented* and *The Sexorcist*.

ELEPHANT MAN, THE
★★★☆ CBS/Fox, 1980, PG, 123 min.
Dir: David Lynch. Cast: Anthony Hopkins, John Hurt, Anne Bancroft, John Gielgud, Wendy Hiller, Freddie Jones, Hannah Gordon, Helen Ryan.

Hauntingly photographed (by Freddie Francis) film version (with no relation to the stage play of the same name) of the famous true story of John Merrick (Hurt), a hideously deformed sideshow freak in Victorian London whose lost humanity is restored by compassionate surgeon Sir Frederick Treves (Hopkins). Hurt and Hopkins are extraordinary as the dignified but grotesque Merrick (great makeup by Christopher Tucker) and the selfless Treves, while many scenes are positively overwhelming in their emotional impact. Still Lynch's best film.

ELIMINATOR, THE
See: *Deadly Games.*

ELVES
★☆ AIP, 1989, R, 96 min.
Dir: Jeff Mandel. Cast: Dan Haggerty, Julie Austin, Deanna Lund, Borah Silver, Mansell Rivers-Bland, Christopher Graham.

Another useless *Gremlins* clone, this one outfitted with an especially unlikely plot about a Nazi scheme to create a Fourth Reich by mating one of the title creatures with teen heroine Austin. Former "Grizzly Adams" star Haggerty is pretty grisly as a drunken department store Santa who tries to save her. Only value here is discovering what lengths former "Land of the Giants" chick Lund will go to land a job.

ELVIRA, MISTRESS OF THE DARK
★★☆ Starmaker, 1988, PG-13, 96 min.
Dir: James Signorelli. Cast: Cassandra Peterson, W. Morgan Sheppard, Daniel Greene, Edie McClurg, Susan Kellerman, Jeff Conaway.

Don't expect much and you may enjoy this horror-comedy featuring the popular TV vixen. Elvira (Peterson) inherits an old New England mansion and a book of supernatural spells from her late aunt, eventually battling both her closed-minded new neighbors and warlock uncle Sheppard, who's after the book. This has more bust jokes per minute than any feature since Jayne Mansfield died but Peterson's pleasing persona and an air of genial amiability make it fun.

EMBRYO
★★ IVE, 1976, R, 104 min. Dir: Ralph Nelson.
Cast: Rock Hudson, Barbara Carrera, Diane Ladd, Roddy McDowall, Anne Schedeen, John Elrich, Jack Colvin, Dr. Joyce Brothers.

This little-remembered camp classic features the Rock in a rare horror film performance as a doctor who develops a way to speed up the growth of a human fetus, creating a beautiful femme Frankenstein (Carrera) from the embryo taken from a suicide victim. Unfortunately, only the fluid from a living fetus keeps Barb from aging into a hideous old hag. Ridiculously earnest, this plays like a TV movie with gore and nudity added. The ending—with a grotesquely withered Carrera giving birth to a mad, babbling Hudson's baby—reaches new heights of tastelessness for a mainstream movie. Retitled *Created to Kill.*

EMPIRE OF THE ANTS
★★ Goodtimes, 1977, PG, 89 min.
Dir: Bert I. Gordon. Cast: Joan Collins, Robert

Lansing, John David Carson, Albert Salmi, Jacqueline Scott, Pamela Shoop, Robert Pine, Brooke Palance.

It's hard to believe that H. G. Wells could have written a novel about a phony real estate development where suckers lured there by the crooked owners are eaten alive by giant irradiated ants—but then, this is a Bert I. Gordon movie! Chinzy special FX rub shoulders with uncomfortable-looking actors mouthing ridiculous dialogue ("I wish I hadn't seen Charlie die like that!" a mud-spattered Collins moans at one point). Better than Gordon's previous Wells farrago, *Food of the Gods*, but not by much.

ENDANGERED SPECIES
★★☆ MGM/UA, 1982, R, 97 min.
Dir: Alan Rudolph. Cast: Robert Urich, JoBeth Williams, Paul Dooley, Hoyt Axton, Peter Coyote, Marin Kanter, Dan Hedaya, Heather Menzies.

Overlooked when first released, this neat combination of political conspiracy thriller and horror film has a rather miscast Urich as a hardened NYC cop investigating a bizarre series of cattle mutilations and grisly murders in a small western town. Were they caused by UFOs? Witchcraft? The Russians? A government cover-up? We never find out. Good work from Williams, cast against type as the town sheriff, but kinda hard to follow. Still, it's worth a look. "Vegas" groupie alert: Urich has an almost full-frontal shower scene about halfway through.

ENDLESS DESCENT
★☆ LIVE, 1989, R, 79 min.
Dir: Juan Piquer Simon. Cast: Jack Scalia, Deborah Adair, Ray Wise, R. Lee Ermey, Ely Pouget, Edmond Purdom.

The search for a lost experimental submarine along the ocean floor leads to an encounter with mutant sea monsters. Another *Deep Star Six/Leviathan* undersea *Alien* spin-off with an interesting cast but cut-rate production values and special effects. Shooting title was *The Rift*.

ENTITY, THE
★★☆ Fox, 1982, R, 125 min.
Dir: Sidney J. Furie. Cast: Barbara Hershey, Ron Silver, Jacqueline Brookes, David Labiosa, George Coe, Alex Rocco, Margaret Blye, Natasha Ryan.

Hershey's gripping performance highlights this well-made, if exploitive, adaptation of Frank De Felitta's novel (supposedly based on a true case) about a young single mother who is repeatedly raped and abused by the invisible force that has begun to haunt her home. Way too long, it loses itself in the second half

in an endless debate between psychiatrist Silver (who thinks Barb is going nuts) and a team of investigating parapsychologists. Worth seeing for Hershey and a handful of interesting FX.

EPITAPH
★ City Lights, 1987, UR, 94 min.
Dir: Joseph Merhi. Cast: Natasha Pavlova, Delores Nascar, Jim Williams, Flint Keller, Linda Tucker-Smith, Liz Kane.

Crummy gore drama about a deranged housewife who commits a series of murders covered up by her loving husband and estranged teen daughter. A really lame and pointless *I Spit on Your Grave* clone with a few graphic effects (like a rat chewing its way through a woman's stomach) to punch up a super-dull narrative.

EQUINOX
★★☆ Wizard, 1969, PG, 80 min.
Dirs: Jack Woods, Mark Thomas McGee. Cast: Edward Connell, Barbara Hewitt, Frank Bonner, Robin Christopher, Fritz Leiber, Jack Woods.

An $8,000 student film that distributor Jack H. Harris picked up for a song, augmented with some new footage shot by Woods and released theatrically in 1970, this concerns four collegians searching for a missing professor (Leiber) and encountering the devil (Woods) and several monsters from another dimension. Amateurish acting and dialogue aside, there are some great effects animation from Jim Danforth and Dave Allen and a fairly imaginative storyline. Co-star Bonner (billed here as Frank Boers, Jr.) later became one of the stars of "WKRP in Cincinnati." Aka *The Beast*.

ERASERHEAD
★★★ RCA/Columbia, 1977, UR, 90 min.
Dir: David Lynch. Cast: Jack Nance, Charlotte Stewart, Allen Josephs, Jeanne Bates, Judith Anna Roberts, Laurel Near.

An almost indescribable filmed nightmare blending horror and dark comedy in its "story"—and I use the term loosely—about a weird retarded couple and their mutant baby. The movie the expression "an acquired taste" was invented for, this is just full to brimming with bizarre images and concepts, creepy characters, and some of the most guaranteed-to-offend scenes this side of John Waters.

ESCAPES
★☆ Prism, 1986, PG, 70 min.
Dir: David Steensman. Cast: Vincent Price, John Mitchum, Shirley O'Key, Todd Fulton, Michael Patton-Hall, Jerry Grisham.

Dull collection of horror and fantasy vignettes introduced by Price. A fisherman becomes the catch; an obnoxious deliveryman becomes trapped in a weird little town; a jogger is stalked by ape-like creatures; an old lady encounters a UFO; a cruel mugger gets his supernatural comeuppance; and a boy watching this video gets caught up in the action. Barely interesting, with stories that would have been rejected by "Tales From the Darkside," cheap technical credits, and Vinnie the P strictly along for the ride.

ESTATE OF INSANITY
★★ VCL, 1964, NR, 88 min.
Dir: Robert Hartford-Davis. Cast: Heather Sears, John Turner, Ann Lynn, Peter Arne, Raymond Huntley, Patrick Troughton, Francis de Wolff, Edina Ronay.

Originally released as *The Black Torment,* this weak Brit gothic chiller wastes a talented cast on a tepid storyline about a young bride (Sears) frightened by bizarre happenings on her husband's estate. Includes all the usual dark-old-house atmospherics, several gratuitous stalker murders, a poor score, and a wholly unconvincing trick ending.

ETERNAL EVIL
★★ Lightning, 1985, R, 85 min.
Dir: George Milhalka. Cast: Karen Black, Winston Reckert, Andrew Bednarsky, Patty Talbot, John Novak, Lois Maxwell.

Confusing psychic thriller about an astral-projecting TV commercial director (Reckert) who may or may not be committing murders while under the influence of a witch (Black) who may or may not be possessed. Got that? This shows some surprising flashes of visual imagination but soon collapses under the weight of its pretensions, not to mention a mean misogynistic streak not quite made up for by the fact that hero Reckert is utterly unsympathetic while sexy villainess Black always engages our emotions. Filmed as *The Blue Man.*

EVICTORS, THE
★★ Vestron, 1979, R, 88 min.
Dir: Charles B. Pierce. Cast: Vic Morrow, Michael Parks, Jessica Harper, Sue Ane Langdon, Dennis Fimple, Bill Thurman.

A couple buy a house in a small Louisiana town and soon strange and mysterious events occur. Is the house haunted or is someone trying to drive them out? A good cast does what it can but the story's "surprises" are pretty obvious, negating the intended suspense, though at least one aspect of the ending provides an unexpected jolt.

EVIL, THE
★★☆ Embassy, 1978, R, 88 min. Dir: Gus Trikonis. Cast: Richard Crenna, Joanna Pettet, Victor Buono, Andrew Prine, Lynne Moody, Cassie Yates, Mary Louise Weller, George O'Hanlon, Jr.

A good, though minor, ghost story told with surprising intensity and attention to detail. An ancient mansion with a violent, mysterious history is being remodeled into a drug rehabilitation center by psychologist Crenna when a strange trap door in the cellar is opened and the house is supernaturally sealed off, trapping eight people within. One by one they're eliminated by the devil (Buono), who lives in a misty netherworld beneath the house. Good acting and some effective humorous touches make this an enjoyable haunted house tale.

EVIL ALTAR
★ Southgate, 1989, R, 90 min. Dir: Jim Winburn. Cast: Robert Z'Dar, Teresa Cooney, John Powers, Tal Armstrong.

Beefcake bad guy Z'Dar plays a sinister satanist in this direct-to-video yawn fest. The usual rituals, murders, and vacuous victims. Don't bother.

EVIL CLUTCH
★★ Rhino, 1988, NR, 84 min. Dir: Andreas Marfori. Cast: Coralina Cataldi Tessoni, Diego Riba, Elena Cantarone, Luciano Crovato, Stefano Molinari.

Lost in the woods, a young couple encounter an evil scientist, a walking corpse, and a beauty with a claw-mouthed, castrating vagina (!!!) in this energetic Italian low-budgeter. Originally titled *Notte nel Bosco: Night in the Woods,* this is nothing if not weird, but it has so much going for it in the way of photography and FX you can't help getting caught up in its weirdness. Not recommended for those who like their movies to be believable.

EVIL DEAD, THE
★★★☆ HBO, 1982, UR, 85 min.
Dir: Sam Raimi. Cast: Bruce Campbell, Ellen Sandweiss, Hal Delrich, Betsy Baker, Sarah York.

Filmed on a shoestring as *Book of the Dead* by a group of energetic young Detroit filmmakers, this high-spirited splatter classic tells of five college students whose weekend at a remote Tennessee mountain cabin is disrupted by an ancient Sumerian demon who possesses the group and transforms them one by one into disfigured zombies. Rough-edged but appealing performances and ridiculously exaggerated gore FX give this the pulpy feel of a horror comic book, and there's some especially invig-

BRUCE CAMPBELL
(1960–)

The handsome Mr. Campbell became a cult star thanks to his bumbling heroics in the *Evil Dead* movies. A first-rate physical comedian, Bruce continues to impress in a whole slew of well-acted low-budget horrors.

The Evil Dead ('83), *Evil Dead II* ('87), *Maniac Cop* ('88), *Moontrap* ('88), *Intruder* ('89), *Darkman* (cameo, '90), *Sundown: The Vampire in Retreat* ('90), *Maniac Cop 2* ('91), *Waxwork II: Lost in Time* ('92), *Lunatics* ('92), *Army of Darkness* ('93), *The Man With the Screaming Brain* (also director, '94).

orating camerawork. Sequels: *Evil Dead II: Dead by Dawn* and *Army of Darkness*.

EVIL DEAD II: DEAD BY DAWN
★★★ Vestron, 1987, R, 84 min. Dir: Sam Raimi. Cast: Bruce Campbell, Sarah Berry, Dan Hicks, Cassie Wesley, Denise Bixler, Richard Domeier.

More amusing than scary, this slicker sequel starts off as a mini-remake (dropping several characters along the way) before continuing Campbell's serio-comic battle with the living dead. Really overreaches itself at times but is such an inspired blend of gross violence and Three Stooges–like humor that it's hard to get mad at. Favorite scene: a screaming Wesley swallowing an errant demon eyeball.

EVIL EYE, THE
See: *Manhattan Baby*.

EVIL MIND, THE
★★☆ Goodtimes, 1935, NR, 69 min. Dir: Maurice Elvey. Cast: Claude Rains, Fay Wray, Jane Baxter, Mary Clare, Ben Field, Donald Calthrop.

Fairly good British thriller with Rains as a phony stage mentalist who suddenly discovers he has real psychic ability; unfortunately, he can only foresee tragedy. Wray fled Hollywood for England to escape typecasting as a horror girl, but here she is anyway, playing Rains' concerned wife. Aka *The Clairvoyant*; remade as *Night Has a Thousand Eyes*.

EVIL OF FRANKENSTEIN, THE
★★☆ MCA/Universal, 1964, NR, 86 min. Dir: Freddie Francis. Cast: Peter Cushing, Peter Woodthrope, Duncan Lamont, Sandor Elés, Katy Wild, Kiwi Kingston.

Okay entry in Hammer's Frankenstein series with Cushing in good form as the Baron, returning to his ruined chateau and reviving his frozen monster (Australian wrestler Kingston in sloppy, Karloffian makeup by Roy Ashton), who falls under the spell of greedy sideshow hypnotist Woodthrope. MCA had the good sense to release the original theatrical print of this film rather than the needlessly padded TV version, making this a must for Hammerphiles.

EVILS OF THE NIGHT
☆ Lightning, 1983, R, 85 min. Dir: Mardi Rustam. Cast: Neville Brand, Aldo Ray, Tina Louise, Julie Newman, John Carradine, Karrie Emerson.

Backwoods boneheads Brand and Ray kidnap young campers and take them to alien bloodsuckers Louise, Newmar, and Carradine living in a crashed spaceship in the woods. This hilariously bad exploitation cheapie is probably the worst film its roster of veteran stars ever appeared in, separately or together—and baby, that's saying a lot!

EVIL SPAWN
★ Camp, 1987, R, 72 min. Dir: Kenneth J. Hall. Cast: Bobbie Bresee, John Carradine, Drew Godderis, John Terrence, Dawn Wildsmith, Pamela Gilbert.

Cheapjack updating of *The Wasp Woman* with the curvaceous Bresee as a fading glamour queen who takes an experimental youth serum that knocks off the years but also turns Bob into a murderous insectoid monster. Junky video nonentity probably shot over an otherwise boring weekend at Bobbie's house, this has lots of blood and boobs but not much else.

EVILSPEAK
★★☆ CBS/Fox, 1982, R, 89 min. Dir: Eric Weston. Cast: Clint Howard, R. G. Armstrong, Joseph Cortese, Claude Earl Jones, Hamilton Camp, Charles Tyner, Haywood Nelson, Lynn Hancock.

Carrie goes to West Point in this watchable, if derivative, shocker about a class nerd (Howard) tormented by macho cadets who avenges himself via a computer hookup with the devil that gives him access to a pack of possessed pigs. Seriously. Some flashy direction (like a severed head in a satanic flashback sequence becoming the soccer ball in a school game in an amazing cut) and a campy cast (though Howard is about 10 years too old for his role—check out the receding hairline) make this nice, sick fun.

EVIL SPIRITS
★★ Prism, 1991, R, 95 min.
Dir: Gary Graver. Cast: Karen Black, Arte Johnson, Michael Berryman, Virginia Mayo, Martine Beswick, Robert Quarry, Anthony Eisley, Yvette Vickers, Bert Mustin, Debra Lamb.

Darkly comic chiller with Black running a boarding home for oddballs whose welfare and pension checks she grabs while most of them end up buried in the backyard. A good cast of veterans (including Mayo, who gets an ax in the head) makes this low-budgeter worthwhile.

EVIL TOONS
★★ Prism, 1991, R, 86 min.
Dir: Fred Olen Ray. Cast: David Carradine, Monique Gabrielle, Suzanne Ager, Madison Stowe, Dick Miller, Arte Johnson.

A quartet of buxom chicks restoring an old mansion accidentally unleash a cartoon monster from an old book in this horror-comic *Roger Rabbit* rip. Good lookin' babes and veteran actors are equally wasted in this silly Ray trifle, which has a monster designed by ace genre critic Chas Balum. Best scene: Miller watching himself in *A Bucket of Blood* and muttering, "How come this guy never won an Academy Award?" Indeed.

EVIL TOWN
★☆ TWE, 1984, R, 88 min.
Dirs: Edward Collins, Peter S. Traynor, and Larry Spiegel. Cast: James Keach, Robert Walker, Dean Jagger, Michele Marsh, Jillian Kessner, Lynda Wiesmeier.

In the best Jerry Warren tradition, this bizarre video hybrid has footage from an unreleased 1974 epic called *God Bless Dr. Shagetz* blended with some new material featuring topless *Playboy* playmate Wiesmeier. The end result is a barely watchable whatsit about mad scientist Jagger's eternal youth experiments conducted on the populace of a small town. Some of the editing is astounding but otherwise the usual hooey.

EXORCISM
★ All Seasons, 1974, R, 90 min.
Dir: Juan Bosch. Cast: Paul Naschy, Maria Perschy, Grace Mills, Maria Kosti, Jorge Torras, Maria Avile.

Lethargic Spanish contribution to the *Exorcist* cycle with Naschy as the obligatory angst-ridden priest trying to help a marble-eyed Mills, who's doing the Linda Blair bit. A real snooze, with the minimal makeup FX saved for the climax, where the evil spirit is driven out of the heroine and into a German shepherd!

EXORCIST, THE
★★★☆ Warner, 1973, R, 121 min.
Dir: William Friedkin. Cast: Ellen Burstyn, Max von Sydow, Lee J. Cobb, Jason Miller, Linda Blair, Kitty Winn, Jack MacGowran, voice of Mercedes McCambridge.

This enormously influential movie singlehandedly changed the genre forever, bringing critical respectability and wide audience acceptance to horror films while at the same time all but crushing the low-budget (mostly British) horror film industry of Hammer, Amicus, and AIP and creating an all-too-quickly boring and repetitive new subgenre: the devil possession pic. Adapted by William Peter Blatty from his novel, this tells of the bizarre illness that befalls young Regan (Blair), the daughter of actress Chris MacNeil (Burstyn). When medicine fails her, Chris turns to the church, particularly troubled young priest Father Karras (Miller), to help her head-spinning, bile-vomiting kid. More effective in its early scenes of quiet understatement than in much of its later sound and fury, this is still a technically brilliant and ground-breaking film with trend-setting makeup FX by Dick Smith, a truly disquieting use of sound and subliminal effects, and bravura vocal acting by McCambridge as the demon's voice.

EXORCIST II: THE HERETIC
★★★ Warner, 1977, R, 117 min.
Dir: John Boorman. Cast: Linda Blair, Richard Burton, Louise Fletcher, Max von Sydow, James Earl Jones, Kitty Winn, Paul Henreid, Ned Beatty.

Boorman's moody, underappreciated follow-up to the Friedkin blockbuster, once considered the ultimate bad sequel, now doesn't look half bad—maybe it's all those lousy, unimaginative sequels released since. The Vatican

---

LINDA BLAIR
(1959–)

This hard-working lass literally turned heads when she first burst upon the screen in *The Exorcist*. The likable, talented Linda has brought her bubbly, pleasant persona to many a film: good, bad, and indifferent.

The Exorcist ('73), *Exorcist II: The Heretic* ('77), *Stranger in Our House* ('78), *Hell Night* ('81), *Grotesque* ('87), *Bad Blood* ('88), *The Chilling* ('88), *Witchery* ('89), *Zapped Again!* ('89), *Repossessed* ('90), *Dead Sleep* ('91).

assigns Burton (in a role meant for Jon Voight) to validate Blair's exorcism and discovers that the demon still resides in the buxom teenager's subconscious. Hard to follow but with some simply stunning photography and special effects (especially at the climax) and an excellent score by Ennio Morricone. Cut to 102 minutes after its premiere, the film has finally been restored to its original length for home video and is well worth reevaluation. Aka *The Heretic.*

EXORCIST III, THE
★★☆ CBS/Fox, 1990, R, 110 min.
Dir: William Peter Blatty. Cast: George C. Scott, Ed Flanders, Brad Dourif, Jason Miller, Nicol Williamson, Viveca Lindfors, Scott Wilson, Nancy Fish, Don Gordon, Zohra Lampert.

Blatty's own *Exorcist* follow-up, based on his novel *Legion,* has Scott as Georgetown detective Kinderman (played in the first film by the late Lee J. Cobb) investigating a series of brutal decapitations. The victims are mostly priests and the M.O. matches that of the infamous Gemini Killer—but he was executed 15 years earlier on the night of Regan MacNeil's exorcism. More a detective story than a true horror film, but Scott's towering presence holds this overly verbose movie together—though the tacked-on exorcism climax is a needless accoutrement. Aka *The Exorcist: 1990* and *Exorcist III: Legion.*

EXORCIST III: LEGION
See: *The Exorcist III.*

EXORCIST: 1990, THE
See: *The Exorcist III.*

EYEBALL
★★ Prism, 1974, R, 86 min.
Dir: Umberto Lenzi. Cast: John Richardson, Martine Brochard, Inez Pellegrin, Silvia Solaré, Georges Riguad, Auretta Gay.

A Spanish Argento imitation about a group of American tourists in Barcelona who are stalked by a maniac in a red rain slicker and gloves who cuts out the eyes of young girls. Routine stuff with plenty of blood, nudity, and lesbian love scenes (the bane of far too many Euro-shockers of this era); the killer's identity is pretty guessable too. Aka *Gatto Rossi in un Labirinto: Red Cat in a Glass Maze* and *The Devil's Eye.*

EYE CREATURES, THE
★ Sinister Cinema, 1965, NR, 80 min.
Dir: Larry Buchanan. Cast: John Ashley, Cynthia Hull, Warren Hammack, Chet Davis, Bill Peck.

Paltry Buchanan remake of *Invasion of the Saucer Men* with Ashley and Hull as a couple of 30-year-old teens who try to thwart an invasion of eyeball-covered aliens with alcohol-based blood. D-grade dumbness with nonexistent production values and junk-shop special effects.

EYE FOR AN EYE, AN
See: *The Psychopath.*

EYE OF THE DEMON
★★ Vidmark, 1987, NR, 96 min.
Dir: Carl Schenkel. Cast: Pamela Sue Martin, Tim Matheson, Barbara Billingsley, Inga Swenson, James B. Sikking, Woody Harrelson, Susan Ruttan, Jeff Conaway.

TV flick originally broadcast as *Bay Coven* about a devil cult on an island off the New England coast. Funny casting (June Cleaver as a witch?) and Pam looks great in a clingy red satin dress, but this is so dull not even a literally explosive ending may rouse you.

EYE OF THE EVIL DEAD
See: *Manhattan Baby.*

EYES OF A STRANGER
★★ Warner, 1981, R, 85 min.
Dir: Ken Wiederhorn. Cast: Lauren Tewes, Jennifer Jason Leigh, John Di Santi, Peter DuPre, Gwen Lewis, Kitty Lunn.

Miami-made slasher with most of its Tom Savini gore cut out before release—so why bother? Tewes is a long way from "The Love Boat" as a TV reporter after rapist-murderer-neighbor Di Santi; Leigh is her deaf-mute kid sister and obvious victim-to-be. Formula thriller.

EYES OF FIRE
★★ Vestron, 1983, R, 86 min. Dir: Avery Crouse. Cast: Dennis Lipscomb, Guy Boyd, Rebecca Stanley, Fran Ryan, Rob Paulsen, Karlene Crockett.

In 1750 western settlers are set upon by Indian demons trying to drive them from their land. Eerie and well cast, this horror-western suffers from a very slow pace and a disjointed narrative that's the obvious result of cutting from the original 108-minute version. Some interesting moments. Aka *Crying Blue Sky.*

EYES OF HELL
See: *The Mask.*

EYES OF LAURA MARS
★★☆ Goodtimes, 1978, R, 103 min.
Dir: Irvin Kerschner. Cast: Faye Dunaway, Tommy

Lee Jones, Brad Dourif, Rene Auberjonois, Raul Julia, Rose Gregorio, Lisa Taylor, Darlanne Fluegel.

Chi-chi highbrow horror with Faye as a glamorous fashion photog whose off-the-wall pics (mixing kinky sex and violence) eerily mirror the crimes of a brutal psycho killer—with whom she shares an unexplained psychic link. Co-scripted by John Carpenter as a vehicle for Barbra Streisand (who sings the theme song, "Prisoner"), this is entertaining but suffers from a confusing storyline, unsympathetic characters, and a dumb ending.

EYES OF THE BEHOLDER
★★ Columbia/TriStar, 1992, R, 90 min. Dir: Lawrence L. Simeon. Cast: Lenny Von Dohlen, Joanna Pacula, Matt McCoy, George Lazenby, Kylie Travis, Charles Napier.

Von Dohlen's gloriously out-of-control acting saves this predictable overdirected psycho flick about a crazoid (Lenny) whose botched brain surgery has turned him into the patient from hell, terrorizing his rich doctor and the doc's chi-chi friends at a party. This one has all the usual exploitation clichés, but Lenny makes it worthwhile.

EYES WITHOUT A FACE
See: *The Horror Chamber of Dr. Faustus.*

FACE AT THE WINDOW, THE
★★ Rhino, 1939, NR, 65 min. Dir: George King. Cast: Tod Slaughter, Marjorie Taylor, John Warwick, Leonard Henry.

More Slaughter shenanigans with Tod as a mad slasher known as the Wolf who uses his half-wit brother as the dreaded "face at the window" to lure his victims to their doom. More unfettered ham from England's untouted original horror star.

FACELESS MONSTER, THE
See: *Nightmare Castle.*

FACE OF FEAR
See: *Peeping Tom.*

FACE OF THE SCREAMING WEREWOLF
★ Sinister Cinema, 1959, NR, 60 min. Dirs: Jerry Warren and Gilberto Martinez Solares. Cast: Lon Chaney, Jr., Yolanda Varela, Yerye Beirute, Tin Tan.

I defy anyone to make any sense out of this U.S.-Mexican hybrid with Lon as a mummy revived by scientist Beirute in a creepy wax museum. The bandages are then removed and—viola!—it's the wolf man complete with the same dark clothes he used to wear in all those Universal flicks in the '40s. Originally a comic chiller starring Tin Tan (who's barely in this version) called *La Casa del Terror: House of Terror,* this minimally dubbed version makes absolutely *no* sense, with pointless scenes of the rampaging wolf man building to a skyscraper-climbing climax that was probably pretty impressive in the original film but here comes out of nowhere and leads to nothing—much like the career of Jerry Warren.

FADE TO BLACK
★★ Media, 1980, R, 100 min. Dir: Vernon Zimmerman. Cast: Dennis Christopher, Linda Kerridge, Tim Thomerson, Norman Burton, Eve Brent Ashe, Gwynne Gilford, Morgan Paull, James Luisi, Marya Small, Mickey Rourke.

Movie buff Christopher freaks and starts dressing up as his favorite screen villains—Karloff, Lugosi, Cagney, Widmark—and begins committing murders; victims include smarmy film producer Paull, hooker Small, and video store co-worker Rourke (in one of his first films). A failed attempt at a ready-made cult film from the director of *The Unholy Rollers,* this suffers from an unlikable central character and an uneven mixture of dark comedy and straight horror. Kerridge is terrific, though, as Christopher's Marilyn Monroe lookalike dream girl. Whatever happened to her, I'd like to know?

FALL BREAK
See: *The Mutilator.*

FALL OF THE HOUSE OF USHER, THE
★☆ Sinister Cinema, 1948, NR, 70 min. Dir: Ivan Barnett. Cast: Gwen Watford, Kay Tendeter, Irving Steen, Vernon Charles, Tony Powell-Bristow, Connie Goodwin.

Amateurish British version of the Edgar Allan Poe classic with Watford as the doomed Madeline and Tendeter as mad brother Roderick, who buries her alive. Certain passages almost resemble *Vampyr* in their stark atmosphere, but cheap production values (is this set in the 19th century or the '40s—it's never made clear) and awful acting by everyone but Watford make this a real strain to endure.

FALL OF THE HOUSE OF USHER, THE

★★★ Goodtimes, 1960, NR, 79 min.
Dir: Roger Corman. Cast: Vincent Price, Mark Damon, Myrna Fahey, Harry Ellerbe.

Released theatrically as *House of Usher*, this beautifully atmospheric adaptation of the Poe tale features Price as hypersensitive Roderick Usher, who lives with his younger sister, Madeline, in a crumbling New England mansion that literally comes apart when they are visited by Madeline's strong-willed fiance. The first of Corman's eight low-cost ($125,000) Poe films, this is somewhat padded and slow and has bland acting from Damon and Fahey but is well written (by Richard Matheson), photographed (by Floyd Crosby), and scored (by Les Baxter) and contains one of Price's most controlled and commanding performances.

FALL OF THE HOUSE OF USHER, THE

★ United, 1979, PG, 101 min.
Dir: James L. Conway. Cast: Martin Laudau, Robert Hays, Charlene Tilton, Ray Walston, Dimitra Arliss.

This awful remake must have cost all of five hundred bucks to cast, shoot, edit, and release. Landau rants and raves as never before as Roderick, who lives with loony sis Arliss and crotchety butler Walston in a cardboard mansion visited by architect Hays and his bride Tilton. It isn't long, then, before Landau buries Arliss alive, she bursts from her coffin, kills Walston, and grapples with Landau as the house is struck by lightning and collapses about them. A miscast, misdirected misfire from Sunn Classics, those nice folks who brought you all those junky pseudo-documentaries and wildlife dramas in the '70s.

FALL OF THE HOUSE OF USHER, THE

See: *The House of Usher.*

FALSE FACE

See: *Scalpel.*

FAN, THE

★★☆ Paramount, 1981, R, 95 min.
Dir: Edward Bianchi. Cast: Lauren Bacall, James Garner, Maureen Stapleton, Michael Biehn, Hector Elizondo, Anna Maria Horsford, Kurt Johnson, Dwight Schultz, Dana Delaney, Griffin Dunne.

Gory, glossy crossbreed of *All About Eve* and *Maniac* with Bacall as a popular film star making her Broadway musical debut who's stalked by a crazed, ardent young fan (Biehn); he mistakes her non-response to his love let-

ters (intercepted as crank mail by secretary Stapleton) as rejection. A fairly accurate version of Bob Randall's cleverly written novel (except for the ending), this tries to be too much like *Dressed to Kill* (right down to the romantic Pino Donaggio music) but *does* showcase Bacall in one of her best latter-day roles.

FANATIC

See: *Die! Die! My Darling!*

FANATIC

See: *The Last Horror Film.*

FANGS OF THE LIVING DEAD

★★ Sinister Cinema, 1968, PG, 94 min.
Dir: Amando de Ossorio. Cast: Anita Ekberg, John Hamilton, Julian Ugarte, Diana Lorys.

In this silly continental vamp romp, Anita is a fashion model who inherits a vampire-infested castle. Originally entitled *Malenka* and aka *La Nipote del Vampiro: The Vampire's Niece*, this was first released in the U.S. as part of the legendary "Orgy of the Living Dead" drive-in triple bill and is very routine, with lots of cleavage and implied lesbianism. Funny dubbing: "Bite, Sylvia, bite!"

FARM, THE

See: *The Curse.*

FATAL ATTRACTION

★★☆ Paramount, 1987, R, 119 min.
Dir: Adrian Lyne. Cast: Michael Douglas, Glenn Close, Anne Archer, Fred Gwynne, Stuart Pankin, Ellen Foley.

A happily married lawyer (Douglas) alone for the weekend has a one-night stand with an unstable blonde (Close), which turns into a nightmare when the girl refuses to let go and begins showing psychotic, knife-wielding tendencies. Wildly overrated, this glossy updating of the far superior *Play Misty for Me* has a knockout performance from Close and a quietly effective one from Archer (as the betrayed wife who, not unexpectedly, emerges as the film's hero) but tries too hard to drum up sympathy for Douglas' basically pretty jerky husband—who doesn't get nearly what he deserves—and has too many obvious horror-suspense setups. The original ending (where Glenn commits suicide and leaves evidence for Mike to be framed for murder—the ultimate revenge!) was cut at the last minute and a routine *Friday the 13th* unstoppable psycho climax substituted. This earlier ending has been included as a supplement to the "Director's Cut" video edition.

FATAL GAMES
★ Vestron, 1984, R, 87 min.
Dir: Michael Elliot. Cast: Sally Kirkland, Lynn
Banashek, Sean Masterson, Michael O'Leary,
Teal Roberts, Melissa Prophet.

A javelin-toting transsexual psycho killer
preys upon a bunch of dim-bulbed athletes at
a private academy for the physically gifted
and mentally handicapped. There are more
babes than blood in this pathetic slasher; it's
sad to see super-talent Kirkland trapped in
drek like this. Look really fast for Linnea
Quigley.

FATAL PULSE
★ Celebrity, 1987, R, 90 min.
Dir: Anthony J. Christopher. Cast: Michelle
McCormick, Ken Roberts, Joe Phelan, Alex Courtney.

Yet another mad slasher goes to work on yet
another sorority house full of buxom bimbettes in yet another direct-to-video waste of
time. Contains the only known recorded incident of death by record album but that's it for
originality.

FEAR
★★☆ Wizard, 1980, R, 95 min.
Dir: Riccardo Freda. Cast: Stefano Patrizi, Anita
Strindberg, Laura Gemser, John Richardson,
Martine Brochard, Silvia Dionisio.

Italian horror pioneer Freda's contribution to
the mad slasher cycle, this has Patrizi as a film
director who visits his mother's old mansion
with several friends, most of whom end up
hacked to death by a shadowy psycho. An
odd mix of stylish, old-fashioned imagery and
modern gore. Original title: *L'Ossessione che
Uccide: Murder Obsession.*

FEAR
★★☆ Vestron, 1989, R, 95 min.
Dir: Rockne O'Bannon. Cast: Ally Sheedy, Michael
O'Keefe, Lauren Hutton, Dina Merrill, Stan Shaw,
John Agar.

Psychic Sheedy becomes linked with a mind-
reading killer called the "Shadow Man" in this
above-average handling of a routine concept.
Good acting by the appealing Sheedy and a
breakneck pace; this falls down only at the
end with a corny climax that manages to rip
off both *Strangers on a Train* and *Horrors of the
Black Museum.*

FEAR, THE
See: *The Gates of Hell.*

FEAR CHAMBER, THE
See: *The Torture Zone.*

FEAR INSIDE, THE
★★☆ Media, 1992, R, 105 min.
Dir: Leon Ichaso. Cast: Christine Lahti, Dylan
McDermott, Jennifer Rubin, David Ackroyd, Thomas
Ian Nicholas, Paul Linke.

Lahti is good in this predictable cable thriller
about an agoraphobic artist held prisoner in
her home by a deranged boarder (Rubin) and
her psychotic boyfriend (McDermott). No surprises but it's professionally put together, with
a plot that has more than a few echoes of the
underappreciated *Lady in a Cage.*

FEAR IN THE CITY OF THE LIVING DEAD
See: *The Gates of Hell.*

FEAR IN THE NIGHT
★★★ Republic, 1972, PG, 94 min. Dir: Jimmy
Sangster, Cast: Peter Cushing, Joan Collins,
Judy Geeson, Ralph Bates.

Sangster manages to wring a few new twists
in his standard drive-her-crazy plot with Geeson as a young bride terrorized at a closed-
down boys school by a maniac with an artificial arm. Atmospheric and well-performed,
this is also available as *Honeymoon of Fear* and
Dynasty of Fear—this latter moniker obviously
inspired by co-star Collins' later TV success.

FEARLESS VAMPIRE KILLERS OR PARDON ME, BUT YOUR TEETH ARE IN MY NECK
★★★☆ MGM/UA, 1967, NR, 107 min.
Dir: Roman Polanski. Cast: Jack McGowran, Sharon
Tate, Ferdy Mayne, Roman Polanski, Alfie Bass,
Terry Downes, Fiona Lewis, Ian Quarrier.

Polanski's stylish send-up of Hammer vampire films with MacGowran as bumbling Professor Abronsius whose attempt to destroy a
Transylvanian vampire cult headed by
debonair Count von Krolock (Mayne) inadver-
tantly causes the spread of vampirism
throughout the world. Like *Abbott and Costello
Meet Frankenstein,* this plays the supernatural
elements perfectly straight, with the humor
arising from the "normal" characters' reaction
to it. Originally released in the U.S. in a heavily re-edited and badly dubbed 98-minute version, the full European print is available on
video.

FEAR NO EVIL
★★☆ Embassy, 1980, R, 99 min.
Dir: Frank LaLoggia. Cast: Stefan Arngrim, Elizabeth
Hoffman, Kathleen Rowe McAllen, Frank Birney,
Daniel Eden, Jack Holland.

Filmed as *Mark of the Beast,* this ambitious low-
budgeter is an interesting variation on themes
similar to those explored in the *Omen* series.

Arngrim is a shy high school kid who turns out to be the anti-Christ, while classmate McAllen is revealed as an archangel sent to destroy him. Surprisingly subtle, with evocative photography and splendid effects. Arngrim first gained attention as the little boy on the "Land of the Giants" TV series.

FEMALE FIEND
See: *Theatre of Death.*

FEMALE PLASMA SUCKERS
See: *Blood Orgy of the She Devils.*

FER-DE-LANCE
★☆ Video Treasures, 1974, NR, 96 min. Dir: Russ Mayberry. Cast: David Janssen, Hope Lange, Ivan Dixon, Jason Evers, Ben Piazza, Charles Robinson.

Contrived TV movie about a group of scientists trapped in a crippled submarine with a horde of poisonous snakes. A good cast does what it can to keep this nonsense afloat but it ain't easy. Aka *Death Drive.*

FIEND
★ Video Unlimited, 1980, NR, 93 min. Dir: Don Dohler. Cast: Don Leifert, Richard Nelson, Elaine White, George Stover.

Cheapo Dohler epic with Leifert as a madman who commits murders for the title creature, an insect-like beastie that feeds on corpses. Amateurish acting, writing, direction, and effects. Aka *Deadly Neighbor.*

FIENDISH GHOULS, THE
See: *Mania.*

FIENDS, THE
See: *Diabolique.*

FIEND WITHOUT A FACE
★★★ Republic, 1957, NR, 74 min. Dir: Arthur Crabtree. Cast: Marshall Thompson, Kim Parker, Kynaston Reeves, Stanley Maxted, Terence Kilburn, James Dyrenforth.

Scientist Reeves' experiments with the materialization of thought lead to the creation of invisible brain-sucking monsters that attack a nearby army base and town. A blast of radiation at the end reveals the fiends to be hideous brain and spinal cord monstrosities. After a slow start, this minor '50s fave really kicks into gear, topping it off with a nightmarish ending that's also one of the first gore scenes in horror film history. See it.

FIEND WITH THE ATOMIC BRAIN
See: *Blood of Ghastly Horror.*

FIEND WITH THE ELECTRONIC BRAIN
See: *Blood of Ghastly Horror.*

FIFTH FLOOR, THE
★☆ Media, 1980, R, 90 min. Dir: Howard Avedis. Cast: Bo Hopkins, Dianne Hull, Mel Ferrer, Julie Adams, Sharon Farrell, Patti D'Arbanville.

A first-rate cast is wasted in this third-rate asylum shocker about a go-go dancer (Hull) railroaded into a madhouse being terriorized by crazed orderly Hopkins (who really outdoes himself here). Despite the potentially sleazy subject matter, this tries for a "respectable" approach to the material that doesn't work at all, making this thing come off far duller than it should be.

FINAL CONFLICT, THE
★★ Fox, 1981, R, 108 min. Dir: Graham Baker. Cast: Sam Neill, Lisa Harrow, Rossano Brazzi, Don Gordon, Barnaby Holm, Mason Adams, Leueen Willoughby, Robert Arden.

Plodding third (and at the time, final) entry in the *Omen* series with Damien (Neill) now in his thirties. The head of his late uncle's corporation, he also takes over his dad's old post of U.S. ambassador to Great Britain while being stalked by an all-monk assassination squad, each armed with one of the sacred daggers of Meggedo. Neill has real charisma as Damien, but the remainder of the cast suffers from a bad case of tired blood; direction and writing are both very uninspired, with few of the usual "creative death" scenes this series is noted for packing much of a wallop. Look for a cameo by Hazel Court during the fox-hunting scene. Aka *Omen III: The Final Conflict* and *The Final Conflict: Omen III.*

FINAL CONFLICT: OMEN III, THE
See: *The Final Conflict.*

FINAL EXAM
★ Embassy, 1981, R, 90 min. Dir: Jimmy Huston. Cast: Cecile Bagdadi, Joel S. Rice, Ralph Brown, Deanna Robbins, Sherry Willis-Birch, John Fallon.

Talky stalker featuring another campus-cruising killer hacking up coeds, frat brothers, and security guards until the inevitable showdown with the lone survivor-heroine. Virtually bloodless, this has next to nothing to recommend it.

FINAL TERROR, THE
★☆ Vestron, 1981, R, 81 min. Dir: Andrew Davis. Cast: Rachel Ward, Daryl Hannah, Adrian Zmed, John Friedrich, Mark Metcalf, Akosua Busia, Lewis Smith, Joe Pantoliano.

Junky backwoods *Deliverance–Friday the 13th* spin-off that probably would never have seen the light of day if not for the contribution of stars-to-be Ward and Hannah. A bunch of unsympathetic simpletons and their vacuous girlfriends take a mountain camping trip and are menaced by a subhuman killer. Same-old-same-old plotting and direction; ludicrous final twist. Aka *Forest Primevil* and *Campsite Massacre.*

FIRESTARTER
★★ MCA/Universal, 1984, R, 115 min.
Dir: Mark L. Lester. Cast: Drew Barrymore, George C. Scott, David Keith, Martin Sheen, Art Carney, Louise Fletcher, Freddie Jones, Heather Locklear, Moses Gunn, Drew Snyder.

Well-cast but lifeless adaptation of the Stephen King novel about a young girl (Barrymore) with the ability to start fires with her mind being sought by government agents out to exploit her power as the ultimate weapon. Barrymore is sweet and her relationship with screen dad Keith is affecting, but the rest of the big-name cast (especially a dazed-looking Scott) seems unclear on what their characters are about, and much of the elaborate special FX work looks tacky and unfinished.

FIRST MAN INTO SPACE
★★☆ Rhino, 1958, NR, 77 min.
Dir. Robert Day. Cast: Marshall Thompson, Marla Landi, Bill Edwards, Robert Ayres, Bill Nagy, Carl Jaffe.

Test pilot Edwards returns from a suborbital flight covered with glittering space dust and driven to kill by an unquenchable thirst for blood. Starkly photographed and legitimately scary, this gripping Brit sci-fi/horror flick (from the makers of *Fiend Without a Face*) has real impact; let down only slightly by some flat performances. The obvious inspiration for the better-known but not better *The Incredible Melting Man.* Aka *Satellite of Blood.*

FIRST POWER, THE
★★ Nelson, 1990, R, 98 min.
Dir: Robert Resnikoff. Cast: Lou Diamond Phillips, Tracy Griffith, Jeff Kober, Dennis Lipscomb, Elizabeth Arlen, Mykel T. Williamson, Carmen Argenziano, Melanie Shatner.

Phillips is an L.A. cop who catches and witnesses the execution of satanic serial killer Kober. It therefore becomes hard for psychic Griffith to convince him that a new spate of similar slayings is the work of Kober, risen from the grave. An overly familiar storyline (with bits of *Shocker, The Exorcist, The Omen,*

and various "Dirty Harry" movies) is given a slight lift thanks to good work from Lou and Jeff and some frantic directorial touches, but this ends up being too predictable for its own good. Shooting title: *Transit.*

FIVE AT THE FUNERAL
See: *House of Terror.*

FIVE GRAVES FOR A MEDIUM
See: *Terror Creatures from the Grave.*

FLATLINERS
★★☆ RCA/Columbia, 1990, R, 111 min.
Dir: Joel Schumacher. Cast: Kiefer Sutherland, Julia Roberts, Kevin Bacon, William Baldwin, Oliver Platt, Kimberly Scott.

Stylish but empty film about five med students who decide to experiment with death: stopping their hearts and then reviving themselves in order to discover what waits on the other side. The horror kicks in when they bring back with them terrible demons from their past. Good-looking, with an attractive young cast but a middle-of-the-road attitude that keeps it from ever being as frightening or imaginative as it should be.

FLESH AND BLOOD SHOW, THE
★★ Video Gems, 1972, R, 85 min.
Dir: Pete Walker. Cast: Jenny Hanley, Ray Brooks, Luan Peters, Judy Matheson, Robin Askwith, Candace Glendenning, Tristan Rogers, Patrick Barr.

Gruesome goulash about a murdering maniac stalking a seaside theatre. When a troupe of actors come there to put on a show, they have a lot more trouble than Judy Garland and Mickey Rooney used to as the hooded fiend begins doing them in. Filled with familiar young faces from the early '70s British horror cinema (not to mention Rogers, a decade before his "General Hospital" success) and a climax originally shown in 3-D, this gore flick is routine at best. Aka *Asylum of the Insane.*

FLESH AND THE FIENDS, THE
See: *Mania.*

FLESHEATER
See: *Revenge of the Living Zombies.*

FLESH EATERS, THE
★★★ Sinister Cinema, 1962, NR, 87 min.
Dir: Jack Curtis. Cast: Martin Kosleck, Rita Morley, Byron Sanders, Barbara Wilkin, Ray Tudor.

Early '60s sicko with veteran movie pervert Kosleck as a crazed marine biologist who has created a form of glittering sea parasite with a taste for human flesh. The definite high point of this early gore piece is the scene where Tudor (hilarious as a beatnik called Omar) drinks a glass of water containing some parasites, which then eat their way out of his stomach! Ouch! Although very cheap, this has some surprisingly good special effects and windswept oceanfront photography (shot on Long Island) to recommend it.

FLESHEATING MOTHERS
★ Academy, 1988, UR, 90 min.
Dir: James Aviles Martin. Cast: Robert Lee Oliver, Donatella Hecht, Valorie Hubbard, Neal Rosen, Terry Hayes.

Tedious would-be camp gore comedy about a suburban neighborhood of bubbly Carol Brady clones turned flesh-lusting Florence Hendersons by some strange virus or another. When these hungry gals call ya' to supper, you'd best pass on it. That goes for the film as well. Not to be confused with *Rabid Grannies*.

FLESH FEAST
★ WesternWorld, 1970, R, 72 min.
Dir: Brad F. Grinter. Cast: Veronica Lake, Phil Philbin, Heather Hughes, Chris Martell, Martha Mischon.

Former '40s fave Lake (she of the peek-a-boo platinum tresses) co-produced this Florida-shot mess, her last film, about a lady scientist whose revolutionary plastic surgery process involves the removal of old skin via an application of flesh-eating maggots. Not really as gross as it probably seemed at the time and really kinda dull; a last-minute plot twist into *They Saved Hitler's Brain* territory, with a cameo by Adolf himself, is more stupid than shocking.

FLESH FOR FRANKENSTEIN
See: *Andy Warhol's Frankenstein*.

FLOWERS IN THE ATTIC
★★ Starmaker, 1987, PG-13, 95 min.
Dir: Jeffrey Bloom. Cast: Louise Fletcher, Victoria Tennant, Kristy Swanson, Jeb Stuart Adams, Lindsay Parker, Ben Ganger, Marshall Colt, Nathan Davis.

Ultra-bland filming of V. C. Andrews' popular supermarket tome about a bunch of sickeningly wholesome blonde moppets locked in the attic of their grandfather's old mansion by their crazy mom (Tennant), who's out to gain the old boy's money. With most of the more controversial elements of the book (i.e., incest) played down, what we're basically left with is a dull TV-type "thriller" with no thrills and not even much in the way of unintended laughs to relieve the tedium. Fletcher does her umpteenth Nurse Ratched bit as the stern grandma; the tacked-on "shocker" ending (featuring an obvious double for Tennant) is really feeble. "Eat the cookie, Mama!"

FLY, THE
★★★ CBS/Fox, 1958, NR, 94 min.
Dir: Kurt Neumann. Cast: David Hedison, Patricia Owens, Vincent Price, Herbert Marshall, Charles Herbert, Kathleen Freeman.

Scientist Hedison (billed here as Al before he changed his name to avoid its joke association with this film) develops a "matter transmitter" he uses to scramble a subject's atoms, send them through the air, and then reassemble them at any given place. Unfortunately, while experimenting on himself, a fly gets into the ointment and Hedison and the insect interchange heads and arms when their atoms are mixed together. A basically silly story (adapted by James "Shogun" Clavell from George Langelaan's *Playboy* piece) gets excellent treatment here, bringing genuine pathos and tension to a tale that, in other hands, would have seemed absolutely ludicrous. Solid acting and effects and an unforgettable ending ("Help me! Help me!"). Price and Marshall had such a hard time being serious they couldn't even face each other for fear of cracking each other up! Remade in 1986; sequels *Return of the Fly* and *Curse of the Fly*.

FLY, THE
★★★★ CBS/Fox, 1986, R, 97 min.
Dir: David Cronenberg. Cast: Jeff Goldblum, Geena Davis, John Getz, Joy Boushel, Les Carlson.

This new version, more a rethinking than a remake, perfectly casts bug-eyed Goldblum as the earnest young scientist experimenting with molecular teleportation. When his atoms are accidentally mixed with those of a fly, Goldblum begins falling apart, slowing metamorphosizing into a grotesque, fly-like monster. Easily Cronenberg's best film, this mixes his legendary taste for the bizarre with a genuinely moving love story that is given credibility by the heartfelt performances of Goldblum and Davis (in her starmaking role). Full of deft, throwaway homages to the original—the famous "Help me!" line is even utilized—and an amusing cameo by the director as a nightmare gynecologist. And remember: "Be afraid; be *very* afraid!"

FLY II, THE
★★ CBS/Fox, 1989, R, 104 min.
Dir: Chris Walas. Cast: Eric Stoltz, Daphne Zuniga, Lee Richardson, John Getz, Harley Cross, Frank Turner, Ann Marie Lee, Gary Chalk.

Another sequel propelled more by financial considerations than any genuine desire to continue the story, this plays mostly like a high-tech rerun of *Return of the Fly*. Stoltz is sympathetic as the genetically superior offspring of Jeff Goldblum and Geena Davis who ages to his twenties in the space of five years and whose inherent fly DNA eventually kicks in and transforms him into the inevitable monster. Well made and with good performances (Getz is amusing in a sardonic cameo), but routine subplots (a romance with Zuniga; evil scientist Richardson out to exploit the fly guy; etc.) and a ridiculously unjustified happy ending (and final twist stolen from *Freaks*) make this just so much standard flypaper.

FOG, THE
★★★ Embassy, 1980, R, 89 min. Dir: John Carpenter. Cast: Adrienne Barbeau, Hal Holbrook, Janet Leigh, Jamie Lee Curtis, John Houseman, Tom Atkins, Nancy Loomis, Charles Cyphers.

Moody ghost story set in a misty California coastal community haunted by the glow-eyed specters of drowned lepers seeking revenge against the descendants of the town's founding fathers. There's a great cast and some good scares and eerie music, but slack pacing and too many logic loopholes keep it from classic status. Carpenter cameos as a church caretaker.

FOG ISLAND
★★ Sinister Cinema, 1945, NR, 72 min. Dir: Terry Morse. Cast: Lionel Atwill, George Zucco, Veda Ann Borg, Jerome Cowan, Sharon Douglas, Ian Keith, John Whitney, Jacqueline de Wit.

A terrific B movie cast is wasted in this poor man's *And Then There Were None* with Zucco luring a motley crew of folk to his remote island manse to do away with them in revenge for his wife's death and his wrongful imprisonment. With typically cheap PRC production values (apart from one startlingly effective effects shot—you'll definitely know it when you see it), the potentially great teaming of Atwill and Zucco ultimately comes to nothing.

FOLKS AT RED WOLF INN, THE
See: *Terror at Red Wolf Inn*.

FOOD OF THE GODS
★★ Vestron, 1976, PG, 88 min. Dir: Bert I. Gordon. Cast: Marjoe Gortner, Pamela Franklin, Ralph Meeker, Ida Lupino, Jon Cypher, Belinda Balaski, Tom Stovall, John McLiam.

One of Mr. B.I.G.'s biggest hits, this laughable adaption of a "portion" of the H. G. Wells novel (previously filmed by Bert as *Village of the Giants*—how did he ever think he could've topped that?) features Marjoe as a macho football player, Pam as a foul-mouthed lady scientist, Ralph as your standard issue greedy bastard, and Ida as a bible-spouting old babe, all battling huge rats, chickens, worms, and wasps made gigantic by the strange substance oozing out of the ground on Lupino's Canadian farm. Beautifully photographed and with the odd good moment but mostly a howl, with some of the best bad dialogue and cheesiest FX you've encountered in years.

FOOD OF THE GODS PART 2
★☆ Avid, 1988, R, 86 min. Dir: Damian Lee. Cast: Paul Coufos, Lisa Schrage, Michael Copeman, Jackie Burroughs, Colin Fox, Frank Pellegrino.

Experiments with a radical growth hormone at a New York university create a pack of huge killer rats. Why anyone would want to make a sequel to *Food of the Gods* is a question too scary to contemplate even here; suffice it to say that this tacky tape peaks when a guy is bitten in the ass while urinating in some bushes and during a climactic rat attack on a team of synchronized swimmers! Aka *Gnaw: Foods of the Gods II*.

FORBIDDEN LOVE
See: *Freaks*.

FORBIDDEN WORLD
★★ Embassy, 1982, R, 77 min. Dir: Allan Holzman. Cast: Jesse Vint, Dawn Dunlap, June Chadwick, Linden Chiles, Fox Harris, Scott Paulin.

 This ultra-cheap New World *Alien* knock-off makes *Galaxy of Terror* look like *Star Wars*. Intergalactic troubleshooter Vint arrives at a genetic research lab on a distant planet just in time to fight a toothy, man-ingesting creature that kills off most of the small cast before eating a cancerous liver and vomiting to death! Just about as tasteless and gauche as it sounds but fun in a brainless sort of way, with lots of grisly makeup effects and a disturbing mixture of female nudity and bestial sex ómuch of it cut to avoid the inevitable X. Shooting title: *Mutant!* Remade as *Dead Space*.

FORCED ENTRY
★ Media, 1975, R, 82 min. Dir: Jim Sotos. Cast: Tanya Roberts, Ron Max, Nancy Allen, Brian Freilino.

Originally released as *The Last Victim*, this mostly bloodless and totally suspenseless stalker movie features Max as a lonely loon who talks to himself a lot and murders women. Tanya, in her film debut, is his ultimate target; Nancy, in *her* film debut, has a small role as a hitchhiker victim. Watching a blank screen is more interesting.

FOREST OF FEAR
See: *Toxic Zombies.*

FOREST PRIMEVIL
See: *The Final Terror.*

FOREVER EVIL
★★ United, 1987, R, 107 min.
Dir: Roger Evans. Cast: Charles Trotter, Red Mitchell, Tracey Huffman, Howard Jacobsen, Diane Johnson, Kent Johnson.

Mitchell is the lone survivor of a demonic attack on a mountain cabin who teams up with Huffman, the only survivor of an earlier demon rampage, and cop Trotter to hunt down the monster responsible: an otherworldly entity known as Yag Kothag. Painfully overlong, this starts out as a bad *Evil Dead* rip-off until it eventually turns into a bad H. P. Lovecraft rip-off. The acting stinks too, but some highly imaginative direction and squishy FX (including the memorable self-abortion of a demon baby) give this a passing grade.

FORGOTTEN ONE, THE
★★☆ Academy, 1989, R, 97 min.
Dir: Phillip Badger. Cast: Terry O'Quinn, Kristy McNichol, Blair Parker, Elisabeth Brooks.

A slow-moving but especially well-acted romantic ghost thriller about an author (O'Quinn) suffering from writer's block who rents an old mansion haunted by a beauteous ghost (Parker) who sees in him the reincarnation of her lost love. A standard plot is given life by an intense O'Quinn, a winsome Kristy, and a surprisingly uncompromising downbeat ending.

4-D MAN, THE
★★ New World, 1959, NR, 85 min.
Dir: Irwin S. Yeaworth, Jr. Cast: Robert Lansing, Lee Meriwether, James Congdon, Robert Strauss, Edgar Stehli, Patty Duke.

A throwback to all those '40s Boris Karloff mad scientist thrillers, this features Lansing as an experimenter who discovers the "fourth dimension," which gives him the ability to pass through any object. His experiments age him prematurely, however, which can be rectified by draining the life force of anyone he

touches. Hampered by too many hokey subplots, but good acting by Lansing and some clever special effects make it minor fun from the makers of *The Blob.* Aka *Master of Terror* and *The Evil Force.*

4TH MAN, THE
★★★ Media, 1979, R, 98 min.
Dir: Paul Verhoeven. Cast: Jeroen Krabbe, Renee Soutendijk, Thom Hoffman, Dolf De Vries, Geert De Jong, Hans Veerman.

This arty Dutch shocker plays like a cross between the work of Brian De Palma and Roman Polanski. A gay alcoholic writer (Krabbe) begins an affair with beautiful blonde hairdresser (Soutendijk). As the relationship progresses, Krabbe develops two obsessions: the first to sleep with Soutendijk's handsome young boyfriend (Hoffman) and the second, and more disturbing, to discover what *really* happened to Renee's three dead husbands. Admirably frank in its presentation (no Hollywood film would feature casual frontal male nudity or homosexual characters who aren't fey sterotypes), this has striking imagery and a shockingly gory twist ending. Even with the poor dubbing it's still well worth seeing. Originally 104 min.

FRANKENHOOKER
★★★ SGE, 1990, UR, 82 min.
Dir: Frank Henenlotter. Cast: James Lorinz, Patty Mullen, Louise Lasser, Charlotte Helmkamp, Shirley Stoler, Joseph Gonzalez.

Electrician Lorinz accidentally decapitates girlfriend Mullen with a lawnmower and thereafter becomes obsessed with restoring her, eventually murdering a group of prostitutes with an explosive batch of crack cocaine and using their best parts to construct a new body for his girl's head. Hilarious parody with great performances from Lorinz and Mullen, cartoony gore, and a lightheartedly sleazy atmosphere that's far less offensive than you'd expect from the synopsis. Lasser, though, is wasted.

FRANKENSTEIN
★★★☆ MCA/Universal, 1931, NR, 70 min.
Dir: James Whale. Cast: Boris Karloff, Colin Clive, Mae Clarke, John Boles, Edward Van Sloan, Dwight Frye.

Whale's classic adaptation of the Mary Shelley novel about an obsessed young scientist (Clive) who brings to life a monster (the unforgettable Karloff) who is driven to kill by a criminal brain. A gothic masterpiece dominated by Whale's moody direction and trenchant sense of humor and Karloff's marvelous child-like performance as the tragic monster. Followed by seven sequels beginning with *Bride of Frankenstein;* current video editions retain several seconds of footage (including the infamous drowning of a little girl) cut from the film's TV prints.

FRANKENSTEIN

★★☆ Thrillervideo, 1972, NR, 128 min.
Dir: Glenn Jordan. Cast: Robert Foxworth, Susan Strasberg, Bo Svenson, Robert Gentry, Heidi Vaughn, John Karlen, Philip Bourneuf, Willie Aames.

Dan Curtis–produced TV version of the Shelley novel with Foxworth good as the obsessed doctor and Svenson even better as the sad and sensitive monster. Marred by cheap video pro-

Boris Karloff defines the horror genre as the monster in Frankenstein *(1931).*

duction values but still the most faithful adaption yet attempted.

FRANKENSTEIN

★★ Video Treasures, 1984, NR, 74 min.
Dir: James Omerod. Cast: Robert Powell, David Warner, Carrie Fisher, John Gielgud, Michael Cochran, Terence Alexander, Susan Woolridge, Edward Judd.

Weak Britain-filmed TV version of the infamous Broadway bomb (one performance only in 1981) with Warner, in scar makeup and a bad haircut, good as the confused, woe-begotten monster but Powell haggard and hammy as Frankenstein and Fisher miscast as his inno-

---

JACK P. PIERCE
(1889–1968)

Universal Studio's ace makeup artist and master monster creator, Pierce headed the company's makeup department from the early '30s through the mid-'40s. His meticulous craftsmanship and attention to detail were legendary and hard on actors—four hours was an average time for makeup application—but this resulted in some of the most convincing creatures ever to lope across a movie screen.

The Monkey Talks ('27), *Dracula* ('31), *Frankenstein* ('31), *Murders in the Rue Morgue* ('32), *The Old Dark House* ('32), *The Mummy* ('32), *The Black Cat* ('34), *Bride of Frankenstein* ('35), *The Werewolf of London* ('35), *The Raven* ('35), *The Invisible Ray* ('36), *Dracula's Daughter* ('36), *Son of Frankenstein* ('39), *Tower of London* ('39), *Black Friday* ('40), *The Mummy's Hand* ('40), *Man-Made Monster* ('41), *The Black Cat* ('41), *The Wolf Man* ('41), *The Ghost of Frankenstein* ('42), *The Mummy's Tomb* ('42), *Frankenstein Meets the Wolf Man* ('43), *Captive Wild Woman* ('43), *The Phantom of the Opera* ('43), *Son of Dracula* ('43), *The Mad Ghoul* ('43), *The Mummy's Ghost* ('44), *Weird Woman* ('44), *Jungle Woman* ('44), *House of Frankenstein* ('44), *Dead Man's Eyes* ('44), *The Mummy's Curse* ('44), *Jungle Captive* ('45), *House of Dracula* ('45), *The Spider Woman Strikes Back!* ('46), *House of Horrors* ('46), *The She-Wolf of London* ('46), *Master Minds* ('49), *Teenage Monster* ('57), *Giant From the Unknown* ('58), *The Devil's Hand* ('58), *Beauty and the Beast* ('63).

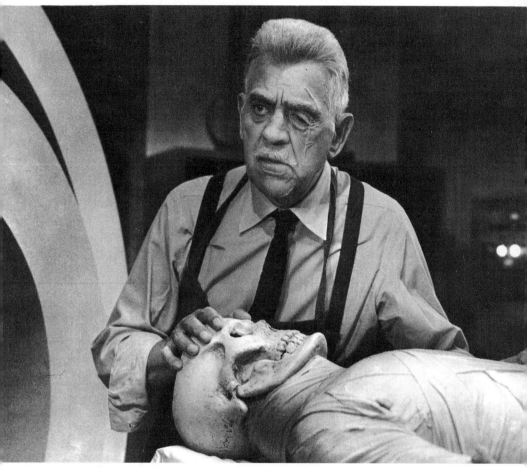

A disfigured Boris Karloff checks his monster for a fever in Frankenstein 1970 *(1958).*

cent fiancee. Flat production values and tape quality make this similar to the 1972 version in everything but acting and story values.

FRANKENSTEIN

★★☆ Turner, 1993, NR, 116 min.
Dir: David Wickes. Cast: Patrick Bergin, Randy Quaid, Fiona Gilles, John Mills, Lambert Wilson, Michael Gothard.

A flawed but interesting new TV version of the story with Bergin as the scientist who clones from himself a deformed monstrosity (Quaid) who is eventually driven to murder by society's rejection. Good acting and make-up, but in its attempt to bring something new to an already done-to-death premise, this tends toward confusion. In a notable performance, Mills brings distinction to the clichéd role of the blind man the monster encounters in his travels.

FRANKENSTEIN AND THE MONSTER FROM HELL

★★☆ Paramount/Gateway, 1973, R, 93 min.
Dir: Terence Fisher. Cast: Peter Cushing, Shane Briant, Madeline Smith, John Stratton, Patrick Troughton, David Prowse.

Hammer's last Frankenstein movie is interesting but compromised in this video edition by being released in an edited ELP-mode version only. The Baron (Cushing) now resides in an asylum where he's aided by an adoring young acolyte (Briant) in the creation of a new monster (Prowse) with a Neanderthal body but the brain of a genius. FX and make-up are weak but this is still worth seeing.

FRANKENSTEIN '80

★ Gorgon, 1973, R, 85 min. Dir: Mario Mancini.
Cast: John Richardson, Gordon Mitchell, Xiro Papas,
Dalila Parker, Renato Romano, Marisa Traversi.

A modern Dr. Frankenstein uses the dreaded
"Schwartz serum" to perfect his ugly, bald
monster, Mosaic. This third-rate Italian addition to the Frankenstein saga is notable mainly
for the first-ever Frankenstein testicle transplant (which Mosaic immediately tries out by
raping a prostitute) but is otherwise just
another gory continental breasts-and-blood job
for completists only. Aka *Frankenstein Mosaic*.

FRANKENSTEIN GENERAL HOSPITAL

☆ New Star, 1988, R, 92 min.
Dir: Deborah Roberts. Cast: Mark Blankfield, Leslie
Jordan, Jonathan Farwell, Kathy Shower, Irwin Keyes,
Lou Cutell.

Awful satire with Blankfield as a modern
descendant of Dr. F trying to build a monster
of his own in the basement of Los Angeles
General Hospital. Considered by many to be
the worst Frankenstein film ever made, it's a
tough point to argue.

FRANKENSTEIN ISLAND

☆ Monterey, 1981, R, 88 min.
Dir: Jerry Warren. Cast: Robert Clarke, Cameron
Mitchell, John Carradine, Katherine Victor, Steve
Brodie, Andrew Duggan.

Junk movie guru Warren remakes his own
anti-classic *Teenage Zombies* with a veteran
cast, a period (sort-of) setting, and a Frankenstein connection. Add to this some nubile
native girls and apparent stock footage of Carradine from some earlier Z epic and you have
…well, let's not get into *that*. Excruciating.

FRANKENSTEIN MEETS THE SPACE MONSTER

★ Prism, 1965, NR, 78 min.
Dir: Robert Gaffney. Cast: Robert Reilly, James Karen,
Nancy Marshall, David Kerman, Marilyn Hanold,
Lou Cutell.

With nothing whatsoever to do with Mary
Shelley's famous creation, this monstrous
mish-mash tells the leisurely story of a disfigured humanoid robot called Frank (Reilly)
who battles Mull, the bug-eyed pet monster of
an alien race who've come to earth to repopu-
late their dying planet with kidnapped beach
bunnies—a popular alien race pastime in
movies like this. Cutell steals it as a lip-smacking alien flunky called Nadir (get it?) and
there's a lot of stock NASA rocket footage to
fast-forward through. Aka *Mars Attacks Puerto
Rico* (where this was filmed) and *Duel of the
Space Monsters*.

FRANKENSTEIN MEETS THE WOLF MAN

★★★ MCA/Universal, 1943, NR, 73 min.
Dir: Roy William Neill. Cast: Lon Chaney, Jr., Bela
Lugosi, Ilona Massey, Patric Knowles, Lionel Atwill,
Maria Ouspenskaya, Dennis Hoey, Dwight Frye.

One of the most entertaining entries in the
Universal series with revived werewolf Larry
Talbot (Chaney) seeking a cure from the late
Dr. Frankenstein, only to find the monster (a
miscast Lugosi) frozen in ice beneath the ruins
of the Frankenstein estate. Fast-paced and fun,
with top makeup, effects, settings, and music.
Marred only by some pre-release editing
removing all mention of the monster's obvious
blindness (left over from the end of *The Ghost
of Frankenstein*), which severely, and rather
unfairly, weakens Bela's performance.

FRANKENSTEIN 1970

★★ Key, 1958, NR, 83 min.
Dir: Howard W. Koch. Cast: Boris Karloff,
Tom Duggan, Jana Lund, Donald Barry,
Charlotte Austin, Mike Lane.

Karloff plays a futuristic descendant of the
original monster maker who tries to recon-
struct and revive his ancestor's creation with
atomic energy while a film crew shoots a horror movie on his estate. Occasionally effective,
especially during its trick opening sequence,
but Karloff overacts badly, the supporting cast
is inadequate, and the monster (swathed in
bandages) looks like he's wearing a bucket
over his head.

FRANKENSTEIN: THE TRUE STORY

★★★ CK Entertainment, 1973, NR, 192 min.
Dir: Jack Smight. Cast: James Mason, Leonard
Whiting, Michael Sarrazin, David McCallum, Jane
Seymour, Nicola Pagett, John Gielgud, Ralph
Richardson, Agnes Moorehead, Michael Wilding,
Margaret Leighton, Tom Baker.

This TV movie is one of the best versions (if
not actually the *true story*) of the Mary Shelley
novel done since *Bride of Frankenstein*—an
obvious inspiration. Whiting is the young med
student who creates beautiful Sarrazin. As
their subsequent relationship begins to take on
definite homosexual overtones, Frankenstein
rejects his creation for his self-righteous
fiancee (Pagett) and the monster begins to
deteriorate both mentally and physically. Soon
Sarrazin falls under the control of the sinister
Mason, who aids Whiting in the construction
of mate Seymour (excellent in one of her earliest roles) but, as per the novel, all ends tragically for all concerned. The Christopher Isher-
wood–Don Bachardy script is full of psycho-
sexual insights usually glossed over in the

143

more conventional retelling, with the story eerily looking forward to the AIDS crisis. The cast of British veterans is first-rate (though Mason overdoes it) and the production trappings are very lavish for a made-for-TV movie.

FRANKENSTEIN'S CASTLE OF FREAKS

★☆ Magnum, 1973, PG, 90 min.
Dir: Robert H. Oliver [Roberto Olivieri]. Cast: Rossano Brazzi, Michael Dunn, Edmund Purdom, Christiane Royce, Semmi Blondell, Alan Collins, Gordon Mitchell, Boris Lugosi.

Brazzi, a long way from singing "Some Enchanted Evening," stars as the good doctor, this time experimenting with a prehistoric Neanderthal man found living on the grounds of his estate (?!). A sort-of second cousin to the equally absurd, though more enjoyable, *Lady Frankenstein*, with an surprisingly large dose of femme nudity for a PG-rated film, Dunn wasted in an embrassing final role as a sex-staved dwarf, and the unforgettable Lugosi as "Ook." Great final moral: "There's a little monster in all of us." Also released as *House of Freaks, Dr. Frankenstein's House of Freaks,* and *The Monsters of Dr. Frankenstein.*

FRANKENSTEIN'S DAUGHTER

★★ Rhino, 1958, NR, 85 min.
Dir: Richard E. Cunha. Cast: John Ashley, Sandra Knight, Donald Murphy, Sally Todd, Harold Lloyd, Jr., John Zaremba, Felix Locher, Wolfe Barzell.

Rock-bottom rip-off of *I Was a Teenage Frankenstein* with Murphy as an egotistical Frankenstein relative living in southern California who creates a female monster from the mangled remains of buxom chippie Todd—the resultant creature looking about as female as Hulk Hogan in heavy lipstick. A surefire laugh riot of lab scenes, pool parties, police investigations, and unbelievable teen romance sure to please the schlockmeisters among us all. British title: *She-Monster of the Night.*

FRANKENSTEIN UNBOUND

★★★ CBS/Fox, 1990, R, 85 min. Dir: Roger Corman.
Cast: John Hurt, Raul Julia, Bridget Fonda, Jason Patric, Nick Brimble, Catherine Rabett.

Futuristic scientist Hurt is accidentally thrust by a time warp back to Lake Geneva, circa 1817, where he encounters both Mary Shelley (Fonda) and her famous characters Victor Frankenstein and his monster—real people on whom she based her novel. An entertaining crossbreed of *Back to the Future* and *Haunted Summer* with a strong cast, interesting story, and offbeat monster makeup (the stitched-

together multicolored eyeballs are most impressive). Corman's first dirrectorial job in 20 years—and his first horror film in 26—this also has pleasing visual nods to his Edgar Allan Poe series.

FREAKMAKER, THE

★★ Vidcrest, 1973, R, 89 min. Dir: Jack Cardiff.
Cast: Donald Pleasence, Tom Baker, Julie Ege, Michael Dunn, Brad Harris, Jill Haworth.

Minor, sometimes nauseating reworking of *Freaks* and *Island of Lost Souls* with Pleasence as a mad British university professor who uses his students as unwitting guinea pigs in his experiments to prove a link between the plant and animal species. Unfortunately, most of the botched results end up on display in Baker's carnival freakshow. This one is slow to start but the cast is in good form and some of Charles Parker's makeups are effective— although, like *Freaks,* this also features a supporting cast of real-life deformed folks. Once seen, "Popeye" is hard to shake. Original release title: *The Mutations.*

FREAKS

★★★☆ MGM/UA, 1932, NR, 62 min. Dir: Tod Browning. Cast: Olga Baclanova, Wallace Ford, Lelia Hyams, Henry Victor, Harry Earles, Daisy Earles.

Browning's chilling classic about circus life, this features Baclanova as a statuesque, cold-hearted aerialist who marries sideshow midget Earles for his money (though where a circus midget would inherit a fortune from is never explained) and then plots to poison him, with his fellow freaks seeking an appropriate revenge. Rarely screened in the States and banned in England for more than 20 years, this disturbing shocker crippled the career of its director and, though stickily acted and rather creaky, is a weird mixture of odd charm and some genuine scares.

FREAKY FAIRY TALES
See: *Deadtime Stories*.

FREDDY'S DEAD: THE FINAL NIGHTMARE
★★☆ New Line, 1991, R, 89 min.
Dir: Rachel Talalay. Cast: Robert Englund, Lisa Zane, Yaphet Kotto, Lezlie Dean, Shon Greenblatt, Elinor Donahue, Roseanne Arnold, Tom Arnold, Alice Cooper, Johnny Depp.

Not really the last installment in the *Nightmare on Elm Street* series (like maybe you thought it *was!*), this is a marginal improvement on parts 4 and 5. Greenblatt is another "last of the Elm Street kids" who has amnesia and thinks he may be Freddy's son, but guess again, Buster, as it turns out to be psychologist Zane, who turns out to be the killer's *daughter* and takes

him on an anticlimactic ending originally shown in 3-D. Inconsistent with others in its series but certainly watchable, though by now Tom and Roseanne are getting to be scarier than Freddy.

FRENZY
★★★ MCA/Universal, 1972, R, 116 min.
Dir: Alfred Hitchcock. Cast: Jon Finch, Barry Foster, Alec McCowen, Barbara Leigh-Hunt, Anna Massey, Vivien Merchant, Billie Whitelaw, Jean Marsh.

Popular Hitchcock shocker about a suave rapist-murderer (Foster) terrorizing London and framing his best friend (Finch) for the killings by targeting his wife (Leigh-Hunt). Masterfully directed but cold and disturbing in its misogyny, this has fine acting from Finch, Foster, and McCowen and some amusing scenes between the latter and his gourmet chef wife Merchant but on the whole isn't up to the master's earlier excursions into the horror genre. Look for Hitch's cameo during the amusing opening sequence.

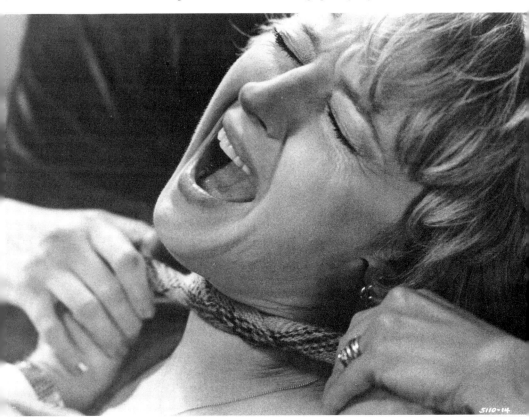

Barbara Leigh-Hunt gets all choked up in Frenzy *(1972).*

Jason contemplates the meaning of life—or is it knife?—in Friday the 13th Part V: A New Beginning *(1985).*

FRIDAY THE 13TH

★★★ Paramount, 1980, R, 95 min.
Dir: Sean S. Cunningham. Cast: Betsy Palmer,
Adrienne King, Harry Crosby, Kevin Bacon,
Laurie Bartram, Jeannine Taylor, Mark Nelson,
Robbi Morgan.

The original summer camp slaughter film, this
is set at fun-filled Camp Crystal Lake, New
Jersey, where an attempted reopening of the
old camp is disrupted by a knife, ax, and
arrow-wielding maniac. Tries to function as a
mystery, but as the killer's identity is pretty
obvious—the character doesn't even appear
on screen until the last 20 minutes—that never
comes off; on the other hand, Tom Savini's
trend-setting gore FX and Palmer's hilariously
outrageous turn make this a seminal slasher
movie. Followed by eight sequels and a completely unrelated TV series.

FRIDAY THE 13TH PART 2

★★☆ Paramount, 1981, R, 87 min.
Dir: Steve Miner. Cast: Amy Steel, John Fuery,
Adrienne King, Stu Charno, Lauren-Marie Taylor,
Russell Todd, Warrington Gillette, Betsy Palmer.

King, the lone survivor of part 1, is dispatched
in her apartment by a mysterious prowler
who then returns to Crystal Lake for more
mayhem and is revealed as a grown and

hooded Jason out to avenge his mom's decapitation. This efficient follow-up is better made
and has an appealing heroine in Steel (the
odds-on favorite *Friday* leading lady), but
much of Carl Fullerton's excellent makeup
work had to be cut to avoid an X rating.

FRIDAY THE 13TH PART 3

★★☆ Paramount, 1982, R, 95 min. Dir: Steve Miner.
Cast: Dana Kimmell, Paul Kratka, Catherine Parks,
Tracie Savage, Larry Zerner, Jeffrey Rogers, Rachel
Howard, Richard Brooker.

Or "Jason's 3-D Adventure." The big guy dons
his now-trademark hockey mask for the first
time as he lays into a bunch of chowderheads
spending the weekend at a farm along the
shores of Crystal Lake. There are mucho stabbings, impalements, electrocutions, and even a
popped eyeball (a great effect in the original 3-
D version) until heroine Kimmell smacks Mr.
Voorhees on the noggin with an ax and then
has a watery encounter with Jason's late mom
(who's mysteriously found her head again). A
nice sense of humor helps this otherwise pretty standard series entry.

FRIDAY THE 13TH—THE FINAL CHAPTER

★★★ Paramount, 1984, R, 91 min. Dir: Joseph Zito.
Cast: Kimberly Beck, Peter Barton, Crispin Glover,

Corey Feldman, Barbara Howard, E, Erich Anderson, Lawrence Monoson, Joan Freeman, Bruce Mahler, Ted White.

Despite the cheater title, this is easily the best of the *Friday* sequels. After a well-edited overview of the first three installments, Jason springs back to life at the local morgue and heads back to Crystal Lake for more teen bashing until the usual female survivor (Beck) and her monster mask-loving kid brother (Feldman in his predrug days) give Jase a fatal taste of his own machete. Excellent makeup FX by Tom Savini (including the ultimate Jason) and an above-average cast make the difference.

FRIDAY THE 13TH PART V: A NEW BEGINNING
★★☆ Paramount, 1985, R, 92 min.
Dir: Danny Steinmann. Cast: Melanie Kinnaman, John Shepherd, Shavar Ross, Richard Young, Carol Lockatell, Juliette Cummins, Debisue Voorhees, Corey Parker, Dick Wieand, Corey Feldman.

Eight years after he helped "kill" Jason, the now teenaged Tommy Jarvis (Shepherd, who's excellent) is sent to a woodsy halfway house for troubled teens, where a hockey-masked maniac goes on a bloody body-count binge. Has Jason returned again? This *Psycho II*–influenced sequel has a spunky heroine in Kinnaman and a very high corpse count but is often needlessly mean-spirited. And your baby sister could guess the "mystery" killer's identity.

FRIDAY THE 13TH PART VI: JASON LIVES!
★★ Paramount, 1986, R, 87 min.
Dir: Tom McLoughlin. Cast: Thom Mathews, Jennifer Cooke, David Kagen, Ron Pallilo, Kerry Noonan, Renée Jones, Tom Fridley, C. J. Graham.

Jason is revived from his grave by a bolt of lighting as a maggot-ridden zombie and goes on yet another killing spree. This routine follow-up restores Jason to his rightful position as slasher par excellence and has a great opening reminiscent of a '60s Hammer film, but Mathews (in the role of Tommy) is awful and the ending is ridiculously contrived. Best scene: Jason taking on a bunch of jerky survivalists.

FRIDAY THE 13TH PART VII: THE NEW BLOOD
★★ Paramount, 1988, R, 88 min.
Dir: John Carl Buechler. Cast: Lar Park Lincoln, Kevin Blair, Terry Kiser, Susan Blu, Kane Hodder, Susan Jennifer Sullivan, Elizabeth Kaitan, Heidi Kozak, Diana Barrows, Bill Butler.

Jason meets *Carrie* in this weakly directed but just-offbeat-enough series entry. The weepy, telekinetic heroine (Lincoln) accidentally resurrects the masked one (Hodder in his first turn as Jason) from Crystal Lake and then spends the rest of the movie trying to put him back. There's zero suspense but the femme cast members are super-pretty ('specially Liz Kaitan); Kiser is his usual, agreeably slimy self; and the Jason makeup is great. The ending, though, reaches new depths of desperation, and *Playgirl*-type hunk hero Blair keeps getting in the way.

FRIDAY THE 13TH PART VIII: JASON TAKES MANHATTAN
★★☆ Paramount, 1989, R, 100 min. Dir: Rob Hedden. Cast: Jensen Daggett, Scott Reeves, Peter Mark Richman, Barbara Bingham, Kane Hodder, V. C. Dupree, Sharlene Martin, Martin Cummins.

Shocked back to life by a charge of electricity, Jason boards a cruise ship for New York, slaughters most of the teen partiers, and trails the few survivors to Manhattan. Slightly better than the two films preceding it, this has good acting and imaginative direction to dress up its familiar body-count scenario. The title, though, is a cheat, as our boy Jason doesn't even reach the Big Apple until the last half hour.

FRIDAY THE 13TH—THE ORPHAN
See: *The Orphan.*

FRIGHT, THE
See: *Visiting Hours.*

FRIGHT HOUSE
★ Studio Entertainment, 1989, R, 110 min. Dir: Len Anthony. Cast: Duane Jones, Al Lewis, Jackie James, Paul Borgese, Jennifer De Lora, Robin Michaels.

This cheap-looking double-header is actually a pair of unfinished projects directed by Anthony, so you get two, two bombs in one. The plots involve campus terrors, including a murderous witch cult and a female vampire professor, and neither is worth the effort. Jones is wasted, while "Grampa Munster" Lewis hams unmercifully.

FRIGHTMARE
See: *Frightmare II.*

FRIGHTMARE
★☆ Vestron, 1982, R, 85 min.
Dir: Norman Thaddeus Vane. Cast: Ferdy Mayne, Luca Bercovici, Jennifer Starrett, Nita Talbot, Leon Askin, Jeffrey Combs.

Mayne's bravura helps along this lopsided flick filmed as *The Horror Star*. Ferdy is a hammy horror actor whose body is stolen from its flashy crypt by a bunch of horror movie–loving college kids. The horror star then returns to life and goes on a murder spree. After a clever, fun first half this becomes just another boring stalker movie.

FRIGHTMARE II
★★☆ Prism, 1974, R, 85 min.
Dir: Pete Walker. Cast: Rupert Davies, Sheila Keith, Deborah Fairfax, Kim Butcher, Paul Greenwood, Leo Genn.

Originally released as simply *Frightmare,* the II was added by Prism to avoid confusion with the previous entry, which was released to video first. In any case, this is one of Brit gore specialist Walker's most brutal and uncompromising films. Fairfax is a girl who agonizes over the release from prison of her murderous, cannibalistic mom and dad (Keith and Davies); soon a series of violent killings starts, but who's responsible? Davies and Keith are all pro as the crazy couple, adding an extra touch of reality to this grim outing. Aka *Once Upon a Frightmare* and *Cover-Up*.

FRIGHT NIGHT
★★★ RCA/Columbia, 1985, R, 105 min.
Dir: Tom Holland. Cast: Chris Sarandon, Roddy McDowall, William Ragsdale, Amanda Bearse, Stephen Geoffreys, Jonathan Strark.

Writer-director Holland helms this fun throwback to a '60s horror second feature with Ragsdale as a teen who comes to believe that his handsome new neighbor (Sarandon) is a vampire. Surprisingly complex character relationships—particularly the young hero's fascination with the clearly bisexual Sarandon, who lives with a male lover but also fangs hookers on the side—puts this a cut above most other '80s vampire flicks, though this doesn't stint on the FX either, coming up with some real eye-poppers during a razzle-dazzle climax. McDowall is in great form as a hammy has-been horror actor pressed into service as a reluctant vampire hunter, but Geoffreys steals it with a manic, Jack Nicholson-ish performance as Ragsdale's best buddy.

FRIGHT NIGHT PART II
★★ IVE, 1989, R, 103 min. Dir: Tommy Lee Wallace. Cast: Roddy McDowall, William Ragsdale, Julie Carmen, Traci Lin, Merritt Butrick, Jonathan Gries, Brain Thompson, Russell Clark.

Routine sequel begins with Ragsdale being convinced by a psychiatrist that the events in

Fright Night were just a delusion—then sexy vampiress Carmen shows up to avenge the death of brother bloodsucker Chris Sarandon. Lush-looking but fairly pointless, with nice FX and telling contributions from McDowall, Carmen, and especially Gries as a cocky werewolf.

FROGS
★★☆ Warner, 1972, PG, 90 min.
Dir: George McGowan. Cast: Ray Milland, Sam Elliott, Joan Van Ark, Adam Rourke, Judy Pace, Lynn Borden.

Enjoyably silly nature-on-a-rampager with Milland as a wealthy southern industrialist whose swampside Florida mansion is besieged by a horde of intelligent frogs who lead their fellow bayou dwellers on a vengeful rampage against Ray and his family for their thoughtless polluting of the area. A first-rate cast is done in by spiders, leeches, snakes, alligators, and snapping turtles in scenes that are genuinely creepy. Much better than you'd think.

FROM A WHISPER TO A SCREAM
See: *The Offspring*.

FROM BEYOND
★★★ Vestron, 1986, R, 85 min.
Dir: Stuart Gordon. Cast: Jeffrey Combs, Barbara Crampton, Ken Foree, Ted Sorel, Carolyn Purdey-Gordon, Bunny Summers.

Freaky follow-up to *Re-animator* from the same creative team. A scientist (Sorel) experimenting with the human pineal gland accidentally unlocks the gateway to another dimension when he mutates through various perverse forms in a search for the ultimate pleasure. Not as gross as *Re-animator* (due in part to some pre-release cutting) and potentially more interesting, this H. P. Lovecraft flick suffers mostly from cramming too many ideas into one storyline. And those who think these films only exploit the female body and sexuality should check out the sequence where muscular Foree is clad only in a *very* revealing pair of wet bikini briefs. The eventual failure of producer Empire Pictures put the kibosh on plans for further Lovecraft adaptions from Gordon with Combs and Crampton—the Roger Corman, Vincent Price, and Hazel Court for a new generation.

FROM BEYOND THE GRAVE
★★★ Warner, 1974, PG, 98 min.
Dir: Kevin Connor. Cast: Peter Cushing, Donald Pleasence, Margaret Leighton, Ian Bannen, David Warner, Lesley-Anne Down, Diana Dors, Ian Ogilvy, Nyree Dawn Porter, Angela Pleasence.

Amicus' last and best anthology, this is centered around a little antique shop run by Cushing, who punishes those who cheat or steal from him by cursing the object taken from the shop. An old mirror harbors the bloodthirsty spirit of Jack the Ripper; a World War II medal instigates a man's encounter with a witch; a snuff box is possessed by a murderous demon; and an ornately carved door leads into a supernatural netherworld. A classy cast and crisp writing (from the stories of R. Chetwynd-Hayes) and direction make this a noteworthy omnibus. Filmed as *Tales From Beyond the Grave* and reissued as *Creatures From Beyond the Grave.*

FROM THE DEAD OF NIGHT
★★ AIP, 1989, NR, 192 min.
Dir: Paul Wendkos. Cast: Lindsay Wagner, Bruce Boxleitner, Robin Thomas, Diahann Carroll, Robert Prosky, Merritt Butrick.

Based on the novel *Walkers* by Gary Brandner, this has Wagner as a woman who survives a near-death experience only to find herself hounded by walking corpses attempting to draw her back over to the "Other Side." Lindsay is her usual vivacious, sympathetic self but the overlong running time works against the creation of suspense, with this TV movie peaking long before it reaches its halfway point.

FROZEN TERROR
★★★ Lightning, 1980, R, 90 min.
Dir: Lamberto Bava. Cast: Bernice Stegers, Stanko Molnar, Roberto Posse, Veronica Zinny.

Bava the younger's first and best effort, this claustrophobic character study has Stegers as a lonely New Orleans divorcee who carries on nightly assignations with the severed head of her late lover, handily kept in the fridge. A weird, elegant mix of twisted psychology and Big Easy atmospherics marred only by a hokey, tacked-on shock ending. Aka *Macabro: Macabre.*

FULL CIRCLE
See: *The Haunting of Julia.*

FULL ECLIPSE
★★★ HBO, 1993, UR, 97 min.
Dir: Anthony Hickox. Cast: Mario Van Peebles, Patsy Kensit, Bruce Payne, Anthony Michael Dennison.

A fast-paced made-for-cable action/horror film about an elite police squad that turns out to consist entirely of werewolves. Dennison is the new recruit (recently bitten) who soon starts sprouting talons out of his knuckles like one of the "X-Men." It doesn't all work, but thanks to a strong cast and imaginative direction this *Lethal Weapon* meets *The Howling* comes off far better than you'd imagine.

FULL MOON HIGH
★★☆ HBO, 1981, PG, 94 min.
Dir: Larry Cohen. Cast: Adam Arkin, Elizabeth Hartman, Ed McMahon, Alan Arkin, Roz Kelly, Kenneth Mars, Joanne Nail, Bill Kirchenbauer, Pat Morita, Demond Wilson.

Cohen's quirky contribution to the early '80s werewolf cycle was this strained but likable comedy about an ageless werewolf (Adam Arkin) who returns to his old high school after 20 years, where he passes himself off as his own son and is shocked by what the passage of time has done to his old friends. A great comic cast makes this obscure flick worth seeking out. The minimal makeup is by Steve Neill.

FULL MOON OF THE VIRGINS
See: *The Devil's Wedding Night.*

FUNERAL HOME
★★ Paragon, 1982, R, 93 min. Dir: William Fruet.
Cast: Lesleh Donaldson, Kay Hawtry, Barry Morse, Dean Garbett, Harvey Atkin, Alf Humphries.

Mild Canadian stalker with Donaldson as a pretty teen who visits grandmother Hawtry's country inn, a former funeral parlor, where guests check in but they don't check out. The usual *Psycho* and *Halloween* clichés. Aka *Cries in the Night.*

FUNHOUSE, THE
★★☆ MCA/Universal, 1981, R, 96 min.
Dir: Tobe Hooper. Cast: Elisabeth Berridge, Cooper Huckabee, Miles Chapin, Largo Woodruff, Kevin Conway, Sylvia Miles, William Finley, Wayne Doba.

Four teens spend the night in a seedy carnival funhouse where they fall victim to a cleft-headed albino who hides his deformity behind the "normality" of a rubber Frankenstein mask. A good cast and gorgeously saturated color photography and set design make up for the unevenness of a screenplay that never bothers to explain far too many of its loose ends and asides to the audience. The opening, spoofing both *Halloween* and *Psycho*, is very amusing.

FURY, THE
★★★ CBS/Fox, 1978, R, 118 min.
Dir: Brian De Palma. Cast: Kirk Douglas, John Cassavetes, Carrie Snodgress, Amy Irving, Andrew Stevens, Fiona Lewis, Charles Durning, Carol Rosson.

De Palma followed his successful *Carrie* with this similar but more elaborate (though ultimately less successful) psychic thriller. Double-crossed government agent Douglas searches for his kidnapped son (Stevens), who's being held by an agency headed by Cassavetes that is out to exploit his psychokinetic abilities. Kirk then teams with the similarly gifted Irving and together they encounter a veritable orgy of bleeding, spinning, and exploding bodies of various cast members. There's good work from Douglas, Cassavetes, Snodgress, and Lewis and a robust score from John Williams, but the plot, adapted by John Farris from his novel, tends toward confusion. The ending, where Cassavetes explodes into a million gory pieces, is a corker. Look for Daryl Hannah, William Finley, and Dennis Franz in small roles.

FURY OF THE WOLF MAN, THE

★☆ Charter, 1971, R, 80 min.
Dir: José Maria Zabalza. Cast: Paul Naschy, Perla Cristal, Veronica Lujan, Michael Rivers.

Low-octane entry in Naschy's werewolf series—the fourth or fifth, it's actually kinda hard to tell. This time Paul returns home from Tibet with his full moon affliction and seeks the help of a lady scientist. She, smitten with Naschy, arranges for the wolf man to slay his unfaithful wife, who later is restored to life as a werewolf herself. The lady lycanthrope angle is the only interesting new wrinkle in this substandard filler.

GALAXY OF TERROR

★★☆ Embassy, 1981, R, 81 min.
Dir: Bruce D. Clark. Cast: Edward Albert, Erin Moran, Ray Walston, Zalman King, Robert Englund, Grace Zabriskie, Sid Haig, Taffee O'Connell.

A weird, badly edited, but entertaining *Alien* clone about a crew of neurotic astronauts searching for survivors of a previous mission to the planet Organthus, who come face-to-face with their worst fears come to life. The plot rarely makes sense (thanks in part to heavy pre-release cutting) and the production values are almost painfully cheapskate (yes, those *are* McDonald's Big Mac boxes lining the

spaceship corridors!), but the real attractions are the moody photography, bizarre settings, and such kickers as O'Connell raped by a slimy 12-foot maggot and Moran's (Joanie on "Happy Days") head exploding! Aka *Mindwarp: An Infinity of Terror* and *Planet of Horrors;* semi-sequel: *Forbidden World.*

GALLERY MURDERS, THE

See: *The Bird With the Crystal Plumage.*

GALLERY OF HORRORS

★ Academy, 1967, NR, 82 min.
Dir: David L. Hewitt. Cast: Lon Chaney, Jr., John Carradine, Rochelle Hudson, Roger Gentry, Karen Joy, Mitch Evans, Vic McGee, Margaret Moore.

Originally released as *Dr. Terror's Gallery of Horrors,* this shoddy rip-off of *Dr. Terror's House of Horrors* has a tuxedoed Carradine linking five comic book-like tales involving a cursed clock; a vampire in 19th-century London; a doctor who rises from the grave as a zombie; three scientists who revive an executed murderer with electricity; and Dracula's encounter with a werewolf. Cardboard sets and amateurish acting—apart from the veteran stars, who should have known better—make this one of the cheesiest anthologies ever, padded with lots of mismatched stock footage from the AIP Poe series. Aka *The Blood Suckers* and *Return From the Past.*

GAMERA

★★ Celebrity, 1965, NR, 79 min.
Dir: Noriaki Yuasa. Cast: Eiji Funakoshi, Michiko Sugata, Harumi Kiritachi, Junichiro Yamashita, Yoshiro Uchida.

Originally titled *Daikaiju Gamera: The Monster Gamera,* this Daiei Company attempt to steal some of Godzilla's thunder was a surprise hit and the first of eight Gamera adventures. The usual atomic testing frees a huge prehistoric flying turtle from an arctic ice tomb, and the monster, dubbed Gamera, heads for Japan to indulge in the usual building toppling until loaded into the nose cone of a rocket and shot into space. Probably the best of its series, this has above-average effects and a semi-serious storyline. Sinister Cinema also has available the padded U.S. release version, *Gammera the Invincible,* with shot-in-America scenes featuring Albert Dekker, Brian Donlevy, John Baragrey, and Diane Findlay.

GAMERA VS. BARUGON

★★ Celebrity, 1966, NR, 101 min.
Dir: Shigeo Tanaka. Cast: Kojiro Hongo, Kyoko Enami, Akira Natsuki, Koiji Fujiyama.

Or *Gamera Part 2*. The titanic turtle returns from space in time to battle Barugon, a freeze-ray-emitting horror born from a huge opal. A surprisingly somber entry in the series. Aka *War of the Monsters*.

GAMERA VS. GAOS

★★ Celebrity, 1967, NR, 87 min.
Dir: Noriaki Yuasa. Cast: Kojiro Hongo, Kichijiro Ueda, Hisayuki Abe, Reiko Kashahara.

More big turtle tomfoolery, this time with Gamera taking on Gaos, an enormous bat-like creature with sonic speed and laser breath. The series really started to get wacky here, mixing in scenes of kid-oriented humor with shots of Gaos eating helpless screaming victims. Aka *Gamera tai Gyaos: Gamera vs. Gyaos* and *Return of the Giant Monsters*.

GAMERA VS. GUIRON

★☆ Celebrity, 1969, NR, 83 min.
Dir: Noriaki Yuasa. Cast: Nobuhiro Kajima, Christopher Murphy, Miyuki Akiyama, Yuko Hamada, Kon Omura, Eiji Funakoshi.

In this goofy entry two young boys are kidnapped by a pair of brain-eating alien babes (named Flobella and Barbella!) whose knife-shaped monster, Guiron, battles Gamera on a distant planet. The odd FX are almost surrealistic, but everything else is a trial for all but the most dedicated Gameraphiles. Aka *Attack of the Monsters*.

GAMERA VS. GYAOS

See *Gamera vs. Gaos*.

GAMERA VS. ZIGRA

★☆ Celebrity, 1971, G, 91 min.
Dir: Noriaki Yuasa. Cast: Eiko Yamani, Reiko Kasahara, Mikiko Tsubouchi, Koji Fujiyama, Isamu Saeki, Arlene Zoellner.

Gamera goes fishing for a gigantic flying shark in this stultifying adventure. One good scene features Gamera playing his theme song on Zigra's spiked back like a xylophone, but otherwise—why bother?

GAMMA 639

See: *Night of the Zombies* (1980).

GAMMERA THE INVINCIBLE

See: *Gamera*.

GANJA AND HESS

See: *Blood Couple*.

GAPPA, THE TRIPHIBIAN MONSTER

See: *Monster From a Prehistoric Planet*.

GARDEN OF THE DEAD

★☆ Video BanCorp, 1972, PG, 85 min.
Dir: John Hayes. Cast: Duncan McLeod, John Dennis, Susan Charney, Marland Proctor, John Dullaghan, Lee Frost.

Obscure companion feature to Hayes' *Grave of the Vampire* about convicts who return from the dead when their common grave is drenched in chloroform—or maybe it was formaldehyde, I wasn't paying that close attention. Pretty dismal. Also out in a drastically shortened version called *Tomb of the Undead*.

GARGOYLES

★★☆ Star Classics, 1972, NR, 73 min.
Dir: B.W.L. Norton. Cast: Cornel Wilde, Jennifer Salt, Grayson Hall, Bernie Casey, Scott Glenn, Woodrow Chambliss.

Archeologist Wilde and photographer daughter Salt encounter a band of living gargoyles in the American Southwest when they come into the possession of a strange skull from the property of murdered desert rat Chambliss. Entertaining TV movie with Emmy-winning monster costumes and an exciting ending pitting the gargoyles against a sheriff's posse and some bikers. "Dark Shadows" Hall steals scenes as an alcoholic motel manageress who ends up hanging upside down from a telephone pole.

GATE, THE

★★ Vestron, 1987, PG-13, 92 min.
Dir: Tibor Takacs. Cast: Stephen Dorff, Christa Denton, Louis Tripp, Kelly Rowan, Jennifer Irwin.

In this slight but popular juvenile thriller, two young boys discover a gateway to hell in their backyard on an otherwise boring afternoon, and the hole spews forth a variety of evil entities. Silly but fun, with impressive low-budget FX and a pleasant young cast.

GATE II, THE

★☆ Columbia/TriStar, 1989, PG-13, 95 min.
Dir: Tibor Takacs. Cast: Louis Tripp, Simon Reynolds, Pamela Seagall, James Villamaire.

Another needless sequel to an only marginally interesting original, this has the now slightly older Tripp taken over by demons who trick our young hero into believing that they will grant his every wish. Didn't the little bonehead learn *anything* from his experiences in part I? Good FX, not much else.

GATES OF HELL, THE

★★☆ Paragon, 1981, UR, 92 min.
Dir: Lucio Fulci. Cast: Christopher George, Katherine

MacColl, Janet Agren, Carlo de Mejo, John Morghen, Daniela Doria.

Originally entitled *Paura nella Citta de Morti Vivente: Fear in the City of the Living Dead*, Fulci's graphic follow-up to his successful *Zombie* is just as gory, if not more so, but not as satisfying. A priest's suicide opens the gates of hell in the New England village of Dunwich, unleashing hordes of brain-squashing ghouls. Lots of intestine barfing and head drilling. Best scene: George rescuing a prematurely buried MacColl from her sealed coffin, his pickax coming dangerously close to her head as it smashes through the casket lid. Aka *City of the Living Dead*.

GENIE OF DARKNESS

★★ Sinister Cinema, 1960, NR, 77 min. Dir: Federico Curiel. Cast: German Robles, Julio Aleman, Domingo Soler, Aurora Alvarado, Mander, Rogelio Jimenez, Fanny Schiller, Rina Valdarno.

The best Nostradamus film (if you can imagine such a thing) but with the worst ending. Nostradamus returns from *The Monster Demolisher* undemolished enough to kill off his arch enemy Igor, fall in love with a pretty actress, and (in the most impressive scene) burn poor Leo's pathetic old mother alive. In the end Professor Duran scatters the ashes from the vampire's coffin to the wind, which will supposedly destroy him. Faster-paced and more complexly plotted than the others in this cheapo series, as such this is moderately enjoyable. Original Mexican title: *Nostradamus y El Genio de las Tinieblas: Nostradamus and the Genie of Darkness*.

GHASTLY ONES, THE

★ Video Home Library, 1969, R, 81 min. Dir: Andy Milligan. Cast: Veronica Radbrook, Hal Belsoe, Eileen Hayes, Don Williams, Maggie Rogers, Richard Romanus.

The first of Milligan's ultra-cheap Staten Island anti-classics, this one concerns a Victorian family being brutally dispatched, one by one, by a greedy heir after the family fortune. There are axings, stabbings, and beheadings galore, but inept technical credits and a never-convincing period setting make it all more funny than shocking or gross. It's amazing that familiar character actor Romanus was encouraged to continue in the business after this inauspicious debut. British title: *Blood Rites*.

GHIDRAH, THE THREE-HEADED MONSTER

★★★ Interglobal, 1964, NR, 85 min. Dir: Inoshiro Honda. Cast: Yosuke Natsuki, Yuriko

Hoshi, Hiroshi Koizumi, Takashi Shimura, Akiko Wakabayashi, Hisaya Ito, Emi Ito, Yumi Ito.

In this good follow-up to *Godzilla vs. Mothra*, the mighty lizard is presented as a hero—albeit a reluctant one—for the first time. When the triple-headed flying dragon Ghidrah arrives on Earth in a meteor, it isn't long before Rodan bursts forth from his volcano resting place and Godzilla rises from the ocean depths and Japan is once again in peril. Fortunately, Mothra and the tiny twin Alilenas persuade Godzilla and Rodan to team up in order to defeat this interloper from space. Solid effects work and a surprisingly complex plot make this one of the best of the Toho monster epics. Original title: *Chikyo Saidaino Kessen: The Biggest Fight on Earth* and also released as *The Greatest Battle on Earth*. Sequel: *Godzilla vs. Monster Zero*.

GHOST, THE

★★★ ABC/Liberty, 1963, NR, 96 min. Dir: Robert Hampton [Riccardo Freda]. Cast: Barbara Steele, Peter Baldwin, Leonard Eliot [Elio Jotta], Harriet White Medin, Umberto Raho, Reginald Price Anderson.

This in-name-only sequel to Freda's *The Horrible Dr. Hichcock* has Steele in one of her best

---

BARBARA STEELE
(1938–)

The sultry First Lady of Fear, La Steele is British born but received her greatest acclaim for her appearances in Italian horror films. Her first starring role was in Mario Bava's seminal *Black Sunday* in 1960; for the rest of the decade she was featured in a variety of continental chillers, usually cast as a perfidiously unfaithful wife or supernatural seductress. In the '70s and '80s Barbara went into semi-retirement, though the haunting actress has re-emerged from time to time to take an occasional role, including that of Dr. Julia Hoffman in Dan Curtis' short-lived prime-time *Dark Shadows* revival in 1991.

Black Sunday ('60), *The Pit and the Pendulum* ('61), *The Horrible Dr. Hichcock* ('62), *The Ghost* ('63), *Castle of Blood* ('63), *The Long Hair of Death* ('64), *Nightmare Castle* ('65), *Terror-Creatures From the Grave* (65), *The She-Beast* ('66), *An Angel for Satan* ('66), *The Crimson Cult* ('68), *They Came From Within* ('76), *Piranha* ('78), *Silent Scream* ('80).

roles as the perfidious wife of Dr. H, who plots with lover Baldwin to murder her hubby, who then seemingly returns from the tomb to drive the conspiring couple to madness and death. A richly photographed *Diabolique*-type Italian chiller, this plays much better than its ordinary-sounding plot line might lead you to suspect. Italian title: *Lo Spettro: The Spectre* and also out as *The Spectre of Dr. Hichcock*.

GHOST BREAKERS, THE
★★★☆ MCA/Universal, 1940, NR, 85 min.
Dir: George Marshall. Cast: Bob Hope, Paulette Goddard, Richard Carlson, Paul Lukas, Anthony Quinn, Willie Best, Noble Johnson, Virginia Brissac.

Hope's best movie, this delightful horror comedy has ol' ski-nose as a sarcastic radio personality who helps beautiful heiress Goddard claim a haunted Cuban castle. Although very funny, this also has glistening atmosphere and Johnson as a towering, scary zombie. The film's success obviously inspired the later Abbott and Costello comic chillers. Remade as *Scared Stiff*.

GHOSTBUSTERS
★★★ RCA/Columbia, 1984, PG, 105 min.
Dir: Ivan Reitman. Cast: Bill Murray, Dan Aykroyd, Sigourney Weaver, Harold Ramis, Rick Moranis, Annie Potts, William Atherton, Ernie Hudson.

This runaway box-office smash is like a multi-million-dollar updating of an old Abbott and Costello movie. When New York City is invaded by weird supernatural forces, centered in a lavish art deco apartment building along Central Park West, the city's only hope is the Ghostbusters: a team of wacky freelance parapsychologists. Some good FX and Murray's winning wise-guy persona are the best things about this somewhat overrated money-maker, which was followed by a cartoon series, lots of toys, and—oh yes—a sequel.

GHOSTBUSTERS 2
★★ RCA/Columbia, 1989, PG, 108 min.
Dir: Ivan Reitman, Cast: Bill Murray, Dan Aykroyd, Sigourney Weaver, Harold Ramis, Rick Moranis, Annie Potts, Ernie Hudson, Peter MacNichol.

Medicore sequel taking place five years later, when the discredited Ghostbusters (sued by the city for the destruction caused to the Big Apple in the original) return to action to prevent a supernatural apocalypse brought about by the restoration of an old painting of an evil sorcerer. Another why-bother follow-up that seems to have been made more because of a contractual obligation than because of any real

want or desire on the part of actors or directors. Too much time is frittered away on the Sigourney's baby subplot, though the FX are as good as ever and MacNicol is hilarious as the marble-mouthed restorer of the cursed canvas.

GHOST CHASERS
★★ Warner, 1951, NR, 69 min.
Dir: William Beaudine. Cast: Leo Gorcey, Huntz Hall, Jan Kayne, Lloyd Corrigan, Philip Van Zandt, Lela Blias, Bernard Gorcey, Billy Benedict.

Another low-brow Bowery Boys horror spoof with the guys visiting the haunted house of a female psychic and encountering a mad scientist and a friendly ghost—no, not Casper. It's okay for series fans and there's good work from Van Zandt as the doc and Corrigan as the ghost.

GHOST FEVER
★☆ Nelson, 1987, PG, 86 min.
Dir: Alan Smithee [Lee Madden]. Cast: Sherman Hemsley, Luis Avalos, Jennifer Rhodes, Deborah Benson, Myron Healey, Pepper Martin.

Slim horror comedy with Hemsley and Avalos as detectives investigating a southern mansion haunted by the ghost of slave trader Martin. Tries hard to be funny but rarely is; this was started in '84 and not finished until '87, with director Madden taking the pseudonymous Smithee credit.

GHOST GALLEON, THE
See: *Horror of the Zombies*.

GHOSTHOUSE
★★ Imperial, 1987, UR, 94 min.
Dir: Humphrey Humbert [Umberto Lenzi]. Cast: Lara Wendel, Greg Scott, Donald O'Brian, Mary Sellars, Ron Houck, Kate Silver.

A pastafied *Poltergeist* shot in and around Boston by an Italian film crew. Strange radio messages emanating from an old Massachusetts mansion bring a group of curious young people to the premises, where they are mostly murdered by a little girl ghost and her possessed clown doll. Good gore but poor dialogue and a bland cast. Up to you.

GHOST IN THE MACHINE
★★ Fox, 1993, R, 92 min.
Dir: Rachel Talalay. Cast: Karen Allen, Chris Mulkey, Wil Horneff, Ted Marcoux, Richard McKenzie.

A dead mass murderer, obsessed with finding and possessing the perfect family, returns as a killer computer virus to haunt single mom Allen and son Horneff in this derivative thriller. Good acting and FX, but the film-makers were clearly unaware that all this had already been done in *Shocker* and *The Stepfather*.

GHOST IN THE NIGHT
See: *Spooks Run Wild*.

GHOST OF FRANKENSTEIN, THE
★★★ MCA/Universal, 1942, NR, 68 min.
Dir: Erle C. Kenton. Cast: Lon Chaney, Jr., Evelyn Ankers, Bela Lugosi, Sir Cedric Hardwicke, Ralph Bellamy, Lionel Atwill, Janet Ann Gallow, Dwight Frye.

In the first of the non-Karloff Frankensteins, Chaney takes over as ol' flat-top is rescued from the dried sulfur pit by pal Ygor (Lugosi). This gruesome twosome then take off for the home of psychiatrist Ludwig Frankenstein (Hardwicke), who's inspired by his father's ghost to put a new brain in the monster's skull. Not as lavish as the first three in the series but far better than its reputation suggests, with solid production values and an outstanding cast—Bela stealing it as the capering Ygor.

GHOST SHIP OF THE BLIND DEAD
See: *Horror of the Zombies*.

GHOSTS IN THE NIGHT
See: *Ghosts on the Loose*.

GHOSTS ON THE LOOSE
★ Goodtimes, 1943, NR, 65 min.
Dir: William Beaudine. Cast: Bela Lugosi, Leo Gorcey, Huntz Hall, Ava Gardner, Bobby Jordan, Minerva Urecal.

There are no ghosts and few laughs in this very weak East Side Kids horror spoof with the boys running into Bela's Nazi spy ring in an eerie old house. The pits. A radiant young Gardner has a small role as the older sister of one of the boys. Aka *Ghosts in the Night* and *The East Side Kids Meet Bela Lugosi*.

GHOST STORIES
See: *Kwaidan*.

Bela Lugosi comforts a plastered Lon Chaney, Jr., in The Ghost of Frankenstein *(1942).*

Boris Karloff plays "Gotcha!" with Dorothy Hyson in The Ghoul *(1933).*

GHOST STORY
See: *Madhouse Mansion.*

GHOST STORY
★★☆ MCA/Universal, 1981, R, 110 min.
Dir: John Irwin. Cast: Fred Astaire, John Houseman, Douglas Fairbanks, Jr., Melvyn Douglas, Patricia Neal, Craig Wasson, Alice Krige, Jacqueline Brookes.

Four elderly New Englanders, haunted by a joint misdeed from their past, are bedeviled by the beauteous Krige, a shape-shifting spirit out for revenge. A handsomely photographed simplification of Peter Straub's mammoth best-seller, this is good to look at but makes little sense and features characters either so unsympathetic or sketchily drawn that you'll end up rooting for the ghost. Superb makeup effects by Dick Smith are all but lost in the editing. Look for Ken Olin of TV's "thirtysomething" in the flashback sequences as a young Houseman.

GHOST TOWN
★★☆ TWE, 1988, R, 85 min.
Dir: Richard Governor. Cast: Franc Luz, Catherine Hickland, Jimmie F. Skaggs, Bruce Glover, Penelope Windust, Laura Schaefer.

Deputy Luz and heiress Hickland are trapped in a dusty ghost town populated by restless spirits and an undead outlaw (Skaggs), who sees in the girl the reincarnation of the chanteuse he loved and murdered a century earlier. Strong on atmosphere, performances, and makeup but weak on pacing and plot, this is probably the best combination of the horror and western genres yet attempted.

GHOST WRITER
★★ Prism, 1989, PG, 91 min. Dir: Kenneth D. Hall. Cast: Audrey Landers, Judy Landers, Anthony Franciosa, Jeff Conaway, David Doyle, Dick Miller.

This transparent ghost comedy (made for theatres but only shown on TV) has Audrey as a writer haunted by the ghost of former Hollywood diva Judy. The cast tries hard, but there are only a handful of laughs and most of the setups and situations are so old they have mold on them.

GHOUL, THE
★★★ Sinister Cinema, 1933, NR, 79 min. Dir: T. Hayes Hunter. Cast: Boris Karloff, Ernest Thesiger, Cedric Hardwicke, Dorothy Hyson, Anthony Bushell, Kathleen Harrison, Ralph Richardson, Harold Huth.

Karloff returned home to England to film this colorful, absurd chiller about an Egyptologist who rises from his tomb to retrieve a valuable scarab stolen from his coffin by his dastardly butler (Thesiger). A fun attempt to cash in on Boris' Hollywood successes, with a good supporting cast and creepy makeup (though it's never explained why Karloff is so weird looking—even before his burial!).

GHOUL, THE
★★☆ Media, 1975, PG, 83 min.
Dir: Freddie Francis. Cast: Peter Cushing, John Hurt, Alexandra Bastedo, Veronica Carlson, Ian McCulloch, Gwen Watford, Stewart Bevan, Don Henderson.

Modest, old-fashioned Brit horror flick about a former cleric (Cushing) with a guilty secret from his past that he keeps hidden away in the attic of his country mansion. When unwary travelers (like the vivacious Carlson) happen by, they end up falling prey to said secret's ravenous hunger for human flesh. The best of a trio of Hammer-like chillers made by Tyburn Films in the mid-'70s, this one benefits from a strong cast, some attractive art direction, and distinctive plot echoes of *Psycho* and *The Reptile*.

GHOULIES
★★ Vestron, 1985, PG-13, 81 min.
Dir: Luca Bercovici. Cast: Peter Liapis, Lisa Pelikan, Michael Des Barres, Jack Nance, Ralph Seymour, Mariska Hargitay, Keith Joe Dick, Bobbie Bresee.

Liapis (who looks like Kyle MacLachlan's creepy brother) inherits an old mansion and a supernatural bible from his satanist father; eventually he is possessed by Dad's spirit and uses the book to summon forth a horde of "ghoulies": ugly little puppets that drool a lot. Routine *Gremlins* clone that never successfully mixes humor and horror, despite a few effective moments (like Bresee as a satanic temptress with a *really long* tongue). The ending is an especial cop-out, though this was successful enough to inspire several direct-to-video follow-ups.

GHOULIES II
★☆ Vestron, 1987, PG-13, 89 min.
Dir: Albert Band [Alfredo Antonini]. Cast: Damon Martin, Kerry Remsen, Royal Dano, Phil Fondacaro, J. Downing, Starr Andreeff, Bill Butler, Anthony Dawson.

Set in a traveling carnival, this dull sequel has the titular terrors hiding out in a funhouse and wrecking havoc on the teen customers. The sideshow milieu gives this some effective atmosphere, but cardboard characters and rubbery effects cause it to wear out its welcome in no time.

GHOULIES III: GHOULIES GO TO COLLEGE
★☆ Vestron, 1990, R, 94 min.
Dir: John Carl Buechler. Cast: Kevin McCarthy, Evan Mackenzie, Griffin O'Neal, Hope Marie Carlton, Marcia Wallace, Kane Hodder.

Third but not, sadly, last in the series, this has the ghoulies running rampant at a college frat house. McCarthy hams it up as a professor who tries to control them and Carlton does a sexy strip, but that may not be enough to keep you around till the end. Aka *Ghoulies Go to College*.

GHOULIES GO TO COLLEGE
See: *Ghoulies III: Ghoulies Go to College*.

GHOUL IN SCHOOL, THE
See: *Werewolf in a Girls Dormitory*.

GIANT CLAW, THE
★☆ Goodtimes, 1957, NR, 74 min.
Dir: Fred F. Sears. Cast: Jeff Morrow, Mara Corday, Morris Ankrum, Robert Shayne, Edgar Barrier, Louis D. Merrill.

A genuine turkey about a gigantic buzzard from outer space flying around the world smashing planes and trains, eating hapless parachutists, and perching atop the Empire State Building. The seasoned B cast act with amazing sincerity, but the effects are among the worst ever seen in a studio-shot Hollywood film, with the puppet bird an absolute riot and lots of stock footage from *The Beast from 20,000 Fathoms*, *It Came from Beneath the Sea*, *Earth vs. the Flying Saucers*, and *War of the Worlds*. Best line: "It's just a bird, a big bird!" Shooting title: *Mark of the Claw*.

GIANT FROM THE UNKNOWN
★★ Media, 1958, NR, 77 min. Dir: Richard E. Cunha. Cast: Edward Kemmer, Sally Fraser, Buddy Baer, Morris Ankrum, Bob Steele, Joline Brand.

Probably Cunha's best film, and that's *still* not saying much, this sometimes effective quickie has Baer as a huge Spanish conquistador who is revived from his swampy grave by a bolt of lighting. He then goes on the usual rampage: axing passersby, carrying off heroine Fraser, and fighting hero Kemmer before toppling from a suspension bridge to his destruction. Typically plotted but with good Jack Pierce makeup and a highly effective climax set during a snowstorm.

GIANT GILA MONSTER, THE
★☆ Rhino, 1959, NR, 74 min.
Dir: Ray Kellogg. Cast: Don Sullivan, Lisa Simone, Shug Fisher, Ken Graham, Ken Knox, Janice Stone.

A bad Elvis clone battles a little dimestore gila monster made to look, via special defects, like —well—a *big* dimestore gila monster knocking over toy cars and a Lionel train set. This amusingly bad companion piece to the far better *The Killer Shrews* has everything: necking teens, a swingin' barn dance, awful songs, and the hero's cute crippled little sister, who seems to have strayed in from some old Shirley Temple movie. All this and Shug Fisher too!

GIANT LEECHES, THE
See: *Attack of the Giant Leeches.*

GIANT SPIDER INVASION, THE
☆ VCL, 1975, PG, 82 min. Dir: Bill Rebane. Cast: Steve Brodie, Barbara Hale, Leslie Parrish, Alan Hale, Robert Easton, Kevin Brodie, Dianne Lee Hart, Bill Williams.

This one you've gotta see for yourself; it's one of the all-time worst. A black hole crashes into Wisconsin(!?) and unleashes a horde of huge spiders born from diamond-encrusted eggs. The terrible moments are legion, mostly supplied by an embarrassed cast of washed-up has-beens and drive-in nobodies and some of the tackiest special effects on record—the main spider is played by a hairy black Volkswagen. Hardly seems like it could have been made in the '70s, but then there's always *A*P*E*.

GIGANTIS, THE FIRE MONSTER
See: *Godzilla Raids Again!*

GINGERBREAD HOUSE, THE
See: *Who Slew Auntie Roo?*

GIRLFRIEND FROM HELL
★★ Avid, 1989, R, 92 min. Dir: Daniel M. Peterson. Cast: Liane Curtis, Dana Ashbrook, James Daughton, James Karen.

Shy Curtis is turned into the school slut when she's demonically possessed in this mild teen horror comedy. "Twin Peaks"' Ashbrook is the nice guy/boyfriend bedeviled by her bold new behavior.

GIRL IN A SWING, THE
★★☆ HBO, 1988, R, 119 min. Dir: Gordon Hessler. Cast: Meg Tilly, Rupert Frazer, Nicholas Le Prevost, Elspet Gray, Helen Cherry, Lorna Heilbron.

Long, slow adaptation of the Richard Abrams novel about a lonely English antiques dealer (Frazer) who marries a mysterious German beauty (Tilly) who's haunted past eventually destroys them. Hauntingly atmospheric and well acted by Tilly, but a dorky, miscast Frazer, needless narration, and far too many soft-core sex scenes muck up this ghost story's overall effectiveness.

GIRLS NITE OUT
★☆ HBO, 1982, R, 92 min. Dir: Robert Deubel. Cast: Julie Montgomery, James Carroll, Hal Holbrook, Rutanya Alda, Suzanne Barnes, David Holbrook.

A psycho dressed as a college's football team mascot (a dancing bear) goes after cheerleaders on a scavenger hunt. Another by-the-numbers slasher with routine murders and wasted appearances by Holbrook (as a campus cop) and Alda. Aka *The Scaremaker.*

GIRL'S SCHOOL SCREAMERS
★★ Media, 1984, R, 85 min. Dir: John P. Finegan. Cast: Mollie O'Mara, Sharon Christopher, Mari Butler, Beth O'Malley, Karen Krevitz, Monica Antonucci.

Philadelphia-shot slasher (filmed as *The Portrait*) about a group of Catholic college coeds falling victim to a mad killer hiding out in an old mansion the school has inherited. After a creepy opening scene featuring a spectral bride right out of *Ghost Story,* this quickly becomes just another predictable bimbos and blades job.

GIRLY
★☆ Prism, 1970, PG, 101 min. Dir: Freddie Francis. Cast: Vanessa Howard, Michael Bryant, Howard Trevor, Ursula Howells, Pat Heyward, Michael Ripper.

This lackluster black comedy (a favorite of director Francis) plays like a British version of TV's "The Addams Family"—only not as funny. A family living in a big old English manor kidnap and kill various "friends" brought home to play with the "children": a teenage brother and sister who act like kids and even sleep in adult-sized cribs. Things take a deadly turn, however, when a new "friend" (Bryant) seduces the entire household, leading to jealousy and murder. The actors and director are consistently superior to their material. Aka *Mumsy, Nanny, Sonny and Girly.*

GNAW: FOOD OF THE GODS II
See: *Food of the Gods Part 2.*

GOD BLESS DR. SHAGETZ
See: *Evil Town.*

GODSEND, THE
★★ Vestron, 1980, R, 86 min. Dir: Gabrielle Beaumont. Cast: Cyd Hayman, Malcolm Stoddard, Angela Pleasence, Patrick Barr, Wilhelmina Green, Joanne Boorman.

Glum familial drama with elements from *The Omen* thrown in for bad measure. A pregnant Pleasence gives birth in the home of total strangers Hayman and Stoddard and then flees. The dopey couple then adopt the newborn girl, who, over the next seven or eight years, eliminates all of her parents's natural children. Starts out strong, but the self-defeating passage of time needed to tell the story cripples all attempts at suspense.

GOD TOLD ME TO

★★★ Charter, 1976, R, 89 min. Dir: Larry Cohen. Cast: Tony LoBianco, Deborah Raffin, Sandy Dennis, Sylvia Sidney, Richard Lynch, Mike Kellin.

In one of Cohen's most bizarre films (and in a career like Larry's, that's saying *a lot!*), NYPD detective LoBianco (who's excellent) investigates a series of brutal, seemingly unrelated murders in which the killers are heretofore ordinary citizens who, when caught, claim that "God told me to!" Unreleased until 1977 and then extensively re-edited, this wonderfully tasteless exercise involves everything from virgin births to alien invaders to the sec-

ond coming, and although it all makes little sense, it's never less than entertaining. Look for the late Andy Kaufman as the cop who goes berserk during the St. Patrick's Day parade. Aka *Demon.*

GODZILLA, KING OF THE MONSTERS

★★★ Paramount/Gateway, 1954, NR, 80 min. Dirs: Inoshiro Honda, Terry Morse. Cast: Raymond Burr, Takashi Shimura, Momoko Kochi, Akira Takarada, Akihiko Hirata, Frank Iwanaga.

In the first and best of the long-running monster series, Tokyo is ravaged for the first time by the towering prehistoric fire hazard, stomping and incinerating the city and its people until reduced to bones by the experimental "oxygen destroyer" of suicidal Dr. Serizawa (Hirata). Modern audiences will undoubtedly be confused by the utter seriousness of this brooding black-and-white classic. Excellent Eiji Tsuburaya special effects, while the added American scenes with Burr cut into the original material work surprisingly well. Followed by no less than 20 sequels, most of which are available on video.

GODZILLA 1985

★★ Starmaker, 1984, PG, 91 min. Dirs: Koji Hashimoto, R. J. Kizer. Cast: Raymond Burr, Ken Tanaka, Shin Takuma, Yusuko Sawaguchi, Yosuke Natsuki, Keiju Kobyashi, Warren Kemmerling, Travis Swords.

This lumbering semi-remake of the 1954 original brings back the big boy for the first time in nearly a decade. Once again Tokyo is in peril, and once again Burr is on hand to comment on the action like a 400-pound Greek chorus. Despite highly touted new and improved special effects (for the first time Godzilla is being played by a mechanical model rather than a guy in a suit), the only discernable difference is that now Godzilla can curl his upper lip. Played too ludicrously straight to be enjoyed even as camp. Followed by *Godzilla vs. Biollante.*

GODZILLA ON MONSTER ISLAND

See: *Godzilla vs. Gigan.*

GODZILLA RAIDS AGAIN!

★★ Goodtimes, 1955, NR, 78 min. Dir: Motoyoshi Odo. Cast: Hiroshi Koizumi, Setsuko Wakayama, Mindru Chiaki, Takashi Shimura.

Toho's second Godzilla movie is also one of the least interesting, with the Big G and a spike-backed creature called Anguris fighting their way through Osaka. Weak effects and heavy-handed "dramatic" subplots abound.

EIJI TSUBURAYA
(1901–1970)

This master of Japanese monster special effects started his career as a cinematographer before becoming head of the Toho Studios special effects department in the '50s. His intricate man-in-a-suit and model cities work in the '50s and early '60s gave way to quicker, cheaper FX in later Toho monster rallies, but his elaborate miniatures and process shots for films like *Godzilla, King of the Monsters* created almost poetic images that remain unsurpassed.

Godzilla, King of the Monsters ('54), *Half Human* ('55), *Gigantis, the Fire Monster* ('55), *Rodan* ('56), *The H-Man* ('58), *Varan the Unbelievable* ('58), *The Human Vapor* ('60), *Mothra* ('61), *King Kong vs. Godzilla* ('63), *Attack of the Mushroom People* ('63), *Godzilla vs. the Thing* ('64), *Dagora, the Space Monster* (64), *Ghidrah, the Three-Headed Monster* ('65), *Frankenstein Conquers the World* ('65), *Monster Zero* ('66), *War of the Gargantuas,* ('67), *Godzilla vs. the Sea Monster* ('67), *Son of Godzilla* ('68), *King Kong Escapes* ('68), *Destroy All Monsters* ('68), *Latitude Zero* ('69), *Godzilla's Revenge* ('69).

Urban renewal, dinosaur style, in Godzilla, King of the Monsters *(1954).*

Original title: *Gojira no Gyaskushu: Godzilla's Counterattack;* first released in the U.S. as *Gigantis, the Fire Monster,* which is still the actual on-screen title of this tape.

GODZILLA'S COUNTERATTACK
See: *Godzilla Raids Again!*

GODZILLA'S REVENGE
★★☆ Paramount/Gateway, 1969, G, 69 min.
Dir: Inoshiro Honda. Cast: Kenji Sahara, Tomonori Yazaki, Machiko Naka, Sachio Sakai.

The *Curse of the Cat People* of the Godzilla series, this entry depicts the trials and tribulations of a lonely latch-key kid who escapes his humdrum everyday world by fantasizing about Godzilla, Minya, and the other residents of Monster Island, his fantasies eventually helping him deal with the school bully and a pair of bumbling bank robbers. The untimely death of effects master Eiji Tsuburaya early in production resulted in the usage of lots of stock footage from earlier films; this was also the first in the series to feature a little kid hero and sometimes bears more than a passing resemblance to *Home Alone!* Harmless fluff, originally known as *Ord Kaiju Daishingeki: All Monsters Attack.*

GODZILLA VS. BIOLLANTE
★★★ HBO, 1989, PG, 104 min.
Dir: Kazurki Omuri. Cast: Kunihiko MItamura, Yoshiko Tanaka, Masanobu Takashima, Megumi Odaka, Toru Minegishi, Yoshiko Kuga.

The best Godzilla movie in years, this direct sequel to *Godzilla 1985* pits the resurrected lizard against a new foe, Biollante, an even bigger monster created via genetic engineering from some Godzilla and plant cells. In keeping with the tone of *G '85,* this is a deadly serious adventure with better-than-usual FX and a strong—if somewhat overstated—environmental message. It was followed by *Godzilla vs. King Ghidrah.*

GODZILLA VS. GIGAN
★★☆ Starmaker, 1972, PG, 89 min.
Dir: Jun Fukuda. Cast: Hiroshi Ishikawa, Yuriko Hishimi, Tomoko Umeda, Minrou Takashima, Kunio Murai, Susumu Fjuita.

Alien cockroaches in human guise invade Earth with their pet monster Gigan (a metal bird with a buzzsaw in his belly); when Godzilla intervenes, Ghidrah is also called into action. Fairly standard '70s Godzilla epic (first released here as *Godzilla on Monster Island*), this is notable for one thing: an alien device that allows Godzilla to talk! Aka *War of the Monsters*.

GODZILLA VS. HEDORAH
See: *Godzilla vs. The Smog Monster*.

GODZILLA VS. MECHAGODZILLA
★★☆ Starmaker, 1974, PG, 84 min.
Dir: Jun Fukuda. Cast: Masauki Daimon, Kazuya Aoyama, Reiko Tajima, Hiroshi Koizumi, Akihiko Hirata, Barbara Lynn.

Toho celebrated Godzilla's 20th anniversary with this colorful free-for-all, throwing in everything from a robot Godzilla to *Planet of the Apes*–type aliens to a James Bond-ish super spy to a big Chinese dog master called King Seesaw. Probably the best Godzilla movie from this period; also known as *Godzilla vs. the Cosmic Monster* and *Godzilla vs. the Bionic Monster*.

GODZILLA VS. MEGALON
★☆ Goodtimes, 1973, PG, 78 min.
Dir: Jun Fukuda. Cast: Katshuhiko Sasaki, Hiroyuki Kawase, Yutaka Hayashi, Kotouro Tomita, Robert Dunham.

The absolute bottom of the Godzilla barrel, this pits our rubbery lizard hero and an Ultra Man–like robot called Jet Jaguar against Megalon, the beetle-like minion of underground bad guys called Seatopians, and a cameoing Gigan. Marred by sub-par effects (apart from a disappearing lake and collapsing dam) and awful dubbing (the kid character sounds like he's on helium).

GODZILLA VS. MONSTER ZERO
★★ Paramount, 1965, NR, 93 min. Dir: Inoshiro Honda. Cast: Nick Adams, Akira Takarada, Kumi Mizuno, Akira Kubo, Keiko Sawai, Jun Tazaki.

Routine Godzilla adventure with a sci-fi slant. Aliens from the mysterious planet X, hidden on the other side of the sun, turn Godzilla and Rodan against Earth after we send the monsters to X to fight Ghidrah—who's also on their side! Hilarious dubbed dialogue makes Adams sound totally ridiculous ("You lousy, stinking rats!" he calls his alien captors at one point). For series fans only. Original title: *Kaiju Kaisenso: Monster Zero*.

GODZILLA VS. MOTHRA
★★★ Paramount, 1964, NR, 87 min.
Dir: Inoshiro Honda. Cast: Akira Takarada, Yuriko Hoshi, Hiroshi Koizumi, Yu Fujiki, Yoshifumi Tajima, Kenji Sahara, Emi Ito, Yumi Ito.

A typhoon washes both Mothra's hugh egg and Godzilla ashore, and Tokyo once again falls victim to the fire-breathing titan. Mothra attempts to stop him but perishes; luckily, her egg hatches and twin larvae emerge to wrap Godzilla in a silky cocoon and send him crashing into the sea. This direct follow-up to *King Kong vs. Godzilla* is easily the best of the sequels, with splendid effects and a plotline that's taken totally straight. Originally released in the U.S. as *Godzilla vs. the Thing*.

GODZILLA VS. THE BIONIC MONSTER
See: *Godzilla vs. Mechagodzilla*.

GODZILLA VS. THE COSMIC MONSTER
See: *Godzilla vs. Mechagodzilla*.

GODZILLA VS. THE SEA MONSTER
★★☆ Interglobal, 1966, NR, 83 min.
Dir: Jun Fukuda. Cast: Akira Takarada, Kumi Mizuno, Toru Watanbe, Hideo Sunazuka, Emi Ito, Yumi Ito.

Fun series entry. On an uncharted island shipwreck survivors encounter a secret military organization and their huge shrimp (there's a contradiction for ya) Ebirah, native slaves, and a comatose Godzilla, who's revived by lightning while the good guys are rescued by guest star Mothra. Undemanding entertainment titled *Nankai No dai Ketto: Big Duel in the North Sea* in Japan and *Ebirah, Horror of the Deep* in England.

GODZILLA VS. THE SMOG MONSTER
★★☆ Warner, 1971, G, 85 min.
Dir: Yoshimitu Bano. Cast: Akira Yamauchi, Hiroyuki Kawase, Toshie Kimura, Toshio Shubaki, Keiko Mari.

In one of his goofiest adventures, Godzilla fights Hedorah, a creature created from pollution, who burns our scaly hero with its acidic blood until the Big G, quite literally, kicks the crap out of him. Besides a ridiculous theme song ("Save the Earth! Find a solution to stop pollution, save the Earth!"), this has animated inserts and oddly arty direction mixing in shots of a sludge choked Tokyo Bay with the battling behemoths. Original title: *Gojira tai Hedorah: Godzilla vs. Hedorah*.

GODZILLA VS. THE THING
See: *Godzilla vs. Mothra.*

GOKE, BODY SNATCHER FROM HELL
See: *Body Snatcher From Hell.*

GOLEM, THE
★★★☆ Sinister Cinema, 1920, NR, 70 min.
Dirs: Paul Wegener, Carl Boese. Cast: Paul Wegener, Lyda Salmanova, Albert Steinruck, Ernst Deutsch, Lothar Muthel, Otto Gebuhr.

One of the most impressive German silent horror films, this features Wegener as the clay statue brought to life by a rabbi hoping to use the walking statue to help his ghetto-dwelling people. Things go awry, however, when the golem falls in love with the rabbi's beautiful daughter (Salmanova). The obvious model for the entire look and much of the plotting of the Universal Frankenstein series, this is imaginatively photographed by later horror film directors Karl Freund and Edgar G. Ulmer. Originally titled *Der Golem, Wie Er In Die Welt Kan: The Golem, How He Came Into the World.*

GOLEM, HOW HE CAME INTO THE WORLD, THE
See: *The Golem.*

GOMAR—THE HUMAN GORILLA
See: *Night of the Bloody Apes.*

GOODNIGHT, GOD BLESS
★ Magnum, 1987, R, 98 min. Dir: John Eyres. Cast: Emma Sutton, Frank Rozelaar Green, Jared Morgan, Jane Price.

Stultifyingly awful Brit stalker about a psycho in priest's garb committing murders at a school playground. As tasteless and terrible as it sounds, this sleazy rip-off of Pete Walker's *The Confessional* should be avoided at all cost.

GOOD SON, THE
★★☆ Fox, 1993, R, 87 min.
Dir: Joseph Ruben. Cast: Macauley Culkin, Elijah Wood, Wendy Crewson, Daniel Hugh-Kelly, David Morse, Jacqueline Brookes.

In this updated sex-change *Bad Seed,* Culkin is an eight-year-old psycho whose evil behavior is observed by cousin Wood, who is, of course, never believed. If the sight of the little *Home Alone* brat cursing, causing traffic accidents, and making attempts on his family's lives isn't enough for you, this only okay thriller really shifts into high gear during a genuinely shocking finale. Too bad the whole movie couldn't have been that good, as it would have rivaled Ruben's classic, *The Stepfather.*

GORE-GORE GIRLS, THE
★★ Midnight, 1971, X, 90 min.
Dir: Herschell Gordon Lewis. Cast: Frank Kress, Amy Farrell, Henny Youngman, Hedda Lubin, Nora Alexis, Emily Eason.

One of the great exploitation titles of all time—too bad the movie itself is only fair. Strippers who work for Henny's Miami club are being gruesomely killed by a masked psycho: throats are slashed, breasts cut off, heads caved in, and in the most memorable instance, a face is deep-fried! Rated X more for its outrageous gore than for sex or skin (there are a few topless shots), despite the poor acting and no-frills production values, you find yourself hooked to this movie all the way to the end, if only from its sheer audacity; just when you think it can't get any more extreme, it does—and then some! Strong stomachs and a perverse sense of humor are recommended. H. G.'s last gore flick, it was re-issued as *Blood Orgy.*

GORGO
★★★ Video Treasures, 1960, NR, 75 min.
Dir: Eugene Lourie. Cast: Bill Travers, William Sylvester, Vincent Winter, Bruce Seton, Joseph O'Conor, Martin Benson.

A 65-foot dinosaur is captured off the coast of Ireland and taken to London, where it's placed on display in Battersea Funfair. Soon after, its 200-foot mom comes roaring into town to reclaim her young, smashing Tower Bridge, Big Ben, and Piccadilly Circus asunder in her quest. One of the best man-in-a-suit monster pics ever, this is basically a remake of Lourie's earlier films *The Beast From 20,000 Fathoms* and *The Giant Behemoth,* with colorful photography, a good cast (Travers and Sylvester, as the two heroes, practically falling in love and forming a nuclear family with adopted son Winter) and totally convincing effects. Aka *The Night the World Shook.*

GORGON, THE
★★★☆ Goodtimes, 1964, NR, 83 min.
Dir: Terence Fisher. Cast: Peter Cushing, Christopher Lee, Barbara Shelley, Richard Pasco, Michael Goodliffe, Patrick Troughton.

Haunting Hammer movie about a turn-of-the-century German village terrorized by Megera, one of the gorgon sisters from ancient Greek myth whose glance can turn you to stone. One of Fisher's best, most underrated pictures, this is like a monster movie version of *Vertigo,* with its mood of tragic love and thwarted desire. It shows its cast in top form, especially the cast-against-type Cushing and Lee as,

BARBARA SHELLEY
(1933–)

British actress and model Shelley became a mainstay at Hammer Studios in the '60s. A truly talented, tall drink of water, Barbara has given notable performances as the haunted heroine of *The Gorgon* and the vampirized Victorian prude in *Dracula, Prince of Darkness*.

Cat Girl ('57), *Blood of the Vampire* ('58), *Village of the Damned* ('60), *Shadow of the Cat* ('61), *The Gorgon* ('64), *Dracula, Prince of Darkness* ('66), *Rasputin, the Mad Monk* ('66), *Five Million Years to Earth* ('68), *Madhouse Mansion* ('74).

respectively, a secretive pathologist and a swashbuckling college professor. The one debit: Roy Ashton's low-budget gorgon makeup.

GORILLA
See: *The Ape*.

GORILLA, THE
★★ Sinister Cinema, 1939, NR, 66 min. Dir: Allan Dwan. Cast: Jimmy Ritz, Harry Ritz, Al Ritz, Anita Louise, Bela Lugosi, Lionel Atwill, Patsy Kelly, Edward Norris.

The Bob Hope comic remake of *The Cat and the Canary* was a runaway hit in '39, so this Ritz Brothers remake of the venerable horror-comedy play (previously filmed in 1927 and 1930) was rushed into production. They shouldn't have bothered. The Ritzes, an acquired taste, aren't very funny, and Bela (as a glowering butler) and Lionel (as an endangered millionaire) are wasted, but comic maid Kelly is good and, though strictly routine, you've seen worse examples of the killer-gorilla-in-an-old-mansion film than this.

GOTHAM
★★☆ Cannon, 1988, R, 96 min. Dir: Lloyd Fouvielle. Cast: Tommy Lee Jones, Virginia Madsen, Frederic Forrest, Colin Bruce, Denise Stephenson, Kevin Jarre.

This fair made-for-cable thriller is what you might have gotten had Mickey Spillane penned *Vertigo*. Jones is a New York P.I. hired to investigate a man's claims that he's being followed by his beautiful wife's ghost (the sultry Madsen). Strong performances and an eerie mood help make watchable this not always easy-to-swallow shocker.

GOTHIC
★★☆ Vestron, 1986, R, 87 min. Dir: Ken Russell. Cast: Natasha Richardson, Gabriel Byrne, Julian Sands, Myriam Cyr, Timothy Spall, Alec Mango.

A predictably bizarre Russell examination of the fateful night in 1816 when Mary Shelley (Richardson) was inspired to write *Frankenstein*. A good-to-look-at but difficult-to-navigate amalgamation of weird images, twisted sexuality, and creepy FX that tends to drag in spots and is limply acted, apart from the radiant Richardson in her screen debut.

GRADUATION, THE
See: *The Prowler*.

GRADUATION DAY
★★ Goodtimes, 1981, R, 96 min. Dir: Herb Freed. Cast: Christopher George, Patch MacKenzie, E. Danny Murphy, E. J. Peaker, Michael Pataki, Billy Hufsey, Linnea Quigley, Vanna White.

After the death of a high school runner during a track meet, her fellow teammates (both male and female) are stalked by a black-gloved psycho who murders them in ridiculously contrived manners. Totally ordinary in terms of story and direction, but check out that cast! You're not gonna come across a bunch like this again in the same film, so for that reason alone you might want to watch.

GRANDMOTHER'S HOUSE
★★ Academy, 1988, R, 85 min. Dir: Peter Rader. Cast: Eric Foster, Kim Valentine, Brinke Stevens, Len Lesser, Ida Lee, Angela O'Neill.

Over the river and through the woods go teen siblings Foster and Valentine, who discover something murderously wrong at their grandparents' home. This wins a few points for trying to be different and, for once, casts cheesecake terror queen Stevens in a straight dramatic role, but in the end it emerges as just another slasher movie.

GRAVE DESIRES
See: *Brides of the Beast*.

GRAVE OF THE VAMPIRE
★★☆ Unicorn, 1972, PG, 89 min. Dir: John Hayes. Cast: William Smith, Michael Pataki, Lyn Peters, Diane Holden, Lieux Dressler, Kitty Vallacher, Eric Mason, Carmen Argenziano.

In this offbeat offshoot from the *Count Yorga* series, a sadistic vampire (Pataki in his best role) passing himself off as a night school professor of the occult is stalked by a son (biker movie regular Smith) conceived in rape in an open grave 25 years earlier. Marred by the usual low-budget gaffes (the opening sequences, set in the '40s, look no different than the remainder of the film) but marked by a nice sense of the bizarre, this features Holden as a coed who (like Louise Allbritton in *Son of Dracula*) loves the supernatural and desperately wants to become a vampire. Aka *Seed of Terror*.

GRAVE ROBBERS FROM OUTER SPACE
See: *Plan Nine From Outer Space*.

GRAVE SECRETS
★★☆ SGE, 1989, R, 88 min. Dir: Donald P. Borchers. Cast: Paul LeMat, Renee Soutendijk, David Warner, Lee Ving, Olivia Barash, John Crawford.

Not bad little ghost tale about an expert in psychic phenomena (LeMat, practically reprising his *Puppetmaster* role) who helps a woman (Soutendijk) who runs a country inn rid it of the violent headless ghost that's haunting the place. Solid performances and imaginative direction bolster a somewhat sluggish storyline and an ending that's a little too pat to fully justify such a complicated buildup.

GRAVESIDE STORY, THE
See: *The Comedy of Terrors*.

GRAVEYARD, THE
See: *Persecution*.

GRAVEYARD SHIFT
★★☆ Virgin Vision, 1986, R, 89 min. Dir: Gerard Ciccoretti. Cast: Silvio Oliviero, Helen Papas, Cliff Stoker, Dorin Ferber, Dan Rose, Kim Cayer.

Nighttime cabbie Oliviero is actually a vampire who romances terminally ill rock video director Papas away from dull husband Stoker. A contrived but stylish direct-to-video vamp pic, this has lots of glitz and good acting from Oliviero and Papas. A nice surprise—there's even a character named Mario Bava! Sequel: *The Understudy: Graveyard Shift II*.

GRAVEYARD SHIFT
★★☆ Paramount, 1990, R, 86 min. Dir: Ralph S. Singleton. Cast: David Andrews, Kelly Wolf, Stephen Macht, Brad Dourif.

Not bad little adaptation of one of Stephen King's first and best short stories, about an old Maine textile mill being terrorized by mutant killer rats. Gritty and grim, it benefits from tough acting and a brooding atmosphere, though the ending disappoints a bit.

GRAVEYARD TRAMPS
See: *Invasion of the Bee Girls*.

GREAT ALLIGATOR, THE
★ Gorgon, 1979, R, 89 min. Dir: Sergio Martino. Cast: Barbara Bach, Mel Ferrer, Claudio Cassinelli, Richard Johnson.

Dumb Italian *Jaws* copy (originally *Il Fume de Grande Caimano: Great Alligator River*) about an African tourist trap terrorized by a huge man-eating gator from local native legend. Not even as good as the simultaneously shot *Screamers*—which uses the same director and much of the same cast—with a bored crew of familiar faces and a monster about as menacing as a big log.

GREATEST BATTLE ON EARTH, THE
See: *Ghidrah, The Three-Headed Monster*.

GREED OF WILLIAM HART, THE
★★ Sinister Cinema, 1948, NR, 78 min. Dir: Oswald Mitchell. Cast: Tod Slaughter, Henry Oscar, Arnold Bell, Jenny Lynn, Winifred Melville, Mary Love.

Slaughter's last movie, this is a cheap but enjoyable Burke and Hare variant, probably made to cash in on *The Body Snatcher*. Scripted by future Hammer director John Gilling, this sees Tod somewhat subdued (for *him* it's subdued), but the basic story of corpse stealing and murder still holds interest. Aka *Horror Maniacs* and *Crimes of the Body Snatchers*; remade as *Mania* and *The Horrors of Burke and Hare*.

GREEN MAN, THE
★★☆ A&E, 1990, NR, 150 min. Dir: Elijah Moshinsky. Cast: Albert Finney, Sarah Berger, Linda Marlowe, Michael Hordern.

This made-for-cable adaptation of a novel by Kingsley Amis has an enormously appealing performance by Finney as the drunken, womanizing owner of a Brit bed-and-breakfast haunted by a sinister ghost, but it's over-long and takes too long to really get going. This is mostly for fans of the star.

GREEN MONKEY
See: *Blue Monkey*.

GREEN SLIME, THE
★★ MGM/UA, 1968, G, 88 min. Dir: Kinji Fukasaku. Cast: Robert Horton, Richard Jaeckel, Luciana Paluzzi, Bud Widom, Ted Gunther, Robert Dunham.

Astronauts destroy an asteroid on a collision course with the earth but return to their space station headquarters with a gooey alien life form that grows into a horde of tentacled, one-eyed monsters. Fairly fun '50s-type sci-fi/

horror with a tad of tension in the first 30 minutes but mostly silly effects, corny dialogue, and acting that would have been an embarrassment to the "Clutch Cargo" TV series. Japanese title: *Gammo Sango Uchu Daisakusen: Death and the Green Slime.* Great theme song: "The gree-een su-lime, slime, slime! The gree-een slime!"

GREMLINS

★★★ Warner, 1984, PG, 106 min.
Dir: Joe Dante. Cast: Zach Galligan, Phoebe Cates, Hoyt Axton, Polly Holliday, Frances Lee McCain, Judge Reinhold, Corey Feldman, Glynn Turman, Scott Brady, Keye Luke, Dick Miller, Jackie Joseph.

Wonderfully demented Christmas movie about a picture-postcard town being trashed by a horde of mischievous little gremlins accidentally born from a teddy bear-like creature called a mogwai. Starts out like a typically cute Spielberg fantasy (he was one of the executive producers) but then flips over into a funny-scary parody of everything from *ET* to *The Birds* and *The Blob,* with terrific performances from the usual great Dante supporting cast of old-timers, lots of in-jokes (spot the references to *The Wizard of Oz, It's a Wonderful Life, Invasion of the Body Snatchers,* and *The Howling*), and super Chris Walas FX that look like the "Twilight Zone" version of "The Muppet Show." This film's fairly high (though fantasized) violence quota led to the creation of the PG-13 rating after protests from parent groups who were too dumb to even notice that this was, in fact, a horror movie and *not* a Disney flick.

GREMLINS 2: THE NEW BATCH

★★☆ Warner, 1990, PG-13, 105 min.
Dir: Joe Dante. Cast: Zach Galligan, Phoebe Cates, John Glover, Christopher Lee, Robert Prosky, Haviland Morris, Robert Picardo, Dick Miller, Jackie Joseph, Keye Luke.

This belated follow-up finds the gremlins taking Manhattan and terrorizing the computer-controlled office tower of millionaire businessman Daniel Clamp (Glover). Where the original was a horror film with comedy scenes, this is a comedy with a few token horror touches. The jokes come thick and fast but, after a while, get to be a bit too much (the inside ones at the expense of the first film come off best). Galligan and Cates are as bland as they were before, but Glover is a joy as the Donald Trump/Ted Turner–like tycoon and Lee is a piss as a stern, gene-splicing mad scientist who simply refuses to be impressed with any of this nonsense. The video version contains a scene that was not in the original theatrical version but is missing a sequence featuring cameos by the likes of Hulk Hogan, Paul Bartel, Belinda Balaski, and Kenneth Tobey—even though they're all still listed in the end credits.

GRIM-PRAIRIE TALES

★★ Academy, 1990, R, 86 min.
Dir: Wayne Coe. Cast: James Earl Jones, Brad Dourif, Lisa Eichorn, William Atherton, Marc McClure, Scott Paulin, Wendy Cooke, Michelle Joyner.

The unctuous Jones is an Old West bounty hunter who spends a night around a campfire spinning scary stories for naive city slicker Dourif. Well cast and sharply photographed, but of the four tales presented, only the second (about a seductress who, quite literally, sucks up her lovers) really comes off, while the others (a violated Indian burial ground; vigilante killer; and haunted gunfighter) are merely passable.

GRIM REAPER, THE

★☆ Media, 1980, R, 81 min.
Dir: Joe D'Amato [Aristide Massaccesi]. Cast: Tisa Farrow, Saverio Vallone, Vanessa Steiger, George Eastman, Zora Kerova, Mark Bodin.

In this fairly dreary Italian mix of stalk-and-slash and cannibal chiller, Farrow is one of several tourists stranded on a remote Greek island with a flesh-munching maniac (Eastman). A really lame combination of explicit gore (some of it cut for an R) and travelogue photography, it was popular enough (in Europe at least) to inspire a sequel: *Monster Hunter.* Aka *Anthropophagous* and *The Anthropophagous Beast.*

GRIP OF THE STRANGLER

See: *The Haunted Strangler.*

GRIZZLY

★★ Media, 1976, PG, 92 min.
Dir: William Girdler. Cast: Christopher George, Andrew Prine, Richard Jaeckel, Joan McCall, Joe Dorsey, Charles Kissinger.

Grisly is the word for this blood-soaked *Jaws* rip-off about a huge prehistoric grizzly bear slaughtering the (mostly female) campers at a Georgia state park. "Rat Patrol" star and *Playgirl* centerfold George defeats the beast with a minimum of trouble. Comparisons with the Spielberg shark show are obvious but unflattering, as this low-budget moneymaker (Girdler's biggest hit) is completely lacking in logic, character, and subtlety. Good locations and a scary opening are the only pluses. Aka *Killer Grizzly.*

GROTESQUE

★☆ Media, 1987, R, 80 min.
Dir: Joe Tornatore. Cast: Linda Blair, Tab Hunter, Guy Stockwell, Donna Wilkes, Brad Wilson, Charles Dierkop, Nels Van Patten, Sharon Hughes, Robert Z'Dar, Luana Patton.

Blair and gal pal Wilkes visit the country cabin of Linda's dad Stockwell (a retired Hollywood makeup man), where everyone is attacked by a gang of vicious overaged punks. Linda is rescued by her horribly deformed brother, who is killed by the surviving punks; they in turn are stalked by Blair's plastic surgeon uncle Hunter. Totally ridiculous *Last House on the Left–Death Wish* hybrid, this is made passably watchable by its eclectic cast and EC comics-style ending; the TV version includes yet *another* twist to the climax not seen in the video edition.

GROWING PAINS

★☆ Thrillervideo, 1980, NR, 50 min.
Dir: Francis Megahy. Cast: Barbara Kellerman, Gary Bond, Matthew Blakstad, Christopher Reilly.

One of the weakest "Hammer House of Horror" entries, this is about a couple who adopt a little boy to replace their dead son, who soon comes to possess his replacement and seek revenge. An uncomfortable mix of pretentiousness and bad taste.

GRUESOME TWOSOME, THE

★★ Sleaziest, 1968, NR, 72 min.
Dir: Herschell Gordon Lewis. Cast: Elizabeth Davis, Chris Martell, Gretchen Welles, Rodney Bedell.

One of the Godfather of Gore's more obscure features, this concerns old lady wigmaker Davis (who looks like Mrs. Bates' ugly sister), who runs a boarding house for college coeds on the side. Son Martell murders said coeds for the material needed for Mom's wigs, which are made of 100% human hair. This wants real hard to be funny and almost is (especially in a genuinely hilarious art movie parody) but, as usual with H.G., the slay's the thing, this time serving up an especially nasty electric carving knife scalping and gross eyeball-popping. If the acting were any broader, they'd knocked the camera over.

GUARDIAN, THE

★★ MCA/Universal, 1990, R, 95 min.
Dir: William Friedkin. Cast: Jenny Seagrove, Carey Lowell, Dwier Brown, Brad Hall, Miguel Ferrer, Natalia Nogulich.

Bland adaptation of Dan Greenberg's novel *The Nanny* about a rich yuppie couple who hire beautiful Brit live-in nurse Seagrove for their newborn baby, only to discover her to be some sort of Druid high priestess who sacrifices infants to an evil tree god. Slickly done and with an impressive turn from Seagrove, but anyone expecting another *Exorcist* from Friedkin had best steer clear.

GUARDIAN OF THE ABYSS

★★☆ Thrillervideo, 1980, NR, 50 min.
Dir: Don Sharp. Cast: Ray Lonnen, Rosalyn Landor, John Carson, Barbara Ewing.

Antiques dealer Lonnen comes into possession of a magical mirror he uses to save pretty Landor from satanic sacrifice. Sharp's sure hand helps make this one of the better "Hammer House of Horror" mini-flicks, with good atmosphere and a strong, if slightly familiar, storyline.

GUILTY AS CHARGED

★★★ Columbia/Tristar, 1991, R, 95 min.
Dir: Sam Irvin. Cast: Rod Steiger, Lauren Hutton, Heather Graham, Isaac Hayes, Zelda Rubinstein, Lyman Ward, Irwin Keyes, Mitch Pileggi.

Steiger is great in the dark-humored tale of a religious fanatic who flips after the murder of his family. When the killers escape the death penalty, Rod kills them himself, as well as others, in a customized electric chair. One of the few recent comedy-horror films that actually works as both, though it runs out of steam before the end.

HACK 'EM HIGH

See: *Cemetery High.*

HALF HUMAN

★★ Rhino, 1955, NR, 70 min.
Dirs: Inoshiro Honda, Kenneth G. Crane. Cast: John Carradine, Akira Takarada, Momoko Kochi, Kenji Kasahara, Akemi Negishi, Morris Ankrum.

An expedition to the mountains of northern Japan encounters a Yeti-like ape creature and its baby. One of Toho's first post-*Godzilla* monster movies, over 30 minutes of footage and most of the dialogue were cut and new scenes and narration with Carradine and Ankrum

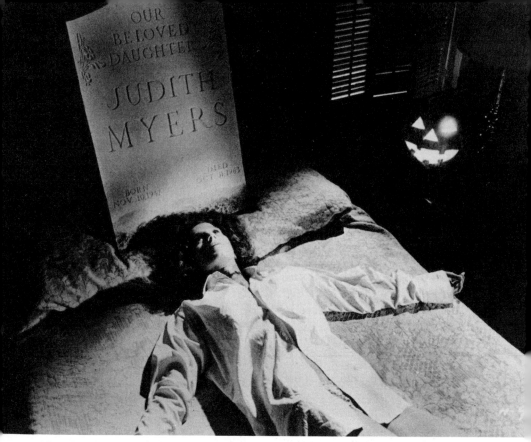

Nancy Loomis gets into the holiday spirit in Halloween *(1978).*

added for the U.S. market in 1958. The results are only fair.

HALLOWEEN

★★★★ Media, 1978, R, 90 min.
Dir: John Carpenter. Cast: Donald Pleasence, Jamie Lee Curtis, Nancy Loomis, P. J. Soles, Charles Cyphers, Kyle Richards, Brian Andrews, Nick Castle.

Carpenter's creepy classic about mad, masked Michael Myers, who escapes from the institution he's been in ever since fatally knifing his babysitting older sister back on Halloween night, 1963. Returning to his boyhood home of Haddonfield, Michael is trailed by his obsessive psychiatrist (Pleasence) while stalking a pretty babysitter (Curtis) and her oblivious friends. This is one of the best, most successful low-budget horror films ever made (costing a mere $350,000, it grossed more than $80 million worldwide), with a beautiful use of widescreen framing (unfortunately lost on the tube) and color composition recalling the films of Mario Bava and Dario Argento. Curtis is warm and appealing in her starmaking role as the besieged heroine, while Pleasence is pure ham as the bug-eyed doc. Followed by three direct sequels, one indirect one, and a veritable avalanche of cheap—and not so cheap—imitations.

JOHN CARPENTER
(1950–)

Carpenter ranks as one of the premier talents of the modern horror film. His low-cost but high-class *Halloween* is a classic example of style over content—the perfect scary movie. All of his films are good-looking, fast-moving, and extremely well-crafted and he has a special affinity for bringing out the best in his actresses.

Eyes of Laura Mars (co-screenplay, '78), *Someone's Watching Me* ('78), *Halloween* ('78), *The Fog* ('80), *Halloween II* (co-producer, co-screenplay, 81), *The Thing* ('82), *Halloween III: Season of the Witch* (co-producer, '82), *Christine* ('83), *Prince of Darkness* ('87), *They Live* ('88), *Memoirs of an Invisible Man* ('92), *Body Bags* (co-director, '93), *In the Mouth of Madness* ('94).

HALLOWEEN II

★★☆ MCA/Universal, 1981, R, 92 min.
Dir: Rick Rosenthal. Cast: Jamie Lee Curtis, Donald Pleasence, Charles Cyphers, Lance Guest, Pamela Susan Shoop, Leo Rossi, Ana-Alicia, Dick Warlock.

This slick but needlessly bloody sequel picks up exactly where the original left off, with Michael Myers stealing a new knife from a neighbor lady watching *Night of the Living Dead* on TV and then heading for the local hospital, where Curtis is recovering from wounds received in the original. Sharply photographed and featuring a better-than-average supporting cast, but awfully pointless and predictable, with graphic murder scenes inspired by the first two *Friday the 13th* movies added in post-production by producer-screenwriter John Carpenter. JLC is wasted.

HALLOWEEN III: SEASON OF THE WITCH

★★☆ MCA/Universal, 1982, R, 98 min.
Dir: Tommy Lee Wallace. Cast: Tom Atkins, Stacey Nelkin, Dan O'Herlihy, Ralph Strait, Jadeen Barbor, Bradley Schachter, Garn Stephens, Maidie Norman.

This in-name-only follow-up owes more to *Invasion of the Body Snatchers* than it does to the first two *Halloween* films. O'Herlihy is spry as an Irish mask maker out to hold a mass sacrifice to ancient Druid gods on Halloween night. How and why this is being done are just two of the many plot loopholes in director Wallace's contrived rewrite of Nigel Kneale's original script. Not as bad as its reputation suggests (with icky Tom Burman makeup effects, including melting faces, decapitations, and one obnoxious little kid whose masked mug explodes in a welter of spiders, roaches, and snakes), although the silly plot (involving everything from robots to remote-controlled Halloween masks to computer chips to Stonehenge) soon collapses under the weight of its own contrivances.

HALLOWEEN 4: THE RETURN OF MICHAEL MYERS

★★ CBS/Fox, 1988, R, 88 min. Dir: Dwight H. Little. Cast: Donald Pleasence, Danielle Harris, Ellie Cornell, Michael Pataki, Beau Starr, Kathleen Kinmont, Sasha Jenson, George P. Wilbur.

Actually, it's really number 3 for Michael, who rises up from the coma he's been in ever since supposedly burning to death at the end of *Halloween II* and returns to Haddonfield to stalk his young niece (Jamie Lee Curtis, now too big a star to appear in films like this, is represented only by photographs). Although graphic violence is mostly played down in favor of suspense, the whole masked-maniac-on-the-

loose scenario is, by now, so hopelessly clichéd that there are virtually no surprises—except maybe how Pleasence's character manages to survive being stabbed and blown up! The climax is fairly taut, but its effect is negated by a twist ending stolen from *Friday the 13th—The Final Chapter*.

HALLOWEEN 5: THE REVENGE OF MICHAEL MYERS

★★ CBS/Fox, 1989, R, 97 min. Dir: Dominique Otherin-Girard. Cast: Donald Pleasence, Danielle Harris, Ellie Cornell, Beau Starr, Wendy Kaplan, Tamara Glynn, Jonathan Chapin, Donald L. Shanks.

The fifth installment of this holiday perennial picks up a year after the conclusion of part 4 with MM escaping the well he fell into and beginning another unchecked rampage with young Jamie (Harris) as main victim-to-be. Darker and more atmospheric than its immediate predecessor, with a dynamite credits sequence of a glittering knife loudly carving up a pumpkin, but also kinda mean-spirited. The nominal female lead is heartlessly killed off early on in a *Psycho*-inspired twist while Michael savagely chops up peripheral characters and the little girl cries and suffers and runs for what seems like an eternity. And the pointless, inconclusive ending hinting at a possible part 6 is a real bummer.

HALLOWEEN PARTY

See: *Night of the Demons*.

HAMMOND MYSTERY, THE

See: *The Undying Monster*.

HAND, THE

★★ Warner, 1981, R, 104 min.
Dir: Oliver Stone. Cast: Michael Caine, Andrea Marcovicci, Annie McEnroe, Bruce McGill, Viveca Lindfors, Rosemary Murphy, Mara Hobel, Pat Corley.

Pretentious updating of the old crawling hand theme with Caine as a cartoonist whose life is destroyed when he loses his drawing hand in a freak auto accident. Saddled with an impossibly selfish wife (Marcovicci), Caine moves to California to take up a teaching position while being haunted by dreams (or are they?) that his severed hand is alive and on a murder spree. Caine is good, even though his character generates little sympathy, but an excellent supporting cast is wasted and the absurd "shocker" ending comes completely out of left field.

HANDS OF A STRANGER

★★☆ Sinister Cinema, 1962, NR, 86 min.
Dir: Newton Arnold. Cast: Paul Lukather, Joan

Harvey, James Stapleton, Larry Haddon, Irish McCalla, Ted Otis, Michael DuPont, Sally Kellerman.

Another version of *The Hands of Orlac,* about a celebrated concert pianist (Stapleton) whose hands are mangled in a taxi crash, forcing surgeons to graft on the mitts of a murderer in police custody killed in the same accident. Soon after, the pianist's sister (Harvey) begins to fear for his sanity as, no longer able to play, he becomes increasingly morose and obsessive, finally turning homicidal. Low-budget but never cheap-looking, with fine camerawork, sharp editing, and a good cast—Kellerman is terrific in an early role as a sexy nurse.

HANDS OF A STRANGLER
See: *The Hands of Orlac* (1961).

HANDS OF ORLAC, THE
See: *Mad Love.*

HANDS OF ORLAC, THE
★★ Sinister Cinema, 1961, NR, 95 min. Dir: Edmond T. Greville. Cast: Mel Ferrer, Christopher Lee, Lucile Saint-Simon, Dany Carrel, Felix Ayler, Donald Wolfit, Basil Sydney, Donald Pleasence.

This presentable adaptation of the familiar tale is more psycho-drama than straight horror film, with a glum Ferrer as the concert pianist who becomes obsessed with the idea that his hands are now those of a recently executed murderer, transplanted onto his wrists after a near-fatal plane crash. Elegant photography by Desmond Dickinson and a showy role for Lee as a flamboyant stage magician give it minor distinction, but a dumb cop-out ending is frustrating. Aka *Hands of a Strangler.*

HANDS OF THE RIPPER
★★★ VidAmerica, 1971, R, 82 min.
Dir: Peter Sasdy. Cast: Eric Porter, Angharad Rees, Jane Merrow, Keith Bell, Dora Bryan, Derek Godfrey.

One of Sasdy's best films, this polished period slasher features the excellent Porter as an early follower of Freud who attempts to help the pretty teen daughter of Jack the Ripper—she is being driven by her father's spirit to commit a rash of brutal murders. The killings themselves are still quite violent, even by today's standards (a maid has her throat slashed by a shard of broken mirror, and a prostitute gets some hatpins driven through her hand and eye), and there's a strong background atmosphere of an Edwardian London populated by sharp-tongued tarts, dirty street urchins, and crooked government officials. First released in the U.S. in a cut version on a twin bill with *Twins of Evil,* the video is of the full Brit print.

HAND THAT ROCKS THE CRADLE, THE
★★☆ Touchstone, 1992, R, 110 min.
Dir: Curtis Hanson. Cast: Rebecca De Mornay, Annabella Sciorra, Matt McCoy, Ernie Hudson, Julianne Moore, John de Lancie.

When a pregnant Sciorra blows the whistle on molesting obstetrition de Lancie and he commits suicide, months later his widow De Mornay is unknowingly employed by our heroine as a nanny for her newborn. Guess what happens? This contrived psycho-thriller was a surprise hit, and although manipulative and unbelievable, it occasionally hits home. Best of all is De Mornay, who gives a bravura performance as the off-her-rocker cradle-rocker. The ending is pure *Friday the 13th.*

HANGING WOMAN, THE
See: *Beyond the Living Dead.*

HANNAH, QUEEN OF THE VAMPIRES
See: *Crypt of the Living Dead.*

HAPPY BIRTHDAY TO ME
★★☆ RCA/Columbia, 1981, R, 110 min.
Dir: J. Lee Thompson. Cast: Melissa Sue Anderson, Glenn Ford, Lawrence Dane, Sharon Acker, Tracy Bregman, Frances Hyland, Jack Blum, Matt Craven, Lisa Langlois, David Eisner.

A sullen-looking Anderson stars in this fairly lavish-looking slasher about a gloved killer doing in the snotty "Top Ten" at the exclusive Crawford Academy. Could the maniac be brain-damaged ex-mental patient Melissa or is someone else stabbing, crushing, and shishkabobbing the cast? Overlong but well acted, with good Tom Burman effects and a notably grisly ending sporting no less than four climactic twists!

HAPPY MOTHER'S DAY, LOVE GEORGE
See: *Run, Stranger, Run.*

HARD TO DIE
★★☆ New Horizons, 1990, R, 76 min.
Dir: Jim Wynorski. Cast: Robyn Harris, Melissa Moore, Lindsay Taylor, Debra Dare, Bridget Carney, Forrest J. Ackerman.

Formerly titled *Tower of Terror,* this agreeably goofy exploiter is like *Die Hard* meets *Friday the 13th* with costumes by Victoria's Secret. Four bimbos working overnight at a high-rise lingerie company are terrorized by a demonically possessed serial killer. It's not great, but worth seeing just for the sight of the lace-clad ladies laying into the mountainous psycho with their high-powered weaponry (conveniently found on the premises), and it's much better than Wynorski's subsequent (and similar) *Sorority House Massacre II.*

HARLEQUIN
See: *Dark Forces.*

HATCHET FOR A HONEYMOON
★★☆ Charter, 1969, PG, 87 min.
Dir: Mario Bava. Cast: Stephen Forsyth, Dagmar Lassander, Laura Betti, Gerald Tichy, Jesus Puente, Alan Collins.

Slight Bava psychological shocker about a crazed fashion designer (Forsyth) with a penchant for hallucinations and chopping up young brides with an ax. When he nails his ever-nagging wife (Betti), her persistent ghost, or perhaps his guilty conscience, leads to his downfall. Originally titled *Il Rosso Segno Della Follia: The Red Sign of Madness* and released in Britain as *Blood Brides,* this has some truly haunting imagery (the killer and one of his victims dancing in a room filled with mannequins; the wife's horrified face reflected in the shiny hatchet blade), though it's often unintentionally funny thanks to some poor dubbing.

HATCHET MURDERS, THE
See: *Deep Red: The Hatchet Murders.*

HAUNTED
★★ United American, 1976, R, 81 min.
Dir: Michael DeGaetano. Cast: Ann Michelle, Aldo Ray, Virginia Mayo, Jim Negele.

This cheap shot-in-Arizona supernatural pic is about a modern Brit gal (the lovely Michelle) who arrives in a small desert town and turns out to be the reincarnation of a suspected witch executed there during Civil War times. A good cast tries to rise above mediocre material.

HAUNTED AND THE HUNTED, THE
See: *Dementia 13.*

HAUNTED HONEYMOON
★★ Orion, 1986, PG, 82 min.
. Dir: Gene Wilder. Cast: Gene Wilder, Gilda Radner, Dom De Luise, Jonathan Pryce, Paul L. Smith, Peter Vaughn.

Silly spoof of all those creaky old-dark-house thrillers from the '30s and '40s with Wilder and Radner as honeymooners terrorized by a warewolf at a gloomy old estate. A few nice bits and an occasionally pleasing homage, but even at only 82 minutes this *drags;* De Luise in a dress is a guaranteed laugh-getter, but he's too underused for this pic's own good.

HAUNTED PALACE, THE
★★★ HBO, 1963, NR, 86 min.
Dir: Roger Corman. Cast: Vincent Price, Debra Paget, Lon Chaney, Jr., Leo Gordon, Frank Maxwell, Elisha Cook, John Dierkes, Milton Parsons, Barboura Morris, Bruno Ve Sota.

Price and wife Paget visit the misty New England coastal village of Arkham, where they move into the hilltop castle they've inherited, and Vinnie is possessed by the vengeful spirit of an executed warlock ancestor. Ostensibly another entry in the Corman-Price-Poe series, this is actually a very effective adaptation of H. P. Lovecraft's *The Case of Charles Dexter Ward,* enlivened by a strong supporting cast, eerie Ronald Stein score, and creepily ambiguous ending.

HAUNTED STANGLER, THE
★★★ MPI, 1958, NR, 78 min.
Dir: Robert Day. Cast: Boris Karloff, Jean Kent, Elizabeth Allen, Anthony Dawson, Vera Day, Tim Turner, Diane Aubrey, Dorothy Gordon.

Karloff is excellent as a reporter investigating a 20-year-old series of showgirl slashings who discovers that an innocent man was hanged for the crimes—and that *he* is the schizophrenic killer! One of the horror great's best latter-day showcases, with Boris effectively twisting himself into the hideous strangler without the aid of a bit of makeup and Kent sassy as an aging showgirl who sings a great song called "Cora." British title: *Grip of the Strangler.*

HAUNTED SUMMER
★★ Cannon, 1988, R, 106 min.
Dir: Ivan Passer. Cast: Eric Stoltz, Laura Dern, Philip Anglim, Alice Krige, Alex Winter.

Like the more flamboyant *Gothic,* this minor melodrama purports to tell what happened at Lake Geneva that fateful summer when Mary Shelley (Krige) was inspired to write *Frankenstein.* Well acted and handsomely produced but dull; Stoltz groupies take note: you get to see him take a full-frontal shower in a waterfall, the *only* shock in this otherwise meandering affair.

HAUNTING, THE
★★★★ MGM/UA, 1963, NR, 112 min.
Dir: Robert Wise. Cast: Julie Harris, Claire Bloom, Richard Johnson, Russ Tamblyn, Lois Maxwell, Fay Compton, Rosalie Crutchley, Diane Clare.

One of the best horror films of the '60s, this multifaceted adaptation of Shirley Jackson's *The Haunting of Hill House* concerns the psychic investigation of an old New England mansion by a parapsychologist (Johnson) and a pair of supernaturally attuned females. One of the women (the superlative Harris) is a lonely spinster who falls under the house's influence and is eventually killed by it—or perhaps commits suicide—feeling that at last she has found a place to "belong." Although the script pulls the old "Are there *really* ghosts or is it all in the heroine's mind?" ploy, the ghost angle is never disproved and, in fact, is *reinforced* at the end, making the so-called "rational" explanation for the haunting anything but the only answer. Beautifully photographed by Davis Boulton, this remains one of the last, best examples of the "terror of the unseen" school of screen horror, brilliantly using distorted camera angles and sound effects in place of the usual gratuitous special FX.

HAUNTING FEAR

★★ Rhino, 1991, R, 87 min.
Dir: Fred Olen Ray. Cast: Brinke Stevens, Jan-Michael Vincent, Karen Black, Jay Richardson, Delia Sheppard, Robert Clarke, Robert Quarry, Michael Berryman.

This alleged version of Poe's "The Premature Burial" is closer to a soft-core episode of HBO's *Tales from the Crypt* series. Stevens is a wealthy wife who has a fear of being buried alive; unfaithful hubby Richardson has a slutty mistress (Sheppard) and a lot of debts. Guess what happens? The lovable cast of low-budget greats enlivens this T&A shocker.

HAUNTING OF HAMILTON HIGH, THE

See: *Hello Mary Lou: Prom Night II.*

HAUNTING OF JULIA, THE

★★★ Magnum, 1976, R, 93 min. Dir: Richard Loncraine. Cast: Mia Farrow, Keir Dullea, Tom Conti, Jill Bennett, Robin Gammell, Cathleen Nesbitt.

Atmospheric adaptation of Peter Straub's first novel, *Julia,* with Farrow as a lonely woman haunted by the accidental death of her young daughter who moves into an eerie London townhouse haunted by the specter of a murderous little girl. Farrow is unforgettable and there's a moody score by Colin Towns, but this may be too slowly paced and downbeat for some. Original title: *Full Circle.*   .

HAUNTING OF MORELLA, THE

★★ New Horizons, 1990, R, 82 min.
Dir: Jim Wynorski. Cast: David McCallum, Nicole Eggert, Christopher Halsted, Lana Clarkson, Maria Ford, Debbie Dutch.

More or less a remake of the first segment from *Tales of Terror,* this Poe derivation deals

with the possession of teen Eggert by her executed witch mom (also Nicole) and her revenge against blind husband/father McCallum. With more cleavage, gratuitous femme nudity, and lesbian scenes than in any movie since the heyday of the early '70s Euro-grindhouse shockers, this has in-jokes galore, including references to *Black Sunday, The Premature Burial, The Haunted Palace, Tomb of Ligeia,* and *Lust for a Vampire.*

HAUNTING OF SARAH HARDY, THE

★☆ Paramount, 1989, NR, 96 min.
Dir: Jerry London. Cast: Sela Ward, Michael Woods, Polly Bergen, Morgan Fairchild.

Sleep-inducing, "Harlequin Romance"–type marginal horror item about a beautiful, pampered young bride (Ward) haunted by the ghost of her mother after moving into the family manse. You could write this one yourself, so why bother watching it?

HAUNTING PASSION, THE

★★ Lorimar, 1983, NR, 96 min.
Dir: Jon Korty. Cast: Jane Seymour, Gerald McRaney, Millie Perkins, Paul Roselli, Ruth Nelson, Ivan Bonar.

Silly tele-movie with Seymour as a sexually unsatisfied housewife (are they kiddin'?) who's seduced away from impotent hubby McRaney by a horny ghost. About as exciting as it sounds, with lots of dreamy photography of steamin' Seymour, and Perkins solid in the obligatory best friend spot.

HAUNTS

★★☆ Video Treasures, 1976, R, 97 min. Dir: Herb Freed. Cast: May Britt, Cameron Mitchell, Aldo Ray, William Gray Espy, Kendall Jackson, E. J. Andre.

Confusing but diverting mix of *Psycho* and *Repulsion* about a frigid middle-aged farm girl (Britt) who is bizarrely affected by a series of brutal rape-murders committed in her small town by a scissors-wielding sicko. Really well-done scenes illustrating the sad waste of Britt's life—accompanied by an especially moving Pino Donaggio score—alternate with a dumb guess-the-killer subplot involving slovenly sheriff Ray. Not for all tastes but a definite curiosity piece with fine acting from Britt. Filmed as *The Veil.*

HAUNTS OF THE VERY RICH

★★ Moonlight, 1972, NR, 72 min.
Dir: Paul Wendkos. Cast: Lloyd Bridges, Cloris Leachman, Edward Asner, Anne Francis, Tony Bill, Donna Mills, Robert Reed, Moses Gunn.

Silly made-for-TV updating of Sutton Vane's *Outward Bound* about a group of people flown to a mysterious resort where, one by one, they discover that they are actually dead and in hell. Lots of dreamy, soft-focus photography and a solid TV movie cast, but even at a scant 72 minutes this begins to wear a bit thin in no time at all, often resembling a horror movie version of "Fantasy Island."

HAZING IN HELL, A
See: *Pledge Night.*

HEAD, THE
★★☆ Sinister Cinema, 1959, NR, 92 min. Dir: Victor Trivas. Cast: Horst Frank, Karin Kernke, Michel Simon, Helmut Schmid, Dieter Eppler, Christiane Maybach.

Sort of like a continental version of *The Brain That Wouldn't Die*, this Germanic oddity concerns the tireless research into the scientific preservation of decapitated heads—a major medical problem the world over. An atmospheric but exceedingly bent little flick that has all of the following: (1) a mad scientist, (2) a beautiful heroine whose hunchbacked body is replaced by that of a murdered stripper, (3) a stalwart (and somewhat dense) hero, (4) an old mansion, (5) a flashy lab, (6) a chubby talking decapitated head, and (7) unintentional guffaws galore. Original title: *Die Nackte und dre Satan: The Naked and Satan* and aka *A Head for the Devil* and *The Screaming Head.*

HEAD FOR THE DEVIL, A
See: *The Head.*

HEADHUNTER
★★ Academy, 1989, R, 92 min. Dir: Francis Schaeffer. Cast: Kay Lenz, Wayne Crawford, Steve Kanaly, June Chadwick, Sam Williams, John Fatooh.

Set in Miami but filmed in South Africa, this routine potboiler features Lenz and Crawford as detectives on the trail of a vicious head-chopping killer who turns out to be a blood-thirsty Nigerian demon. There's a good climax (featuring scenes from the Z classic *The Hideous Sun Demon*), but it's a long, dull wait to get to it.

HEADHUNTER, THE
See: *The Avenger.*

HEAD THAT WOULDN'T DIE, THE
See: *The Brain That Wouldn't Die.*

HEAR NO EVIL
★★ Fox, 1993, R, 97 min. Dir: Robert Greenwald. Cast: Marlee Matlin, D. B. Sweeney, Martin Sheen, John C. McGinley, Christina Carlesi, Marge Redmond.

Hearing-impaired Oscar-winner Matlin is a deaf woman menaced by psychos who are after a rare coin in this mechanical change-of-affliction rip-off of *Wait Until Dark*. The cast is talented but they can't do much with such thin material. What's next, a mute girl terrorized in *Speak No Evil*?

HEARSE, THE
★★ Media, 1980, PG, 97 min. Dir: George Bowers. Cast: Trish Van Devere, Joseph Cotten, David Gautreaux, Donald Hotton, Med Flory, Perry Lang.

Minor haunted house melodrama with Trish moving into her late aunt's country house and finding herself shadowed by a sinister black 1953 Packard hearse driven by a man with a disfigured face. A few laughs, a few jolts, with Trish in fine form and Cotten funny as a cantankerous old lawyer who wants the house for himself.

HEART OF MIDNIGHT
★★☆ Virgin Vision, 1988, R, 93 min. Dir: Mathew Chapman. Cast: Jennifer Jason Leigh, Peter Coyote, Denise Dumont, Gale Mayron, Frank Stallone, Brenda Vaccaro.

Kinky thrills with Leigh as the twitchy inheritor of a boarded-up New Orleans sex palace who finds herself haunted by strange manifestations from the past when she tries to reopen the place as a trendy night club. Leigh (one of the best, most underrated actresses of her generation) is excellent, the supporting cast is in fine form, and there's plenty of lush photography and art direction, but this has an ending that'll have you either scratching your head in confusion or rewinding to see what you missed.

HEARTSTOPPER
★★☆ Tempe, 1989, R, 90 min. Dir: John Russo. Cast: Kevin Kindlin, Moon Zappa, Tom Savini, Michael J. Pollard.

Based on Russo's novel *The Awakening*, this decent low-budgeter is about a vampire from the Revolutionary War (Kindlin) revived in modern times to seek victims, fall in love with Zappa, and be pursued by cop Savini—who also provided the gory FX. Imaginative and well acted, this sometimes resembles George Romero's *Martin*.

HE KNOWS YOU'RE ALONE
★★☆ MGM/UA, 1980, R, 94 min. Dir: Armand Mastroianni. Cast: Caitlin O'Heaney, Don Scardino, Elizabeth Kemp, Patsy Pease, Tom Rolfing, Lewis Arlt, Tom Hanks, Dana Barron.

Bride-to-be O'Heaney (having second thoughts about her upcoming nuptials to her jerky boyfriend) is stalked by psycho Arlt, who has been knifing brides ever since being left at the altar years before. Standard stalker: efficiently shot and with good performances from O'Heaney, Scardino (as a jilted beau trying to get back in her good graces), and Oscar-winner Hanks (as a pompous psych major who thinks horror films are dumb). Too bad the plot holds so few surprises, though the trick ending *does* provide a jolt. Filmed as *Blood Wedding*.

HELLBOUND: HELLRAISER II

★★☆ New World, 1988, UR, 97 min. Dir: Tony Randel. Cast: Clare Higgins, Ashley Laurence, Imogen Boorman, Kenneth Cranham, William Hope, Doug Bradley, Sean Chapman, Barbie Wilde.

This ambitious, if somewhat confused, sequel sees plucky Kirsty (the lovely Laurence) sent to a mental hospital following the bizarre events of the original film. It turns out, though, that the institution is run by the sinister Dr. Channard (Cranham) who has long been fascinated by the legend of the Cenobites and is using a mute teen with an obsession for puzzles to reopen the dreaded "Lament Configuration." Good performances from Laurence, Cranham, and most especially the seductively sinister Higgins as Kirsty's evil stepmom Julia and some imaginative effects work help distract the viewer from a pointlessly overcomplicated plot full of extraneous explanations and amazing coincidences. Aka *Hellraiser II: Hellbound* and also out in a heavily cut R version.

HELL CREATURES

See: *Invasion of the Saucer Men.*

HELL HIGH

★ Prism, 1986, R, 83 min.
Dir: Douglas Grossman. Cast: Maureen Mooney, Christopher Cousins, Christopher Stryker, Millie Prezioso, Jason Brill, Kathy Rossetter.

Unpleasant *I Spit on Your Grave* rip-off about a quartet of high schoolers whose prank against an unbalanced teacher (Mooney) ends in her near death and bloody retaliation. The characters are moronic, and gratuitous plot elements are stolen from everything from *Carrie* to *Porky's*. When, oh when, will the exploiters stop making this junk? Aka *Raging Fury* and *Real Trouble*.

HELLHOLE

★☆ RCA/Columbia, 1985, R, 95 min.
Dir: Pierre de Moro. Cast: Judy Landers, Ray Sharkey,

Mary Woronov, Marjoe Gortner, Terry Moore, Edy Williams.

An interesting cast (to state the obvious) wastes its efforts in this trashy clone of *The Fifth Floor* with sexy Landers as a gal who witnessed mom's murder, blocked it out, and is now in an asylum where she's menaced by crazed Sharkey and evil Woronov. So sleazy you might want to give the TV a good scrubbing after watching it.

HELL HOUSE

See: *Carnage.*

HELLMASTER

★★ AIP, 1992, R, 90 min. Dir: Douglas Schulze. Cast: John Saxon, David Emge, Amy Raasch, Eric Kingston, Suzanne Labatt, Ron Ashton.

Saxon is a college professor whose experimental drug turns students into murderous ghouls—the lead one looks like *Hellraiser's* Pinhead sans pins. Ordinary budget thriller aka *They* and *Soulstealer*.

HELL NIGHT

★★☆ Video Treasures, 1981, R, 100 min. Dir: Tom DeSimone. Cast: Linda Blair, Vincent Van Patten, Peter Brophy, Jenny Neumann, Suki Goodman.

Blair and friends spend the night in creepy old Garth Manor as part of a sorority-fraternity hazing and are stalked by a deformed killer haunting the place. Predictable but well-made slasher with less explicit gore than usual but some fair suspense and Linda in good, personable form.

HELLO MARY LOU: PROM NIGHT II

★★☆ Virgin Vision, 1987, R, 92 min. Dir: Bruce Pittman. Cast: Michael Ironside, Wendy Lyon, Lisa Shrage, Justin Louis, Richard Monette, Brock Simpson.

Bitchy prom queen Mary Lou (Shrage) is killed in a freak accident on prom night 1957; 30 years later she returns to possess modern prom queen hopeful Lyon. Some great FX (like a blackboard transformed into a swirling black whirlpool) and Shrage's campy bravura carry this in-name-only sequel, which proved popular enough to inspire a sequel of its own. Best line: "It's Linda Blairsville!" Filmed as *The Haunting of Hamilton High*.

HELLRAISER

★★★☆ New World, 1987, R, 93 min. Dir: Clive Barker. Cast: Andrew Robinson, Clare Higgins, Ashley Laurence, Sean Chapman, Robert Hines, Doug Bradley.

British horror author extraordinaire Barker made his directorial debut with this gripping

Doug Bradley makes a point as Pinhead in Hellraiser *(1987).*

tale about a group of creatures called Cenobites: sadomasochistic demons from another dimension who enter into our world through a weird oriental puzzle box called the "Lament Configuration." When a man (Chapman) is skinned alive by the Cenobites, he is accidentally brought back to life by a drop of blood and convinces his sister-in-law/lover (Higgins) to bring him men, whose skin he needs to be whole again. Crystalline color photography and interestingly drawn characters dominate this rewardingly complex but gruesome film. Sequel: *Hellbound: Hellraiser II* and *Hellraiser III: Hell on Earth.*

HELLRAISER II: HELLBOUND
See: *Hellbound: Hellraiser II.*

HELLRAISER III: HELL ON EARTH
★★★ Paramount, 1992, UR, 96 min.
Dir: Anthony Hickox. Cast: Terry Farrell, Doug Bradley, Paula Marshall, Kevin Bernhardt, Ken Carpenter, Ashley Laurence.

In this second sequel Farrell is a New York TV reporter who battles the resurrected Pinhead (Bradley) and the demons of her own past. Bradley gets more screen time here than in either of the earlier *Hellraisers* and makes the most of it with a beautifully arch and amusing performance as the dreaded Pope of Hell. Farrell and Marshall (as a young punkette also caught up in the action) are also good, while Laurence has a cameo on videotape. Better than *Hellbound* andequal to the original.

HENRY: PORTRAIT OF A SERIAL KILLER
★★★☆ MPI, 1986, UR, 82 min. Dir: John McNaughton. Cast: Michael Rooker, Tracy Arnold, Tom Towles, Ray Atherton, Kurt Naebig, Eric Young.

Rooker is Henry, an amiable Chicago psycho killer who, aided by roommate Towles, videotapes various murders until the friends are pulled apart by the latter's sister (Arnold). A near-brilliant documentary-style shocker, this has excellent acting, fine direction, and a script full of more heart-breakingly true moments than in a dozen more pretentious "straight" features. Be warned, however, that this is one of the most unsettling movies you're ever gonna see, with a grim atmosphere that clings to you like moss on a rock.

HEX
See: *The Shrieking.*

H. G. WELLS' NEW INVISIBLE MAN
See: *The New Invisible Man.*

HIDDEN, THE
★★★ Media, 1987, R, 97 min. Dir: Jack Sholder. Cast: Kyle MacLachlan, Michael Nouri, Clu Gulager,

---

CLIVE BARKER
(1950–)

Barker is a British horror author, screenwriter, and director who became one of the main propagators of the so-called "splatterpunk" movement of the '80s. Probably the most talented and creative horror writer of today, he has the ability to mix sharp characterizations, bizarre ideas, and graphic sex and violence into genuinely disturbing tales of dark horror.

Transmutations ('86), *Rawhide Rex* ('87), *Hellraiser* (also director, '87), *Hellbound: Hellraiser II* (original characters, '88), *Nightbreed* (also director, '90), *Hellraiser III: Hell on Earth* (original characters, '92), *Candyman* (original story, "The Unbidden," '92).

Claudia Christian, Ed O'Ross, Clarence Felder, Catherine Cannon, Chris Mulkey.

Slam-bang combo of your typical '80s buddy/cop movie with an alien-invasion horror flick. Seemingly normal, everyday citizens begin violent crime waves and turn out to be possessed by an alien entity with a passion for fast cars, loud music, and lots of heavy-duty artillery. Although somewhat murky where motivation is concerned, this moves like gangbusters and is sparked by first-rate acting (particularly MacLachlan as an alien bounty hunter in human form and Nouri as his reluctant cop-partner) and a winning sense of the absurd.

HIDDEN II, THE

★★ New Line, 1993, R, 89 min. Dir: Seth Pinsker. Cast: Raphael Sbarge, Kate Hodge, Jovin Montanaro, Christopher Murphy, Michael Weldon, Tony Di Benneto.

Fifteen years after its original rampage, the gooey, insect-like alien from *The Hidden* spawns a new horde of offspring that prey on patrons of a new-wave dance club and are hunted by extraterrestrial cop Sbarge. This bland sequel is pretty negligible, with an overabundance of scenes of the alien critters either being swallowed or barfed up by the supporting cast and an unbelievable romance between Sbarge and heroine Hodge—he doesn't know how to use a toothbrush but he *does* know how to have sex!

HIDDEN ROOM OF 1,000 HORRORS

See: *The Tell-Tale Heart.*

HIDE AND GO SHRIEK

★ New Star, 1987, R, 90 min. Dir: Skip Schoolnik. Cast: George Thomas, Donna Baltron, Brittain Frye, Bunky Jones, Scott Kubay, Annette Sinclair.

Boring stalker about a bunch of high school hoseheads who spend the night in a furniture store, play hide and seek, have sex, and get murdered by a mystery killer who may or may not be the store's creepy nightwatchman. Lousy acting by a cast of deserved unknowns, slack pacing, and bargain-basement FX sink this from the start.

HIDEOUS SUN DEMON, THE

★☆ Rhino, 1959, NR, 74 min. Dirs: Robert Clarke, Tom Boutross. Cast: Robert Clarke, Patricia Manning, Nan Peterson, Patrick Whyte, Fred La Porta, Peter Similuk.

A Z classic with Clarke as an alcoholic scientist transformed by radiation into a werelizard: he gets scaly whenever touched by the rays of the sun. A fairly clever concept gets especially clunky handling, with silly rubber monster makeup and Clarke overacting like never before—he makes Lon Chaney, Jr., look like Laurence Olivier. There *is* a fairly tense climax set atop a huge oil storage tank, though. British title: *Blood on His Lips.*

HIDER IN THE HOUSE, THE

★★☆ Vestron, 1989, R, 109 min. Dir: Matthew Patrick. Cast: Gary Busey, Mimi Rogers, Michael McKean, Bruce Glover.

Busey is terrific in this medium thriller about a psychiatric out-patient who builds a private room for himself in the attic of a family's new home. Busey then falls in love with the wife (Rogers, Tom Cruise's ex) and begins a campaign to win her affections—even resorting to murder to do so. Though the plot is contrived to the point of absurdity, the always winning ways of Busey and Rogers help us overlook this.

HIGH DESERT KILL

★★☆ MCA/Universal, 1989, NR, 96 min. Dir: Harry Falk. Cast: Chuck Connors, Anthony Geary, Marc Singer, Micah Grant, Deborah Anne Mansey, Lori Birdsong.

T. S. Cook (*The China Syndrome*) scripted this fair made-for-cable movie, which starts out as a semi-remake of *Deliverance* about three city guys and a grizzled guide on a hunting trip and then turns into a semi-remake of *The Thing* as an alien monster systematically possesses and kills them off. You've seen worse.

HIGHWAY TO HELL

★★ Hemdale, 1990, R, 93 min. Dir: Ate de Jong. Cast: Patrick Bergin, Chad Lowe, Kristy Swanson, Richard Farnsworth, Lita Ford, Pamela Gidley, Jerry Stiller, Anne Meara, Gilbert Gottfried, Kevin Peter Hall, C. J. Graham, Jarrett Lennon.

This horror-fantasy has a good cast and some excellent ideas but never quite jells. Teen lovers Lowe and Swanson run off to elope, but Kristy is kidnapped by mutant-demon cop Graham (who played Jason in *Friday the 13th VI*) and carried off to hell. Chad follows and must do battle there with devil Bergin. Much is played for laughs, but this really isn't a comedy; it's mostly for curious fans of the terminally weird.

HILLBILLYS IN A HAUNTED HOUSE

★ United, 1967, NR, 86 min. Dir: Jean Yarbrough. Cast: Basil Rathbone, Lon Chaney, Jr., John Carradine, Ferlin Huskey, Joi Lansing, Don Bowman, Linda Ho, George Barrows.

Unbelievably bad mix of hoary haunted house clichés and echo-chambered country music about a trio of Nashville nitwits spending the night in a dilapidated mansion also inhabited by spies Rathbone, Chaney, and Carradine (not to mention the gorilla from *Konga*). A pathetic last effort for a frail-looking Rathbone, this climaxes a full 15 minutes before the actual ending, allowing for plenty of endless musical numbers at a low-budget version of the Grand Ole Opry.

HILLS HAVE EYES, THE

★★★☆ Vestron, 1977, R, 87 min.
Dir: Wes Craven. Cast: Susan Lanier, Robert Houston, Dee Wallace, Russ Grieve, Virgina Vincent, James Whitworth, Janus Blythe, Michael Berryman.

One of Craven's best films is a gory look at the family unit in which a "white bread" Cleveland family run afoul of a tribe of cannibal-killers in the desert. Mom and Dad are both killed, but ultimately the teen kids turn the tables and survive—in the end turning out to be even more savage than their attackers. Almost unbearably tense and scary in spots, with Craven beautifully capturing the isolation and loneliness of the desert location and an effective undercurrent of black humor mostly lacking from Wes' previous hit, *The Last House on the Left*. Berryman is a standout as the most likable weird of the Hill family.

HILLS HAVE EYES PART II, THE

★ HBO, 1983, R, 88 min.
Dir: Wes Craven. Cast: Tamara Stafford, Kevin Blair, John Laughlin, Janus Blythe, Robert Houston, Michael Berryman, Colleen Riley, John Bloom.

It's hard to believe that Craven himself could be responsible for this truly awful sequel to his classic *The Hills Have Eyes*, but here's the evidence. Playing like a bad *Friday the 13th* rip-off, this has a band of teen dirt bikers stranded in the same spot where the first film took place and set upon by the last two remaining members of the mutant Hill family. Full of dumb character behavior, flashback padding (even the dog has a flashback!), and ragged editing (the ultimate fates of two of the main charaters are left completely up in the air), this rates as one of the most ill-conceived sequels ever.

HITCHER, THE

★★☆ HBO, 1986, R, 97 min. Dir: Robert Harmon. Cast: Rutger Hauer, C. Thomas Howell, Jennifer Jason Leigh, Jeffrey DeMunn.

In this nihilistic but compelling slasher variant, nice kid Howell picks up menacing hitchhiker Hauer but manages to push him out of the car when he brandishes a knife. Later Hauer begins a series of gory killings, leaving enough evidence behind to put the blame on Howell—seemingly in revenge for his rejection of him. Rarely believable (and slightly homophobic and anti-female as well) but also highly suspenseful, with Hauer's terrific performance and director Harmon's way with bizarre imagery (like a severed finger turning up in an order of french fries) a formidable double act.

HITCHHIKER, THE

★★☆ Lorimar, 1985–88, NR, 90 min. per tape
Dirs: Roger Vadim, Paul Verhoeven, Mai Zetterling, Michael Hodges, Phillip Noyce, others. Cast: Karen Black, Harry Hamlin, Gary Busey, Margot Kidder, Willem Dafoe, Kirsty Alley, Geraldine Page, Susan Anspach, Darren McGavin, Tom Skerritt, Stephen Collins, Robert Vaughn, Barry Bostwick, Sybil Danning, Jenny Seagrove, Page Fletcher.

Twisty made-for-cable anthology with three episodes per tape. The casts are consistently excellent, but the stories themselves—involving the usual ghosts, voodoo curses, mad killers, and ironic revenge—tend to be a bit uneven.

HOBGOBLINS

★ TWE, 1988, PG-13, 89 min.
Dir: Rick Sloane. Cast: Tom Bartlett, Paige Sullivan, Steven Boggs, Kelly Palmer, Billy Frank.

Yet another irritating micro-budgeted *Gremlins*, this one features furry little hand puppets creating havoc at a movie studio and dance club. Makes *Ghoulies* look like *Aliens*.

HOLD THAT GHOST

★★★☆ MCA/Universal, 1941, NR, 86 min.
Dir: Arthur Lubin. Cast: Bud Abbott, Lou Costello, Joan Davis, Richard Carlson, Evelyn Ankers, Marc Lawrence, Mischa Auer, The Andrews Sisters.

One of A&C's best films, this slick and entertaining old-dark-house comedy is funnier and fresher than most comedies made today. Bud and Lou inherit an old country inn from a murdered gangster and stay there one stormy night. Beautifully effective photography and settings back up a splendid supporting cast (Davis steals it as a professional radio screamer). Funniest scene: Bud and Lou arguing over the meaning of the expression "a figure of speech."

HOLLYWOOD CHAINSAW HOOKERS

★★ Camp, 1987, R, 75 min. Dir: Fred Olen Ray.
Cast: Gunnar Hansen, Linnea Quigley, Jay

Richardson, Michelle Bauer, Dawn Wildsmith, Dennis Mooney.

Perky Quigley, the Goldie Hawn of gore, is a teenage runaway who gets mixed up with both Hollywood prostitution *and* a psychotic cult of chainsaw worshippers lorded over by *Texas Chainsaw Massacre*'s own Leatherface Hansen. Funnier than it sounds, this one will appeal to fans of senseless bloodshed and bare breasts; the title alone should be enough to keep everyone else clear.

HOLLYWOOD MEATCLEAVER MASSACRE, THE
See: *Meatcleaver Massacre.*

HOLLYWOOD STRANGLER
See: *Don't Answer the Phone.*

HOLOCAUST 2,000
★★ Vestron, 1977, R, 102 min. Dir: Alberto De Martino. Cast: Kirk Douglas, Simon Ward, Agostina Belli, Anthony Quayle, Virginia McKenna, Alexander Knox, Adolfo Celli, Romolo Valli.

Originally released to U.S. theatres as *The Chosen*, this gory Italian *Omen* rip-off casts Douglas as a millionaire industrialist who discovers that his son (Ward) is the anti-Christ and out to start a nuclear apocalypse. Lots of gory death scenes (a man beheaded by a helicopter blade is the most memorable) and an interesting cast, but the plot is dull and there are too many silly Kirk nude scenes.

HOLY TERROR
See: *Alice, Sweet Alice.*

HOMEBODIES
★★★ 1974, Nelson, PG, 96 min.
Dir: Larry Yust. Cast: Paula Trueman, Frances Fuller, William Hanson, Ian Wolfe, Ruth McDevitt, Peter Brocco, Linda Marsh, Douglas Fowley.

Shot in Cincinnati, Ohio, this rewardingly weird little thriller concerns six elderly residents of a condemned tenement building who turn to murder to avenge themselves upon those who evicted them. A great cast of old-timers and a clever plot keep this baby moving at a good clip.

HOME FOR THE HOLIDAYS
★★★ Starmaker, 1972, NR, 74 min. Dir: John Llewellyn Moxey. Cast: Sally Field, Eleanor Parker, Julie Harris, Jessica Walter, Jill Haworth, Walter Brennan.

Estranged sisters Field, Parker, Walter, and Haworth visit their dying dad (Brennan) for Christmas. After his claims that his new wife (Harris) is poisoning him are mostly ignored, some psycho in a rain slicker and Playtex Living Gloves begins decimating the clan with a handy pitchfork. This highly entertaining made-for-TV yuletide massacre movie has a top cast in fine form (Parker is outstanding, especially in her final scene), efficient direction, and a memorable score by George Tipton.

HOME, SWEET HOME
★ Vestron, 1980, R, 84 min.
Dir: Nettie Peña. Cast: Jake Steinfeld, Sallee Elyse, Peter de Paula, Vanessa Shaw.

This worthless holiday hacker has beefcake-to-the-stars Steinfeld on a rantin' rampage as a musclehead out to fatally fuck up a family's Thanksgiving dinner. Please place the appropriate turkey joke here.

HONEYMOON KILLERS, THE
★★★ Vestron, 1969, R, 108 min.
Dir: Leonard Kastle. Cast: Tony LoBianco, Shirley Stoler, Doris Roberts, Mary Jane Higby.

Based on the true exploits of the notorious "Lonely Hearts Killers," in which an overweight nurse and her gigolo boyfriend robbed and murdered a series of well-to-do old maids, this cheap but well-made little shocker has fine performances and a nice semi-documentary flavor. Filmed as *The Lonely Hearts Killers.*

HOOK CULT MURDERS, THE
See: *The Phyx.*

HORRIBLE DR. HICHCOCK, THE
★★★ Republic, 1962, NR, 76 min.
Dir: Robert Hampton [Riccardo Freda]. Cast: Barbara Steele, Robert Flemyng, Montgomery Glenn, Maria Teresa Vianello, Harriet White Medin.

Steele, her exquisite face pressed against a rain-washed window, her limpid eyes wide with shock, is the ideal heroine for this sado-sexual European horror hit. Flemyng is the title physician, a closet necrophile who may have killed his first wife with a death-semblance formula during their sexual "funeral games" and might also do the same to new bride Barbara. Rich color photography and beautiful atmosphere highlight this Italian chiller, which was somewhat cut down for U.S. consumption (Sinister Cinema has available an uncut 83-minute print titled *The Terror of Dr. Hichcock*). Aka *Raptus: Rapture* and *The Horrible Secret of Dr. Hichcock*; sequel: *The Ghost.*

HORRIBLE HOUSE ON THE HILL, THE
See: *Devil Times Five.*

HORRIBLE SECRET OF DR. HICHCOCK, THE
See: *The Horrible Dr. Hichcock.*

HORROR AND SEX

See: *Night of the Bloody Apes.*

HORROR CASTLE

See: *The Virgin of Nuremberg.*

HORROR CHAMBER OF DR. FAUSTUS, THE

★★★☆ Sinister Cinema, 1959, NR, 84 min.
Dir: Georges Franju. Cast: Pierre Brasseur, Alida Valli, Edith Scob, Juliette Mayniel, Beatrice Altariba, François Guerin.

Franju's classic about a mad surgeon kidnapping young girls and cutting off their faces to restore the lost beauty of his china-masked daughter is an almost perfect blend of poetry and subtle horror. Beautifully austere photography and settings help distract from the painfully unelegant dubbed dialogue, while the plot echoes elements of *Psycho* (shot after this but released first) and contains one of the earliest widely seen gore shots (when doctor Brasseur removes the face of lovely Mayniel). Sinister also has available the original 92-minute version, *Les Yeux Sans Visage: Eyes Without a Face,* in French with subtitles. Highly recommended.

HORROR CREATURES OF THE PREHISTORIC PLANET

See: *Horror of the Blood Monsters.*

HORROR EXPRESS

★★★ Goodtimes, 1972, PG, 86 min.
Dir: Gene [Eugenio] Martin. Cast: Christopher Lee, Peter Cushing, Telly Savalas, Silvia Tortosa, Alberto de Mendoza, Julio Pena, Helga Line, Jorge Rigaud.

What starts out as just another Lee-Cushing gothic horror movie quickly turns into an off-beat, flamboyant mix of *Murder on the Orient Express* and *The Thing.* Lee is an archeologist who unearths a fossilized ape man in 1906 China and returns with it to the west aboard the Trans-Siberian Express. Once the trip is underway, however, the creature is reactivated by a once-dormant alien life force and begins absorbing the minds of various passengers, reducing them to blank-eyed corpses with smooth, empty brains. Lee and Cushing (as a scientific rival) are in top form, while Savalas is fun in a small role as a crazed Cossack. Originally called *Panico en el Transiberiano: Panic on the Trans-Siberian Express,* this Spanish chiller is strengthened by good direction and an interesting premise.

HORROR HIGH

See: *The Twisted Brain.*

HORROR HOSPITAL

★★☆ MPI, 1973, R, 90 min. Dir: Antony Balch.
Cast: Michael Gough, Robin Askwith, Vanessa Shaw, Ellen Pollack, Dennis Price, Skip Martin.

Gough has a field day in this camp Brit mad-doctor flick about a resort that's actually a cover for the zombie-making activities of evil Dr. Storm (Gough). Full of great silly touches (like a limo with retractable machetes used for handy decapitations) and a great supporting turn from Martin as Gough's dwarf assistant. Aka *The Computer Killers.*

HORROR HOTEL

★★★☆ Sinister Cinema, 1960, NR, 76 min.
Dir: John Moxey. Cast: Christopher Lee, Betta St.

MILTON SUBOTSKY
(1921–1991)

The co-founder of England's Amicus Productions and Hammer's chief rival, American-born Subotsky produced and often wrote and edited an entire series of entertaining anthology horror flicks in the '60s and '70s, utilizing as inspiration such diverse material as the writings of Robert Bloch and R. Chetwynd-Hayes, and EC comics. After Amicus folded in 1977, Subotsky continued to work within the genre, although none of his productions were up to the sleek enjoyability of his earlier work.

Horror Hotel (co-producer, original story, '60), *Dr. Terror's House of Horrors* (co-producer, screenplay, '65), *The Skull* (co-producer, screenplay, '65), *The Psychopath* (co-producer, '66), *The Deadly Bees* (co-producer, '67), *Torture Garden* (co-producer, '68), *Scream and Scream Again* (co-producer, '70), *The Mind of Mr. Soames* (co-producer, '70), *The House That Dripped Blood* (co-producer, '71), *I, Monster* (co-producer, screenplay, '71), *Tales From the Crypt* (co-producer, screenplay, '72), *Asylum* (co-producer, screenplay, '72), *Vault of Horror* (co-producer, screenplay, '73), *—And Now the Screaming Starts!* (co-producer, '73), *From Beyond the Grave* (co-producer, '74), *Madhouse* (co-producer, '74), *The Beast Must Die* (co-producer, '74), *The Land That Time Forgot* (co-producer, '75), *The Uncanny* (co-producer, original stories, '77), *Dominique* (co-producer, '79), *The Monster Club* ('81), *Cat's Eye* (co-producer, '85), *Maximum Overdrive* (co-producer, '86), *Sometimes They Come Back* (co-producer, '91).

Christopher Lee gets crossed in Horror of Dracula *(1958).*

John, Dennis Lotis, Patricia Jessel, Venetia Stevenson, Valentine Dyall.

Super low-budget British film (produced by Milton Subotsky several years before forming his Amicus company) about a coed (Stevenson) who comes to a misty New England village in order to check into its history of witchcraft and ends up being sacrificed by a coven headed by the local inn proprietress (Jessel), who's the reincarnation of an executed witch. The beautifully misty atmosphere and strong plot (in which the heroine is killed halfway through and then replaced by another girl who almost meets the same fate, as in the simultaneously shot *Psycho*) help make this a minor classic of the '60s. Original title: *City of the Dead*.

HORROR HOTEL MASSACRE
See: *Eaten Alive.*

HORROR MAN
See: *The Tell-Tale Heart.*

HORROR MANIACS
See: *The Greed of William Hart.*

HORROR OF DRACULA
★★★★ Warner, 1958, NR, 81 min.
Dir: Terence Fisher. Cast: Peter Cushing, Christopher Lee, Michael Gough, Melissa Stribling, Carol Marsh, John Van Eyssen, Valerie Gaunt, Miles Malleson.

In the first and best of Hammer's Dracula series, Lee is superb as the seductive count, swooping low over the repressed Victorian ladies who become his all-too-willing victims. Cushing is equally fine as the tireless Dr. Van Helsing, who tracks the vampire king until their final, classic struggle in the rays of the morning sun. Sharply directed by Fisher, with a trim Jimmy Sangster script and dynamic James Bernard score, this is, simply put, one of the very best. Originally titled *Dracula* and followed by eight sequels.

HORROR OF FRANKENSTEIN, THE
★★☆ Republic, 1970, R, 91 min. Dir: Jimmy Sangster.

entist's black comic maid discovers the means to destroy them. This is the kind of movie that's probably more entertaining this way than if it had been done competently, with lots of stilted acting and the "Zombie Stomp" sung by the Del-Aires. Originally released to video in a cut version, Admit One's print restores the missing gore. Aka *Invasion of the Zombies.*

HORROR OF THE BLOOD MONSTERS

★ VidAmerica, 1970, PG, 85 min.
Dir: Al Adamson. Cast: John Carradine, Robert Dix, Vicki Volante, Joey Benson, Jennifer Bishop, Bruce Powers, Britt Semand, voice of Brother Theodore.

Adamson does a Jerry Warren with this confused hilarity about a space mission to a distant planet that scientists believe is the source of a vampire plague currently terrorizing the world. Once on the planet, astronauts (led by a cranky Carradine) encounter tinted stock footage from *One Million B.C.* and reams of tinted footage from a heretofore unheard-of Filipino vampire-caveman epic. A cinematic jigsaw, this has hammy opening narration by Theodore, Semand as a lady astronaut in white vinyl go-go boots, and a totally incongruous "PG" heavy-breathing sex scene in a room full of props left over from *Dracula vs. Frankenstein.* Aka *Vampire Men of the Lost Planet, Creatures of the Prehistoric Planet, Horror Creatures of the Prehistoric Planet,* and *Space Mission of the Lost Planet.*

HORROR OF THE WEREWOLF

See: *Night of the Howling Beast.*

HORROR OF THE ZOMBIES

★★ VidAmerica, 1974, R, 90 min. Dir: Amando de Ossorio. Cast: Maria Perschy, Jack Taylor, Carlos Lemos, Manuel de Blas, Barbara Rey, Blanca Estrada.

A group of gorgeous models and their friends board a mysterious, mist-enshrouded old galleon, which they discover to be inhabited by the ghoulish, blind, and bloodthirsty Knights Templar. Fair third entry in de Ossorio's "Blind Dead" series, this is reasonably atmospheric, but the model of the phantom galleon used throughout the film looks like it belongs in some kid's bathtub. The gore is fairly restrained, apart from the dismemberment of Rey (cut from some prints). Original title: *El Buque Maldito: The Ghost Galleon* and aka *Ghost Ship of the Blind Dead* and *Ship of Zombies.*

HORROR ON SNAPE ISLAND

See: *Tower of Evil.*

HORROR PLANET

★★☆ Embassy, 1981, R, 92 min. Dir: Norman J.

TERENCE FISHER
(1904–1980)

The guiding force behind the look and feel of the classic Hammer films, this hard-working Brit director helped revitalize the horror genre in the late '50s. Although Fisher was another underappreciated genre talent whose work was mostly scorned in its day, nearly all of his gothics have beautifully withstood the test of time.

Stolen Face ('52), *The Curse of Frankenstein* ('57), *Horror of Dracula* ('58), *The Revenge of Frankenstein* ('58), *The Hound of the Baskervilles* ('59), *The Man Who Could Cheat Death* ('59), *The Mummy* ('59), *The Stranglers of Bombay* ('60), *Brides of Dracula* ('60), *The Two Faces of Dr. Jekyll* ('60), *The Curse of the Werewolf* ('61), *The Phantom of the Opera* ('62), *Sherlock Holmes and the Deadly Necklace* ('63), *The Horror of It All* ('64), *The Gorgon* ('64), *The Earth Dies Screaming* ('64), *Dracula, Prince of Darkness* ('66), *Island of Terror* ('66), *Frankenstein Created Woman* ('67), *The Devil's Bride* ('68), *Frankenstein Must Be Destroyed!* ('69), *Frankenstein and the Monster from Hell* ('73).

Cast: Ralph Bates, Kate O'Mara, Veronica Carlson, Dennis Price, Joan Rice, Graham James, Jon Finch, David Prowse.

Not another sequel to Hammer's classic *The Curse of Frankenstein,* this is actually a modestly funny black comic remake. Bates as the young baron is more interested in deflowering the local female population than in creating monsters, though he somehow finds the time to construct a bald, flat-headed bozo (Prowse, later to play Darth Vader in *Star Wars*) in a bandage bikini. Harmless fluff with a solid cast and some amusing bits; originally billed with *Scars of Dracula.*

HORROR OF PARTY BEACH, THE

★☆ Admit One, 1964, NR, 72 min.
Dir: Del Tenney. Cast: John Scott, Alice Lyon, Allen Laurel, Eulabelle Moore, Marilyn Clark, The Del-Aires.

A classic of ineptitude combining a Frankie-and-Annette beach party movie with a monster cautionary tale on the horrors of atomic waste. Said waste, dumped off the coast of a swingin' Connecticut teen beach, turns a couple of skulls into seven-foot sea monsters with hot dogs in their mouths, which quickly attack beach bunnies and slumber parties until a sci-

Warren. Cast: Judy Geeson, Robin Clarke, Jennifer Ashley, Stephanie Beacham, Steven Grieves, Heather Wright, Barry Houghton, Victoria Tennant.

Gory, British-made *Alien* clone about astronauts being killed by a lady scientist (Geeson) who was raped by a scaly extraterrestrial and is about to give birth to its mutant offspring. Although contrived in the extreme, the story moves at a brisk pace and the cast is above average, especially Geeson, who brings far more poignancy and bravura to her role than you might normally expect. Original title: *Inseminoid*.

HORROR RISES FROM THE TOMB
★★☆ Charter, 1972, R, 88 min. Dir: Carlos Aured. Cast: Paul Naschy, Helga Line, Emma Cohen, Vic Winner, Cristina Suriana, Luis Ciges.

One of Naschy's most brutal and entertaining efforts, this plays like a gore version of the '50s favorite *The Thing That Couldn't Die*. A decapitated sorcerer (Naschy) possesses a lookalike descendant in order to revive his executed mistress (Suriana) and rejoin his head to his body. A rather top-heavy plot is kept moving via plenty of interesting twists, gruesome killings, and the odd touch of unintended humor (especially at the climax).

HORRORSCOPE
See: *976-Evil*.

HORROR SHOW, THE
★☆ MGM/UA, 1989, R, 90 min.
Dir: James Isaac. Cast: Lance Henriksen, Brion James, Rita Taggart, Deedee Pfeiffer, Aron Eisenberg, Thom Bray, Matt Clark, Terry Alexander.

This pathetic rip-off of the *Nightmare on Elm Street* films has cop Henriksen haunted by dreams (or are they?) of recently executed mass-murderer Max Jenke (James). Actually, it is just a disguised third entry in the feeble "House" series (released abroad as *House III: The Horror Show*), with variable FX wasted on a trite storyline. Henriksen, though, underplays well as the haunted here; James, on the other hand, is pure ham as the giggly, sub-Freddy villain.

HORRORS OF BURKE AND HARE, THE
★★ New World, 1971, R, 91 min. Dir: Vernon Sewell. Cast: Harry Andrews, Derren Nesbitt, Glynn Edwards, Dee Shenderey, Yootha Joyce, Alan Tucker, Françoise Pascal, Yutte Stensgaard.

Veteran hack Sewell helms this tacky remake of *Mania* (originally titled *Burke and Hare*) with emphasis this time less on the body snatching than on the bodies of prostitutes Pascal and Stensgaard. Andrews, however, rises above all in an excellent turn as Dr. Knox.

HORRORS OF SPIDER ISLAND
★★ Sinister Cinema, 1959, NR, 76 min. Dir: Jamie Nolan [Fritz Bottger and Alex D'Arcy]. Cast: Helga Frank, Alex D'Arcy, Barbara Valentin, Harald Maresch.

An irresistibly cheesy German-Yugoslavian concoction about a planeload of showgirls and their agent (D'Arcy) stranded on a spider-infested island where the agent is transformed by an arachnid bite into a grotesque spider-monster. It takes a while for this thing to get going, but once it does, it rivals the unintended hilarity of the best of Ed Wood. There's papier-mâché makeup and a brief skinny-dipping scene that was quite daring for the time. Aka *Ein Toter Hing im Netz: A Corpse Hangs in Web* and *It's Hot in Paradise*.

HOSPITAL MASSACRE
★★ MGM/UA, 1981, R, 88 min. Dir: Boaz Davidson. Cast: Barbi Benton, Chip Lucia, Jon Van Ness, Den Surles, Gay Austin, John Warner Williams.

Playboy Playmate of the Year and former Hugh Hefner squeeze Benton stars in this hospital slasher, in which she is stalked by a masked scalpel-wielding crazy out to avenge a long-ago Valentine's Day humiliation. Pointless in the extreme, with routine gore murders and nude scenes. Aka *Be My Valentine, or Else!*, *X-Ray*, and *Ward 13*.

HOSPITAL OF TERROR
★★ VidAmerica, 1977, R, 88 min.
Dir: Al Adamson. Cast: Jill Jacobson, Geoffrey Land, Marilyn Joi, Mary Kay Pass.

Originally released as *Nurse Sherri*, this is one of Adamson's more presentable pics, a credible *Carrie* rip about a young nurse (Jacobson) possessed by the spirit of a patient who died on a hospital's operating table and is out to get revenge on those he holds responsible. Poorly produced but surprisingly well acted. TV title: *Beyond the Living*.

HOUND OF THE BASKERVILLES, THE
★★★ Key, 1939, NR, 80 min.
Dir: Sidney Lanfield. Cast: Basil Rathbone, Nigel Bruce, Richard Greene, Wendy Barrie, Lionel Atwill, John Carradine, Morton Lowry, Mary Gordon.

The first and one of the best of 14 Sherlock Holmes mysteries starring Rathbone and Bruce, this one is based on Sir Arthur Conan Doyle's most famous story, with Holmes up against the ghosty legend of the "Hound of Hell." A strong cast and flavorful photography

BASIL RATHBONE
(1892–1967)

Born Philip St. John Basil Rathbone in Johannesburg, South Africa, Rathbone was a distinguished stage actor who became a top Hollywood bad guy before his fortuitous casting as Sherlock Holmes in 1939's *The Hound of the Baskervilles*. Although he later claimed to resent the type casting that resulted from his Holmes association (including specializing in horror films in the last years of his life), this fine actor effortlessly made the role forever his own.

Love From a Stranger ('37), *Son of Frankenstein* ('39), *The Hound of the Baskervilles* ('39), *The Adventures of Sherlock Holmes* ('39), *The Mad Doctor* ('41), *The Black Cat* ('41), *Sherlock Holmes Faces Death* ('43), *The Spider Woman* ('44), *The Scarlet Claw* ('44), *The Pearl of Death* ('44), *The House of Fear* ('45), *The Woman in Green* ('45), *The Black Sleep* ('56), *The Magic Sword* ('62), *Tales of Terror* ('62), *The Comedy of Terrors* ('64), *Queen of Blood* ('66), *The Ghost in the Invisible Bikini* ('66), *Autopsy of a Ghost* ('67), *Hillbillies in a Haunted House* ('67).

and settings make this one of Hollywood's best treatments of the Holmes mystique, and it's still the best of the many versions of *Hound*. The controversial final line, "Watson, the needle!" kept this out of circulation for years.

HOUND OF THE BASKERVILLES, THE
★★★ MGM/UA, 1959, NR, 86 min.
Dir: Terence Fisher. Cast: Peter Cushing, Christopher Lee, Andre Morell, Marla Landi, Francis De Wolff, Ewen Solon, Miles Malleson, David Oxley.

Good Hammer remake abandons much of the original's plot but still manages to remain faithful to the Conan Doyle spirit, with Cushing an energetic Holmes and Morell an intelligent, understated Watson. Beautifully photographed on gorgeous sets; Osley steals it in the opening flashback as the lustful Sir Hugo Baskerville.

HOUNDS OF ZAROFF, THE
See: *The Most Dangerous Game*.

HOUSE
★★ New World, 1986, R, 92 min.
Dir: Steve Miner. Cast: William Katt, George Wendt, Richard Moll, Kay Lenz, Mary Stavin, Susan French.

Slick-looking but hopelessly juvenile haunted house comedy with Katt as an author of horror stories who retires to his aunt's mansion to write a "serious" novel about his Vietnam experiences, only to be teased and tormented by a horde of playful spirits. Full of rubbery monsters and flat humor (though Wendt is amusing as a nosy neighbor), this film is a clutter of disparate elements that never come together, yet it was somehow popular enough to inspire three sequels. Lenz is utterly wasted in the thankless role of Katt's bitchy ex-wife.

HOUSE II: THE SECOND STORY
★☆ New World, 1987, PG-13, 88 min.
Dir: Ethan Wiley. Cast: Arye Gross, Jonathan Stark, Royal Dano, Lar Park Lincoln, John Ratzenberger, Bill Maher, Amy Yasbeck, Devon Devasquez.

A clever title masks an awful, inept sequel. An immature bonehead (Gross) with a bitch of a girlfriend (Lincoln) and a buffoon of a best buddy (Stark) inherits an old mansion and soon after resurrects his prospector great-grandfather (Dano), who owns a crystal skull with supernatural powers. Although this is good-looking and has some great FX, it is killed by unlikable characters it shoves down our throats, as well as annoyingly out-of-place western and fantasy film touches. Dano is good, though.

HOUSE III: THE HORROR SHOW
See: *The Horror Show*.

HOUSE IV: HOME DEADLY HOME
★★ RCA/Columbia, 1991, R, 93 min.
Dir: Lewis Abernathy. Cast: Terri Treas, William Katt, Scott Burkholder, Denny Dillon, Melissa Clayton, Dabbs Greer, Ned Romero, John Santucci.

Katt and Treas inherit an old house in the desert. Katt is killed in a car crash and Treas and daughter-in-a-wheelchair Clayton move into the house, which proves to be haunted—wotta surprise! The only *House* "sequel" to have at least *something* to do with the original (Katt plays the same character as he did in that film but with a new wife and daughter), this is played mostly straight by its comic cast and has all the usual haunted house bits—and an ending that goes so far as to rip off *Ghost!*

HOUSE BY THE CEMETERY, THE
★★☆ Vestron, 1981, UR, 78 min.
Dir: Lucio Fulci. Cast: Katherine MacColl, Paolo Malco, Giovanni Frezza, Ania Pieroni, Dagmar Lassander, Giovanni de Nardi.

College professor Malco, wife MacColl, and young son Frezza move into an old grave-

Fangs for the memories: Nancy Barrett in House of Dark Shadows *(1970).*

yard-side house outside Boston in which the basement harbors the living dead remains of the ageless, evil Dr. Freudstein (de Nardi). Densely atmospheric, with elements borrowed from everything from *The Turn of the Screw* to *The Shining*, this gory tidbit is one of Fulci's most interesting films. The U.S. prints are badly edited, however, with two sequences shown out of order!

HOUSE BY THE EDGE OF THE PARK, THE
★★ Vestron, 1981, R, 91 min. Dir: Ruggero Deodato. Cast: David Hess, Annie Belle, John Morghen, Lorraine DeSelle, Christain Borromeo.

Bored yuppies pick up street people Hess and Morghen and take them to a fancy party, little realizing that Hess is a crazed psychopath. Low on gore and kinda dull at first, but once *Last House on the Left* star Hess starts stalking, this Italian yawner finally kicks into gear.

HOUSE BY THE LAKE, THE
See: *Death Weekend.*

HOUSE IN MARSH ROAD, THE
★★ Sinister Cinema, 1960, NR, 70 min. Dir:Montgomery Tully. Cast: Patricia Dainton, Tony Wright, Sandra Dorne, Derek Aylward.

This compact Brit low-budgeter (shown on TV as *Invisible Creature*) is about a writer (Wright) whose murderous intentions against his wife (Dainton) are foiled by the actions of a mysterious poltergeist. It's fairly tense but also

somewhat silly, with Dorne as Wright's mistress, who wears a dress to match the tacky wallpaper in her living room.

HOUSEKEEPER, THE
★★ Warner, 1986, R, 96 min. Dir: Ousama Rawi. Cast: Rita Tushingham, Ross Petty, Shelley Peterson, Jackie Burroughs, Jessica Steen, Jonathan Crombie.

Tushingham excels in this otherwise ponderous Canadian adaptation of Ruth Rendell's novel *A Judgement in Stone* (the original title). A repressed, dyslexic British housekeeper working for a rich, pampered American family murders anyone who discovers the truth about her affliction. Good-looking, but too many unsympathetic characters make it rough going.

HOUSE OF BLOOD
See: *Mansion of the Doomed.*

HOUSE OF CRAZIES
See: *Asylum.*

HOUSE OF DARK SHADOWS
★★★★ MGM/UA, 1970, PG, 96 min. Dir: Dan Curtis. Cast: Jonathan Frid, Joan Bennett, Grayson Hall, Kathryn Leigh Scott, Roger Davis, Nancy Barrett, John Karlen, Thayer David, Louis Edmonds, David Henesy.

In this stylish film version of the popular TV serial, vampire Barnabas Collins (played

---

DAN CURTIS
(1928–)

Curtis is a TV producer-director best known as the creator of *Dark Shadows* and a string of popular '70s TV flicks, including the highly rated *The Night Stalker*. His films are fast-paced and fun but tend to look a bit too much alike.

The Strange Case of Dr. Jekyll and Mr. Hyde (producer, '68), *House of Dark Shadows* ('70), *Night of Dark Shadows* ('71), *The Night Stalker* (producer, '72), *The Night Strangler* ('73), *Frankenstein* (producer, '73), *The Norliss Tapes* ('73), *The Picture of Dorian Gray* (producer, '73), *Dracula* ('74), *Shadow of Fear* (producer, '74), *The Invasion of Carol Enders* (producer, '74), *Scream of the Wolf* ('74), *The Turn of the Screw* ('74), *Trilogy of Terror* ('75), *Burnt Offerings* ('76), *Dead of Night* ('77), *Curse of the Black Widow* ('77), *Intruders* ('92).

superbly by Frid) is released from his chained coffin by handyman Karlen and arrives at the estate of Collinwood in Maine, where he passes himself off to his modern descendants as a visiting cousin from England. When he meets governess Maggie Evans (Scott), Barnabas sees in her the reincarnation of his lost love, Josette, and begins planning a vampire wedding in a misty, cobweb-strewn crypt. Beautifully shot on location in Tarrytown, New York, this remains one of the best vampire films of its era, with fine performances, fast-paced direction, and terrific early makeup work from Dick Smith. Sequel: *Night of Dark Shadows*.

HOUSE OF DEATH

☆ Vestron, 1981, R, 89 min.
Dir: David Nelson. Cast: Susan Kiger, Martin Tucker, Jody Kay, Jennifer Chase.

Fifth-rate slasher trash with a black-gloved, machete-slinging psycho hacking up teenagers during a carnival's visit to a small North Carolina town. It is terribly acted, written, and directed and has a musical score better suited to an episode of "The Brady Bunch." Aka *Death Screams* and *Night Screams*.

HOUSE OF DOOM

See: *The Black Cat*.

HOUSE OF DOOM

See: *House of Psychotic Women*.

HOUSE OF DRACULA

★★☆ MCA/Universal, 1945, NR, 67 min.
Dir: Erle C. Kenton. Cast: Lon Chaney, Jr., John Carradine, Martha O'Driscoll, Onslow Stevens, Lionel Atwill, Jane Adams, Glenn Strange, Skelton Knaggs.

Dedicated scientist Stevens tries to use modern science to cure the Universal monsters. He succeeds, temporarily, with the Wolf Man (Chaney) but is tainted by Dracula's (Carradine) blood and transforms into a Jekyll-and-Hyde madman who revs up the Frankenstein monster (Strange) one more time. The last of Universal's serious monster rallies, this is unusual for any number of reasons—beginning with the fact that Dracula himself is killed off only halfway through a Dracula movie!—and despite its cheapness (lots of stock footage, stock settings, and stock music), it is a slight improvement over the previous year's *House of Frankenstein*. Best scene: Carradine beguiling nurse O'Driscoll as she plays "Moonlight Sonata" on the piano.

HOUSE OF EVIL

See: *Dance of Death*.

HOUSE OF EVIL

See: *The House on Sorority Row*.

HOUSE OF EXORCISM, THE

★★ Gorgon, 1975, R, 93 min.
Dir: Mickey Lion [Mario Bava]. Cast: Telly Savalas, Elke Sommer, Robert Alda, Alida Valli, Sylva Koscina, Alessio Orano.

Bava's exquisite chiller *Lisa and the Devil* is mutilated into yet another post-*Exorcist* vomit fest, with the film's original demon-reincarnation plot (involving doubles, the devil in human form, mannequins, and gruesome murder) now related in flashback by a toad-spitting Sommer to priest Alda (who was not featured in the original film). That some of the Bava brilliance managed to survive (like a marvelous scene where Orano brings his bedridden wife a piece of cake and the camera pulls back to reveal the woman's rotted corpse and a room full of moldy, crumbling slices of cake on tiny china plates) is a tribute to the great director. The haunting theme, "Concerto of Aranjuez," later turned up as background music in Ricardo Montalban's Cordova commercials. Aka *The Devil in the House of Exorcism*.

HOUSE OF FEAR, THE

★★★ Key, 1945, NR, 69 min.
Dir: Roy William Neill. Cast: Basil Rathbone, Nigel Bruce, Dennis Hoey, Aubrey Mather, Paul Cavanagh, Harry Cording, Holmes Herbert, Sally Shepherd.

Good entry in the Rathbone Holmes series with a plot quite similar to Agatha Christie's *And Then There Were None* (filmed the same year). Holmes and Watson visit the gloomy Scottish mansion that's the headquarters of the "Good Comrades" club, whose members are being murdered and mutilated by a mysterious maniac. Solid mystery-horror with an atypical ending, in that Watson (Bruce) is the first to solve the crimes!

HOUSE OF FRANKENSTEIN

★★☆ MCA/Universal, 1944, NR, 70 min.
Dir: Erle C. Kenton. Cast: Boris Karloff, Lon Chaney, Jr., John Carradine, J. Carrol Naish, Anne Gwynne, Lionel Atwill, George Zucco, Elena Verdugo, Peter Coe, Glenn Strange.

Dr. Gustav Niemann (Karloff) escapes from prison one stormy night with hunchbacked cellmate Daniel (Naish) and uses the front of a traveling Chamber of Horrors to seek revenge on his enemies. Along the way he revives Count Dracula (Carradine) by removing the wooden stake from his skeleton and defrosts the Wolf Man (Chaney) and the Frankenstein

GLENN STRANGE
(1899–1973)

This New Mexico cowboy–rodeo star–stuntman was plucked from obscurity by Universal to play the Frankenstein Monster in their all-star monster rally *House of Frankenstein*. Coached by co-star Boris Karloff, Strange was successful enough in the role (in his own way) to get to play the part twice more, most notably in *Abbott and Costello Meet Frankenstein*. In the decade before his death, Glenn was best known to TV fans as Sam the bartender on *Gunsmoke*.

The Mad Monster ('42), *The Black Raven* ('43), *The Monster Maker* ('44), *House of Frankenstein* ('44), *House of Dracula* ('45), *Abbott and Costello Meet Frankenstein* ('48), *Master Minds* ('49).

monster (Strange) from an ice cavern beneath the ruins of the old Frankenstein estate. This fun-filled Universal monster mash has excellent performances from Chaney and Naish and a flavorful score by Hans J. Salter to help distract you from the contrivances of its script.

HOUSE OF FREAKS
See: *Frankenstein's Castle of Freaks.*

HOUSE OF MADNESS
See: *Dr. Tarr's Torture Dungeon.*

HOUSE OF MORTAL SIN
See: *The Confessional.*

HOUSE OF PSYCHOTIC WOMEN
★★ VidAmerica, 1973, R, 84 min.
Dir: Carlos Aured. Cast: Paul Naschy, Diana Lorys, Eva Leon, Maria Perschy, Eduardo Calvo, Ines Morales.

Ex-con Naschy takes a job as handyman for three sex-starved, slightly demented sisters living in a house whose neighborhood is being terrorized by a psycho who likes to murder blue-eyed blondes and hack out their eyes. Naschy's version of a Dario Argento thriller (originally called *Los Ojos Azules de la Muneca Rota: Blue Eyes of the Broken Doll*), this is fairly well done on its own weird terms, though by the time you find out whodunit you probably won't care anymore. TV title: *House of Doom.*

HOUSE OF SEVEN CORPSES, THE
★★☆ Video Gems, 1973, PG, 88 min.
Dir: Paul Harrison. Cast: John Ireland, Faith Domergue, John Carradine, Charles Macauley, Carole Wells, Jerry Strickler.

Enjoyable small-scale thriller (shot in Salt Lake City) about a low-budget movie company making a horror film at creepy old Beale Manor, where an actress reading from the Tibetan Book of the Dead revives a murderous walking corpse. The good cast has fun with their showy parts (especially Macauley), and there's an interesting use of library music (mostly from "The Outer Limits") mixed with original choral work, as well as some genuine jolts (particularly when the ghoul's shadow seems, for a moment, to be part of a gnarled tree).

HOUSE OF TERROR
See: *Face of the Screaming Werewolf.*

HOUSE OF TERROR
★☆ Media, 1972, R, 90 min.
Dir: Sergei Goucharoff. Cast: Jennifer Bishop, Arell Blanton, Jacqueline Hyde, Mitchell Gregg.

Cheapo Hitchcock imitation with sexy nurse Bishop marrying patient Gregg after the mysterious death of wife Hyde. Later the wife's lookalike sister shows up, followed by murder galore. Good performance from the underrated Hyde, but this is otherwise a waste. John "Bud" Cardos directed second unit. Aka *Five at the Funeral.*

HOUSE OF THE BLACK DEATH
★ Loonic, 1965, NR, 80 min.
Dirs: Harold Daniels, Reginald Le Borg, Jerry Warren. Cast: Lon Chaney, Jr., John Carradine, Andrea King, Tom Drake, Dolores Faith, Jerome Thor, Katherine Victor, Sabrina.

Cardboard monstrosity—culled from footage contributed by three different directors!—about the cursed Desarde family, who are dominated by voodoo, witchcraft, and lycanthropy. A haphazard melange of werewolves, go-go-dancing witches, Chaney with horns, you name it. Most of the veteran cast look sick or drunk or both. Aka *Night of the Beast* and *Blood of the Man Devil.*

HOUSE OF THE DARK STAIRCASE
See: *A Blade in the Dark.*

HOUSE OF THE LIVING DEAD
★ Interglobal, 1973, PG, 87 min. Dir: Ray Austin. Cast: Mark Burns, Shirley Ann Field, David Oxley, Margaret Inglis, Dia Sydow, Lynee Maree.

Mail-order bride Field finds terror at her fiance's African veldt estate, which is haunted by his mad brother, who likes to collect the souls of animals and people (just *how* is never explained) and store them in colored glass jars. This plodding, preposterous potboiler was shot in South Africa and was the best argument for sanctions *I* could ever think of. Original title: *Dr. Maniac.*

HOUSE OF THE LONG SHADOWS

★★☆ MGM/UA, 1983, PG, 101 min.
Dir: Pete Walker. Cast: Vincent Price, Christopher Lee, Peter Cushing, John Carradine, Desi Arnaz, Jr., Sheila Keith, Julie Peasgood, Richard Todd.

The grand old men of horror are in grand form in this otherwise lackluster version of Earl Derr Biggers' *Seven Keys to Baldpate* about a mystery writer (a grotesquely miscast Arnaz) who stumbles upon a bizarre family reunion while trying to write a novel in a creaky old Welsh mansion. Contrived, to say the least, and with an annoying twist ending, it is still worth seeing as the only film to feature Price, Lee, Cushing, and Carradine together and in such fine form.

HOUSE OF USHER

See: *The Fall of the House of Usher.*

HOUSE OF USHER, THE

★ RCA/Columbia, 1989, R, 91 min.
Dir: Alan Birkinshaw. Cast: Oliver Reed, Donald Pleasence, Romy Windsor, Rufus Swart, Norman Coombes, Anne Stradi.

Ludicrous new version of the Poe classic with Windsor as the fiancee of Usher boy Swart. When they visit the family manse (which looks like it's constructed from sets left over from *Suspiria*), he is buried alive and she is raped by brooding Uncle Reed, who wants her to carry on the Usher line (why didn't he just let her marry his nephew, who was also, after all, an Usher?). Since this peaks during a nude man's castration via hungry rat, Poe purists needn't fear its straying from the original text. Really, really bad. Aka *The Fall of the House of Usher.*

HOUSE OF WAX

★★★☆ Warner, 1953, NR, 88 min.
Dir: Andre de Toth. Cast: Vincent Price, Phyllis Kirk, Frank Lovejoy, Carolyn Jones, Paul Picerni, Roy Roberts, Paul Cavanagh, Charles Bronson.

Price became a genre superstar thanks to his role in this remake of *Mystery of the Wax Museum,* about a sculptor who loses both his face and his life's work in an insurance-scam fire. He replaces the former with a life-like mask and the latter by dipping the corpses of murder victims in wax. One of the few remakes to improve on its original, this has lots of gaslight and shadow atmospherics, a great supporting cast (Jones as a giggly early victim, Bronson as Price's hulking, mute manservant), and fun 3-D effects (in the theatrical version, anyway), including the infamous paddle-ball man.

HOUSE OF WHIPCORD

★★ IVE, 1974, R, 86 min.
Dir: Pete Walker. Cast: Barbara Markham, Patrick Barr, Ray Brooks, Ann Michelle, Penny Irving, Sheila Keith, Dorothy Alison, Robert Tayman.

One of Walker's better known but less effective chillers, this features Markham as the sadistic warden of an unauthorized women's prison where the female "criminals" are tortured and abused by the psychotic staff. There is a *Psycho* protagonist switch and a typically robust performance from prison guard Keith (the Shelley Winters of Great Britain) but otherwise not much.

HOUSE ON HAUNTED HILL

★★★☆ Fox, 1958, NR, 75 min.
Dir: William Castle. Cast: Vincent Price, Carol Ohmart, Richard Long, Alan Marshall, Carolyn Craig, Elisha Cook, Julie Mitchum, Leona Anderson.

Castle's best gimmick shocker, this has a delightfully urbane Price as suave millionaire Frederick Loren, who invites five people to spend the night in an eerie, supposedly haunted old mansion in return for $10,000 apiece—if they survive the night. This is a thoroughly enjoyable little number with a falling chandelier, clutching hands, a ceiling that drips blood, a severed head in the closet, a skeleton in the basement, an acid vat in the wine cellar, an ugly old witch on roller skates, well—it just goes on and on. Originally released in "Emergo"—a silly trick where, during a climactic scene, a plastic skeleton on a wire was flown over the audience's heads. Favorite line, Price to perfidious wife Ohmart: "Remember the fun we had when you poisoned me?"

HOUSE ON SKULL MOUNTAIN, THE

★☆ CBS/Fox, 1974, PG, 85 min.
Dir: Ron Honthaner. Cast: Victor French, Janee Michelle, Jean Durand, Mike Evans, Xernona Clayton, Ella Woods.

Dull blaxploitation horror shot in Atlanta. Relatives gather for a will reading in an old mansion where the voodoo-practicing butler (Durand) does them in, one by one. A justly forgotten oddity of the mid-'70s that's no credit to familiar TV faces French ("Highway to Heaven") and Evans ("The Jeffersons").

WILLIAM CASTLE
(1914–1977)

Born William Schloss, this master of crass gimmicks and outrageous showmanship worked on the stage and in radio with everyone from Bela Lugosi to Orson Welles before starting as a dialogue director at Columbia in the '40s. A decade later he tried his hand at the horror genre with a cheapo *Diabolique* variant called *Macabre*, which he produced and directed. Though barely memorable, the film's advertising gimmick of offering a Lloyds of London insurance policy to patrons in case of death by fright caught on with the public and inspired Bill to make an entire series of low-budget B&W horrors sporting such hokey trimmings as "Emergo," "Percepto," and "Illusion-O." His best film as director is the great *House on Haunted Hill*. He later produced Roman Polanski's classic *Rosemary's Baby* and the often-forgotten TV series *Ghost Story*. The cigar-chomping Castle can often be seen in cameos in several of his films.

Macabre ('58), *House on Haunted Hill* ('58), *The Tingler* ('59), *13 Ghosts* ('60), *Homicidal* ('61), *Mr. Sardonicus* ('61), *The Old Dark House* ('63), *13 Frightened Girls* ('63), *Strait-Jacket* ('64), *The Night Walker* ('65), *I Saw What You Did!* ('65), *Let's Kill Uncle!* ('66), *Rosemary's Baby* (producer, '68), *Shanks* ('74), *Bug* (producer, '75).

HOUSE ON SORORITY ROW, THE

★★☆ Vestron, 1982, R, 91 min. Dir: Mark Rosman. Cast: Kathryn NcNeil, Eileen Davidson, Lois Kelso Hunt, Christopher Lawrence, Janis Zido, Robin Meloy, Harley Kozak, Jodi Draigie.

A bungled prank leads to the death of a stern sorority house mother, who is avenged by her mad, deformed son, who systematically slaughters all but one of the girls involved. Surprisingly satisfying entry in the madman-and-coed genre directed with flourish by former Brian De Palma assistant director Rosman. With pleasing echoes of *Diabolique* and the work of Mario Bava, good performances, and a lush score by Richard Band. British title: *House of Evil*.

HOUSE ON STRAW HILL, THE

★☆ New World, 1975, R, 84 min. Dir: James Kenelm Clarke. Cast: Udo Kier, Linda Hayden, Fiona Richmond,, Patsy Smart.

Distasteful suspense chiller about a neurotic mystery author (Kier) whose country retreat is invaded by a sexy new secretary (the ever-sultry Hayden), who masturbates a lot and harbors a deadly secret. With more skin than blood, this looks like a soft-porn flick with a few gory murders added for the horror market. Aka *Exposé* and *Trauma*.

HOUSE THAT BLED TO DEATH, THE

★★☆ Thrillervideo, 1980, NR, 50 min. Dir: Tom Clegg. Cast: Rachel Davies, Nichollas Ball, Brian Croucher, Emma Ridley, Pat Maynard.

Above-average "Hammer House of Horror" segment about a family who move into a suburban house haunted by the memory of a gory knife murder. Fun *Amityville Horror*–like premise topped by a wicked double-twist ending.

HOUSE THAT DRIPPED BLOOD, THE

★★★ Prism, 1971, PG, 97 min. Dir: Peter Duffell. Cast: Christopher Lee, Peter Cushing, Ingrid Pitt, Jon Pertwee, Denholm Elliott, Nyree Dawn Porter, Tom Adams, Joanna Dunham, Chloe Franks, John Bennett.

Taut Amicus anthology scripted by Robert Bloch about a mysterious country mansion with an eerie influence on its various occupants. Elliott is a writer menaced by a character from his imagination; Cushing is a retired businessman haunted by a beautiful waxworks figure; Lee is a stern father convinced that his angelic little daughter is a witch; and Pertwee is a hammy horror film star transformed into a genuine vampire by an old black cloak. Good fun, with the final episode especially enjoyable, thanks to the humorous performances of Pertwee and the voluptuous Pitt.

HOUSE THAT VANISHED, THE

★☆ Video Treasures, 1973, R, 98 min. Dir: Joseph [José] Larraz. Cast: Andrea Allan, Karl Lanchbury, Maggie Walker, Peter Forbes-Robinson, Judy Matheson, Annabella Wood.

Transparent Brit stalker about a model who witnesses a murder in a country house her boyfriend was planning to rob. When the couple return to the house, it seems to have disappeared—as does the boyfriend soon after. A bad mystery with more skin than splatter, some clumsy red herrings, and an obvious killer. Aka *Scream and Die* and *Psycho Sex Fiend*.

HOUSE WHERE DEATH LIVES, THE

See: *Delusion*.

HOUSE WHERE EVIL DWELLS, THE

★★ MGM/UA, 1982, R, 88 min. Dir: Kevin Connor.
Cast: Edward Albert, Susan George, Doug McClure,
Amy Barrett, Mako Hattori, Toshiyuki Sasaki, Toshiya
Maruyama, Henry Mitowa.

An American family move into a lovely little
house outside Kyoto, Japan, which they discover is haunted by the ghosts of a love triangle who died in a bloody murder-suicide incident over 100 years earlier. A sharp-looking
but predictable haunted house tale, this has an
interesting setting and unexpectedly gory
murders but phony special effects and a needlessly high sex and nudity quotient. If you've
ever wanted to see McClure with his pants off,
this is the horror film for you.

HOW AWFUL ABOUT ALLAN

★★ Edde Entertainment, 1970, NR, 72 min.
Dir: Curtis Harrington. Cast: Anthony Perkins, Julie
Harris, Joan Hackett, Kent Smith, Robert H. Harris.

This is one of Harrington's enjoyable, atmospheric TV movies, adapted by *Baby Jane*
author Henry Farrell from his own novel.
Perkins is good in the tailor-made role of a
man suffering from hysterical partial blindness after the accidental death of his father.
Harris is his embittered, disfigured sister, and
Hackett the old girlfriend out to rekindle the
flame. Guess which one is trying to drive

Tony mad with stories of a shadowy boarder
in the house who may or may not exist and
may or may not be out to kill him? This has
plot elements looking forward to *Psycho II* and
effectively claustrophobic photography and
set design.

HOWLING, THE

★★★☆ Embassy, 1981, R, 90 min. Dir: Joe Dante.
Cast: Dee Wallace, Patrick Macnee, Dennis Dugan,
Christopher Stone, Belinda Balaski, Kevin McCarthy,
John Carradine, Slim Pickens, Elisabeth Brooks,
Robert Picardo, Dick Miller, Kenneth Tobey.

Wallace is an L.A. TV reporter recovering
from an assault who's sent by pop psychologist Macnee to a northern California retreat
that turns out to be a haven for neurotic werewolves. A deft mixture of state-of-the-art FX
and self-deprecating humor, this John
Sayles–scripted adaptation of the Gary Brandner book is highlighted by numerous in-jokes
(half the characters are named after various
horror film directors), a great supporting role
for Miller as an occult bookstore owner ("The
Manson people used to hang around here and
shoplift!"), and groundbreaking Rob Bottin
makeups. Followed by five in-name-only
sequels.

HOWLING II, THE

★ HBO, 1985, R, 87 min. Dir: Philippe Mora.

*Christopher Stone ponders
the miracle of body waxing
in* The Howling *(1981).*

Cast: Christopher Lee, Sybil Danning, Annie McEnroe, Rep Brown, Marsha A. Hunt, Ferdy Mayne.

Dispiritingly awful sequel picking up at the funeral of the Dee Wallace character, at which her brother (Brown) is approached by occult expert Lee (in one of his worst roles), who seeks his aid in stamping out the werewolf cult once and for all. Grimy photography ruins the effect of on-location photography in Czechoslovakia; cheap-looking makeup FX make the werewolves look like gorillas. Even Danning's formidable nude scenes don't help. Aka *Howling II: Your Sister Is a Werewolf* and *Howling II: Stirba, Werewolf Bitch.*

HOWLING II: STIRBA, WEREWOLF BITCH
See: *The Howling II.*

HOWLING II: YOUR SISTER IS A WEREWOLF
See: *The Howling II.*

HOWLING III, THE
★☆ Vista, 1987, PG-13, 94 min.
Dir: Philippe Mora. Cast: Barry Otto, Imogen Annesley, Dasha Blahova, Max Fairchild, Ralph Cotterill, Leigh Biolos, Frank Thring, Michael Pate.

A scientist doing research on werewolves discovers a tribe of marsupial lycanthropes living in the Australian outback; one pretty werewolf lass (Annesley) moves to Sydney, where she's immediately cast in the lead of a cheap horror opus called *Shapeshifters Part 8!* A sometimes amusing but overall tiresome semi-spoof with werewolf ballerinas, werewolf nuns, but not many laughs. Aka *Howling III: The Marsupials.*

HOWLING III: THE MARSUPIALS
See: *The Howling III.*

HOWLING IV: THE ORIGINAL NIGHTMARE
★★ IVE, 1988, R, 91 min. Dir: John Hough. Cast: Romy Windsor, Michael T. Weiss, Antony Hamilton, Suzanne Severeid, Lamya Derval, Dennis Folbigge.

Another needless *Howling* sequel, this is a virtual remake of the original, with Windsor as a gothic novelist recovering from overwork who moves with husband Weiss to a small town where everyone turns out to be a werewolf. Shot in South Africa, this dull entry is flatly acted and directed but has some good makeups by Steve Johnson showcased in the last 20 minutes or so.

HOWLING V: THE REBIRTH
★★ IVE, 1989, R, 96 min. Dir: Neal Sundstrom. Cast: Philip Davis, Victoria Catlin, Elizabeth Shé, Mary Stavin, Ben Cole, Stephanie Faulkner.

A group of international tourists are invited to the reopening of a Hungarian castle closed for 500 years, where they are stalked and murdered by a werewolf. Borrowing much of its plot from *The Beast Must Die,* this beautifully photographed (on actual Budapest locations) entry in the semi-series isn't as trite as the three that proceeded it but isn't gonna win any awards, either. A good-looking but unknown (except for Stavin) cast do well by their stock characters, but the werewolf is barely glimpsed.

HOWLING VI: THE FREAKS
★★☆ LIVE, 1991, R, 102 min.
Dir: Hope Perello. Cast: Brendan Hughes, Michele Matheson, Bruce Martyn Payne, Sean Gregory Sullivan, Carol Lynley, Antonio Fargas.

The best of the sequels, by default, has a sensitive performance from Hughes as a young werewolf coveted as a new sideshow attraction by evil vampire circus-owner Payne. A richer than usual storyline (borrowing much from *Something Wicked This Way Comes*) and a good supporting cast (though Lynley is wasted) and makeup give you hope that they might finally get it right again—around about *Howling 124.*

HOW TO MAKE A MONSTER
★★☆ RCA/Columbia, 1958, NR, 73 min.
Dir: Herbert L. Strock. Cast: Robert H. Harris, Paul Brinegar, Gary Conway, Gary Clarke, Heather Ames, Malcolm Atterbury, Morris Ankrum, Thomas B. Henry, Robert Shayne, John Ashley.

Clever semi-sequel to both *I Was a Teenage Werewolf* and *I Was a Teenage Frankenstein* with mad AIP makeup man Harris flipping out when he learns that new studio heads have decided to switch from the production of teen horror films to teen musicals. He then hypnotizes the young actors playing the teenage Frankenstein and werewolf characters in their last epic and commands them to kill the horror-hatin' execs. Fast and fun, with lots of heavy-duty overacting from a bug-eyed Robert H. and Ashley popping up for a brief musical number.

HUMAN EXPERIMENTS
★ VidAmerica, 1979, R, 82 min. Dir: Gregory Goodell. Cast: Linda Haynes, Geoffrey Lewis, Aldo Ray, Jackie Coogan, Ellen Travolta, Lurene Tuttle.

Another boring horror-in-an-asylum number with country singer Haynes wrongly sent to an institution where doc Lewis conducts bizarre behavioral experiments. Not even the promise of this campy cast is enough to make you watch. Aka *Beyond the Gate.*

HUMAN MONSTER, THE

★★★ United, 1939, NR, 75 min. Dir: Walter Summers. Cast: Bela Lugosi, Greta Gynt, Hugh Williams, Edmon Ryan, Wilfrid Walter, Alexander Field.

One of Bela's most underrated efforts, this British shocker (originally called *The Dark Eyes of London* and adapted from the book by Edgar Wallace) has him at his diabolical best as a master criminal who, in the guise of a gentle soup kitchen reverend, is running a successful insurance scam in which those insured in Bela's name are murdered by his hulking blind henchman (Walter) and then thrown in the Thames, so that the deaths are thought to be accidental drownings. Murky photography and some unfunny "comic relief" notwithstanding, this Lugosi flick can stand with his best work in the genre. Remade as *The Dead Eyes of London*.

HUMANOIDS FROM THE DEEP

★★★ Warner, 1980, R, 78 min. Dir: Barbara Peeters. Cast: Doug McClure, Ann Turkel, Vic Morrow, Cindy Weintraub, Anthony Penya, Denise Galik, Lynn Theel, Meegan King.

This funny, gross New World *Alien–Creature From the Black Lagoon* hybrid features hopped-up sea monsters spawned by mutant DNA mutilating men and raping women in a small northern California fishing village. It has a good cast and great low-budget Rob Bottin FX, but the rape angle may be too offensive for some—the nudity and bestiality reportedly added by another director after Peeters completed her cut. The ending is not recommended for viewing by pregnant women. Aka *Beneath the Darkness* and *Monster*.

HUMONGOUS

★☆ Embassy, 1981, R, 93 min. Dir: Paul Lynch. Cast: Janet Julian, David Wallace, Janit Baldwin, John Wildman, Joy Boushel, Layne Coleman.

Another annoying slasher in which a bunch of stupid teens become stranded on a Canadian island haunted by a huge retarded killer who worships his mother's corpse and kills them all except heroine Julian. Not an honest moment of horror or suspense occurs in the entire picture; only Baldwin impresses as the hero's sarcastic sister.

HUNCHBACK OF NOTRE DAME, THE

★★★☆ Goodtimes, 1923, NR, 93 min. Dir: Wallace Worsley. Cast: Lon Chaney, Patsy Ruth Miller, Norman Kerry, Ernest Torrence, Brandon Hurst, Raymond Hatton, Tully Marshall, Kate Lester.

Chaney is great as Quasimodo in this impressive early version of Victor Hugo's novel. Although dated as most silents seem today, this still has the epic sweep and melodramatic flourishes for which it was famous, with good atmosphere and convincing makeup and set design. Best scene: Chaney scudding along the facade of the cathedral and then hanging upside down from a gargoyle to thumb his nose at the crowd below!

HUNCHBACK OF NOTRE DAME, THE

★★★★ Turner, 1939, NR, 117 min. Dir: William Dieterle. Cast: Charles Laughton, Maureen O'Hara, Sir Cedric Hardwicke, Thomas Mitchell, Edmond O'Brien, Alan Marshall, Walter Hampden, Harry Davenport, Helene Whitney, George Zucco.

Superb remake with Laughton unforgettable as the twisted hunchbacked bellringer who falls for gypsy girl O'Hara and saves her from wrongful execution for murder and witchcraft. One of the great films of the 1930s, with a powerful cast, solid script, impressive sets and photography, and a beautiful score by Alfred Newman.

HUNCHBACK OF NOTRE DAME, THE

★★★ Vidmark, 1982, NR, 96 min. Dir: Michael Tuchner. Cast: Anthony Hopkins, Lesley-Anne Down, Derek Jacobi, John Gielgud, Robert Powell, Gerry Sundquist, David Suchet, Roland Culver.

Solid TV remake underplaying the usual epic qualities in favor of character relationships. Hopkins is sadly affecting as Quasimodo, while Gielgud is amusing in a cameo as the court's chief torturer and Down is the most gorgeous Esmeralda ever.

HUNCHBACK OF THE MORGUE, THE

See: *The Rue-Morgue Massacres*.

HUNGER, THE

★★☆ MGM/UA, 1983, R, 96 min. Dir: Tony Scott. Cast: Catherine Deneuve, David Bowie, Susan Sarandon, Cliff De Young, Beth Ehlers, Dan Hedaya, Ann Magnuson, William Dafoe.

Stylish but empty adaptation of the Whitley Strieber novel about a beautiful, ageless vampiress (Deneuve) living in a chic apartment in New York's Sutton Place who claims blood specialist Sarandon as a lover when current paramour Bowie begins to rot away. Cold and distant but certainly good to look at, though the lesbian subplot looks like an upscale version of one of Hammer's "Karnstein" flicks and the twist ending is stolen from *Daughters of Darkness*. Excellent Dick Smith makeup effects are all but wasted, thanks to poor coverage.

"Is that Joan Crawford I hear?" asks Bette Davis in Hush . . . Hush, Sweet Charlotte *(1965).*

HUNGRY WIVES
See: *Season of the Witch.*

HUNTER'S BLOOD
★★ Nelson, 1987, R, 101 min. Dir: Robert C. Hughes. Cast: Sam Bottoms, Kim Delaney, Clu Gulager, Joey Travolta, Ken Swofford, Mayf Nutter.

In this low-brow *Deliverance* rehash with horror overtones, a group of city folks take an Oklahoma hunting trip and end up falling victim to the usual backwoods psychopaths. A good cast, some suspense, and lots of gore, but too familiar to build much tension.

HUNT TO KILL
See: *The White Buffalo.*

HUSH . . . HUSH, SWEET CHARLOTTE
★★★☆ Key, 1965, NR, 132 min.
Dir: Robert Aldrich. Cast: Bette Davis, Olivia de Havilland, Joseph Cotten, Agnes Moorehead, Cecil Kellaway, Mary Astor, Victor Buono, Bruce Dern, William Campbell, George Kennedy.

Originally intended as a honeydewed follow-up to Aldrich's *Whatever Happened to Baby Jane?* (to be called *Whatever Happened to Cousin Charlotte?*), this was to reunite Bette Davis and Joan Crawford, but Joan bailed out early on and was replaced by de Havilland, turning this instead into a kind of macabre sequel to *Gone With the Wind* gone seriously wacky. Davis is an aging southern belle haunted by visions of brutally murdered Dern, who was beheaded some 30-plus years before. It couldn't be that cousin Livie and family doc Joe Cotten are out to drive her nuts for her scratch, could it? Long but nicely atmospheric and very welled acted (especially by de Havilland, in a classic performance of evil masked by sweet gentility), this has a memorably gory hatchet murder.

HYSTERIA
★★ MGM/UA, 1965, NR, 85 min.
Dir: Freddie Francis. Cast: Robert Webber, Lelia Goldoni, Jennifer Jayne, Anthony Newlands, Maurice Denham, Peter Woodthorpe.

Utterly routine Hammer suspense film with amnesiac Webber implicated in a brutal knife murder in a shower—where else? Good cast and photography, but an obvious script and brassy, obnoxious musical score make it a bore.

HYSTERICAL

★☆ Media, 1983, PG, 86 min.
Dir: Chris Bearde. Cast: Bill Hudson, Mark Hudson, Bret Hudson, Cindy Pickett, Richard Kiel, Julie Newmar, Bud Cort, Robert Donner, Charlie Callas, Murray Hamilton, Keenan Wynn, Clint Walker.

Dumb-dumb spoof of everything from *Jaws* to *Friday the 13th* with TV's Hudson Brothers as ghostbusters out to exorise a lighthouse haunted by ghost Newmar. You might laugh once, you might twice, but any more than that would be too much to ask of this painfully unfunny farce. A good cast wasted.

I BURY THE LIVING

★★☆ Goodtimes, 1958, NR, 76 min. Dir: Albert Band [Alfredo Antonini]. Cast: Richard Boone, Theodore Bikel, Peggy Maurer, Herb Anderson, Howard Smith, Robert Ostrerloh.

Boone is the new manager of a cemetery who discovers that he can kill by remote control when he sticks a black pin into a map of the reserved plots meant to sport white ones. Trying to undo the several deaths he's caused, Boone then removes the black pins to replace them with white ones and. . . . Eerie and effective for its first hour, this low-budgeter ultimately collapses under the weight of one of the most annoyingly contrived "surprise" endings in horror history, spoiling much of the mood it so successfully builds up in the early going. Still worth seeing, though, for its atmosphere and the skillful performances of Boone and Bikel.

ICED

★ Prism, 1988, R, 86 min. Dir: Jeff Kwitney. Cast: Debra Deliso, Doug Stevenson, Lisa Loring, Joseph Alan Johnson, Ron Kologie, Elizabeth Gorcey.

A sort-of slasher *Big Chill* in which an obnoxious bunch of former college friends are lured to a remote mountain condo where they indulge in sex, drugs, and bad practical jokes until a mysterious killer mercifully begins doing them in via ski pole, hunting knife, and

king-sized icicle. Sharply photographed but peopled with doltish characters and enough girl-guy nudity to qualify it as soft porn. As one babe puts it about a bad drive-in flick: "It's the kind of movie where you only watch the screen if someone is naked or getting killed." Indeed.

I DISMEMBER MAMA

★ Video Treasures, 1972, R, 85 min.
Dir: Paul Leder. Cast: Zooey Hall, Geri Reischl, Joanna Moore Jordan, Greg Mullavey, Marlene Tracy, Frank Whiteman.

Hall is a woman-hating psycho with a big-time Oedipus complex who escapes from an asylum and begins a killing spree while falling in love with an 11-year-old girl. Pretty awful, this was originally called *Poor Albert and Little Annie* before its infamous retitling, though Mama is at no point actually dismembered. I guess they just couldn't resist it.

I DON'T WANT TO BE BORN

See: *The Devil Within Her.*

I DRINK YOUR BLOOD

★★ Flamingo, 1971, R, 83 min. Dir: David Durston.
Cast: Bhaskar, Jadine Wong, Ronda Fultz, Elizabeth Marner-Brooks, Richard Bowler, Lynn Lowry.

This infamous stomach-turner—trimmed by five minutes to avoid an X rating—was one of the first horror films to be influenced by *Night of the Living Dead* and was originally paired with the more sedate *I Eat Your Skin* in a memorable drive-in double bill. A kid gets revenge on the devil-worshipping hippies who gave his granddad an LSD cocktail by feeding them meat pies injected with rabies, turning them into homicidal maniacs. Still quite bloody but not especially compelling, with cheesy acting and direction.

I EAT YOUR SKIN

★ ☆ Rhino, 1964, PG, 82 min.
Dir: Del Tenney. Cast: William Joyce, Heather Hewitt, Betty Hyatt Linton, Dan Stapleton, Walter Coy, Robert Stanton.

When Jerry Gross needed a co-feature for his *I Drink Your Blood* in 1971, he pulled this unreleased hunk of celluloid out of the woodwork. A mad doctor conducting cancer cure experiments on a Caribbean island creates a horde of bug-eyed, crud-faced zombies instead. Though there's a bit of gore this isn't nearly as gruesome as its title suggests. The acting, on the other hand, is as gruesome as it gets. Aka *Voodoo Blood Bath* and *Zombies.*

IF IT'S A MAN, HANG UP!
★★★ IVE, 1975, NR, 72 min.
Dir: Shaun O'Riordan. Cast: Carol Lynley,
Tom Conti, Gerald Harper, Paul Angelis.

Here's a superior Brian Clemens–scripted TV
horror with Lynley in top form as a leggy
fashion model stalked by a black-gloved psycho peeping Tom–obscene phone caller. It's
genuinely suspenseful, with attention paid to
detail and a wholly surprising surprise
ending.

IGOR AND THE LUNATICS
☆ Video Treasures, 1985, UR, 79 min.
Dir: Billy Parolini. Cast: Joseph Eero, Joe Niola,
T. J. Michaels, Mary Ann Schacht.

Called the worst movie of all time by "Entertainment Tonight" (now there's recommendation for ya), this minimalistic gore job is pretty
bad even so. The "plot" concerns a bunch of
former hippies avenging themselves on the
small-town simps who sent them to prison.
The "highlight" is a girl sliced in half length-
wise, which shows you just how bad this
home-video-quality stinker really is. Makes
Plan Nine look like *Alien*.

I LOVE TO KILL
See: *Impulse* (1974).

I, MADMAN
★★ Media, 1989, R, 88 min.
Dir: Tibor Takacs. Cast: Jenny Wright, Clayton
Rohner, Randall William Cooke, Steven Memel,
Stephanie Hodge, Bruce Wagner.

Bookstore clerk Wright becomes obsessed
with a creepy old horror novel whose villainous main character (makeup man Cooke in a
gruesome face of his own design) seems to
have entered into the real world. An interesting premise gets mangled thanks to flip handling and too many dumb attempts at black
humor. The leads are personable enough, but
their characters generate little sympathy.

I MARRIED A MONSTER FROM OUTER SPACE
★★★ Paramount, 1958, NR, 78 min.
Dir: Gene Fowler, Jr. Cast: Tom Tryon, Gloria Talbott,
Ken Lynch, John Eldredge, Valerie Allen,
Maxie Rosenbloom.

A camp classic title masks a fairly sober feminist variation on *Invasion of the Body Snatchers*.
Beloved B babe Talbott has her best role as a
sexually unfulfilled newlywed who discovers
that dull groom Tryon (later the author of *The
Other* and *Harvest Home*) is actually a member
of an apparently homosexual alien race who
have come to earth and taken on human form

to reluctantly mate with our women to
advance their dying species. Low-key lighting,
tense situations, and some gruesome special
effects make this a minor gem.

I MARRIED A WEREWOLF
See: *Werewolf in a Girl's Dormitory.*

I'M DANGEROUS TONIGHT
★★☆ MCA/Universal, 1990, R, 92 min.
Dir: Tobe Hooper. Cast: Anthony Perkins, Madchen
Amick, Corey Parker, Dee Wallace-Stone, Mary Frann,
R. Lee Ermey, Natalie Schafer, William Berger.

One of Hooper's better recent endeavors, this
made-for-cable Cornell Woolrich adaptation
involves a scarlet Aztec ceremonial robe with
a murderous influence on whoever wears it.
When college coed Amick restyles the robe as
a party gown, campus havoc erupts. Well cast
and legitimately eerie in spots, but things
begin to unravel after the midway point, with
a good final twist punching up an otherwise
limp wrap-up.

IMMORTAL MONSTER, THE
See: *Caltiki, The Immortal Monster.*

IMPULSE
★ IVE, 1974, PG, 82 min.
Dir: William Grefe. Cast: William Shatner,
Ruth Roman, Jennifer Bishop, Harold Sakata,
Kim Nicholas, James Dobson.

A bewigged Bill is a polyester-clad lady's man
and part-time psycho killer whose activities
are caught on to by the obnoxious young
daughter of his latest conquest. Clumsy Hitchcock references—a *Marnie*-inspired flashback;
a cracked, *Psycho*-esque title; and the casting of
Strangers on a Train star Roman—and Shatner's hilarious histrionics figure prominently
in the execution of this Florida-lensed cheapo,
which has similarities to the later *The Stepfather*. Also known as *I Love to Kill* and *Want a
Ride, Little Girl?*

IMPULSE
★★ Vestron, 1984, R, 91 min. Dir: Graham Baker.
Cast: Tim Matheson, Meg Tilly, Hume Cronyn,
Amy Stryker, John Karlen, Bill Paxton.

Passable updating of George Romero's *Crazies*
premise with the toxic poisoning of a small
town's milk supply turning everyone into
sociopathic maniacs. A good cast and photography, but sluggish pacing and a ridiculously
out-of-nowhere ending hurt.

INCENSE FOR THE DAMNED
See: *Bloodsuckers.*

INCREDIBLE INVASION, THE
See: *Alien Terror.*

INCREDIBLE MELTING MAN, THE
★★ Orion, 1977, R, 85 min.
Dir: William Sachs. Cast: Alex Rebar, Burr De Benning, Myron Healey, Ann Sweeny, Michael Alldredge, Lislie Wilson, Rainbeaux Smith, Janus Blythe.

Mindless throwback to '50s flicks like *First Man Into Space* with Rebar as an astronaut who returns from a trip to Saturn with a strange degenerative disease: he is literally melting away and is driven to consume human flesh to temporarily forestall the inevitable. Flat direction and a ridiculously contrived story are made palatable by Rick Baker's incredibly moist FX (the most goo in any pre-*Alien* movie award goes here) and the vivaciousness of ever-lovely scene-stealer Smith. Future Oscar-winning director Jonathan Demme has a small acting role.

INCREDIBLE TORTURE SHOW, THE
See: *Bloodsucking Freaks.*

INCREDIBLE 2-HEADED TRANSPLANT, THE
★★☆ Trans Atlantic, 1971, PG, 88 min.
Dir: Anthony Lanza. Cast: Bruce Dern, Pat Priest, Casey Kasem, John Bloom, Albert Cole, Berry Kroeger, Larry Vincent, Jack Lester.

One of Dern's last and funniest exploitation films before he hit the "Big Time" casts him as a loony scientist experimenting with cranial transplants who grafts the head of a psychotic criminal onto the body of his mountainous retarded handyman. The resultant double-header then escapes, kills several teenagers, and carries off Bruce's long-suffering wife Priest (TV's Marilyn Munster). A so-so make-up job is made up for by an ultra-campy cast (including diminutive "Top 40" host Kasem as the hero) and the appropriately named theme song "It's Incredible."

INCREDIBLY STRANGE CREATURES WHO STOPPED LIVING AND BECAME MIXED-UP ZOMBIES, THE
★★☆ Camp, 1963, NR, 82 min.
Dir: Ray Dennis Steckler. Cast: Cash Flagg [Ray Dennis Steckler], Brett O'Hara, Carolyn Brandt, Sharon Walsh, Atlas King, Madison Clarke, Erina Enyo, Jack Brady.

This infamously titled exploiter is a lot better than you might expect, with good color and imaginative cinematography. Happy-go-lucky beatnik Jerry (producer-director Steckler under his nom-de-thesp Cash Flagg) is turned into a hypnotized killer by warty carnival fortune teller Madame Estrella (O'Hara), who keeps her disfigured cast-off lovers locked in a closet for no other reason than so they can escape and kill her at the climax. Certainly ambitious for such a low-budget affair, with lots of silly, arty directorial touches, lengthy (and out of place) dance numbers, fairly effective makeup, and plenty of laughs. Reissued as *Teenage Psycho Meets Bloody Mary.*

INCUBUS, THE
★★☆ Vestron, 1981, R, 92 min.
Dir: John Hough. Cast: John Cassavetes, Kerrie Keane, John Ireland, Erin Flannery, Duncan McIntosh, Helen Hughes, Harvey Atkin, Mitch Martin.

Based on the book by Ray Russell, this Canadian film tells of a series of brutal rape-murders sweeping a small Wisconsin town which turn out to be the work of a hideous, incredibly endowed demon known as an incubus. Routinely structured and sports a totally unbelievable surprise ending, but strong direction from Hough and a quirky performance from Cassavetes make what, in other hands, might have been a fairly unsavory little movie quite watchable indeed.

INDESTRUCTIBLE MAN, THE
★★ Sinister Cinema, 1956, NR, 70 min.
Dir: Jack Pollexfen. Cast: Lon Chaney, Jr., Marian Carr, Casey Adams, Robert Shayne, Ross Elliott, Stuart Randall.

Fairly somber mix of gangsters and horror that sometimes resembles Lon's early hit *Man-Made Monster.* Chaney is executed killer "Butcher" Benton, who is brought back to life after his electrocution by an injection from scientist Shayne and then sets out to hunt down the gang members who betrayed him. Has its good points and bad, the worst being the awful "Dragnet"-style narration. "McHale's Navy" star Joe Flynn has a small part as Shayne's assistant.

INDIAN SCARF, THE
★★ Sinister Cinema, 1963, NR, 85 min.
Dir: Alfred Vohrer. Cast: Heinz Drache, Gisela Uhlen, Klaus Kinski, Eddi Arent, Corny Collins, Elizabeth Flickenschildt.

This loose adaptation of Edgar Wallace's *The Frightened Lady* gathers the usual bunch of heirs at the usual creepy old manor where they're stalked and strangled by the usual psycho killer who's after all the money. The usual German krimi with a typical turn from Kinski as a bug-eyed drug addict and all-around red herring.

INFERNAL IDOL, THE
See: *Craze.*

INFERNO
★★★☆ Key, 1980, R, 106 min.
Dir: Dario Argento. Cast: Leigh McClosky, Irene Miracle, Daria Nicolodi, Elenora Giorgi, Alida Valli, Sacha Pitoeff, Gabriele Lavia, Veronica Lazar.

Argento's follow-up to his masterwork *Suspiria* is a subtler, more subdued affair. Poetess Miracle investigates the history of her pink and violet New York apartment building, built in homage to the powerful witch "Mother of Darkness," and is brutally decapitated for her trouble. Later brother McCloskey arrives from Rome to avenge her and nearly suffers a similar fate. With its nonlinear, dream-like plotting and vague, insubstantial characters, this is more like a series of lush set-pieces than an actual movie, a fact that may have prompted distributor 20th Century-Fox to shelve it for five years before finally releasing it direct-to-video. Wimpoid Leigh is the weakest hero in the Argento filmography and much of the action is frustratingly vague, but see it for the haunting visuals (like Miracle swimming through a flooded ballroom, the last work of the great Mario Bava) and suspenseful setups (the rat attack on crippled bookseller Pitoeff), casebook examples on how to make a good, atmospheric horror film. Music by Keith Emerson.

INFERNO OF THE LIVING DEAD
See: *Night of the Zombies* (1981).

INFESTED
★★★ Republic, 1993, R, 85 min.
Dir: Tony Randel. Cast: Rosalind Allen, Peter Scolari, Ami Dolenz, Seth Green, Ray Oriel, Alfonso Ribiero, Barry Lynch, Michael Medeiros.

Formerly (and better) titled *Ticks,* this spirited throwback to a '50s Saturday matinee monster flick deals with a group of city folk trapped in a mountain cabin by a horde of oversized (but not giant) bloodsucking mutant ticks. A solidly crafted little monster movie with first-rate writing, direction, acting, and FX.

INITIATION, THE
★★ New World, 1983, R, 97 min.
Dir: Larry Stewart. Cast: Daphne Zuniga, Vera Miles, Clu Gulager, James Read, Frances Peterson, Marilyn Kagen.

Another fill-in-the-blanks slasher with more sorority hopefuls stalked by yet another psychotic mystery murderer: in this case knifing and hatcheting victims in a mall closed for the night. Acting, plotting, and direction are all standard, despite some surface gloss and some recognizable faces.

INITIATION OF SARAH, THE
★★ Goodtimes, 1978, NR, 91 min.
Dir: Robert Day. Cast: Kay Lenz, Shelley Winters, Tony Bill, Morgan Brittany, Morgan Fairchild, Tisa Farrow, Robert Hays, Kathryn Crosby.

Predictable TV rip-off of *Carrie* with Lenz good as the bookish scapegoat for a bunch of elitist bitches at a California college. Our heroine pledges the least popular sorority, whose weird house mother (Winters) trains her to use her telekinetic powers against her tormentors. Shelley is always fun doing her "crazy mama" bit and the supporting cast is exceptional, but they're all wasted on a tacky, derivative production more interested in seeing how much semi-nudity and how many wet blouses it can get away with than in trying to generate suspense.

INNER SANCTUM
★★ RCA/Columbia, 1991, R, 90 min.
Dir: Fred Olen Ray. Cast: Tanya Roberts, Margaux Hemingway, Joseph Bottoms, Valerie Wildman, Bill Butler, Bret Clark, Suzanne Ager, Jay Richardson.

Ray goes the erotic thriller route with this slick but confused vid flick. Roberts (my favorite "Charlie's Angel") does a hilarious Cathy Moriarity impression as a sexy nurse caught up in one of those everyone's-trying-to-kill-everyone-else-for-their-money plotlines. It's sort of a low-rent Brian De Palma movie further hampered by a ridiculously out-of-nowhere ending—Fred reportedly ran out of money before he could finish the film properly. Lots of simulated sex and body-double nudity too.

INNOCENT BLOOD
★★★ Warner, 1992, R, 112 min.
Dir: John Landis. Cast: Anne Parillaud, Robert Loggia, Anthony La Paglia, Don Rickles, Kim Coates, Angela Bassett, Frank Oz, Tom Savini, Ted Raimi, Dario Argento, Linnea Quigley, Forrest J. Ackerman.

Although a comic combo of *The Godfather* and *The Hunger* might not sound like such a hot idea, *American Werewolf* director Landis pulls it off with style and aplomb. *La Femme Nikita's* slinky Parillaud is a sexy vampire who puts the bite on Pittsburgh crime boss Loggia, turning him into a Mafia neck-muncher out to take over the town. Loggia is aces as the undead don, and there are plenty of knowing homages—every time someone turns on a TV an old horror film is playing—though it drags a bit before wrapping things up in high style. Loads of cameos, the funniest being Linnea's as a screaming nurse.

INNOCENT PREY
★★ Vidmark, 1983, R, 100 min. Dir: Colin Eggleston. Cast: P. J. Soles, Martin Balsam, Kit Taylor, John Warnock, Debisue Voorhees.

Soles' perky charm is about the only distinguishing factor in this routine stalker movie, which is quite similar to the later *Sleeping With the Enemy*. P. J. flees a crazy boyfriend for a new life in Sydney, Australia, and just when she gets her act together, guess who's stalking? Totally predictable; P. J. deserves a better showcase than this.

INN OF THE DAMNED
★☆ Wizard, 1974, NR, 125 min. Dir: Terry Bourke. Cast: Judith Anderson, Alex Cord, Michael Craig, Joseph Furst, Tony Bonner, Carla Hoogeveen.

Dull Australian thriller with Anderson and Furst the proprietors of an outback inn where guests have a habit of getting brutally bumped off. Veteran actress Anderson tries, but this is otherwise a totally boring experience.

INN OF THE FRIGHTENED PEOPLE
See: *Terror Under the House.*

INQUISITION
★★ Video City, 1976, R, 94 min. Dir: Jacinto Molina. Cast: Paul Naschy, Monica Randall, Richardo Merino, Toni Isbert.

Naschy's debut as director (under his real name) is a typically violent tale of witch hunting and torture in 16th-century France. Some eerie moods and a clever twist ending, but otherwise unremarkable.

INSECT, THE
See: *Blue Monkey.*

INSEMINOID
See: *Horror Plant.*

IN THE COLD OF THE NIGHT
★☆ Republic, 1990, NR, 113 min. Dir: Nico Mastorakis. Cast: Jeff Lester, Adrienne Sachs, David Soul, Tippi Hedren.

Mastorakis' entry in the tired "erotic thriller" subgenre, this has Lester as a guy suffering from recurring nightmares in which he murders a beautiful woman (Sachs) whom he's never met. Guess who quickly turns up in his life for real and, wouldn't ya know it, they fall in love. But will Jeff's nastier dreams come true as well? It's predictable and trite, with

Hedren popping in long enough to have a nasty avian encounter and collect a quick paycheck. Also available in an R version.

IN THE GRIP OF THE MANIAC
See: *The Diabolical Dr. Z.*

IN THE GRIP OF THE SPIDER
See: *Web of the Spider.*

IN THE SHADOW OF KILIMANJARO
★☆ IVE, 1986, R, 97 min. Dir: Raju Patel. Cast: Timothy Bottoms, John Rhys-Davies, Irene Miracle, Michele Carey, Leonard Trolley, Patty Foley.

Based on a true incident that occurred in 1983, this gory clone of *Jaws* and *The Birds* tells of thirst-crazed baboons attacking and killing people during an African drought. A stilted cast and phony-looking gore scenes dominate this subpar nature-runs-amoker.

INTO THE BADLANDS
★★ MCA/Universal, 1991, NR, 91 min. Dir: Sam Pillsbury. Cast: Bruce Dern, Mariel Hemingway, Helen Hunt, Dylan McDermott, Lisa Pelikan, Andrew Robinson.

Dern is a sardonic bounty hunter who acts as the main link between a trio of Old West tales of irony and horror. An outlaw (McDermott) begins a doomed affair with a dying bar girl (Hunt); two women (Hemingway and Pelikan) are trapped by a pack of slavering wolves in a desolate mountain cabin; and the bounty hunter himself is haunted by the corpse of an innocent man he mistakenly killed. An okay anthology with a fine cast.

INTRUDER
★★☆ Paramount, R, 83 min. Dir: Scott Spiegel. Cast: Elizabeth Cox, Dan Hicks, Renee Estevez, David Byrnes, Sam Raimi, Ted Raimi.

Routinely plotted but energetically directed slasher about a supermarket night crew murdered by a psycho who may or may not be the crazed ex-boyfriend of the pretty head checkout girl. Likable characters, interesting camera placement, and a carload of cameos ("Green Acres" fans take note), but Paramount cut the violence heavily to ensure an R, robbing this film of most of its spectacular KNB FX work. Shooting title: *Night Crew: The Final Checkout.*

INTRUDER WITHIN, THE
★★☆ TWE, NR, 91 min. Dir: Peter Carter. Cast: Chad Everett, Jennifer Warren, Joseph Bottoms, Rochne Tarkington, James Hayden, Lynda Mason Green.

Enjoyable made-for-TV *Alien* spin-off with workers on an offshore oil rig being terrorized by a hideous creature dredged up from the ocean floor. A familiar plot, but the likable cast and good creature design by James Cummins and Henry Golas make it fun. Aka *Panic Offshore* and *The Lucifer Rig*.

INVADERS FROM MARS
★★★ Nostalgia Merchant, 1953, NR, 78 min.
Dir: William Cameron Menzies. Cast: Jimmy Hunt, Helena Carter, Arthur Franz, Leif Erickson, Hillary Brooke, Morris Ankrum, Milburn Stone, Robert Shayne.

A young boy (Hunt) witnesses a spaceship land in his backyard but can't convince anyone of the truth, probably because everyone in town, his parents included, has been turned into a zombie by the invaders. Imaginative direction from ace production designer Menzies makes this one of the best-remembered alien invasion films of the '50s, with wonderfully tacky Martians (complete with zippers up their backs) and a double-twist ending borrowed from *Dead of Night*. Remade in 1986.

INVADERS FROM MARS
★★ Video Treasures, 1986, PG, 93 min.
Dir: Tobe Hooper. Cast: Hunter Carson, Karen Black, Louise Fletcher, Timothy Bottoms, Laraine Newman, James Karen, Bud Cort, Christopher Allport.

In this mostly ineffectual remake, millions of dollars' worth of glossy FX gum up the works of the simple B-movie plot of a boy who tries to stop the Martian invasion of his small town. Fletcher is hilarious as a Miss Gultch–like schoolteacher, and Black revives all those great old *Trilogy of Terror* facial ticks, but this is mostly a missed opportunity. The original film's Jimmy Hunt has a brief cameo as a policeman.

INVASION OF CAROL ENDERS, THE
★★ MPI, 1974, NR, 69 min.
Dir: Burt Brinckerhoff. Cast: Meredith Baxter, Christopher Connolly, Charles Aidman, John Karlen, George Di Cenzo, James Storm.

A cheapie Dan Curtis–produced TV movie with Baxter as a hospital patient possessed by the spirit of a murdered fellow patient. There is good acting in this otherwise routine videotaped late-night fodder.

INVASION OF THE ANIMAL PEOPLE
★ Loonic, 1960, NR, 73 min.
Dirs: Virgil Vogel, Jerry Warren. Cast: John Carradine, Barbara Wilson, Robert Burton, Sten Gester.

Just to prove he doesn't pick only on the Mexican cinema, Warren re-edits and films U.S. inserts for this Swedish monster movie about a huge bigfoot-like beast let loose on the Scandinavian countryside by some alien invaders. Carradine narrates the tale from a single set. Positively coma-inducing. Aka *Terror in the Midnight Sun*.

INVASION OF THE BEE GIRLS
★★☆ Nelson, 1973, R, 85 min.
Dir: Denis Sanders. Cast: William Smith, Anitra Ford, Victoria Vetri, Cliff Osmond, Wright King, Ben Hammer.

Nicholas Meyer wrote this funny feminist parable in which the neglected wives of a group of dull scientists get a new lease on life via nuclear power. Radiation and special bee's wax turn them into beautiful human queen bees who kill their husbands during sex. Scenes of naked women smeared with gooey bee's wax and then covered with live bees are *very* strange, and there's lots of hilarious dialogue and a great exploitation cast headed by biker movie veteran Smith. Aka *Graveyard Tramps*.

INVASION OF THE BLOOD FARMERS
★ Regal, 1972, PG, 77 min.
Dir: Ed Adlum. Cast: Norman Kelly, Tanna Hunter, Bruce Detrick, Paul Craig-Jennings, Richard Erickson, Cynthia Fleming.

A bad taste classic! Druids masquerading as dirt farmers drain the blood of everyone they can get their hands on in order to find the proper type needed to revive their queen and ensure their own immortality. A no-budget wonder, this has pitiful acting, outrageously overdone sound effects for the blood-draining scenes, and beautifully saturated color photography. And don't miss the opening, in which an off-screen narrator does a ridiculously bad James Mason imitation.

INVASION OF THE BODY SNATCHERS
★★★★ Republic, 1956, NR, 80 min.
Dir: Don Siegel. Cast: Kevin McCarthy, Dana Wynter, Larry Gates, Carolyn Jones, King Donovan, Virginia Christine, Jean Willes, Ralph Dumke, Whit Bissell, Richard Deacon.

Brilliant '50s allegorical horror film in which the entire population of a sleepy California town is replaced by alien pods that copy an individual, drain his mind and memory while he sleeps, and then replace him or her with an emotionless double. The '50s "Red scare" and postwar obsession with conformity and "normal values" are savagely satirized (the pods make better citizens than the people they're replacing), but the film is quite frightening as well, with an unforgettable climax in which

Kevin McCarthy and Dana Wynter ponder a pod on the pool table in Invasion of the Body Snatchers *(1956).*

lone survivor McCarthy stumbles along the highway at night shouting at passing cars: "They're here, they here; you're next, you're next!" The "happy ending" framing device with Bissell and Deacon was added at the last minute against director Siegel's wishes and was removed from some reissue prints. Based on the novel *The Body Snatchers* by Jack Finney; remade in 1978 and in 1993 as *Body Snatchers*.

INVASION OF THE BODY SNATCHERS
★★★☆ MGM/UA, 1978, PG, 115 min.
Dir: Philip Kaufman. Cast: Donald Sutherland, Brooke Adams, Leonard Nimoy, Jeff Goldblum, Veronica Cartwright, Art Hindle, Lelia Goldoni, Kevin McCarthy, Don Siegel, Robert Duvall.

Terrific remake of the '50s classic, with the pods this time in San Francisco, their seeds falling from the sky during a rainstorm. Seventy-two hours later all but one resident of the city has been transformed into an emotionless cypher. Kaufman directs with assurance:

scenes brim with both tension and humor, with the self-actualizing '70s attacked just as thoroughly as the Commie-baiting '50s were in the original. Top-flight acting, creepy make-up FX (making explicit what the first film only hints at), and a subtle use of sound effects help make this one of the best remakes ever, with amusing guest roles for McCarthy, Siegel, and Duvall.

INVASION OF THE FLESH HUNTERS
★★☆ Vestron, 1980, R, 91 min.
Dir: Anthony Dawson [Antonio Margherti]. Cast: John Saxon, Elisabeth Turner, John Morghen, Cindy Hamilton, May Heatherley, Venantino Venantini.

Saxon is excellent as a Vietnam vet infected with a weird form of cannibal-rabies in this shot-in-Atlanta Italian *Dawn of the Dead–Apocalypse Now* combo. John, two old army buddies (including Morghen of *The Gates of Hell* and *Make Them Die Slowly*), and an infected nurse bite several people and then take to the sewers for a final showdown with the police. Not as

JOHN SAXON
(1935–)

Born Carmine Orrico, this one-time male model starred in a number of popular teen flicks in the '50s before turning to horror with films shot in the U.S., Italy, England, and Canada. Working with everyone from Bava to Argento, Saxon has a classiness and self-deprecating sense of humor that always shine through, even the thinnest-drawn characters.

The Evil Eye ('62), *Queen of Blood* ('66), *Blood Beast From Outer Space* ('66), *Black Christmas* ('75), *The Bees* ('78), *Beyond Evil* ('80), *Blood Beach* ('81), *Cannibals in the Streets* ('81), *Unsane* ('83), *A Nightmare on Elm Street* ('84), *A Nightmare on Elm Street 3: Dream Warriors* ('87), *My Mom's a Werewolf* ('88), *Death House* (also director, '88), *Welcome to Spring Break* ('89), *Blood Salvage* ('89), *The Arrival* ('91), *Hellmaster* ('92), *A Nightmare on Elm Street 7* ('94).

bad as you might think, though all current prints are severely cut from the unrated theatrical version, the dubbed dialogue winning the Howard Stern gratuitous cursing award. Original title: *Cannibal Apocalypse* and aka *Cannibals in the Streets*.

INVASION OF THE SAUCER MEN
★★☆ Columbia/TriStar, 1957, NR, 68 min. Dir: Edward L. Cahn. Cast: Steve Terrell, Gloria Castillo, Frank Gorshin, Lyn Osborn, Raymond Hatton, Russ Bender, Scott Peters, Ed Nelson.

Enjoyable serio-comic sci-fi/horror about a teenagers' lovers' lane invaded by diminutive aliens with eyes on their hands and alcohol-based blood. Terrell (the sort of hip teen who always wears a coat and tie) and Castillo are the young couple out to stop them. Has some surprisingly grisly moments for what's basically just a farce. British title: *Hell Creatures;* remade as *The Eye Creatures.*

INVASION OF THE VAMPIRES
★★ Sinister Cinema, 1962, NR, 78 min. Dir: Miguel Morayta. Cast: Carlos Agosti, Erna Martha Bauman, Rafael Etienne, Bertha Moss, Raoul Farell, Adrias Roel.

In this sequel to *The Bloody Vampire,* the evil Count Frankenhausen (Agosti) is finally done in via a lance through the heart—but his death causes his already staked minions to rise up as lumbering zombies! The dubbed dialogue is worse than ever, with everyone standing around arguing about what a terrible situation this all is. But there is some nice, moody photography, and the scenes of the revived staked zombies marching about are surprisingly creepy.

INVASION OF THE ZOMBIES
See: *The Horror of Party Beach.*

INVASION OF THE ZOMBIES
See: *City of the Walking Dead.*

INVISIBLE AGENT
★★ MCA/Universal, 1942, NR, 80 min. Dir: Edwin L. Marin. Cast: Jon Hall, Ilona Massey, Peter Lorre, Sir Cedric Hardwicke, J. Edward Bromberg, Albert Basserman.

The fourth and weakest entry in Universal's *Invisible Man* series, this horror-as-war-propaganda item features Hall (in the same role as John Sutton in *The Invisible Man Returns*) pressed into service by the Allies to use his invisibility serum to spy on the Nazis. The cast is first-rate, but John Fulton's Oscar-nominated special effects are surprisingly unimpressive.

INVISIBLE DEAD, THE
★ Wizard, 1970, R, 79 min. Dir: Peter Chevalier. Cast: Howard Vernon, Britt Crava, Fred Sanders.

Another sequel to *The Awful Dr. Orlof* (but without Jess Franco? What gives?) originally called *Orloff and the Invisible Man.* This time the doc (Vernon) creates an invisible blood-drinking monster that likes to rape naked women. As depressing as it sounds. Aka *Love Life of the Invisible Man.*

INVISIBLE GHOST, THE
★★☆ Sinister Cinema, 1941, NR, 64 min. Dir: Joseph H. Lewis. Cast: Bela Lugosi, Polly Ann Young, John McGuire, Clarence Muse, Terry Walker, Betty Compson.

Bela's first Monogram production has an awful excuse for a script (some hogwash about a guy hypnotized into killing by the presence of his amnesiac wife), but strong work from Lugosi in one of his few roles as a kind, decent man (albeit one who commits murders on the side, but then nobody's perfect). Effectively creative direction from cult fave Lewis makes this consistently watchable. Aka *The Phantom Killer.*

INVISIBLE KID, THE
★☆ Media, 1987, PG, 96 min. Dir: Avery Crounse. Cast: Jay Underwood, Karen Black, Wally Ward, Chynna Phillips, Mike Genovese, Brother Theodore.

Transparent nerd comedy with Underwood as your standard-issue high school loser who invents an invisibility formula he uses for all the obvious purposes (like sneaking into the girls' locker room). With its mild PG rating, this sidesteps most of the usual exploitation touches (like nudity and gore) for a kinder, gentler approach that's just plain dull. Black is especially strident and unpleasant as the kid's mom.

INVISIBLE MAN, THE

★★★☆ MCA/Universal, 1933, NR, 71 min.
Dir: James Whale. Cast: Claude Rains, Gloria Stuart, William Harrigan, Henry Travers, Una O'Connor, Forrester Harvey, E. E. Clive, Dwight Frye, John Carradine, Walter Brennan.

A delightfully dark comic version of the H. G. Wells book about a chemist (Rains) who discovers a formula for invisibility which renders him both unseeable and insane—the drug

A bandaged Claude Rains outlines his evil plans for Gloria Stuart in The Invisible Man *(1933).*

JOHN P. FULTON
(1902–1965)

One of the pioneers of movie special effects, Fulton headed Universal Pictures' special effects department from the early '30s to the mid-'40s. His effects for the classic *The Invisible Man* have rarely been bettered. Fulton won an Oscar for parting the Red Sea in Cecil B. De Mille's *The Ten Commandments* in 1956.

Frankenstein ('31), *Murders in the Rue Morgue* ('32), *The Invisible Man* ('33), *Bride of Frankenstein* ('35), *The Werewolf of London* ('35), *The Invisible Ray* ('36), *Dracula's Daughter* ('36), *Son of Frankenstein* ('39), *The Invisible Man Returns* ('40), *The Invisible Woman* ('41), *Man-Made Monster* ('41), *The Black Cat* ('41), *The Wolf Man* ('41), *The Ghost of Frankenstein* ('42), *Invisible Agent* ('42), *Night Monster* ('42), *Captive Wild Woman* ('43), *Son of Dracula* ('43), *Calling Dr. Death* ('43), *Weird Woman* ('44), *The Scarlet Claw* ('44), *The Invisible Man's Revenge* ('44), *Ghost Catchers* ('44), *Dead Man's Eyes* ('44), *House of Frankenstein* ('44), *The Mummy's Curse* ('44), *House of Dracula* ('45), *Pillow of Death* ('46), *The Naked Jungle* ('54), *I Married a Monster From Outer Space* ('58), *The Colossus of New York* ('58).

transforming him into a megalomaniacal killer. Great dialogue ("We'll start with a few murders; great men, little men—just to prove we show no distinction!") and outstanding special effects by John Fulton help make this one of the great horror films of the '30s. Rains is brilliant and seen only once, in the last few seconds.

INVISIBLE MAN RETURNS, THE
★★★ MCA/Universal, 1940, NR, 81 min.
Dir: Joe May. Cast: Vincent Price, Nan Grey, Sir Cedric Hardwicke, John Sutton, Cecil Kellaway, Alan Napier.

A solid sequel to Universal's original *Invisible Man* movie, this has Price in his first leading horror role as a man wrongly accused of his brother's murder, who escapes from prison using the old invisibility formula of Dr. Sutton's late brother, Claude Rains. In this disembodied form, Price then tracks down the real killer. Solid John Fulton special effects and an excellent cast make this one of the best sequels of its sequel-saturated decade.

INVISIBLE RAY, THE
★★★ MCA/Universal, 1936, NR, 80 min.
Dir: Lambert Hillyer. Cast: Boris Karloff, Bela Lugosi, Frances Drake, Frank Lawton, Walter Kingsford, Beulah Bondi, Violet Kemble Cooper, Frank Reicher.

Solid Karloff-Lugosi co-starrer with Boris as a scientist who becomes contaminated with radiation from a fallen meteor, glowing in the dark and bringing instant death to anyone he touches. Lugosi is a fellow scientist who tries to cure him. Impressive special effects and photography highlight this early mixture of gothic horror and modern science fiction.

INVISIBLE STRANGLER, THE
★ Video Treasures, 1976, PG, 85 min.
Dir: John Florea. Cast: Robert Foxworth, Stefanie Powers, Elke Sommer, Sue Lyon, Leslie Parrish, Marianna Hill, Mark Slade, Cesare Danova.

Filmed as *The Astral Factor* and barely released, this banal rip-off of the slightly better (and certainly funnier) *Psychic Killer* stars Foxworth as a convicted murderer who uses supernatural studies to make himself invisible so he can escape his cell and romp around strangling women. A surprisingly well-known cast trashes their collective reputation in this tripe.

INVISIBLE WOMAN, THE
★★★ MCA/Universal, 1941, NR, 72 min.
Dir: A. Edward Sutherland. Cast: Virginia Bruce, John Barrymore, John Howard, Charlie Ruggles, Oscar Homolka, Margaret Hamilton, Edward Brophy, Shemp Howard, Donald McBride, Charles Lane, Maria Montez, Anne Nagel.

An amusing, well-cast comedy, this has Bruce as a fashion model who becomes the test subject for eccentric scientist Barrymore's invisibility machine. Virginia first uses her new transparency to torment creepy boss Lane but eventually becomes a hero when she saves Barrymore and boyfriend Howard from gangsters after the invention. Good comic turns from Bruce, Barrymore (who was allegedly drunk through most of this), and Ruggles (as a butler who takes an elaborate pratfall about two seconds into the movie) and some interesting new twists on the familiar effects sequences make this a fun, offbeat entry in the series.

INVITATION TO HELL
★★ SVS, 1984, NR, 95 min.
Dir: Wes Craven. Cast: Robert Urich, Joanna Cassidy, Susan Lucci, Kevin McCarthy, Patty McCormack, Joe Regalbuto, Barret Oliver, Soleil Moon Frye, Nicholas Worth, Virginia Vincent.

In this fair Craven tele-film (clearly patterned after *Poltergeist*), Urich discovers that the local health club is built over an entranceway to hell and that its owner (daytime TV siren Lucci) is a seductive succubus. Hampered by network censorship but has a talented cast and some stylish flourishes. Filmed as *The Club*.

ISLAND, THE

★ MCA/Universal, 1980, R, 114 min.
Dir: Michael Ritchie. Cast: Michael Caine, David Warner, Angela Punch-McGregor, Don Henderson, Frank Middlemass, Jeffrey Frank.

Caine, the hardest-working man in show business, stars in this repellent adaptation of the Peter Benchley novel about modern-day psychopathic pirates terrorizing the Bermuda Triangle. Caine curses a lot, Warner jabbers a lot, Punch-McGregor wears a faceful of mud, and Frank is an obnoxious brat of a kid you'd like to feed to the sharks. Oh, and did I mention how much I really dislike this mess?

ISLAND CLAWS

★ Vestron, 1980, PG, 82 min.
Dir: Herman Cardenas. Cast: Robert Lansing, Nita Talbot, Barry Nelson, Steve Hanks, Jo McDonnell, Martina Deignan.

Lansing may have thought *Empire of the Ants* was a bad career move, but this one *really* takes the crab cake. Nuclear radiation turns Florida crabs into huge monsters made out of plaster which snap up a few members of the supporting cast until take-charge guy Bob decides to pitch in. You've probably seen worse, but I wouldn't waste too much time dwelling on it. Aka *Night of the Claw*.

ISLAND OF DR. MOREAU, THE

★★ Goodtimes, 1977, PG, 98 min. Dir: Don Taylor.
Cast: Burt Lancaster, Michael York, Barbara Carrera, Nigel Davenport, Richard Basehart, Nick Cravat.

A bland, miscast remake of the '30s classic *Island of Lost Souls* based on the novel by H. G. Wells. Lancaster is a scientist busy turning the animals of a tropical island into quasi-human beings, thanks to his radical surgical technique. York is a shipwrecked sailor who is also experimented on; in this case evolution is reversed, changing him to semi-animal. Beautifully photographed but with rubbery-looking makeup FX. Carrera's role makes little sense because pre-release cutting omitted a shock ending that's her entire character's reason for being!

ISLAND OF LIVING HORROR

See: *Brides of the Beast*.

ISLAND OF LOST SOULS

★★★★ MCA/Universal, 1932, NR, 70 min.
Dir: Erle C. Kenton. Cast: Charles Laughton, Bela Lugosi, Richard Arlen, Lelia Hyams, Arthur Hohl, Kathleen Burke.

Most '30s horror films are more entertaining than truly frightening, but this controversial version of H. G. Wells' *The Island of Dr. Moreau* (the author hated it) is still pretty strong stuff and may be the greatest horror film of its decade. As Dr. Moreau, Laughton is masterful in his impeccable white suits as he takes the animals of his remote tropical island home and transforms them via surgery into pathetic quasi-human beings. Lugosi is interesting in a disappointingly small role as the hirsute "Sayer of the Law"; Arlen less so as the typically bland '30s leading man Laughton hopes to mate with sultry "Panther Woman" Burke. The shocking climax, set in the infamous "House of Pain," is unforgettable. Banned in England for 20 years and rarely seen on TV, this was remade far less successfully as *The Island of Dr. Moreau*.

ISLAND OF TERROR

★★★ MCA/Universal, 1966, NR, 87 min.
Dir: Terence Fisher. Cast: Peter Cushing, Edward Judd, Carole Gray, Eddie Byrne, Sam Kydd, Niall MacGinnis.

This is a great '60s horror sleeper about cancer cure experiments on a tiny island off the coast of Ireland that accidentally produce tentacled, turtle-like monsters called Silicates, which suck the bone marrow from their victims. A fine cast in top form, coupled with tense, scary direction and really gross sound effects, help make this the best low-budget Brit monster movie since *Fiend Without a Face*.

ISLAND OF THE ALIVE

See: *It's Alive III: Island of the Alive*.

ISLAND OF THE TWILIGHT PEOPLE

See: *The Twilight People*.

ISLE OF THE DEAD

★★★☆ Turner, 1945, NR, 72 min.
Dir: Mark Robson. Cast: Boris Karloff, Ellen Drew, Marc Cramer, Katherine Emery, Alan Napier, Jason Robards, Sr., Helene Thimig, Skelton Knaggs.

One of the most underrated Val Lewton chillers, this does for vampires what *Cat People* did for werewolves, *I Walked With a Zombie* did for the living dead, and *The Seventh Victim* did for witches—that is, give them a sense of dark poetry and soul. Karloff is excellent, both menacing and charming, as a Greek general trapped by the plague in 1912 with a diverse group of people on a cemetery-surmounted island that the locals fear is a haven for vampires—a legend seemingly made a reality when a woman is prematurely buried and rises from her tomb. Dankly atmospheric, this has one unforgettable moment when the woman buried alive suddenly screams out from the confines of her water-dripping mausoleum.

ISLE OF THE FISHMEN
See: *Screamers.*

ISLE OF THE SNAKE PEOPLE
See: *Cult of the Damned.*

I SPIT ON YOUR GRAVE
★ VidAmerica, 1978, R, 100 min.
Dir: Meir Zarchi. Cast: Camille Keaton, Eron Tabor, Richard Pace, Anthony Nichols, Gunter Kleeman.

One of the most infamous titles of all time, this no-frills revenge melodrama would've sunk without a trace had not a couple of high-minded critics condemned it to high heaven on TV, thus creating a ready-made army of geeky curiosity seekers. Keaton (Buster's grand-niece) is a pretty writer on vacation in the woods who's raped *twice* by a quartet of backwoods cretins, flips out, and then begins stalking and hacking her attackers to death. So much for the plot. Totally inept. Original title: *Day of the Woman.*

IT
★★★ Warner, 1990, NR, 192 min.
Dir: Tommy Lee Wallace. Cast: Richard Thomas, John Ritter, Annette O'Toole, Harry Anderson, Tim Reid, Dennis Christopher, Tim Curry, Olivia Hussey, Richard Masur, Michael Cole.

In this mammoth, thoroughly entertaining TV adaptation of Stephen King's lengthy tome, a small New England town is terrorized by a demon who takes the human form of clown Curry and feeds on young children. Can a group of successful but unhappy, screwed-up adults who once battled the monster as kids finally destroy the beast for good? The first half of this well-crafted tele-movie is more suspenseful and scary than the second, which tends to get a bit silly as it heads for its climax. The casting is excellent. Aka *Stephen King's It.*

IT CAME FROM BENEATH THE SEA
★★☆ Goodtimes, 1955, NR, 78 min.
Dir: Robert Gordon. Cast: Kenneth Tobey, Faith Domergue, Donald Curtis, Ian Keith, Dean Maddox, Jr., Harry Lauter.

Atomic testing revives a gigantic prehistoric octopus, which crushes a few ships and then attacks San Francisco. Formula '50s monster movie—talky, but with the usual powerhouse Ray Harryhausen FX to make it worth your time. Budget note: the producers were so tight-fisted, Ray could only give his monster five tentacles of the requisite eight!

IT CAME FROM THE LAKE
See: *Monster.*

IT CAME WITHOUT WARNING
See: *Without Warning.*

IT CONQUERED THE WORLD
★★☆ RCA/Columbia, 1956, NR, 68 min.
Dir: Roger Corman. Cast: Peter Graves, Beverly Garland, Lee Van Cleef, Sally Fraser, Russ Bender, Dick Miller, Jonathan Haze, Paul Blaisdell.

Minor Corman classic with Van Cleef as a scientist obsessed with his communication with the dreaded cucumber monster from Venus—a fiendish creature out to conquer the world through mind control and the draining away of earth's energy sources. Totally preposterous but lots of fun, with a zippy pace and some terrifically ripe dialogue delivered with aplomb by Garland. Remade as the infamous *Zontar, The Thing From Venus.*

IT HAPPENED AT LAKEWOOD MANOR
See: *Ants!*

IT HAPPENED AT NIGHTMARE INN
See: *Nightmare Hotel.*

IT LIVES AGAIN!
★★ Warner, 1978, R, 90 min.
Dir: Larry Cohen. Cast: Frederic Forrest, Kathleen Lloyd, John Ryan, John Marley, Andrew Duggan, Eddie Constantine, James Dixon, Dennis O'Flaherty.

"The *It's Alive!* baby is back—only now there are three of them!" screamed the ads. Big deal. Ryan, dad of the killer infant in *It's Alive!*, approaches pregnant Lloyd and husband Forrest, who are about to give birth to another mutant. Ryan and friends want to protect the baby, but evil government scientists are—surprise! surprise!—out to perform dastardly experiments on it, as they have to others in their control. The acting has to be seen to be believed (Ryan is, if anything, even more whacked out than he was in the first movie, if such a thing is possible), while Cohen tends to telegraph every shock well before it happens. Definitely the weakest of the three killer baby flicks. Aka *It's Alive! 2.*

IT LIVES BY NIGHT
See: *The Bat People.*

"IT'S ALIVE!"
☆ Sinister Cinema, 1968, NR, 80 min.
Dir: Larry Buchanan. Cast: Tommy Kirk, Shirley Bonne, Bill Thurman, Annabelle McAdams, Corveth Austerhouse.

A staple of late-night and early-morning TV for years, this tells the laughable tale of three people imprisoned in a cave in the Ozarks by a madman with a pet dinosaur. This cracker then babbles on and on until the monster (a tacky creation first seen in *Creature of Destruction*) finally shuts him up by eating him. Filmed for about 98 cents, with pathetic acting and technical credits, this was allegedly based on a Richard Matheson short story called "Being."

IT'S ALIVE!
★★☆ Warner, 1974, PG, 91 min.
Dir: Larry Cohen. Cast: John Ryan, Sharon Farrell, Andrew Duggan, Michael Ansara, Guy Stockwell, Robert Emhardt, James Dixon, William Wellman, Jr.

The movie that put Cohen on the map (well, on every horror fan's map), this is about the birth of a killer mutant infant who terrorizes Los Angeles. The basically absurd storyline is handled with commendably straight faces (though Ryan gets to be a bit much), and Rick Baker's clever (though only vaguely glimpsed) makeup design is excellent. Bernard Her-

---

LARRY COHEN
(1938–)

One of the most imaginative, off-the-wall auteurs to specialize in the genre, Larry created the underrated '60s TV series *The Invaders,* and hit the big time (of sorts) when his best-known film, *It's Alive!,* became an unexpected box-office hit upon re-release in 1977. Cohen's films are full of weird ideas and strange comedy and he always makes excellent use of some of our more eclectic actors.

Daddy's Gone A-Hunting (screenplay, '69), *Bone* ('72), *It's Alive!* ('74), *God Told Me To* ('77), *It Lives Again!* ('78), *Full Moon High* ('81), *Q* ('82), *The Stuff* ('85), *It's Alive III: Island of the Alive* ('86), *Return to Salem's Lot* ('87), *Maniac Cop* (producer, 88), *Wicked Stepmother* ('89), *Maniac Cop 2* (producer, '90), *The Ambulance* ('91), *Maniac Cop 3* (producer, '92).

---

rmann composed the eerie score. Followed by *It Lives Again!* and *It's Alive III: Island of the Alive.*

IT'S ALIVE! 2
See: *It Lives Again!*

IT'S ALIVE III: ISLAND OF THE ALIVE
★★☆ Warner, 1986, R, 94 min.
Dir: Larry Cohen. Cast: Michael Moriarty, Karen Black, Laurene Landon, Gerrit Graham, Macdonald Carey, James Dixon, Patch Mackenzie, Neal Israel.

Moriarty is amusingly sincere as the dad of a mutant baby sent by the government to live with several others of its kind on a remote island. Five years later an expedition to the island discovers that the tots age three times normal speed and are now rowdy teens who've developed a taste for human flesh. Slick and silly, this has strong acting, good use of the louma crane, and effective recreations of Rich Baker's original makeup design by Steve Neill. Aka *Island of the Alive.*

IT! THE TERROR FROM BEYOND SPACE
★★★ MGM/UA, 1958, NR, 68 min.
Dir: Edward L. Cahn. Cast: Marshall Thompson, Shawn Smith, Kim Spalding, Ann Doran, Dabbs Greer, Paul Langton, Robert Bice, Ray "Crash" Corrigan.

The sole survivor of the first manned mission to Mars is charged in the deaths of his fellow crew members, although the real killer is a bloodthirsty alien creature that has stowed away on the rescue ship and is now stalking new victims. The obvious model for *Alien* (not to mention *Aliens*), this has a dull cast but very creepy atmosphere and a tension that is not dispelled even by the fact that, when finally revealed, "It" is little more than stuntman Corrigan in a baggy rubber suit. This is a genuinely scary movie.

IVANNA
See: *Blood Castle.*

I WALKED WITH A ZOMBIE
★★★★ Turner, 1943, NR, 69 min.
Dir: Jacques Tourneur. Cast: Frances Dee, Tom Conway, James Ellison, Christine Gordon, Edith Barrett, James Bell, Darby Jones, Sir Lancelot.

If *White Zombie* is the voodoo movie equivalent of a fairy tale, then this is the voodoo movie as tone poem. A young nurse (Dee) travels to Haiti to care for a plantation owner's ailing wife (Gordon) who turns out to be a zombie. Using *Jane Eyre* as inspiration, this is a film of remarkably rich moods and unusually strong characterizations for the period, with an especially imaginative use of sound. A far more complex movie than the title indicates.

I WANT HER DEAD
See: *W.*

I WAS A TEENAGE FRANKENSTEIN
See: *Teenage Frankenstein.*

I WAS A TEENAGE WEREWOLF
★★★☆ RCA/Columbia, 1957, NR, 76 min.
Dir: Gene Fowler, Jr., Cast: Michael Landon, Yvonne Lime, Whit Bissell, Tony Marshall, Dawn Richard, Barney Phillips, Ken Miller, Guy Williams.

This ingenious Herman Cohen production, a sort of *Werewolf Without a Cause,* was the first film ever to tap directly into the huge teen horror market and become a monster hit. Landon is first-rate as an underachieving high school hothead being treated by psychiatrist Bissell. Whit, seeing in Mike the perfect subject for his experiments in mental regression, sends the kid on a psychic trip into the past, triggering off the beast within and unleashing a letter-jacketed wolf boy on the neighborhood. Sincere acting and genuine tension make the difference in a film far better than its laughingstock title would allow you to believe, with excellent makeup by Philip Scheer.

HERMAN COHEN
(1930–)

This young producer really had his finger on the pulse of the nation when he created *I Was a Teenage Werewolf* and began slanting his low-budget horror features toward the youth audience. In the '60s and '70s he began to expand his horizons with slightly larger budgets and big-name performers like Joan Crawford and Jack Palance, but his goofy AIP flicks are what will be best remembered.

Bela Lugosi Meets a Brooklyn Gorilla ('52), *Target Earth!* ('54), *I Was a Teenage Werewolf* ('57), *I Was a Teenage Frankenstein* ('57), *Blood of Dracula* ('57), *How to Make a Monster* ('58), *Horrors of the Black Museum* ('59), *The Headless Ghost* ('59), *Konga* ('61), *Black Zoo* ('63), *A Study in Terror* ('66), *Berserk!* ('68), *Trog* ('70), *Craze* ('74), *Crocodile* ('80), *Watch Me When I Kill* ('81).

JACK'S BACK
★★★ Paramount, 1988, R, 96 min.
Dir: Rowdy Herrington. Cast: James Spader, Cynthia Gibb, Jim Haynie, Robert Picardo, Rod Loomis, Rex Ryon.

Quirky little suspenser about a carbon-copy Ripper slashing prostitutes in modern L.A. When med student Spader catches on to the Ripper's activities, he is murdered and his death is avenged by his twin brother (Spader again), who had a psychic link with his dead sibling. Written and directed with considerably more freshness than you'd imagine, this has a good dual lead performance from the likable Spader and plot twists that are clever enough to seem like logical developments of plot rather than gratuitous surprises.

JACK'S WIFE
See: *Season of the Witch.*

JACK THE RIPPER
★★☆ Sinister Cinema, 1959, NR, 88 min.
Dirs: Robert S. Baker, Monty Berman. Cast: Lee Patterson, Eddie Byrne, Betty McDowall, Ewen Solon, John Le Mesurier, Barbara Burke.

Jimmy Sangster scripted this fictionalized treatment of the Ripper murders, which producer Joseph E. Levine unsuccessfully attempted to ballyhoo into a major US hit à la his *Hercules.* The notorious slasher is revealed as a deranged doctor out to get the tart whose rejection drove his son to suicide; the killer is eventually crushed beneath an elevator in a scene shown in color. Gritty but effective, this has none of the surface glossiness of the Hammer films it was shot to cash in on. Sinister's print is of the original British version, complete with Stanley Black's moody score—replaced in the U.S. cut by Pete Rugolo's brassy jazz.

JACK THE RIPPER
★☆ Vestron, 1976, R, 89 min.
Dir: Jess [Jesus] Franco. Cast: Klaus Kinski, Josephine Chaplin, Andreas Mankopff, Herbert Fux, Lina Romay, Ursula von Wiese.

Kinski's manically obsessed performance is the only reason to endure this tasteless version of the story with krazy Klaus as a humanitarian doctor driven to carve up London streetwalkers who remind him of his hooker mom. Charlie Chaplin's daughter Josephine is also on hand as the ballerina who risks her life to catch Jack—an idea pinched from Franco's first hit, *The Awful Dr. Orloff*. Good photography and bloody FX—eyes, hands, and breasts are mutilated at regular intervals—with a juxtaposition of violence and sex that's highly disturbing. The dubbing is horrible.

JACK THE RIPPER

★★★ Lorimar, 1988, NR, 192 min.
Dir: David Wickes. Cast: Michael Caine, Jane Seymour, Armand Assante, Susan George, Ray McAnally, Lysette Anthony, Edward Judd, Michael Gothard.

This lavish TV movie pays tribute to the 100th anniversary of the Ripper murders. Caine is in good form here as the Scotland Yard man on the case. This often looks like a slasher film made for *Masterpiece Theatre*, with lots of classy Brit actors going toe to toe with flashing knives, splashing blood, and the odd severed body part or two. Seymour is wasted as a police sketch artist (a fictional character, natch) who aids Caine, while Assante has hammy fun as actor Richard Mansfield, who was playing Dr. Jekyll and Mr. Hyde on stage at the time and who was a major suspect in the killings.

JACOB'S LADDER

★★★ LIVE, 1990, R, 113 min.
Dir: Adrian Lyne. Cast: Tim Robbins, Elizabeth Pena, Danny Aiello, Matt Craven, Jason Alexander, Macauley Culkin.

Fatal Attraction's Lyne helms this stylish metaphysical chiller with Robbins excellent as a postal worker haunted by bizarre, frightening visions that may or may not be the result of drug experiments conducted on him while serving in Vietnam. Often confusing but worth working with; highlighted by an eerie atmosphere and creepy *An Occurrence at Owl Creek Bridge*–inspired twist ending.

JADE MASK, THE

★★ MGM/UA, 1945, NR, 66 min.
Dir: Phil Rosen. Cast: Sidney Toler, Mantan Moreland, Edwin Luke, Hardie Allbright, Janet Warren, Dorothy Granger, Edith Evanson, Frank Reicher.

Charlie Chan (Toler) is called in to investigate the murder of an inventor (Reicher), whose mist-enshrouded mansion is then seemingly stalked by the walking dead. Standard B fare

---

KLAUS KINSKI
(1926–1991)

One of the most intense actors *ever*, this Polish-born performer (real name Klaus Gunther Naksynski) made an international name for himself by appearing in several well-received Werner Herzog films in the '70s. Unhappy with his fame as a star of horror movies ("horrible movies," Klaus called them), he nonetheless added his distinctive presence to many in Germany, England, and the U.S. from the '60s to the '80s. He was also the father of the gorgeous Nastassja.

The Avenger ('60), *The Dead Eyes of London* ('61), *The Black Abbot* ('61), *The Door With Seven Locks* ('62), *The Indian Scarf* ('63), *Circus of Fear* ('67), *Creature With the Blue Hand* ('67), *Justine* ('68), *Venus in Furs* ('69), *Count Dracula* ('70), *Web of the Spider* ('70), *Slaughter Hotel* ('71), *Death Smiles on a Murderer* ('73), *Jack the Ripper* ('76), *Nosferatu, the Vampyre* ('79), *Schizoid* ('80), *Venom* ('82), *Creature* ('85), *Crawlspace* ('86), *Nosferatu in Venice* ('89).

---

with a familiar-faced cast and the usual hard-to-swallow "rational" explanation for the spookier plot devices.

JASON GOES TO HELL: THE FINAL FRIDAY

★★★ New Line, 1993, UR, 90 min.
Dir: Adam Marcus. Cast: John LeMay, Kari Keegan, Kane Hodder, Erin Gray, Billy Green Bush, Steven Culp, Allison Smith, Steven Williams, Kipp Marcus, Julie Michaels.

The alleged last bash for everyone's favorite gore goalie, this cleverly bumps the masked one off in the pre-credits sequence and then spends most of the rest of its running time with various folk being possessed by Jason's murderous spirit *Hidden*-style. This earns points for trying something different with the series but sometimes tends toward murkiness—both dramatically and visually—while the cast is excellent. The ending is effective but the final twist (involving a cameo by a certain gloved slasher) is strictly for laughs. The unrated tape has very graphic FX and some surprising frontal male nudity, while the R-rated cut is much drier.

JASON LIVES!: FRIDAY THE 13TH PART VI

See: *Friday the 13th Part VI: Jason Lives!*

Jason (Kane Hodder) rakes in more profits in Jason Goes to Hell: The Final Friday *(1993).*

JAWS
★★★★ MCA/Universal, 1975, PG, 124 min.
Dir: Steven Spielberg. Cast: Roy Scheider, Robert Shaw, Richard Dreyfuss, Lorraine Gary, Murray Hamilton, Jeffrey Kramer, Susan Backlinie, Chris Rebello, Jay Mello, Carl Gottlieb.

The most financially successful horror film ever made, this colossal hit scared beach-goers out of the water for many a season and made Spielberg a major Hollywood player. When a pretty midnight bather is gobbled up by a great white shark in the waters off the Long Island resort town of Amity, the local sheriff (Scheider) employs a marine biologist (Dreyfuss) and an old salt (Shaw) to hunt the hungry monster down. With obvious debts to both *Moby Dick* and *Creature From the Black Lagoon,* Spielberg manages to craft a tense and genuinely scary movie that goes far beyond the framework of Peter Benchley's rather mediocre best-seller to touch the place hidden deep within us all that fears the darkness beneath the water's placid surface. Beautifully photographed by Bill Butler, seamlessly edited by Verna Fields, and robustly scored by Oscar winner John Williams, this was followed by three sequels and schools of contrived imitations.

JAWS 2
★★☆ MCA/Universal, 1978, PG, 117 min.
Dir: Jeannot Szarc. Cast: Roy Scheider, Lorraine Gary, Murray Hamilton, Jeffrey Kramer, Joseph Mascolo, Ann Dusenberry, Donna Wilkes, Keith Gordon.

Three years after the original shark attacks off the Amity coast, sheriff Scheider becomes convinced that another great white is on the prowl. Slick but pointless, this plays like a sort-of *Jaws Blanket Bingo,* with a boatload of silly teens added to the plot for the shark—this one sporting a *Phantom of the Opera* disfigured face—to swallow whole. Szarc, who inherited this white elephant after Universal fired original director John Hancock for not following the formula of the first film, does his best to raise a few goosebumps; perky Dusenberry stands out in a crowded supporting cast.

JAWS 3
★★ MCA/Universal, 1983, PG, 97 min.
Dir: Joe Alves. Cast: Dennis Quaid, Bess Armstrong, Louis Gossett, Jr., Simon MacCorkindale, Lea Thompson, John Putch.

A Florida marine park where one of the grown sons of the sheriff from the first two *Jaws* films works is crashed by a huge shark searching for its captive baby, with tourists and park workers high on the menu. Released theatrically as *Jaws 3-D* and originally conceived as a comedy (*Jaws 3: People 0*), this patchwork combination of *Gorgo* and *Revenge of the Creature* (co-scripted by Richard Matheson) is good for a few cheap thrills and a couple of laughs—especially in the original 3-D version—but frankly, if you've seen one shark movie. . . .

JAWS 3-D
See: *Jaws 3.*

JAWS OF DEATH
★★ Media, 1976, PG, 93 min. Dir: William Grefe. Cast: Richard Jaeckel, Jennifer Bishop, Harold Sakata, John Chandler.

Run-of-the-mill post-*Jaws* thriller revamps the plotline of *Stanley* with sharks instead of snakes. Shark-loving Jaeckel avenges himself on the fishermen he feels are harming his finny friends by reducing them to fish food. Jaeckel is typically enthusiastic as the crazed "hero." Shown on TV as *Mako: The Jaws of Death.*

JAWS OF SATAN
★☆ MGM/UA, 1980, R, 87 min. Dir: Bob Claver. Cast: Fritz Weaver, Gretchen Corbett, Jon Korkes, Norman Lloyd, Diana Douglas, Christina Applegate.

Priest Weaver battles a satanically possessed king cobra (the film's shooting title) in this laughable *Jaws-Exorcist* pastiche. The cast plays it ridiculously straight (even a prepubescent, pre-"Married With Children" Applegate), and there's a clearly evident pane of glass separating the snake from its victims—a boo-boo also apparent in the mega-buck *Raiders of the Lost Ark.*

JAWS THE REVENGE
★★ MCA/Universal, 1987, PG-13, 90 min.
Dir: Joseph Sargent. Cast: Michael Caine, Lorraine Gary, Lance Guest, Mario Van Peebles, Karen Young, Lynn Whitfield.

This fourth and presumably last installment in the big fish series offers solid acting from Caine and beautiful Bahamian locations—and that's about it. The ludicrous script has Gary (who did little or nothing in the original *Jaws* and *Jaws 2*) as the widow of sheriff Roy Scheider, who was smart enough to croak between pictures. She fears that great white sharks have a personal vendetta against her family when one kills her younger son and then follows her to the Caribbean. The Universal tour shark is scarier.

JEKYLL & HYDE . . . TOGETHER AGAIN
★ Paramount, 1982, R, 87 min. Dir: Jerry Berlson. Cast: Mark Blankfield, Bess Armstrong, Tim Thomerson, Krista Errickson, George Chakiris, Cassandra Peterson.

A one-joke comedy that can't even make *that* joke funny, this pathetic drug culture rip-off of *The Nutty Professor* features Blankfield as a nerdy chemist who snorts a cocaine-like powder and transforms into a hairy, obnoxious swinger. Offensive most of the time, pathetic the rest; R. L. Stevenson must have *really* spun in his grave over this baby.

JENNIFER
★★ Vestron, 1978, PG, 90 min. Dir: Brice Mack. Cast: Lisa Pelikan, Bert Convy, Nina Foch, John Gavin, Jeff Corey, Wesley Eure, Amy Johnston, Louise Hoven.

In this slow-moving *Carrie* copy, Pelikan is a lonely scholarship student at an exclusive girls school who is tormented by both her cruel peers and a religious fanatic dad (Corey) and who uses her psychic power over snakes to seek a slithery revenge. Totally predictable but well acted, with director Mack playing up psychological suspense over more overt shocks. Retitled *Jennifer, the Snake Goddess* for TV.

JENNIFER 8
★★☆ Paramount, 1992, R, 126 min. Dir: Bruce Robinson. Cast: Andy Garcia, Uma Thurman, Lance Henriksen, Kathy Baker, John Malkovich, Kevin Conway, Lenny Von Dohlen, Graham Beckel.

Garcia is a cop who becomes obsessed with the idea that a serial killer is preying on blind women in a snowy northwestern community. Thurman is the sightless music teacher who becomes the maniac's next target. This overlong but well-acted murder mystery pushes all the usual buttons and contains all the usual homages (to *Wait Until Dark, See No Evil, Jagged Edge,* and others) but never builds the way it should and has an ending that falls rather flat.

JENNIFER, THE SNAKE GODDESS
See: *Jennifer.*

JESSE JAMES MEETS FRANKENSTEIN'S DAUGHTER
★☆ Embassy, 1965, NR, 82 min.
Dir: William Beaudine. Cast: John Lupton, Narda Onyx, Estelita, Cal Bolder, Steven Geray, Jim Davis.

Actually, it's the baron's *granddaughter* who encounters the famous outlaw, transplanting an artificial brain of her own creation into the head of Jesse's wounded buddy Hank, whom she redubs Igor for some unknown reason—I guess Hank just isn't a good name for a monster. A companion piece to the simultaneously shot *Billy the Kid vs. Dracula,* this silly horror-oater needs the bravura of a Carradine to put it over, something this dull cast never does.

JITTERS, THE
★★ Prism, 1988, R, 80 min. Dir: John Fasano. Cast: Sal Viviano, Marilyn Tokuda, James Hong, Frank Dietz.

The director (and some of the cast) of *Black Roses* strikes back with this marginally better tale of vampires on the loose in San Francisco's Chinatown. A cross between *The Lost Boys* and *Big Trouble in Little China,* the film features good makeup and some imaginative touches but awful acting and uneven technical credits.

JOEY
See: *Making Contact.*

JUDGEMENT DAY
★☆ Magnum, 1989, PG-13, 88 min.
Dir: Ferde Grofe. Cast: Cesar Romero, Monte Markham, Peter Mark Richman, Kenneth McLeod, David Anthony Smith, Gloria Hayes.

In this atmospheric but dull Mexican flick, a pair of U.S. tourists (McLeod and Smith) stumble into a sleepy south-of-the-border town called Santana, where once each year the devil and his whip-wielding minions rule.

Yawn-inducing non-thriller salvaged by a few nice images (a ruined hilltop tower) and good work from Romero in the Vincent Price role.

JUDGEMENT IN STONE, A

See: *The Housekeeper*.

JUNIOR

★ Starmaker, 1984, R, 80 min. Dir: Jim Henley. Cast: Linda Singer, Suzanne DeLaurentiis, Jeremy Ratchford, Michael McKeever.

Absolutely irredeemable *Chainsaw Massacre* rip about a pair of ex-con tootsies who run afoul of maniac Ratchford, who worships his crazy mom—played by a guy in drag! With more T&A than gore-n-grue, this has little to offer the serious slaughter fan.

JURASSIC PARK

★★☆ MCA/Universal, 1993, PG-13, 126 min. Dir: Steven Spielberg. Cast: Sam Neill, Laura Dern, Jeff Goldblum, Richard Attenborough, Ariana Richards, Joseph Mazzello, Wayne Knight, Samuel L. Jackson, Bob Peck, Martin Ferrero.

The biggest box-office hit of all time, this lengthy adaptation of the Michael Crichton best-seller wants to be the *King Kong* of the '90s but, despite state-of-the-art FX, just doesn't cut it. Attenborough is a billionaire who creates an island resort park inhabited by genetically engineered dinosaurs. When scientists Neill, Dern, and Goldblum (not to mention Attenborough's grandkids, Richards and Mazzello) visit the island, sabotage and a power failure result in the prehistoric beasts going on a rampage. Compared to the graphic nature of Crichton's book, this pulls far too many of its punches to be as scary or suspenseful as it could be and makes a major dramatic mistake by turning its main menace (a thundering Tyrannosaurus Rex) into a hero! The *ET* influence lives on. On the plus side are a first-rate cast, beautiful location photography, and the above-mentioned computer-generated and full-scale model FX. The John Williams score is so familiar-sounding, though, he ought to sue himself for plagiarism.

JUST BEFORE DAWN

★★★ Paragon, 1980, R, 90 min. Dir: Jeff Lieberman. Cast: George Kennedy, Deborah Benson, Chris Lemmon, Gregg Henry, Jamie Rose, Mike Kellin, Ralph Seymour, John Hunsaker.

In the Oregon mountains a group of young people who are checking out a parcel of land one of them has inherited is set upon by a pair of huge, deformed, in-bred hillbilly twins. Lieberman's variation on *The Hills Have Eyes*,

this starts off looking routine but quickly distinguishes itself thanks to distinct characterizations and a genuine feel of backwoods helplessness and menace. Another interesting genre piece from the underrated Lieberman.

JUSTINE, OR THE MISFORTUNES OF VIRTUE

See: *Deadly Sanctuary*.

JUVENATRIX

See: *The Rejuvenator*.

KEEP, THE

★★ Paramount, 1983, R, 96 min. Dir: Michael Mann. Cast: Scott Glenn, Alberta Watson, Jurgen Prochnow, Ian McKellen, Robert Prosky, Gabriel Byrne.

F. Paul Wilson's strikingly original novel about Nazi stormtroopers versus a Dracula-like vampire in his Transylvanian fortress gets butchered but good in this moody, muddled mix of H. P. Lovecraft, *Alien, Raiders of the Lost Ark*, and *They Saved Hitler's Brain*. The actors are all saddled with so many different accents and dialects that much of the dialogue is incomprehensible, while the plot, with the revived vampire altered into some sort of personification of evil or something, is riddled with holes big enough to drive a Panzer division through. Visually interesting, though, with imagery recalling everything from *Beauty and the Beast* to *Exorcist II* and an impressive monster costume designed by Nick Maley.

KEEPER, THE

★ Interglobal, 1976, PG, 88 min. Dir: Tom Drake. Cast: Christopher Lee, Sally Gray, Tell Schrieber, Ross Vezarian.

Lee is the only reason to endure this inept Canadian shocker about an asylum administrator who forces his charges to sign over their money to him; he then kills them and any stray relatives who may protest the new will. Shoddy and slow, with poor supporting performances and flat direction; *Bedlam* this ain't.

KEEP MY GRAVE OPEN

★ Unicorn, 1979, R, 78 min. Dir: S. F. Brownrigg. Cast: Camilla Carr, Gene Ross, Stephen Toblowsky, Ann Stafford, Annabelle McAdams, Bill Thurman.

The director of *Don't Look in the Basement* returns with this obtuse psycho-thriller about a woman (Carr) who imagines that she's her own long-missing brother and uses a sword to kill guys who make passes at her. This shot-in-Texas obscurity has a twist ending that makes absolutely no sense at all.

KILL AND GO HIDE
See *The Child.*

KILL, BABY, KILL!
★★★ Sinister Cinema, 1966, NR, 83 min.
Dir: Mario Bava. Cast: Erika Blanc, Giacomo Rossid Stuart, Fabienne Dali, Gianni Vivaldi, Piero Lulli, Max Lawrence.

A dumb title masks one of Bava's eeriest chillers, about a Transylvanian village cursed by a mad baroness (Dali) who haunts the place with the ghost of her young daughter. Beautifully photographed in rich color, this boasts haunting images that obviously inspired the great Fellini while shooting his segment for the Poe anthology *Spirits of the Dead.* Originally titled *Operazione Paura: Operation Fear,* this was re-released in the early '70s as *Curse of the Living Dead* as part of the infamous "Orgy of the Living Dead" triple bill drive-in package.

KILLBOTS
See: *Chopping Mall.*

KILLER BATS
See: *The Devil Bat.*

KILLER BEHIND THE MASK
See: *Savage Weekend.*

KILLER FISH
★☆ Key, 1978, R, 101 min. Dir: Anthony M. Dawson [Antonio Margheriti]. Cast: Lee Majors, Karen Black, James Franciscus, Margaux Hemingway, Marisa Berenson, Gary Collins, Dan Pastorini, Anthony Steffen.

This soggy action-adventure-horror film is an obvious, and far inferior, rip-off of the superior *Piranha*—itself a rip-off of *Jaws,* making this a rip-off's rip-off! A valuable cache of stolen gems is lost at the bottom of a piranha-filled South American lake that the thieves, some bad and some not so bad, foolishly brave to retrieve their loot. Tensionless and contrived but worth a look for its tremendous cast—I mean, Karen, Margaux, and Marisa all in the same movie—the mind boggles! Shown on TV as *Deadly Treasure of the Piranha.*

KILLER GRIZZLY
See: *Grizzly.*

KILLER IN EVERY CORNER, A
★★ Thrillervideo, 1974, NR, 73 min.
Dir: Malcolm Taylor. Cast: Joanna Pettet, Patrick Magee, Max Wall, Eric Flynn, Don Henderson.

Routine Brian Clemens–scripted Brit TV chiller with Magee as a college psych professor who invites some students to his home for a weekend of experimental junior psychology; things turn ugly when someone begins a murder spree. Magee's usual professionalism and the always welcome freshness of Pettet make this videotaped production a harmless watch.

KILLER KLOWNS FROM OUTER SPACE
★★☆ Media, 1988, PG-13, 86 min.
Dir: Stephen Chiodo. Cast: Grant Cramer, Suzanne Snyder, John Vernon, Royal Dano, John Allen Nelson.

Bozos from beyond the stars traveling in a circus-tent flying saucer and using popcorn and cotton candy weapons menace small-town simpletons in this funny, visually imaginative spoof of '50s teen horror. It has solid makeup and effects work and the usual droll Vernon histrionics; be sure to stick around to the very end for the hilarious music video after the end credits.

KILLER ORPHAN
See: *The Orphan.*

KILLER PARTY
★★☆ Key, 1984, R, 91 min.
Dir: William Fruet. Cast: Elaine Wilkes, Sherry Willis-Burch, Joanna Johnson, Martin Hewitt, Ralph Seymour, Paul Bartel, Alicia Fleer, Woody Brown.

Better-than-average actors and production values dress up this Canadian-shot slasher. A sorority sister (Johnson) attending an annual April Fool's Day costume bash at the campus "haunted house" is possessed by the spirit of a vengeful frat brother and goes on a killing spree, inexplicably clad in a deep-sea diving suit. Filmed as *The April Fool* and also briefly known as *Fool's Night,* this was shelved until '86, when MGM cut out most of the gore and gave it a brief regional release. It gets the most out of its appealing trio of femme leads (particularly Sigourney Weaver lookalike Wilkes) and funny Bartel cameo, with sharply drawn characters and situations provided by scripter Barney (*Friday the 13th—The Final Chapter*) Cohen.

KILLER SHREWS, THE
★★☆ Sinister Cinema, 1959, NR, 70 min.
Dir: Ray Kellogg. Cast: James Best, Ingrid Goude, Baruch Lumet, Ken Curtis, Gordon McLendon, Alfredo De Soto.

Despite a rock-bottom budget and monsters that look like refugees from the local pound, there is some genuine tension as well as shocks to be found in this shot-in-Texas cheapskate classic. Scientific experiments on a remote island turn harmless little rodents into fanged, greyhound-sized beasts with a taste for human flesh—which they taste at every given opportunity. Not nearly as bad as you've probably heard, and featuring some especially grisly sound effects, it's much better than its original co-feature, *The Giant Gila Monster*.

KILLERS OF THE CASTLE OF BLOOD

See *Blood Castle*.

KILLER TOMATOES STRIKE BACK!

★ Fox, 1990, NR, 90 min.
Dir: John De Bello. Cast: John Astin, Rick Rockwell, Crystal Carson, Steve Lundquist.

Nobody asked them back but the tomatoes return anyway, with mad scientist Astin continuing his experiments with the deadly veggies. I know tomatoes are really fruits, but deadly fruits somehow don't sound as impressive. Either way this one's for John Astin fans only.

KILLER WITH 2 FACES, THE

★★ Moonlight, 1974, NR, 72 min.
Dir: John Scholz-Conway. Cast: Donna Mills, Ian Hendry, David Lodge, Roddy McMillan, Susan Drury, Robin Parkinson.

Mills is attracted to charming Hendry, little realizing that he has a murderous twin, recently escaped from an asylum, with a penchant for strangling women. Guess which brother she ends up trapped with in a remote country house? Familiar crazy twin thriller, the weakest of three Brian Clemens shockers Donna made for Brit TV.

KILLING HOUR, THE

★★ CBS/Fox, 1981, R, 97 min.
Dir: Armand Mastroianni. Cast: Perry King, Elizabeth Kemp, Kenneth McMillian, Norman Parker.

A pretty artist (Kemp) finds herself drawing the likenesses of women just before they're murdered by a psycho in contact with a local TV talk show host (King). Soon the artist begins sketching her *own* murdered features. Will she be the next victim? Routinely plotted and directed psychic thriller along *Eyes of Laura Mars* lines, this was shelved for three years before being released direct-to-video and is predictable right down to the twist ending. TV title: *The Clairvoyant*.

KILLING KIND, THE

★★☆ Paragon, 1973, R, 95 min. Dir: Curtis Harrington. Cast: Ann Sothern, John Savage, Ruth Roman, Cindy Williams, Luana Anders, Sue Bernard.

Obscure but interesting Harrington thriller with handsome Savage miscast as a 21-year-old virgin wrongly accused of rape who leaves prison with a murderous hatred of women. It figures, then, that his overprotective mom (Sothern, looking like the Goodyear Blimp in a hostess gown) should run a boarding house just swimmin' with women. The impressive supporting cast includes Williams in an early, negative role as a pushy boarder and Anders as a repressed librarian neighbor, a character later recreated by Carrie Snodgress in semi-sequel *The Attic*.

KINDRED, THE

★★☆ Media, 1987, R, 92 min. Dirs: Jeffrey Obrow, Stephen Carpenter. Cast: Rod Steiger, Kim Hunter, David Allen Brooks, Talia Balsam, Amanda Pays, Timothy Gibbs, Peter Frenchette, Julia Montgomery.

Fun throwback to a '50s Saturday afternoon monster flick combining elements from *Basket Case* and *The Boogens* with *CHUD*-like makeup effects. Hunter is briefly on hand as a dying genetic researcher whose old house harbors a gooey secret beneath its floorboards: a mutant life form created by splicing the cells of her son with those of a fish. Also involved are Steiger (in an ill-fitting hairpiece) and the lovely Pays as a girl who grows gills. A *big* improvement on Obrow-Carpenter's debut feature *The Dorm That Dripped Blood*.

FAY WRAY
(1907–)

The original scream queen, Fay was born in Canada but raised in California. She made her film debut in several comedy shorts and eventually graduated to prestigious films for directors like Erich von Stroheim and Josef von Sternberg. Her casting as the in-hand lady love of the great ape in *King Kong* typecast her in horror roles, but she continued as a successful character actress in movies and TV right through the 1960s.

Doctor X ('32), *The Most Dangerous Game* ('32), *Mystery of the Wax Museum* ('33), *The Vampire Bat* ('33), *King Kong* ('33), *Black Moon* ('34), *Below the Sea* ('34), *The Clairvoyant* ('35).

The world's Mightiest Monster is Broadway bound in **King Kong** *(1933).*

KING COBRA

See: *Jaws of Satan.*

KINGDOM OF THE SPIDERS

★★★ Goodtimes, 1977, PG, 94 min.
Dir: John "Bud" Cardos. Cast: William Shatner,
Tiffany Bolling, Woody Strode, Altovise Davis,
Natasha Ryan, Lieux Dressler, David McLean,
Marcy Lafferty.

Driven into a frenzy when pesticides kill off
their natural food supply, hordes of tarantulas
begin attacking the residents of a small Arizona desert community. This likable low-budget *Jaws* cash-in is well handled by journey-
man jack-of-all-trades director Cardos, with
Shatner giving an enjoyably relaxed, playful
(and non-hammy) performance as the local
vet. Much better than you'd think.

KING KONG

★★★★ Turner, 1933, NR, 100 min.
Dirs: Merian C. Cooper, Ernest B. Schoedsack.
Cast: Fay Wray, Robert Armstrong, Bruce Cabot,
Frank Reicher, Sam Hardy, Noble Johnson,
James Flavin, Victor Wong.

The definitive monster-on-a-rampage movie,
this is a classic not only of the horror film but
of the cinema itself. We all know the story: a
documentary filmmaker travels with his crew
to an uncharted island inhabited by prehistoric beasts ruled by a huge ape called Kong.
Kong falls for the woman (Wray) left to him as
a sacrifice by worshipping natives; battles
dinosaurs; is captured and taken to New York,
where he escapes; reclaims his bride; and dies
in a fall from the summit of the Empire State
Building. Rarely has there been so convincing
a fantasy creation on the screen as Kong—ET
being one of the few exceptions—with Willis
O'Brien's dated but still effective, not to mention charming, animation giving the great
gorilla and his fellow monsters the sort of life
and personality sadly lacking from today's
multimillion-dollar special effects extravagan-
zas. Corny performances and Max Steiner's
great score add to the fun. Remade in 1976;
sequel: *Son of Kong.*

KING KONG

★★ Paramount, 1976, PG, 134 min.
Dir: John Guillermin. Cast: Jessica Lange, Jeff Bridges,

Charles Grodin, John Randolph, René Auberjonois, Ed Lauter, John Agar, Rick Baker.

This over-hyped, over-produced, over-everything $24 million remake remains one of the most ill-conceived and unimaginative films of the '70s. Beautiful Hawaiian locations and Lange's spirited debut performance—she's still trying to live this down—are the sole high spots of this near-parody, with Kong (Baker in a convincing ape costume and cable-controlled mask) shipped to New York by a greedy oil company as their new corporate symbol. Predictably, he escapes and kidnaps Lange before doing a swan dive from the top of the World Trade Center. That this thing copped an Oscar for its mediocre effects work is, perhaps, the biggest joke of all. Still, this is better than its sequel. Best line: "Who do you think went through here, some guy in an ape suit?"

KING KONG LIVES!

★ Lorimar, 1986, PG-13, 104 min.
Dir: John Guillermin. Cast: Linda Hamilton, Brian Kerwin, John Ashton, Peter Michael Goetz.

This incredibly inept sequel to the '76 Kong shows how the great ape really didn't die after his fall from the World Trade Center (!!!!) but is alive and well thanks to a tank-sized artificial heart and blood transfusions from the recently discovered, and equally colossal, Lady Kong. Cut-rate effects and cloying attempts at sentimentality dominate this needless production, whose greatest sin among many is in utterly wasting the lovely and talented Hamilton—Kong doesn't even get to pick her up! Script echoes of earlier Kong movies, Mighty Joe Young, Konga, and Escape From the Planet of the Apes (from which this movie's ending was stolen) do little to help.

KING KONG VS. GODZILLA

★★☆ Goodtimes, 1963, NR, 90 min.
Dirs: Inoshiro Honda, Thomas Montgomery. Cast: Michael Keith, James Yagi, Tadao Takashima, Mie Hama, Kenji Sahara, Harry Holcombe.

Godzilla rises again—for the first time in color—when an atomic sub bumps into his iceberg tomb. Meanwhile, a Tokyo TV sponsor sends a couple of knuckleheads to a distant island to capture the legendary King Kong. Kong fights a huge, slimy octopus; gets stoned on some fermented berry juice; is taken to Japan and there escapes; ravages Tokyo; carries off Hama; and eventually battles the mighty lizard high atop Mt. Fuji. The effects run hot and cold—the octopus scenes are pretty creepy—but this time the dubbing is purposely funny ("King Kong won't make a mon-

key out of us!") and it's all good-natured fun. Take note: in the longer Japanese version, it's home-boy Godzilla and not Kong who emerges victorious!

KING OF THE ZOMBIES

★★ Sinister Cinema, 1941, NR, 66 min. Dir: Jean Yarbrough. Cast: Dick Purcell, Joan Woodbury, John Archer, Henry Victor, Mantan Moreland, Patricia Stacey.

A wooden Victor stars as a Dracula-caped mad doctor creating zombies on a remote island in this rock-bottom Monogram madness. Luckily, Moreland is on hand to lend his considerable comic skills, and he steals the movie handily away from his dull co-stars with his ceaseless banter and comic asides—he's at his best when he thinks that he has become a zombie. If you have to see it at all, see it for Mantan.

KISS, THE

★★ RCA/Columbia, 1988, R, 98 min. Dir: Pen Densham. Cast: Joanna Pacula, Meredith Salenger, Mimi Kuzyk, Jan Rubes, Nicholas Kilbertus, Pamela Collyer, Shawn Levy, Sabrina Boudot.

This stylish but absurd supernatural thriller casts Pacula as a fashion model suffering from a hereditary demonic curse in the form of a serpent-like parasite she must pass on to teenage niece Salenger with a kiss. This slender plot is padded with several superfluous Omen-like death scenes; voodoo rituals involving a topless, undulating Joanna; and a silly demon-cat familiar. Frantic editing, some nice effects (except for that darn cat), and Kuzyk as a spunky neighbor who takes on Pacula during a cluttered climax keep this humming.

KISS AND KILL
See: Against All Odds.

KISS FROM EDDIE, A
See: The Arousers.

KISS OF DEATH
See: Against All Odds.

KISS OF THE BEAST
See: Meridian: Kiss of the Beast.

KRONOS
See: Captain Kronos, Vampire Hunter.

KWAIDAN

★★★ ☆ Sinister Cinema, 1964, NR, 160 min. Dir: Masaki Kobayashi. Cast: Rentaro Mikuni, Keiko Kishi, Katsuo Nakamura, Ganemon Nakamura, Michiyo Aratama, Tatsuya Nakadai, Kanjiro Nakamura, Noburo Nakaya.

Visually stunning collection of Japanese period horror tales—the title translates as *Ghost Stories*—adapted from the works of Lafacadio Hearn. A man leaves his faithful wife for another woman, returns to her years later, and discovers her to be a ghost; a traveler is permitted to survive his encounter with a beautiful vampire if he agrees never to speak of her existence; a minstral's body is covered in magical symbols to protect him from evil spirits; and a samurai is possessed after drinking from a teacup containing a warrior's ghost. Overlong, but the haunting atmosphere—each segment is set during a different season of the year—and a beautiful use of color and set design impart a genuine feeling of the supernatural. Some prints run 125 minutes with the second story cut; this episode was the obvious inspiration for the third segment in *Tales From the Darkside: The Movie.*

LABYRINTH
See: *A Reflection of Fear.*

LADY BEWARE
★★☆ IVE, 1987, R, 108 min. Dir: Karen Arthur. Cast: Diane Lane, Michael Woods, Cotter Smith, Tyra Ferrell, Peter Nevargic, Edward Penn.

Steamy erotic thriller with Lane as a sexy window dresser whose provocative department store displays attract the attention of psycho-peeping Tom Woods. Starts off as just your average stalker but then goes off into some intriguing, if not always plausible, directions all its own before settling down to a predictable but satisfying hunter-becomes-the-hunted turn-the-tables climax.

LADY FRANKENSTEIN
★★☆ Embassy, 1972, R, 83 min. Dir: Mel Welles. Cast: Joseph Cotten, Sara Bay, Mickey Hargitay, Paul Muller, Peter Whiteman, Herbert Fux.

When Baron Frankenstein (Cotten) is crushed to death by his latest creation, his sexy surgeon daughter (Bay) makes a monster of her own—a super-powerful creature designed both to avenge her father *and* to satisfy her insatiable lust. This funny Italian imitation of

Hammer's *The Horror of Frankenstein* manages to predate *Andy Warhol's Frankenstein* in its queasy mixture of sex and gore and is oddly entertaining, almost in spite of itself. A late-night TV favorite since the mid-'70s, you have to see it uncut on tape in order to get the full effect of its ludicrous sex-on-the-operating-table climax.

LADY IN A CAGE
★★★ Paramount, 1964, NR, 93 min. Dir: Walter Grauman. Cast: Olivia de Havilland, Ann Sothern, James Caan, Jennifer Billingsley, Jeff Corey, Rafael Campos.

In this underrated '60s psycho-thriller, de Havilland is a pampered poetess trapped in a private elevator in her home by a broken hip and a power failure, where she is terrorized by a trio of brutal thugs led by Caan in his film debut. One of the first films of its era to comment directly on the increasing violence of its time, this is dominated by de Havilland's excellent performance as she slides slowly from smug self-import into hate-filled savagery. Much better than you may have heard, with a very violent ending.

LADY IN WHITE
★★☆ Virgin Vision, 1988, PG-13, 113 min. Dir: Frank LaLoggia. Cast: Lukas Haas, Len Cariou, Katherine Helmond, Alex Rocco, Jason Presson, Renata Vanni, Angelo Bertolini, Joelle Jacob.

In 1962 doe-eyed Haas is locked overnight on Halloween in his school's cloak room, where he spies the ghost (Jacob) of a little girl murdered there 10 years earlier and becomes the target of the still-uncaught killer. Sometimes admired, this slowly paced film has good atmosphere and performances but is riddled with plot holes and features a "mystery killer" whose identity is so obvious he may as well be wearing a neon sign.

LAIR OF THE WHITE WORM
★★★ Vestron, 1988, R, 93 min. Dir: Ken Russell. Cast: Amanda Donohue, Hugh Grant, Catherine Oxenberg, Sammi Davis, Peter Capaldi, Stratford Johns.

Russell's deliciously absurd adaptation of Bram Stoker's last novel, this features Donohue in a magnificent performance as a hilariously sarcastic high priestess of an ancient snake cult out to hold a virgin sacrifice to the legendary huge white serpent living in the caverns beneath her English estate. One of the uneven Russell's most underappreciated works, this has enough gore, campy dialogue, sexual-religious imagery, and scenes of the luscious Oxenberg in her underwear for a full evening's entertainment and then some.

LAKE OF THE LIVING DEAD
See: *Zombie Lake.*

LAMP, THE
See: *The Outing.*

LAND OF THE MINOTAUR
★★ Interglobal, 1976, PG, 85 min.
Dir: Costa Corryiannis. Cast: Peter Cushing, Donald Pleasence, Luan Peters, Costus Skouras, Nikos Verlakis, Vanna Revilli.

Cushing is a Carpathian baron living on a Greek island where he heads up a cult that sacrifices bleach-blonde babes in hot pants to a huge fire-breathing minotaur statue. Originally titled *The Devil's Men,* this prettily photographed but dull British-Greek co-production is buoyed by a dapper Peter, an amusing Pleasence as a heroic priest, and an eerie Brian Eno score. Aka *Minotaur.*

LAND THAT TIME FORGOT, THE
★★ Video Treasures, 1975, PG, 90 min.
Dir: Kevin Connor. Cast: Doug McClure, Susan Penhaligon, John McEnery, Keith Barron, Anthony Ainley, Bobby Parr.

Lackluster Amicus dinosaur pic based on the Edgar Rice Burroughs novel about a group of WWI shipwreck survivors picked up by a German submarine who end up on a lost continent of cavemen and prehistoric beasts somewhere near the South Pole. Mild fun hampered by routine scripting and acting and poor special effects—the monsters are all portrayed by clumsy, unconvincing mock-ups. Sequel: *The People That Time Forgot.*

LAND UNKNOWN, THE
★★ MCA/Universal, 1957, NR, 78 min.
Dir: Virgil Vogel. Cast: Jack Mahoney, Shawn Smith, William Reynolds, Henry Brandon, Phil Harvey.

A naval expedition at the South Pole discovers a humid air pocket hovering above a misty valley inhabited by dinosaurs, man-eating plants, and the half-mad survivor of a previous expedition. This routine lost-world-and-dinosaurs epic has imaginative photography and art direction, but the life-size mock-up and man-in-a-suit monsters aren't always effective. It's somewhat similar to the later Amicus film *The People That Time Forgot.*

LAST DINOSAUR, THE
★★ Edde Entertainment, 1976, NR, 94 min.
Dirs: Alex Grasshoff and Tom Kotani. Cast: Richard

Boone, Joan Van Ark, Steven Keats, Luther Rackley, Tatsu Nakamura, Mamiya Seka.

A passable "lost world" film made in Japan by an American company, this was released in the U.S. directly to TV. Boone is a wealthy adventurer who discovers the existence of a prehistoric world beneath the North Pole and mounts an expedition to hunt down the only creature on Earth he has yet to conquer—a Tyrannosaurus Rex. Good FX and acting give this predictable monster flick a slight lift.

LAST HORROR FILM, THE
★★ Video Treasures, 1982, R, 87 min.
Dir: David Winters. Cast. Caroline Munro, Joe Spinell, Judd Hamilton, Devin Goldenberg, David Winters, Mary Spinell.

A junky but surprisingly watchable semi-follow-up to *Maniac* set at the Cannes Film Festival, where crazed cabbie and would-be filmmaker Spinell stalks scream queen Munro, whose entourage is being brutally murdered—but by whom? The real-life festival background adds a flavorful backdrop to this cheesy slasher opus—everyone from Karen Black to Robin Leech turns up at one point or another—with big Joe giving another of his no-holds-barred thespic exercises matched blow for blow by his dear ol' mom in a cameo as herself. Also titled *Fanatic.*

LAST HOUSE ON THE LEFT, THE
★★☆ Vestron, 1972, R, 81 min. Dir: Wes Craven.
Cast: David Hess, Lucy Grantham, Sandra Cassel, Fred Lincoln, Jeramie Rain, Marc Sheffler.

Craven's directorial debut was this infamous stomach-turner about a gang of low-lifes who kidnap, torture, rape, and kill a pair of teenage girls, only to feel the even more violent wrath of the parents of one of their victims. A powerful, though repellent, examination of the day-to-day violence in American lives, like it or not, this drive-in remake of Ingmar Bergman's *The Virgin Spring*—which Craven improved on in his second, similar film *The Hills Have Eyes*—is hard to ignore. Available from Vestron in two versions: an "uncut" 81-minute print with some snippets of gore cut out in the late '70s restored, and a "softer" 80-minute cut.

LAST HOUSE ON THE LEFT, PART II, THE
See: *Bay of Blood.*

LAST MAN ON EARTH, THE
★★☆ Sinister Cinema, 1961, NR, 86 min.
Dir: Sidney Salkow. Cast: Vincent Price, Franca Bettoia, Emma Danieli, Giacomo Rossi Stuart.

No one, including star Price, has ever had much nice to say about this Rome-shot first film version of Richard Matheson's classic novel *I Am Legend,* but in all fairness, it's not half bad. Vinnie is badly miscast as the heroic scientist who's seemingly the sole human survivor of a worldwide plague of vampirism, but the gloomy atmosphere of lonely, deserted streets is well caught and there are some genuinely nightmarish scenes of the vampires attacking Price's boarded-up house which were obviously one of the inspirations behind George Romero's classic *Night of the Living Dead.* Remade as *The Omega Man.*

LAST RITES
See: *Dracula's Last Rites.*

LAST SLUMBER PARTY, THE
★ United, 1987, UR, 80 min. Dir: Stephen Tyler. Cast: Jay Jensen, Nancy Meyer, Joann Whitley, Paul Ameud.

Still another psycho killer goes after still more underdressed tootsies in this totally needless *Slumber Party Massacre* rip that somewhat anticipates the later *Dr. Giggles* and has still another *Dead of Night*–inspired final twist. Not even as good as *SPM III.*

LAST VICTIM, THE
See: *Forced Entry.*

LAST WAVE, THE
★★★ Rhino, 1977, PG, 103 min. Dir: Peter Weir. Cast: Richard Chamberlain, Olivia Hammett, David Gulpilil, Frederick Parslow, Vivean Gray, Nanjiwara Amagula.

One of Aussie director Weir's best, this haunting chiller has a strong performance from Chamberlain as a Sydney lawyer who defends a group of young aborigines on a murder charge and begins having bizarre, prophetic dreams involving a huge tidal wave. Spellbinding imagery and sharp, hypnotic editing help make this one of the best, most underrated horror films of the '70s, with a devastating final shot.

LEATHERFACE: THE TEXAS CHAINSAW MASSACRE III
★★☆ RCA/Columbia, 1989, R, 80 min. Dir: Jeff Burr. Cast: Kate Hodge, Ken Foree, Bill Butler, R. A. Mihailoff, Viggo Mortensen, Joe Unger.

Not so much another sequel, this is more of a remake of the first movie, with Leatherface (Mihailoff) living with a new family of down-home cannibals and preying on a young yuppie couple traveling across Texas. Vivid char-acters and sharp dialogue contributed by scripter David Schow make this an improvement on part 2, but multiple MPAA cuts leave much of the storyline incoherent. Foree steals it as a likable survivalist whose ultimate survival makes little sense; *'Saw 2* heroine Caroline Williams has a brief cameo.

LEECH WOMAN, THE
★★☆ MCA/Universal, 1960, NR, 77 min. Dir: Edward Dein. Cast: Coleen Gray, Grant Williams, Gloria Talbott, Phillip Terry, John Van Dreelen, Estelle Hemsley, Kim Hamilton, Arthur Batanides.

Once again I buck the general consensus by admitting that I actually kinda like this last low-budget monster film from Universal Pictures. Gray is great as an aging doctor's wife given a new lease on life by an African potion derived from blood and the male pineal glands she digs out of her victims with a weird hook-ring. Without the potion, Coleen keeps aging back into a hag who gets uglier and uglier each time. It's marred somewhat by a rushed ending and too many unsympathetic characters, but still worth catching for Gray's performance alone.

LEGACY, THE
★★☆ MCA/Universal, 1978, R, 100 min. Dir: Richard Marquand. Cast: Katharine Ross, Sam Elliott, Roger Daltry, Charles Gray, Lee Montague, Hildegard Neil, Margaret Tyzack, John Standing.

Architects Ross and Elliott are stranded by a motorcycle accident at the British manor of wealthy satanist Standing, who is murdering his coven of jet-set followers in order to prepare the way for the reincarnation of his mother (Ross). Though limply plotted, this slick, silly *Omen*-like shocker has a classy cast; zesty murder scenes (flames engulf Gray; Neil is impaled on shards from a broken mirror; Who front man Daltry suffers a bungled tracheotomy), and enough early tension (not to mention a rear-view Elliott nude shot) to make it eminently watchable. TV title: *The Legacy of Maggie Walsh.*

LEGACY OF BLOOD
See: *Blood Legacy.*

LEGACY OF MAGGIE WALSH, THE
See: *The Legacy.*

LEGEND LIVES!, THE
See: *Madman.*

LEGEND OF BLOOD CASTLE, THE
★★ Interglobal, 1972, R, 82 min. Dir: Jorgé Grau. Cast. Lucia Bosé, Ewa Aulin,

Espartaco Santoni, Silvano Tranquili, Ana Furra, Franca Grey.

Dull version of the Elisabeth Bathoray legend, perhaps made to cash in on Hammer's *Countess Dracula*. Bosé shows the proper air of desperation as the middle-aged countess who tries to recapture her lost youth by bathing in virgin's blood, but there's little else in this Euro-potboiler to recommend. Sickening scenes of a pigeon attacked by a falcon and two small boys torturing a live bat with fire seem real, not faked, adding to this film's overall clammy feeling. Aka *Blood Ceremony* and *Female Butcher*.

LEGEND OF HELL HOUSE, THE

★★★ CBS/Fox, 1973, PG, 93 min.Dir: John Hough. Cast: Roddy McDowall, Pamela Franklin, Gayle Hunnicutt, Clive Revill, Roland Culver, Michael Gough.

Strong Richard Matheson–scripted adaption of his novel *Hell House* about psychic researchers investigating the "Mt. Everest of Haunted Houses," the infamous Belasco House. A scientist (Revill) believes that the force inhabiting the manse is merely unchanneled energy, while a mental medium (Franklin) is convinced that the entity is the ghost of the son of the house's debauched owner. Good acting, solid production values, and special effects, but the ending seems like a big buildup to nothing.

LEGEND OF SPIDER FOREST, THE

★☆ Media, 1971, R, 88 min. Dir: Peter Sykes. Cast: Simon Brent, Neda Arneric, Derek Newark, Sheila Allen, Gerard Heinz, Gertan Klauber.

Originally titled *Venom*, this silly Brit thriller concerns English tourist Brent's encounter with "Spider Goddess" Arneric in the forests

---

PAMELA FRANKLIN
(1949–)

Pert Pam started her career as a British child actress, most notably in '61's *The Innocents*, before coming to America and establishing herself as a scream queen with such efforts as *Necromancy* and *The Legend of Hell House* (her best). Sadly though, by the late '70s she had all but vanished from TV and film work.

The Innocents ('61), *The Nanny* ('65), *Our Mother's House* ('67), *And Soon the Darkness* ('70), *Necromancy* ('72), *The Legend of Hell House* ('73), *Satan's School for Girls* ('73), *Screamer* ('74), *Terror From Within* ('74), *Food of the Gods* ('76).

---

of Bavaria, who turns out to be the front for some inane neo-Nazi plot. This looks like a bad episode of "The Avengers" but without the charm of Patrick Macnee and Diana Rigg to carry it through.

LEGEND OF THE BAYOU

See: *Eaten Alive.*

LEGEND OF THE 7 GOLDEN VAMPIRES, THE

★★☆ Sinister Cinema, 1974, R, 88 min. Dir: Roy Ward Baker. Cast: Peter Cushing, Julie Ege, David Chiang, Robin Stewart, Shih Szu, John Forbes-Robertson.

Hammer's last Dracula movie was this oddly entertaining blend of vampires and kung fu with the count (weakly impersonated by Forbes-Robertson when Christopher Lee withdrew from the part) possessing the body of an evil Chinese high priest and heading up a deadly cult of masked, rotted vampires battled by Dr. Van Helsing (Cushing), who's on a lecture tour of China. Much better than you'd imagine; also released as *Dracula and the 7 Golden Vampires* and, in a heavily cut version, as *The Seven Brothers Meet Dracula.*

LEGEND OF THE WEREWOLF

★★ Media, 1975, PG, 86 min. Dir: Freddie Francis. Cast: Peter Cushing, Ron Moody, Hugh Griffith, David Rintoul, Lynn Dalby, Roy Castle, Renee Houston, Michael Ripper.

Fair updating of Hammer's *Curse of the Werewolf* with Rintoul as an orphan raised by wolves who becomes an assistant zoo keeper in Paris and begins a series of lycanthropic killings targeting the patrons of prostitute Dalby, whom he loves. Good acting and storyline go unsupported by cheap-looking production values and a never-convincing period setting.

LEGEND OF THE WOLF WOMAN

★ United, 1976, R, 84 min. Dir: Rino [Salvatore] di Silvestro. Cast: Annik Borel, Frederick Stafford, Dagmar Lassander, Renato Rossini.

Ludicrous Spanish pic (originally *La Lupa Mannera: Wolf Woman* with Borel as Daniela: a buxom babe whose voracious sexual appetite causes her to become a werewolf. Why? I don't know. Lots of low-grade laughs. Aka *She Wolf.*

LEGEND OF WITCH HOLLOW, THE

See: *The Witchmaker.*

LEONOR

★★ CBS/Fox, 1975, R, 90 min. Dir: Juan Buñuel. Cast: Liv Ullmann, Michel Piccoli, Ornella Mutti, Antonio Ferrandis.

Ullmann, of all people, stars as a 14th-century noblewoman whose satanic pact allows her to rise from her crypt after her death to plague husband Piccoli and new bride Mutti. This baroque oddity, directed by the son of Spanish cinema giant Luis Buñuel, seems a strange vehicle indeed for the queen of Swedish angst flicks. I guess Barbara Steele was out of town that week.

LEOPARD MAN, THE
★★★ Turner, 1943, NR, 66 min.
Dir: Jacques Tourneur. Cast: Dennis O'Keefe, Margo, Jean Brooks, Isabel Jewell, James Bell, Margaret Landry, Tula Parma, Abner Biberman.

Sharp adaptation of Cornell Woolrich's seminal stalker novel *Black Alibi* about a psycho killer who uses an escaped panther as cover for a series of murders in a tiny New Mexico village. The solid Val Lewton production is distinguished by smart characterization and classic scare scenes. Those familiar with the novel will note that in the film another character entirely is revealed as the surprise killer.

LEPRECHAUN
★ Vidmark, 1993, R, 92 min.
Dir: Mark Jones. Cast: Warwick Davis, Jennifer Aniston, Ken Olandt, Mark Holton, Robert Gorman, John Sanderford.

The luck of the Irish really ran out when they made this pathetic flick about a diminutive demon from the Emerald Isle (Davis) who's after the jarheads he thinks stole his pot o' gold. Davis is amusing, but everything else about this nonsensical cross between *Child's Play* and *Finian's Rainbow* is too annoying to be funny. This was followed by a sequel(!!!): *Leprechaun II: Bride of Leprechaun.* "I'm the Leprechaun, and I want me pot o' gold!"

LESBIAN TWINS
See: *The Virgin Witch.*

LET'S SCARE JESSICA TO DEATH
★★★ Paramount, 1971, PG, 88 min.
Dir: John Hancock. Cast: Zohra Lampert, Barton Heyman, Mariclare Costello, Kevin O'Connor, Gretchen Corbett, Alan Manson.

Interesting low-key tale about a fragile ex-mental patient (the stunning Lampert) who moves with her musician husband into a Connecticut farmhouse that she comes to believe is haunted by a female vampire. Moody and deliberately paced, with lots of marvelous little details in both atmosphere and plot (Jessica makes tracings of gravemarkers she decorates her bedroom with, while her husband drives a hearse), this is far superior to most other low-budget horrors being made at the same time. Only the generic multiple-shock ending comes as a letdown.

LEVIATHAN
★★☆ MGM/UA, 1989, R, 97 min.
Dir: George Pan Cosmatos. Cast: Peter Weller, Richard Crenna, Amanda Pays, Daniel Stern, Lisa Eilbacher, Ernie Hudson, Hector Elizondo, Meg Foster.

Although still no great shakes, this is probably the best of the half-dozen "terror in the deep" underwater horror/sci-fi features released in '89. Deep-sea miners discover a derelict Russian sub called *Leviathan,* whose contaminated vodka supply begins mutating the miners, as it did the Russian crew, into hideous creatures. No surprises but a good cast and strong production values. Amazingly, both this and the similar *Deepstar Six* sport exactly the same surprise endings. Coincidence?

LIES
★★★ Key, 1983, R, 93 min.
Dirs: Ken and Jim Wheat. Cast: Ann Dusenberry, Bruce Davison, Clu Gulager, Gail Strickland, Terence Knox, Bert Remsen, Dick Miller, Douglas Leonard.

Underrated mystery-horror with the always terrific Dusenberry as an actress fired from a cheap slasher film for not exposing her breasts. ("I'm an actress, *not* a stripper," she tells producer Miller. "What's with this actress crap?" the great one retorts. "This is a fuckin' horror film!") She is hired to star in a movie about a mad heiress and ends up involved in an elaborate plot to steal an inheritance. Plot twists predating both *Body Double* and *Dead of Winter* and an all-pro cast of underappreciated thesps make this a truly enjoyable little thriller. Best scene: the hanging in the elevator shaft.

LIFE FOR A LIFE, A
See: *The Witching.*

LIFEFORCE
★★ Vestron, 1985, R, 101 min. Dir: Tobe Hooper.
Cast: Steve Railsback, Peter Firth, Frank Finlay, Mathilda May, Patrick Stewart, Michael Gothard.

Murky mix of horror and sci-fi derived from Colin Wilson's novel *Space Vampires* (also the shooting title). Railsback heads an expedition to explore Halley's Comet and discovers a derelict spacecraft in the comet's tail containing nude alien vampires (headed by gorgeous May) who suck the life force, not the blood, of

A young Jodie Foster stars as The Little Girl Who Lives Down the Lane *(1976).*

their victims. A watchable but ridiculous movie that throws everything but the kitchen sink into its bizarre plot.

LIFT, THE
★★☆ Media, 1983, R, 98 min.
Dir: Dick Maas. Cast: Huub Stapel, Willeke Van Ammeroog, Josine Van Dalsum, Hans Veerman, Ab Alsopoel, Hans Dagelet.

A horror movie about a killer elevator? Sounds dumb, but this tongue-in-cheek Dutch thriller works pretty well. When people in a high-rise office tower begin meeting strange, violent ends in a computerized lift, a company repairman and a pretty reporter investigate, discovering that the elevator was programmed by a mad scientist and has living human cells as a part of its mechanical makeup. Rarely plausible and atrociously dubbed, but some of the scenes work up some nice, suspenseful moments, and the rich color photography gives the film a fun, comic-book feel.

LINK
★☆ HBO, 1986, R, 103 min. Dir: Richard Franklin. Cast: Terence Stamp, Elisabeth Shue, Steven Pinner, Richard Garnett, David O'Hara, Kevin Lloyd.

Fizzled thriller that tries to be a simian version of *The Birds.* Shue is the pretty student-assistant of mad primotogist Stamp, whose experiments at increasing the intelligence of chimpanzees turns his chief subject, called Link, into a superior-minded killer. No suspense and few thrills, this is enlivened only by the antics of the Ray Berwick–trained chimps, with Link played by an orangutan in unconvincing chimp makeup. Even *The Ape Man* is more fun than this.

LISA
★★ MGM/UA, 1989, PG-13, 91 min. Dir: Gary Sherman. Cast: Cheryl Ladd, Staci Keanan, D. W. Moffett, Tanya Fenmore, Jeffrey Tambor, Julie Cobb.

Repressed by a too-strict mom, 14-year-old Lisa (Keanan) plays phone games by anonymously calling up guys she thinks are cute. Inadvertently she dials a woman-stalking psycho known as the "Candlelight Killer" and places her mom (Ladd) in terrible danger. Modest updating of William Castle's *I Saw What You Did,* with good playing and a haunting saxophone score, but plotted too obviously to offer up much suspense.

LISA AND THE DEVIL
See: *The House of Exorcism.*

LISA, LISA
See: *The California Axe Massacre.*

LITTLE GIRL WHO LIVES DOWN THE LANE, THE
★★★ Vestron, 1976, PG, 91 min.
Dir: Nicholas Gessner. Cast: Jodie Foster, Martin Sheen, Alexis Smith, Scott Jacoby, Mort Shuman.

Enchanting, low-key chiller with Foster as a fiercely independent 13-year-old living alone in a small Canadian town who masks the deaths of her parents and kills anyone who attempts to disrupt her solitary lifestyle. Despite her difficult role, Jodie always engages sympathy, as does Jacoby as the lame teenage magician who helps her in her plan, while Smith as an elitist bitch and Sheen as her child-molester son are effectively villainous. Sharp little thriller.

LITTLE MONSTER
★★ Vestron, 1989, PG, 100 min.
Dir: Richard Alan Greenberg. Cast: Brad Savage, Howie Mandel, Daniel Stern, Margaret Whitton,

Ben Savage, Rick Ducommun, Amber Barretto, Frank Whaley.

Weak kid-oriented horror-comedy in the *Beetlejuice* mode with Savage as a boy who finds a weird but friendly monster (Mandel, in silly makeup) living under his bed. Muddled and uninvolving but reasonably well made, with a manic Mandel and cutesy-pie Savage.

LITTLE SHOP OF HORRORS, THE
★★★☆ Goodtimes, 1960, NR, 70 min.
Dir: Roger Corman. Cast: Jonathan Haze, Jackie Joseph, Mel Welles, Dick Miller, Myrtle Vail, Jack Nicholson.

The best two-day movie ever made! One rainy weekend Corman and company decided to slap together this robust black comedy–monster movie, and the result is one of the funniest movies ever made. Haze is Seymour Krelboined, the doltish apprentice in a skid-row flower shop ("Lots plants—cheap!" reads a sign), who creates a hybrid plant from a venus fly-trap. Unfortunately, "Audrey Junior" (named for girlfriend Joseph) develops a taste for human blood ("Feed me!" it demands), leading poor Seymour into a string of klutzy murders. Great dialogue ("You're another Luther Glendale!" coos an impressed Joseph while shop owner Welles, when asked if "Audrey Junior" has a scientific name, comments, "Yes, of course, but who could denounce it?") is provided by scripter Charles B. Griffith, and classic performances are contributed by Welles, Miller (as a flower-eating customer), and Nicholson in a legendary cameo as masochistic dental patient Wilbur Force ("Oh, God!" he cries when Haze, disguised as a dentist, stops drilling, "don't stop now!"). A great, incredibly cheap classic later adapted into the off-Broadway musical, which itself was filmed in 1986. Aka *The Passionate People Eater.*

LITTLE SHOP OF HORRORS, THE
★★☆ Warner, 1986, PG-13, 92 min.
Dir: Frank Oz. Cast: Rick Moranis, Ellen Greene, Steve Martin, Vincent Gardenia, Bill Murray, John Candy, Jim Belushi, voice of Levi Stubbs.

An elaborate, rather overblown film version of the off-Broadway musical version of the 1960 classic, with Moranis as skid-row flower shop schnook Seymour who develops a new breed of flesh-and-blood-devouring plant. Lots of big-star cameos (Martin and Murray are hilarious as a sadistic dentist and his pain-loving patient), but Greene steals it hands down as sweet, squeaky-voiced Audrey. Enjoyable, but overloaded with too many state-of-the-art spe-

cial FX and lacking a hard edge in its more good-natured inspiration—though this actually substituted a last-minute happy ending in place of the play's more downbeat conclusion.

LIVER EATERS, THE
See: *Spider Baby.*

LIVING COFFIN, THE
★☆ Sinister Cinema, 1958, NR, 72 min.
Dir: Fernando Medez. Cast: Gaston Santos, Maria Duval, Pedro d'Aquillon, Hortensia Santovena.

A Mexican *Premature Burial* with Santovena as an old lady who is obsessed with being buried alive and, of course, is, returning from the grave for the usual revenge. More low-grade south-of-the-border silliness.

LIVING DEAD, THE
See: *Cult of the Damned.*

LIVING DEAD AT MANCHESTER MORGUE, THE
★★★ AEE, 1974, R, 86 min. Dir: Jorgé Grau.
Cast: Arthur Kennedy, Ray Lovelock, Christine Galbo, Aldo Massasso.

This is a cut version of Spanish director Grau's underrated shot-in-Britain *Night of the Living Dead* cash-in, *Non Si Seve Profanare ol Sonne die Morte: Let Sleeping Corpses Lie,* first released in the U.S. as *Don't Open the Window.* An experimental sound wave machine being used to fight an insect infestation in rural England accidentally revives the recently deceased as flesh-lusting ghouls, although most of their subsequent mayhem is blamed by boneheaded Irish cop Kennedy on counter-culture types Lovelock and Galbo. Grau brilliantly contrasts the lushly green English countryside with the gory activities of the walking dead (though the two most infamous scenes—involving a disemboweled policeman and a nurse whose breast is torn off—have been eliminated from this print). There's an unsettling use of stereophonic sound, giving this an impact few of the innumerable post–*Dawn of the Dead* zombie flicks would attain. Aka *Breakfast at Manchester Morgue.*

LIVING HEAD, THE
★★ Sinister Cinema, 1961, NR, 75 min.
Dir: Chano Ureta. Cast: Ana Luisa Peluffo, Abel Salazar, German Robles, Antonio Raxell.

The decapitated head of an ancient Aztec ruler and his mummified high priest are brought to Mexico City, where the head commands the mummy to begin killing off the archeologists who brought them there. Needlessly talky addition to the lengthy roster of Mexi-monster films; some interesting scenes but dubbing ruins most of it.

LOCK YOUR DOORS
See: *The Ape Man.*

LODGER, THE
★★★ Sinister Cinema, 1926, NR, 73 min. Dir: Alfred Hitchcock. Cast: Ivor Novello, June, Marie Ault, Arthur Chesney, Malcolm Keen.

Hitchcock's first suspense movie, this atmospheric adaptation of the Marie Belloc-Lowndes novel features Novello as the new boarder in the home of a couple whose daughter's jealous boyfriend suspects of being a mass murderer known as the "Avenger." Great scenes include a shot up through a floor to show Novello pacing above and an exciting final chase, but the contrived happy ending (forced on Hitch by the studio, just as in *Suspicion* 15 years later) doesn't ring true. Aka *The Lodger: A Story of the London Fog.*

LODGER: A STORY OF THE LONDON FOG, THE
See: *The Lodger.*

LONELY HEARTS KILLERS, THE
See: *The Honeymoon Killers.*

LONE WOLF
★★ Prism, 1988, R, 97 min. Dir: John Callas. Cast: Dyann Brown, Kevin Hart, Jamie Newcomb, Anne Douglas, Jeff Hart, Tom Henry.

Direct-to-video werewolf chiller obviously inspired by *Silver Bullet,* about a bunch of teenagers trying to ascertain the identity of the brutal full-moon murderer plaguing their small town. Not as good as the same production team's *Mind Killer* but better than most of those awful *Howling* sequels, with good makeup and effective humor and shocks.

LONG DARK NIGHT, THE
See: *The Pack.*

LONG DARK NIGHT, THE
See: *Blind Fear.*

LONG HAIR OF DEATH, THE
★★★ Sinister Cinema, 1964, NR, 94 min. Dir: Anthony Dawson [Antonio Margheriti]. Cast: Barbara Steele, Giorgio Ardisson, Halina Zalewska, Robert Rains, Jean Rafferty, Laureen Nuyan.

Steele's splendid presence dominates this obscure Euro-shocker about a woman who returns from the grave both to avenge her death at the hands of a sadistic count and to save her sister from a similiar fate. Strong photography full of arresting images and an ironic ending that predates that of *The Wicker Man* add to the atmosphere.

LONG NIGHT OF TERROR, THE
See: *Castle of Blood.*

LONG WEEKEND
★★☆ Media, 1977, NR, 95 min. Dir: Colin Eggleston. Cast: John Hargreaves, Briony Behets, Mike McEwen, Michael Atkins.

This offbeat Australian thriller is like a more serious version of *Frogs.* Bickering couple Hargreaves and Behets spend a weekend in the wilderness and, after destroying much of their environment, are destroyed themselves when nature strikes back. Sometimes this is unintentionally funny, but it's legitimately scary and suspenseful as well.

LOOKER
★★ Warner, 1981, PG, 90 min. Dir: Michael Crichton. Cast: Albert Finney, Susan Dey, James Coburn, Leigh Taylor-Young, Dorian Harewood, Tim Rossovich, Darryl Hickman, Kathryn Witt.

Beverly Hills plastic surgeon Finney discovers that several of his patients, all beautiful models, have been murdered and replaced by computer-generated clones being used for subliminal TV advertising. This very silly sci-fi/horror thriller started out as a comedy and should have stayed that way; halfway through production it was switched to a straight thriller, but there are few thrills, though plenty of laughs, thanks to a confusing story and an embarrassed-looking cast. Some nice sets, though.

LORELEI'S GRASP, THE
See: *When the Screaming Stops!*

LOST BOYS, THE
★★☆ Warner, 1987, R, 97 min. Dir: Joel Schumacher. Cast: Jason Patric, Corey Haim, Jami Gertz, Kiefer Sutherland, Dianne Wiest, Edward Herrmann, Corey Feldman, Barnard Hughes.

Moderately successful vampire variation on *Peter Pan* about a band of teen vampires who won't grow up and try to convert hunky Patric to their ageless click. Lots of glitz and flash, lots of handsome young performers, and lots of loud rock music do not a good movie necessarily make. This one has its moments (including a slam-bang climax) but on the whole these MTVampires lack, eh, bite.

LOST CONTINENT, THE
★★ Sinister Cinema, 1951, NR, 83 min.
Dir: Sam Newfield. Cast: Cesar Romero, Hillary Brooke, Hugh Beaumont, John Hoyt, Whit Bissell, Acquanetta, Chick Chandler, Sid Melton.

A routine *Lost World*–type movie about a downed atomic rocket traced to a mysterious mountain inhabited by prehistoric beasts, this has an exceptional B cast (though the ladies are wasted in nonparticipatory roles). The effects by Augie Lohman are only so-so; the dinosaur sequences are tinted green.

LOST PLATOON
★ AIP, 1988, R, 83 min. Dir: David A. Prior.
Cast: David Parry, William Knight, Stephen Quadros, Sean Heyman, Michael Wayne, Michiko.

I can hear the producer now: "*Platoon* was a big hit, right? *The Lost Boys* was a big hit too, right? Well, why not *combine* the two? A Vietnam vampire movie! Think of it!" Then again, don't. Another dumbbell direct-to-vid fang opera without even its unusual setting to recommend it.

LOST WORLD, THE
★★★ Goodtimes, 1925, NR, 60 min. Dirs: Harry O. Hoyt, William Dowling. Cast: Wallace Beery, Bessie Love, Lewis Stone, Lloyd Hughes, Arthur Hoyt, Bull Montana, Alma Bennett, Finch Smiles.

Available today only in this heavily cut version (the original ran 108 minutes), this silent precursor to *King Kong* is based on the Arthur Conan Doyle story of Professor Challenger's (Beery) discovery of a South American plateau inhabited by prehistoric beasts. The non-monster footage is awkwardly acted and directed, but Willis O'Brien's special effects are still impressive for their times—especially during the escaped brontosaur's climactic rampage through the streets of London. Remade in 1960 and 1993.

LOVE AT FIRST BITE
★★☆ Orion, 1979, PG, 96 min. Dir: Stan Dragoti.
Cast: George Hamilton, Susan Saint James, Richard Benjamin, Arte Johnson, Dick Shawn, Sherman Hemsley, Isabel Sanford, Eric Laneuville.

Silly but popular Dracula spoof with Hamilton surprisingly good in a film-long Lugosi imitation as a love-smitten count who comes to New York City to search out the fashion model he has fallen in love with. Johnson (as Renfield) is great and there are some very funny moments ("What do you want from him, blood?"), but some unfortunate racist and sexist sterotypes cheapen the overall effectiveness.

LOVE AT STAKE
★★☆ Nelson, 1988, R, 86 min.
Dir: John Moffitt. Cast: Barbara Carrera, Patrick Cassidy, Kelly Preston, Bud Cort, Dave Thomas, Stuart Pankin, Georgia Brown, Anne Ramsey.

Spoof of Salem witch trials with Carrera as a real witch who wreaks havoc while the dim-witted locals burn innocents under the auspices of greedy mayor Thomas and judge Pankin, who are after their victims' land. Surprisingly funny, Mel Brooks–like comedy with sexy Carrera in good form and Thomas and Pankin often very amusing; the one-joke story drags a bit, though. Filmed as *Burnin' Love.*

LOVE EXORCIST, THE
See: *Daddy's Deadly Darling.*

LOVE FROM A STRANGER
★★☆ Sinister Cinema, 1937, NR, 90 min.
Dir: Rowland V. Lee. Cast: Basil Rathbone, Ann Harding, Binnie Hale, Bruce Seton, Bryan Powley, Joan Hickson.

Rathbone's floridly over-the-top performance distinguishes this Agatha Christie thriller about a pretty girl (Harding) who wins a fortune and is rushed into marriage by suave Basil who, not surprisingly, turns out to be a maniac. Static early Brit shocker is not without interest; Rathbone and director Lee reteamed two years later for *Son of Frankenstein.*

LOVE FROM A STRANGER
★★ Nelson, 1947, NR, 81 min. Dir: Richard Whorf.
Cast: Sylvia Sidney, John Hodiak, Ann Richards, John Howard, Isobel Elsom, Philip Tonge.

Routine remake with the always interesting Sidney as the lady who fears that her perfect new hubby (Hodiak) is a psycho who's planning to kill her and bury her in the basement. Well acted but slow; might've worked better (and probably did) as a half-hour episode of "Alfred Hitchcock Presents."

LOVE LIFE OF THE INVISIBLE MAN
See: *The Invisible Dead.*

LOVE MANIAC
See: *The Blood of Ghastly Horror.*

LOVE ME DEADLY
★★ Video Gems, 1972, R, 93 min.
Dir: Jacques le Certe. Cast: Mary Wilcox, Lyle Waggoner, Christopher Stone, Timothy Scott.

This really sick flick features the bodacious Wilcox as a voluptuous necrophilic babe who falls for handsome lunk Waggoner (the old Carol Burnett co-star and *Playgirl*'s first nude celeb) and becomes involved in the activities of a bisexual satanist/mortician who embalms people alive. Has the look and feel of a typical early '70s grind-house item but with the sort of off-the-wall touches (like a frontally nude male prostitute seduced by the mortician onto an embalming table a full decade before a very similiar heterosexual encounter in *Re-Animator*) you don't usually find in these cheap creepers.

LOVERS BEYOND THE TOMB
See: *Nightmare Castle.*

LOVE TRAP
See: *Curse of the Black Widow.*

LUCIFER PROJECT, THE
See: *Barracuda.*

LUCIFER RIG, THE
See: *The Intruder Within.*

LUCKY STIFF
★★☆ RCA/Columbia, 1988, R, 82 min.
Dir: Anthony Perkins. Cast: Joe Alaskey, Donna Dixon, Jeff Kober, Morgan Sheppard, Barbara Howard, Charles Frank, Leigh McCloskey, Fran Ryan.

Amusing black comedy with Alaskey as a nice fat guy who can't understand what knockout Dixon sees in him—that is, until she takes him home to meet her family of hillbilly cannibals. Uneven, but full of funny gags and a likable cast going full tilt. Filmed as *Mr. Christmas Dinner.*

LURKERS
☆ Media, 1987, R, 90 min.
Dir: Roberta Findlay. Cast: Christine Moore, Gary Warner, Marina Taylor, Carissa Channing.

Another junky Findlay flick (and maybe her worst) with Moore as a girl haunted by her mom's death and various evil spirits out to claim her for satan. Badly acted, written, and directed, with an ending that is about 90 minutes too far from the beginning.

LUST FOR A VAMPIRE
★★☆ Republic, 1971, R, 91 min.
Dir: Jimmy Sangster. Cast: Ralph Bates, Barbara Jefford, Suzanna Leigh, Michael Johnson, Yutte Stensgaard, Mike Raven.

Lesbian vampire Mircalla Karnstein (Danish dish Stensgaard) is revived by the blood of a peasant girl and goes on a rampage at a girls' finishing school next door to her ruined family estate. This colorful, somewhat contrived sequel to *The Vampire Lovers* has lots of need-

lessly goofy touches (like a pop song called "Strange Love" droning on during a sex scene) but has a spirited cast and clever ending to recommend it. TV title: *To Love a Vampire.*

LUST OF THE VAMPIRE
See: *The Devil's Commandment.*

LYCANTHROPUS
See: *Werewolf in a Girls Dormitory.*

MACABRA
See: *Demonoid.*

MACABRE
See: *Frozen Terror.*

MACABRE SERENADE
See: *Dance of Death.*

MAD BUTCHER, THE
★☆ Magnum, 1971, R, 81 min.
Dir: John [Guido] Zurli. Cast: Victor Buono, Brad Harris, Karin Field, Franca Polcelli.

Buono is bueno in this otherwise tacky Euro-shocker about an obese Viennese butcher who murders his wife, brother-in-law, and a local prostitute and then grinds them into sausages. An uncomfortable blend of black comedy and straight horror, this has surprisingly little blood but plenty of female skin. Original title: *Il Stranglatore de Vienna: The Strangler of Vienna* and aka *Meat is Meat.*

MAD DOCTOR OF BLOOD ISLAND, THE
★☆ Magnum, 1969, R, 88 min.
Dirs: Gerardo de Leon, Eddie Romero. Cast: John Ashley, Angelique Pettyjohn, Ronald Remy, Alicia Alonso, Ronaldo Valdez, Tony Edmunds.

This zoom-happy sequel to *Brides of the Beast* has more nasty doings on Blood Island, this time under the auspices of evil Dr. Lorca (Remy), who turns a local landowner into the hideous Chlorophyll Monster, who runs around dismembering nude Filipino chicks. Ashley plays a different character than he did in *Brides* but the result is the same; Pettyjohn gets some practice for her later nosedive into porn (as Heaven St. John) by letting John undress and paw her in a cave. All this sex really gets in the way of the lurching direction and phony gore, a tactic reversed in the sequel, *Beast of Blood*. TV title: *Tomb of the Living Dead*.

MADHOUSE

★★★ HBO, 1974, PG, 91 min. Dir: Jim Clark. Cast: Vincent Price, Peter Cushing, Robert Quarry, Adrienne Corri, Natasha Pyne, Linda Hayden.

Price's *Sunset Boulevard* casts him as an aging horror star (is this type casting, or what?) whose attempted comeback on English TV is thwarted by a skull-masked psycho killing folks in manners based on Price's old "Dr. Death" movies. Not up to either *The Abominable Dr. Phibes* or *Theatre of Blood*, but this loose adaptation of Angus Hall's novel *Devilday* has a fine cast, a couple of good scares, lots of film clips from the AIP Poe series to represent the fictional "Dr. Death" movies, and a totally off-the-wall ending. Filmed as *The Revenge of Dr. Death*.

MADHOUSE

★★ Virgin Vision, 1981, R, 92 min. Dir: Ovidio G. Assotitis. Cast: Trish Everly, Dennis Robertson, Michael Macrae, Richard Baker.

Routine slasher filmed by Italians in Savannah, Georgia, about a pretty teacher (Tina Louise lookalike Everly) who fears that her mad, disfigured twin sister has escaped from the asylum and is on a killing spree. Good-looking but derivative, with characters so unpleasant and a maniac whose motivation is so absurd that it's hard to care.

MADHOUSE MANSION

★★☆ Continental, 1974, PG, 86 min. Dir: Stephen Weeks. Cast: Marianne Faithfull, Larry Dann, Murray Melvin, Vivian Mackerall, Penelope Keith, Barbara Shelley.

An extremely odd but interesting India-shot haunted house film about three old college friends investigating an old manor house haunted by Edwardian spirits caught in a time warp and a child's doll with homicidal tendencies. After a strained first half of bungled comedy, this settles down into a tense little exercise in sustained chills with a good performance by Faithfull and a very creepy ending. Original title: *Ghost Story*.

MAD LOVE

★★★ MGM/UA, 1935, NR, 67 min. Dir: Karl Freund. Cast: Peter Lorre, Colin Clive, Frances Drake, Ted Healy, Sara Haden, Edward Brophy.

PETER LORRE
(1904–1964)

One of the great movie villains of the '30s and '40s, Lorre (born in Hungary as Laszlo Lowenstein) was a popular stage actor in Berlin when he made his sensational screen debut as the pathetic child murderer in Fritz Lang's *M*. After working for Alfred Hitchcock in England, Lorre came to the States, where he made his Hollywood debut in *Mad Love* and subsequently became a popular member of the Warner Brothers stock company, often teamed with Sidney Greenstreet in a variety of mysteries and melodramas. In the '60s a more rotund Peter made a minor comeback in several Roger Corman flicks.

M ('30), *Mad Love* ('35), *Stranger on the Third Floor* ('40), *You'll Find Out* ('40), *The Face Behind the Mask* ('41), *Invisible Agent* ('42), *The Boogie Man Will Get You* ('42), *The Beast With Five Fingers* ('46), *Tales of Terror* ('62), *The Raven* ('63), *The Comedy of Terrors* ('64)

Impressive version of Maurice Renard's *The Hands of Orlac* (this film's British title). Lorre is great in his first American role as bald, glow-eyed Dr. Gogol, a famed surgeon who replaces the mangled hands of pianist Orlac (Clive) with those of executed knife murderer Brophy in a bizarre plan to win the love of Orlac's actress wife (Drake). Slick MGM production values, creative direction and photography, and a splendid cast make this a top-notch mad doctor flick. Remade as *The Hands of Orlac* and *Hands of a Stranger*.

MADMAN

★☆ HBO, 1982, R, 88 min. Dir: Joe Giannone. Cast: Alexis Dubin [Gaylen Ross], Tony Fish, Harriet Bass, Seth Jones, Jan Claire, Alex Murphy.

Blatant *Friday the 13th* rip-off with another summer camp stalker after another bunch of boring teen counselors he chops up in a variety of ways. Giannone manages some impressive-looking setups, but an unimaginative script and mostly amateurish acting keep this film entrenched with all the dozens of other slasher also-rans. Also released as *The Legend Lives*, *Madman Marz*, and *Campfire Tale*.

MADMAN MARZ

See: *Madman*.

MADMEN OF MANDORAS
See: *They Saved Hitler's Brain.*

MAD MONSTER, THE
★★ Sinister Cinema, 1942, NR, 76 min.
Dir: Sam Newfield. Cast: George Zucco,
Anne Nagel, Johnny Downs Glenn Strange.

Zucco flares his nostrils once again as Dr.
Lorenzo Cameron, a discredited scientist who
proves his claim that blood can be transfused
between different species by injecting half-wit
handyman Strange with wolf's blood; the
result is a werewolf George uses to dispatch
his scientific adversaries. Zucco is always fun
in this sort of role and there's some good
misty atmosphere on hand, but, as usual with
these PRC cheapies, the supporting cast, plotting, and direction are all barely adequate at
best.

MAFU CAGE, THE
See: *My Sister, My Love.*

MAGIC
★★ Embassy, 1978, R, 106 min.
Dir: Richard Attenborough. Cast: Anthony Hopkins,
Ann-Margret, Burgess Meredith, Ed Lauter,
David Ogden Stiers, Jerry Hauser.

There's nothing particularly magical about
this predictable ventriloquist-and-his-dummy
thriller with Hopkins as a timid voice throw-
er–magician who lives vicariously through his
foul-mouthed puppet who may or may not be
committing murders. Hopkins and Ann-Margret (as a hometown girl he had a hopeless
crush on in high school) are good and Meredith even better as Hopkins' sagacious manager, but this routine version of William Goldman's novel (most of which was told from the
dummy's point-of-view!) never really takes
off. Memorable harmonica-dominated score
by Jerry Goldsmith, though.

MAJORETTES, THE
★☆ Vestron, 1987, R, 93 min.
Dir: Bill Hinzman. Cast: Kevin Kindlin,
Terrie Godfrey, Mark V. Jericky, Sueanne Seamens,
Denise Holt, Carl Hetrick.

A hooded killer is hacking high school
majorettes in this lackluster slasher filmed in
Pittsburgh by several *Night of the Living Dead*
veterans, including director Hinzman (who
played the graveyard zombie) and writer John
Russo, who scripted from his own novel.
Badly acted and poorly paced, this switches
gears every 15 minutes or so and lacks a
strong, central heroine figure. The 93 minutes
seem more like 193.

MAKE THEM DIE SLOWLY
★★☆ Thrillervideo, 1980, UR, 92 min.
Dir: Umberto Lenzi. Cast: John Morghen, Lorianne
de Selle, Brian Redford, Zora Kerowa, Robert
Kerman, Richard Bolla.

One of the most infamous titles of all time, this
is the best known of the Italian jungle-cannibal
subgenre and about as violent a movie as
you're ever gonna see. Students de Selle, Redford, and Kerowa are in the Colombian jungles to disprove the theory of cannibalism
amongst the locals, who are befriended by
cruel drug dealer Morghen. When he rapes
and murders a native girl her tribe seeks
revenge by capturing the outsiders and torturing, killing, and eating them. Only Lorianne
survives. Although not as bad as it's supposed
to be, with a genuine feeling of fear and
unease, it's the gore you've come to see and
gore you get—everything from impaled
breasts to castration to brain eating and
more—all presented in a plain, uncompromising manner that makes Herschell Gordon
Lewis look like George Cukor. Original title:
Cannibal Ferox.

MAKING CONTACT
★☆ Starmaker, 1985, PG, 79 min.
Dir: Roland Emmerich. Cast: Joshua Morrell,
Eva Kryll, Tammy Shields, Jan Zierold,
Barbara Klein, Jerry Hall.

Overly derivative German shocker in which a
young boy obsessed by the death of his father
falls under the influence of a possessed ventriloquist's dummy—which looks alarmingly
like Ronald Reagan! Ideas are pinched liberal-
ly from *Poltergeist, Dead of Night, Psycho, E.T.,*
and a host of others, while the score sounds
like ersatz John Williams. Made interesting
only by some good FX and that creepy little
gipper devil doll. Original title: *Joey.*

MAKO: JAWS OF DEATH
See: *Jaws of Death.*

MALEDICTION, THE
See: *Satan's Princess.*

MAMA DRACULA
★ TWE, 1980, R, 91 min. Dir: Boris Szulzinger.
Cast: Louise Fletcher, Maria Schneider, Marc-Henri
Wajnberg, Alexander Wajnberg, Jimmy Shuman,
Jess Hahn.

Lame vampire comedy with Fletcher (doing a
bad Lugosi accent) as the countess who stays
forever young by bathing in the blood of virgins. Sounds funny so far, right? Well made
but utterly lacking in entertainment value, this

makes *Love at First Bite* look like *The Fearless Vampire Killers.*

MAN AND HIS MATE

See: *One Million B.C.*

MAN AND THE MONSTER, THE

★★ Sinister Cinema, 1958, NR, 72 min.
Dir: Rapheal Baledon. Cast: Abel Salazar, Martha Roth, Enrique Rambel, Ofelia Guilman.

A pianist sells his soul to the devil for the ability to play like a concert master. Unfortunately, every time he plays, he transforms into a hairy monster. A Carnegie Hall booking could be tough. Like most Mexican horror films, this takes real dedication to sit through. There's a great, scary beginning, but things sort of peter out later on.

MAN BEAST

★★ Rhino, 1956, NR, 72 min.
Dir: Jerry Warren. Cast: Rock Madison, Virginia Maynor, Tom Maruzzi, Lloyd Nelson, George Skaff.

This is unusual: a Jerry Warren film without any Mexican movie stock footage! And it's actually fairly interesting! An expedition to the Himalayas not only encounters the infamous abominable snowman but also discovers that one of its members is a half-breed yeti whose mother was kidnapped by the creatures many years before. Atmospheric night photography and an air of eerie desolation make this easily Warren's most accomplished picture. Originally co-billed with *Godzilla, King of the Monsters.*

MANHATTAN BABY

★★ Lightning, 1983, R, 87 min.
Dir: Lucio Fulci. Cast: Christopher Connelly, Martha Taylor, Brigitta Boccole, Giovanni Frezza, Cinzia De Ponti, Laurence Welles.

The daughter of an American Egyptologist falls under the influence of a strange, eye-embossed amulet that can open the gateway into a supernatural netherworld. One of Fulci's most restrained, and dull, efforts, this has some nice photography and an effective scene where a man is clawed to death by stuffed birds suddenly come to life, but it has too many coy in-jokes (like a babysitter named Jamie Lee) and really stints on the red stuff when compared to some of the earlier flicks from the grand old man of Italian splatter. Original title: *L'Occio del Male: The Evil Eye* and aka *The Possessed* and *Eye of the Evil Dead.*

MANIA

★★★ Goodtimes, 1960, NR, 91 min.
Dir: John Gilling. Cast: Peter Cushing, Donald

DONALD PLEASENCE
(1919–)

A bald Brit character actor, Pleasence became a somewhat reluctant horror star in the '70s and by the '80s was firmly established as the master of conveying bug-eyed neurosis, even in his heroic parts! Horror fans know him best as Dr. Sam Loomis, the monomaniacal Michael Myers hunter in the *Halloween* series.

Mania ('60), *Circus of Horror* ('60), *The Hands of Orlac* ('61), *No Place Like Homicide* ('61), *Eye of the Devil* ('67), *Raw Meat* ('72), *Tales That Witness Madness* ('73), *Dr. Jekyll and Mr. Hyde* ('73), *From Beyond the Grave* ('74), *The Mutations* ('74), *Escape From Witch Mountain* ('75), *The Devil Within Her* ('75), *Land of the Minotaur* ('76), *The Uncanny* ('77), *Night Creature* ('78), *The Dark Secret of Harvest Home* (narrator, '78), *Halloween* ('78), *Dracula* ('79), *The Monster Club* ('81), *Halloween II* ('81), *Alone in the Dark* ('82), *The Devonsville Terror* ('83), *Terror in the Aisles* ('84), *Creepers* ('85), *Nothing Underneath* ('86), *Spectres* ('87), *Prince of Darkness* ('87), *Phantom of Death* ('87), *Halloween 4: The Return of Michael Myers* ('88), *Buried Alive* ('88), *Nosferatu in Venice* ('89), *Halloween 5: The Revenge of Michael Myers* ('89), *Ten Little Indians* ('89), *The House of Usher* ('89), *Shadows and Fog* ('92).

Pleasence, June Laverick, Dermot Walsh, George Rose, Billie Whitelaw, John Cairney, Renee Houston.

Originally released as *The Flesh and the Fiends,* this gritty low-budget version of the Burke and Hare story works quite well, thanks to Cushing's incisive performance as Dr. Knox, the early 19th-century Edinburgh surgeon who employs the murderous body snatchers as "specimen" gatherers for his lectures. Good atmosphere, with settings and photography often recalling Hogarth engravings. Aka *The Fiendish Ghouls* and *Psycho-Killers.*

MANIAC

☆ Sinister Cinema, 1934, NR, 51 min.
Dir: Dwain Esper. Cast: Bill Woods, Horace Carpenter, Ted Edwards, Phyllis Diller, Thea Ramsey, Jennie Dark.

You've never seen anything like this zero-budgeted '30s exploitation shocker, which pretends to be both an adaptation of Edgar Allan Poe's "The Black Cat" *and* a serious documentary on insanity. Yeah, right. A loon (Woods) kills the mad doctor he works for and, in a fit of schizophrenic guilt, takes on his personality after bricking up the doc's corpse behind a cellar wall. Truly awful but worth noting for its surprising bursts of gory violence and femme nudity—something you don't usually expect to find in an old-fashioned B horror film (this one played in "Adults Only" theaters). This Phyllis Diller, by the way, is not *the* Phyllis Diller—she can't be *that* old. Don't miss the cat's eyeball-eating scene!

MANIAC

★★☆ RCA/Columbia, 1963, NR, 86 min.
Dir: Michael Carreras. Cast: Kerwin Mathews, Nadia Gray, Liliane Brousse, Donald Houston, George Pastell, Justine Lord.

Yet another Hammer *Psycho* derivation, this one photographed in a thick gray light on location in France's Camargue district. Mathews is an American tourist who has affairs with both a voluptuous inn proprietress and her pretty teen stepdaughter and aids in breaking their husband-father out of the local asylum, thus unknowingly unleashing a blowtorch-toting terror on the community. Fairly predictable for the most part, this *does* sport a fairly shocking surprise-twist ending and has good acting.

MANIAC

★☆ Media, 1981, UR, 87 min.
Dir: William Lustig. Cast: Joe Spinell, Caroline Munro, Gail Lawrence, Kelly Piper, Rita Montone, Tom Savini.

Spinell is Frank Zito, a crazed NYC serial killer with a powerful mother fixation who stalks the city killing and scalping young women whose hair he uses to adorn the female mannequins he keeps in his apartment. This is a nonstop orgy of ultra-gory killings, underdeveloped characters (most of whom exist solely to be slaughtered), and totally unbelievable plot twists (we're actually expected to accept the unlikely idea that gorgeous Munro would actually want to date greasy, slobbering Spinell). The *only* reason you might want to endure this is for the opportunity to see some of Tom Savini's most unrestrained and realistic FX work. Otherwise, it's only for the most die-hard of slasher and Caroline completists.

MANIAC COP

★★☆ TWE, 1988, R, 85 min.
Dir: William Lustig. Cast: Tom Atkins, Bruce Campbell, Laurene Landon, Richard Roundtree, William Smith, Sheree North, Victoria Caitlin, Robert Z'Dar.

A disfigured psycho in a 48-long police uniform commits multiple murders in Manhattan, slashing and strangling dozens until revealed to be a brain-damaged ex-cop long thought dead by the authorities. A watchable mix of slasher and action adventure clichés, with a clever Larry Cohen script and a typically full-tilt performance from Atkins. The unexpected death of the film's most likable character and one of those annoying inconclusive endings do it the most damage.

MANIAC COP 2

★★☆ LIVE, 1990, R, 87 min.
Dir: William Lustig. Cast: Robert Davi, Claudia Christian, Bruce Campbell, Laurene Landon, Michael Lerner, Leo Rossi, Clarence Williams III, Robert Z'Dar.

Solid sequel with undead killer cop Cordell (Z'Dar) back in action, offing surviving officers Campbell and Landon and then teaming up with psycho stripper-strangler Rossi. The rare sequel, in that it's equal to, if not better than, its inspiration, this has a great cast (many of them successfully cast against type), terrific action, and enough inventive plot twists to keep it from ever becoming just another tepid rehash.

MANIAC COP 3: BADGE OF SILENCE

★★ Academy, 1992, R, 85 min.
Dirs: William Lustig and Joel Soisson. Cast: Robert Davi, Caitlin Dulany, Gretchen Becker, Jackie Earl Haley, Robert Forster, Julius Harris, Paul Gleason, Robert Z'Dar.

The butcher in blue returns for this third outing in which he avenges the comatose condition of a tough female cop (Becker) with whom he's unaccountably fallen in love. The usual off-the-wall casting and bizarre touches help this uneven and unnecessary sequel, whose myriad production headaches are plainly evident in the finished product.

MANITOU, THE

★★☆ Charter, 1978, PG, 103 min.
Dir: William Girdler. Cast: Tony Curtis, Susan Strasberg, Michael Ansara, Stella Stevens, Burgess Meredith, Ann Sothern, Jon Cedar, Paul Mantee.

A silly but fun *Exorcist*-type thriller in which a tennis-ball-sized tumor growing on the neck of a girl (Strasberg) turns out to be a fetus harboring the reincarnation of an evil Indian medicine man. As ludicrous as it all sounds, the plot (derived from the novel by Graham Masterton) is handled with assurance by Girdler (who died tragically shortly after this film's completion); the cast has a ball (especially Curtis as a phony mystic confronted for the first time by real supernatural power); and at least two scenes (the seance and birth sequences) pack a real punch.

MAN'S BEST FRIEND
★★☆ New Line, 1993, R, 87 min.
Dir: John Lafia. Cast: Ally Sheedy, Lance Henriksen, Frederic Lehne, William Sanderson, Robert Costanzo, Trula M. Marcus.

Sheedy is a TV newsgal whose exposé on vivisectionist Henriksen's lab puts her in contact with Max, a genetically engineered super-dog with a nasty psychotic streak that comes to the fore when Ally innocently frees Max and takes him home. This enjoyable combo of *Cujo* and *The Terminator* has good acting from Sheedy and Henriksen and some real suspense, only stumbling at the end with one of the goofiest deus ex machinas since Argento handed a chimp a straight razor at the climax of *Creepers.*

MANSION OF THE DOOMED
★☆ United, 1976, R, 85 min. Dir: Michael Pataki. Cast: Richard Basehart, Gloria Grahame, Trish Stewart, Lance Henriksen, Vic Tayback, Arthur Space.

An ocular rehash of *The Horror Chamber of Dr. Faustus.* Basehart reaches a new career low as Dr. Chaney, a kindly eye surgeon who tries to restore the sight of blinded daughter Stewart by kidnapping people and removing their eyes for unsuccessful transplants. Despite gory makeups and some zesty touches from veteran sleaze actor and director Pataki, it's too depressing to be much fun. Also released as *Eyes, The Eyes of Dr. Chaney, Terror of Dr. Chaney, Massacre Mansion,* and *House of Blood.*

MANSTER, THE
★☆ Sinister Cinema, 1972, NR, 72 min. Dirs: George P. Breakstone, Kenneth G. Crane. Cast: Peter Dyneley, Jane Hylton, Satoshi Nakamura, Terri Zimmern.

This Japanese-American co-production proudly stands head and shoulders above most others in the ever-popular "so bad it's good" sweepstakes on sheer weirdness value alone. Yank reporter Dyneley interviews Japanese scientist Nakamura who, just for the hell of it, injects him with his experimental serum. The next thing you know, Pete develops an eye on his shoulder that grows into a hideous second head, his original noggin sprouts fangs and hair, and he ultimately splits in two! Tacky and gross and with haphazard editing—but ya gotta see that splitting-in-half scene! You won't be a complete person until you do. Aka (appropriately enough) *The Split.*

MAN THEY COULD NOT HANG, THE
★★☆ Goodtimes, 1939, NR, 63 min.
Dir: Nick Grindé. Cast: Boris Karloff, Lorna Gray, Robert Wilcox, Roger Pryor, Don Beddoe, Ann Doran.

The first of Karloff's four Columbia mad doctor flicks, this features elements predating the *Dr. Phibes* films. Boris is a scientist who's sentenced to die for the murder of a young assistant he hoped to revive with his experimental artificial heart. After his execution, Karloff is restored to life by the heart and then begins stalking the judge, lawyers, and jury he holds responsible for his hanging. Like the similar *The Man With Nine Lives,* this uncannily predicts an experiment that someday would become a scientific reality. Karloff performs with his usual elan, while Grindé directs with flair on a stringent budget.

MAN WHO CAME FROM UMMO, THE
See: *Dracula vs. Frankenstein.*

MAN WHO CHANGED HIS MIND, THE
See: *The Man Who Lived Again.*

MAN WHO HAUNTED HIMSELF, THE
★★ HBO, 1970, PG, 94 min.
Dir: Basil Dearden. Cast: Roger Moore, Hildegarde Neil, Olga Georges-Picot, Anton Rodgers, Freddie Jones, Thorley Walters.

Dull retread of the "Alfred Hitchcock Presents" episode "The Case of Mr. Pelham," with Moore as a London businessman tormented by his "inner self" and released from his subconscious when he dies for a moment on a hospital operating table. Slow and confusing, but with a solid Brit supporting cast—especially Jones as a logic-minded psychiatrist. Favorite Moore line: "I'm not James Bond of Her Majesty's secret service, you know!"

MAN WHO LIVED AGAIN, THE
★★☆ Sinister Cinema, 1936, NR, 64 min.
Dir: Robert Stevenson. Cast: Boris Karloff, Anna Lee, John Loder, Frank Cellier, Donald Calthrop, Cecil Parker.

Karloff is cast in a typical role as a scientist who develops a process to transfer brain waves from one person to another and switches his own mind to the body of his pretty assistant's young beau. This British flick (originally *The Man Who Changed His Mind*) is interesting but plays its fantastic material too seriously, without the bombastic, tongue-in-cheek quality of Karloff's similar Hollywood endeavors. Aka *The Brain Snatcher* and *Dr. Maniac.*

MAN WITHOUT A FACE, THE
See: *Circus of Fear.*

MAN WITH THE SYNTHETIC BRAIN, THE
See: *Blood of Ghastly Horror.*

MAN WITH THE X-RAY EYES, THE
See: *X—The Man With X-Ray Eyes.*

MAN WITH TWO BRAINS, THE
★★☆ Warner, 1983, R, 90 min. Dir: Carl Reiner. Cast: Steve Martin, Kathleen Turner, David Warner, Paul Benedict, Merv Griffin, voice of Sissy Spacek.

In this amiable mad doctor comedy, Martin is his usual manic self as the world's foremost brain surgeon who marries a beautiful harridan (Turner) but later falls in love with a disembodied brain (voiced by Spacek). Will he ever bring together the mind he loves with the body he lusts for? There are the usual leering sex jokes but also surprising sweet spots. Turner is positively glorious as the sluttiest bitch in screen history, while Merv contributes a memorable turn in a *Dressed to Kill* parody. Best line: "Into the mud, scum queen!"

MAN WITH TWO HEADS, THE
★ Midnight, 1972, R, 80 min.
Dir: Andy Milligan. Cast: Denis DeMarne, Julia Stratton, Gay Field, Jacqueline Lawrence.

Typically grimy Milligan effort combining *Dr. Jekyll and Mr. Hyde* and *The Manster.* This time Dr. Jekyll's formula gives him a second, monstrous head and generously increases his sex drive as well as his lust for blood. The usual awful acting and phony period settings are augmented by a surprising amount of sex and skin; in this instance, two heads are definitely *not* better than one.

MARDI GRAS FOR THE DEVIL
★★ Prism, 1992, R, 93 min. Dir: David A. Prior. Cast: Robert Davi, Lesley-Anne Down, Michael Ironside, John Amos, Margaret Avery, Lydie Denier.

Formerly called *Night Trap*, this is set in New Orleans and pits cop Davi against satanic serial killer Ironside, who dashes about in high-powered scenes clearly influenced by the old *Kolchak: The Night Stalker* TV show. This action-horror piece is moderately watchable but seriously wastes an excellent cast—particularly the ever-lovely Down.

MARDI-GRAS MASSACRE
★ Paragon, 1976, R, 97 min. Dir: Jack Weis. Cast: Curt Dawson, Gwen Arment, Laura Misch, Wayne Mack.

This totally inept gore flick (filmed as *Crypt of Dark Secrets*) is an unofficial remake of *Blood Feast* with a crazed Aztec high priest (in place of BF's crazed Egyptian high priest) slicing out hookers' hearts in order to revive an ancient goddess. A couple of messy heart-ripping scenes in this badly acted, nearly interminable mess.

MARIA MARTEN
See: *Murder in the Red Barn.*

MARK OF DEATH, THE
See: *Creature of the Walking Dead.*

MARK OF THE BEAST
See: *Fear No Evil.*

MARK OF THE DEVIL
★★ Edde Entertainment, 1970, R, 96 min. Dir: Michael Armstrong. Cast: Herbert Lom, Udo Kier, Olivera Vuco, Reggie Nalder, Gaby Fuchs, Herbert Fux.

Best known for its advertising ("Rated V for Violence!") and "Stomach Distress Bag" giveaway, this gory German rip-off of *The Conqueror Worm* (originally known as *Hexen Bis Auf Blut Gequalt: Witches Tortured Till They Bleed*) has Lom as an impotent nobleman who takes out his sexual frustration on young women wrongly accused, tortured, and executed for witchcraft. Although not quite as gruesome as it seemed at the time, this is still so tasteless overall—with rape, torture, and witch burnings aplenty—that it's still pretty hard to endure, lacking the humorous touches that make Herschell Gordon Lewis' gore flicks so weirdly watchable. Aka *Witches* and *Burn, Witch, Burn.*

MARK OF THE DEVIL PART II
★ Video Dimensions, 1972, R, 88 min.
Dir: Adrian Hoven. Cast: Anton Diffring, Erica Blanc, Jean-Pierre Zola, Reggie Nalder.

"Exorcism be damned!" the ads cried. This inevitable follow-up is basically just a slightly altered remake with Diffring this time and countess Blanc the victim of his cruel tortures. Scenes are borrowed from both its inspiration and Ken Russell's *The Devils,* but the results are too dull and passionless to provide much interest. The late, great Diffring was better served elsewhere. Original title: *Hexen Geschandet und zu Tode Gequalt: Witches Tortured Till They Die.*

MARK OF THE VAMPIRE
★★★ MGM/UA, 1935, NR, 61 min.
Dir: Tod Browning. Cast: Lionel Barrymore, Bela Lugosi, Elizabeth Allen, Lionel Atwill, Jean Hersholt, Henry Wadsworth, Donald Meek, Carol Borland.

Bela Lugosi and Carol Borland strike a classic pose in Mark of the Vampire *(1935).*

A remake of the lost Lon Chaney silent *London After Midnight*, this unjustly neglected MGM *Dracula* cash-in is one of the most enjoyable horrors of the '30s. Gorgeously photographed by James Wong Howe and with marvelously atmospheric set design, this film is often criticized for its cop-out ending (where the vampires haunting a Czechoslovakian village turn out to be part of a plot to catch a murderer—oops, I gave it away!) but this can be easily forgiven in light of its incredible visual strengths. Filmed as *Vampires of Prague*.

MARS ATTACKS PUERTO RICO
See: *Frankenstein Meets the Space Monster*.

MARSUPIALS: HOWLING III, THE
See: *The Howling III*.

MARTIN
★★★☆ HBO, 1977, R, 95 min.
Dir: George A. Romero. Cast: John Amplas, Lincoln Maazel, Christine Forrest, Tom Savani, Elayne Nadeau, George A. Romero.

Amplas is quite capable as the misanthropic title character of this unique modern vampire tale written and directed by Romero. Martin is a sexually confused, lonely teenager who lives in a dying Pennsylvania steel town and lives out his fantasies of being a vampire by attacking women with razor blades and drinking their blood. More difficult and complex than any of Romero's other horror films, with Amplas' performance and Savini's realistic gore FX helping to transcend the deficiencies of some weak supporting performances and poor sound recording.

MARY, MARY, BLOODY MARY
★☆ Continental, 1975, R, 92 min.
Dir: Juan Lopez Moctezuma. Cast: Cristina Ferrare, John Carradine, David Young, Helena Rojo.

Years before she started doing TV diet commercials, fashion plate Ferrare starred in this Mexican vampire-gore flick. As Mary, Cristina displays little relish as she moves from victim to victim, stabbing them in the neck with a sharpened hair clip while being hunted by her aged, guilt-ridden dad—Carradine wasted yet again in a small role completed by an unconvincing double in the best *Plan Nine From Outer Space* tradition. Very poor.

MASK, THE
★★ Rhino, 1961, NR, 83 min.
Dir: Julian Roffman. Cast: Paul Stevens, Claudette Nevins, Bill Walker, Anne Collings.

Some imaginative 3-D sequences (thankfully preserved in this video edition) highlight this otherwise ordinary Canadian shocker about a psychiatrist who comes into possession of an ancient Aztec mask that causes bizarre hallucinations and drives him to murder. Scenes of hooded satanists, a rotting ghoul, and a girl with a skull face are pretty creepy and punch up a slim storyline that's indifferently acted and directed. Aka *Eyes of Hell* and *The Spooky Movie Show* and sort of remade in 1994.

MASK OF FU MANCHU, THE
★★★ MGM/UA, 1932, NR, 67 min. Dir: Charles Brabin. Cast: Boris Karloff, Myrna Loy, Karen Morley, Lewis Stone, Charles Starrett, Jean Hersholt.

Entertaining adaptation of the Sax Rohmer novel with Karloff and Loy well cast as the evil Fu and his seductive, sadistic daughter. The plot involves a search for the lost treasure of Ghengis Khan and features plenty of ripe dialogue (some of it unfortunately cut from this otherwise pristine video edition), glitzy

MGM production values, imaginative tortures, and hunky Starrett dressed in a diaper and treated like a brainless sex object by Loy. Does Camille Paglia know about this?

MASK OF THE DEMON

See: *Black Sunday.*

MASKS OF DEATH

★★☆ Lorimar, 1984, PG, 82 min.
Dir: Roy Ward Baker. Cast: Peter Cushing, John Mills, Anne Baxter, Ray Milland, Anton Diffring, Susan Penhaligon, Gordon Jackson, James Cossins.

Marginally horrific Sherlock Holmes adventure with the great P.I. (Cushing) coming out of retirement on the brink of WWI to investigate a trio of deaths in which the victims were literally frightened to death. A sadly aged Cushing is surprisingly sharp and delightful as Holmes but the story is snail-paced, with the mystery solved almost as an afterthought. Still has its moments, though. TV title: *Sherlock Holmes and the Masks of Death.*

MASQUE OF THE RED DEATH, THE

★★★★ Orion, 1964, NR, 88 min.
Dir: Roger Corman. Cast: Vincent Price, Hazel Court, Jane Asher, David Weston, Patrick Magee, Nigel Green, Skip Martin, John Westbrook.

Devil-worshipper Price seals himself and his followers away in his 15th-century Italian castle when plague ravages the area, everyone eventually failing victim to the disease during an orgiastic masked ball. The pinnacle of Corman's Poe cycle, this was shot on a lavish (for him) six-week schedule on sets left over from *Becket* and is exquisitely lensed in lush colors by ace cinematographer and later director Nicolas Roeg. Price is excellent, by turns both campy *and* restrained, and the supporting cast (especially Court) is outstanding.

MASQUE OF THE RED DEATH, THE

★★ MGM/UA, 1989, R, 82 min.
Dir: Larry Brand. Cast: Patrick Macnee, Adrian Paul, Clare Hoak, Tracy Reiner, Jeff Osterhage, Maria Ford.

Needless remake of the Corman classic with Paul as the dour 15th-century nobleman who attempts to escape the plague by hiding both himself and his friends away in his hilltop fortress—until the red death himself (Macnee) arrives on the scene. Although the period is well caught, bland acting (apart from Macnee in basically an extended cameo) and slow pacing make this little more than a minor rehash lacking both the scope and panache of the '64 version—which was probably budgeted half of this one.

ROGER CORMAN
(1926–)

The king of the quickies, this ingenious director graduated from '50s Z favorites like *It Conquered the World* and *The Wasp Woman* to his color and wide-screen Edgar Allan Poe adaptations in the '60s, the best of which was *The Masque of the Red Death*. After leaving the director's chair in the '70s, Corman headed both New World and Concorde–New Horizons Pictures. He later returned to directing with *Frankenstein Unbound*.

Monster From the Ocean Floor (producer, '54), *The Day the World Ended* ('56), *It Conquered the World* ('56), *Attack of the Crab Monsters* ('57), *Not of This Earth* ('57), *The Undead* ('57), *The Viking Women and the Sea Serpent* ('57), *Teenage Caveman* ('58), *The Wasp Woman* ('59), *A Bucket of Blood* ('59), *House of Usher* ('60), *The Little Shop of Horrors* ('60), *Creature From the Haunted Sea* ('61), *The Pit and the Pendulum* ('61), *The Premature Burial* ('62), *Tales of Terror* ('62), *Tower of London* ('62), *The Raven* ('63), *The Terror* ('63), *Dementia 13* (producer, '63), *X—The Man With X-Ray Eyes* ('63), *The Haunted Palace* ('64), *The Masque of the Red Death* ('64), *Tomb of Ligeia* ('65), *Queen of Blood* (producer, '66), *Piranha* (producer, '78), *Humanoids from the Deep* (producer, '80), *Galaxy of Terror* (producer, '81), *Forbidden World* (producer, '82), *Not of this Earth* (producer, '88), *The Masque of the Red Death* (producer, '89), *The Haunting of Morella* (producer, '90), *Watchers II* (producer, '90), *Frankenstein Unbound* ('90), *Dead Space* (producer, '91), *Dracula Rising* (producer, '92), *Carnosaur* (producer, '93).

MASQUE OF THE RED DEATH, THE

★☆ RCA/Columbia, 1990, R, 93 min.
Dir: Alan Birkinshaw. Cast: Herbert Lom, Brenda Vaccaro, Frank Stallone, Michelle McBride, Christine Landé, Simon Poland.

Poe's haunting tale of death and decadence becomes just another slasher movie as wealthy Lom holds a masked ball at a Bavarian castle crashed by a scarlet-robed masked maniac. Attractive photography and set design and arch performances from Lom and (especially) Vaccaro highlight this third and arguably best of Harry Alan Towers' updated Poe flicks filmed in South Africa in 1988–89.

MASSACRE AT CENTRAL HIGH

★★★ MCA/Universal, 1976, R, 88 min. Dir. Renee Daalder. Cast: Derrel Maury, Andrew Stevens, Kimberly Beck, Robert Carradine, Steve Bond, Rainbeaux Smith, Ray Underwood, Lani O'Grady.

Maury, the new kid at inner-city hellhole Central High, is brutalized and crippled by the ruling gang he later seeks a gruesome vengeance upon. This surprisingly potent mix of *Death Wish* and *To Sir, With Love* has horror and slasher overtones boosted by clever plotting and a great exploitation cast of the oldest high school seniors since *Blackboard Jungle.*

MASSACRE MANSION

See: *Mansion of the Doomed.*

MASSACRE MANSION

See: *The Nesting.*

MASTER OF TERROR

See: *The 4-D Man.*

MAUSOLEUM

★★☆ Embassy, 1983, R, 96 min.
Dir: Michael Dugan. Cast: Bobbie Bresee, Marjoe Gortner, La Wanda Page, Norman Burton, Maurice Sherbanee, Laura Hippe.

Humorous, inventive *Exorcist*-like exploiter with Bresee possessed and mutated by a sexually voracious demon who causes her to seduce and murder several people. Clever John Buechler makeup for the she-demon includes breasts with snarling, fanged faces, while Page ("Sanford and Son"'s Aunt Esther) steals it as a nervous maid with the best line: "There's some strange shit goin' on in this house!"

MAXIMUM OVERDRIVE

★ Lorimar, 1986, R, 97 min.
Dir: Stephen King, Cast: Emilio Estevez, Laura Harrington, Pat Hingle, Yeardley Smith, John Short, Ellen McElduff, Holter Graham, Marla Maples.

Since most authors claim that it's unimaginative and talent-barren directors who screw up their work when it's brought to the screen, King has no one but himself to blame for this lumbering mess. Based on his excellent short story "Trucks," this has a bunch of repulsive characters trapped in a southern truck stop by murderous machines given independent life when the earth passes through the tail of a rogue comet. Full of stupid inconsistencies—Why are cars unaffected by the comet when all the other machines go wild?—and annoying toilet humor, this throws away a terrific premise and harrowing FX work in a misguided bid to become the *Plan Nine From Outer Space* of the 1980s. And yes, that's *the* Marla as an early victim.

MEATCLEAVER MASSACRE

★ United, 1976, R, 87 min.
Dir: Evan Lee. Cast: Christopher Lee, Larry Justin, J. Arthur Craig, James Habif, Robert Clark, Alisa Beaton.

Grade-Z *Texas Chainsaw Massacre* rip-off with Lee's intro footage totally unrelated and probably meant for another movie entirely. A professor of the occult seeks revenge on the young thugs who killed his family through a pact with a powerful demon. Odd flashes of imagination occasionally shine through this otherwise depressing waste of celluloid. Aka *Hollywood Meatcleaver Massacre* and *Revenge of the Dead.*

MEAT IS MEAT

See: *The Mad Butcher.*

MEDUSA TOUCH, THE

★★☆ Avid, 1978, PG, 109 min.
Dir: Jack Gold. Cast: Richard Burton, Lee Remick, Lino Ventura, Harry Andrews, Marie-Christine Barrault, Jeremy Brett, Michael Hordern, Derek Jacobi, Alan Badel, Gordon Jackson.

Burton is a hoot as John Morlar, a writer whose psychic powers can bring about only tragedy ("I have a gift for dee-zaw-ster!" he intones) and is nearly murdered by his psychiatrist (Remick) after he causes a jumbo jet to crash into a London office tower. A gory, funny, entertaining mating of *Carrie* with your typical '70s Irwin Allen–type disaster movie, this has a distinguished cast, some *Omen*-style death scenes, and laughs galore.

MEETING AT MIDNIGHT

★★☆ MGM/UA, 1944, NR, 64 min.
Dir: Phil Rosen. Cast: Sidney Toler, Mantan Moreland, Frances Chan, Joseph Crehan, Jacqueline de Wit, Helen Beverly.

Originally released as *Black Magic*, this moody Monogram Charlie Chan flick features a rare appearance by number-one daughter Frances, who involves Dad with a murder committed during a seance. Effective light and shadow work and pleasing Moreland comic relief.

MEPHISTO WALTZ, THE

★★★ CBS/Fox, 1971, R, 108 min.
Dir: Paul Wendkos, Cast: Alan Alda, Jacqueline Bisset, Barbara Parkins, Curt Jurgens, Bradford Dillman, William Windom, Kathleen Widdoes, Pamelyn Ferdin.

Good post–*Rosemary's Baby* occult thriller with gorgeous Jackie (in her best-ever role) discovering that her journalist husband (Alda, in his last pre-"M.A.S.H." role) has been taken over by the soul of master pianist cum satanist Jurgens. Lots of soul-switching, arty direction, and frantic camerawork are found in this creepy adaptation of the Fred Mustard Stewart novel.

MERIDIAN: KISS OF THE BEAST

★★ Paramount, 1990, R, 86 min.
Dir: Charles Band. Cast: Sherilyn Fenn, Malcolm Jamieson, Charlie Spradling, Hilary Mason, Phil Fondacaro, Vernon Dobtcheff.

Soft-core sex-horror (a sort-of *Last Tango in Transylvania*) with "Twin Peaks" chick Fenn as an Italian princess who falls in love with Jamieson, a carnival performer suffering from a werewolf-like curse. Beautifully photographed and scored, but with the main focus on nudity and sex, the horror elements (including Greg Cannom's so-so beast design) get short-changed. Shown on cable as *Kiss of the Beast*.

MESA OF LOST WOMEN

☆ Sinister Cinema, 1952, NR, 69 min.
Dir: Herbert Tevos, Ron Ormond. Cast: Jackie Coogan, Richard Travis, Mary Hill, Tandra Quinn, Angelo Rossitto, Katherine Victor.

One of the very worst, this laugher concerns the experiments of evil Dr. Aranya (Coogan, Uncle Fester himself in a cheesy beard) who is trying to create a race of spider women. Incredibly inept on all counts; the two guys who helmed this mess make Ed Wood look like John Ford. Aka *Lost Women of Zarpa*.

MESMERIZED

★★ Vestron, 1985, PG, 93 min.
Dir. Michael Laughlin. Cast: Jodie Foster, John Lithgow, Michael Murphy, Harry Andrews, Dan Shor.

Dull New Zealand–set psychological melodrama with Foster as the young bride of weird, middle-aged Lithgow, whose strange behavior drives her to murder. A good cast is wasted on inadequate material based on a true story. Aka *My Letter to George* and *Shocked*.

MESSIAH OF EVIL

★★☆ Video Gems, 1973, R, 89 min. Dir: Willard Huyck. Cast: Marianna Hill, Michael Greer, Joy Bang, Anitra Ford, Royal Dano, Elisha Cook.

Haunting, ahead-of-its-time *Night of the Living Dead* spin-off from George Lucas writers Huyck and Gloria Katz. Lovely Hill arrives in a creepy California coastal town searching for artist dad Dano and becomes witness to a takeover by cannibalistic ghouls. Though often

confusing, this has some truly remarkable scenes—Ford's discovery of a crowd of ghouls eating raw meat in a brightly lit supermarket; Bang surrounded by ghouls in a movie theatre; the attack on a beach house by shadowy figures bursting through a skylight—and interesting atmosphere. Also out as *Dead People, Return of the Living Dead, Revenge of the Screaming Dead,* and *The Second Coming*.

METEMPSYCHO

See: *Tomb of Torture.*

METEOR MONSTER

★☆ Sinister Cinema, 1957, NR, 65 min.
Dir: Jacques Marquette. Cast: Anne Gwynne, Gloria Castillo, Stuart Wade, Gilbert Perkins.

Better known as *Teenage Monster,* this junky '50s schlock horror, set in a small western town, has former Universal leading lady Gwynne as the mother of a teen turned into a werewolf-like monster after being struck by a meteor. Gwynne and ace makeup man Jack Pierce really hit the skids here, as this depressing no-budgeter isn't even good for many laughs. Aka *Monster on the Hill.*

MIAMI GOLEM

See: *Miami Horror.*

MIAMI HORROR

★ Panther, 1987, R, 90 min. Dir: Martin Herbert [Alberto de Martino]. Cast: David Warbeck, John Ireland, Laura Trotter, Lawrence Loddi.

Another Italian non-thriller with Warbeck as a TV reporter who gets mixed up with evil Ireland's (badly dubbed) plot to use a creepy-looking alien baby creature for world conquest. Just a lot of running around. Original title: *Miami Golem.*

MICROWAVE MASSACRE

★★ Rhino, 1979, R, 76 min.
Dir: Wayne Berwick. Cast: Jackie Vernon, Loren Schein, Claire Ginsberg, Lou Ann Webber.

Comedian Vernon stars in this moderate black comedy about a hen-pecked hubby who murders bitchy wife Ginsberg, chops her up, wraps her in foil, and pops her in the freezer. When he accidentally cooks a bit of her in the microwave and eats it, he develops a taste for female flesh. Tacky, but Jackie makes it minor fun.

MIDNIGHT

★★ Vidmark, 1981, R, 88 min. Dir: John Russo.
Cast: Lawrence Tierney, Melanie Verliin, John Amplas, Robin Walsh, John Hall, Charles Jackson.

Russo directs this low-budget adaptation of his own novel with runaway teens Verliin, Hall, and Jackson captured by a family of rural blood-drinking psychos who worship their mother's corpse. Starts too slowly and ends too abruptly, and too many likable characters meet bad ends (even more so in the book), but there are some effective moments and pleasing echoes of *The Texas Chainsaw Massacre* and *The Hills Have Eyes*. Aka *Backwoods Massacre*. Followed by a sequel.

MIDNIGHT

★ SVS, 1989, R, 85 min.
Dir: Norman Thaddeus Vane. Cast: Lynn Redgrave, Tony Curtis, Steve Parrish, Karen Witter, Frank Gorshin, Rita Gam, Gustav Vintas, Wolfman Jack.

Redgrave has her worst role ever (and that's counting her Weight Watchers commercials) as a tacky Elvira-type TV horror hostess. When her show is canceled and those responsible start dying, guess who's blamed? Annoying horror comedy dominated by obnoxious characters and unfunny situations.

MIDNIGHT HOUR, THE

★★ Vidmark, 1985, NR, 96 min. Dir: Jack Bender. Cast: Shari Belafonte-Harper, LeVar Burton, Lee Montgomery, Michelle Pfeiffer, Jonna Lee, Cindy Morgan, Kevin Morgan, Kevin McCarthy, Dick Van Patten.

Slight TV movie obviously patterned after Michael Jackson's "Thriller" video. A bunch of over-the-hill high school students accidentally revive a graveyard full of vampires, werewolves, zombies, and ghouls one Halloween night, and the creatures rampage through their small town. Good makeups and a charming performance from Lee as a '50s teenybopper who returns from the grave to party.

MIGHTY JOE YOUNG

★★★ Turner, 1949, NR, 94 min.
Dir: Ernest B. Schoedsack. Cast: Terry Moore, Ben Johnson, Robert Armstrong, Frank McHugh, Regis Toomey, Lora Lee Michel.

It's no *King Kong* but this well-loved, $2 million, three-years-in-the-making animated monster movie is still a lot of fun. Moore is a pretty teenager living on an African ranch with her 10-foot-tall pet gorilla, Joe. Armstrong, sending up his *Kong* role, is the showman who takes them to Hollywood to appear at an African-themed night club. All goes well until the caged and lonely Joe gets drunk and wrecks the club; he is ordered destroyed but is spared when he rescues his mistress and some children from an orphanage fire. Although it won an effects Oscar, the stop-motion work

was so expensive it never again was given this free a rein in a Hollywood production—all but killing the career of effects master Willis O'Brien. Available in both B&W and color, the Turner prints restore the red tint to the climactic scenes in the monochrome edition not seen since the original release. Look for familiar faces like Nestor Paiva, Irene Ryan, Charles Lane, and Ellen Corby in bit parts.

MIKEY

★★☆ Imperial, 1991, R, 91 min.
Dir: Dennis Dimster-Denk. Cast: Brian Bonsall, Josie Bissett, Ashley Laurence, Lyman Ward, John Diehl, Mimi Craven, Whitby Hertford, David Rogue.

The Adoption may have been a title better suited to this suspenser about a psycho nine-year-old (Bonsall) who keeps offing his adoptive families. This borrows lots from *The Stepfather—The Stepson?*—and has a rather cruel streak, not to mention one of those annoying here-we-go-again endings. But it also has some real scares and a chilling performance from young Bonsall—whose character on TV's *Family Ties* was notable for going from infant to age five in the space of a single summer.

MILL OF THE STONE MAIDENS

See: *Mill of the Stone Women.*

MILL OF THE STONE WOMEN

★★☆ Paragon, 1960, NR, 93 min.
Dir: Giorgio Ferroni. Cast: Pierre Brice, Scilla Gabel, Dany Carrel, Wolfgang Preiss.

Exquisitely atmospheric continental horror film based on a story from "Flemish Tales." A dedicated doctor (Preiss) with typical mad scientist daughter problems must drain the life force of various young women to keep her alive. These tootsies then petrify into stone statues used to decorate a carousel powered by the doc's windmill home. An interesting package of arresting visuals and overworked clichés. Aka *Mill of the Stone Maidens* and *Drops of Blood.*

MILPITAS MONSTER, THE

★★ VCI, 1976, PG, 81 min. Dir: Robert L. Burrill. Cast: Priscilla House, Douglas Hagdohl, Scott A. Henderson, Scott Parker.

A toxic waste–spawned creature menaces the California town of Milpitas. Pleasant low-budget amateur spoof of every monster movie cliché you can mention.

MINDKILLER

★★☆ Prism, 1987, PG-13, 86 min.
Dir: Michael Krueger. Cast: Joe McDonald,

Christopher Wade, Shirley Ross, Kevin Hart, Diana Calhoun, Tom Henry.

Experimenting with expanding the power of his mind, a nerdy librarian (McDonald) develops incredible mental abilities, but eventually his brain bursts from his head as a *Fiend Without a Face*–like monster. Better than you'd imagine, this video potboiler boasts solid performances, a witty script, and excellent makeup FX.

MINDWARP: AN INFINITY OF TERROR
See: *Galaxy of Terror.*

MINISTER'S MAGICIAN, THE
See: *Dark Forces.*

MINOTAUR
See: *Land of the Minotaur.*

MIRROR, MIRROR
★★ Academy, 1991, R, 104 min.
Dir: Marina Sargenti. Cast: Karen Black, Rainbow Harvest, Yvonne De Carlo, William Sanderson, Kristin Dattilo, Ricky Paull Goldin.

Harvest is a teen tootsie who dresses like Winona Ryder in *Beetlejuice* and falls under the spell of an ornate old mirror containing a demon who helps her to off her enemies *Carrie*-style. Routine teen-angst chiller filler with numerous deaths but not much in the way of character involvement, this video flick is rife with ideas borrowed from countless other shockers.

MISERY
★★★ Nelson, 1990, R, 107 min.
Dir: Rob Reiner. Cast: James Caan, Kathy Bates, Lauren Bacall, Richard Farnsworth, Frances Sternhagen, Graham Jarvis.

His legs crushed by a terrible car accident, romance novelist Paul Sheldon (Caan) is cared for in a snow-bound house by nurse Annie Wilkes (Bates). Odd to begin with, Annie soon turns out to be a psychotically obsessed fan of Sheldon's work out to avenge the death of Misery, her favorite character, who has been killed off in his latest book. Skillfully assembled by Reiner, this basically one-set, two-character adaptation of Stephen King's novel has terrific work from Caan and Oscar winner Bates and is a nice blend of tension and dark humor. Only a needless shock movie postscript holds it back.

MISS DEATH
See: *The Diabolical Dr. Z.*

MOLE PEOPLE, THE
★★ MCA/Universal, 1956, NR, 76 min. Dir: Virgil Vogel. Cast: John Agar, Cynthia Patrick, Hugh Beaumont, Alan Napier, Nestor Paiva, Phil Chambers.

In this stodgy Universal programmer, Agar and Beaumont discover an underground civilization of Sumerian albinos and their hideous slaves—the Mole folk of the title. Despite some creepy scenes of people being pulled down into a sand pit and good monster makeup, this is still one of the company's weakest '50s flicks. The downbeat ending is especially unfortunate.

MOM
★★☆ TWE, 1990, R, 96 min.
Dir: Patrick Rand. Cast: Jeanne Bates, Mark Thomas Miller, Mary McDonough, Stella Stevens, Brion James, Claudia Christian.

TV newsman Miller's life is turned upside down when his elderly mother (Bates) is transformed into a cannibalistic werewolf by blind boarder James. This funny semi-spoof (somewhat anticipating *Dead Alive* but not nearly as outrageous) has good work from James, veteran Bates, and a still sexy Stevens (as a hooker-victim) but the offbeat premise doesn't sustain itself.

MONKEY SHINES: AN EXPERIMENT IN FEAR
★★ Orion, 1988, R, 113 min.
Dir: George A. Romero. Cast: Jason Beghe, John Pankow, Kate McNeil, Joyce Van Patten, Christine Forrest, Janine Turner.

Disappointing psychological thriller with Beghe unsympathetic as a handsome college athlete who is paralyzed in an accident and given a specially trained monkey called Ella to act as his "helping hand." Trouble is, Ella has been treated with a mind-expanding drug derived from human brain fluid that transforms her into a murderous extension of her master's helpless rage. Slack and wordy but with excellent turns from Pankow (as the scientist who experiments on the monkey), Van Patten (as the hero's grasping mom), and Forrest (Mrs. Romero, as a persnickety nurse). Filmed as *Ella.*

MONSTER
☆ Academy, 1978, PG, 77 min.
Dirs: Kenneth Hartford, Herbert L. Strock. Cast: Jim Mitchum, John Carradine, Philip Carey, Anthony Eisley, Andrea Hartford, Glen Hartford.

In this rock-bottom epic, a puppet sea monster terrorizes Colombian villagers in a town fringing the polluted lake that spawned it. *Jaws* clichés rub shoulders with *Exorcist* excesses while a carload of has-beens look as though they're unsure whether their paychecks are gonna clear. Unreleased for several years after its completion, it should have stayed that way. Aka *Monsteroid, Monster, The Legend That Became a Terror,* and *It Came From the Lake.*

MONSTER A GO-GO

☆ United, 1965, NR, 70 min.
Dirs: Bill Rebane, Sheldon Seymour [Herschell Gordon Lewis]. Cast: Phil Morton, June Travis, George Perry, Lois Brooks, Henry Hite.

Another one of those ya-gotta-see-it-to-believe-it! numbers started by Rebane and made "releasable" by ole H.G. under a pseudonym. Hite, "The World's Tallest Man," is an astronaut turned into a scarred giant by outer space radiation. Filmed as *Terror at Halfday,* this flatfooted foolishness has all the charm of a 70-minute rectal examination.

MONSTER BARAN, THE

See: *Varan the Unbelievable.*

MONSTER CLUB, THE

★★☆ Thrillervideo, 1981, PG, 97 min.
Dir: Roy Ward Baker. Cast: Vincent Price, Donald Pleasence, John Carradine, Britt Ekland, Stuart Whitman, Simon Ward, Richard Johnson, Barbara Kellerman, Patrick Magee, James Laurenson, Lesley Dunlop, Anthony Valentine.

Price is a garrulous vampire who takes horror author Carradine to a London disco for the supernatural set, where three strange tales are related. Laurenson is a shadmock, a creepy guy with a fatal whistle; family man vampire Johnson is stalked by dedicated monster hunter Pleasence; and horror film director Whitman finds real terror in a town populated entirely by ghouls. Never released theatrically in America, this Amicus-type anthology, produced by Milton Subotsky, is fun but should have been much better considering the talent involved. The stories themselves are merely fair, with the framing device—featuring musical numbers by Night, The Pretty Things, UB 40, and others—providing the most enjoyment.

MONSTER DEMOLISHER, THE

★☆ Sinister Cinema, 1960, NR, 85 min.
Dir: Federico Curiel. Cast: German Robles, Julio Aleman, Domingo Soler, Aurora Alvarado, Mander, Rogelio Jimenez.

Nostradamus returns, whether you want him to or not, in this tedious sequel to *The Curse of Nostradamus.* This time the bearded one uses a murderous convict to do his evil bidding and

is battled by both Professor Duran and long-time family nemesis Igor de Kradek. In the end he is apparently, but not actually, destroyed by a sound-wave device fatal to bats and vampires. Original title: *Nostradamus y El Destructor de Monstruos: Nostradamus and the Destroyer of Monsters;* sequel: *Genie of Darkness.*

MONSTER DOG

★ TWE, 1986, NR, 84 min. Dir: Clyde Anderson [Carlos Aured]. Cast: Alice Cooper, Victoria Vera, Carlos Sanurio, Pepita James.

Aging rockers must have it as bad as has-been fashion models and athletes if Coop was forced to appear in this drekky Spanish horror film. A rock star and his entourage shoot a video in an old castle and somebody begins turning into a werewolf—or monster dog. Guess who? Another direct-to-vid embarrassment.

MONSTER FROM A PREHISTORIC PLANET

★★ Orion, 1967, NR, 90 min.
Dir: Haruyasu Noguchi. Cast: Tamio Kawaji, Yoko Yamamoto, Yuji Okada, Koji Wada, Tatsuya Fuji.

Gorgo, Japanese style. Explorers on a Kong-type island discover a man-sized prehistoric reptile-bird they take back with them to Tokyo. Its hundred-foot mom and dad then turn up, engage in the usual city-stomping, rescue their kid, and return home. The usual stuff. Aka *Daikyaju Gappa: The Monster Gappa* and *Gappa—The Triphibian Monster.*

MONSTER FROM GREEN HELL

★ Rhino, 1957, NR, 71 min.
Dir: Kenneth Crane. Cast: Jim Davis, Barbara Turner, Robert E. Griffin, Eduardo Cianelli, Vladimir Sokoloff.

A missile crash in Africa causes wasps to be transformed into gigantic native-munching monsters by a radiation leak. Maybe the worst of the '50s big-bug movies, with clumsy special effects, colorless acting, and lots of jungle stock footage from *Stanley and Livingstone.*

MONSTER FROM MARS

See: *Robot Monster.*

MONSTER FROM THE OCEAN FLOOR

★☆ Vidmark, 1954, NR, 64 min.
Dir: Wyott Ordung. Cast: Anne Kimball, Stuart Wade, Dick Pinner, Jonathan Haze, Inez Palange.

Roger Corman produced this low-budget chiller (his first) with Kimball as a lady scientist who investigates sea monster reports in a sleepy Mexican village and ends up encountering a cyclopian octopus. Not much, but it cost next to nothing ($12,000) and turned a quick profit, paving the way for many later, better Corman pics.

MONSTER FROM THE SURF

See: *The Beach Girls and the Monster.*

MONSTER GAPPA, THE

See: *Monster From a Prehistoric Planet.*

MONSTER HIGH

★ RCA/Columbia, 1989, R, 90 min.
Dir: Rudiger Poe. Cast: Dean Iandoli, Diana Frank, David Marriot, David Bloch.

Lousy horror comedy about alien invaders taking over a high school attended by the usual sex-starved idiots. High school's a bad enough experience without all these stupid teen movies making matters worse. Flunk it.

MONSTER HUNTER

★☆ Lightning, 1981, R, 91 min.
Dir: Peter Newton [Aristide Massaccesi]. Cast: George Eastman, Annie Belle, Ian Danby, Edmund Purdom, Katja Berger.

This unwanted sequel to *The Grim Reaper* is just another rip-off of *Halloween*. Eastman is back as the unstoppable, cannibalistic killer who rampages through a hospital and later menaces the bedridden heroine whose little brother thinks he's the boogeyman. Purdom is a priest out to destroy the monster in this sub-par neapolitan gore grab-bag. Aka *Anthropophagus II* and *Absurd*.

MONSTER IN THE CLOSET

★★☆ Lorimar, 1986, PG, 87 min.
Dir: Bob Dahlin. Cast: Donald Grant, Denise DuBarry, Claude Akins, John Carradine, Paul Dooley, Howard Duff, Henry Gibson, Donald Moffat, Stella Stevens, Kevin Peter Hall.

Fun monster movie spoof about a closet-dwelling creature who feasts (off-screen) on the guest cast while reporter Grant and teacher DuBarry try to stop it. Silly-looking but surprisingly amusing, with one of the funniest touches being that the monster (Hall) turns out to be gay—no wonder he wants out of the closet!

MONSTER MAKER, THE

★★ Sinister Cinema, 1944, NR, 62 min.
Dir: Sam Newfield. Cast: J. Carrol Naish, Ralph Morgan, Wanda McKay, Tala Birell, Terry Frost, Glenn Strange.

Mad doctor Naish lusts for pretty McKay. When denied her hand by her concert pianist dad Morgan, Naish injects him with a chemi-

Heads up! It's The Monster of Piedras Blancas *(1958).*

cal that induces acromegaly. Good acting in the lead roles make this PRC rip-off of *The Raven* mildly interesting. Skimpy sets and overly dark photography, but Morgan's plight is made to seem genuinely tragic, while Naish savors his purple dialogue with relish.

MONSTER MEETS THE GORILLA, THE
See: *Bela Lugosi Meets a Brooklyn Gorilla.*

MONSTER OF LONDON CITY, THE
★★ Sinister Cinema, 1964, NR, 87 min. Dir: Edwin Zbonek. Cast: Hansjorg Felmy, Marianne Koch, Dietmar Schonherr, Chariklia Baxevanos.

Felmy, a stage actor appearing as Jack the Ripper at London's Edgar Allan Poe theater, becomes the chief suspect when a new series of streetwalker slayings sweep Whitechapel. Routine German krimi, with both hokey and lurid touches, from a story by Bryan Edgar Wallace.

MONSTER OF PIEDRAS BLANCAS, THE
★★ Republic, 1959, NR, 71 min. Dir: Irvin Berwick. Cast: Les Tremayne, Jeanne Carmen, Don Sullivan, Forrest Lewis, John Harmon, Frank Avridson.

A hideous, man-sized sea creature, cared for by a lonely lighthouse keeper, commits several ghastly murders in a small seaside community. Fair *Creature From the Black Lagoon* variant with good makeup, a few scares (including a surprisingly gory beheading), and lots of clichés.

MONSTER OF TERROR
See: *Die, Monster, Die!*

MONSTER OF THE WAX MUSEUM
See: *Nightmare in Wax.*

MONSTEROID
See: *Monster.*

MONSTER ON THE CAMPUS
★★☆ MCA/Universal, 1958, NR, 76 min. Dir: Jack Arnold. Cast: Arthur Franz, Joanna Moore, Judson Pratt, Troy Donahue, Nancy Walters, Whit Bissell, Helen Westcott, Ross Elliott.

Arnold brings tension and some real scares to this somewhat contrived '50s monster flick. Franz is a college professor contaminated by the irradiated blood of a prehistoric coelacanth fish and transformed into a murderous Neanderthal man. Despite good acting and some surprising bursts of violence (women dragged about by their hair and a guy getting a hatchet in the face), this is one of those movies in which suspense is wholly derived from char-

acters behaving as stupidly as possible. The rubbery ape-man makeup is very similar to the Mr. Hyde design from *Abbott and Costello Meet Dr. Jekyll and Mr. Hyde.*

MONSTERS
★★☆ Lorimar, 1988–91, NR, 60 min. per tape. Dirs: Michael Gornick, Ted Gershuny, Debra Hill, Warner Shook, Ernest Farino, Bette Gordon, others. Cast: David McCallum, Linda Blair, Adrienne Barbeau, Darren McGavin, Mary Woronov, Ashley Laurence, Robert Lansing, Jerry Stiller, Imogene Coca, Laraine Newman, Tempest Bledsoe, Fritz Weaver, Anne Meara, Meatloaf.

Double-billed episodes from the fun companion series to "Tales From the Darkside." Production values are faulty, but good makeup FX (each story is, as the title indicates, centered around a monster) and talented casts of familiar faces make many of these shows—involving vampires, zombies, demons, aliens, and other such folk—extremely watchable.

MONSTERS FROM THE MOON
See: *Robot Monster.*

MONSTER SHOW, THE
See: *Freaks.*

MONSTER SNOWMAN, THE
See: *Half Human.*

MONSTERS OF TERROR
See: *Dracula vs. Frankenstein* (1969).

MONSTERS OF THE NIGHT
See: *The Navy vs. The Night Monsters.*

MONSTER SQUAD, THE
★★☆ Vestron, 1987, PG-13, 82 min. Dir: Fred Dekker. Cast: Andre Gower, Robby Kiger, Brent Chalem, Ryan Lambert, Ashley Bank, Michael Faustino, Stephen Macht, Duncan Regehr, Tom Noonan, Mary Ellen Trainor.

A bunch of monster movie-loving kids discover that their small southern town has been invaded by Dracula himself (Regehr), who's leading several other supernatural superstars in the search for a magical amulet. Not up to Dekker's debut film, *Night of the Creeps,* but still worthwhile, with excellent Stan Winston makeups and a minimum of cloying Spielbergian cuteness. Noonan is especially memorable as a friendly Frankenstein monster.

MONSTER THAT CHALLENGED THE WORLD, THE
★★☆ MGM/UA, 1957, NR, 83 min. Dir: Arnold Laven. Cast: Tim Holt, Audrey Dalton,

Hans Conreid, Casey Adams, Mimi Gibson, Gordon Jones.

Unique full-scale model FX and a nice sense of atmosphere distinguish this formula '50s monster movie inspired by *Them!* An earthquake unleashes huge prehistoric mollusks that terrorize a naval base along California's Salton Sea. It's somewhat slow in spots, but good acting from Conreid and a straightforward, documentary-style approach to the story make this one of the more enjoyable creature features of its decade.

MONSTER, THE LEGEND THAT BECAME A TERROR
See: *Monster.*

MONSTER WALKED, THE
See: *The Monster Walks.*

MONSTER WALKS, THE
★★ Kino, 1932, NR, 63 min.
Dir: Frank R. Staryer. Cast: Rex Lease, Vera Reynolds, Sheldon Lewis, Mischa Auer, Martha Mattox, Sleep n' Eat [Willie Best].

Heiress Reynolds is menaced by a crazed ape and its equally unhinged keeper (Auer). Cheapie early '30s shocker rescued from obscurity by video. Not as good as Strayer's *The Vampire Bat* but fair fun for nostalgia-minded horror fans. Aka *The Monster Walked.*

MONSTER YONGKARI
See: *Yongary, Monster from the Deep.*

MONSTER ZERO
See: *Godzilla vs. Monster Zero.*

MONSTROSITY
★ Sinister Cinema, 1964, NR, 70 min.
Dir: Joseph Mascelli. Cast: Frank Gerstle, Erika Peters, Marjorie Eaton, Judy Bamber, Frank Fowler, Lisa Lang.

Better known by its TV title, *The Atomic Brain,* this bottom-of-the-barrel baby has it all: brain transplants, zombies, dog men, cat women, over-the-hill gigolos, and a bunch of odd characters sporting the most improbable foreign accents imaginable. Old lady Eaton wants surgeon Gerstle to transplant her brain into the body of sexy young Peters, but it ends up in a black cat instead. The cat then sets off Gerstle's atomic reactor, which blows sky high, killing everyone but Erika. Cinematographer-turned-director Mascelli composes a couple of nice shots, but everything else is clearly not to be taken seriously.

MOON OF THE WOLF
★★☆ Goodtimes, 1972, NR, 74 min.
Dir: Daniel Petire. Cast: David Janssen, Barbara Rush, Bradford Dillman, John Beradino, Geoffrey Lewis, Royal Dano.

Every time the full moon rises over the Louisiana bayou country, someone is mysteriously torn to pieces as if by some powerful beast. It couldn't be a werewolf, could it? That's what sheriff Janssen tries to find out in this not-bad TV movie based on the novel by Leslie H. Whitten. Janssen's amiable charm helps a lot, though the wolf man isn't fully seen until the last 15 minutes or so and the makeup is kinda skimpy.

MORTUARY
★★ Vestron, 1981, R, 91 min.
Dir: Howard Avedia. Cast: Mary McDonough, Christopher George, Lynda Day George, David Wallace, Bill Paxton, Alvy Moore.

Familiar low-rent slasher with McDonough, formerly of "The Waltons," menaced by a cloaked madman who dispatches his victims with embalming tools. The Georges, particularly Lynda Day, who looks absolutely smashing in a low-cut black negligee, are wasted, but Paxton gives a winning performance as the mystery killer—oops, sorry!

MORTUARY ACADEMY
★★ RCA/Columbia, 1989, R, 86 min.
Dir: Michael Schroeder. Cast: Christopher Atkins, Lynn Danielson, Perry Lang, Tracey Walter, Paul Bartel, Mary Woronov, Cesar Romero, Wolfman Jack.

The Brothers Grimm (Atkins and Lang) are forced to take a course at their family's Mortuary Academy in order to inherit it in this mostly lame horror-comedy along *Police Academy* lines. It isn't much, but Bartel and Woronov are always a delight, even in minor fare like this.

MORVINI'S VENOM
See: *Night of the Cobra Woman.*

MOST DANGEROUS GAME, THE
★★★ Goodtimes, 1932, NR, 63 min.
Dirs: Ernest B. Schoedsack, Irving Pichel. Cast: Joel McCrea, Fay Wray, Leslie Banks, Robert Armstrong, Hale Hamilton, Noble Johnson.

Sportsman McCrea is shipwrecked on an island lorded over by mad Russian count Banks, who hunts humans as prey and collects their severed heads as trophies. The first and best version of Richard Connell's classic short story "The Hounds of Zaroff," this was filmed by many of the *King Kong* team on some of the same jungle sets. Banks gives an outstanding performance as the cruel count, forever fondling his forehead dueling scar. British title: *The Hounds of Zaroff*.

MOST DANGEROUS MAN ALIVE, THE
★★☆ Vestron, 1958, NR, 81 min.
Dir: Allan Dwan. Cast: Ron Randell, Debra Paget, Elaine Stewart, Anthony Caruso, Gregg Palmer, Morris Ankrum.

Veteran director Dwan and a solid cast add spark to this routinely structured horror/gangster flick similar to *The Indestructible Man*. Hood Randell is exposed to an atomic blast and becomes an unkillable man of steel, avenging himself on double-crossing partner Caruso and girlfriend Paget. Good action shocker with grim performances.

MOTEL HELL
★★☆, MGM/UA, 1980, R, 102 min.
Dir: Kevin Connor. Cast: Rory Calhoun, Paul Linke, Nina Axelrod, Nancy Parsons, Wolfman Jack, Elaine Joyce.

Rambunctious semi-spoof with Calhoun as the owner of the rundown Motel Hello (the "o" on the sign is burned out) whose guests are butchered for ingredients for "Farmer Vincent Fritters." A grinning Rory is in great form and Joyce is marvelous as a sadomasochistic motel guest with a taste for whips, but overall this tends to be more silly than funny. The chainsaw duel finale is exciting.

MOTHER RILEY MEETS THE VAMPIRE
See: *My Son, The Vampire*.

MOTHER'S DAY
★★☆ Video Treasures, 1980, NR, 90 min.
Dir: Charles Kaufman. Cast: Nancy Hendrickson, Deborah Luce, Tiana Pierce, Holden McGuire, Billy Ray McQuade, Rose Ross.

Former college chums Hendrickson, Luce, and Pierce find their weekend-in-the-woods reunion disrupted by hillbilly maniacs who commit rape and murder to impress their crazed mother. Some insightful characterizations and subtle social comment distinguish this gory women-in-jeopardy film, making it far less offensive than many others of its ilk.

MOTHRA
★★☆ Goodtimes, 1961, NR, 90 min. Dir: Inoshiro Honda. Cast: Franky Sakai, Kyoko Kagawa, Ken Uehara, Hiroshi Koizumi, Emi Ito, Yumi Ito.

An expedition to a strange island discovers a pair of singing miniature twin princesses called the Alilenas. Brought to Tokyo, they are

---

ISHIRO [INOSHIRO] HONDA
(1911–1993)

The premier director of Japanese monster films for more than 20 years, Honda was the star director at Toho Studios and the guiding hand behind the successful careers of Godzilla, Mothra, Rodan, and other stars. On the other end of the scale, Ishiro also worked with Akira Kurosawa on projects like *Ran* and *Dreams*.

Godzilla, King of the Monsters ('54), *Half Human* ('55), *Rodan* ('56), *The H-Man* ('58), *Varan, the Unbelievable* ('58), *The Human Vapor* ('60), *Mothra* ('62), *King Kong vs. Godzilla* ('63), *Attack of the Mushroom People* ('63), *Godzilla vs. the Thing* ('64), *Dagora, the Space Monster* ('65), *Ghidrah, the Three-Headed Monster* ('65), *Frankenstein Conquers the World* ('65), *Monster Zero* ('66), *War of the Gargantuas* ('67), *King Kong Escapes* ('68), *Destroy All Monsters* ('68), *Latitude Zero* ('69), *Godzilla's Revenge* ('69), *Yog, Monster From Space* ('70), *Terror of Mechagodzilla* ('76).

---

exploited by a ruthless showman until rescued by their god: a huge caterpiller called Mothra. Colorful and enjoyable Japanese monster film with elaborate but unconvincing effects. Mothra and the girls returned in several Godzilla series entries.

MOUNTAINTOP MOTEL MASSACRE
★☆ Starmaker, 1983, R, 95 min.
Dir: Jim McCullough, Jr. Cast: Anna Chappell, Bill Thurman, Will Mitchel, Virginia Loridans, Major Brock, Amy Hill.

It's hard to believe that anyone would shelve a movie with a title like this for three years, but New World did, finally cutting it loose in '86. The titular lodgings, which make the Bates Motel look like a five-star establishment, are a string of shacks run by crazy Chappell, who has been recently released from an asylum and sickles most of the cast. Sometimes funny but mostly dull slasher with lots of phony gore FX.

MOVIE HOUSE MASSACRE
★ Active, 1984, NR, 75 min.
Dir: Alice Raley. Cast: Mary Woronov, Jonathan Blakely, Lynne Darcy, Cynthia Hartline.

Grindingly bad slasher about a movie theater, closed after a series of gory killings, that's reopened and menaced by a cheerleader-stalking maniac. Only an appearance by the terrific

MARY WORONOV
(1940–)

This leggy exploitation goddess started her career in experimental films for Andy Warhol in the early '60s before graduating to Roger Corman New World quickies in the '70s. A genuine talent, she brings a wonderful sense of sardonic sexiness to even the most limiting of roles.

Silent Night, Bloody Night ('72), *Sugar Cookies* ('73), *Seizure* ('74), *Hollywood Boulevard* ('76), *Eating Raoul* ('82), *Night of the Comet* ('84), *Hellhole* ('85), *Movie House Massacre* ('85), *Nomads* ('86), *Terrorvision* ('86), *Chopping Mall* ('86), *Warlock* ('89), *Mortuary Academy* ('89), *Watchers II* ('90).

Woronov distinguishes this tacky no-budget effort.

MR. CHRISTMAS DINNER
See: *Lucky Stiff.*

MR. FROST
★★☆ SVS, 1990, R, 92 min. Dir: Philip Setbon. Cast: Jeff Goldblum, Alan Bates, Kathy Baker, Jean-Pierre Cassel.

Goldblum's electrifying performance as an imprisoned mass murderer trying to convince psychiatrist Baker that he's really the devil highlights this medium psychological thriller with supernatural overtones. An interesting but poorly paced misfire, this has some striking similarities to the almost simultaneously released *The Exorcist III.*

MR. WRONG
See: *Dark of the Night.*

MS. 45
★★★ IVE, 1981, R, 84 min. Dir: Abel Ferrara. Cast: Zoe Tamerlis, Steve Singer, Jack Thibeau, Darlene Stuto, Peter Yellen, Jimmy Laine [Abel Ferrara].

Ferrara followed his less-than-great *Driller Killer* with this excellent action-horror-revenge flick. Thana (Tamerlis) flips after being raped twice on the same night and begins murdering every man she meets. Sharp direction and a powerful performance from the seductive Tamerlis make this better than all of Charles Bronson's *Death Wish* movies combined. Aka *Angel of Vengeance.*

MULTIPLE LISTINGS
See: *Open House.*

MUMMY, THE
★★★☆ MCA/Universal, 1932, NR, 73 min. Dir: Karl Freund. Cast: Boris Karloff, Zita Johann, David Manners, Edward Van Sloan, Arthur Byron, Bramwell Fletcher, Noble Johnson, Leonard Mudie.

One of Karloff's best performances highlights this romantic thriller clearly inspired by *Dracula* and *Svengali.* In 1922 archeologists open the tomb of a mummy called Im-Ho-Tep who is accidentally returned to life by the Scroll of Thoth. Ten years later the mummy, now in the guise of an ancient scientist called Ardath Bey, oversees the excavation of the crypt of his beloved Princess Anckes-en-Amon, whose reincarnation he sees in a beautiful modern girl. Arresting direction by cameraman Freund, beautiful images, and a fine supporting cast make this a true horror classic. Followed by several quickie mummy flicks in the '40s and remade by Hammer in 1959.

MUMMY, THE
★★★ Warner, 1959, NR, 87 min. Dir: Terence Fisher. Cast: Peter Cushing, Christopher Lee, Yvonne Furneaux, Eddie Byrne, Felix Ayler, Raymond Huntley, George Pastell, Michael Ripper.

Hammer had the good sense to turn this remake of the classic original into an amalgamation of story elements from *all* the Universal mummy movies, resulting in a colorful, entertaining blend. Lee is powerful as the living dead Kharis, bandaged guardian of the tomb of his beloved Princess Ananka, who rises from a misty swamp to deal out an ancient revenge against those who defiled her tomb. Equally good is Cushing as the son of the chief archeologist and Furneaux as Cushing's wife and possible Ananka reincarnation. Somewhat slowly paced, but good action highlights and gorgeous color photography carry it through.

MUMMY AND THE CURSE OF THE JACKALS, THE
☆ Academy, 1969, NR, 80 min. Dir: Oliver Drake. Cast: Anthony Eisley, John Carradine, Marliza Pons, Robert Alan Browne, Maurine Dawson, Saul Goldsmith.

Long forgotten and unacknowledged, this clunker has to be seen to be fully appreciated. Eisley stars as a Las Vegas–based Egyptologist who is cursed by a beautiful, perfectly preserved princess (Pons) into changing nightly into a werewolf-like jackalman. Meanwhile, Pons' guardian mummy rises up to pointlessly

Bramwell Fletcher watches Boris Karloff get all wrapped up as The Mummy *(1932).*

knock off a couple of strippers before taking on the jackalman in an absurd climax. Poor acting and silly scenes abound, especially when the tubby mummy and immobily masked jackalman rampage through a crowd of Vegas gamblers on the strip who barely notice them. Movies don't come any crummier than this.

MUMMY'S CURSE, THE

★★☆ MCA/Universal, 1944, NR, 60 min.
Dir: Leslie Goodwins. Cast: Lon Chaney, Jr., Virginia Christine, Peter Coe, Kay Harding, Martin Kosleck, Dennis Moore, Kurt Katch, Holmes Herbert.

The last (and, oddly enough, one of the better) of the Kharis movies relocates the action in the Louisiana bayou country (even though the mummy was last seen sinking into a bog in New England) and takes place 25 years after

the incidents in *The Mummy's Ghost*—1969 this ain't. Anyway, a new high priest (Coe) and his creepy assistant (Kosleck) reanimate Kharis (Chaney), who takes off after the reincarnated Ananka (Christine, who three decades later would find fame on TV coffee commercials as Mrs. Olson). A flavorful atmosphere and Kosleck's usual perverted villainy make this a kick to watch. The scene where Ananka revives from the swamp is the best.

MUMMY'S GHOST, THE

★★☆ MCA/Universal, 1944, NR, 60 min.
Dir: Reginald Le Borg. Cast: Lon Chaney, Jr., John Carradine, Ramsay Ames, Robert Lowery, Barton MacLane, George Zucco, Frank Reicher, Claire Whitney.

Kharis (Chaney) rises yet again, this time searching for the reincarnation of his beloved

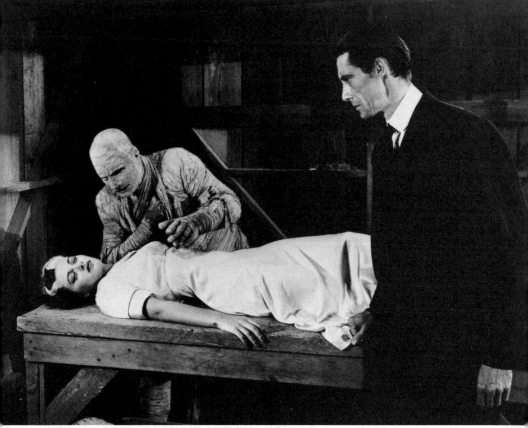

A jealous John Carradine watches Lon Chaney, Jr., go for Ramsay Amers in a big way in The Mummy's Ghost *(1944).*

Princess Ananka. She turns out to be a pretty Egyptian exchange student (Ames, in a role intended for Acquanetta) at the local college. Carradine's intense high priest and an unexpected downbeat ending are the best parts of this otherwise routine sequel.

MUMMY'S HAND, THE
★★★ MCA/Universal, 1940, NR, 66 min.
Dir: Christy Cabanne. Cast: Dick Foran, Peggy Moran, Wallace Ford, George Zucco, Cecil Kellaway, Eduardo Cianelli, Charles Trowbridge, Tom Tyler.

The first of the Kharis-the-mummy series has Foran heading an expedition searching for the lost tomb of Princess Ananka and encountering its living-dead guardian (Tyler) in the care of tana leaf-brewing high priest Zucco. This one's the best of the bunch; it has a fast pace, a fun cast, and impressive sets left over from James Whale's campy adventure epic *Green Hell.* Sequels: *The Mummy's Tomb, The Mummy's Ghost,* and *The Mummy's Curse.*

MUMMY'S REVENGE, THE
★★ Unicorn, 1973, R, 93 min.
Dir: Carlos Aured. Cast: Paul Naschy, Rina Otolina, Jack Taylor, Helga Line, Maria Silva, Luis Davila.

Naschy has a dual role as the murderous mummy of an evil pharaoh called Amanotef and its guardian high priest. When the mummy is unearthed, he follows the usual trail of killing his unearthers and stalking the reincarnation of his wife. Ho-hum. Some good atmosphere and bloody violence but too slow and as badly dubbed as they come.

MUMMY'S TOMB, THE
★★☆ MCA/Universal, 1942, NR, 59 min.
Dir: Harold Young. Cast: Lon Chaney, Jr., Elyse Knox, John Hubbard, Turhan Bey, Dick Foran, Wallace Ford, George Zucco, Mary Gordon, Frank Reicher, Virginia Brissac.

The second in the Kharis series, and the first with Chaney in the lead, relocates the action back in the states in Mapleton, Massachusetts, where the bandaged one bumps off all those responsible for bringing the body of Princess Ananka to America. The film is routinely plotted and has too much stock footage, but the photography, music, and cast are first-rate. This video print, however, is missing the scene where Kharis strangles sweet old Gordon (Mrs. Hudson in the Basil Rathbone Sherlock Holmes series).

GEORGE ZUCCO
(1886–1960)

Zucco was an English stage and screen actor who, like Lionel Atwill, became typecast as a second-string horror star in the 1940s. The distinguished Zucco was adept at playing monster-making mad doctors and tana leaf-brewing high priests, but he was never really happy with most of his Hollywood work. Although it has been often reported that he died insane, believing himself to be one of his own mad movie characters, the Zucco family firmly denies this little bit of Hollywood Babyloney.

The Cat and the Canary ('39), *The Hunchback of Notre Dame* ('39), *The Adventures of Sherlock Holmes* ('39), *The Mummy's Hand* ('40), *The Monster and the Girl* ('41), *The Mad Monster* ('42), *Dr. Renault's Secret* ('42), *The Mummy's Tomb* ('42), *Dead Men Walk* ('43), *The Black Raven* ('43), *The Mad Ghoul* ('43), *Voodoo Man* ('44), *The Mummy's Ghost* ('44), *House of Frankenstein* ('44), *Fog Island* ('45), *The Flying Serpent* ('46), *Scared to Death* ('47), *Who Killed Doc Robin?* ('48).

MUMSY, NANNY, SONNY, AND GIRLY
See: *Girly.*

MUNCHIES
★☆ MGM/UA, 1987, PG, 82 min.
Dir: Bettina Hirsch. Cast: Harvey Korman, Charles Stratton, Nadine Van Der Velde, Alix Elias, Paul Bartel, Robert Picardo.

Yet another needless *Gremlins* cash-in with another pack of furry puppets going on another comic rampage. Korman (in a dual role), Bartel, and Picardo are funny, but this is mainly for those who want something to make *Critters* look like the height of originality.

MUNSTERS' REVENGE, THE
★★ MCA/Universal, 1981, NR, 96 min.
Dir: Don Weis. Cast: Fred Gwynne, Yvonne De Carlo, Al Lewis, Jo McDonnell, K. C. Martel, Sid Caesar, Peter Fox, Howard Morris.

TV's munstrous family from 1313 Mockingbird Lane return in this routine tele-movie (from that period when countless popular shows from the '60s were being revived) that pits them against mad scientist Caesar. If you liked the show you might like this, though McDonnell and Martel are sad substitutes for

Pat Priest and Butch Patrick. At least it's better than "The Munsters Today."

MURDER BY DECREE
★★★ Embassy, 1979, PG, 124 min.
Dir: Bob Clark. Cast: Christopher Plummer, James Mason, Donald Sutherland, Geneviève Bujold, David Hemmings, Susan Clark, Anthony Quayle, John Gielgud, Frank Finlay, Teddi Moore.

Plummer and Mason are exceptional as Sherlock Holmes and Dr. Watson in this thriller that pits them against Jack the Ripper—whose true identity Holmes eventually uncovers. A superior mystery-horror, it is strikingly similar to *A Study in Terror*, with post-Watergate touches. Bujold is unforgettably sad as the tormented heroine, while Clark directs the horror scenes with the same sort of acumen he exhibited in *Black Christmas.*

MURDER BY MAIL
See: *Schizoid.*

MURDER BY NATURAL CAUSES
★★★☆ Lorimar, 1979, NR, 96 min.
Dir: Robert Day. Cast: Hal Holbrook, Katharine Ross, Barry Bostwick, Richard Anderson, Jeff Donnell, Victoria Carroll.

Terrific TV thriller with Ross as the frustrated wife of famed mentalist Holbrook who plots with lover Bostwick to dispose of her hubby by scaring him to death. Superb performances and clever script complications make this one of the most impressive tele-thrillers ever written by "Columbo" creators Richard Levison and William Link. Great final line.

MURDER BY PHONE
★★ Warner, 1980, R, 79 min.
Dir: Michael Anderson. Cast: Richard Chamberlain, John Houseman, Sara Botsford, Barry Morse, Robin Gammell, Gary Reineke.

Well-made but ridiculous Canadian thriller about a madman who uses sound waves to commit murder over the phone, the vibrations causing the victims to explode. As dumb as they come, but slickly directed and featuring a cast who clearly weren't taking any of this nonsense seriously. Aka *Bells, Hell's Bells,* and *The Calling.*

MURDER IN THE RED BARN
★★☆ Rhino, 1935, NR, 67 min. Dir: George King. Cast: Tod Slaughter, Sophie Stewart, Eric Portman, Ann Trevor, D. J. Williams, Clare Greet.

Slaughter's first and best film was this lurid but fun dramatization of a famous true British murder case. A girl is murdered by a jealous suitor (guess who?) and her corpse is buried in the family barn; later her mother dreams of the killing and digs up her daughter's body! The Todmeister is at his best here as the opportunistic killer ("Don't you trust me, Maria?" he has the colossal nerve to coo at one point), making this the one to see in the Slaughter filmography. Britist title: *Maria Marten or the Murder in the Red Barn*.

MURDER MANSION

★★ Embassy, 1972, PG, 86 min.
Dir: Francisco Lara Polop. Cast: Ana Gade, Andres Resino, Evelyn Stewart, Anna Lisa Nardi, Eduardo Fajardo, Ingrid Garbo.

Atmospheric but routinely plotted Spanish chiller about a group of travelers stranded by fog at a supposedly haunted mansion. The heroine (Gade) is terrorized by various ghosts and vampires until the obvious twist ending. So familiar that, even if you've neven seen it before, you'll swear you have.

MURDER MOTEL

★★ IVE, 1974, NR, 72 min. Dir: Malcolm Taylor. Cast: Robyn Millan, Ralph Bates, Edward Judd, Derek Francis.

This Brian Clemens–penned TV *Psycho* rip-off is about a girl investigating the disappearance of her embezzler brother from an eerie backwater motel. Sound familiar? It's complete with a shot of blood spiraling down the bathroom drain and Brit horror vets Bates and Judd. The best thing about the film is its psychedelic credits sequence!

MURDER OBSESSION

See: *Fear*.

MURDERS IN THE RUE MORGUE

★★☆ MCA/Universal, 1932, NR, 60 min.
Dir: Robert Florey. Cast: Bela Lugosi, Sidney Fox, Leon Ames, Brandon Hurst, Noble Johnson, Arlene Francis.

After being bumped from Universal's original production of *Frankenstein*, director Florey and star Lugosi ended up with this flamboyant booby prize. It bears little resemblance to Poe but *does* contain one of Bela's most enjoyable out-of-control performances as the crazed early Darwinian Dr. Mirakle. Fox is the virginal lass Lugosi hopes to mate with his pet ape Erik in order to prove a link between the species. This *Cabinet of Dr. Caligari*–inspired period piece is a bit creaky 'round the edges but still worth seeing for Bela and some surprisingly grisly touches. A young John Huston provided additional dialogue!

MURDERS IN THE RUE MORGUE

★★☆ Vestron, 1971, PG, 87 min.
Dir: Gordon Hessler. Cast: Jason Robards, Christine Kaufmann, Herbert Lom, Lilli Palmer, Michael Dunn, Adolfo Celli, Maria Perschy, Peter Arne.

One of Hessler's better pictures, this could have been a great *Nightmare on Elm Street*–type dreams vs. reality piece before AIP mucked it up in the editing. In 19th-century Paris, Robards' Grand Guinol company is putting on a production of the Poe tale while members of the company are being murdered by disfigured former member Lom. Kaufmann is the terrified actress whose strange dreams (originally meant to be perceived as part of the actual action) lead to the killer's identity and motivation. Robards is hammy in a role probably meant for Vincent Price, but the rest of the cast underplays nicely.

MURDERS IN THE RUE MORGUE

★★ Vidmark, 1986, NR, 92 min.
Dir: Jeannot Szwarc. Cast: George C. Scott, Rebecca De Mornay, Val Kilmer, Ian McShane.

Handsome but plodding TV remake with Scott as a retired Parisian police inspector who amuses himself by casually investigating a brutal double murder. Eventually he becomes embroiled in the case and discovers the killer to be a crazed ape. Good-looking photography and set design, but the plot has enough padding for two Roger Corman movies, the romantic leads are miscast, and the monster ape looks like a *Greystoke* reject. Still, Scott manages to maintain interest.

MUTANT!

See: *Forbidden World*.

MUTANT

★★☆ Vestron, 1984, R, 100 min.
Dir: John "Bud" Cardos. Cast: Wings Hauser, Bo Hopkins, Jennifer Warren, Jody Medford, Lee Montgomery, Cary Guffey.

Brothers Hauser and Montgomery are stranded in a small southern town where the residents are falling victim to toxic waste, being transformed into blue-faced zombies. Sounds pretty ordinary, but a good cast (headed by the always wacky Wings) and expert action direction from Cardos make this exceptional. Shooting title: *Night Shadows*.

MUTATIONS, THE

See: *The Freakmaker*.

MUTILATOR, THE

★ Vestron, 1983, NR, 86 min. Dir: Buddy Cooper.

Cast: Matt Mitler, Ruth Martinez, Jack Chatham, Bill Hitchcock, Connie Rogers, Frances Raines.

Junky, gore-encrusted regional slasher movie with Mitler and college friends stalked by psycho Chatham at a remote condo. After just about everyone has been killed, the maniac is revealed as Matt's vengeful dad and he's bumped off by herione Martinez. No-frills production with inept photography and editing but some pretty graphic FX for gorehounds. Filmed as *Fall Break.*

MY BEST FRIEND IS A VAMPIRE
★★ HBO, 1988, PG, 89 min.
Dir: Jimmy Huston. Cast: Robert Sean Leonard, Evan Mirand, Cheryl Pollack, David Warner, René Auberjonois, Fannie Flagg.

Run-of-the-mill teen monster comedy with Leonard as a delivery boy bitten by a seductive lady vampire, his transformation endangering his budding relationship with pretty Pollack. Pleasant actors and some funny situations, but an odd subplot equates vampirism with homosexuality and runs against the grain of the rest of the movie.

MY BLOODY VALENTINE
★★☆ Paramount, 1981, R, 91 min.
Dir: George Mihalka. Cast: Paul Kelman, Lori Hallier, Neil Affleck, Keith Knight, Cynthia Dale, Alf Humphreys.

A psycho in miner's garb terrorizes the village of Valentine's Bluff on St. Valentine's Day, cutting out his victims' hearts with a pickax. Sharp photography and an effective score distinguish this holiday slash fest, though jerky characters and MPAA-cut gore scenes are occasionally annoying. Best scene: the killing in the laundromat.

MY BOYFRIEND'S BACK
★★ Touchstone, 1993, PG-13, 85 min.
Dir: Bob Balaban. Cast: Traci Lind, Andrew Lowery, Bob Dishy, Paul Dooley, Edward Herrmann, Mary Beth Hurt, Cloris Leachman, Austin Pendleton.

Shy guy Lowery dies before he can take pretty Lind to the prom, returning from the grave as a zombie to keep the date. This harmless horror-comedy has a good cast but doesn't leave much of an impression. Produced by *Friday the 13th*'s Sean Cunningham, this was originally called *Johnny Zombie* until Touchstone decided that it was beneath them to release a movie with the word zombie in the title.

MY DEMON LOVER
★☆ RCA/Columbia, 1987, PG-13, 86 min.
Dir: Charles Loventhal. Cast: Scott Valentine,

Michelle Little, Arnold Johnson, Robert Trebor, Alan Fudge, Gina Gallego.

Feeble horror-comedy with Valentine as an obnoxious NYC street musician who is cursed to become a demonic monster whenever sexually aroused. Some good makeups (many of them barely glimpsed) are the only reason to sit through this laughless clinker, which looks like an extended bad epsiode of "Monsters."

MY LETTER TO GEORGE
See: *Mesmerized.*

MY MOM'S A WEREWOLF
★★ Prism, 1989, PG, 84 min. Dir: Michael Fischa.
Cast: Susan Blakely, John Saxon, Katrina Caspary, John Schuck, Ruth Buzzi, Marilyn McCoo.

Neglected housewife Blakely begins an affair with pet shop owner Saxon, little realizing that he is a werewolf. After she's bitten, can teen daughter Caspary and gypsy fortune teller Buzzi help? Tame TV-type comedy with a seasoned cast having fun and a couple of laughs.

MY SISTER, MY LOVE
★★ Wizard, 1978, R, 98 min. Dir: Karen Arthur. Cast: Lee Grant, Carol Kane, James Olson, Will Geer.

Strange psychological horror film with Grant and Kane as sisters who live together in their late father's African mansion. Lee is an astromoner having an affair with co-worker Olson, while Carol is an artist who raises apes in a cage and has an incestuous lesbian desire for her sis, leading to madness and death. Not for all tastes and often hard to follow, but the ladies are first-rate. Aka *The Mafu Cage* and *Deviation.*

MY SON, THE VAMPIRE
★★☆ Sinister Cinema, 1952, NR, 74 min.
Dir: John Gilling. Cast: Bela Lugosi, Arthur Lucan, Dora Bryan, Richard Wattis, Maria Mercedes, Philip Leaver.

This infamous Brit quickie is actually Bela's best '50s film. He's genuinely funny as a mad scientist who thinks he's a vampire and plots to conquer the world with his all-powerful robot until undone by old Irish washerwoman Mother Riley (Lucan, a once-popular English drag performer). Lucan's scenes verge on the grotesque, but Lugosi belies the years and steals the show. Originally *Old Mother Riley Meets the Vampire* and aka *Mother Riley Meets the Vampire* and *Vampire Over London.*

MYSTERIOUS INVADER, THE
See: *The Astounding She Monster.*

LIONEL ATWILL
(1885–1946)

This crisp British stage and screen actor had a lucrative Hollywood career in the '30s and '40s as a popular second-string horror star. Whether mad scientist or stalwart burgomaster or police inspector, Atwill (whose private life of alleged sexual carousing was quite infamous) could always be counted on to give it his considerable all.

Doctor X ('32), *The Vampire Bat* ('33), *Mystery of the Wax Museum* ('33), *Murders in the Zoo* ('33), *The Sphinx* ('34), *Mark of the Vampire* ('35), *Son of Frankenstein* ('39), *The Hound of the Baskervilles* ('39), *The Gorilla* ('39), *Man-Made Monster* ('41), *The Ghost of Frankenstein* ('42), *The Mad Doctor of Market Street* ('42), *The Strange Case of Dr. RX* ('42), *Night Monster* ('42), *Sherlock Holmes and the Secret Weapon* ('43), *Frankenstein Meets the Wolf Man* ('43), *House of Frankenstein* ('44), *Fog Island* ('45), *House of Dracula* ('45).

MYSTERIOUS ISLAND
★★★RCA/Columbia, 1961, NR, 101 min.
Dir: Cy Endfield. Cast: Michael Craig, Joan Greenwood, Gary Merrill, Michael Callan, Beth Rogan, Herbert Lom.

Some great Ray Harryhausen special effects and a truly wonderful Bernard Herrmann score highlight this fine monster fantasy about Civil War soldiers and two shipwrecked women stranded on an island inhabited by huge animals. When the island's volcano threatens to erupt, the group is rescued by none other than Captain Nemo (Lom in a rather effective cameo). Solid adaptation of Jules Verne's sequel to *Twenty Thousand Leagues Under the Sea.*

MYSTERIOUS MR. WONG
★★ Sinister Cinema, 1935, NR, 60 min.
Dir: William Nigh. Cast: Bela Lugosi, Wallace Ford, Arline Judge, Fred Warren, Lotus Long, Robert Emmet O'Connor.

Lugosi is a Chinese warlord with a Hungarian accent in this cheapo rip-off of *The Mask of Fu Manchu.* Bela is after the legendary 12 coins of Confucius, and wisecracking reporters Ford and Judge try to stop him. This is very cheesy-looking and full of insulting ethnic slurs, but Bela is always a kick.

MYSTERY OF THE WAX MUSEUM
★★★ MGM/UA, 1933, NR, 77 min.
Dir: Michael Curtiz. Cast: Lionel Atwill, Fay Wray, Glenda Farrell, Frank McHugh, Allen Vincent, Gavin Gordon, Arthur Edmund Carewe, Edwin Maxwell.

For many years a lost film, this early Technicolor "classic" shows its age badly and is actually inferior to its better-known remake, *House of Wax.* On the plus side, though, Atwill gives his best performance as a mad, disfigured sculptor who was burned in a fire in the wax museum and disguises his scars with a wax mask; he is recreating the statues lost in the fire by dipping the corpses of murder victims in hot wax. Also great are Farrell as a plucky, wisecracking reporter (a cliché usually stumbled over in these creaky early melodramas) and Wray in her usual screaming heroine spot. "Your face, it was wax! You fiend!"

MY WORLD DIES SCREAMING!
See: *Terror in the Haunted House.*

NAIL GUN MASSACRE
★ Magnum, 1985, R, 90 min.
Dirs: Bill Leslie, Terry Lofton. Cast: Rocky Patterson, Michelle Meyer, Ron Queen, Beau Leland.

You mean, it actually took *two* guys to direct this derivative junk about a helmeted hacker with a nail gun killing macho construction jerks and their bimbettes? Apparently so, which is the only out-of-the-ordinary element in this lackluster, surprisingly bloodless late entry in the power-tool-of-death subgenre.

NAKED AND SATAN, THE
See: *The Head.*

NAKED JUNGLE, THE
★★★ Paramount, 1954, NR, 95 min.
Dir: Byron Haskin. Cast: Charlton Heston, Eleanor Parker, William Conrad, Abraham Sofaer.

Heston stars as a repressed, blunt-jawed South American rancher who must battle both strong-willed mail-order bride Parker *and* millions of voracious, man-eating soldier ants in this creepy critter flick produced by sci-fi fave George Pal. Bear with a slow first half, though; after that, this really kicks.

NATIONAL LAMPOON'S CLASS REUNION
★ Video Treasures, 1982, R, 84 min.
Dir: Michael Miller. Cast: Gerrit Graham, Shelley Smith, Fred McCarren, Stephen Furst, Zane Buzby, Michael Lerner, Miriam Flynn, Jacklyn Zeman, Blackie Dammett, Anne Ramsey.

Pathetically unfunny slasher spoof with an Unknown Comic–like paper-bag-headed killer bumping off the 1972 graduating class of Lizzie Borden High at their 10-year class reunion. Comes alive for about two minutes during an on-target Diana Ross and the Supremes number, but other than that this is the pits, with a potentially exceptional comic cast utterly wasted, particularly Ramsey as a cafeteria worker who has to cut her lasagna with a chainsaw.

NATURE'S MISTAKES
See: *Freaks.*

NAVY VS. THE NIGHT MONSTERS, THE
★ Paragon, 1966, NR, 87 min.
Dir: Michael A. Hoey. Cast: Mamie Van Doren, Anthony Eisley, Bobby Van, Pamela Mason, Phillip Terry, Bill Gray, Russ Bender, Kaye Elhardt.

Walking, man-eating trees terrorize the personnel of an uncommonly tropical Antarctic naval base in this enjoyable junky Z flick. All the guys fight over Mamie; the extras try not to trip over the awesomely fake painted backdrops and cardboard set decorations (including monsters that look like bloated rhubarb); and the hero's actually named Charlie Brown! Funnier than anything Blake Edwards ever made.

NEAR DARK
★★★☆ HBO, 1987, R, 93 min.
Dir: Kathryn Bigelow. Cast: Adrian Pasdar, Jenny Wright, Lance Henriksen, Bill Paxton, Tim Thomerson, Jenette Goldstein, Joshua Miller, Marcie Leeds.

Terrific, vastly underrated black comic chiller mixing up components from the vampire, western, and biker genres into a high-powered brew. Pasdar is a likable, if rather dumb, Oklahoma farm boy who is seduced into a life of nomadic vampirism by undead teen temptress Wright, one of the "Family": a band of vampires that travels in a van throughout the American Southwest in search of fresh blood. Sparked by strong performances (Henriksen and Paxton are sheer perfection), great dialogue, and excellent imagery (hazy moons, blazing suns, and multicolored sunrises and sunsets), this ignored minor gem is worthy of rediscovery.

NECROMANCER
★☆ Forum, 1989, R, 88 min. Dir: Dusty Nelson. Cast: Elizabeth Kaitan, Russ Tamblyn, John Tyler, Rhonda Durton, Stan Hurwitz, Lois Masten.

Dull, predictable, supernatural revenge flick with the luscious Kaitan as an acting student who avenges her brutal rape through supernatural powers gained via possession from witch Masten. Former *tom thumb* Tamblyn is wasted as a horny teacher.

NECROMANCY
See: *The Witching.*

NECROPOLIS
★ Vestron, 1987, R, 77 min.
Dir: Bruce Hickey. Cast: Leeanne Baker, Jacquie Fitz, Michael Conte, William K. Reed.

Three-hundred-year old witch Baker, who sports *six* breasts, no less, murders street people while disguised as a punk hoodlum in this rock-bottom Empire Pics cheapie. A pointless, plotless waste of time that's not even good for laughs. For mutant mammary muttonheads only.

NEEDFUL THINGS
★★☆ New Line, 1993, R, 120 min.
Dir: Fraser C. Heston. Cast: Max von Sydow, Ed Harris, Bonnie Bedelia, Amanda Plummer, J. T. Walsh, Valri Bromfield, Shane Meier, Lisa Blount.

Another watchable but forgettable Stephen King movie, from an equally readable but forgettable novel, with von Sydow as the satanic owner of an antique store in the Maine community of Castle Rock, where all hell, quite literally, breaks loose. This plays better as a black comedy than a horror film and has an uncredited influence from the Amicus film *From Beyond the Grave,* but it is held together by Heston's assured direction and a very good cast—with von Sydow a real delight as spooky, sardonic Leland Gaunt.

NEIGHBOR, THE
★★ Academy, 1993, R, 93 min.
Dir: Rodney Gibbons. Cast: Rod Steiger, Linda Kozlowski, Ron Lea, Frances Bay, Bruce Boa, Jane Wheeler.

Another entry in the increasingly tiresome "Fill-in-the-blank From Hell" horror subgenre, this one offers up a surprisingly subdued Steiger as an evil obstetrician out to terminate the pregnancy of neighbor Kozlowski. Why? Because she reminds Rod of his late mom, who died during childbirth, that's why. Formula shot-in-Canada thriller with few surprises.

NEKROMANTIK
★★★ Film Threat, 1989, UR, 71 min.
Dir: Jorg Buttgereit. Cast: Daktari Lorenz, Beatrice M., Harold Lundt, Susa Kohlstaedt, Heike Surban.

This German-made grotesquery is one of the most unforgettable film-watching experiences ever. Lorenz is part of an accident clean-up crew obsessed with death and decay. When he brings home a male corpse, he and necrophilic girlfriend M. have sex with it, Beatrice becoming so infatuated that she eventually runs off with the cadaver! This sends Daktari on a bloody murder spree that ends in an amazingly sickening scene of suicidal self-abuse. Clearly one of the sickest films ever, but Buttgereit is no hack; he brings a powerful semi-documentary feel to this, making it often resemble *Henry, Portrait of a Serial Killer* crossed with *Love Me Deadly*. Recommended—but only for the most adventurous of viewers.

NEKROMANTIK 2: RETURN OF THE LOVING DEAD
★★☆ Film Threat, 1991, UR, 100 min.
Dir: Jorg Buttgereit. Cast: Monika M., Mark Reeder, Simone Spore, Wolfgang Muller.

Obviously, Buttgereit could *never* top the depravity of the original, but this follow-up certainly tries. Monika M. now takes over the role played in part one by Beatrice M., digging up her late boyfriend's corpse and trying to get new beau Reeder interested in her gross hobby. Fans of the first will know exactly what to expect—everyone else might be better off watching a rerun of "Full House."

NEON MANIACS
★☆ Vestron, 1986, R, 91 min.
Dir: Joseph Mangine. Cast: Alan Hayes, Leilani Sarelle, Donna Locke, Victor Elliot Brandt.

Monsters who can't stand water—and yet live in rainy San Francisco—battle teens armed with water pistols in this silly low-budgeter directed by cinematographer Mangine. Slick but dumb, with lots of blood, comic-book colors, and rubbery creatures.

NERVOSUS
See: *Revenge in the House of Usher.*

NEST, THE
★★★ MGM/UA, 1988, R, 88 min. Dir: Terence H. Winkless. Cast: Robert Lansing, Lisa Langlois, Franc Luz, Terri Treas, Stephen Davies, Jack Collins.

Mutant flesh-eating cockroaches terrorize the residents of a small island off the Washington coast in this fun, dark-humored tale from Roger Corman's Concorde Pictures. The film

is sparked by a good cast playing believable, sometimes quite funny characters, as well as a strong script and very icky effects, some of them obviously inspired by David Cronenberg's *Fly* remake. Treas steals it as a lady scientist turned on by bug bites.

NESTING, THE
★★☆ Warner, 1981, R, 103 min.
Dir: Armand Weston. Cast: Robin Groves, Christopher Loomis, Michael David Lally, John Carradine, Gloria Grahame, Bill Rowley.

Agoraphobic novelist Groves moves into a strange octagonal house in upstate New York, which she discovers is a former brothal haunted by the ghosts of murdered prostitutes. This elegant cheapie is boosted by a solid, intriguing screenplay and a nice role for a still sexy Grahame in, sadly, her last film. Filmed as *Phobia* and reissued, in a cut version, as *Massacre Mansion.*

NETHERWORLD
★★ Paramount, 1991, R, 84 min. Dir: David Schmoeller. Cast: Michael Bendetti, Denise Gentile, Holly Floria, Anjanette Comer, Robert Sampson.

This is a sleek but uninvolving voodoo thriller. Bendetti inherits a New Orleans estate and gets mixed up with supernatural harlot Gentile, who's out to revive his dead dad (Sampson). It has the odd good moment and effect (like a gratuitous flying stone hand) but is nearly ruined by an annoying hero in need of a good hair wash.

NEW INVISIBLE MAN, THE
★★ Sinister Cinema, 1957, NR, 94 min.
Dir: Alfredo B. Cravenna. Cast: Arturo de Cordova, Ana Luisa Peluffo, Augusto Benedico, Raul Meraz.

Fair Mexican-made semi-remake of *The Invisible Man Returns* with de Cordova falsely accused of murder and turning invisible to catch the real culprit. Mediocre special effects and crummy dubbing detract from the overall effect. Aka *H. G. Wells' New Invisible Man* and *The Invisible Man in Mexico.*

NEW KIDS, THE
★☆ RCA/Columbia, 1985, R, 90 min.
Dir: Sean S. Cunningham. Cast: Shannon Presby, Lori Loughlin, James Spader, John Philbin, Vincent Grant, Eric Stoltz.

Unsuccessful crossbreed of the teen slasher and vigilante genres. Brother and sister Presby and Loughlin are the new kids in town menaced by a sadistic gang led by Philbin. When they attempt rape, the siblings plot a gory comeuppance. A halfway exciting climax in an abandoned amusement park does little to help.

NEWLYDEADS, THE

★☆ City Lights, 1988, UR, 76 min. Dir: Joseph Merhi. Cast: Jim Williams, Jean Levine, Jay Richardson, Scott Kaske, Roxanne Michaels, Captain Mike.

Cheesy video gore job about a Lake Arrowhead honeymoon lodge owner who kills an amorous transvestite and years later is haunted on his own honeymoon by the crossdresser's vengeful ghost. Occasionally amusing, especially Captain Mike as a perpetually drunken preacher, but too tacky and annoying to make for truly compelling viewing.

NEW YEAR'S EVIL

★☆ Paragon, 1980, R, 85 min. Dir: Emmett Alston. Cast: Roz Kelly, Kip Niven, Chris Wallace, Grant Cramer, Louisa Moritz, Jed Mills, Taffee O'Connell, Teri Copley.

A less than great throwback to those bygone days when no holiday was safe from the makers of mad slasher movies. Kelly stars as the obnoxious, self-centered host of a televised punk New Year's Eve party ("New Year's Rockin' Eve" this ain't) menaced by phone by a loon out to kill a woman every time a different U.S. time zone reaches midnight. Guess who's gonna get it at 12 o'clock California time? With bad music, little blood, and a predictable twist ending, this is saved only by Moritz's sweet performance as a ditzy blonde.

NEW YORK RIPPER, THE

★ Vidmark, 1982, R, 85 min. Dir: Lucio Fulci. Cast: Jack Hedley, Almanta Keller, Palo Malco, Alexandra Delli Colli, Howard Ross, Daniela Doria.

Fulci's worst horror film is an awful melange of slasher clichés about a duck-voiced—that's what I said, duck-voiced!— maniac carving up Manhattan babes for maybe the flimsiest excuse any of these movies has ever forced upon an unsuspecting world. Violently antifemale (the scene where a semi-nude Doria has her eyeball and nipple slashed with a razor blade borders on pornographic), with lousy dubbing, muddy color, crummy gore effects, and an abrasive musical score. Aka *The Ripper.*

NEXT!

★★Interglobal, 1971, R, 81 min. Dir: Luciano Martino. Cast: Edwige Fenech, Alberto de Mendoza, Cristina Airoldi, George Hilton, Ivan Rassimov.

Another routine continental slasher film. Eurohorror vet Fenech is the busty heroine menaced by a razor-killer in Vienna who may or may not be her estranged husband. Strictly second-rate. Aka *Lo Strano Vizio della Signora Wardh: The Strange Weakness of Mrs. Ward, The Next Victim,* and *Blade of the Ripper.*

NEXT OF KIN

★★ Media, 1982, R, 86 min. Dir: Tony Williams. Cast: Jackie Kerin, John Jarratt, Alex Scott, Gerda Nicolson, Charles McCallum, Bernadette Gibson.

Kerin inherits a retirement home from her late aunt and tries running the establishment until a mysterious killer begins picking the residents off one by one. This New Zealand–made maniac movie has some stylish flourishes and offbeat touches (with many of the victims wizened geriatrics rather than the usual bouncy teens) before it collapses into yet another *Friday the 13th*–inspired bloodbath.

NEXT VICTIM, THE

See: *Next!*

NEXT VICTIM, THE

★★Thrillervideo, 1974, NR, 72 min. Dir: James Omerod. Cast: Carroll Baker, T. P. McKenna, Maurice Kaufman, Ronald Lacey, Brenda Cavendish, Max Mason.

Predictable Brian Clemens–penned tele-chiller with Baker as a wheelchair-bound lady left alone for the weekend in her nearly deserted apartment building. Naturally, there's a crazed strangler on the loose, and equally naturally, they meet head on. Forgettable, though helped a lot by Baker's sincere, sympathetic performance.

NIGHT ANDY CAME HOME, THE

See: *Deathdream.*

NIGHT ANGEL

★★☆ Fries, 1989, R, 87 min. Dir: Dominique Otherin-Girard. Cast: Isa Anderson, Karen Black, Linden Ashby, Debra Feuer, Doug Jones, Helen Martin, Gary Hudson, Sam Hennings.

The seductive Anderson stars as Lilith, Adam's first wife, who was kicked out of the Garden of Eden and is now an evil entity personifying wanton lust. When she turns up as a cover girl for *Siren* magazine, all hell, quite literally, breaks loose. Though it looks like *Lair of the White Worm* meets *The Kiss,* this actually plays much better than you'd expect, although it suffers from a dearth of unsympathetic characters (apart from the ageless Black) and a ragged series of MPAA cuts. Aka *Deliver Us From Evil.*

NIGHTBREED

★★★ Video Treasures, 1990, R, 101 min.
Dir: Clive Barker, Cast: Craig Sheffer, Anne Bobby, David Cronenberg, Charles Haid, Hugh Quarshie, Hugh Ross, Doug Bradley, John Agar.

Barker's flawed but ambitious adaptation of his novella *Cabal* features hunky Sheffer as a guy framed for a series of brutal murders actually committed by his mad psychiatrist (director Cronenberg, who gives a fantastic debut acting performance). Haunted by dreams of a strange world called Midian (located under an old cemetery), Sheffer flees there, where he becomes some sort of monster messiah following his death. Disjointed but with a terrific cast, imaginative visuals, and excellent makeup design for the monstrous denizens of Midian.

NIGHT CALLER

See: *Night Caller From Outer Space.*

NIGHT CALLER FROM OUTER SPACE

★★ SVS, 1965, NR, 84 min. Dir: John Gilling. Cast: John Saxon, Patricia Haines, Maurice Denham, Alfred Burke, Jack Watson, Barbara French.

Beautiful girls answering a provocative ad in *Bikini Girl* magazine are abducted by a hideous alien in this serviceable Brit thriller. Moody photography and one shocking twist near the end, but otherwise routine. Aka *Night Caller* and *Blood Beast From Outer Space.*

NIGHT CHILD

See: *What the Peeper Saw.*

NIGHTCOMERS, THE

★★ Embassy, 1971, R, 95 min.
Dir: Michael Winner. Cast: Marlon Brando, Stephanie Beacham, Harry Andrews, Thora Hird, Verna Harvey, Christopher Ellis, Anna Palk.

Brando, in his last lesser film before *The Godfather* made him a big star all over again, stars as the brutish Quint in this prequel to Henry James' *The Turn of the Screw.* Often unintentionally funny, but Beacham is fine as the tormented governess Miss Jessel, and there's some nice photography and an unexpectedly gory climax. Sometimes admired; often not.

NIGHT CREATURE

★ VCI, 1977 R, 82 min.
Dir: Lee Madden. Cast: Donald Pleasence, Nancy Kwan, Ross Hagen, Jennifer Rhodes, Lesley Fine.

Boring Filipino "thriller" with Pleasence miscast as a macho sportsman hunting a killer panther on his private island. Kwan is wasted and Hagen awful as the wiseguy here—a role

he never would have gotten if he hadn't produced the film! Aka *Out of the Darkness.*

NIGHT CREW: THE FINAL CHECK OUT

See: *Intruder.*

NIGHT CRIES

★★ VCL, 1978, NR, 96 min. Dir: Richard Lang. Cast: Susan Saint James, Michael Parks, William Conrad, Cathleen Nesbitt, Jamie Smith Jackson, Dolores Dorn.

Sleepy TV flick with Saint James as a distraught lady claiming to be receiving psychic messages from her dead baby. Saint James is appealing and there are some eerie passages, but in the main too slow and derivative.

NIGHT EVELYN CAME OUT OF THE GRAVE, THE

★★ Sinister Cinema, 1972, R, 99 min.
Dir: Emilio P. Miraglia. Cast: Anthony Steffen, Mariana Mafatti, Erika Blanc, Rod Murdock, Giacomo Rossi Stuart, Umberto Raho.

Steffen is a British lord recently released from an asylum who is obsessed with his late wife, Evelyn. After he marries lovely Mafatti, it seems that Evelyn rises from the grave to harass the newlyweds into becoming newlydeads. This confusing Italian chiller is highlighted by Blanc as a stripper who uses a velvet-lined coffin in her act. Aka *La Notte Che Evelyn Usci Dalla Tomba: The Night That Evelyn Left the Tomb, The Night She Rose From the Tomb,* and *Sweet to Be Kissed, Hard to Die.*

NIGHT EYES

See: *Deadly Eyes.*

NIGHTFLYERS

★☆ IVE, 1987, R, 89 min.
Dir: T. C. Blake [Robert Collector]. Cast: Catherine Mary Stewart, Michael Praed, Lisa Blount, John Standing, Michael Des Barres, Hélène Udy.

Astronauts investigating some strange phenomena discover that their spaceship has a murderous life of its own. Feeble adaptation of a good story by George R.R. Martin, with solid production values wasted on yet another tired *Alien* hybrid with touches of *2001* and *The Legend of Hell House.*

NIGHT GALLERY

★★★ MCA/Universal, 1969, NR, 98 min.
Dirs: Boris Sagal, Steven Spielberg, Barry Shear. Cast: Joan Crawford, Roddy McDowall, Richard Kiley, Ossie Davis, Barry Sullivan, Sam Jaffe, Tom Bosley, George Macready, Norma Crane, Barry Atwater.

Rod Serling scripted and hosted this entertaining TV film, which served as the pilot for the later series. McDowall murders rich uncle Macready for his money, only to be haunted to death by a macabre painting; Crawford is a heartless blind dowager who buys bum Bosley's eyes in time to see the New York blackout; and Kiley is a Nazi war criminal who discovers the secret of astral projection in a South American art gallery. The EC comics-type first segment is best, though first-time director Spielberg brings some style to the second (helped tremendously by Crawford in one of her best performances). Only the pretentious last story doesn't come off. Aka *Rod Serling's Night Gallery.*

NIGHT GAME

★☆ HBO, 1989, R, 94 min. Dir: Peter Masterson. Cast: Roy Scheider, Karen Young, Richard Bradford, Lane Smith.

A series of murders is investigated by Texas detective Scheider, who discovers that the hook-handed maniac times his killings to coincide with Houston Astros night games. Offbeat but routinely structured pseudo-thriller with few surprises.

NIGHT GOD SCREAMED, THE

★★ United, 1971, PG, 85 min. Dir: Lee Madden. Cast: Jeanne Crain, Alex Nicol, Daniel Spelling, Barbara Hancock, Dawn Cleary, James B. Sikking.

Forties star Crain goes the *Baby Jane* route as a minister's wife who testifies against the hippies who killed her husband and is marked for murder. Later a hooded figure menaces Jeanne while she looks after the teen kids of her new employer. Crain's poise and the sleazy atmosphere are at odds throughout, but the double-shock ending is great. Aka *Scream* and *Nightmare House.*

NIGHT HAIR CHILD

See: *What the Peeper Saw.*

NIGHT HAS EYES, THE

★★ Goodtimes, 1942, NR, 79 min. Dir: Leslie Arliss. Cast: James Mason, Joyce Howard, Wilfred Lawson, Tucker McGuire, Mary Clare.

Subdued Brit chiller with Mason as a moody composer, shell-shocked in the war, who may be committing murders near his moor-bound manor. Overdoes it a bit on misty atmosphere and McGuire makes for annoying "comic" relief, but Mason gives a typically good performance. Aka *Terror House.*

NIGHT IN THE CRYPT

See: *One Dark Night.*

NIGHT LIFE

★★ MCA/Universal, 1989, NR, 96 min. Dir: Daniel Taplitz. Cast: Ben Cross, Maryam D'Abo, Keith Szarabajka, Camile Saviola, Oliver Clark, Glenn Shadix.

Blasé TV vamp comedy with D'Abo as a gorgeous bloodsucker in modern Mexico City who romances blood doctor Szarabajka while being pursued by undead ex-husband Cross—who would go on to play Barnabas Collins in the short-lived "Dark Shadows" revival. Plays like a comic remake of *To Die For,* and an unfunny one at that, with only a good cast and some unusual locations to give it any life.

NIGHT LIFE

★★☆ RCA/Columbia, 1990, R, 86 min. Dir: David Acrombie. Cast: Scott Grimes, Cheryl Pollack, John Astin, Anthony Geary, Darcy DeMoss, Alan Blumenfeld.

Wisecracking teen mortuary assistant Grimes and mechanic girlfriend Pollack are terrorized by lightning-revived high school zombies in this lightweight but enjoyable teenage horror-comedy. Good acting (with Astin cast against type as Grimes' cruel mortician uncle) and some effective makeup, though, curiously, the horror elements don't kick in until the last half hour or so.

NIGHTMARE

★ Continental, 1981, UR, 89 min. Dir: Romano Scavolini. Cast: Baird Stafford, Sharon Smith, C. J. Cooke, Mik Cribben, Danny Ronen, Kathleen Ferguson.

An ex-mental patient (who looks like a deranged Dick Van Dyke) chops his way from New York to Florida as he searches for his estranged wife and young kids—his son eventually inheriting his murderous ways. Take away the gruesome slashings (the makeup was initially, and falsely, accredited to Tom Savini) and you've got a badly acted TV movie about a boring, dysfunctional family with an especially bratty and annoying son. Put them back in and you've got one of the cheesiest and sleaziest stalker movies of its era. Aka *Nightmares in a Damaged Brain* and *Blood Splash.*

NIGHTMARE AT NOON

★☆ Republic, 1988, R, 96 min. Dir: Nico Mastorakis. Cast: George Kennedy, Bo Svenson, Wings Hauser, Kimberly Beck, Brion James.

An almost too good to be true exploitation cast is mostly wasted in this flat thriller "inspired" by George Romero's *The Crazies.* A town's contaminated water supply turns just plain folks into just plain maniacs; Svenson leads a small band of the unthirsty to possible safety. Unfortunately, this one never lives up to its potential.

NIGHTMARE AT SHADOW WOODS
See: *Blood Rage*.

NIGHTMARE CASTLE
★★★ Sinister Cinema, 1965, NR, 81 min.
Dir: Allan Grunewald [Mario Caiano]. Cast: Barbara Steele, Paul Muller, Helga Line, Lawrence Clift, Rik Battaglia, John McDouglas.

Robust Steele vehicle with Babs as the unfaithful wife of doctor Muller who disfigures both wifey and her lover, cuts out their hearts, and then cremates them. Later Muller marries his emotionally unbalanced sister-in-law (Steele in a blonde wig), who believes she's going even crazier when sis and her lover begin haunting the estate. Barbara excels in a typical dual role, while the pale gray photography and Ennio Morricone's richly romantic music create a marvelous mood. Original title: *Amanti D'Oltretomba: Lovers Beyond the Tomb*: British title: *The Faceless Monster*.

NIGHTMARE CITY
See: *City of the Walking Dead*.

NIGHTMARE HOTEL
★★☆ Sinister Cinema, 1973, R, 92 min.
Dir: Eugenio Martin. Cast: Judy Geeson, Aurora Bautista, Esperanza Roy, Victor Alcazar, Lone Fleming, Blanca Estrada.

Geeson comes to a Spanish hotel searching for her missing sister, only to discover that the sisters who own it are psychopaths who murder the young women staying at their establishment they feel are morally irresponsible sluts. Good acting (especially Bautista as the more crazed of the sisters, who curses the "loose" women around her while spying on skinny-dipping teenagers and sleeping with a teen busboy), but it becomes increasingly silly as it nears conclusion, finally ending on a ridiculously abrupt note. Originally *Una Vela Para el Diabolo: A Candle For the Devil* and also out as *Nightmare Inn* and *It Happened at Nightmare Inn*.

NIGHTMARE HOUSE
See: *Scream, Baby, Scream!*

NIGHTMARE HOUSE
See: *The Night God Screamed*.

NIGHTMARE IN A CONTAMINATED CITY
See: *City of the Walking Dead*.

NIGHTMARE INN
See: *Nightmare Hotel*.

NIGHTMARE IN WAX
★☆ Interglobal, 1967, PG, 95 min.
Dir: Bud Townsend. Cast: Cameron Mitchell, Anne Helm, Scott Brady, Berry Kroeger, Victoria Carroll, Phillip Baird, Hollis Morrison, John Cardos.

The utimate bad Cameron Mitchell movie! Cam plays a fire-scarred Hollywood makeup man now running the Movieland Wax Museum. Little does anyone, except the audience, suspect, but several of the "displays" are actually kidnapped actors given a paralizing drug. A shoestring *House of Wax* with plenty of laughs and the umpteenth *Dead of Night*–inspired trick ending. Aka *Monster of the Wax Museum* and *Crimes of the Wax Museum*.

NIGHTMARE MAKER
See: *Night Warning*.

NIGHTMARE OF TERROR
See: *Demons of the Mind*.

NIGHTMARE OF TERROR
See: *Tourist Trap*.

NIGHTMARE ON ELM STREET, A
★★★☆ Video Treasures, 1984, R, 91 min.
Dir: Wes Craven. Cast: Heather Langenkamp. John

CAMERON MITCHELL
(1918–1994)

Born Cameron Mizell in Pennsylvania's Dutch country, Mitchell made his Broadway debut in *Death of a Salesman* but a decade later was appearing in all manner of cheap horror and exploitation pix. Cam's best genre film is Mario Bava's classic *Blood and Black Lace*; his nadir, probably the tacky *The Toolbox Murders*, in which he croons "Motherless Child" like nobody's business.

Gorilla at Large ('54), *Face of Fire* ('59), *Blood and Black Lace* ('65), *Man-Eater of Hydra* ('66), *Nightmare in Wax* ('67), *Autopsy of a Ghost* ('67), *Haunts* ('76), *The Toolbox Murders* ('78), *The Swarm* ('78), *Screamers* ('78), *Silent Scream* ('80), *Without Warning* ('80), *The Demon* ('81), *Frankenstein Island* ('81), *Blood Link* ('83), *Night Train to Terror* (incorporated scenes from the unreleased *Cataclysm*, '85), *The Tomb* ('86), *The Offspring* ('87).

WES CRAVEN
(1941–)

One of the major exploitation directors of the '70s and '80s and the father of Freddy Krueger, Craven makes films that are low in budget but usually high in imagination. Not at his best in studio-backed, big-bucks bonanzas, he has made a welcome return to independent filmmaking in recent years.

The Last House on the Left ('72), *The Hills Have Eyes* ('77), *Stranger in Our House* ('78), *Deadly Blessing* ('81), *Swamp Thing* ('82), *The Hills Have Eyes Part 2* ('84), *Invitation to Hell* ('84), *A Nightmare on Elm Street* ('84), *Chiller* ('85), *Deadly Friend* ('86), *A Nightmare on Elm Street 3: Dream Warriors* (co-screenplay, 87), *The Serpent and the Rainbow* ('88), *Shocker* ('89), *Night Vision* ('90), *The People Under the Stairs* ('91), *A Nightmare on Elm Street 7* ('94).

Saxon, Ronee Blakley, Robert Englund, Amanda Wyss, Johnny Depp, Nick Corri, Charles Fleischer.

Craven's best is an imaginative variation on the early '80s teen slasher formula. Four teens are tormented by identical dreams involving a disfigured fiend in a fedora, striped sweater, and razor-tipped glove. When all her friends start dying, smart girl Langenkamp discovers the dream monster to be one Fred Krueger (Englund, in a star-making role), a child molester and murderer who was torched by the neighborhood parents when released from jail on a technicality. In order to defeat the vengeful nightmare killer, Heather must try to bring him out of her dreams into the real world. The best of its popular series, this gets a lot of mileage out of a limited budget, showcasing Craven's raw, muscular direction at its best. Only the silly "Setting things up for the sequel" ending mars an otherwise perfect tale.

NIGHTMARE ON ELM STREET 2: FREDDY'S REVENGE, A

★★ Video Treasures, 1985, R, 85 min.
Dir: Jack Sholder. Cast: Mark Patton, Kim Myers, Robert Englund, Clu Gulager, Hope Lange, Robert Rusler, Marshall Bell, Sydney Walsh.

A new family move into the house previously occupied by Heather Langenkamp's family, and the shy teen son (Patton) falls under the influence of Freddy. It seems Mr. Krueger wants the lad as a vehicle through which he can reenter the world and controls Patton by

exploiting his repressed homosexuality and trying to get rid of gal pal Myers. This FX-heavy follow-up has a good supporting cast wasted on dumb characters and a plot that attempts to turn the pizza-faced Freddy into a comic anti-hero, a ploy that led the way to Fred becoming a pop icon of the late '80s. Child molester and kid killer as superstar? Who'da thunk it?

NIGHTMARE ON ELM STREET 3: DREAM WARRIORS, A

★★★ Video Treasures, 1987, R, 97 min.
Dir. Chuck Russell. Cast: Heather Langenkamp, John Saxon, Robert Englund, Patricia Arquette, Craig Wasson, Brooke Bundy, Priscilla Pointer, Larry Fishburne, Rodney Eastman, Jennifer Rubin, Dick Cavett, Zsa Zsa Gabor.

The best of the *Nightmare* sequels pits the now grown-up Langenkamp (in a awkward but affecting performance) against the ubiquitous Freddy, training a group of suicidal, nightmare-tormented teens to battle the gloved one as "Dream Warriors." Great special effects and nice humorous touches help overcome a somewhat uneven screenplay (co-written by Wes Craven) and flaccid, disappointing ending. The TV scene (with cameos by Cavett and Gabor) is a special hoot.

NIGHTMARE ON ELM STREET 4: THE DREAM MASTER, A

★★☆ Video Treasures, 1988, R, 93 min.

ROBERT ENGLUND
(1950–)

The human embodiment of razor-clawed Freddy Krueger, Englund went from obscure dramatic actor to horror sensation with the success of the *Nightmare on Elm Street* series. His natural panache and good sense of humor make him the closest thing we have to a modern-day Karloff or Lugosi.

Eaten Alive ('76), *Mind Over Murder* ('79), *Galaxy of Terror* ('81), *Dead & Buried* ('81), *A Nightmare on Elm Street* ('84), *A Nightmare on Elm Street 2: Freddy's Revenge* ('85), *A Nightmare on Elm Street 3: Dream Warriors* ('87), *A Nightmare on Elm Street 4: The Dream Master* ('88), *976-Evil* (director, '89), *A Nightmare on Elm Street 5: The Dream Child* ('89), *The Phantom of the Opera* ('89), *Freddy's Dead: The Final Nightmare* ('91), *Dance Macabre* ('91), *Night Terrors* ('93), *A Nightmare on Elm Street 7* ('94).

Heather Langenkamp gives Robert Englund a taste of his own glove in A Nightmare on Elm Street 3: Dream Warriors *(1987).*

Dir: Renny Harlin. Cast: Robert Englund, Lisa Wilcox, Tuesday Knight, Danny Hassel, Andras Jones, Brooke Theiss, Toy Newkirk, Rodney Eastman, Brooke Bundey, Hope Marie Carlton.

Number 4 for Freddy is a definite drop in quality from the previous outing, though it does have its moments. Krueger is inexplicably revived when a dog pisses hellfire on his grave(!?). He then bumps off all the surviving "Dream Warriors" from the last film and ends up fighting a girl called Alice (Wilcox) who ultimately defeats him by releasing the souls of all his victims. Slick-looking, but tries so hard to be funny that it forgets to be frightening, taking it as about as far from Wes Craven's original scary concept as it was gonna get.

NIGHTMARE ON ELM STREET 5: THE DREAM CHILD, A

★★ Video Treasures, 1989, UR, 90 min.
Dir: Stephen Hopkins, Cast: Robert Englund, Lisa Wilcox, Danny Hassel, Kelly Jo Minter, Erika Anderson, Joe Seeley.

Freddy number 5 is dark, gritty, and grim— and also pretty pointless. Wilcox finds her unborn baby possessed by ol' fingerblades and, once again, must battle him as he, once again, begins murdering her friends in their sleep. This tries to return to the scary spirit of the original but really doesn't succeed; too many Freddy games, fan clubs, and TV shows have pretty much dulled his edge for good. Add to this a phony *For Keeps*–style view of teen pregnancy and a flashy but dull retread of the last film's climax and you end up with little more than a needless rehash. Also available in the slightly less gruesome original theatrical R version. Followed by *Freddy's Dead: The Final Nightmare.*

NIGHTMARE ON THE 13TH FLOOR

★★ Paramount, 1990, R, 85 min. Dir: Walter Grauman. Cast: Michele Greene, James Brolin, Louise Fletcher, John Karlen, Terri Treas, Alan Fudge.

A pretty but dopey magazine writer (Greene) doing a story on a posh L.A. hotel called the Wessex discovers the existence of an unknown

13th floor haunted by an ax-wielding satanist who kills for immortality. Gory but goofy cable chiller with a pro cast doing what they can to enliven the routine proceedings. More laughs than anything else.

NIGHTMARES
See: *Cathy's Curse.*

NIGHTMARES
See: *Stage Fright* (1982).

NIGHTMARES
★★☆ MCA/Universal, 1983, R, 99 min.
Dir: Joseph Sargent. Cast: Cristina Raines, Emilio Estevez, Lance Henriksen, Veronica Cartwright, Richard Masur, Mariclare Costello, Louis Giambalvo, Billy Jacoby, Moon Zappa, Bridgette Anderson, Albert Hague, William Sanderson.

A tetrology of tales in the "Night Gallery" vein with Raines as a housewife menaced by a slasher; Estevez as an arcade-game-obsessed teen who battles one for his life; Henriksen as a priest whose faith is tested by a satanic truck; and Cartwright and Masur as an unhappily married couple whose home is invaded by a jumbo-sized rat. Originally made for TV but released to theaters first (with a gory murder added to the beginning to snag an R rating), this isn't half bad, though it suffers the consequences of putting its best, scariest tale first and its longest, silliest one last.

NIGHTMARES IN A DAMAGED BRAIN
See: *Nightmare.*

NIGHTMARE SISTERS
★ TWE, 1987, R, 82 min. Dir: David De Coteau. Cast: Linnea Quigley, Brinke Stevens, Michelle Bauer, Hal Havins, Sandy Brooke, Timothy Kaufman.

No-budget cheesecake horror with Linnea et al. as a trio of sorority babes possessed by a sexually active demon who turns these repressed wallflowers (Linnea, Brinke, and Michelle as repressed wallflowers?) into sexy succubi who kill via fellatio. Nothing to recommend for anyone other than girl-watchers and fans of cheap makeup FX; this is for Linnea-lusters alone. The cable TV version is heavily doctored.

NIGHT OF A THOUSAND CATS
★ Paragon, 1972, R, 83 min.
Dir: René Cardona, Jr. Cast: Anjanette Comer, Hugo Stiglitz, Zulma Faiad, Christa Linder.

Dopey Mexican non-thriller with Stiglitz as a wealthy playboy with a castle equipped with a cellar pit full of flesh-eating kitties and a tro-phy room sporting glass cases containing human heads. The lovely Comer (badly dubbed) is a bored housewife who stumbles into this mess and just barely escapes becoming cat chow. Moderately gory but padded to the max with lots of dull travelog footage of Acapulco. Also out in a heavily cut version called *Blood Feast.*

NIGHT OF BLOODY HORROR
★☆ Paragon, 1970, R, 77 min.
Dir: Joy N. Houck, Jr. Cast: Gerald McRaney, Gaye Yellen, Herbert Nelson, Evelyn Hendricks, Charlotte White, Lisa Dameron.

A young and balding McRaney ("Major Dad") stars in this New Orleans–shot slasher about a moody guy given to psychedelic blackouts whose busty girlfriends have a bad habit of getting knifed and axed to death. Cheap, bloody psycho-thrills surprisingly similar to Pete Walker's '70s Brit slashers and sporting a trick ending so obvious you'd have to be comatose not to guess it.

NIGHT OF DARK SHADOWS
★★☆ MGM/UA, 1971, PG, 93 min.
Dir: Dan Curtis. Cast: David Selby, Kate Jackson, Lara Parker, Grayson Hall, John Karlen, Nancy Barrett, James Storm, Thayer David.

Selby and Jackson (in their film debut) inherit Collinwood and move in, only to be haunted by the ghost of the powerful witch Angelique (Parker). Okay sequel to *House of Dark Shadows*, benefiting from the same beautiful locations and fine cast, though the plotting (resembling one of the TV series' "parallel time" plotlines) leaves something to be desired. Filmed as *Curse of Dark Shadows* while the TV show was in its final weeks; a third *DS* film was planned but never made.

NIGHT OF TERROR
See: *Buriel Ground.*

NIGHT OF THE BEAST
See: *House of the Black Death.*

NIGHT OF THE BLIND DEAD
See: *Tombs of the Blind Dead.*

NIGHT OF THE BLOOD BEAST
★★ Sinister Cinema, 1958, NR, 65 min.
Dir: Bernard L. Kowalski. Cast: Michael Emmet, Angela Greene, John Baer, Ed Nelson, Georgianna Carter, Tyler McVey.

An astronaut returns from space with an alien stowaway and a bun in the oven: the monster has implanted its offspring in our hero, mak-

Kate Jackson and David Selby investigate the catacombs of Collinwood in Night of Dark Shadows *(1971).*

ing him the world's first pregnant man! Violent (the monster rips its victims' heads off) and funny (mostly thanks to Emmet's hilarious, angst-ridden performance as the mama-to-be), this AIP cheapie is flatly made but oddly compelling.

NIGHT OF THE BLOODY APES
★ MPI, 1968, R, 81 min.
Dir: René Cardona. Cast: Armando Silvestre, Norma Lazareno, José Elias Moreno, Carlos Lopez Moctezuma, Noelia Noel, Agustin Martinez.

Full-color remake of the Mexican classic *Doctor of Doom* with Silvestre as a doctor who saves the life of his dying son by giving him the heart of a gorilla. Sonny survives but begins turning into an ape-like rapist-murderer. Silvestre tries to fix this by giving him a kidnapped girl's heart, but for some unknown reasons the ape-ish behavior continues. Luckily, heroine Lazareno, a lady wrestler, puts a stop to all this while investigating the disappearance of her sister—the reluctant female

heart doner. Totally lacking the sweet innocence of earlier Mexican horrors, this substitutes gross open heart surgery shots and lots of topless ladies and, frankly, it's no improvement. Originally titled *Horror y Sexo: Horror and Sex* and aka *The Horrible Human Beast* and *Gomar—The Human Gorilla.*

NIGHT OF THE CLAW
See: *Island Claws.*

NIGHT OF THE COBRA WOMAN
★★ Embassy, 1972, R, 77 min.
Dir: Andrew Meyer. Cast: Joy Bang, Marlene Clark, Roger Garrett, Vic Diaz, Rosemarie Gil, Slash Marks.

In the Philippines, a beautiful nurse is bitten by a Firebrand cobra and mutates into an ageless snake woman who secretes venom, sheds her skin, and drains the vitality of her lovers during sex. Likable, if clumsy, performances and interesting locations highlight this slithery distillation of *Cult of the Cobra* histrionics and *Apocalypse Now* atmospherics for Joy Bang completists everywhere. Filmed as *Morvini's Venom.*

NIGHT OF THE COMET

★★☆ Video Treasures, 1984, PG-13, 94 min.
Dir: Thom Eberheardt. Cast: Catherine Mary Stewart, Kelli Maroney, Robert Beltran, Geoffrey Lewis, Mary Woronov, Sharon Farrell.

Wacky horror/sci-fi/comedy with Stewart and Maroney as Valley Girl sisters who survive a worldwide catastrophe in which a passing comet has reduced most of the world's population to piles of red dust. They battle the few other survivors (most of whom have become cannibalistic zombies) and fight over last eligible guy Beltran. Funny without being forced and scary without being inconsistent, this is held together by its zesty cast, with Farrell contributing an especially hilarious cameo in the first 10 minutes.

NIGHT OF THE CREEPS

★★★ HBO, 1986, R, 88 min.
Dir: Fred Dekker. Cast: Jason Lively, Steve Marshall, Jill Whitlow, Tom Atkins, Allan J. Kayser, Bruce Solomon, Wally Taylor, Dick Miller.

It's hard not to get a kick out of this spirited in-jokester about an alien slug with the ability to burrow into a person's brain where it lays its egg and turns the host into a zombie with a soon-to-be-exploding head. A lovingly wrought melange of likable college student heroes; Pillsbury Doughboy aliens; Romeroesque walking corpses; Cronenbergian bursting brain pans; hip genre jokes; a pretty love theme; and Dick Miller too. An unsung minor classic, the cable TV version features director Dekker's *original* ending not present in the theatrical and video versions. Aka *Creeps* and *Homecoming Night.*

NIGHT OF THE DARK FULL MOON

See: *Silent Night, Bloody Night.*

NIGHT OF THE DEATH CULT

★★ SVS, 1975, R, 88 min. Dir: Amando de Ossorio. Cast: Victor Petit, Maria Kosti, Sandra Mozarowsky, Julie James, José Antonio Calvo.

Fourth, final, and dullest entry in de Ossorio's untouted "Blind Dead" series. A dopey young couple move to a small seaside community terrorized by the skeletal Knights Templar, who choose the wife as their next sacrificial victim. When the ghouls' idol is ultimately destroyed, they crumble to bloody piles of bones. Eerie blue lighting and Anton Abril's Gregorian chanting score are atmospheric, but the film as a whole is padded and repetitious,

with Calvo's village idiot about as subtle as SCTV's Bruno the hunchback. Original title: *La Noche de los Gaviotas: Night of the Seagulls.*

NIGHT OF THE DEMON

See: *Curse of the Demon.*

NIGHT OF THE DEMON

See: *The Touch of Melissa.*

NIGHT OF THE DEMON

★★ VCII, 1979, R, 95 min.
Dir: James C. Wesson. Cast: Michael J. Cutt, Joy Allen, Bob Collins, Jodi Lazirus, Melanie Graham, Lynn Eastman.

Silly but viewable bigfoot-gore movie. College prof Cutt and several students investigate monster rumors in the North Woods and end up encountering a murderous man-beast and the half-crazed girl who bore its mutant child. Hilariously bloody: intestines are ripped out, bodies mutilated, and in the funniest scene, a man's penis is torn off! Yow! The acting is pretty funny too, though the pace is too solemn and slow to make this the definitive bad bigfoot-gore movie. Better luck next time, guys.

NIGHT OF THE DEMONS

★★☆ Republic, 1988, UR, 89 min.
Dir: Kevin S. Tenney. Cast: Linnea Quigley, Mimi Kincade, Cathy Podwell, William Gallo, Lance Fenton, Hal Havins.

Pleasantly formulaic '80s horror pic with a bunch of overaged high school hosers holding a Halloween party in an abandoned mortuary. When an evil force is unleashed from the basement, the partiers are transformed into purple-faced demons. More fun than Tenney's initial success—the overrated *Witchboard*—with slick photography and good Steve Johnson makeup FX; too bad the characters are so obnoxious. Linnea does some remarkable new things with a tube of lipstick. Filmed as *Halloween Party;* also out in an R version. Followed by a sequel.

NIGHT OF THE GHOULS

★☆ Rhino, 1958, NR, 69 min.
Dir: Edward D. Wood, Jr. Cast: Kenne Duncan, Duke Moore, Tor Johnson, Valda Hansen, John Carpenter, Paul Marco, Jeannie Stephens, Criswell.

Quite a legend has been built up around this long-shelved Wood tour-de-farce. Unreleased due to unpaid lab bills, this was rumored to be a sequel to *Plan Nine From Outer Space* and to feature Lon Chaney, Jr., and Vampira in the cast. Neither is true. Actually, this is an excruciatingly dull follow-up to *Bride of the Monster* with Duncan as fake spiritualist "Dr. Acula" (oh, please!), who holds phony seances in Bela Lugosi's old house (despite the fact that it burned to the ground in *Bride*) while a fire-scarred Johnson lumbers around in the background. Criswell narrates from a coffin and there's an EC comics–type ending in which walking corpses rise up to seek revenge. Easily Woodsie's weakest "classic," originally titled *Revenge of the Dead*.

NIGHT OF THE HOWLING BEAST

★★ Super, 1975, R, 87 min. Dir: Miguel Iglesias Bonns. Cast: Paul Naschy, Grace Mills, Silvia Solar, Gil Vidal, Luis Induni, Veronica Miriel.

Another Naschy Waldemar the werewolf opus. This time he's in Tibet, where he encounters cannibalistic wolf women, an evil warlord whose kinky mistress likes to flay young ladies alive (until she's stabbed in a most unmentionable place), and a yeti who kidnaps Wal's girlfriend. Lots of great bad dialogue ("You're not an ordinary woman—you've got personality!"), lots of gore and action, and some unexpectedly beautiful snowy imagery. Original title: *La Maldicion de la Bestia: Curse of the Beast* and aka *The Werewolf and the Yeti* and *Horror of the Werewolf*.

NIGHT OF THE HUNTER

★★★☆ MGM/UA, 1955, NR, 93 min. Dir: Charles Laughton. Cast: Robert Mitchum, Shelley Winters, Lillian Gish, Evelyn Varden, Peter

"They're coming to get me, Barbara!" Night of the Living Dead *(1968)*.

Graves, Don Beddoe, James Gleason, Gloria Castillo, Billy Chapin, Sally Jane Bruce.

Mitchum gives one of his greatest performances as a sadistic, woman-hating, ex-con preacher who marries and murders widow Winters and then pursues her young children, whom he believes know the whereabouts of bank loot stolen by their father. Blunted by an overly arty approach, but overall Laughton's direction (his first and only time behind the camera) has moments of brilliance, while Mitchum makes for one of the most memorably menacing psychos in horror movie history. Remade for TV in 1991.

NIGHT OF THE LIVING DEAD

★★★★ Goodtimes, 1968, NR, 95 min. Dir: George A. Romero. Cast: Judith O'Dea, Duane Jones, Russell Streiner, Karl Hardman, Marilyn Eastman, Keith Wayne, Judith Ridley, Krya Schon.

Romero's classic debut tale of the dead rising up as flesh-eating ghouls hasn't lost any of its power, even after more than 25 years, and remains (like the same decade's *Psycho*) a model for the genre for many years to come. A small group of people trapped in a boarded-

---

GEORGE A. ROMERO
(1940–)

Born in the Bronx, New York, Romero has become the horror auteur of Pittsburgh since directing his classic *Night of the Living Dead* in 1968. One of the few directors around who uses graphic gore as part of the storytelling process rather than for its own exploitive sake, Romero makes films that are always heavy with ideas and social consciousness but are never less than entertaining.

Night of the Living Dead ('68), *Season of the Witch* ('72), *The Crazies* ('73), *Martin* ('77), *Dawn of the Dead* ('79), *Creepshow* ('82), *Day of the Dead* ('85), *Creepshow 2* (screenplay, '87), *Monkey Shines: An Experiment in Fear* ('88), *Two Evil Eyes* (co-director, '90), *Tales From the Dark Side: The Movie* (co-screenplay, '90), *Night of the Living Dead* (screenplay, '90), *The Dark Half* ('93), *Unholy Fire* ('94).

up Pennsylvania farmhouse battle the zombies *and* each other until (in a shocking ending for its time) no one survives. Stark black-and-white photography and mostly amateurish performances give it the feel of a documentary, while the fear and unease it generates (especially in the first half) remain undiminished. Still the Pittsburgh filmmaker's finest achievement, followed by a pair of sequels, carloads of rip-offs, and the 1990 remake.

NIGHT OF THE LIVING DEAD

★★★ RCA/Columbia, 1990, R, 88 min.
Dir: Tom Savini. Cast: Patricia Tallman, Tony Todd, Tom Towles, McKee Anderson, Bill Butler, Katie Finneran, Bill Moseley, Heather Mazur.

Surprisingly, this mostly needless remake of the classic original comes off quite well and even manages to wrangle a few new twists in its familiar story. Once again, bickering survivors hole up in a farmhouse while hordes of cannibalistic ghouls try to get them; only this time the heronie (Tallman) is a Sigourney Weaver type who gets stronger as things get more desperate, and gore is played down in favor of action and dark humor. Good performances from Tallman, Todd, and Towles and promising direction from makeup maestro Savini make this far more than just a redundant rehash.

NIGHT OF THE SEAGULLS

See: *Night of the Death Cult.*

NIGHT OF THE ZOMBIES

☆ Interglobal, 1980, R, 88 min. Dir: Joel M. Reed.
Cast: Jamie Gillis, Samantha Grey, Ryan Hilliard, Ron Armstrong, Juni Kulis, Alphonso DeNoble.

The director of *Bloodsucking Freaks* strikes back with this putrid tale of the CIA vs. a plot to take over the world with Nazi zombies left over from WWII. A lousy rip-off of the above-average cheapie *Shock Waves,* with porn star Gillis proving he can act better with his clothes off. Aka *Gamma 639.*

NIGHT OF THE ZOMBIES

☆ Vestron, 1981, UR, 99 min.
Dir: Bruno Mattei. Cast: Margit Evelyn Newton, Frank Garfield, Selan Karay, Robert O'Neil, Gaby Renom.

The only positive thing you can say about this enormously stupid Spanish/Italian *Dawn of the Dead* clone is that it almost makes the preceding entry look good. Soldiers and TV reporters are attacked by cannibal ghouls in New Guinea, but mostly all we get to do is watch endless stock nature footage from some National Geographic special and listen to the unsympathetic cast argue a lot. Technically primitive, this has lousy dubbing and Play-Dough makeup FX. Aka *Inferno di Morti Viventi: Inferno of the Living Dead* and *Zombie Creeping Flesh.*

NIGHT SCHOOL

★★ Warner, 1981, R, 88 min. Dir: Kenneth Hughes. Cast: Rachel Ward, Leonard Mann, Drew Snyder, Joseph R. Sicari, Annette Miller, Karen MacDonald.

Slick but routine slasher with Ward (in her big screen debut) as one of the several students at a Boston women's college menaced by a head chopper in black leather motorcycle garb and helmet. Nothing you haven't seen before, with lots of snide black humor redeemed by solid photography, Ward's beauty, and a good twist ending. British title: *Terror Eyes.*

NIGHT SCREAMS

See: *House of Death.*

NIGHT SHADOWS

See: *Mutant.*

NIGHT STALKER, THE

★★★☆ CBS/Fox, 1972, NR, 73 min.
Dir: John Llewellyn Moxey. Cast: Darren McGavin, Carol Lynley, Simon Oakland, Ralph Meeker, Barry Atwater, Claude Akins, Kent Smith, Charles McGraw, Larry Linville, Elisha Cook.

Dan Curtis produced this popular TV shocker in which McGavin gives a classic portrayal as reporter Carl Kolchak. When a series of showgirl killings sweep Las Vegas, Kolchak discovers the murderer to be an 80-year-old Hungarian vampire named Janos Skorzeny (Atwater) but has a hard time convincing the authorities, who either think he's crazy or are afraid he might be right. Terrifically paced, with the horror of the pasty-faced, fanged Atwater well played off the neon glitz of Vegas and successful touches of humor and social satire. Followed by a sequel, *The Night Strangler,* and a TV series: "Kolchak: The Night Stalker."

NIGHT STALKER, THE

★★☆ MCA/Universal, 1974, NR, 100 min.
Dirs: Rudolph Borchert, David Chase. Cast: Darrin McGavin, Simon Oakland, Ruth McDevitt, Kathleen Nolan, Suzanne Charney, William Daniels, Jan Murray, Beatrice Colan, Ken Lynch, Mickey Gilbert.

This offers two of the better episodes from the often silly "Kolchak: The Night Stalker" TV series, with McGavin battling a reincarnation of Jack the Ripper and a reactivated female victim of the vampire he fought in the original

CURTIS HARRINGTON
(1922–)

A stylish director of psychological thrillers, Harrington started his career with experimental shorts before directing his first horror feature, *Night Tide*, for Roger Corman's Filmgroup company. Although many of his later films were made for TV, Harrington brings an individual look and mood to them, which puts them in a category far removed from their more nondescript brethren.

Night Tide ('61), *Queen of Blood* ('66), *Games* ('67), *How Awful About Allan* ('70), *What's the Matter with Helen?* ('71), *Who Slew Auntie Roo?* ('72), *The Killing Kind* ('73), *The Cat Creature* ('73), *Killer Bees* ('74), *The Dead Don't Die* ('75), *Ruby* ('77), *Devil Dog: The Hound of Hell* ('78).

Night Stalker TV movies. McGavin's boundless charm and a fun supporting cast make this an enjoyable double feature.

NIGHT TIDE
★★★☆ Sinister Cinema, 1961, NR, 84 min.
Dir: Curtis Harrington. Cast: Dennis Hopper, Linda Lawson, Luana Anders, Gavin Muir, Marjorie Eaton, Cameron.

Impressive directorial bow for Harrington, in which he remakes *Cat People* as the tale of a lonely sailor (Hopper) who falls in love with a phony carnival mermaid (Lawson) who claims to be descended from the legendary sirens. When he investigates her past, Hopper discovers that all of Lawson's previous boyfriends met a watery grave. Harrington's fascination for nuance and detail and strong work from Hopper, Lawson, and Anders make this haunting little movie one of the most fascinating low-budget chillers of the 1960s. Look fast for Bruno Ve Sota.

NIGHT TRAIN TO TERROR
★☆ Video Treasures, 1985, R, 93 min.
Dirs: John Carr, Jay Schlossberg-Cohen, Philip Marshak, Gregg Tallas, Tom McGowan. Cast: John Phillip Law, Cameron Mitchell, Richard Moll, Marc Lawrence, Meredith Haze, Ferdy Mayne, Faith Clift, Robert Bristol, Rick Barnes, Sharon Ratcliff.

Really weird patchwork anthology made up from an unfinished feature (the first segment) and two shortened direct-to-video releases (*Death Wish Club* and *The Nightmare Never Ends* aka *Cataclysm*), this is one of the strangest flicks you're ever gonna come across. God and the devil argue over the souls of three people while holed up in a cramped train compartment adjoining a room where a bunch of disco-dancing aerobics airheads gyrate endlessly to the same awful song. The three stories involve a private clinic dealing in black market organ transplants; a decadent "Death" club; and a lady doctor who discovers that an ageless Nazi war criminal is actually the anti-Christ. Haphazard and confusing, but it *does* have lots of gory FX, an interesting cast (some of them appearing in more than one role), and a consistently off-the-wall script by Philip Yordan.

NIGHT VISITOR, THE
★★ United, 1971, PG, 102 min.
Dir: Laslo Benedek. Cast: Liv Ullman, Max von Sydow, Trevor Howard, Per Oscarsson, Rupert Davies, Andrew Keir.

Bergman regulars Ullman, von Sydow, and Oscarsson in an arty slasher movie about a mad axman? Yup, and it's pretty dumb. Max is incarcerated for a murder he didn't commit and every night escapes from prison in his underwear and, with his trusty hatchet, brings grisly justice to those who framed him. Uplifted somewhat by its evocative snowy landscapes (filmed in Sweden and Denmark) and the professionalism of its cast, this is still a waste. Produced by Mel Ferrer and aka *Salem* and *Salem Come to Supper*; the von Sydow and Ullman roles were originally intended for Christopher Lee and Barbara Steele.

NIGHT VISITOR
★★ MGM/UA, 1990, R, 93 min.
Dir: Rupert Hitzig. Cast: Derek Rydall, Teresa Vander Woude, Elliott Gould, Allen Garfield, Richard Roundtree, Shannon Tweed, Brooke Bundey, Michael J. Pollard.

By-the-numbers teen horror with a plot structure ripped off from *Fright Night*. Rydall is an annoying high school prankster who discovers that least favorite teacher Garfield is a satanic serial killer but, of course, no one believes him. Neither would you. This has a fairly lush look, but the interesting supporting cast is wasted in dull roles.

NIGHT WALK
See: *Deathdream*.

NIGHT WALKER, THE
★★★ MCA/Universal, 1965, NR, 86 min.
Dir: William Castle. Cast: Barbara Stanwyck, Robert Taylor, Lloyd Bochner, Judi Meredith, Rochelle Hudson, Hayden Rourke.

Robert Bloch scripted this bizarre Castle thriller about a wealthy widow (Stanwyck, about as vulnerable a target for terror as your average pro linebacker) haunted by reality-bending dreams of her dead, disfigured, blind hubby (Rourke, Dr. Bellows on "I Dream of Jeannie") and a phantom lover (Bochner) who seems to have entered into the real world. A florid, corny, but entertaining shocker that seems to have influenced *A Nightmare on Elm Street.*

NIGHT WARNING

★★☆ Thorn/EMI, 1982, R, 92 min.
Dir: William Asher. Cast: Bo Svenson, Susan Tyrell, Jimmy McNichol, Julia Duffy, Britt Leach, Marcia Lewis, Steve Eastin, Bill Paxton.

What could have been just another cheap slasher (filmed as *Butcher, Baker, Nightmare Maker*) is enlivened considerably by the acting abilities of Svenson and Tyrell. Susan is a loon who fakes a rape when she kills a TV repairman for not complying with her advances and Bo is a homophobic sheriff who's convinced that Tyrell's nephew McNichol is a gay killer who murdered the guy in a fit of homosexual jealousy. In any case, this ain't your average stab fest. Also out as *Nightmare Maker* and *Thrilled to Death.*

NIGHT WATCH

★★★ Fox Hills, 1973, PG, 99 min.
Dir: Brian G. Hutton, Cast: Elizabeth Taylor, Laurence Harvey, Billie Whitelaw, Robert Lang, Tony Britton, Linda Hayden.

Liz is excellent in her only horror flick (so far) as a pampered heiress who keeps claiming to see dead bodies in the boarded-up old mansion next to her London townhouse. Is Liz nuts? Is a psycho killer really waiting to strike? It couldn't be that husband Harvey and best friend Whitelaw are lovers and are trying to get Liz out of the way? Nah! Complete with almost constant thunderstorms, plush settings, and lush music, this has a very gory shock climax often trimmed on TV.

NIGHTWING

★☆ RCA/Columbia, 1979, PG, 105 min.
Dir: Arthur Hiller. Cast: Nick Mancuso, Kathryn Harrold, David Warner, Stephen Macht, Strother Martin, George Clutesi.

Absurd adaptation of the Martin Cruz Smith novel about a plague of vampire bats overrunning the American Southwest. Even worse than *The Swarm,* this has ludicrous scenes of silly-looking actors running from Carlo Rambaldi's bat puppets (which are so dumb-looking they hardly appear) augmented by lots of dull "romantic" scenes involving Mancuso and Harrold. Beautiful photography and one of Warner's great ranting performances are the only reasons to endure this guano.

NIGHTWISH

★☆ Vidmark, 1988, UR, 92 min. Dir: Bruce R. Cook.
Cast: Clayton Rohner, Alisha Das, Elizabeth Kaitan, Jack Starrett, Bob Tessier, Brian Thompson.

A college professor lures four students to a remote house ostensibly for some dream research work but actually to take part in some alien breeding experiments with ectoplasmic extraterrestrials. This annoyingly plotted shocker shifts gears too often and rarely makes sense; it tries to get away with its incomprehensibility by ultimately claiming to take place in the cluttered mind of its terrified main character. Gruesome but dumb.

976-EVIL

★☆ RCA/Columbia, 1989, R, 104 min.
Dir: Robert Englund. Cast: Stephen Geoffreys, Sandy Dennis, Patrick O'Bryan, Maria Rubell, Jim Metzler, Lezlie Dean, J. J. Cohen, Robert Picardo.

Englund's directoral debut is this generic combination of *Nightmare on Elm Street* and *Carrie* clichés about a high school nerd (a typecast Geoffreys) who gains supernatural power when he taps into a 976 dial-the-devil service. The basic idea had potential, but Englund's uninspired handling of it (not to mention confusing continuity and hammy acting) makes this a real chore to sit through. It was released theatrically at 88 minutes, but the additional footage only makes matters worse. Aka *Horrorscope.*

976-EVIL II: THE ASTRAL FACTOR

★★ Vestron, 1992, R, 90 min. Dir: Jim Wynorski.
Cast: Patrick O'Bryan, Debbie James, Rene Assa, Brigitte Nielsen, Philip McKeon, Leslie Ryan, Monique Gabrielle, George "Buck" Flower.

Unlike most direct-to-video sequels, this actually *does* follow up on the storyline of Robert Englund's less-than-great '89 original. O'Bryan returns for an encore to try to put a stop to all those 800 calls from hell, but the main plot concerns James as a bouncy blonde coed attending a community college whose dean (Assa) is an astral-projecting serial killer. This routine *House*-inspired nonsense has one great, from-out-of-nowhere moment when a girl (Ryan) watching *It's a Wonderful Life* on TV gets sucked into the action, the movie then turning into *Night of the Living Dead*—the ultimate public-domain video nightmare!

NINTH CONFIGURATION, THE
★★☆ New World, 1980, R, 105 min.
Dir: William Peter Blatty. Cast: Stacy Keach, Scott
Wilson, Jason Miller, Ed Flanders, Neville Brand,
Robert Loggia, Richard Lynch, Moses Gunn,
Tom Atkins, Joe Spinell.

Considered by some to be a brilliant directorial debut, Blatty's screen adaptation of his
novel *Twinkle, Twinkle, Killer Kane* (also the
shooting title) is difficult but interesting.
Keach stars as an army psychologist who
begins manipulating the patients at a remote
military insane asylum that looks like a gothic
castle. Eventually, and not unexpectedly, he
proves to be far crazier than any of his
charges. An impressive all-male cast (many of
them in their only respectable production
from the period) and some clever direction
make this offbeat film worth seeing, though
it's not quite as good as some would have it.
Originally 140 minutes.

NOCTURNA
★ Media, 1979, R, 85 min. Dir: Harry Tampa.
Cast: Nai Bonet, John Carradine, Yvonne DeCarlo,
Tony Hamilton, Brother Theodore, Sy Richardson.

Would-be disco diva Bonet produced this
tacky vanity job in which she plays the dance-
obsessed granddaughter of the aged count
(Carradine in his last turn as the vampire
king). When Nocturna flees to New York to
take up with the musician she loves, Dracula
arrives to break things up. A dated, badly
directed embarrassment for John, Yvonne, and
the always delightful Theodore. As for Nai . . .
who cares. Aka *Nocturna, Dracula's Granddaughter*.

NOCTURNA, DRACULA'S GRANDDAUGHTER
See: *Nocturna*.

NOMADS
★★ Paramount, 1986, R, 93 min.
Dir: John McTiernan. Cast: Lesley-Anne Down,
Pierce Brosnan, Anna-Maria Montecelli,
Adam Ant, Mary Woronov, Nina Foch,
Jeannie Elias, Frances Bay.

Down is a Los Angeles emergency room doctor who becomes possessed by the spirit of
French anthropologist Brosnan (in an atrocious accent) and through him discovers the
existence of the Nomads: evil supernatural
spirits disguised as leather-clad punks.
Though attractively photographed and showing good work from Down, Woronov, and
Elias, this is too muddled and obscure to build
much of a fan following. McTiernan later
struck gold with *Predator* and *Die Hard*.

NO PLACE LIKE HOMICIDE
See: *What a Carve Up!*

NO PLACE TO HIDE
★★☆ Video Treasures, 1981, NR, 95 min.
Dir: John Llewellyn Moxey. Cast: Kathleen Beller,
Mariette Hartley, Keir Dullea, Arlen Dean Snyder.

Jimmy Sangster scripted this slick, familiar-
looking, lady-in-distress thriller about a pretty
art student (Beller) being stalked by a masked
maniac no one will believe really exists. When
Beller is apparently killed, the twists begin.
No real surprises (the ending is right out of
Dressed to Kill), but with a few eerie scenes and
a skillful cast.

NOSFERATU
★★★★ Goodtimes, 1922, NR, 63 min.
Dir: F. W. Murnau. Cast: Max Schreck, Gustav von
Waggenheim, Greta Schroder, Alexander Granach,
Ruth Landshoff, John Gottowt, G. H. Schnell.

With the names changed to avoid copyright
payment (it didn't work—Bram Stoker's
widow still sued), this first version of *Dracula*
is still one of the best. Schreck is unforgettably
creepy as the vampire Count "Orlok" who
sweeps through the German town of Bremen
like the plague, claiming many victims until
the heroine (Schroder) takes it upon herself to
destroy him. Although some of the techniques
have dated badly (fast motion and negative
printing), the atmosphere of death and disease
and Schreck's stiff, corpse-like presence make
this an early horror classic and maybe the
best, the most atypical, of the German silent
horror films. Original title: *Nosferatu: Eine
Symphonie des Grauens: Nosferatu: A Symphony
of Horror*.

NOSFERATU: A SYMPHONY OF HORROR
See: *Nosferatu*.

NOSFERATU, THE VAMPYRE
★★☆ CBS/Fox, 1979, PG, 107 min.
Dir: Werner Herzog. Cast: Klaus Kinski, Isabelle
Adjani, Bruno Ganz, Roland Topor, Walter Ladengast,
Martje Grohmann.

Overrated remake of the silent classic with
Kinski made up to look like Max Schreck as
the rat-like Dracula. There are some beautiful,
fairy-tale-like images and unsettling scenes of
swarming, plague-infested rats (check out the
scene where a dying family has a final meal
together while the vermin carpet the ground
around them), but a funereal pace and hilariously overblown performances make it mostly
a sharp-looking misfire. A shorter, English-
language version was also released but with-

drawn in favor of this superior(?) German-speaking subtitled print.

NOSTRADAMUS AND THE DESTROYER OF MONSTERS
See: *The Monster Demolisher.*

NOSTRADAMUS AND THE GENIE OF DARKNESS
See: *Genie of Darkness.*

NOTHING BUT THE NIGHT
See: *The Devil's Undead.*

NOTHING UNDERNEATH
★★☆ SVS, 1985, R, 94 min.
Dir: Carlo Vanzina. Cast: Donald Pleasence, Tom Schanley, Renee Simonsen, Nicola Perring, Marie McDonald, Catherine Noyes.

Stylish but contrived Euro-slasher. A Wyoming forest ranger (Schanley) investigates the disappearance of his fashion model twin sister from a hotel in Milan, Italy, and eventually encounters a scissors-wielding maniac with a grudge against models. Good-looking and fairly diverting, this has homages to Bava, Argento, and De Palma, as well as a rich, sub–*Body Double* score by Pino Donaggio.

NOT OF THIS EARTH
★★MGM/UA, 1988, R, 80 min.
Dir: Jim Wynorski. Cast: Traci Lords, Arthur Roberts, Roger Lodge, Ace Mask, Lenny Juliano, Michael Delano.

By-the-numbers remake of the 1957 Roger Corman film, obviously slapped together to take advantage of Lords' then notoriety as an underaged porn star. It's the same plot with Roberts (coming on like Mr. Spock on "Star Trek") as the alien vampire after human blood, with the added attractions of topless bimbos and cheap special effects. Try to count how many times you can see the camera crew reflected in various car doors.

NOW I LAY ME DOWN TO DIE
See: *Dream No Evil.*

NURSE SHERRI
See: *Hospital of Terror.*

NUTTY PROFESSOR, THE
★★☆ Paramount, 1963, NR, 107 min.
Dir: Jerry Lewis. Cast: Jerry Lewis, Stella Stevens, Del Moore, Kathleen Freeman, Henry Gibson, Celeste Yarnall, Francine York, Julie Parrish.

Even non-Lewis lovers should get a kick out of this *Dr. Jekyll and Mr. Hyde* spoof, consid-

ered by his fans to be his greatest triumph. A buck-toothed college prof (Lewis) takes a formula that turns him, not into a monster, but into an annoyingly suave ladies man who looks amazingly like Dean Martin! Though no classic, it's still much better than you might imagine, with Lewis not nearly as irritatingly manic as he can be.

OASIS OF THE ZOMBIES
★ Wizard, 1982, R, 94 min.
Dir: A. M. Frank [Jesus Franco]. Cast: Manuel Gelin, France Jordan, Jeff Montgomery, Lina Romay, Doris Regina, Henry Lambert.

Another Nazi zombie flick, this one is set in the north African desert, where people searching for Rommel's lost treasure of gold encounter its living dead guardians. More entertaining than the similar *Zombie Lake* (but then again, watching paint dry would be more entertaining than *Zombie Lake*) but of the same paltry school. Originally known as *Le Tresor des Morts Vivants: Treasure of the Living Dead* and reissued as *Bloodsucking Nazi Zombies* (cool title!), this has one nice image of zombies marching across a sand dune set against a bright orange sky, but little else.

OBLONG BOX, THE
★★☆ HBO, 1969, PG, 91 min.
Dir: Gordon Hessler. Cast: Vincent Price, Christopher Lee, Hilary Dwyer, Alastair Williamson, Sally Geeson, Rupert Davies, Peter Arne, Uta Levka.

Modest addition to American International's Poe cycle with Price as an Englishman whose mad brother (Williamson) is suffering from a disfiguring African curse. When the latter is buried alive, his coffin is violated by body snatchers in the employ of a local doctor (Lee) and he rises from his coffin to don a red velvet mask and go on a rampage of throat slittings. Originally to be directed be Michael Reeves (who committed suicide shortly before the start of production), this has a lot of diverse elements that never jell and wastes both Price and Lee (who share only a single scene). The shock surprise ending, though, is genuinely jolting.

OBSESSION

★★☆ Goodtimes, 1976, PG, 98 min.
Dir: Brian De Palma. Cast: Cliff Robertson, Geneviève Bujold, John Lithgow, Sylvia "Kuumba" Williams, Wanda Blackman, Stanley J. Reyes.

Vertigo revisited with Robertson as a New Orleans businessman who loses his wife and daughter during a bungled kidnapping and 20 years later encounters his wife's apparent reincarnation in a Rome church. Guess who she really is. Lots of artsy camera moves and far-fetched plot twists in the Paul Schrader script but heartfelt acting from Robertson and Bujold and a haunting score by Bernard Herrmann make it worth watching. Shelved by Columbia, it was finally released to cash in on the success of De Palma's next film, *Carrie*.

OBSESSION: A TASTE FOR FEAR

★☆ Imperial, 1987, R, 88 min.
Dir: Picco Raffanini. Cast: Virginia Hey, Gerard Daimon, Carlo Mucari, Teagan Clive, Carin McDonald, Eva Grimaldi.

Slick-looking but ugly-edged Italian giallo about a bisexual "video artist" (Hey) investigating the brutal murder of one of her models (a femme body builder who makes Brigette Nielsen look like Betty White) and coming up against the usual black-gloved psycho killer. Romano Albani's lush photography is a definite plus, but this is peopled with far too many obnoxious, hedonistic weirdos played by a talent-dry cast resembling everyone from George Michael to Pat Paulson.

OCTAMAN

★☆ Prism, 1971, PG, 79 min. Dir: Harry Essex. Cast: Kerwin Mathews, Pier Angeli, Jeff Morrow, Jerome Guardino, Buck Kartalian, David Essex.

Shoddy, unofficial remake of *Creature From the Black Lagoon* directed by one of that film's screenwriters. A scientific expedition in Mexico encounters a ludicrous half-man, half-octopus creature (designed by a very young Rick Baker) that takes a liking to heroine Angeli (who committed suicide during production) and carries her off. More sad than funny, though the cast should receive some sort of award for managing to keep straight faces during the silly attack scenes.

OFFERINGS

★ Southgate, 1989, R, 94 min.
Dir: Christopher Reynolds. Cast: Loretta Leigh Bowman, Elizabeth Greene, G. Michael Smith, Jerry Brewer.

Tedious gore flick about a cannibalistic madman who returns to his hometown after a decade to mutilate the teens who humiliated him as a child, sending various organs and body parts to Bowman as "love offerings." This offers third-rate acting and gore FX.

OFFSPRING, THE

★★☆ IVE, 1987, R, 100 min.
Dir: Jeff Burr. Cast: Vincent Price, Clu Gulager, Cameron Mitchell, Susan Tyrell, Terry Kiser, Rosalind Cash, Harry Caesar, Martine Beswick, Angelo Rossitto, Lawrence Tierney.

An especially gruesome anthology film linked by Price as the town librarian of Oldfield, Tennessee, a hamlet dominated by evil. Vinnie spins tales for investigating reporter Tyrell involving a necrophilic nerd and the birth of a zombie baby; a hermit with eternal life; a carnival glass eater suffering a voodoo curse; and sadistic, corpse-worshipping Civil War children. A good cast of genre pros and some creepy Rob Burman makeups make this worthwhile. Price acted kinda ashamed of his participation herein, but it's a lot better than some of his other later ventures into horror. Filmed as *From a Whisper to a Scream*.

OF UNKNOWN ORIGIN

★★☆ Warner, 1983, R, 88 min.
Dir: George P. Cosmatos. Cast: Peter Weller, Shannon Tweed, Jennifer Dale, Lawrence Dane, Kenneth Welsh, Louis Del Grande.

For its first three-quarters this Canadian man vs. rat shocker, about a New York yuppie whose posh brownstone is invaded by an extra-large rodent of unusual strength and intelligence, unreels with surprising wit and assurance. Unfortunately, it overreaches itself in the last 20 minutes or so, becoming increasingly ridiculous until it falls flat with a silly ending. Weller is excellent, even though his character is too smug to inspire much sympathy, and Cosmatos does a good job at suggesting the rat's malevolent presence through quick cutting and extreme close-ups of eyes, claws, and a tail. From the novel *The Visitor* by Chauncey G. Parker III.

OLD MOTHER RILEY
MEETS THE VAMPIRE

See: *My Son, The Vampire*.

OMEGA MAN, THE

★★ Warner, 1971, PG, 98 min. Dir: Boris Sagal. Cast: Charlton Heston, Anthony Zerbe, Rosalind Cash, Paul Koslo, Lincoln Kilpatrick, Eric Laneuville.

Pretentious, overly symbolic remake of *The Last Man on Earth* with macho Heston blasting pasty-faced ghouls as, seemingly, the last "normal" man left after a strange global plague. Eventually he meets a spirited black girl (Cash, who's delightful) for some heavy-handed racial statements, and after she becomes a ghoul Chuck dies in a bloody, Christ-like posture. Occasionally good images and effective action, but too many dated early '70s touches (hippies, anti-Vietnam sentiments, and so on) make it too silly to take seriously.

OMEN, THE

★★★☆ Fox, 1976, R, 111 min. Dir: Richard Donner. Cast: Gregory Peck, Lee Remick, David Warner, Billie Whitelaw, Harvey Stephens, Patrick Troughton, Holly Palance, Leo McKern.

The best of the post-*Exorcist* devil movies, this is also the first and best of its own series. American diplomat Peck and wife Remick adopt a newborn baby boy at a Rome hospital, only to discover five years later in London that the brat is actually the anti-Christ and responsible for a series of bizarre deaths: a hanging, impalement via church spire, and decapitation by a sheet of plate glass, among others. High on atmosphere, with a classy cast and an Oscar-winning score by Jerry Goldsmith. Followed by *Damien—Omen II, The Final Conflict,* and *Omen IV: The Awakening.*

OMEN II, THE
See: *Damien—Omen II.*

Brat from hell Harvey Stephens manhandles Lee Remick in The Omen *(1976).*

OMEN III: THE FINAL CONFLICT
See: *The Final Conflict*.

OMEN IV: THE AWAKENING
★☆ Fox, 1991, NR, 91 min.
Dirs: Jorge Montesi and Dominique Otherin-Girard.
Cast: Faye Grant, Michael Woods, Asia Vieria,
Michael Lerner, Megan Leitch, Ann Hearn.

This mostly worthless fourth entry tells of a
rich, politically inclined couple whose adopted
daughter turns out to be the child of Damien
Thorn—presumably the result of his brief
affair with the heroine of *The Final Conflict*.
This is so inept that it takes nearly 80 minutes
to establish the facts of the brat's birth, which
the audience knows from the start, and seriously misuses snatches from Jerry Goldsmith's
tremendous scores for the first three *Omens*.
Only a sincere performance from Grant and a
memorable death-by-wrecking-ball for Lerner
make this TV movie worth a glance.

ONCE BITTEN
★★ Vestron, 1985, PG-13, 93 min. Dir: Howard
Storm. Cast: Lauren Hutton, Jim Carrey, Karen
Kopins, Cleavon Little, Thomas Ballatore, Skip Lackey.

Hutton's presence adds stature to this otherwise minor vampire comedy. Lauren is a
beautiful undead countess who needs the
blood of a male virgin to survive and chooses
a high school nerd (*Ace Ventura*'s Carrey) as
her next victim. Too derivative of *Porky's* and
Love at First Bite to develop much of personality of its own, though when sexy Lauren or
campy Little (as Hutton's fey manservant who
also has an eye for Carrey) are on hand, it's
never dull.

ONE BODY TOO MANY
★★☆ Hal Roach, 1944, NR, 75 min.
Dir: Frank McDonald. Cast: Jack Haley, Jean Parker,
Bela Lugosi, Douglas Fowley, Blanche Yurka,
Lyle Talbot.

A fun cast distinguishes this routine '40s old-
dark-house comedy. Haley (the Tin Woods-
man from *The Wizard of Oz*) is a bumbling
door-to-door salesman mistaken for a private
eye and hired to discover which of an eccentric millionaire's relatives bumped him off.
Bela steals it as a suspicious butler whose cups
of poisoned coffee are forever being refused
by other members of the cast.

ONE DARK NIGHT
★★☆ HBO, 1983, PG, 88 min.
Dir: Tom McLoughlin. Cast: Meg Tilly, Adam West,
Melissa Newman, Robin Evans, David Mason Daniels,
Elizabeth Daily.

Meg is a high schooler whose club initiation
stunt has her spending the night in a mausoleum also occupied by some reanimated
corpses under the control of a recently
interred psychic called Raymar. Not bad, with
good zombie effects by Tom and Ellis Burman
and a sparkling performance from the winsome Tilly. Aka *Rest in Peace* and *A Night in
the Crypt*.

ONE DEADLY OWNER
★★☆ Thrillervideo, 1973, NR, 72 min.
Dir: Ian Fordyce. Cast: Donna Mills, Jeremy Brett,
Robert Morris, Laurence Payne.

Better than usual ITC videotaped TV chiller
with Mills a fashion model compelled to buy a
creamy white Rolls Royce she discovers to be
haunted by the ghost of its previous owner. Of
the three Brian Clemens–scripted thrillers
Donna made for ITC, this is easily the best; the
mystery is fairly obvious but the way in which
the conclusion is arrived at is pretty clever and
there are a couple of good chills, the best a
sudden, sourceless scream in the car.

ONE MILLION B.C.
★★☆ Nostalgia Merchant, 1940, NR, 80 min.
Dirs: Hal Roach, Hall Roach, Jr., D. W. Griffith. Cast:
Victor Mature, Carole Landis, Lon Chaney, Jr., John
Hubbard, Mamo Clarke, Nigel de Brulier.

This silly pseudo-documentary about the early
days of man works better as a monster movie
than a history lesson. Mature became a major
beefcake star thanks to his role here as cave
guy Tumak, who falls for pretty Landis as
Loana, a member of a rival tribe. These crazy
kids must then battle dinosaurs, warring
tribes, and an erupting volcano in order to stay
together. The magnified-lizard trick photography turned up in dozens of B through Z
movies over the next 20 years, while a heavily
made-up Chaney makes his horror debut as
Mature's *father!* Much of Griffith's footage—
including the cave people speaking perfect
English—was cut before release. Remade by
Hammer as the Raquel Welch–Ray Harryhausen vehicle *One Million Years B.C.*

ONE STEP BEYOND
★★☆ Video Specials, 1959–61, NR, 60 min. per
tape. Dir: John Newland. Cast: Joan Fontaine,
Warren Beatty, William Shatner, Christopher Lee,
Cloris Leachman, Donald Pleasence, Patrick Macnee,
Louise Fletcher, Anton Diffring, Elizabeth
Montgomery, Robert Lansing, Patty McCormick.

Episodes from Newland's popular supernatural series with storylines built around various
forms of psychic phenomena (with some of

the stories based on actual case histories). Somewhat stodgy and static-looking, but several shows (notably the ones featuring Lee, Leachman, Macnee, and McCormick) are quite good and casting throughout is excellent.

ONIBABA
★★★☆ Connoisseur, 1965, NR, 105 min.
Dir: Kaneto Shindo. Cast: Nobuko Otowa, Jitsuko Yoshimura, Kei Sato, Taiji Tonomura, Jukichi Uno.

Bravura Japanese period horror about two women, a mother and a daughter-in-law, who kill deserting soldiers and sell their armor for profit, throwing the bodies into a nearby pit. When the younger woman falls in love with one of their potential victims, the older uses a hideous demon mask taken from a disfigured soldier to scare the young man away. The plan backfires horribly, however, when the mask gets stuck to the mother's face, forcing her daughter-in-law to smash it revealing . . . Beautifully done, with sharp photography and eerie scenes of the women luring soldiers to their doom through the tall, wavering reeds. Aka *The Hole, The Demon,* and *Devil Woman.*

OPEN HOUSE
★★ Prism, 1987, R, 97 min.
Dir: Jag Mundhra. Cast: Joseph Bottoms, Adrienne Barbeau, Rudy Ramos, Mary Stavin, Scott Thompson Baker, Darwyn Swalve.

By-the-numbers slasher. A radio psychologist (Bottoms) keeps receiving weird phone calls from a giggly, dog-food-eating serial killer who's been offing various female real estate agents in the area; Bottoms' girlfriend Barbeau (a real estate lady, natch) is high on the list of victims. The cast tries, but this is all too tired and predictable to be of much interest, even with some fairly sensationalistic murders. Filmed as *Multiple Listings.*

OPERA
See: *Terror at the Opera.*

OPERATION FEAR
See: *Kill, Baby, Kill.*

ORACLE, THE
★★ USA, 1985, R, 94 min.
Dir: Roberta Findlay. Cast: Caroline Capers Powers, Roger Neil, Pam La Testa, Victoria Dryden, Chris Maria DeKoron, Dan Lutzky.

Not bad for a Findlay film, perhaps because someone else wrote it, this somewhat antici-pates the better-known *Witchboard* in its tale of a beautiful girl who falls under the influence of a haunted ouija board. Lots of gooey FX, though a stalker subplot doesn't quite fit in with the rest of the proceedings.

ORCA
★★☆ Paramount, 1977, PG, 92 min.
Dir: Michael Anderson. Cast: Richard Harris, Charlotte Rampling, Will Sampson, Bo Derek, Keenan Wynn, Robert Carradine.

Harris is a guilt-ridden fisherman who harpooned the pregnant mate of a killer whale that is now seeking a deadly revenge on the sea captain and his crew. After the *King Kong* remake, this Dino De Laurentiis–financed *Jaws* copy didn't look too promising but really isn't all *that* bad. With equal helpings of the touching and the absurd, this features Rampling as a chi-chi marine biologist sporting an endless wardrobe right out of *Vogue,* and Derek in her first important film role as a girl whose leg is bitten off by Orca. Aka *Orca, The Killer Whale.*

ORCA, THE KILLER WHALE
See: *Orca.*

ORGASMO
See: *Paranoia.*

ORGY OF THE DEAD
☆ Rhino, 1966, NR, 90 min.
Dir: A. C. Stephen. Cast: Cast: Criswell, Fawn Silver, Pat Barrington, William Bates, Texas Starr, Bunny Glaser.

Laughably dated horror-nudie with a screenplay by none other than Ed Wood! A young couple (Barrington and Bates) are held prisoner in a graveyard where the "Prince of Darkness" (Criswell) passes judgment on various female "sinners" portrayed by a bevy of busty, topless strippers. Truly awful, but so boneheadedly absurd as to be almost likable in a perverse sort of way. Aka *Orgy of the Vampires* and *Revenge of the Dead.*

ORGY OF THE VAMPIRES
See: *Orgy of the Dead.*

ORIGINS UNKNOWN
See: *Alien Predator.*

ORLOFF AND THE INVISIBLE MAN
See: *The Invisible Dead.*

ORPHAN, THE
★ Rhino, 1979, R, 80 min. Dir: John Ballard. Cast: Mark Owens, Peggy Feury, Joanna Miles, Donn Whyte, Eleanor Stewart, Afolabi Ajayi.

Unattractive, *Omen*-like shocker loosely derived from the story "Srendi Vashtar" by Saki. Did young Owens—suffering from severe headaches and mental blackouts—kill Mom and Dad? What do you think? Do you care? I didn't. For the record, Janis Ian sings the melancholy theme song, and heretofore respected acting coach Feury sullies her reputation as the kid's aunt. Aka *Friday the 13th—The Orphan* and *Killer Orphan*.

OTHER, THE

★★★ CBS/Fox, 1972, PG, 100 min.
Dir: Robert Mulligan. Cast: Uta Hagen, Diana Muldaur, Chris Udvarnoky, Martin Udvarnoky, Victor French, Portia Nelson, Jenny Sullivan, John Ritter.

Evocative filming of Tom Tryon's best-seller about a young boy dominated by the evil spirit of his dead twin brother, who learned the secret of astral projection from their Russian immigrant grandma (Hagen). Occasionally overburdened with needless symbolism and rather obvious in its mystery (the novel worked better here) but boosted by its pristine photography, rich 1930s period detail, fine cast, and lovely Jerry Goldsmith score.

OTHER HELL, THE

★☆ Vestron, 1980, R, 88 min.
Dir: Stefan Oblowsky. Cast: Franca Stoppi, Carlo de Mejo, Francesca Carmeno, Frank Garfield.

Madness, murder, and demonic possession in a convent. This low-grade Italian clone of *The Exorcist* and *The Devils* was released to theaters briefly as *Guardian of Hell*.

OUTER LIMITS, THE

★★★☆ MGM/UA, 1963–65, NR, 52 min. per tape
Dirs: Gerd Oswald, John Brahm, Leonard Horn, Byron Haskin, others. Cast: Martin Landau, Cliff Robertson, Robert Culp, Sally Kellerman, William Shatner, Donald Pleasence, Miriam Hopkins, David McCallum, Shirley Knight, Bruce Dern, Nick Adams, Warren Oates, Carroll O'Connor, Joanna Frank, Simon Oakland, Grace Lee Whitney.

Although usually categorized a sci-fi, this early '60s TV fave has many horror episodes (similar in style to the old "Thriller" show with Boris Karloff in style) as well. Notable installments include "The Man Who Was Never Born" with Landau and Knight, "The Zanti Misfits" with Dern, "The Sixth Finger" with McCallum, and "Fun and Games" with Adams, and all figure among the most uniquely directed and photographed and scariest stories ever broadcast on network television.

OUTING, THE

See: *Scream.*

OUTING, THE

★☆ Avid, 1987, R, 87 min. Dir: Tom Daley. Cast: Deborah Winters, James Huston, Andra St. Ivanyi, Scott Blankston, Danny H. Daniels, Mark Mitchell.

No, it's not the Tom Cruise story. Actually, this is another lackluster teen-kill pic (filmed as *The Lamp*) with at least one novel twist: the killer, in this case, is a demonic genie riled from his magical lamp by the bimbo heroine. Poor acting, limp writing, and routine makeup FX are enlivened only by one great scene where the nominal hero has his throat torn out by the teeth of a suddenly reactivated mummy.

OUT OF CONTENTION

★★ Eagle Crest, 1972, NR, 73 min.
Dir: Herschell Daugherty. Cast: Elizabeth Montgomery, George Maharis, Eileen Heckart, Sue Ane Langdon.

Montogomery brings a needed touch of class to this TV movie originally shown as *The Victim* with Liz terrorized by a prowling killer while searching for her missing sister at a storm-lashed country cottage. Routine stuff; the same story was first done as an episode of "Thriller" (called "The Storm") with Nancy Kelly.

OUT OF SIGHT, OUT OF MIND

★★ Prism, 1990, R, 91 min.
Dir: Greydon Clark. Cast: Susan Blakely, Edward Albert, Lynn-Holly Johnson, Wings Hauser.

Blakely is good in this otherwise ordinary woman-in-jeopardy flick as a mother losing her young daughter to a sinister cult that years later comes back after her. One of exploitation director Clark's more respectable efforts, this still isn't much.

OUT OF THE BODY

★★ SVS, 1988, R, 90 min.
Dir: Brian Trenchard-Smith. Cast: Mark Hembrow, Tessa Humphries, Shane Briant, Carrie Zivetz.

A musician in Sydney, Australia, dreams of women being murdered by an eye-gouging killer just before it happens. Naturally, no one, including several victims-to-be, believes him when he tries to prevent the killings. A dull supernatural stalker movie, this has unappealing characters and little suspense.

OUT OF THE DARK

★★☆ RCA/Columbia, 1988, R, 88 min.

Dir: Michael Schroeder. Cast: Karen Black, Cameron Dye, Lynn Danielson, Bud Cort, Geoffrey Lewis, Tracey Walter, Divine, Paul Bartel, Tab Hunter, Lainie Kazan, Starr Andreeff, Silvana Gallardo.

Odd but likable semi-spoof of De Palma/Argento–style thrillers with a clown-masked maniac offing the babes who work for Black's 976 phone service, "Suite Nothings." It has a terrifically quirky cast (including the divine Divine in his final role as a Hitchcock looka-like detective), but its black humor and more stylish moments are often negated by the ordinariness of its routine stalk-and-slash structure.

OUT OF THE DARKNESS
See: *Night Creature.*

OVAL PORTRAIT, THE
★ Parade, 1973, PG, 86 min.
Dir: Rogelio Gonzalez, Jr. Cast: Wanda Hendrix, Barry Coe, Gisele Mackenzie, Barney O'Sullivan.

Dull Mexican-made Poe adaptation about a girl possessed by a bride whose spirit has been inhabiting the portrait done of her by her mad artist-husband. Slow and meandering, with flat acting, poorly dubbed dialogue, and unimaginative direction; it doesn't climax so much as it just simply ends, with no problems solved and no questions answered. The Les Baxter score only serves to remind you how good Roger Corman's Poe films are.

OVEREXPOSED
★★ MGM/UA, 1990, R, 83 min.
Dir: Larry Brand. Cast: Catherine Oxenberg, David Naughton, Karen Black, Jennifer Edwards, William Bumiller, John Patrick Reger.

Oxenberg is a soap actress whose bitchy character's activities attract the attention of a psycho fan who is out to drive her crazy and is murdering her co-stars with an acid-laced cold cream. Starts out by making some interesting statements on the price of celebrity and the schizo nature of acting but quickly becomes just another scare-the-pretty-girl number (though quite well done on its obviously small budget) with far too many superfluous characters and a silly surprise maniac in Freddy Krueger makeup.

OVER MY DEAD BODY
See: *The Brain* (1962).

PACIFIC HEIGHTS
★★☆ CBS/Fox, 1990, R, 103 min.
Dir: John Schlesinger. Cast: Michael Keaton, Melanie Griffith, Matthew Modine, Beverly D'Angelo, Laurie Metcalf, Mako, Nobu McCarthy, Tippi Hedren.

Yups Griffith and Modine rent the first floor of their Frisco brownstone to smoothy Keaton, who turns out to be a psychotic tenant from hell. A mechanical suspense film with a top cast and promising premise, this is marred by unsympathetic characters and plot twists with all the freshness of a stale pretzel. Still, Keaton is terrific as the sort of guy who couldn't get a room at the Bates Motel.

PACK, THE
★★ Warner, 1978, PG, 99 min.
Dir: Robert Clouse. Cast: Joe Don Baker, Hope Alexander-Willis, Richard B. Schull, R. G. Armstrong, Bibi Besch, Ned Wertimer.

A pack of dogs abandoned on a remote vacation island by some thoughtless visitors become savage killers menacing the terrified locals. Routine entry in the *Birds–Jaws* nature-on-the-rampage genre, this has all the usual situations augmented by a good cast and photography. Aka *The Long, Dark Night.*

PALE BLOOD
★★ RCA/Columbia, 1990, R, 93 min.
Dir: V. V. Dachin Hsu. Cast: George Chakiris, Wings Hauser, Pamela Ludwig, Diana Frank, Darcy De Moss, Earl Garnes.

Chakiris is a sullen, relatively heroic vampire who teams with psychic private eye Ludwig to catch a blood-draining killer who may—or may not—be one of the undead. The always over-the-top Hauser is a video artist who's involved in the murders. There's a slim cast and not much action but the interestingly directed item has attractive color, some clever gags (like a sleeping-bag-style zip-up portable coffin), and a cameo by Sybil Danning.

PANDEMONIUM
★★ MGM/UA, 1982, PG, 82 min.
Dir: Alfred Sole. Cast: Tom Smothers, Carol Kane, Candy Azzara, Debralee Scott, Marc McClure, Judge

Reinhold, Tab Hunter, Eve Arden, Eileen Brennan, Donald O'Connor, Kaye Ballard, Paul Ruebens.

Sole (*Alice, Sweet Alice*) helmed this inconsequential slasher spoof set at a coed cheerleader camp stalked by a mystery maniac who struck there once before 20 years earlier. Smothers is a Canadian Mountie out to crack the case and Kane a telekinetic cheerleader high on the killer's list. Filmed as *Thursday the 12th* (the title was changed to avoid confusion with *Saturday the 14th*), this features super players frittered away on inferior material and pointless guest roles (though both Arden and Brennan, the latter in an on-target Piper Laurie take-off, are fun) with an occasionally effective zing at the likes of *Carrie, Halloween, Friday the 13th,* and *Dressed to Kill.*

PANGA
See: *Curse III: Blood Sacrifice.*

PANIC
See: *The Tell-Tale Heart.*

PANIC AT LAKEWOOD MANOR
See: *Ants!*

PANIC OFFSHORE
See: *The Intruder Within.*

PANIC ON THE TRANS-SIBERIAN EXPRESS
See: *Horror Express.*

PAPERHOUSE
★★★ Vestron, 1988, PG-13, 94 min.
Dir: Bernard Rose. Cast: Charlotte Burke, Glenne Headly, Ben Cross, Elliott Spiers, Gemma Jones, Sarah Newbold.

Burke is an imaginative 11-year-old English lass who escapes her unhappy home life by retreating into a dark fantasy world she eventually comes to share with crippled Spiers, whom she's never met. The feature debut of rock video specialist Rose (who would go on to direct *Candyman*), this is overrated by some but has excellent acting from young Burke and is, for the most part, an effective blend of fantasy, horror, and sentiment.

PARANOIA
★ Republic, 1968, X, 91 min.
Dir: Umberto Lenzi. Cast: Carroll Baker, Lou Castel, Colette Descombes, Tino Carraro.

Baker gasps and moans her way through this dumb Italian sex-horror film (originally rated X, it would easily win an R today). She plays a wealthy lady whose affair with handsome Castel is complicated by the arrival of his "sis-ter" Descombes and a series of pseudo-scary happenings at her remote villa. Clumsy shock effects and inept direction redeemed only by a hilarious *deus ex machina* at the climax. Also titled *Orgasmo.*

PARASITE
★☆ Paramount, 1982, R, 85 min.
Dir: Charles Band. Cast: Robert Glaudini, Demi Moore, Vivian Blaine, Luca Bercovici, Al Fann, Cherie Currie.

Mostly just an inept combination of *Alien* and *Mad Max,* this cheapie made money thanks to its being one of the first 3-D films of the '80s. Mainly, though, it's a less-than-thrilling scare job about a scientist (Glaudini) experimenting with a flesh-eating parasite in a dusty desert town, the beastie chowing down on various lunk-headed locals. Unmemorable apart from a very gruesome shot of one of the parasites bursting from Blaine's head and leaping off the screen—an effect totally lost in the 2-D tape. Demi's film debut.

PARASITE MURDERS, THE
See: *They Came From Within.*

PARENTS
★★ Vestron, 1989, R, 82 min.
Dir: Bob Balaban. Cast: Randy Quaid, Mary Beth Hurt, Sandy Dennis, Bryan Madorsky, Graham Jarvis, Juno Mills-Cockell.

Unfocused black comedy about a strange little boy (Madorsky) living in '50s suburbia who discovers that his TV sitcom-like parents are actually murderous cannibals. Quaid is great as the creepy Ward Cleaver-ish dad in omnipresent tie and sweater, and he's matched by Hurt as the frilly, color-coordinated mom, but young Madorsky gives a badly negative performance, making it hard to care *what* happens to him, good or bad. Balaban borrows heavily from Kubrick and Argento (one shot of the camera whooshing from the cellar through the house and out the roof is a doozy) but shows little style of his own.

PAROXISMUS
See: *Venus in Furs.*

PARTS: THE CLONUS HORROR
★★ Vestron, 1979, PG, 90 min.
Dir: Robert S. Fiveson. Cast: Tim Donnelly, Paulette Breen, Peter Graves, Dick Sargent, Keenan Wynn, Lureen Tuttle.

Fair low-budget thriller about a guy (Donnelly) who discovers that he and many others are actually clones bred for use in keeping a select group of politicians forever healthy and youthful-looking (the Ronald Reagan story?). A watchable mix of horror and conspiracy thriller from the late '70s mini-glut of clone movies. Aka *The Clonus Horror*.

PARTY LINE

★☆ SVS, 1988, R, 91 min.
Dir: William Webb. Cast: Richard Hatch, Shawn Weatherly, Leif Garrett, Greta Blackburn, Richard Roundtree, James O'Sullivan.

Annoying thriller with Garrett and Blackburn as a brother-and-sister psycho team who murder folks they lure into their clutches through a 976 dating service. Tacky and badly cast, with Blackburn over the top as the loony sis.

PAST MIDNIGHT

★★☆ Columbia/TriStar, 1991, R, 100 min.
Dir: Jan Eliasberg. Cast: Rutger Hauer, Natasha Richardson, Clancy Brown, Guy Boyd, Ernie Lively, Tom Wright.

Richardson and Hauer fall in love in rainy, picturesque Oregon—but he's just been released from prison after serving time for the knife murder of his pregnant girlfriend and she's his social worker. This suspenser is well made and acted but fairly pat and predictable, though the ending *does* build up to a couple of fair shocks. And the music is *very* over-wrought.

PATRICK

★★☆ Edde Entertainment, 1978, PG, 96 min.
Dir: Richard Franklin. Cast: Susan Penhaligon, Robert Thompson, Robert Helpmann, Bruce Barry, Rod Mullinar, Julia Blake.

Enjoyable Australian version of *Carrie* with touches of *Psycho* and *Coma*. Poor Patrick (Thompson) has been in a coma ever since he electrocuted his mom and her lover, but he hasn't just been lying around; quite the contrary, as he's developed a powerful telekinetic ability he uses to control the life of his pretty new nurse (Penhaligon). Despite the handicap of dubbed-in American accents, the characters are refreshingly realistic and Franklin builds suspense well, despite a couple of awkward moments—including the obligatory *Carrie*-esque final jolt.

PEARL OF DEATH, THE

★★★ Key, 1944, NR, 68 min. Dir: Roy William Neill. Cast: Basil Rathbone, Nigel Bruce, Evelyn Ankers, Miles Mander, Dennis Hoey, Rondo Hatton.

First-rate entry in Universal's Sherlock Holmes series. The master detective investigates the theft of the priceless Borgia pearl and

EVELYN ANKERS
(1918–1988)

This blonde and beautiful Chilean-born British actress was the Kate Hepburn to Lon Chaney, Jr.'s Spencer Tracy in various '40s B horror features. Basically misused by Universal Pictures, despite the odd triumph (*The Wolf Man, The Pearl of Death*), Ankers retired from the screen in 1960 and settled in Hawaii with actor-husband Richard Denning.

Hold That Ghost ('41), *The Wolf Man* ('41), *The Ghost of Frankenstein* ('42), *Sherlock Holmes and the Voice of Terror* ('42), *Captive Wild Woman* ('43), *Son of Dracula* ('43), *The Mad Ghoul* ('43), *Weird Woman* ('44), *The Pearl of Death* ('44), *The Invisible Man's Revenge* ('44), *Jungle Woman* ('44), *The Frozen Ghost* ('45).

comes up against the spine-snapping maniac "the Hoxton Creeper" (Hatton). Good work from Ankers as a villainess with a penchant for disguise and Hatton as the lumbering Creeper—a character whose popularity led to the acromegalic Hatton's brief stardom in second features like *House of Horrors* and *The Brute Man*.

PEEPING TOM

★★★☆ Admit One, 1960, NR, 101 min.
Dir: Michael Powell. Cast: Carl Boehm, Moira Shearer, Anna Massey, Maxine Audley, Esmond Knight, Shirley Ann Field, Michael Goodliffe, Brenda Bruce.

Trashed by just about every critic who saw it back in the 1960 and first released in the U.S. three years later in a badly butchered version, this psycho classic has only just recently begun to get the favorable attention it deserves. Boehm is hauntingly good as a young photographer obsessed with filming the women he murders at the moment of death, a madness instilled in him by his crazed psychiatrist father (director Powell in a cameo). Careful photography and settings give this the true atmosphere of late '50s Brit sub-pornography (wanton tarts and "nudie" models) in all its grunginess. All but ruining the career of its distinguished director (*The Red Shoes*), this is one of the unsung horror masterworks of its era. TV title: *Face of Fear*.

PEOPLE THAT TIME FORGOT, THE

★★☆ Embassy, 1977, PG, 90 min.
Dir: Kevin Connor. Cast: Patrick Wayne, Doug

McClure, Sarah Douglas, Dana Gillespie, Thorley Walters, Shane Rimmer, Milton Reid, David Prowse.

Amicus' last production, this sequel to*The Land That Time Forgot* is something of an improvement. Wayne leads an expedition via biplane to find the lost McClure and battles dinosaurs, cavemen, and a tribe of head-hunters who worship an erupting volcano. The FX range from some unconvincing dinosaur mock-ups to some good matte paintings to one-time David Bowie squeeze Gillespie in a tight fur bra. There's also a more pronounced sense of humor, which never hurts in pictures like this.

PEOPLE TOYS
See: *Devil Times Five.*

PEOPLE UNDER THE STAIRS, THE
★★☆ MCA/Universal, 1991, R, 102 min.
Dir: Wes Craven. Cast: Brandon Adams, Everett McGill, Wendy Robie, A. J. Langer, Ving Rhames, Kelly Jo Minter.

Young Adams helps his older sister's boyfriend (Rhames) rob their wealthy landlords, only to discover they are dangerous psychopaths who've imprisoned a number of young people in the basement of their creepy house. This ambitious but badly flawed film tries to say something significant about those who heartlessly exploit the underclasses, but that gets mostly buried within the confines of a campy, somewhat unbelievable storyline that keeps trying to get you to take it seriously even when it's spoofing itself. An excellent cast and solid production values help make this one of Craven's most professional-looking films, but the script definitely could have used another polish.

PERFECT BRIDE, THE
★★☆ Fox, 1991, R, 92 min.
Dir: Terrence O'Hara. Cast: Sammi Davis, Kelly Preston, Linden Ashby, John Agar.

In this surprisingly suspenseful made-for-cable chiller, Davis is excellent as a pretty, psychotic bride-to-be not above murder to help assuage those nasty prenuptial jitters. Preston is her future sister-in-law who suspects the truth. The plot is pretty obvious, but the movie is fun, with Agar stealing it as Preston's dottering granddad.

PERSECUTION
★☆ Media, 1974, PG, 92 min.
Dir: Don Chaffey. Cast: Lana Turner, Ralph Bates, Trevor Howard, Olga Georges-Picot, Suzan Farmer, Patrick Allen, Ronald Howard, Mark Weavers.

This absurd, often unpleasant psychological thriller has Lana as a pant-suited harridan who makes life miserable for her son (Bates) while lavishing affection on her beloved cat. When the cat causes the deaths of his wife and baby son, Ralph flips and gives Mom her debasing comeuppance. The first and worst of a trio of Tyburn productions designed to emulate the look and feel of '60s Hammer films, this is a disaster on almost every level, with only Bates' fine performance standing out. Turner considers this her worst—and she should know. Also released as *Sheba, The Terror of Sheba* and *The Graveyard.*

PET SEMATARY
★★☆ Paramount, 1989, R, 101 min.
Dir: Mary Lambert. Cast: Dale Midikiff, Denise Crosby, Fred Gwynne, Brad Greenquist, Blaze Berdahl, Miko Hughes.

Stephen King's bleakest novel is adapted to the screen by the author himself with only middling results. When his toddler son Gage is killed in a freak accident, Dr. Louis Creed (Midikiff) inters him in an ancient Indian burial mound with life-giving properties just beyond the neighboring "pet sematary," only to have the kid return as a blade-wielding vessel of pure evil. Starts too slowly and ends too quickly to establish the proper balance between the workaday normality of its characters and their final descent into the supernatural. The actors fail to connect with their characters (apart from the delightful Gwynne), and the storyline takes every predictable turn possible (even for those who haven't read the book). Just the same, there *is* some compensation—namely, solid photography, good make-up FX, and several effective—if often cruel—shocks.

PET SEMATARY TWO
★★ Paramount, 1992, R, 100 min.
Dir: Mary Lambert. Cast: Edward Furlong, Anthony Edwards, Clancy Brown, Jared Rushton, Darlanne Fluegel, Jason McGuire.

Another needless sequel from the director of the original. Teenager Furlong, mourning the accidental death of horror star mom Fluegel, gets caught up in the corpse-raising carryings on at the ol' Indian burial ground, with obvious results. The film is slow and mean-spirited, but the performers (especially Brown as the sadistic local sheriff) are good and the makeup FX are well done.

PHANTASM
★★☆ Embassy, 1979, R, 87 min. Dir: Don Coscarelli. Cast: Angus Scrimm, Michael Baldwin, Bill

Thornbury, Reggie Bannister, Kathy Lester, Lynn Eastman, Susan Harper, Terrie Kalbus.

This nonsensically convoluted shocker concerns the weird happenings at Morningside mortuary where the sinister "Tall Man" (Scrimm) is robbing graves and committing murder, shrinking his victims into undead dwarves for use as slave labor in another dimension. Totally ridiculous but with some effective gore and inventive effects (particularly the brain-drilling silver sphere), this features a funny-menacing performance from the glowering Scrimm. Its box-office success led to the inevitable *Phantasms II* and *III*.

PHANTASM II
★★ MCA/Universal, 1988, R, 96 min.
Dir: Don Coscarelli. Cast: Angus Scrimm, Reggie Bannister, James Le Gros, Paula Irvine, Samantha Phillips, Kenneth Tigar.

Another '80s sequel, this plays not so much as a follow-up than as a bigger-budgeted remake. Tall Man Scrimm is back in action again, this time battled by two survivors of the earlier film plus a psychic girl who catches on to his activities. All the highlights of the first film are replayed with *three* silver spheres this time, but as usual, bigger doesn't always mean better. Despite some visual cleverness, this rehash hasn't much to offer beyond a few derivative thrills and had to be heavily cut in order to avoid an X.

PHANTOM FROM SPACE
★☆ Goodtimes, 1953, NR, 72 min. Dir: W. Lee Wilder. Cast: Ted Cooper, Rudolph Anders, Noreen Nash, James Seay, Harry Landers, Dick Sands.

Dull sci-fi/horror opus about an alien in diving suit and helmet terrorizing people in Los Angeles' Griffith Park and proving himself invisible when he doffs his duds to escape the army and police investigators. Sleep-inducing non-thriller with the phantom unimaginatively revealed at the end as a bikini-clad muscleman in a bald cap.

PHANTOM FROM 10,000 LEAGUES, THE
★★ Sinister Cinema, 1955, NR, 75 min. Dir: Dan Milner. Cast: Kent Taylor, Cathy Downs, Michael Whalen, Helene Stanton, Philip Pine, Vivi Janiss.

Creature From the Black Lagoon was the obvious inspiration for this moody Z flick about a uranium-spawned sea mutant terrorizing a California coastal town. Bleak photography and a mournful score give the film atmosphere, but the dumb-looking monster is revealed too early and too often to be either scary or convincing.

PHANTOM KILLER. THE
See: *The Invisible Ghost.*

PHANTOM KILLER, THE
★★ Sinister Cinema, 1942, NR, 61 min. Dir: William Beaudine. Cast: Dick Purcell, Joan Woodbury, John Hamilton, Mantan Moreland.

Routine Monogram cheapie remade from *The Sphinx* with Hamilton (Perry White on the old "Superman" TV series) in Lionel Atwill's role as twins—one a deaf-mute, the other a psychotic killer. Pretty missable, though any horror film with Moreland comic relief can't be all bad.

PHANTOM OF DEATH
★★ Vidmark, 1987, R, 91 min. Dir: Ruggero Deodato. Cast: Michael York, Donald Pleasence, Edwige Fenich, Mapi Galan, Fabio Sartos, Antonella Ponziani.

Typical Italian stalker with York as a concert pianist who is deranged by a premature aging disease and begins slashing women with a bushido blade. Derivative of Cronenberg's *Fly* remake and several Argento films (notably *Unsane*), this has lush sets and costumes and creative camerawork to spare but is not as personal as some of Deodato's earlier shockers. York is good, but Pleasence merely walks through his familiar police inspector role.

PHANTOM OF SOHO, THE
★★ Sinister Cinema, 1963, NR, 97 min. Dir: Franz Josef Gottlieb. Cast: Dieter Borsche, Barbara Rutting, Hans Sohnker, Elisabeth Flickenschildt.

Run-of-the-mill German krimi based on the book *Murder by Proxy* by Bryan Edgar Wallace. Scotland Yard investigates a series of murders committed by a figure shrouded in a hooded cloak and wearing a skull mask—the phantom of the title. The mystery's solution is interesting but comes too late to make much difference. Mainly for completists.

PHANTOM OF TERROR
See: *The Bird With the Crystal Plumage.*

PHANTOM OF THE MALL: ERIC'S REVENGE
★★ Fries, 1989, R, 90 min. Dir: Richard Friedman. Cast: Derek Rydall, Kari Whitman, Morgan Fairchild, Ken Foree, Rob Estees, Pauly Shore.

Or *I Was a Teenage Phantom of the Opera.* The fire-scarred ex-boyfriend (Rydall) of pretty but vapid Whitman haunts the ventilator system of the newly constructed shopping mall where she works, occasionally emerging to commit a pointless gore murder or two. Casting TV

The great Lon Chaney in his most famous role as The Phantom of the Opera *(1925).*

bimbette Fairchild as a big-city mayor tosses credulity out the window on page one, making this film's "Sweet Valley High" approach to teen romance seem positively believable in contrast. A few gory thrills but zip suspense, as the obnoxious victims practically have "Kill Me" tattooed on their foreheads.

PHANTOM OF THE OPERA, THE

★★★☆ Goodtimes, 1925, NR, 75 min.
Dir: Rupert Julian. Cast: Lon Chaney, Mary Philbin, Norman Kerry, Arthur Edmund Carewe, John Saint Polis, Snitz Edwards, Gibson Gowland, Virginia Pearson.

This first and best movie version of the classic Gaston Leroux tale is also one of the best silent horror films ever made. Chaney is unforgettable as the skull-faced Erik, who courts a lovely young singer at the Paris opera house from behind a blank mask; only becoming a monster when rejection and the hatred of others drive him to it. Chaney directed many of his own scenes, and most leave an everlasting impression: his gliding into a masked ball as Poe's "Red Death"; the abduction of heroine Philbin through the glistening black catacombs beneath the opera house; and, of course, the famous unmasking, which, believe it or not, still packs a jolt today. If Chaney had made only one movie in his career to remembered for, this would have been it. Some scenes were originally shown in an early Technicolor process, and the film was also reissued in a part-talkie version. It was remade in '43, '62, '83, '89, '90, and as both *The Phantom of Hollywood* and *Phantom of the Paradise*—not to mention Andrew Lloyd Whatshisname's overpraised Broadway musical version.

PHANTOM OF THE OPERA, THE

★★★ MCM/Universal, 1943, NR, 92 min.
Dir: Arthur Lubin. Cast: Claude Rains, Susanna Foster, Nelson Eddy, Edgar Barrier, Jane Farrar, Fritz Feld, Leo Carillo, Hume Cronyn.

This richly appointed semi-musical remake disappoints in only one area: not enough horror. Rains is excellent as a kindly violinist crippled by arthritis who tries to kill the publisher he suspects of stealing his masterwork and has a tray of etching acid thrown in his face. Later he dons a mask and cloak and becomes the dreaded Phantom of the Opera and fatherly protector of an aspiring young soprano (Foster). An Oscar winner for sets and color photography, this takes a while to get going but, once under way, does builds suspense nicely to its highly dramatic falling chandelier sequence. The phantom makeup, though, is very tame.

LON CHANEY
(1886–1930)

The silent cinema's legendary "Man of a Thousand Faces," Chaney used his natural talent for mime (the result of growing up with deaf-mute parents) and ability with makeup to create some of the most memorable horror characters of the silent era. In 1957, James Cagney starred in a sudsy and mostly fictional bio-pic, *The Man of a Thousand Faces.*

A Blind Bargain ('22), *The Hunchback of Notre Dame* ('23), *The Monster* ('25), *The Phantom of the Opera* ('25), *The Unholy Three* ('25), *The Unknown* ('27), *London After Midnight* ('27), *West of Zanzibar* ('28), *The Unholy Three* (Chaney's only sound film, '30).

PHANTOM OF THE OPERA, THE

★★ RCA/Columbia, 1989, R, 89 min.
Dir: Dwight H. Little. Cast: Robert Englund, Jill Schoelen, Alex Hyde-White, Bill Nighy, Stephanie Lawrence.

Handsome-looking but confusing slasher movie remake of the venerable horror classic. Modern singer Schoelen is transported by a hit on the head back to late-19th-century London, where she encounters a murderous composer (Englund) who lives beneath the opera house and hides his fire-fried face behind a mask of human skin. Shot on location in Budapest, this often has the look of an old Hammer film, though its needlessly gory trimmings (including a diva's head in a punch bowl) and Englund's Oliver Reed–like whispering performance could and should have been under more control.

PHANTOM OF THE PARADISE

★★★ CBS/Fox, 1974, PG, 91 min. Dir: Brian De Palma. Cast: Paul Williams, William Finley, Jessica Harper, Gerrit Graham, George Memmoli.

A flop when first released, this campy rock-n-roll updating of *The Phantom of the Opera* is in some ways similar to *The Rocky Horror Picture Show* and infinitely better. Finley has appeal as a timid rock composer whose greatest work and later his face are destroyed by evil impresario Williams. Disfigured by a record press, Finley then dons an owl-like mask to become the murderous phantom haunting Williams' rock palace, the Paradise. This mostly resembles the '62 Hammer version, but De Palma is quite clever at recycling the usual story elements, while Williams' songs are amusingly dated (apart from the pretty love ballad sung by Harper) and Graham steals it as swishy heavy-metal boy Beef.

PHANTOM SHIP, THE

★★ Sinister Cinema, 1936, NR, 64 min. Dir: Denison Clift. Cast: Bela Lugosi, Shirley Grey, Arthur Margetson, Dennis Hoey.

Static film version of the infamous disappearance of the crew of the *Marie Celeste*—possibly blamed on the madness of crazed seaman Lugosi. Apart from being a prophetic collaboration between Bela and a young Hammer Films, this pseudo-chiller has little going for it beyond the odd eerie moment. British title: *The Mystery of the Marie Celeste*.

PHASE IV

★★☆ Paramount, 1973, PG, 86 min. Dir: Saul Bass. Cast: Nigel Davenport, Lynne Frederick, Michael Murphy, Alan Gifford, Helen Horton, Robert Henderson.

Ace title designer Bass made his directorial debut with this good-to-look-at but confusing variation on the nature-runs-amok genre. Scientists Davenport and Murphy study the bizarre behavior of ants in the Arizona desert and discover that they have mutated into an intelligent new species out to subjugate all of mankind and take command of the planet. Striking compositions and good color, with Ken Middleham's magnified ant photography far scarier than most any B-movie special effect you could mention. Too bad the plot finally flips out at the end with an unsatisfying Zen climax.

PHENOMENA

See: *Creepers.*

PHOBIA

★☆ Paramount, 1980, R, 90 min. Dir: John Huston. Cast: Paul Michael Glaser, Susan Hogan, John Colicos, Alexandra Stewart, Lisa Langlois, David Eisner.

I'll bet you didn't know that Huston directed a big budget horror movie starring "Starsky and Hutch" hero Glaser, did you? That's because this stupid movie was barely released, even in the big horror year of 1980. Glaser is laughably miscast as a psychiatrist whose group therapy patients are dying from their worst fears come true. People are drowned, crushed, blown up, bitten by snakes, and topple from tall buildings while Dr. Glaser desperately tries to figure out what's going on. You will much sooner than he does, so why bother sticking around?

PHOBIA

See: *The Nesting.*

PICNIC AT HANGING ROCK

★★★ Vestron, 1975, PG, 110 min. Dir: Peter Weir. Cast: Rachel Roberts, Dominic Guard, Helen Morse, Jackie Weaver, Vivean Gray, Kristy Child.

While picnicking near a legendary rock outcropping in the Australian outback, a teacher and three girls from an exclusive finishing school disappear. Was it murder? Witchcraft? Alien abduction? We never find out, though one of the girls does resurface with no memory of her experience. This gossamer-fine tale of sunlight and terror is one of Weir's best early features and is based on a true incident.

PICTURE MOMMY DEAD

★☆ Charter, 1966, NR, 82 min. Dir: Bert I. Gordon. Cast: Don Ameche, Martha Hyer, Zsa Zsa Gabor, Susan Gordon, Maxwell Reed, Wendell Corey, Signe Hasso, Anna Lee.

Pathetic *Baby Jane*–type shocker about a troubled teen (Gordon, daughter of guess who?) bedeviled by both an evil stepmother (Hyer in one of her patented bitch roles) and the ghost of her murdered mama (a pre-arrest Gabor). Alternately bland and absurd, with clumsy shock scenes and an exceptionally campy cast utterly wasted.

PICTURE OF DORIAN GRAY, THE

★★★☆ MGM/UA, 1945, NR, 110 min. Dir: Albert Lewin. Cast: Hurd Hatfield, George Sanders, Angela Lansbury, Donna Reed, Peter Lawford, Lowell Gilmore, Richard Fraser, voice of Sir Cedric Hardwicke.

Glossy MGM adaptation of the Oscar Wilde novel about a handsome but soulless young aristocrat (Hatfield) who remains forever young while his portrait ages and corrupts in his stead. Hatfield is bland but Sanders (as the epigram-spouting Sir Henry) and Lansbury (as the tragic Sibyl) are marvelous, while the shock sequences showing the portrait in full color have real impact. Remade in 1970 (as *Dorian Gray*), 1973, and 1983 (as *The Sins of Dorian Gray*).

PICTURE OF DORIAN GRAY, THE

★★☆ Thrillervideo, 1973, NR, 128 min. Dir: Glenn Jordan. Cast: Shane Briant, Nigel Davenport, Charles Aidman, Linda Kelsey, Vanessa Howard, Fionnuala Flanagan, John Karlen, Brendan Dillon.

This stark Dan Curtis TV version won't win any awards for direction or photography, but it remains a solid, well-acted videotape production of the Oscar Wilde tale. Hammer star Briant is perfect as the beautiful and remote Dorian and Kelsey (later of "The Lou Grant Show") is fresh and appealing, but it's stolen by Davenport as the cynical Sir Harry, giving this usually detached actor a chance to really let go and have fun.

PIECES
★★ Vestron, 1983, UR, 85 min.
Dir: Juan Piquer Simon. Cast: Christopher George, Lynda Day George, Edmund Purdom, Paul L. Smith, Ian Sera, Frank Brana.

If you're a fan of unadulterated sleaze, you can't go wrong with this unintentionally hilarious Spanish slasher set at a Boston college beset by a chainsaw-toting terror out to create a human jigsaw puzzle by carving up coeds. From the flashback opening (set in the '40s but featuring a push-button phone) to the ridiculous double-shock ending (in which randy hero Sera is castrated by the grisly human puzzle come to life—whoops, sorry!), this is a guaranteed piss for all gross-out and Mr. and Mrs. George completists. Original title: *A Mil Gritos en la Noche: 1,000 Cries Has the Night.*

PIGS
See: *Daddy's Deadly Darling.*

PIN . . .
★★★ Video Treasures, 1988, R, 103 min.
Dir: Sandor Stern. Cast: David Hewlett, Cyndy Preston, Terry O'Quinn, John Ferguson, Hélène Udy, Patricia Collins.

Subtle and effective Canadian psychological thriller about a repressed doctor's son (Hewlett) who suffers from delusions that a life-sized anatomical doll called Pin (short for Pinocchio) is alive and killing those who come between the lad and his sexy sister (Preston). Despite excellent performances (particularly O'Quinn of *The Stepfather* as another malevolent parental figure) and sharp cinematography, this downbeat tale is marred by an unbelievably happy ending—except for a terrifically creepy *Psycho*-esque final shot.

PIRANHA
★★★ Warner, 1978, R, 89 min.
Dir: Joe Dante. Cast: Bradford Dillman, Heather Menzies, Kevin McCarthy, Keenan Wynn, Barbara Steele, Dick Miller, Belinda Balaski, Melody Thomas, Bruce Gordon, Paul Bartel.

Steven Spielberg's favorite *Jaws* rip-off, this finny foolishness has Dillman and Menzies unknowingly unleashing a school of mutant piranha into a Texas river, where they munch a bunch of fishermen, buxom bikini chicks, and cute little kiddie campers. Although bloody and scary in parts, this plays better as a spoof, with a superior B cast abetted by a funny John Sayles script and all the usual Dante winks. Who could ask for anything more? How about Steele as a svelte lady scientist with great cheekbones and an arched eyebrow? Miller as a Texas con man with a Brooklyn accent? Bartel as a bitchy head camp counselor? A beach bunny reading *Moby Dick*? It just never stops.

PIRANHA II: FLYING KILLERS
See: *Piranha II: The Spawning.*

PIRANHA II: THE SPAWNING
★☆ New Line, 1981, R, 84 min.
Dir: James Cameron. Cast: Tricia O'Neil, Steve Marachuk, Lance Henriksen, Ricky G. Paull, Ted Richert, Leslie Graves.

This Brazil-shot in-name-only job features *flying* piranha killing off folks at a Club Med type of resort. Super-bloody, it shows few flashes of the sort of talent Cameron would later display in *The Terminator* and *Aliens* but can be dopey fun if you catch it in the right mood. Aka *Piranha II: Flying Killers* and *The Spawning.*

PIT, THE
☆ New World, 1982, R, 92 min. Dir: Lew Lehman. Cast: Sammy Snyders, Jeannie Elias, Sonja Smits, Laura Hollingsworth, Andrea Swartz, Gerald Jordan.

The pits. This bargain basement bungler has to be seen to be believed, as an obnoxious brat (Snyders) carries on boring conversations with his possessed teddy bear while feeding neighbors and family members to a pitful of voracious ape-like creatures. Dramatically unfocused (the babysitting heroine is bumped off halfway through) and with silly *Dr. Who*–style monsters, this yawner has a kinda amusing twist ending but I doubt you'll wait around for it. Shooting title: *Teddy.*

PIT AND THE PENDULUM, THE
★★★☆ Goodtimes, 1961, NR, 80 min.
Dir: Roger Corman. Cast: Vincent Price, Barbara Steele, John Kerr, Luana Anders, Antony Carbone, Patrick Westwood.

Kerr is an Englishman visiting brother-in-law Price's Spanish castle to investigate the death of sister Steele, a death faked by the unfaithful wife, who is out to drive hubby mad—not counting on his obsession with his inquisitor father and his various torture devices. The film is a triumph of atmosphere and mood over plot and performance: Price is hammy, Kerr wooden, and Steele underused, but the settings, photography, and special effects reach incredible heights of effectiveness for such an inexpensive production.

PIT AND THE PENDULUM, THE
★★★ Paramount, 1990, R, 97 min.
Dir: Stuart Gordon. Cast: Lance Henriksen, Rona De Ricci, Jonathan Fuller, Oliver Reed, Jeffrey Combs, Tom Towles, Frances Bay, Carolyn Purdey-Gordon.

A solid remake in which Henriksen is outstanding as the torturer Torquemada who, during the Spanish Inquisition, rules Toledo and nearly destroys newlyweds De Ricci and Fuller: she has her tongue cut out and is buried alive while he's strapped beneath the title device. Grim but funny, with plenty of Gordon's trademark black humor ("Go torture some heretics!" Henriksen barks at an underling at one point, while witch Bay, upon being told that there isn't time to torture her before burning her sighs, "Thanks, anyway"). Reed is hilarious as a pompous envoy of the Pope who ends up bricked behind a wall à la *The Cask of Amontillado.*

PLANET OF BLOOD
★★☆ Star Classics, 1966, NR, 78 min.
Dir: Curtis Harrington. Cast: Basil Rathbone, John Saxon, Judi Meredith, Dennis Hopper, Florence Marley, Forrest J. Ackerman.

Originally released as *Queen of Blood,* this is a cheap but watchable horror/sci-fi hybrid about an expedition to Mars that encounters a shipwrecked lady alien with green skin (Marley) who turns out to be an extraterrestrial vampire. Harrington blends his original material well with some special effects footage derived from some Russian space opus and the cast is pretty interesting for this sort of zero-budgeted affair, but the pacing is awfully sluggish, with the real action not beginning until the last 20 minutes or so.

PLANET OF HORRORS
See: *Galaxy of Terror.*

PLANET OF THE VAMPIRES
★★★ Orion, 1965, NR, 86 min.
Dir: Mario Bava. Cast: Barry Sullivan, Norma Bengell, Angel Aranda, Evi Marandi, Fernando Villena, Franco Andrei.

Vincent Price and Barbara Steele discuss an amicable divorce in The Pit and the Pendulum *(1961).*

Bava revolutionized the European sci-fi film with this atmospheric chiller, which has all the usual gothic mood but just happens to take place in an outer space. Two spaceships land on an alien world where they discover a derelict ship containing the skeletons of a bizarre alien race, and crewmen are possessed by disembodied beings after death and transformed into vampires. Bava directs this slight tale with assurance: pools of brilliant red and blue light and lots of rolling fog covering the obvious limited set and often tacky effects work. One of the secondary inspirations behind *Alien,* this was originally called *Terrore Nello Spazio: Terror in Space* and is shown on TV as *The Demon Planet.*

PLAN NINE FROM OUTER SPACE
★★★ Nostalgia Merchant, 1958, NR, 79 min.
Dir: Edward D. Wood, Jr. Cast: Bela Lugosi, Vampira, Tor Johnson, Lyle Talbot, Gregory Walcott, Mona MacKinnon, Dudley Manlove, Joanna Lee, Duke Moore, Criswell.

Criswell introduces this grade Z masterpiece about an alien invasion by ham actors in flying hubcaps who raise the dead of a cardboard cemetery in the form of Lugosi (using footage from an unfinished vampire movie and an unconvincing double), TV horror hostess Vampira, and ex-wrestler Johnson. Easily Wood's most watchable (and infamous) hunk-a-junk of filmcraft, this lacks logic, cohesion, talent, and intelligence, and is a hell of a lot funnier than many intentional so-called comedies. As the man says, "There comes a time in every man's life when he cannot believe what his eyes can see." Indeed. Shooting title: *Grave Robbers From Outer Space.*

PLAYGIRL KILLER
★ New World, 1969, NR, 90 min.
Dir: Erick Santamaria. Cast: William Kerwin, Jean Christopher, Neil Sedaka, Andree Champayne, Mary Lou Collier.

This hilariously bad Canadian trash was never released to U.S. theatres but has been haunting our late shows since the early '70s as *Decoy for Terror.* Kerwin (who as Thomas Woods appeared in several H. G. Lewis classics— what a career!) stars as a psycho artist who murders his female models in order to make them stand still. The true highlight of this nonsense, though, is "Mr. Breaking Up Is Hard To Do" himself, who tries to be sexy (I said *tries* to be) as a singer involved with one of Bill's victims, sings two awful songs, and holds in his gut a lot while wearing a bathing suit. What some guys won't do to stay in the public eye between hits!

PLAY MISTY FOR ME
★★★ MCA/Universal, 1971, R, 102 min.
Dir: Clint Eastwood. Cast: Clint Eastwood, Jessica Walter, Donna Mills, John Larch, Jack Ging, Irene Hervey.

Eastwood directs himself for the first time as a late night disc jockey whose casual affair with a pretty fan (Walter) turns ugly when he dumps her for old flame Mills and Jess begins showing an unhealthy interest in sharp cutlery. The obvious model for the better known but less effective *Fatal Attraction,* even after 20 years this still packs plenty of punch, with Walter giving the standout performance of her checkered career as the wild-eyed and oddly sympathetic psycho. Marred only by a dippy romantic interlude between Eastwood and Mills set to Roberta Flack's "The First Time Ever I Saw Your Face," which grinds this otherwise fast-paced film to a needless five-minute standstill. Look for frequent Eastwood director Don Siegel in a cameo as a bartender.

PLAYROOM
★ Republic, 1989, R, 86 min.
Dir: Manny Coto. Cast: Lisa Aliff, Christopher McDonald, Jamie Rose, James Purcell, Aron Eisenberg, Vincent Schiavelli.

This sharply lensed but stupid direct-to-vid release suffers from one of the worst premises ever: a young archeologist leads an expedition to an ancient Yugoslavian tomb ostensibly to find a valuable treasure but actually to search for his childhood friend—the ghost of a sadistic boy prince (a sort of young Vlad the Impaler). A cast of especially irritating characters (the sort who have sex in a musty crypt as though it were a cheap motel room) and a stupid *Child's Play*–derived climax involving the prince's diminutive reanimated corpse spouting anachronistic wisecracks make this about as much fun as a dentist's waiting room. Aka *Schizo.*

PLEASE DON'T EAT MY MOTHER
★ Video Dimensions, 1971, R, 98 min.
Dir: Carl Monson. Cast: Buck Kartalian, Rene Bond, Alicia Friedland, Lyn Lundgren.

This forgotten soft-porn remake of *Little Shop of Horrors* features Kartalian as a middle-aged, virginal mama's boy who buys a talking carnivorous plant to which he feeds his Mom. Later he spies on various sexy dames and then feeds them to the toothy plant as well. This one tries to be humorous but isn't very; the coy skin and sex scenes are very badly dated. Aka *Glump.*

PLEDGE NIGHT
★ Imperial, 1988, R, 87 min.
Dir: Paul Ziller. Cast: Todd Eastland, Shannon McMahon, Joey Belladonna, Will Kempe, Arthur Joseph Lundquist, Cecilia Wilde.

Filmed as *A Hazing in Hell,* this aggressively awful campus slasher has Lundquist as a frat guy possessed by a murdered '60s hippie and offing boneheaded pledges. This cheap New York–lensed flick had almost all of its moist gore FX cut to get an R rating, rendering it almost totally boring and worthless.

PLUMBER, THE
★★☆ Media, 1978, NR, 77 min.
Dir: Peter Weir. Cast: Judy Morris, Ivar Kants, Robert Coleby, Candy Raymond.

Amusing dark comedy about a woman (the excellent Morris) who is terrorized by a demented plumber (Kants) who turns her bathroom into a Three Stooges–like nightmare while constantly badgering her with a slick combination of menace and charm. Made for Australian TV, this is another offbeat horror item from Weir before he went Hollywood. Aka *The Mad Plumber.*

POISON IVY
★★ New Line, 1992, R, 91 min.
Dir: Katt Shea Ruben. Cast: Drew Barrymore, Sara Gilbert, Tom Skerritt, Cheryl Ladd.

This minor teen variation on the *Hand That Rocks the Cradle* formula presents Barrymore as a lethal Lolita who worms her way into schoolmate Gilbert's dysfunctional Beverly Hills family and exploits and destroys them. Drew is good in her first "grownup" role, but there isn't much in the way of suspense or excitement until near the end.

POLTERGEIST
★★★☆ MGM/UA, 1982, PG, 114 min.
Dir: Tobe Hooper. Cast: JoBeth Williams, Craig T. Nelson, Beatrice Straight, Heather O'Rourke, Oliver Robins, Dominique Dunne, Zelda Rubinstein, James Karen.

An ordinary California tract home family get mixed up in the supernatural when it turns out that their house has been built upon an ancient cemetery; vengeful ghosts communicate through a TV set and abduct the family's youngest daughter into another dimension. The candy-coated influence of co-writer-producer Steven Spielberg is much in evidence, but this sweetness is well tempered by Hooper's more cynical horror-in-the-heartland approach, resulting in the best of both worlds and one of the most intense and scary PG-rated films ever made. Solid acting, top FX, and a nice, unobtrusive sense of humor help make this one of the best horror flicks of the '80s.

POLTERGEIST II: THE OTHER SIDE
★★ MGM/UA, 1986, PG-13, 90 min.
Dir: Brian Gibson. Cast: JoBeth Williams, Criag T. Nelson, Heather O'Rourke, Oliver Robins, Zelda Rubinstein, Geraldine Fitzgerald, Will Sampson, Julian Beck.

This modest, somewhat unnecessary sequel finds the Freeling family now living with Grandma (Fitzgerald). When the old lady dies, little O'Rourke begins getting calls from her on a toy telephone while the entire family must contend with a ghostly minister (Beck) who wants to draw the girl back over to the "other side." Hurt by forced humor and a ridiculous ending (in which things best kept off-screen in the original are ludicrously visualized), but sincere acting and a gruesome scene involving the aptly named "Vomit Monster" make it fair fun.

POLTERGEIST III
★★☆ MGM/UA, 1988, PG-13, 97 min.
Dir: Gary Sherman. Cast: Tom Skerritt, Nancy Allen, Heather O'Rourke, Zelda Rubinstein, Lara Flynn Boyle, Kip Wentz, Richard Fire, Nate Davis.

High-tech variation on an overworked theme with O'Rourke (who died during filming) relocated at her aunt and uncle's (Allen and Skerritt) Chicago high-rise, where the evil Reverend Kane (Davis, replacing the late Julian Beck) makes one last attempt to claim her. Interesting visually, this uses reflections in glass, chrome, and water as the gateway into the netherworld, a Valhalla of ice and mist, but is saddled with dumb characters, needless subplots, and cheapie FX work. Better than II, but only just.

POOR ALBERT AND LITTLE ANNIE
See: *I Dismember Mama.*

POPCORN
★★☆ RCA/Columbia, 1991, R, 91 min.
Dirs: Mark Herrier, Alan Ormsby. Cast: Jill Schoelen, Tom Villard, Tony Roberts, Dee Wallace-Stone, Ray Walston, Derek Rydall, Kelly Jo Minter, Karen Witter.

Film students holding an all-night horrorthon at an ornate old theatre are murdered by a disfigured psycho avenging the loss of his face. Although the plot is standard slasher silliness (the villain is one part Freddy Krueger/one part Dr. Phibes), the films-within-the-film (spoofing cheap '50s horror flicks like *Begin-*

ning of the End and *The Indestructible Man*) are inspired and the cast quite likable—and only *some* of them die, in a departure from the usual collegiate slaughter movie in which body count reigns over all. The uncredited Ormsby directed the three mock horrorthon features and wrote the script as "Tod Hackett."

PORTRAIT, THE
See: *Girls School Screamers.*

POSSESSED, THE
★★ Unicorn, 1977, NR, 74 min. Dir: Jerry Thorpe. Cast: James Farentino, Joan Hackett, Claudette Nevins, Ann Dusenberry, Harrison Ford, Eugene Roche, Diana Scarwid, P. J. Soles.

Passable TV *Exorcist* clone with Farentino as a priest who survives a near-death experience to try and help the owners of a private girls school bedeviled by a demon. A good cast saves this studiously silly flick with Hackett as the possessed headmistress who vomits out the inventory of a hardware store and Ford as a horny teacher who goes up in flames.

POSSESSED, THE
See: *Manhattan Baby.*

POSSESSION
★★ Vestron, 1981, R, 80 min.
Dir: Andrzej Zulawski. Cast: Isabelle Adjani, Sam Neill, Heinz Bennett, Margit Carstensen.

Badly butchered art shocker—cut from 127 minutes!—mixing sex, politics, religion, and horror into a very muddled brew. Adjani copped a best actress award at the Cannes Film Festival as a demented Berlin housewife who gives birth to a slimy, tentacled monster she then makes her lover, much to the bafflement of secret agent husband Neill—not to mention the audience. The cool blue lighting and Carlo Rambaldi's creature are worth noting, but in the future the art-house filmmakers should leave the genre to the exploitation boys.

POSSESSION OF JOEL DELANEY, THE
★★★ Paramount, 1972, R, 105 min.
Dir: Waris Hussein. Cast: Shirley MacLaine, Perry King, Michael Hordern, Lovelady Powell, Barbara Trentham, David Elliot, Lisa Kohane, Miriam Colon.

Good adaptation of Ramona Stewart's novel about a Manhattan socialite (MacLaine) whose younger brother (King) is possessed by the spirit of a Puerto Rican decapitation murderer. Hussein manages to create a genuinely unsettling mood and there are good performances

from the stars—plus some surprisingly gory moments that include a memorable severed-head-on-the-fridge scene. Great twist ending.

POWER, THE
★★ Vestron, 1983, R, 84 min.
Dirs: Jeffrey Obrow, Stephen Carpenter. Cast: Susan Stokey, Warren Lincoln, Lisa Erickson, Chad Christian, Ben Gilbert, J. Dinan Myretetus.

Low-budget possession shocker about various college town citizens falling under the influence of an old statuette representing the Aztec deity Destacatyl. Good makeups by Matthew Mungle but technically sloppy, with poor acting and witless dialogue.

PRANKS
See: *The Dorm That Dripped Blood.*

PREDATOR
★★☆ CBS/Fox, 1987, R, 107 min.
Dir: John McTiernan. Cast: Arnold Schwarzenegger, Carl Weathers, Elpidia Carrillo, Bill Duke, Jesse Ventura, Sonny Landham, R. G. Armstrong, Kevin Peter Hall.

Arne and the boys are mercenaries on a rescue mission in Central America who run afoul of a murderous intergalactic hunter after human trophies. This slick mix of action adventure and sci-fi/horror owes a lot to the Z classic *Without Warning* (Hall played the monster in that one too) and delivers all the goods expected of it without ever stretching its cinematic muscles beyond the obvious. Starts slowly but eventually blossoms into the sort of big-screen kick McTiernan would later perfect in *Die Hard.*

PREDATOR 2
★★☆ CBS/Fox, 1990, R, 108 min.
Dir: Stephen Hopkins. Cast: Danny Glover, Gary Busey, Maria Conchita Alonso, Rueben Blades, Bill Paxton, Robert Davi, Morton Downey, Jr., Kevin Peter Hall.

Effective follow-up finds another "Predator" in L.A. circa 1997, with cop Glover battling both this deadly alien *and* rival street gangs. Action packed, though overlong, with good work from Glover and (especially) a manic Paxton to offset the obnoxious Downey and a plot that makes little sense. Look for the *Alien* in-joke near the climax.

PREMATURE BURIAL, THE
★★★ Vestron, 1962, NR, 80 min.
Dir: Roger Corman. Cast: Ray Milland, Hazel Court, Richard Ney, Heather Angel, Alan Napier, John Dierkes, Dick Miller, Brendan Dillon.

HAZEL COURT
(1926–)

A red-haired Brit actress who became Hammer Films' first glamour gal, Court later moved to the U.S., where she appeared in several of Roger Corman's Poe films and in TV series like *Alfred Hitchcock Presents*, *Thriller*, and *The Twilight Zone*. Also a talented artist, she's married to director Don Taylor, whose credits include *The Island of Dr. Moreau* and *Damien—Omen II*.

Ghost Ship ('52), *Devil Girl from Mars* ('54), *The Curse of Frankenstein* ('57), *The Man Who Could Cheat Death* ('59), *Dr. Blood's Coffin* ('61), *The Premature Burial* ('62), *The Raven* ('63), *The Masque of the Red Death* ('64), *The Final Conflict* (cameo, '81).

Shot apart from the other entries in the Corman-Poe series (note the absence of Vincent Price), this is a serious, moody tale about a medical student (Milland) who is obsessed with the idea that he will someday follow in his father's footsteps and be buried alive. Though he builds for himself a special vault to prevent premature interment, Milland is buried alive just the same—and later erupts from his grave a murdering madman. Good acting and a haunting score by Ronald Stein (derived from the ballad "Molly Malone") make this a solid entry in the Edgar Allan Poe sweepstakes, with Court at her most ravishing, even amongst the misty graves and tombstones.

PREMONITION, THE
★★☆ Embassy, 1976, PG, 94 min. Dir: Robert Allen Schnitzer. Cast: Sharon Farrell, Jeff Corey, Richard Lynch, Edward Bell, Ellen Barber, Danielle Brisebois.

This sometimes admired Mississippi-shot psychic thriller has much of the atmosphere of the old Val Lewton thrillers—and many of their drawbacks. Farrell is the mother of an adopted daughter kidnapped by her crazed natural mother and uses her latent supernatural abilities to get her back. Outstanding performances from Farrell and Barber (as the battling moms) and Lynch (as Barber's carnival lover) and a nice creepy mood, but too many needless subplots and sticky attempts at "human drama" create hurtful dull stretches.

PRETTYKILL
★ Warner, 1987, R, 95 min.
Dir: George Kaczender. Cast: David Birney,

Season Hubley, Susannah York, Yaphet Kotto, Suzanne Snyder, Germaine Houde.

A classy cast is wasted in this sleazy slasher about a cop (Birney) with a hooker girlfriend (Hubley) he uses to catch a psycho streetwalker eliminator. Pathetically unsuspenseful and with ludicrous plot twists, this makes *Stripped to Kill* look like *Dressed to Kill*.

PRETTY POISON
★★★☆ CBS/Fox, 1968, NR, 89 min.
Dir: Noel Black. Cast: Anthony Perkins, Tuesday Weld, Beverly Garland, John Randolph, Dick O'Neill, Ken Kercheval.

This bizarre but eminently enjoyable black comic thriller is one of the best psychological horror films of the '60s. Perkins is perfect as a fantasizing pyromaniac who becomes infatuated with teen cheerleader Weld, little realizing that she's more dangerous then he is! A sharp script by Lorenzo Semple, Jr., taut direction, and fabulous acting from Tony, Tuesday, and Bev Garland (as Tuesday's bitchy mom) help make this a definite don't miss.

PREY, THE
★ New World, 1980, R, 80 min.
Dir: Edwin Scott Brown. Cast: Debbie Thureson, Steve Bond, Lori Lethin, Jackie Coogan, Gary Goodrow, Carel Struycken.

Dull *Friday the 13th* clone featuring a huge forest-fire-disfigured killer gypsy (played by Struycken of "Twin Peaks" and *The Addams Family*) murdering the usual bunch of over-aged teens. A real yawn, with poor acting from a bunch of photogenic no-talents (including *Playgirl* model and soap star Bond) and

BEVERLY GARLAND
(1926–)

Two decades before Sigourney Weaver, Garland (born Beverly Fessenden) was the original scream queen with guts. A popular Roger Corman player in the '50s, in the '60s Bev successfully moved into character acting and was a regular on both *My Three Sons* and *The Scarecrow and Mrs. King*.

The Neanderthal Man ('53), *It Conquered the World* ('56), *Curucu, Beast of the Amazon* ('56), *Not of This Earth* ('57), *The Alligator People* ('59), *Stark Fear* ('62), *Twice-Told Tales* ('63), *Pretty Poison* ('68), *The Mad Room* ('69).

lots and *lots* of close-ups of bugs crawling on rocks and tree branches.

PREY OF THE CHAMELEON
★★★ Prism, 1992, R, 91 min.
Dir: Fleming B. Fuller. Cast: Daphne Zuniga, James Wilder, Alexandra Paul, Don Harvey.

The serial killer genre has become rather glutted of late (especially on TV), but this cable chiller clearly stands out from the pack. Zuniga is terrific as a psycho who butchers victims of both sexes and then impersonates them. Wilder is her next intended target and Paul his police officer ex-girlfriend, who catches on. This is very well done, with strong acting and direction and shocking bursts of violence.

PRIME EVIL
★★ Starmaker, 1988, R, 86 min.
Dir: Roberta Findlay. Cast: William Beckwith, Christine Moore, Tim Gail, Max Jacobs, Mavis Harris, Gary Warner, Ruth Collins, Amy Brentano.

A demonic cult of priests and nuns hold the virgin sacrifice of a loved one every 13 years for wealth, power, and immortality. Our impossibly goody-goody social worker heroine (Moore) discovers that she's next on the sacrificial hit parade, thanks to evil grandpa Jacobs. Very slick-looking for Findlay, with a strong *Omen–Rosemary's Baby* storyline and a gooey-mouthed gargoyle monster designed by Ed French, but this has the usual bad acting, dopey dialogue, and boring college kid characters to contend with as well.

PRINCE OF DARKNESS
★★☆ MCA/Universal, 1987, R, 101 min.
Dir: John Carpenter. Cast: Donald Pleasence, Lisa Blount, Jameson Parker, Victor Wong, Dennis Dun, Susan Blanchard, Anne Howard, Ann Yen, Dirk Blocker, Alice Cooper.

Carpenter's muddled but interesting combination of *The Exorcist, The Thing,* and *Five Million Years to Earth* bears more than an uncredited passing similarity to Nigel Kneale's excellent Brit TV movie *The Stone Tapes.* Priest Pleasence summons a team of scientists to study the slimy contents of an old canister discovered beneath a Los Angeles church. The canister turns out to contain the liquified remains of the devil, and drinking this liquid brings about the demonic possession of several members of the group. Carpenter has all the ingredients here for a classic horror film but fails to make them jell into a coherent whole. Scenes involving melting faces, swarming bugs, and the devil's hand have impact but lack the proper dramatic build-up. A good cast tries hard, but most must deal with underdeveloped characters.

PRINCESS OF DARKNESS
See: *Satan's Princess.*

PRISON
★★★ New World, 1988, R, 102 min.
Dir: Renny Harlin. Cast: Lane Smith, Viggo Mortensen, Chelsea Field, Lincoln Kilpatrick, Andre De Shields, Arlen Dean Snyder.

This surprisingly potent tale of horror in the big house is Empire Pictures' best film after *Re-Animator.* Smith is the new warden at a recently reopened state pen where the ghost of a wrongly executed prisoner goes on the rampage. Solid acting, atmospheric lensing, and an almost overwhelming air of menace make this one of the best low-budget horrors of the '80s.

PRIVATE EYES, THE
★★ New World, 1980, PG, 92 min. Dir: Lang Elliott. Cast: Tim Conway, Don Knotts, Trisha Noble, Bernard Fox, Grace Zabriskie, John Fujoika.

Conway and Knotts try to be Abbott and Costello in this kiddie-oriented horror spoof about a pair of bumbling detectives investigating several murders in an eerie old house. There are a few scattered laughs and sexy Noble is diverting, but the "surprise" climax is obvious from the get-go.

PRIVATE PARTS
★★☆ MGM/UA, 1972, R, 86 min. Dir: Paul Bartel. Cast: Ayn Ruymen, Lucille Benson, John Ventantonio, Laurie Main, Stanley Livingston, Ann Gibbs.

Partly successful black comic/horror set at a seedy L.A. hotel run by daffy Benson. When pretty teen niece Ruymen visits, she becomes the obsession of photographer cousin Ventantonio, who pastes a photo of her face on his plastic love doll and may be responsible for several murders. Bartel manages good atmosphere in the hotel, but the blend of comedy, skin, and psycho-shocks is an uneven one, with a twist ending right out of *Homicidal.*

PROFILE OF TERROR
See: *The Sadist.*

PROMISE OF RED LIPS, THE
See: *Daughters of Darkness.*

PROM NIGHT
★★☆ Virgin Vision, 1980, R, 91 min.
Dir: Paul Lynch. Cast: Jamie Lee Curtis, Leslie Nielsen, Antoinette Bower, Casey Stevens, Eddie Benton, Michael Tough, David Mucci, Robert Silverman.

JLC is at her best in this derivative and dumb but quite presentable slasher about a hooded killer avenging a young girl's death by slaying those responsible at their high school prom. Girls scream, a head rolls on the dance floor, and Jamie struts her stuff in a hilariously out-of-place *Saturday Night Fever* disco sequence—though she later proves her acting mettle in her final confrontation with the killer. Followed by three kind-of sequels: *Hello Mary Lou: Prom Night II*, *Prom Night III: The Last Kiss*, and *Prom Night IV: Deliver Us From Evil*.

PROM NIGHT III: THE LAST KISS

★★ IVE, 1989, R, 95 min.
Dirs: Ron Oliver and Peter Simpson. Cast: Courtney Taylor, Tim Conlon, Cyndy Preston, David Stratton, Jeremy Ratchford, Dylan Neal.

Another campy in-name-only sequel with evil Mary Lou (now played by Taylor) returning to Hamilton High to seduce a young hunk (likable Conlon) away from his annoyingly cute girlfriend (Preston) while bumping off his enemies, including a biology teacher, guidance counselor, and school bully. Amusing but uneven, with Taylor (in gore makeup resembling wet Rice Krispies) a weak substitute for wicked Lisa Schrage and too many *Nightmare on Elm Street* borrowings.

PROM NIGHT IV: DELIVER US FROM EVIL

★☆ LIVE, 1991, R, 93 min.
Dir: Clay Borris. Cast: Nikke de Boer, Joy Tanner, Alden Kane, Alle Ghadban.

This *very* slow "sequel" returns to the slasher roots of the first *Prom Night* and borrows large chunks from *The Confessional* and *Prince of Darkness* but adds nothing of its own. A mad priest stalks four very dull teens who bypass their prom for a private sex and booze party. As usual, all but the heroine bite it before her inevitable confrontation with Father Psycho. This shot-in-Canada stalker is professionally put together but way dull. "Here's to Jamie Lee Curtis!"

PROPHECY

★★ Paramount, 1979, PG, 102 min.
Dir: John Frankenheimer. Cast: Robert Foxworth, Talia Shire, Armand Assante, Richard Dysart, Victoria Racimo, George Clutesi.

During the shooting of this film, Frankenheimer was quoted as saying that he wanted to make the scariest horror movie ever. So what happened? Instead we get this foolishness about industrial pollution in the Maine woods turning bears into gooey-faced mutants, with elements from *Gorgo*, *Grizzly*,

and *Tell Them Willie Boy Is Here* worked in as well. Thumping direction, hammy, overwrought performances, and hokey FX provide much laughter but few scares. The photography (with Oregon substituting for Maine) is nice, though.

PROWLER, THE

★★☆ VCII, 1981, R, 88 min. Dir: Joseph Zito.
Cast: Farley Granger, Vicky Dawson, Christopher Goutman, Lawrence Tierney, Cindy Weintraub, Thom Bray.

Better-than-usual formula maniac movie about a jilted WW II soldier who killed his former fiancee and her new beau with a pitchfork during a college graduation dance in the '40s. When the dance is held again after a 35-year hiatus, the gruesome killings begin again. Great Tom Savini FX include a girl pitchforked in the shower; a guy getting a bayonet through the skull; and a climactic exploding head. Dawson is a sympathetic heroine; Richard Einhorn composed the excellent score. Aka *The Graduation* and *Rosemary's Killer*.

PSYCHIC, THE

★★☆ Video Treasures, 1978, R, 89 min.
Dir: Lucio Fulci. Cast: Jennifer O'Neill, Marc Porel, Gabriele Ferzatti, Evelyn Stewart.

This Italian quickie bears all the earmarks of a rip-off of the better-known *Eyes of Laura Mars* but was actually made first. Hollywood steals from Fulci? Anyway, this isn't too bad, with O'Neill appealing as an heiress with psychic flashes of a murder in a country house which may or may not have already occurred. A gripping opening following a woman's suicidal descent down a cliff and a neat twist ending (reused by Lucio in his version of *The Black Cat*) are the best parts. The original title was *Seito Note in Mero: Six Black Notes*.

PSYCHIC

★★☆ Vidmark, 1992, R, 92 min.
Dir: George Milhalka. Cast: Zach Galligan, Catherine Mary Stewart, Michael Nouri, Albert Shultz.

An entertaining but fairly predictable made-for-cable chiller, this one's about a college student with ESP (Galligan) who tries to stop a slasher before he gets to the female professor (Stewart) Zach has foreseen will be the next target. Good acting, direction, and photography help you overlook this film's familiar-sounding plot.

PSYCHIC KILLER

★★ Embassy, 1975, PG, 90 min. Dir: Ray Danton.
Cast: Jim Hutton, Julie Adams, Paul Burke, Nehemiah

Persoff, Aldo Ray, Neville Brand, Della Reese, Rod Cameron, Whit Bissell, Mary Wilcox.

This terrific junk thriller with an "all star" cast has to be seen to be believed. A still-boyish Hutton is an ex-mental patient who uses astral projection to leave his body (under police surveillance) and murder those who put him away for the killing of his mother. Good casting includes Ray as a detective, Reese as a sassy welfare mom, Bissell as a horny old doctor, and Brand as a butcher chopped up in his own machinery and helps distract you from the flat-footed direction and general sleazy atmosphere. Aka *The Kirlian Force.*

PSYCHO

★★★★ MCA/Universal, 1960, R, 108 min.
Dir: Alfred Hitchcock. Cast: Anthony Perkins, Janet Leigh, Vera Miles, John Gavin, Martin Balsam, John McIntyre, Simon Oakland, Frank Albertson, Vaughn Taylor, Patricia Hitchcock.

The most famous and imitated horror film of them all, this was conceived by the master of suspense as both a black joke on his audience and an attempt to ride the crest of the low-budget shockers just coming into vogue at the time. Leigh stars, but not for long, as a Phoenix, Arizona, secretary who embezzles $40,000 and then makes the mistake of lodging at the creepy Bates Motel, where she has a fatal bathroom encounter with the owner's deranged "mother." Whole volumes have been written on this movie, the best remem-

Tony Perkins goes Psycho *(1960).*

ROBERT BLOCH
(1917–)

A prolific screen and story writer who created *Psycho*, Bloch has penned literally hundreds of short horror tales, many of them adapted to the screen in a variety of compendium flicks in the '60s and '70s. A clever wordsmith, he's not above going for the most outrageous sick puns to cap his entertaining stories.

Psycho (original novel, '60), *The Couch* ('61), *The Cabinet of Caligari* ('62), *Strait-Jacket* ('64), *The Night Walker* ('65), *The Skull* (original story, '65), *The Psychopath* ('66), *The Deadly Bees* ('67), *Torture Garden* ('68), *The House That Dripped Blood* ('71), *Asylum* ('72), *The Cat Creature* ('73), *The Dead Don't Die* ('75), *Psycho II* (original characters, '83), *Psycho III* (original characters, '86), *Psycho IV: The Beginning* (original characters, '90).

bered and most popular work of the most famous director of all time. Joseph Stefano adapted Robert Bloch's novel, which was itself inspired by real-life Wisconsin maniac and ghoul Ed Gein. Bernard Herrmann's memorably spiky soundtrack is still being ripped off by various horror and suspense film composers. Perkins would later return as lovable looney Norman Bates in three sequels more than 20 years and did a memorable plug for the "Norman Bates School of Motel Management" on the original "Saturday Night Live."

PSYCHO II

★★☆ MCA/Universal, 1983, R, 113 min.
Dir: Richard Franklin. Cast: Anthony Perkins, Vera Miles, Meg Tilly, Robert Loggia, Dennis Franz, Claudia Bryar, Hugh Gillin, Lee Garlington.

Surprisingly potent sequel picking up 22 years later with Norman Bates (the ever twitchin' Tony) released from an asylum and returning to the old homestead, where a new rash of

ANTHONY PERKINS
(1932–1992)

This tall, boyish-looking actor was a minor leading man of the '50s whose career was forever altered when Alfred Hitchcock cast him as knife-wielding mama's boy Norman Bates in his seminal 1960 film, *Psycho*. After that Tony was hopelessly typecast, though he resisted genre identification until the '80s, when he embarked on a series of *Psycho* sequels and a good-natured spoofing of his own image.

Psycho ('60), *The Fool Killer* ('65), *Pretty Poison* ('68), *How Awful About Allan* ('70), *Someone Behind the Door* ('71), *Psycho II* ('83), *The Sins of Dorian Gray* ('83), *Psycho III* (also director, '86), *Destroyer* ('88), *Lucky Stiff* (director, '89), *Edge of Sanity* ('89), *Daughter of Darkness* ('90), *I'm Dangerous Tonight* ('90), *Psycho IV: The Beginning* ('90), *A Demon in My View* ('91), *In the Deep Woods* ('92).

killings occur—seemingly committed by Norman's mom, risen from the dead. Written by Tom Holland, this is a well-crafted mixture of black humor and slasher horror but gets a little out of hand as it nears its confusing conclusion—and runs about 10 minutes too long. The blade-down-the-throat scene is a highlight; look for the Hitchcock cameo in Mrs. Bates' bedroom.

PSYCHO III
★★★ MCA/Universal, 1986, R, 92 min.
Dir: Anthony Perkins. Cast: Anthony Perkins, Diana Scarwid, Jeff Fahey, Roberta Maxwell, Hugh Gillin, Lee Garlington, Juliette Cummins, Katt Shea Ruben.

Perkins' underrated directing debut is the best of the *Psycho* sequels. The homicidal idyll at the Bates Motel is disrupted once again when Norman takes on a smarmy assistant manager (Fahey) and rents a room to a winsome Marion Crane lookalike (Scarwid), a suicidal ex-nun with whom he falls in love. Tony's assured direction includes deft homages to *Vertigo, Frenzy,* and *Deep Red* and the cast is excellent. Plus, there's an emotional impact to much of Charles Edward Pogue's script that gives the characters and story far more depth than one would usually find in your average third-hand follow-up.

PSYCHO IV: THE BEGINNING
★★ MCA/Universal, 1990, R, 96 min. Dir: Mick

Garris. Cast: Anthony Perkins, Olivia Hussey, Henry Thomas, CCH Pounder, Donna Mitchell, Warren Frost, Thomas Schuster, Sharen Camille.

Or *Norman Bates: The Wonder Years.* Scripted by Joseph Stefano, this well-intentioned but laborious prequel to the Hitchcock classic has a reformed Norman (Perkins) once again out of the bug house and reminiscing about his past with a radio talk show host (Pounder) doing a special on matricide. The best scenes in this fourth chapter depict the malevolent Mama Bates (a great if cast-against-type Hussey) tormenting teen Norman (*ET*'s Thomas, bearing an uncanny resemblance to Perkins), all leading to his homicidal breakdown. The setting-things-up-for-another-sequel ending (*Norman's Baby?*) is the weakest link.

PSYCHO A-GO-GO
See: *The Blood of Ghastly Horror.*

PSYCHO COP
★ Southgate, 1989, R, 87 min.
Dir: Wallace Potts. Cast: Bobby Ray Shafer, Jeff Qualle, Palmer Lee Todd, Dan Campbell, Cynthia Guyer, Linda West.

Six teenagers with the personality of Play-Dough spend the weekend at a country house where they are stalked by a devil-worshipping loon in a police uniform. This totally inept slasher has a couple of moist killings but really putrid acting—Shafer as the chortling title character makes Tom Arnold look like Tom Cruise, while the three "teen" guy victims look like they'd be more at home in a gay porn flick. The direction is flat and the script is truly senseless. Followed by a sequel(!!!).

PSYCHO GIRLS
★★ MGM/UA, 1985, R, 92 min.
Dir: Gerard Ciccoritti. Cast: John Haslett Cuff, Darlene Mignacco, Agi Gallus, Rose Graham.

Tongue-in-cheek low-budget slasher about a psycho-housekeeper whose wrongly committed sister escapes from the asylum to terrorize her sister's rich employers in revenge. Tries hard to be funny, but general amateurishness makes it little more than a half-amusing misfire. Ciccoritti's second feature, *Graveyard Shift,* is much more successful.

PSYCHO KILLERS
See: *Mania.*

PSYCHOMANIA
★★☆ Sinister Cinema, 1963, NR, 90 min.
Dir: Richard Hilliard. Cast: Lee Phillips, Shepperd

Strudwick, Jean Hale, Margot Hartman, James Farentino, Sylvia Miles, Dick Van Patten, Kaye Elhardt.

Del Tenney co-wrote and co-produced this *Psycho*-influenced, made-in-Connecticut thriller directed by the cinematographer of his *The Horror of Party Beach* and *The Curse of the Living Corpse*. A vicious knife murderer is terrorizing the coeds at a private girls college and all the evidence points to moody artist Phillips, who's prone to blackouts and was once suspected in the death of his father. With some stylish moments and a surprisingly upscale cast, this thriller is fairly gory for its time. It usually airs on TV in a cut version, so this uncut video may be worth seeking out. Aka *Violent Midnight*.

PSYCHOMANIA
★★☆ Goodtimes, 1971, PG, 89 min.
Dir: Don Sharp. Cast: George Sanders, Beryl Reid, Nicky Henson, Mary Larkin, Robert Hardy, Ann Michelle.

Odd but likable British horror-comedy about the leader (Henson) of a motorcycle gang called the Living Dead who makes a pact with the devil for eternal life. After committing suicide, he roars out of his grave on his bike (buried with him by his thoughtful gang) and convinces his friends to join him in real living death. With weirdly elegant music and set design, this film features Sanders as a butler who turns out to be the devil in disguise and Reid as Henson's devoted mum who conducts seances on the side. Aka *The Death Wheelers*.

PSYCHOPATH
★☆ Fox Hills, 1973, R, 85 min. Dir: Larry Brown. Cast: Tom Basham, Gretchen Kanne, Henry Olek, Margaret Avery.

Basham's bizarrely committed performance as a kiddie show host who flips and begins murdering his fans' abusive parents is all this slightly offensive cheapie has going for it. Strange murders, overwrought acting, and unintentional hilarity reign supreme in this seldom-seen exploiter. Aka *An Eye for an Eye*.

PSYCHO SEX FIEND
See: *The House That Vanished*.

PSYCHOS IN LOVE
★★ Wizard, 1987, UR, 87 min.
Dir: Gorman Bechard. Cast: Carmine Capobianco, Debi Thibeault, Frank Stewart, Cecilia Wilde, Donna Davidge, Ruth Collins.

A gross psycho-slasher parody that almost succeeds. Capobianco is Joe, a grape-hating woman-killer who meets Kate (Thibeault), whose grape-hating and man-murdering ways result in an instant attraction. Old-fashioned romance and a high body count are the obvious results. Often hits the mark, but an overall self-consciousness makes it look like an overlong "Saturday Night Live" skit.

PSYCHO SISTERS
★★ Prism, 1972, PG, 76 min.
Dir: Reginald LeBorg. Cast: Susan Strasberg, Faith Domergue, Sydney Chaplin, Charles Knox Robinson, Kathleen Freeman, Steve Mitchell.

Modest C-grade psychological thriller with Strasberg and Domergue as the title siblings, each trying to drive the other insane for an inheritance. Dated by its trendy mod touches but worth seeing for fans of its veteran leading ladies—Faith has a nearly topless shower scene. TV title: *So Evil, My Sister*.

PULSE
★★ RCA/Columbia, 1987, PG-13, 91 min.
Dir: Paul Golding. Cast: Cliff De Young, Roxanne Hart, Joey Lawrence, Charles Tyner, Myron Healey, Matthew Lawrence.

Young Lawrence (several years before his teen idol phase on TV's "Blossom"), forced to live with estranged dad De Young and new stepmom Hart, comes to believe that evil forces are controlling the house's electricity and turning the appliances against the occupants. This well-meaning but dull electrician's variation on *Poltergeist* has good macro-photography and a creepy role for Tyner as an old coot with all the answers but is too silly for its own good.

PUMPKINHEAD
★★★ MGM/UA, 1988, R, 86 min.
Dir: Stan Winston. Cast: Lance Henriksen, Jeff East, Cynthia Bain, John DiAquino, Kerry Remsen, Joel Hoffman.

Atmosphere-heavy tale of a group of young dirt bikers who accidentally kill a farmer's young son; the farmer (Henricksen) seeks revenge by having a backwoods hag summon up Pumpkinhead, a bloodthirsty demon, to dispatch them. A solid cast (Henriksen is at his best) and first-rate creature FX make this an impressive, if predictably plotted, directorial debut for makeup man Winston. Aka *Vengeance: The Demon;* followed by a sequel.

PUPPETMASTER
★★☆ Paramount, 1989, R, 90 min.
Dir: David Schmoeller. Cast: Paul LeMat, Irene Miracle, William Hickey, Jimmie F. Skaggs, Robin Frates, Barbara Crampton.

Entertaining variation on the *Trilogy of Terror–Child's Play* killer doll theme about a group of psychics being stalked and murdered around an old hotel (situated in Hitchcock's mythical Bodega Bay) by a band of murderous, living puppets. Fun but uninvolving, this has a totally out-of-place kinky sex subplot and a cast that alternately sends it up and plays it straight. The FX work is great, with David Allen's puppet creations clever enough to charm as well as chill.

PUPPETMASTER II
★★ Paramount, 1990, R, 89 min.
Dir: David Allen. Cast: Elizabeth MacLellan, Collin Bernsen, Steve Welles, Gregory Webb, Charlie Spradling, Nita Talbot.

The puppets are back (this time joined by a flame-throwing new friend) to revive their dead creator and bump off a group of college psychic investigators. This slimly plotted sequel boasts more great FX work, but dull characters (apart from the always terrific Talbot) and a slow pace make it seem longer than it is. Funniest scene: Bernsen's (brother of "L.A. Law" star Corbin) bare-assed battle with flame-thrower.

PUPPETMASTER III: TOULON'S REVENGE
★★☆ Paramount, 1991, R, 82 min.
Dir: David De Coteau. Cast: Guy Rolfe, Richard Lynch, Sarah Douglas, Ian Abercrombie, Walter Gotell, Michelle Bauer.

This prequel traces the story of puppeteer Toulon's (Rolfe) creation of his little friends and their vengeance against the Nazis when Gestapo officer Lynch murders Toulon's beloved wife (Douglas, in a rare sympathetic turn). This third entry in the series is potentially the best, with a more interesting cast and plotting and some familiar Universal backlot settings. The little guys' franchise possibilities, though, have been pretty much played out.

PUPPETMASTER 4
★★ Paramount, 1993, R, 80 min.
Dir: Jeff Burr. Cast: Gordon Currie, Chandra West, Guy Rolfe, Jason Adams, Teresa Hill, Stacie Randall.

A young scientist (Currie) experimenting with the creation of artificial intelligence gets caught up in the battle between Andre Toulon's puppets and some hellish totems. This fourth installment starts out looking like it will be the best yet—the totems look like an H. R. Giger version of the *Trilogy of Terror* fetish doll—but halfway through, it sputters out into an inconclusive setup for Part 5. And

the evil demon character looks like a Sid & Marty Kroft version of the monster from *The Keep.*

PUZZLE OF THE GOLDEN TRIANGLES, THE
See: *Circus of Fear.*

PYX, THE
★★☆ Prism, 1973, R, 111 min.
Dir: Harvey Hart. Cast: Christopher Plummer, Karen Black, Donald Pilon, Jean-Louis Roux, Yvette Brind'Amour, Lee Broker.

Plummer is a detective investigating the murder of prostitute Black and comes up against a black magic cult in this slow but well-directed Canadian thriller from the helmer of the great but forgotten '60s shocker *Dark Intruder.* Aka *The Hook Cult Murders.*

Q
★★★ MCA/Universal, 1982, R, 92 min.
Dir: Larry Cohen. Cast: Michael Moriarty, Candy Clark, David Carradine, Richard Roundtree, James Dixon, Malachy McCourt.

One of Cohen's best films, this tongue-in-cheek monster romp features Moriarty in a hilarious performance (one he's used a few too many times since) as a petty crook who stumbles upon the culprit behind a series of grisly murders in Manhattan: the Aztec demon god Quetzecoatl, who's built his nest atop the Chrysler Building. Full of tacky charm, explicit gore, and off-the-wall humor, not to mention the oddly affecting title critter brought to life via limited but charmingly old-fashioned effects animation. British title: *The Winged Serpent.*

QUEEN OF BLOOD
See: *Planet of Blood.*

QUEEN OF THE CANNIBALS
See: *Dr. Butcher, M.D.*

QUEEN OF THE GORILLAS
See: *The Bride and the Beast.*

RABID

★★☆ Warner, 1977, R, 90 min.
Dir: David Cronenberg. Cast: Marilyn Chambers, Frank Moore, Joe Silver, Howard Ryshpan, Patricia Gage, Susan Roman.

Cronenberg's peculiar take on the vampire genre, this features porn star Chambers as a motorcycle accident victim whose life is saved by an experimental skin graft with an unexpected side-effect: a hankering for blood she sucks from her victims through a fleshy syringe she's developed in her armpit. Those she attacks become rabid zombies who threaten Montreal. Scenes of these zombies oozing yellow guck from their eyes and mouths and attacking folks on subways or in shopping malls are quite funny, hampering the attempts at horror, though there's a genuinely unsettling operating room sequence. Chambers is quite good too. Aka *Rage*.

RABID GRANNIES

★ Media, 1989, R, 86 min. Dir: Emmanuel Kervyn. Cast: Danielle Daven, Anne Marie Fox, Jack Mayar, Françoise Moens, Elliot Lison.

A mysterious package transforms a pair of gentle grannies into nasty nannas with a taste for human flesh. Typical Troma tripe for only the most desperate. Not to be confused with *Flesh Eating Mothers*.

RACE WITH THE DEVIL

★☆ CBS/Fox, 1975, PG, 88 min.
Dir: Jack Starrett. Cast: Peter Fonda, Warren Oates, Loretta Swit, Lara Parker, R. G. Armstrong.

Two couples who witness a satanic ceremony are pursued across Texas by the vengeful cult. Stupid combo of *Rosemary's Baby* and your typical '70s drive-in car crash movie with next to nothing to recommend it apart from its talented cast. The ending will make you scream—but only in frustration.

RAGE

See: *Rabid*.

RAGING FURY

See: *Hell High*.

RAISING CAIN

★★☆ MCA/Universal, 1992, R, 91 min.
Dir: Brian De Palma. Cast: John Lithgow, Lolita Davinovich, Steven Bauer, Gregg Henry, Frances Sternhagen, Mel Harris.

It's hard to get a handle on this confusing, often self-derivative De Palma shocker, but once you do it can be a lot of fun. Lithgow is typically great as a child psychologist obsessed with his young daughter and dominated by his behaviorist father and psycho twin brother, who may or may not exist. Davinovich is his oblivious wife, tempted into an affair with a man she briefly knew (platonically) in the past. There are unexpected homages to *Peeping Tom, Ghost Story, The 4th Man,* and *Unsane* and a scary replay of De Palma's empty shoes bit from *Dressed to Kill.*

RAMPAGE

★★☆ Paramount, 1987, R, 97 min.
Dir: William Friedkin. Cast: Michael Biehn, Alex McArthur, Deborah van Valkenburgh, Nicholas Campbell, Grace Zabriskie, Billy Green Bush, John Harkins, Art La Fleur.

Shelved for five years and then severely re-edited, this intense, well-directed thriller concerns the gory career of serial killer McArthur and attorney Biehn's attempts at proving him sane enough to go to trial after his capture. Riveting performances and strong-armed direction make this worth seeing, but the restructuring and cutting (from 118 minutes) for its brief '92 release are clearly evident, blunting the film's overall effectiveness.

RAPTURE

See: *The Horrible Dr. Hichcock.*

RATS, THE

See: *Deadly Eyes.*

RATS, THE

★ Video Treasures, 1983, NR, 97 min.
Dir: Vincent Dawn [Bruno Mattei].
Cast: Richard Raymond, Alex McBride, Richard Cross, Ann Gisel Glass, Janna Ryann.

Remember that obscure all-star thriller *Chosen Survivors* about post-nuclear war survivors vs. rabid vampire bats? Well, this Italian flick retells virtually the same story with man-eating rats in place of bats. In any case this is an undigestible melange of bad dubbing and bad taste.

RATS ARE COMING! THE WEREWOLVES ARE HERE!, THE

☆ Midnight, 1972, R, 92 min. Dir: Andy Milligan.

BELA LUGOSI
(1882–1956)

Born Bela Blasko in Lugos, Hungary, Bela was a fairly successful stage star in Budapest before traveling to Berlin, where he made several silents (as Arisztid Olt), and then on to America and Broadway. Learning English phonetically, he landed the lead in the Broadway production of *Dracula* and was eventually cast in Universal's movie version following the death of Lon Chaney, originally set to star. Although he scored a major success, Lugosi was forever typecast as a horror man, only occasionally breaking out in a '30s comedy or two. By the '40s he was hopelessly trapped in grade B or worse cheapies; a decade later morphine addiction (resulting from treatment of a recurring WWI injury) and a series of ill-advised career moves reduced poor Bela to commitment to a state hospital (where he was cured) and appearances in Ed Wood movies. A much better actor than his detractors would have you believe, Lugosi is often the sole saving grace of more than a dozen lamentable quickies.

Janus-Faced ('20), *The Devil Worshippers* ('20), *The Thirteenth Chair* ('29), *Dracula* ('31), *Murders in the Rue Morgue* ('32), *White Zombie* ('32), *Island of Lost Souls* ('33), *The Death Kiss* ('33), *Night of Terror* ('33), *The Black Cat* ('34), *Mark of the Vampire* ('35), *The Raven* ('35), *The Invisible Ray* ('36), *The Phantom Ship* ('36), *Son of Frankenstein* ('39), *The Human Monster* ('39), *Black Friday* ('40), *You'll Find Out* ('40), *The Devil Bat* ('41), *The Black Cat* ('41), *The Invisible Ghost* ('41), *Spooks Run Wild* ('41), *The Wolf Man* ('41), *Black Dragons* ('42), *The Ghost of Frankenstein* ('42), *The Corpse Vanishes* ('42), *Night Monster* ('42), *Bowery at Midnight* ('42), *Frankenstein Meets the Wolf Man* ('43), *The Ape Man* ('43), *Ghosts on the Loose* ('43), *Return of the Vampire* ('44), *Voodoo Man* ('44), *Return of the Ape Man* ('44), *One Body Too Many* ('44), *The Body Snatcher* ('45), *Zombies on Broadway* ('45), *Genius at Work* ('46), *Scared to Death* ('47), *Abbott and Costello Meet Frankenstein* ('48), *My Son, the Vampire* ('52), *Bela Lugosi Meets a Brooklyn Gorilla* ('52), *Bride of the Monster* ('55), *The Black Sleep* ('56), *Plan Nine From Outer Space* ('56).

Bela Lugosi and a stuffed friend who justifies the title of The Raven *(1935).*

Cast: Hope Stansbury, Jacqueline Skarvelis, Ian Innes, Berwick Kaler, Noel Collins, Joan Ogden.

As bad as anything you've ever seen, this awful "Dark Shadows" rip-off about a family of Victorian werewolves had its rat footage added at the last minute to cash in on Willard. With or without it, this dull-as-dishwater opus (the werewolves don't even show up until the last 10 minutes) may be Milligan's worst. Even *Werewolves on Wheels* is better! Shooting title: *Curse of the Full Moon.*

RATTLERS
★ Media, 1975, PG, 82 min.
Dir: John McCauley. Cast: Sam Chew, Elizabeth Chauvet, Tony Ballen, Dan Priest, Al Dunlap, Darwin Jostin.

Plodding *Jaws*-inspired thriller about nerve gas–contaminated rattlesnakes terrorizing the populace of a small Mojave Desert community. Absurd plotting (the hero and heroine, searching for the snakes, spend most of their time in a tent in the wilderness while the rattlers are busy killing off people in town), poor acting, and bland, PG-rated violence dominate. One creepy image of a girl attacked by snakes in her bathtub later turned up again in *Deadly Blessing.*

RAVEN, THE

★★★ MCA/Universal, 1935, NR, 61 min.
Dir: Louis Friedlander [Lew Landers]. Cast: Bela Lugosi, Boris Karloff, Irene Ware, Lester Matthews, Samuel S. Hinds, Ian Wolfe.

Guignol at its grandest with Lugosi in his definitive mad doctor performance. As Dr. Richard Vollin, Bela is a brilliant surgeon with two obsessions: the pretty dancer (Ware) whose life he saved and the works of Edgar Allan Poe. When denied the already engaged girl's hand by her stuffy dad (Hinds) (a nice plot twist suggests that Bela and Irene might have ended up together if not for the interference of others), Bela flips and, aided by hideously disfigured helpmate Karloff, subjects Hinds to his homemade "pit and the pendulum" in his mansion's basement. Fast and furious and a must for Lugosiphiles; his only co-starrer with Boris in which *he* had the leading role.

RAVEN, THE

★★★ Goodtimes, 1963, NR, 85 min.
Dir: Roger Corman. Cast: Vincent Price, Peter Lorre, Boris Karloff, Hazel Court, Jack Nicholson, Olive Sturgess.

Not a remake of the Lugosi-Karloff "version" but a delightful spoof of the entire Corman-Price-Poe cycle. Price, Lorre, and Karloff are rival sorcerers in 15th-century England who use their magical skills to battle for supremacy while Peter changes back and forth from raven to human form and trades quips with a young Nicholson (as his son) and Court (in dangerously low-cut gowns) looks on in vague interest. All the expected clichés are given a gentle poke in the ribs by Richard Matheson's clever script, while the special effects are quite elaborate-looking for such a cheap production. Favorite line, Lorre to Price upon entering a musty family crypt: "Hard place to keep clean, huh?"

RAWHEAD REX

★★ Vestron, 1986, R, 89 min. Dir: George Pavlou. Cast: David Dukes, Kelly Piper, Nial O'Brien, Ronan Wilmot, Niall Tobin, Heinrich von Buenau.

Rawhead Rex, a huge pagan god from pre-Christian history, is revived when his ancient grave is disturbed and goes on a bloody rampage through the quiet Irish countryside. Good photography and an elaborate (if overexposed) monster design highlight this otherwise routine Clive Barker adaptation.

RAZORBACK

★★★ Warner, 1984, R, 94 min.
Dir: Russell Mulcahy. Cast: Gregory Harrison, Arkie Whiteley, Bill Kerr, Judy Morris, Chris Haywood, David Argue.

Surprisingly effective porcine Australian version of *Jaws* with hunky Harrison as an American tourist vengefully hunting the colossal razorback boar that killed his wife. Flashy direction by rock video vet Mulcahy, excellent pacing, welcome homages to Tobe Hooper and Dario Argento, and a briefly glimpsed, though well-executed, title monster designed by Bob McCarron make this an unexpected find.

REAL TROUBLE

See: *Hell High.*

RE-ANIMATOR

★★★☆ Vestron, 1985, NR 86 min.
Dir: Stuart Gordon. Cast: Jeffrey Combs, Barbara Crampton, Bruce Abbott, David Gale, Robert Sampson, Carolyn Purdey-Gordon.

H. P. Lovecraft would have a hard time recognizing his episodic gem "Herbert West—Re-Animator" as it is presented here, but everyone else should be made aware that this is one of the funniest, bloodiest, cleverest gore fests of the '80s. Experiments at reviving the dead at good ol' Miskatonic University turn the dean into a zombie, a professor into a sex-starved severed head, and an autopsy room full of cadavers into an army of living dead maniacs. Lots of great comic dialogue ("Who's going to believe a talking head? Get a job in a sideshow!"), gung-ho performances, and some of the grossest FX ever make this a must-see for gorehounds everywhere. Once seen, the "head" scene is hard to shake. Sequel: *Bride of Re-Animator.* Also out in a slightly restructured R version.

RED-BLOODED AMERICAN GIRL

★★☆ Paramount, 1988, R, 89 min.
Dir: David Blyth. Cast: Christopher Plummer, Heather Thomas, Andrew Stevens, Lydie Denier, Kim Coates, Andrew Jackson.

Blood researcher Stevens is lured to the high-tech private clinic of vampire Plummer, who infects Thomas with a new strain of vampirism in order to induce Stevens to find a cure for the condition. A trim, somewhat tongue-in-cheek vamp flick, this has similarities to the underrated *Thirst;* strong turns from Plummer, Thomas, and Stevens; and an inventive, intelligent, and kinky screenplay by Alan Moyle.

REDEEMER, THE

See: *Class Reunion Massacre.*

REDEEMER, SON OF SATAN, THE

See: *Class Reunion Massacre.*

RED HANGMAN, THE

See: *The Bloody Pit of Horror.*

RED HOUSE, THE

★★☆ Goodtimes, 1947, NR, 95 min.
Dir: Delmer Daves. Cast: Edward G. Robinson,
Lon McCallister, Judith Anderson, Allene Roberts,
Julie London, Rory Calhoun.

Minor but well-done horror mystery with
Robinson as a crippled farmer who warns
people away from the supposedly haunted
Oxhead Woods and the mysterious red house
within. When Edward G.'s sister and niece
disregard him, tragedy strikes. A nice mood of
dank swamps and misty forests and especially
fine acting from Robinson and a typically
stern Anderson make this worth watching.

RED LIPS, THE

See: *Daughters of Darkness.*

REDNECK ZOMBIES

★☆ TWE, 1988, R, 83 min.
Dir: Pericles Lewnes. Cast: Lisa De Haven, W. E.
Benson, William W. Decker, James Housely.

Crude rural horror comic with toxic-contami-
nated moonshine transforming hillbillies into
the living dead. When a busload of your usual
Friday the 13th–type teens amble by, the
expected mayhem erupts. Another Troma
waste of time, this is hampered even further
by having most of its gore cut for an R.

RED SIGN OF MADNESS, THE

See: *Hatchet for a Honeymoon.*

RED WOLF INN

See: *Terror at Red Wolf Inn.*

REFLECTING SKIN, THE

★★★ LIVE, 1990, R, 106 min.
Dir: Philip Ridley. Cast: Jeremy Cooper, Viggo
Mortensen, Lindsay Duncan, Duncan Fraser,
Sheila Moore, David Longworth.

Set in the post-WWII 1940s, this haunting
British chiller concerns American farmboy
Cooper's obsession with widowed neighbor
Duncan whom he thinks is a vampire after his
older brother (Mortensen). Eerie and very well
acted, this gets bogged down in too many odd
subplots and runs about a reel too long but,
for the most part, is a brave and perceptive

little film about the horrors of childhood (both
real and imagined).

REFLECTION OF FEAR, A

★★☆ RCA/Columbia, 1972, PG, 89 min.
Dir: William A. Fraker. Cast: Robert Shaw, Sally
Kellerman, Sondra Locke, Mary Ure, Signe Hasso,
Mitchell Ryan.

Muddled but visually interesting psycho-
shocker about a repressed teenager (Locke)
whose split personality and homicidal tendencies take over when her divorced dad (Shaw)
arrives to visit with a new fiancee (Kellerman).
Good direction from cinematographer Fraker
and a first-string cast, but the plot twists are
pretty obvious, including the *Homicidal*-in-
reverse surprise climax. Aka *Labyrinth* and
Autumn Child.

REFLECTIONS OF MURDER

★★★ Republic, 1974, NR, 97 min.
Dir: John Badham. Cast: Tuesday Weld, Joan Hackett,
Sam Waterston, Michael Lerner, Lucille Benson,
R. G. Armstrong, Lance Kerwin, John Levin.

In this excellent TV remake of *Diabolique,* the
wife and mistress (Hackett and Weld) of a
cruel private school headmaster (Waterston)
drown him in a bathtub and are later haunted
by his apparent ghost. Fine acting and taut,
atmospheric direction make this an above-
average rehash of a classic chiller.

REFRIGERATOR, THE

★★☆ Monarch, 1991, R, 86 min.
Dir: Nicholas Jacobs. Cast: Julia McNeal, David
Simonds, Angel Caban, Phyllis Sanz.

This fun little cheapie, shot in Lower Manhattan, has McNeal and Simonds as a young couple who come to New York to find fame and
fortune and end up battling a possessed major
appliance. It sounds dumber than dumb and
takes its silly premise *very* seriously, but director Jacobs manages to balance the shocks and
laughs (most of them intentional) quite well,
making this the most enjoyable shot-in-Man-
hattan splatter film since the original *Basket
Case.*

REINCARNATE, THE

★★ Wizard, 1971, PG, 99 min. Dir: Don Haldane.
Cast: Jack Creley, Jay Reynolds, Trudy Young,
Terry Tweed, Hugh Webster, Gene Tyburn.

Creley is a dying occultist who wishes to reincarnate his soul in the body of younger artist
Reynolds in this dull Canadian flick. Some
interesting touches but marred by hammy
acting and a draggy plot—even more so in
the 122-minute theatrical version.

REINCARNATION OF PETER PROUD, THE

★★ Video Treasures, 1975, R, 104 min.
Dir: J. Lee Thompson. Cast: Michael Sarrazin,
Jennifer O'Neill, Margot Kidder, Cornelia Sharpe,
Paul Hecht, Tony Stefano, Debralee Scott,
Steve Franken.

Contrived adaptation of Max Ehrlich's novel
about a California college prof (Sarrazin) who
discovers that he is the reincarnation of a
wealthy hunk murdered in the '40s by his
unhappy wife (Kidder). Complications arise
when Sarrazin falls in love with O'Neill, the
daughter of his former incarnation. An eerie
score by Jerry Goldsmith and good work from
Kidder, but otherwise flat acting and an overall lack of suspense sink this like a stone. *Playgirl* centerfold Stefano appears mostly nude as
Sarrazin's former self.

REJUVENATOR, THE

★★★ SVS, 1988, R, 87 min. Dir: Brian Thomas Jones.
Cast: Vivian Lanko, John MacKay, James Hogue,
Katell Pleven, Jessica Dublin, Marcus Powell.

Lanko is terrific in this fun updating of *The
Leech Woman* about an aging movie queen
made younger by a scientist's serum derived
from human brain fluid. Trouble starts when
the formula turns out to have an only temporary effect and Lanko periodically begins turning into a hideous hag who needs the fresh
brain fluid of murder victims to regain her
youth and beauty. Good Ed French makeups
and a solid supporting cast add to the effectiveness. Check it out. Aka *Rejuvenatrix* and
Juvenatrix.

REJUVENATRIX

See: *The Rejuvenator.*

RELENTLESS

★★☆ RCA/Columbia, 1989, R, 92 min. Dir: William
Lustig. Cast: Judd Nelson, Robert Loggia, Leo Rossi,
Meg Foster, Patrick O'Bryan, Angel Tompkins.

Obnoxious Brat Packer Nelson is wholly convincing in his best role as an L.A. Police Academy dropout who freaks and decides to show
the force just how much smarter than them he
is by beginning a series of knife murders—his
victims chosen at random from the phone book.
Spends too much time with its clichéd young
cop/old cop team subplot and wastes the contribution of underrated screen goddess Foster
but, like *Maniac Cop,* shows Lustig's considerable growth as a filmmaker and is often quite
suspenseful. Followed by a pair of sequels.

RELENTLESS 2: DEAD ON

See: *Dead On: Relentless 2.*

RELENTLESS 3

★★ New Line, 1993, R, 84 min. Dir: James Lemmo.
Cast: Leo Rossi, William Forsythe, Signy Coleman,
Tom Bower.

This third film in the series has detective Rossi
on the trail of a new psycho (Forsythe, creepily effective here) who scalps and slashes his
victims and sends pieces of tattooed skin to
the police. Part 3 is nastier than the first two
parts, but it was badly edited just before
release and Meg Foster is sorely missed.

REPOSSESSED

★★☆ LIVE, 1990, PG-13, 84 min.
Dir: Bob Logan. Cast: Linda Blair, Leslie Nielsen,
Ned Beatty, Anthony Starke, Lana Schwab,
Thom J. Sharp.

Moderately funny *Exorcist* spoof made legitimate thanks to Blair's good-natured send-up
of her most famous role and Nielsen's as ever
satirical elan as the exorcist who comes out of
retirement when housewife Linda is repossessed by the demon who once inhabited her
as a child. Like *Airplane* (its obvious inspiration), this has a bad joke for every good one
(but *try* not to laugh when Nielsen imitates
Billy Idol, Robert Palmer, and Elton John) but
gets by on the high spirits of its two lead performers, with Linda proving herself an adept
comedienne.

REPULSION

★★★★ Studio Entertainment, 1965, NR, 105 min.
Dir: Roman Polanski. Cast: Catherine Deneuve,
Yvonne Furneaux, Ian Hendry, Patrick Wymark,
John Fraser, Renee Houston.

After *Psycho,* this is the best psychological horror film of the '60s. Deneuve is unforgettable
as a beautiful young manicurist whose obsessive fear of sex causes her mind to crumble
when left alone in her apartment by promiscu-
ous sister Furneaux. Polanski's first English-
language feature, this has the odd awkward
moment but still maintains its considerable
impact, thanks to Deneuve's performance,
Gilbert Taylor's photography, and some still
quite potent shocks. Look for the director as a
spoon player on a street corner.

REQUIEM FOR A VAMPIRE

See: *Dungeon of Terror.*

REST IN PEACE

See: *One Dark Night.*

REST IN PIECES

★ IVE, 1987, R, 90 min. Dir: Joseph Braunstein
[José Larraz]. Cast: Dorothy Malone, Scott Thompson

Baker, Lorin Jean Vail, Jack Taylor, Patty Sheppard, Jeffrey Segal.

Atrocious Spanish-U.S. co-production about a couple who inherit an estate from their suicidal aunt (Malone) inhabited by the ghosts of various suicide victims who want the wife to join them. Gory but tedious, with especially awful performances—Malone included.

RESURRECTED, THE
★★★ LIVE, 1991, R, 105 min.
Dir: Dan O'Bannon. Cast: Chris Sarandon, John Terry, Jane Sibbett, Robert Romanus, Jewel Shepard.

O'Bannon's first directorial job since *Return of the Living Dead* is this solidly gothic remake of Corman's *The Haunted Palace* based on Lovecraft's "The Case of Charles Dexter Ward." Terry is a private eye hired by Sibbett to find missing husband Sarandon—who turns out to be involved in experiments to reanimate the dead and is under the influence of a warlock ancestor also played by Chris. This blends its clipped, Dashiell Hammett–like main character with Lovecraft's horrors surprisingly well, adding crisp cinematography, bizarre makeup FX, and a beautifully modulated performance by Sarandon.

RESURRECTION SYNDICATE, THE
See: *The Devil's Undead.*

RETRIBUTION
★★ Virgin Vision, 1987, R, 109 min.
Dir: Guy Magar. Cast: Dennis Lipscomb, Leslie Wing, Hoyt Axton, Suzanne Snyder, Jeff Pomerantz, George Murdock.

Routine low-budget possession pic with Lipscomb (in an awful hairpiece) as a wimpy suicidal artist inhabited by the vengeful spirit of a murdered gangster out to get his killers. Goes overboard on character development (most aren't worth developing) and smoky atmospherics, with a twist ending borrowed from *The Possession of Joel Delaney.*

RETURN
★★ Academy, 1985, R, 82 min.
Dir: Andrew Silver. Cast: Karlene Crockett, John Walcutt, Anne Francis, Frederic Forrest.

Minor reincarnation movie with Crockett as an heiress who discovers that boyfriend Walcutt (the family gardener) is her grandfather reborn and the key to her family's darkest secret. Francis and Forrest bring much-needed spark to this slight tale.

RETURN FROM THE PAST
See: *Gallery of Horrors.*

RETURN OF COUNT YORGA, THE
★★★ Orion, 1971, PG, 97 min.
Dir: Bob Kelljan. Cast: Robert Quarry, Mariette Hartley, Roger Perry, Yvonne Wilder, Walter Brooke, George Macready, Edward Walsh, Rudy De Luca, Craig T. Nelson, Michael Pataki.

Fun, effective—if somewhat predictable—sequel, with the Count (the ever-sardonic Quarry) beguiled by San Francisco orphanage worker Hartley and sending his harem of fanged followers to slaughter her family in a great *Night of the Living Dead*–inspired sequence. Later he hypnotizes Mariette into falling in love with him while fiance Perry tries to rescue her. An entertaining, higher-budgeted follow-up with good acting, a diverse supporting cast, and a nice mix of laughs and scares. Favorite scene: Yorga watching *The Vampire Lovers* on TV.

RETURN OF DRACULA, THE
★★★ MGM/UA, 1958, NR, 77 min.
Dir: Paul Landres. Cast: Francis Lederer, Norma Eberhardt, Ray Striklyn, Virginia Vincent, Greta Gransted, Gage Clarke, John Wengraf, Jimmie Baird.

A vampiric *Shadow of a Doubt,* this clever '50s low-budget shocker has the suave Lederer as the Count, who murders a Balkan artist and enters the U.S. using his identity. In California, Drac moves in with the all-American Mayberry family whose teen daughter (Eberhardt) soon falls under his spell. This is surprisingly sober and straightforward for its time (even with the teenage hero and heroine), and has excellent performances from Lederer, Eberhardt, and Vincent (as a blind girl who becomes a sighted vampiress who turns into a white wolf). There are also some nice directorial touches (like a flash of color during the penultimate staking scene).

RETURN OF MR. H, THE
See: *They Saved Hitler's Brain.*

RETURN OF SWAMP THING, THE
★★ RCA/Columbia, 1989, PG-13, 86 min.
Dir: Jim Wynorski. Cast: Louis Jourdan, Heather Locklear, Sarah Douglas, Dick Durock, Ace Mask, Monique Gabrielle.

A real vegged-out sequel to the Wes Craven original with an even swampier thing (a returning Durock) falling for the bimbette daughter (Locklear, cast to type) of arch nemesis Arcane (Jourdan, whose reappearance here after his death at the end of part one is barely explained). Goofy fun in the TV "Batman" vein, this has some impressive mutant monsters, but the fat little kid character has all the talent and likability of a tree stump. Gabrielle's welcome presence helps a lot, as always.

RETURN OF THE ALIENS: THE DEADLY SPAWN

★★☆ Continental, 1983, R, 79 min.
Dir: Douglas McKeown. Cast: Charles George Hildebrandt, Tom De Franco, Richard Lee Porter, Jean Tafler, Karen Tigne.

A meteorite crashes near a storm-bound house that is soon after invaded by blind alien tadpoles with incredible bridgework and big appetites who find their victims through sound. This literally bargain basement item (half of it takes place in a dark cellar) is enlivened by cutely grotesque monsters, incredibly gory killings, and a refreshingly unobnoxious little kid hero. Briefly shown in theatres as simply *The Deadly Spawn*.

RETURN OF THE APE MAN

★★ Cinemacabre, 1944, NR, 60 min.
Dir: Phil Rosen. Cast: Bela Lugosi, John Carradine, Frank Moran, Judith Gibson, Michael Ames, Mary Currier.

Laugh-filled Monogram lunacy with Lugosi and Carradine as scientists who revive a prehistoric man they find frozen in arctic ice (made of plastic). Bela thinks the ape guy (Moran in visible BVDs) needs a new brain, so he thoughtfully gives it John's. Despite the cranial improvements, the prehistoric troublemaker still goes on his expected rampage: killing Bela, carrying off heroine Gibson, and dying in the obligatory fire. George Zucco, originally meant to play the ape man after the brain transplant, is credited but does not appear, while Bela and Long John make the most of their overacting opportunities. Good Lugosi line at a boring party: "Some people's brains would never be missed!" Despite the title, this has no connection to Bela's earlier *Ape Man* non-hit.

RETURN OF THE EVIL DEAD

★★ JTC, 1973, R, 87 min.
Dir: Amando de Ossorio. Cast: Tony Kendall, Fernando Sanchez, Esperanza Roy, Lone Fleming, Frank Brana, Loretta Tovar.

Number 2 in de Ossorio's Spanish "Blind Dead" series has the sightless ghouls disrupting a Portuguese village's centennial celebration. Highlighted by Sanchez's robust, funny performance as the town's shifty mayor and a really creepy, suspense-filled ending. Original title: *El Ataque de los Muertos Sin Ojos: Attack of the Blind Dead*.

Danielle de Metz wishes she had a No-Pest strip in Return of the Fly *(1959).*

RETURN OF THE FLY

★★☆ CBS/Fox, 1959, NR, 80 min.
Dir: Edward L. Bernds. Cast: Vincent Price, Brett Halsey, David Frankham, Danielle De Metz, John Sutton, Dan Seymour.

Adequate sequel that should have been called *Son of the Fly*. Price returns as the brother of the original *Fly* experimenter whose son (Halsey) revives Dad's old teleportation experiments with predictable results. Moody and even a bit scary in spots, this has less sentiment than the original and a colorful sense of the absurd. The fly makeup is better this time out, though a silly guinea pig man has to be seen for itself.

RETURN OF THE GIANT MONSTERS

See: *Gamera vs. Gaos*.

RETURN OF THE KILLER TOMATOES

★★ New World, 1988, PG, 98 min.
Dir: John DeBello. Cast: John Astin, Anthony Starke, Karen Mistal, George Clooney, Steve Lundquist.

In this silly but watchable sequel to *Attack of the Killer Tomatoes,* Astin is a looney scientist out to create human-tomato hybrids and pretty Mistal is his first big success. Not as awful as it might seem, with Astin giving his typically wigged-out performance.

RETURN OF THE LIVING DEAD
See: *Messiah of Evil.*

RETURN OF THE LIVING DEAD
★★★ HBO, 1985, R, 90 min.
Dir: Dan O'Bannon. Cast: Clu Gulager, James Karen, Don Calfa, Thom Mathews, Beverly Randolph, Linnea Quigley, Miquel Nunez, Jewel Shepard.

Hilarious horror comic semi-sequel to *Night of the Living Dead.* A canister containing a zombie is discovered in the basement of a medical supplies warehouse. When a strange gas escapes the canister, it mixes with rain and soaks the ground of an ancient cemetery, reviving the corpses therein as brain-munching zombies. A fast pace, terrific comic acting (including Linnea in her star-making role), and an inventive and funny script are marred only by an abrupt, unsatisfying ending.

RETURN OF THE LIVING DEAD PART II
★☆ Lorimar, 1988, R, 88 min. Dir: Ken Wiederhorn. Cast: James Karen, Thom Mathews, Marsha Deitlein, Dana Ashbrook, Michael Kenworthy, Suzanne Snyder.

LINNEA QUIGLEY
(1958–)

The Goldie Hawn of gore, Linnea is a bubbly, delightful presence who often only needs to appear for a brief moment in a film to enhance its entertainment value. Though she has yet to get a vehicle truly worthy of her talents, prime Quigley can be glimpsed in both *Return of the Living Dead* and *Night of the Demons.*

Psycho From Texas ('74), *Don't Go Near the Park* ('80), *Graduation Day* ('81), *The Black Room* ('83), *Fatal Games* (bit, '84), *Silent Night, Deadly Night* ('84), *Return of the Living Dead* ('85), *Creepozoids* ('87), *Sorority Babes in the Slimeball Bowl-O-Rama* ('87), *Nightmare Sisters* ('87), *Night of the Demons* ('88), *A Nightmare on Elm Street 4: The Dream Master* (bit, '88), *Dead Heat* (TV version, '88), *Drive-In Madness* ('88), *Linnea Quigley's Horror Workout* ('89), *Murder Weapon* ('89), *Sexbomb* ('89), *Blood Church* ('90), *Innocent Blood* (cameo, '92), *Pumpkinhead II* ('93).

This totally unnecessary sequel plays closer to a remake with another barrel of zombie-spawning gas raising another squadron of living dead who this time attack a *Poltergeist*-like tract home development. Slickly made but *really* lame; the Michael Jackson throwaway gag near the end provides the sole laugh.

RETURN OF THE LIVING DEAD PART III
★★☆ Vidmark, 1993, UR, 96 min.
Dir: Brian Yuzna. Cast: Mindy Clarke, J. Trevor Edmund, Kent McCord, Sarah Douglas, Basil Wallace, Pia Reyes.

Against all odds, this third installment is a vast improvement on spoofy part II and almost as good as the original. Army brat Edmund brings his accidentally killed girlfriend Clarke back to life with the zombie-making gas now being experimented on by the military. Mindy spends the rest of the movie trying to resist the urge to munch on J.T.'s brain. Thoughtfully put together and refreshingly downbeat, this has good acting and makeup FX. It is also out in a less graphic R version.

RETURN OF THE VAMPIRE
★★☆ Goodtimes, 1943, NR, 69 min.
Dir: Lew Landers. Cast: Bela Lugosi, Frieda Inescort, Nina Foch, Roland Varno, Miles Mander, Matt Willis.

Bela is bloodsucker Armand Tesla who is revived during the London Blitz and seeks revenge on doctor Inescort who once drove an iron spike through his heart. Foch is the beautiful girl Lugosi chooses as a mate. Stolid but entertaining Columbia imitation of a Universal horror film, this has lots of mist, Willis as a werewolf helpmate, and a memorably grisly climax with Bela's face melting in the sunlight.

RETURN OF THE WOLF MAN
See: *The Craving.*

RETURN TO HORROR HIGH
★★ New World, 1987, R, 95 min.
Dir: Bill Froelich. Cast: Lori Lethin, Brendan Hughes, Vince Edwards, Alex Rocco, Scott Jacoby, Maureen McCormick, Philip McKeon, Richard Brestoff.

Silly comic slasher about a sleazy film company making a sleazy movie at a high school closed down after a gruesome mass murder. When the killings are recreated, the maniac reappears for more real-life mayhem—or maybe not. Too confusingly constructed (the ending makes almost no sense) to be of more than only passing interest, though there are good turns from Rocco (as the producer who shouts, "Everyone likes a good gross-out!")

and McCormick (of "The Brady Bunch") as a lady cop who gets sexier as she gets bloodier.

RETURN TO SALEM'S LOT
★★☆ Warner, 1987, R, 100 min.
Dir: Larry Cohen. Cast: Michael Moriarty, Richard Addison Reed, Samuel Fuller, Andrew Duggan, June Havoc, Evelyn Keyes, Ronee Blakley, James Dixon.

A weird, to say the extreme least, semi-sequel to Tobe Hooper's film version of the Stephen King novel. Moriarty is an anthropologist who moves with his bratty teen son (Reed) to the little New England hamlet dominated by vampires. Though marred by dimestore FX, this has some good laughs, and cult director Fuller is a hoot as a rascally old Nazi hunter who, in a pinch, can turn fearless vampire killer as well.

REVENGE
See: *Terror Under the House.*

REVENGE
★ United, 1986, R, 100 min.
Dir: Christopher Lewis. Cast: Patrick Wayne, John Carradine, Bennie Lee McCowan, Stephanie Knopka.

Boring filmed sequel to the shot-on-video *Blood Cult* with Wayne avenging his brother's death in the first film by battling the cult of murderous dog-worshippers (fronted by Carradine in another two-scene cameo). Technically superior to its predecessor but just as dull, with lots of cut-rate gore FX and awful acting. The "surprise" ending makes utterly no sense at all.

REVENGE IN THE HOUSE OF USHER
☆ Edde Entertainment, 1983, R, 93 min.
Dir: A. M. Franck [Jesus Franco]. Cast: Howard Vernon, Robert Foster, Lina Romay, Dan Villers, Jean Tolzak, Joan Verly.

Awful adaptation of the Edgard [sic] Allan Poe tale about crazed Dr. Usher (Vernon) who drains the blood of young girls in order to preserve his dying daughter while dictating his memoirs (illustrated through black-and-white flashbacks from *The Awful Dr. Orlof!*). Ridiculous dialogue ("Anything else, sir?" Usher's manservant asks. "Yes, drop dead!" he replies!), anachronistic period detail, and terrible effects (the fall of the house is accomplished by shaking the camera while wood splinters off camera and somebody drops a couple of Lego blocks on the ground) make this Franco at his worst—and buddy, *that's* bad! Originally titled *El Hunimiento de la Casa Usher: The Fall of the House of Usher* and shown on TV as *Nervosus.*

REVENGE OF THE BLOOD BEAST
See: *The She Beast.*

REVENGE OF THE COLOSSAL MAN
See: *War of the Colossal Beast.*

REVENGE OF THE CREATURE
★★★ MCA/Universal, 1955, NR, 81 min.
Dir: Jack Arnold. Cast: John Agar, Lori Nelson, John Bromfield, Nestor Paiva, Dave Willock, Clint Eastwood, Brett Halsey, Ricou Browning.

The Gill-Man is captured and brought to a Florida aquarium where scientists Agar and Nelson begin to experiment on him. When the creature falls in love with Lori, he escapes his chains and terrorizes Jacksonville in search of his lady. Arnold's follow-up to his classic *Creature From the Black Lagoon* isn't as imaginative but has lots of action (apart from a dull middle section), some surprisingly potent violence, and a scary pre-*Psycho* motel shower scene.

REVENGE OF THE DEAD
See: *Meatcleaver Massacre.*

REVENGE OF THE DEAD
See: *Night of the Ghouls.*

REVENGE OF THE DEAD
See: *Orgy of the Dead.*

REVENGE OF THE DEAD
★★ Vestron, 1983, R, 98 min. Dir: Pupi Avati.
Cast: Gabriele Lavia, Anne Conovas, Paolo Tanziana, Cesare Barbetti.

Writer Lavia discovers a spell for raising the dead on an old typewriter ribbon and, hoping to use it as the basis for a new novel, accidentally calls up a horde of zombies. This offbeat variation on the usual Italian walking dead movie is interesting but uninvolving viewing, with far less splatter than you'd expect from the advertising art. Aka *Zedar.*

REVENGE OF THE LIVING ZOMBIES
★ Magnum, 1988, UR, 88 min.
Dir: Bill Hinzman. Cast: Bill Hinzman, Leslie Ann Wick, John Mowod, Kevin Kindlin, Denise Morrone, Lisa Smith.

Hinzman, who played the graveyard ghoul in the classic *Night of the Living Dead,* directs and plays a similar role in this virtual remake with a group of young clods trapped in another farmhouse by another pack of voracious zombies. Not too swift, with poor acting and some truly abysmal technical credits. Aka *Flesheater.*

REVENGE OF THE SAVAGE BEES
See: *Terror Out of the Sky.*

REVENGE OF THE SCREAMING DEAD
See: *Messiah of Evil.*

REVENGE OF THE STEPFORD WIVES
★★ Embassy, 1980, NR, 91 min.
Dir: Robert Fuest. Cast: Sharon Gless, Arthur Hill, Julie Kavner, Don Johnson, Audra Lindley, Mason Adams.

Mediocre tele-movie follow-up to the theatrical feature with Gless as a cocky TV reporter investigating stories about the weird behavior of the women of Stepford and stumbling upon their awful secret—a secret inconsistent with those revealed in the first and third (*The Stepford Children*) films in this series. Gless and Kavner are good, but Johnson (whose minor contribution is played up big-time on the video box) is annoying as Kavner's stupid husband. The direction is surprisingly anonymous, considering some of the other genre credits of the usually stylish Fuest.

REVENGE OF THE VAMPIRE
See: *Black Sunday.*

REVOLT OF THE DEMONS
See: *Revolt of the Zombies.*

REVOLT OF THE ZOMBIES
★☆ Sinister Cinema, 1936, NR, 65 min.
Dir: Victor Halperin. Cast: Dean Jagger, Dorothy Stone, Roy D'Arcy, Robert Noland, George Cleveland, Teru Shimada.

Penny-pinching semi-sequel to *White Zombie* with Jagger a poor Lugosi substitute as a Cambodian zombie master who commands a group of walking dead soldiers during World War I. Unlike the fairy tale–like *White Zombie*, this tries to merge its horror with the real world and it just doesn't work, emerging as one of the dumber disappointments of the original '30s horror cycle. Aka *Revolt of the Demons.*

RIFT, THE
See: *Endless Descent.*

RING OF TERROR
★☆ Sinister Cinema, 1962, NR, 80 min.
Dir: Clark L. Paylow. Cast: George Mather, Esther Furst, Austin Green, Joseph Conway.

The pay *must* have been low on this early '60s nonentity about a fearless med school student (Mather) who accepts a bet to steal a ring from the finger of a soon-to-be-interred corpse. An

"Alfred Hitchcock Presents"–like story dragged out to feature length. Your sister's baby shower video packs more entertainment value.

RIPPER, THE
See: *The New York Ripper.*

RIPPER, THE
★☆ United, 1986, UR, 101 min.
Dir: Christopher Lewis. Cast: Tom Schreier, Mona Van Pernis, Tom Savini, Wade Tower, Andrea Adams, Bennie Lee McCowan.

Savini's five-minute cameo in *Exorcist* contacts in the title role and some really graphic FX are the sole distinguishing factors of this shot-on-video slasher. A college prof (Schreier) comes into possession of Jack the Ripper's ring and, predictably, is possessed by him and begins a series of murders. From the makers of *Blood Cult*, this is marginally better but it's a narrow margin.

ROAD GAMES
★★☆ Embassy, 1981, R, 100 min.
Dir: Richard Franklin. Cast: Stacy Keach, Jamie Lee Curtis, Marion Edward, Grant Page.

A sort of *Rear Window* on wheels down under with Keach as an existential trucker in Australia whose hobby of observing his fellow travelers gets him mixed up with perennial girl-on-the-run JLC and a maniac who beheads his female victims with a guitar string. Good photography, strong lead performances, and a nice sense of self-deprecating humor dress up this artsy slasher from the director of *Psycho II*.

ROBOT MONSTER
★☆ Rhino, 1953, NR, 63 min.
Dir: Phil Tucker. Cast: George Nader, Claudia Barrett, Selena Royle, John Mylong, Gregory Moffett, Pamela Paulson, George Barrows, voice of John Brown.

After *Plan Nine From Outer Space*, this 3-D monstrosity is the funniest bad movie ever made. Ro-Man, an alien who looks suspiciously like a gorilla in a diving helmet, tries to conquer the earth with a bubble machine and stock footage from *One Million B.C.* That is, until he gets a load of Barrett, one of the last six people left alive after Ro-Man's attack, in a tight blouse. Totally terrible and totally amazing, with priceless dialogue, hilarious plot complications, and a surprisingly robust score, courtesy of Elmer Bernstein. Also released as *Monster From Mars* and *Monsters From the Moon.*

ROBOT VS. THE AZTEC MUMMY, THE
★★ Goodtimes, 1957, NR, 65 min.
Dir: Rafael Portillo. Cast: Ramon Gay, Rosita Arenas, Crox Alvarado, Luis Aceves Castaneda.

In this second sequel to *The Aztec Mummy* (U.S. re-edited version: *Attack of the Mayan Mummy*), the evil Dr. Krupp (Alvarado), known to his friends as "The Bat," creates a tin-can robot with a human brain to battle the ragtag Aztec Mummy and force the bandaged one into revealing the site of his hidden treasure. The Aztec Mummy series was probably the dumbest concocted by the Mexican horror film industry, but this is far from the worst entry, with loads of fun and hokey elements. Original title: *La Momia Azteca contra el Robot Humano: The Aztec Mummy vs. the Human Robot.*

ROCK 'N' ROLL NIGHTMARE
★ Academy, 1987, PG-13, 83 min.
Dir: John Fasano. Cast: Jon-Mikl Thor, Jillian Peri, Frank Dietz, Dave Lane, Teresa Simpson, Liane Abel.

Another bad combo of crappy rock music and worse horror, this features *Ghoulie*–like puppet demons, *Evil Dead*–inspired camera placement, and muscle-head rocker wannabe Thor as a hero who dresses more like a Chippendale's dancer than a musician. Yech! TV title: *The Edge of Hell.*

ROCKULA
★☆ Cannon, 1989, PG-13, 90 min.
Dir: Luca Bercovici. Cast: Dean Cameron, Tawny Fere, Toni Basil, Bo Diddley, Thomas Dolby.

Flat horror comedy with Cameron as a Dracula descendent who falls in love with rock musician Fere. What follows are some less than hilarious "comic" hijinks. For Bo Diddley movie buffs only.

ROCKY HORROR PICTURE SHOW, THE
★★★ CBS/Fox, 1975, R, 95 min.
Dir: Jim Sharman. Cast: Tim Curry, Susan Sarandon, Barry Bostwick, Richard O'Brien, Nell Campbell, Meatloaf, Patricia Quinn, Charles Gray.

This eternally popular cult movie derived from O'Brien's play *The Rocky Horror Show* is either great fun or really, really dumb, depending on your point of view. Curry is hilarious as transvestite mad scientist Frank N. Furter, and there are good turns from Sarandon, Campbell, and Meatloaf, but this can only really be appreciated en masse at one of its midnight art house showings. Sequel: *Shock Treatment.*

RODAN
★★☆ Paramount/Gateway, 1956, NR, 72 min.
Dir: Inoshiro Honda. Cast: Kenji Sawara, Yumi Shirakawa, Akihiko Hirata, Akio Kobori.

One of the best Japanese creature features, this deals with a pair of huge flying monsters born from prehistoric eggs ravaging the world. Intricate special effects and a creepy opening third set in a small Japanese mining village help this a lot. The longer Japanese version was called *Radon* and this is also known as *Rodan, The Flying Monster.*

RODAN, THE FLYING MONSTER
See: *Rodan.*

ROSEMARY'S BABY
★★★★ Paramount, 1968, R, 137 min.
Dir: Roman Polanski. Cast: Mia Farrow, John Cassavetes, Ruth Gordon, Sidney Blackmer, Maurice Evans, Ralph Bellamy, Angela Dorian, Patsy Kelly, Elisha Cook, Charles Grodin.

William Castle produced Polanski's classic adaptation of Ira Levin's novel about a young Manhattan housewife (Farrow) impregnated with the devil's spawn thanks to a pact made by her actor husband (Cassavetes) with the witch cult next door (in return, he is to have professional success). Long but utterly involving, with excellent performances (Gordon won an Oscar as tacky witch Minnie) and a subtle approach to the material that the explicitness of an *Exorcist* would have ruined. TV sequel: *Look What's Happened to Rosemary's Baby.*

ROSEMARY'S KILLER
See: *The Prowler.*

RUBY
★★☆, United, 1977, R, 84 min.
Dir: Curtis Harrington. Cast: Piper Laurie, Stuart Whitman, Roger Davis, Janit Baldwin, Crystin Sinclair, Len Lesser.

An absurd but enjoyable exploitation mix of *Carrie, The Exorcist,* and *The Godfather* set at a '50s drive-in specializing in horror films (like *Attack of the 50-Foot Woman*). If you thought Laurie pulled out all the stops in *Carrie,* wait till you see her go it as the title character here, a former gun moll who is haunted by her slain lover who possesses their autistic teen daughter (Baldwin) while murdering former gangsters now working at the drive-in. The plot, as you can tell, is incredibly complicated to no good end, but Harrington drenches everything in his usual soft-focus photography and mock-nostalgic period detail, making for a fun low-budget thriller. Beware the drastically recut

"Woody, is that you?" Mia Farrow in Rosemary's Baby *(1968).*

TV version with all the violence edited out and talky new scenes (directed by Stephanie Rothman) added, a version credited to "Allen Smithee."

RUDE AWAKENING
★★ Thrillervideo, 1980, NR, 50 min. Dir: Peter Sasdy. Cast: Denholm Elliott, James Laurenson, Pat Heywood, Lucy Gutteridge.

Elliott's performance highlights this routine "Hammer House of Horror" episode about a henpecked real estate agent who escapes his humdrum life through dreams that end up being more real to him than actual reality. Moderately engrossing.

RUE MORGUE MASSACRES
★★☆ All Seasons, 1972, R, 82 min. Dir: Javier Aguirre. Cast: Paul Naschy, Rossana Yanni, Alberto Dalbes, Maria Perschy, Vic Winner, Maria Elena Apron.

Better known as *El Jorobada de la Morgue: The Hunchback of the Morgue*, this is one of Naschy's goriest, funniest, most entertaining Spanish monster flicks. The overly complex plot involves a hunchbacked Swiss morgue attendant named Gotho (Paul) who loves a girl dying of tuberculosis. After she kicks, Gotho begins stealing bodies and murdering folks for a mad doc (Winner) who needs corpses to feed his creation—a living blob of matter—on condition that the scientist then restore the dead girl to life. Very, very violent and more than a little silly, this features the infamous scene where Naschy is attacked and actually bitten by real rats he then sets on fire.

RUNESTONE, THE
★★★ LIVE, 1991, R, 102 min. Dir: Willard Carroll. Cast: Peter Riegert, Joan Severance, Alexander Godonov, William Hickey, Mitchell Laurence, Tim Ryan, Chris Young, Lawrence Tierney.

Lively monster flick, adapted from a novella by Mark E. Rogers, about an ancient runestone unearthed from a Pennsylvania mine which unleashes a long-fingered Norse demon to possess archeologist Laurence and go on a rampage through Manhattan. This is fairly lavish-looking, with a well-orchestrated *Omen*-esque score by David Newman and a nice cast headed by Riegert as a foul-mouthed, candy-munching cop. Lance Anderson's monster design is merely adequate and the film lacks true suspense (no matter how many extras the monster knocks off, you *know* the heroes are never in any *real* danger), but overall this yields a nice surprise.

RUN, STRANGER, RUN
★★★ RCA/Columbia, 1973, PG, 90 min.
Dir: Darren McGavin. Cast: Patricia Neal, Cloris Leachman, Bobby Darin, Ron Howard, Tessa Dahl, Kathie Brown, Joe Mascolo, Simon Oakland.

Released to theatres as *Happy Mother's Day, Love George,* this all-star splatter film was way ahead of its time. Howard—halfway between playing Opie Taylor and Richie Cunningham—is an adopted teen who turns up in a tiny Nova Scotia fishing village searching for his natural parents. His arrival triggers off not only the usual soap opera melodramatics but a string of brutal knife and cleaver murders as well. Terrific performances, beautiful locations, and solid direction from actor McGavin make this sadly overlooked thriller a real video find.

RUSH WEEK
★☆ RCA/Columbia, 1990, R, 96 min.
Dir: Bob Bralver. Cast: Pamela Ludwig, Dean Hamilton, Roy Thinnes, Gregg Allmann, Kathleen Kinmont.

Yet another campus psycho flick with Ludwig as a reporter posing as a student and after the killer. Thinnes' broad performance as the school dean and a memorable decapitation climax are all that'll hold your attention.

SADIST, THE
★★☆ Rhino, 1963, NR, 81 min.
Dir: James Landis. Cast: Arch Hall, Jr., Helen Hovey, Marilyn Manning, Richard Alden, Don Russell.

Hall (so awful as the teen hero of *Eegah!*) is creepily convincing as a young psycho who, along with gal pal Manning, holds three schoolteachers hostage. Threats lead to torture, which leads to murder, which leads to a final confrontation between Arch and sole sur-

vivor Hovey. Cheap but compelling, with effective B&W photography by Vilmos Zsigmond. Aka *Profile of Terror.*

SALEM
See: *The Night Visitor.*

SALEM COME TO SUPPER
See: *The Night Visitor.*

SALEM'S LOT
★★★ Warner, 1979, NR, 184 min.
Dir: Tobe Hooper. Cast: David Soul, James Mason, Bonnie Bedelia, Lance Kerwin, Lew Ayres, Ed Flanders, Geoffrey Lewis, Marie Windsor, Elisha Cook, Fred Willard, Clarissa Kaye, Reggie Nalder.

Originally releasd to video in a shortened version dubbed *Salem's Lot: The Movie,* this is the full, uncut print of this TV film based on one of Stephen King's earliest and best novels. Troubled novelist Soul returns to his boyhood Maine home to exorcise some personal demons and ends up battling the Nosferatu-like vampire (Nalder) who's just moved into the *Psycho*-esque house on the hill. Sometimes looks like a Hammer Films version of *Peyton Place* with its huge cast of screwed-up characters and snarling vampires, yet there are some excellent scenes—the child vampire scratching at the window; the resurrection of Kaye; the murder of Flanders—and a great performance from Mason as the vampire's erudite familiar whose impeccable exterior (like that of the mysterious Marsden House) masks a grotesquely corrupted reality. Sequel: *Return to Salem's Lot.*

SAMSON IN THE WAX MUSEUM
★★ Sinister Cinema, 1963, NR, 85 min.
Dir: Alfonso Corona Blake. Cast: Santo, Norma Mora, Fernando Oses, José Luis Jimenez.

Mexico's premier masked wrestler Santo (known as Samson in the English-language version) battles a mad doctor and his living wax creations in this *House of Wax* knock-off. Silly but atmospheric. Original title: *El Santo en el Museo de Cera: Santo in the Wax Museum.*

SAMSON VS. THE VAMPIRE WOMEN
★★☆ Sinister Cinema, 1961, NR, 89 min.
Dir: Alfonso Corona Blake. Cast: Santo, Lorena Velasquez, Maria Duval, Fernando Oses.

The first and best of a series of popular Mexican wrestler horror films (originally titled *El Santo contra las Mujeres Vampiros: Santo vs. the Vampire Women*) with masked hero Santo coming up against statuesque vampire queen Valasquez and her handmaidens. Dumb fun with lots of mist, cobwebs, coffins, and punch-outs.

SANTA
See: *Christmas Evil.*

SANTA SANGRE
★★☆ Republic, 1989, NC-17, 118 min.
Dir: Alejandro Jodorowsky. Cast: Axel Jodorowsky, Blanca Guerra, Sabrina Dennison, Guy Stockwell, Thelma Tixou, Adan Jodorowsky.

Bizarre horror-art film from gifted Spanish director Jodorowsky. Young Axel Jodorowsky is a circus performer who acts as the arms of his armless mother, committing a series of brutal murders for her as well. Imagine a cross between *Psycho* and *Freaks* with the atmosphere of *Fellini Satyricon* and this might be the result. Gorgeous color, opulent sets, gruesome violence, indifferent dramatics. Also out in a cut R version.

SANTO IN THE WAX MUSEUM
See: *Samson in the Wax Museum.*

SANTO VS. THE VAMPIRE WOMEN
See: *Samson vs. the Vampire Women.*

SATANIC RITES OF DRACULA, THE
★★☆ ABC/Liberty, 1973, R, 87 min. Dir: Alan Gibson. Cast: Christopher Lee, Peter Cushing, Joanna Lumley, Freddie Jones, Michael Coles, William Franklyn, Barbara Yu Ling, Valerie Van Ost.

Lee's last stand as Hammer's Dracula (though the series still had one more entry, *The Legend of the 7 Golden Vampires,* to go) is another uneven modern vampire tale, though a slight improvement on its predecessor, *Dracula A.D. 1972.* Prof. Van Helsing (Cushing) is called in to investigate the involvement of several government officials with a black magic coven he discovers to be fronted by a revived Dracula who's now out to destroy the entire world via a deadly bacteria. This owes more to Ian Fleming, Sax Rohmer, and "The Avengers" than it does to Bram Stoker, but it does boast the usual fine turns from the Brit horror boys (though Chris has even less screen time than he did in *A.D. 1972*) and a few clever innovations in the usual vampire clichés to recommend it for Hammer completists. First released in the U.S. in a cut version called *Count Dracula and His Vampire Bride;* shooting title: *Dracula Is Dead and Well and Living in London.*

SATANIK
★★ Sinister Cinema, 1968, NR, 80 min.
Dir: Piero Vivarelli. Cast: Magda Konopka, Julio Pena, Armando Calvo, Umberto Raho, Mimma Ippoliti.

Familiar-looking Spanish-Italian potboiler with Konopka as an ugly babe made beautiful by a magic potion. Needless to say, the effect is only temporary and, equally needless to say, Magda becomes a grotesque crone who must kill to become pretty again. Visually interesting but dramatically hollow.

SATAN'S CHEERLEADERS
★★ Interglobal, 1977, PG, 92 min.
Dir: Greydon Clark. Cast: John Ireland, Yvonne DeCarlo, John Carradine, Jack Kruschen, Sydney Chaplin, Jacqueline Cole, Kerry Sherman, Sherry Marks.

Sexy high school cheerleaders run afoul of Ireland's rural satanic cult looking for a virgin to sacrifice—boy, did they pick the wrong girls! Disappointing exploitation pic (considering the subject matter and cast) with a PG rating that pretty much puts the kibosh on any potential gore, nudity, or fun. Carradine puts in about his ten-thousandth cameo appearance in a low-budget horror movie.

SATAN'S CLAW
See: *The Blood on Satan's Claw.*

SATAN'S PRINCESS
★☆ Paramount, 1989, R, 90 min. Dir: Bert I. Gordon. Cast: Robert Forster, Lydie Denier, Caren Kaye, Ellen Geer, Jack Carter, Leslie Huntley.

Sexy Denier has a near-definitive role as a murderous succubus in this otherwise dreadfully lame Gordon opus (his first in many a moon). Forster is once again cast as a burned-out detective assigned a bizarre murder case; comic Carter appears briefly in the prologue as a monk(?!); while the demon, in her true form, looks like she frequents the same hairdresser as the alien in *Predator.* Lots of gratuitous nudity and lesbianism too. Aka *The Malediction* and *Princess of Darkness.*

SATAN'S SCHOOL FOR GIRLS
★★☆ Prism, 1973, NR, 74 min.
Dir: David Lowell Rich. Cast: Pamela Franklin, Roy Thinnes, Kate Jackson, Jo Van Fleet, Lloyd Bochner, Jamie Smith Jackson, Gwynne Gilford, Cheryl Ladd.

Perky Pam investigates her sister's suicide by enrolling in her college, the exclusive Salem Academy, which she discovers to be a hotbed of witchcraft and satanic activity. Somewhat similar to the later *Suspiria,* though less flamboyant, this TV flick has a good cast (including two "Charlie's Angels"-to-be) and all the usual scenes of windswept nights, corridor-roaming heroines, and climactic holocausts you expect from this sort of enterprise.

SATAN'S SISTER
See: *The She-Beast.*

SATAN'S SKIN
See: *The Blood on Satan's Claw.*

SATELLITE OF BLOOD
See: *First Man Into Space.*

SATURDAY THE 14TH
★★☆ Embassy, 1981, PG, 75 min.
Dir: Howard R. Cohen. Cast: Richard Benjamin, Paula Prentiss, Severn Darden, Jeffrey Tambor, Kari Michaelson, Kevin Brando, Nancy Lee Andrews, Rosemary DeCamp.

Despite the punning title, this isn't a spoof of slasher movies but an old-fashioned haunted house comedy. Benjamin, Prentiss, and family move into the scary old house they've inherited and almost immediately find themselves knee deep in various vampires, demons, and monsters all after some ancient "Book of Evil" secreted somewhere in the house. Too silly for words, but a good comic cast and funny gags put this squarely in the "So dumb it's fun" category.

SATURDAY THE 14TH STRIKES BACK!
★☆ MGM/UA, 1988, PG, 78 min.
Dir: Howard R. Cohen. Cast: Jason Presson, Julianne McNamara, Ray Walston, Patty McCormack, Avery Schreiber, Rhonda Aldrich, Leo Gordon, Michael Berryman.

A real low-concept follow-up with another dumbbell family (headed by Schreiber and McCormack—one of the oddest pairings in screen history) moving into yet another haunted house where they encounter still more cut-rate creatures from beyond. A spook comedy that's not even good for laughs—now *that's* sad.

SATURN 3
★★ CBS/Fox, 1980, R, 88 min.
Dir: Stanley Donen. Cast: Kirk Douglas, Farrah Fawcett, Harvey Keitel, Douglas Lambert.

Lush but laughable *Alien* rip-off about a psychotic astronaut (Keitel) and his killer robot menacing idyllic space lovers Douglas and Fawcett. Donen, an otherwise talented director, seems completely at a loss about what to do with all this sex and gore in space; despite heavy pre-release cutting, it moves at a snail's pace, with performances that are a total embarrassment (Kirk takes the cake in a role that requires him to be nude in every other scene). Good production values and special effects are the sole saving grace in yet another

non-event for Farrah fans—though the lady would eventually prove her acting ability some years later.

SAVAGE BEES, THE
★★★ USA, 1976, NR, 91 min.
Dir: Bruce Geller. Cast: Ben Johnson, Gretchen Corbett, Michael Parks, Horst Buchholz, Paul Hecht, James Best.

Most killer-bee movies are real stingers but this modest and well-produced TV film is the pleasant exception. The ever-reliable Johnson is a Louisiana sheriff investigating a child's bizarre death that turns out to be the work of a swarm of African killer bees that eventually attack the New Orleans Mardi Gras. The attack scenes are suprisingly potent for a telemovie, including some grisly makeup, and the entire affair manages to build suspense quite well to a clever, offbeat ending. Sequel: *Terror Out of the Sky.*

SAVAGE INTRUDER
★★☆ Unicorn, 1968, R, 90 min.
Dir: Donald Wolfe. Cast: Miriam Hopkins, John David Garfield, Gale Sondergaard, Lester Matthews, Florence Lake, Joe Besser.

It's really weird to see some of the veteran performers in this low-octane psycho-gore-thriller with Garfield (son of the great John) as a Hollywood gigolo who leeches off faded stars like Hopkins. This little-seen oddity is worth a look for its cast and some fairly inept dismemberment murders. Aka *Hollywood Horror House* and *The Comeback.*

SAVAGE WEEKEND
☆ Paragon, 1976, R, 86 min.
Dir: David Paulsen. Cast: Christopher Allport, Marilyn Hamlin, James Doerr, Kathleen Heaney, David Gale, William Sanderson.

A group of dumb city slickers spend a weekend of horrors at a country house where a maniac in a fright mask eliminates most of them via garroting and hanging, a hatpin in the head, stabbing, and chainsawing. Useless, inept slasher film with awful acting (though both Gale and Sanderson would prove themselves later), lots of needless sex and nudity, and the most consistently visible boom mike in movie history. Aka *The Upstate Murders* and *Killer Behind the Mask;* not released until 1980.

SCALPEL
★★☆ Charter, 1976, R, 95 min.
Dir: John Grissmer. Cast: Robert Lansing, Judith Chapman, Arlen Dean Snyder, David Scarroll, Sandy Martin.

Uneven but underrated horror-mystery with Lansing as a plastic surgeon who transforms disfigured go-go dancer Chapman into the replica of his long-missing daughter as part of an inheritance scam. An entertaining minor '70s thriller, this has strong performances and plot echoes of *Diabolique* and *Vertigo*. Original title: *False Face*.

SCALPS
★ Continental, 1983, R, 82 min.
Dir: Fred Olen Ray. Cast: Kirk Alyn, Carroll Borland, Jo Ann Robinson, Richard Hench, Barbara Magnusson, Forrest J. Ackerman.

Another low-budget stalker-gore film, although this time there's a supernatural slant: the stalker is possessed by an ancient Indian demon and scalps as well as stabs most of the cast. Alyn (the original movie Superman), *Mark of the Vampire* star Borland, and "Famous Monsters" Ackerman are around for cameos; the plotting steals mostly from *Friday the 13th* and *The Manitou* and there's a twist ending right out of *The Possession of Joel Delaney*. Ray's sort-of homage to *Death Curse of Tartu*, this is very bloody and very bad.

SCANNER COP
★★☆ Republic, 1993, R, 94 min.
Dir: Pierre David. Cast: Daniel Quinn, Darlanne Fluegel, Richard Lynch, Brion James, Hilary Shepard, Richard Grove, Mark Rolston, Cyndi Pass.

The series takes an interesting, commercial new turn with this entry in which a rookie L.A. cop (Quinn) uses his scanner abilities to battle bad guy Lynch, a neurologist hypnotizing his patients into murdering anyone they see in a police uniform! Modest but well done, with lots of action, flashy performances, and the requisite exploding heads.

SCANNERS
★★★ Embassy, 1981, R, 103 min.
Dir: David Cronenberg. Cast: Jennifer O'Neill, Patrick McGoohan, Stephen Lack, Michael Ironside, Lawrence Dane, Robert Silverman.

Cronenberg's best-known early shocker, this concerns a race of telepaths known as Scanners; good Scanner Lack is pressed into service by scientist McGoohan to battle bad Scanner Ironside, who likes to make people's heads explode. Weakened in part by Lack's ineffectual casting and a jumbled storyline but pulled through by strong performances from McGoohan and Ironside, solid direction, and some of the most graphic FX ever seen in an R-rated film, including a knockout ending supervised by makeup maestro Dick Smith.

SCANNERS 2: THE NEW ORDER
★★☆ Media, 1991, R, 104 min.
Dir: Christian Duguay. Cast: Deborah Raffin, David Hewlett, Vlasta Varna, Yvan Pontoni, Isabelle Mejias, Tom Butler.

Not bad sequel with Hewlett as the Scanner son of the original's Jennifer O'Neill and Stephen Lack who attempts to stop a crew of evil Scanners from taking over the world. This follow-up delivers everything expected of it, from exploding heads to bursting blood vessels, with Hewlett doing a good job in the lead role.

SCANNERS 3: THE TAKEOVER
★★ Republic, 1992, R, 100 min.
Dir: Christian Duguay. Cast: Liliana Komorowka, Steve Parrish, Valerie Valos, Daniel Pilon, Collin Fox, Peter Wright.

Komorowka's outlandish turn highlights this second sequel. Liliana is a repressed Scanner who takes an experimental drug to stop her migraines but is instead transformed into a monomaniacal seductress out to take over the world. Parrish is her pacifist brother who seeks to assuage his destructive Scanner tendencies by attending a Buddhist monastery in a hilarious *Kung Fu*–inspired subplot. This is hard to take seriously, but it has enough violence and bloodshed to keep you interested. Followed by *Scanner Cop*.

SCARECROWS
★★★ Forum, 1988, UR, 83 min.
Dir: William Wesley. Cast: Victoria Christian, Michael Simms, Ted Vernon, Richard Vidan, Kristina Sanborn, B. J. Turner.

Genuinely creepy zombie variant about several robbers and the father and teen daughter they've taken hostage stranded in a remote farmhouse where a trio of living scarecrows kill them one by one, turning them into straw-stuffed cadavers. An almost unbearably tense atmosphere and fairly graphic, if but sparingly used, FX help overcome awkward, if enthusiastic, acting and dialogue and some repetitive action near the middle. Also available in a cut R version.

SCARED STIFF
★★ Paramount, 1953, NR, 108 min.
Dir: George Marshall. Cast: Dean Martin, Jerry Lewis, Lizabeth Scott, Carmen Miranda, George Dolenz, Dorothy Malone, William Ching, Paul Marion.

Weak Martin and Lewis remake of the great Bob Hope scare comedy *The Ghost Breakers*. Dean as a radio crooner and Jerry as his valet help heiress Scott claim a Cuban castle haunted by zombies and ghosts. Overlong and only sporadically funny (thanks mainly to Miranda); Bing Crosby and Bob Hope make a joint gag appearance.

SCARED STIFF

★☆ Republic, 1986, R, 84 min.
Dir: Richard Friedman. Cast: Andrew Stevens, Nicole Fortier, David Ramsey, Mary Page Keller, Josh Segal, Jakie David.

Slow-moving low-budgeter about a pop singer and her young son who move with her psychiatrist lover into an old antebellum southern mansion haunted by the ghost of a voodoo-accursed slave trader. Rambling and poorly structured, with hammy performances and rubbery makeup effects.

SCARED TO DEATH

★☆ Sinister Cinema, 1946, NR, 67 min.
Dir: Christy Cabanne. Cast: Bela Lugosi, George Zucco, Douglas Fowley, Joyce Compton, Nat Pendleton, Molly Lamont, Gladys Blake, Angelo Rossitto.

Bela's only color horror film is a cheapy Monogram-like mystery shocker narrated in flashback by a woman's corpse! Lugosi is a Dracula-like stage magician, Zucco a sinister psychiatrist, Fowley an annoying wise-cracking reporter, Pendleton a dumb comic-relief cop, etc. There's a loud obnoxious musical score, and the addition of color adds nothing to these uninspired dark old house goings-on. Shooting title: *Accent on Horror.*

SCARED TO DEATH

★★☆ Video Treasures, 1980, R, 93 min.
Dir: William Malone. Cast: John Stinson, Diana Davidson, Toni Janotta, Jonathan David Moses, Walter Edmiston, Pamela Bowman.

This poverty-row *Alien* is surprisingly witty and fun. The Syngenor, a genetic mutant that feasts on human spinal fluid, terrorizes the sewers of Los Angeles while being hunted by cynical private detective Stinson. Too long but the plot manages to work in knowing homages to *The Fly* and *Carrie,* and there's a likable cast and a good (if familiar-looking) monster designed by director Malone. Sequel: *Syngenor.*

SCARLET CLAW, THE

★★★ Key, 1944, NR, 74 min.
Dir: Roy William Neill. Cast: Basil Rathbone, Nigel Bruce, Gerald Hamer, Paul Cavanagh, Kay Harding, Arthur Hohl, Miles Mander, Victoria Horne.

One of the best entries in Universal's Sherlock Holmes series has Holmes and Watson attend-

ing a Canadian occult convention when they're retained by a woman the same night she's slain by the legendary marsh monster who's long been haunting the misty village of La Morte Rouge. Moody and well plotted, with a bravura performance from familiar-faced character actor Hamer working overtime in a triple role.

SCARLET CLUE, THE

★★☆ MGM/UA, 1945, NR, 65 min.
Dir: Phil Rosen. Cast: Sidney Toler, Benson Fong, Mantan Moreland, Helen Devereaux, Robert Homans, Virginia Brissac, I. Stanford Jolley, Janet Shaw.

Probably the best of Monogram's Charlie Chan series, this has the detective on the trail of a monster-masked killer terrorizing a radio and television station. Fast paced and solidly constructed, with a striking elevator murder similar to one in Argento's *Cat O'Nine Tails* and a truly surprising surprise killer.

SCARLET EXECUTIONER, THE

See: *The Bloody Pit of Horror.*

SCARLET HANGMAN, THE

See: *The Bloody Pit of Horror.*

SCARS OF DRACULA

★★☆ Thorn/EMI, 1970, R, 95 min.
Dir: Roy Ward Baker. Cast: Christopher Lee, Jenny Hanley, Dennis Waterman, Christopher Matthews, Patrick Troughton, Michael Gwynn, Wendy Hamilton, Michael Ripper.

One of the weakest Hammer Draculas conversely features more Lee than ever before; revived by bat's blood, the Count stabs and bites the supporting cast until hit by a bolt of lightning. Cardboard sets and chintzy, bat-on-a-string special effects sink much of this, though Hanley and Waterman are one of Hammer's most likable young romantic couples and there's more sex and blood than in any other Hammer Drac pic. Originally released with *The Horror of Frankenstein.*

SCHIZO

★★ Interglobal, 1976, R, 109 min.
Dir: Pete Walker. Cast: Lynne Frederick, John Leyton, Stephenie Beacham, John Fraser, Jack Watson, Queenie Watts.

Frederick—Peter Sellars' last wife—is an ice-skating star whose new marriage to lawyer Leyton is disrupted by mysterious stalker Watson and a string of gruesome killings: throats are slashed, a head bashed in, and a knitting needle is driven through a woman's skull and out one of her eyes. But who's the murderer? Typical Walker splatter movie, with good acting but a slow pace and a surprise ending wholly negated by the film's title! Aka *Amok* and *Blood of the Undead*.

SCHIZO
See: *Playroom*.

SCHIZOID
★☆ MCA/Universal, 1980, R, 88 min.
Dir: David Paulsen. Cast: Klaus Kinski, Marianna Hill, Craig Wasson, Donna Wilkes, Christopher Lloyd, Richard Herd, Joe Regalbuto, Flo Gerrish.

A scissor slasher begins picking off members of psychiatrist Kinski's therapy group while sending paste-up letters to group member Hill, a newspaper advice columnist. This poorly directed maniac movie has an above-average cast utterly wasted and a twist ending you can see coming from a long way off. Better than Paulsen's first feature, *Savage Weekend*, but then what wouldn't be? Original title: *Murder by Mail*.

SCHLOCK
See: *The Banana Monster*.

SCHOOLGIRL KILLER
★★☆ AIR, 1968, PG, 82 min.
Dir: Anthony Dawson [Antonio Margheretti].
Cast: Michael Rennie, Mark Damon, Eleanor Brown, Sally Smith, Ludmilla Lvova, Alan Collins.

This is a standard but fun neopolitan shocker about a crazed, cross-dressing strangler on the loose at a fashionable girls school. Well photographed and scored, this lacks the atmospherics of a Bava (originally set to direct) or Argento but is reasonably well done, with Smith stealing it as a spy-crazy student who saves the day. Originally known as *Sette Vergini per il Diavolo: Seven Virgins for the Devil* and first released in the U.S. as *The Young, the Evil and the Savage*.

SCHOOL THAT COULDN'T SCREAM, THE
★★ Sinister Cinema, 1972, R, 107 min. Dir: Massimo Dallamano. Cast: Fabio Testi, Cristina Galbo, Joachim Fuchsberger, Karin Baal, Camille Keaton.

Originally called *Cosi Avette Fatto a Solange?: What Have You Done to Solange?*, this Italian stalker movie in the Argento mold deals with a series of gruesome murders at a girls school following the disappearance of a pregnant student (Keaton, of *I Spit on Your Grave* fame) after a botched amateur abortion. Tasteless in the extreme (the female victims are stabbed in the vagina) but with a fair amount of suspense

and some imaginative photography—by Joe D'Amato!

SCISSORS
★★ Paramount, 1991, R, 105 min. Dir: Frank De Felitta. Cast: Sharon Stone, Steve Railsback, Ronny Cox, Michelle Phillips, Vicki Frederick.

Sleek B movie with Stone as an emotionally fragile young woman (who restores old dolls as a hobby) tormented and trapped into taking the fall for a vicious murder by some mysterious nemesis. It's overlong and has an obvious "surprise" ending and clumsy red herrings, but the cast makes it worthwhile.

SCREAM
See: *The Night God Screamed*.

SCREAM
★ Vestron, 1981, R, 81 min. Dir: Bryon Quisenberry. Cast: Pepper Martin, Hank Worden, John Ethan Wayne, Julie Marine, Alvy Moore, Gregg Palmer, Woody Strode, Bobby Diamond.

The veteran cast members are utterly wasted in this bargain basement *Friday the 13th* offshoot about campers getting slaughtered in a spooky ghost town. Gains its one star for casting older actors rather than the usual witless teens in pivitol roles but still awful. Originally titled *The Outing* and not to be mistaken for the goofy killer genie movie of the same name.

SCREAM AND DIE
See: *The House That Vanished*.

SCREAM AND SCREAM AGAIN
★★★ Orion, 1970, PG, 94 min.
Dir: Gordon Hessler. Cast: Vincent Price, Christopher Lee, Peter Cushing, Judy Huxtable, Michael Gothard, Alfred Marks, Christopher Matthews, Judi Bloom, Peter Sallis, Uta Levka.

Intriguingly offbeat mix of vampires, fascists, and mad science based on the book *The Disoriented Man* by Peter Saxton. Three disinvolved storylines concerning a militaristic political state, a Frankensteinian private clinic, and go-go girls falling victim to a bloodsucking murderer all come together in the last 15 minutes at the home of sympathetic mad doctor Price. The three horror superstars all have basically supporting roles and share no scenes (though Price and Lee meet briefly at the climax), with Marks stealing it as the no-nonsense detective investigating the vampire killings. Best scene: Gothard, made up to resemble Mick Jagger, tearing off his own hand to escape police handcuffs. Originally co-billed with *The Dunwich Horror*.

William Marshall buys it again in Scream, Blacula, Scream! *(1973).*

SCREAM, BABY, SCREAM

★☆ Regal, 1969, R, 83 min.
Dir: Robert L. Emery. Cast: Ross Harris, Eugenie Wingate, Chris Martell, Suzanne Stuart, Larry Swanson.

Florida-lensed clinker with Swanson as a mad artist who paints only ugliness and disfigures his models for just the right look. On occasion offbeat enough to provide marginal interest, but mostly just badly acted drivel with papier-mâché makeup effects. Aka *Nightmare House.*

SCREAM, BLACULA, SCREAM!

★★☆ Orion, 1973, PG, 95 min.
Dir: Bob Kelljan. Cast: William Marshall, Pam Grier, Don Mitchell, Richard Lawson, Michael Conrad, Barbara Rhodes, Craig T. Nelson, Nicholas Worth.

Adequate follow-up to *Blacula* lacks much of what made the original so special, substituting instead lots of action and campy humor. Mamuwalde (the magnificent Marshall) is reincarnated from his bones during a voodoo ritual and hopes to use the powers of a beautiful priestess (Grier in an uncomfortable lady-in-distress spot) to effect a cure of his vampiric condition. The usual early '70s vampire movie routines.

SCREAM BLOODY MURDER

★ United, 1972, R, 86 min. Dir: Marc B. Ray.
Cast: Fred Holbert, Leigh Mitchell, Robert Knox, Ron Bastone, Suzette Hamilton, Charles Reynolds.

A hook-handed teen has an Oedipal fixation on Mom (he lost his hand while killing Dad with a tractor for love of same), but eventually offs her and his new stepdad while trying to have a relationship with a slightly older artist-cum-prostitute. Advertised as the movie you'll need a blindfold to watch, which might've helped. There are, however, two funny moments: when our maniac attacks an old lady who then proceeds to beat the shit outta him with her canes and when the killer whines to the heroine: "I buy you groceries and art stuff and kill people for you but do you appreciate it? No!" Aka *Claw of Terror.*

SCREAMERS

★☆ Embassy, 1978, R, 83 min.
Dirs: Sergio Martino, Miller Drake. Cast: Barbara Bach, Richard Johnson, Joseph Cotten, Mel Ferrer, Cameron Mitchell, Claudio Cassinelli, Beryl Cunningham, Eunice Bolt.

On an uncharted island Johnson exploits the mutant fish men created by scientist Cotten until Cotten's beautiful daughter Bach leads them in revolt. Originally a finny Italian *Island of Dr. Moreau* rip-off called *L'Isola Degli Uomini Pesci: Island of the Fish Men,* this was tricked up for U.S. release with a new opening sequence featuring Ferrer and Mitchell and gory make-up inserts provided by Chris Walas. Ironically, these accoutrements provide the film with its only life, with everything rapidly going downhill from there. Also released as *Island of the Mutations* and *Something Waits in the Dark;* the same basic cast and crew were also responsible for the even less interesting *The Great Alligator.*

SCREAM FOR HELP

★☆ Lorimar, 1984, R, 90 min.
Dir: Michael Winner. Cast: Rachael Kelly, Marie Masters, David Allen Brooks, Lolita Lorre, Rocco Sisto, Corey Parker.

Terrible melodrama with Kelly as a teenager who suspects that Mom's new hubby has murderous intentions against them. Of course he *does,* but no one listens to Rach until it's almost too late. Surprisingly similar to *The Stepfather* but not half as good, with shrill acting and an annoying musical score from '60s rocker John Paul Jones.

SCREAMING DEAD, THE

★ Wizard, 1972, R, 84 min.
Dir: Jess [Jesus] Franco. Cast: Dennis Price, Howard Vernon, Britt Nichols, Anne Libert, Alberto Dalbes, Mary Francis, Luis Barboo, Fernando Bilbao.

Originally called *Dracula contra Frankenstein: Dracula Against Frankenstein* and aka *Dracula, Prisonnier de Frankenstein: Dracula, Prisoner of Frankenstein,* this is the tireless Señor Franco's queasy tribute to the Universal monster rallies of the '40s. A toasted-looking Price as Dr. F. revives a green-faced Vernon as Drac; Nichols is the vampire's bride, Barboo a necrophilic hunchback, and Bilbao a poor man's Frankenstein's monster. A tacky French-Spanish mix of traditional monster film elements with some soft-core sex and gore, though most of the eroticism has been edited out of the U.S. version.

SCREAMING HEAD, THE

See: *The Head.*

SCREAMING SKULL, THE

★★☆ Sinister Cinema, 1958, NR, 68 min.
Dir: Alex Nicol. Cast: John [William] Hudson, Peggy Webber, Russ Conway, Tony Johnson, Alex Nicol.

This sometimes quite scary low-budgeter gives its familiar plot a lift through interesting

execution. Widower Hudson brings wealthy new bride Webber, just recovering from a nervous breakdown, to the eerie southern mansion where wifey number one cashed in her chips. Soon wifey number two begins seeing and hearing a screeching human skull all around the place. Not surprisingly, this turns out to be part of a drive-her-crazy plot perpetuated by Webber that goes terribly awry (for him, anyway) when his dead first spouse decides to *really* get into the act. Solid acting and photography and a very unnerving atmosphere of misty ponds and shrieking peacocks give this film minor distinction.

SCREAM OF FEAR

★★★ RCA/Columbia, 1961, NR, 81 min.
Dir: Seth Holt. Cast: Susan Strasberg, Ann Todd, Ronald Lewis, Christopher Lee.

The first and best of a half-dozen *Psycho* and *Diabolique* B&W thrillers from Hammer, this features Strasberg as a wheelchair-bound heiress terrorized by her father's ambulatory corpse at a remote French villa. A first-rate shocker, this has excellent acting, creamy photography, an edgy score, and a famiiar twist ending topped by a double twist guaranteed to throw you for a loop. Original British title: *A Taste of Fear.*

SCREAM OF THE DEMON LOVER

See: *Blood Castle.*

SCREAMS OF A WINTER NIGHT

★★ United, 1979, R, 91 min.
Dir: James L. Wilson. Cast: Matt Borel, Gil Glasgow, Patrick Byers, Mary Agen Cox, Robin Bradley, Beverly Allen.

Shoestring anthology shot by semi-professionals in the wilds of Louisiana. College friends tell scary campfire tales involving a Bigfoot type menacing lover's lane; a haunted dormitory; and a frigid coed knife murderess. The storytellers then end up falling victim to an Indian wind demon. Bland presentation and acting, though the final moments are surprisingly potent.

SCREAMTIME

★★ Vestron, 1983, R, 89 min.
Dir: Al Beresford. Cast: Robin Bailey, Ann Lynn, Ian Saynor, Yvonne Nicholson, Dora Bryan, Jean Anderson, David Van Day, Vincent Russo, Michael Gordon, Marie Scinto.

Mediocre Brit anthology (with a connecting device shot in New York) about two guys who steal three horror videos—about a mad puppeteer; a woman who has visions of murder in her new home; and a robber undone by his victims' living garden gnomes—and end up paying for it big time when elements from the films enter the real world. The first and third segments are dumb and dull, respectively, but the second (similar to the Hammer TV film *In Possession*) has its moments—including a truly shocking twist ending.

SEANCE ON A WET AFTERNOON

★★★☆ VidAmerica, 1964, NR, 111 min.
Dir: Bryan Forbes. Cast: Kim Stanley, Richard Attenborough, Mark Eden, Nanette Newman, Patrick Magee, Judith Donner.

Stanley and Attenborough are magnificent in this downbeat psychological thriller. Stanley is a phony medium who arranges for husband Attenborough to kidnap a wealthy couple's young daughter so that she can later use her psychic "power" to find her. Things go terribly wrong, however, when the child dies and hubby wants out of his increasingly disturbed wife's schemes. A beautifully maintained air of tension and suspicion, sharp photography, and genuinely electrifying acting all add up to make this one of the top British films of the 1960s.

SEA SERPENT, THE

★ Lightning, 1984, PG, 92 min.
Dir: Gregory Greens [Amando de Ossorio].
Cast: Ray Milland, Timothy Bottoms, Taryn Power, Jared Martin, Gerard Tichy, Jack Taylor.

Milland played his last role in this corny conception about a huge eel terrorizing the Spanish seacoast. *Blind Dead* auteur de Ossorio wisely took a pseudonymous credit for this laughable drek featuring the worst special effects since *The Giant Claw*. If the cast wasn't so good, this could have been the *A*P*E* of the '80s.

SEASON OF THE WITCH

★★ Vista, 1971, R, 89 min.
Dir: George A. Romero. Cast: Jan White, Ray Laine, Anne Muffly, Joedda McClain.

Romero's weakest film is marred even further by heavy editing—from 130 minutes!—and the world's dullest cast. White is an unhappily married housewife who discovers feminism and witchcraft in swingin' early '70s Pittsburgh. Worth seeing for Romero completists but too heavy-handed and dull to give anyone else much to get excited over. Aka *Jack's Wife* and *Hungry Wives*.

SECRET OF DORIAN GRAY, THE

See: *Dorian Gray*.

SECRET OF DR. ORLOFF, THE

See: *Dr. Orloff's Monster*.

SECT, THE

See: *The Devil's Daughter*.

SEDDOCK

See: *Atom-Age Vampire*.

SEDDOCK, SON OF SATAN

See: *Atom-Age Vampire*.

SEDUCTION, THE

★☆ Video Treasures, 1982, R, 103 min.
Dir: David Schmoeller. Cast: Morgan Fairchild, Michael Sarrazin, Andrew Stevens, Vince Edwards, Colleen Camp, Joanne Linville.

Fairchild is totally unsympathetic as a pampered TV newswoman stalked by ardent fan Stevens in this glossy Brian De Palma wannabe thriller. With credulity chucked out the window from the get-go (hunk Stevens clearly would never be turned down by anyone as superficial as Fairchild's character), all we're left with are boring scenes of Morgan in her bathtub, Morgan in her pool, Morgan in her Jacuzzi, ad nauseum. Good support from Edwards, Camp, and Linville and a mock Pino Donaggio score by Lalo Schifrin are all this baby has going for it. Shooting title: *The Romance*.

SEEDPEOPLE

★ Paramount, 1992, R, 82 min.
Dir: Peter Manoogian. Cast: Sam Hennings, Andrea Roth, Dane Witherspoon, Holly Fields.

Pathetic rip-off of *Invasion of the Body Snatchers* about seedpods from outer space possessing people in a remote California valley—sound familiar? Another Charles Band bummer with some of the worst special effects since *The Green Slime*.

SEE NO EVIL

★★★ Goodtimes, 1971, PG, 90 min.
Dir: Richard Fleischer. Cast: Mia Farrow, Dorothy Alison, Robin Bailey, Diane Grayson, Norman Eshley, Brian Rawlinson, Paul Nicholas, Christopher Matthews.

Mia is great in this tense mix of *Psycho* and *Wait Until Dark* about a blind girl whose family is slaughtered by a vicious killer while she's out horseback riding. Mia then returns to a house full of corpses she cannot see and a maniac after an incriminating ID bracelet. Edge-of-your-seat thrills until a somewhat slack final third; nice autumnal photography and a pretty Elmer Bernstein score. Trivia buffs: this was the last first-run feature to play New York's Radio City Music Hall. Written by Brian Clemens; original British title: *Blind Terror*.

SEIZURE
★★★ Starmaker, 1974, PG, 94 min.
Dir: Oliver Stone. Cast: Jonathan Frid, Martine Beswick, Christina Pickles, Joe Sirola, Hervé Villechaize, Troy Donahue, Mary Woronov, Anne Meacham.

Controversial Oscar winner Stone's directorial debut was this offbeat Canadian shocker about a famed horror novelist (Frid) tormented by a recurring nightmare of torture and murder that seems to be coming true. Somewhat confused in places and ultimately offering up one ending too many, but sharp photography and a strong, eclectic cast (with outstanding performances from Frid and Beswick) make it worthwhile. Originally co-billed with *The Beast Must Die;* reissued as *Queen of Evil.*

SENDER, THE
★★★ Paramount, 1982, R, 92 min.
Dir: Roger Christian. Cast: Kathryn Harrold, Zeljko Ivanek, Shirley Knight, Paul Freeman.

Understated psychic thriller with Ivanek as a suicidal amnesiac who turns a mental hospital upside down with his ability to project his nightmares into the minds of others. Worth catching for its haunting atmosphere and fine acting—especially Knight as Ivanek's mom, who may or may not be a ghost.

SENSUOUS VAMPIRES
See: *Vampire Hookers.*

SENTINEL, THE
★★☆ MCA/Universal, 1977, R, 92 min.
Dir: Michael Winner. Cast: Cristina Raines, Chris Sarandon, Martin Balsam, John Carradine, José Ferrer, Ava Gardner, Arthur Kennedy, Burgess Meredith, Sylvia Miles, Deborah Raffin, Eli Wallach, Christopher Walken.

Slick, all-star *Exorcist*-like shocker with Raines as a New York fashion model who discovers that her Brooklyn Heights brownstone is built upon the gateway to hell. One of the goriest big-budget films of the '70s, this has a memorably sick climax mixing in real life freaks with Dick Smith makeup FX to portray the denizens of Hades. Look for Beverly D'Angelo, Jeff Goldblum, William Hickey, and Tom Berenger in small parts. Avoid the heavily doctored TV version of this adaptation of Jeffrey Konvitz's novel.

SERPENT AND THE RAINBOW, THE
★★☆ MCA/Universal, 1988, R, 97 min.
Dir: Wes Craven. Cast: Bill Pullman, Cathy Tyson, Zakes Mokae, Paul Winfield, Michael Gough, Brent Jennings, Theresa Merritt, Dey Young.

This uneven combination of voodoo horror and *Raiders of the Lost Ark* dare-doing wasn't quite the breakthrough film Craven had hoped for. Bland Pullman is an archeologist sent to Haiti by a U.S. pharmaceutical firm to learn the secret of zombie-making. Trouble begins when Pullman runs afoul of politico Mokae, who also happens to be a powerful voodoo master. Although good-looking, with most of the casting astute (Tyson, Mokae, Winfield, Gough), overall this remains something of a misfire.

SERVANTS OF TWILIGHT
★★★ Vidmark, 1991, R, 96 min.
Dir: Jeffrey Obrow. Cast: Bruce Greenwood, Belinda Bauer, Grace Zabriskie, Jack Kehoe, Jarrett Lennon, Carel Strycken, Kelli Maroney, Jilliam McWhirter.

The best of the admittedly nothing to brag about film adaptations of the work of Dean R. Koontz, this well-plotted variation on *The Omen* tells of a private detective (Greenwood) hired by a distraught mom (Bauer) to protect her young son from a religious sect out to kill the kid because they believe him to be the anti-Christ. Good acting (especially from the always crazed Zabriskie as the sect leader) and a truly surprising twist ending make the difference in this modest but well-done shot-in-Canada effort. Aka *Dean R. Koontz's Servants of Twilight.*

7 BROTHERS MEET DRACULA, THE
See: *The Legend of the 7 Golden Vampires.*

SEVEN DEATHS IN THE CAT'S EYE
★★ Prism, 1973, R, 86 min. Dir: Anthony Dawson [Antonio Margheriti]. Cast: Jane Birkin, Anton Diffring, Sergé Gainsbourg, Venantino Venantini, Françoise Christophe, Hiram Keller.

Margheriti's obscure entry in the early '70s weirdly titled Argento-esque giallo subgenre features Birkin as an heiress involved with murder and a possessed cat in an old Scottish castle. A confusing Italian non-thriller with the great Diffring (as the sinister butler) dubbed by someone else.

7 DOORS OF DEATH
★★★ Thrillervideo, 1981, R, 80 min.
Dir: Lewis Fuller [Lucio Fulci]. Cast: Katherine MacColl, David Warbeck, Sarah Keller, Veronica Lazar.

VAL LEWTON
(1904–1951)

The Russian-born producer of a whole series of model psychological horror films for RKO Radio Pictures in the '40s, Lewton made films that were often overly arty and pretentious, but many are among the most impressive horror films of their decade. Directed by the likes of Jacques Tourneur and Robert Wise, they use shadow and suggestion in place of Universal Pictures' more blatant monster makeup and often effectively turn established horror myths on their head. The best of his films were *I Walked With a Zombie*, *The Seventh Victim*, and *The Body Snatcher*.

Cat People ('42), *I Walked With a Zombie* ('43), *The Leopard Man* ('43), *The Seventh Victim* ('43), *The Ghost Ship* ('43), *Curse of the Cat People* ('44), *The Body Snatcher* ('45), *Isle of the Dead* ('45), *Bedlam* ('46).

This heavily cut version of Fulci's masterpiece *L'Adela: The Beyond,* though often confusing, is still worth seeing. A rip-off/homage to *Inferno* and *The Sentinel*, this has MacColl inheriting an old New Orleans hotel built upon one of the seven earthly gateways to hell—is that counting the one in Brooklyn Heights in *The Sentinel*? When a handyman knocks open a mysterious door in the basement, all manner of shocking things happen, including several gruesome murders—via acid, killer spiders, and a rusty spike in a wall—and the usual zombie invasion. Though obviously shot on the cheap, this has moments of true surreal beauty, a sepia-tinted opening paying tribute to Corman's *The Haunted Palace,* and an incredible shot of light shining through a hole blasted through the head of a little girl zombie (snipped for the sake of an R). Italian version runs 86 minutes.

SEVENTH SIGN, THE
★★ RCA/Columbia, 1988, R, 97 min.
Dir: Carl Schultz. Cast: Demi Moore, Michael Biehn, Juergen Prochnow, John Heard, Peter Friedman, Manny Jacobs, Akousha Busia, John Taylor.

Hokey end-of-the-world thriller that looks like an old post-*Omen* script someone found stuffed in a drawer for a decade. Moore is affecting as a pregnant woman who begins to fear that the upcoming birth of her child and the string of bizarre catastrophes currently plaguing the world are signals of the apocalypse—fears that are reinforced by her enigmatic boarder Prochnow. Occasionally powerful imagery offsets the often ridiculous dialogue and situations, with everything culminating in a disappointing cop-out ending.

SEVENTH VICTIM, THE
★★★★ Turner, 1943, NR, 71 min.
Dir: Mark Robson. Cast: Tom Conway, Kim Hunter, Jean Brooks, Hugh Beaumont, Evelyn Brent, Isabel Jewell, Erford Gage, Elizabeth Russell.

Teenage Hunter visits New York's Greenwich Village searching for missing older sister Brooks and encounters a cult of devil worshippers who've marked former member Jean for death. This outstanding Val Lewton production is one of the darkest, most downbeat films ever to come out of Hollywood, with a suffocating atmosphere of hopelessness and gloom, scenes that clearly inspired both *Rosemary's Baby* and *Psycho*, and a shattering final scene that's unforgettably subtle and chilling. "Perry Mason" secretary Barbara Hale can be seen briefly on a subway car.

SEVEN VIRGINS FOR THE DEVIL
See: *Schoolgirl Killer.*

SEVERED ARM, THE
★ Interglobal, 1973, R, 92 min.
Dir: Gary Adelman. Cast: Deborah Walley, Paul Carr, Roy Dennis, Marvin Kaplan.

When a group of guys are trapped in a cave-in, they get mighty hungry and draw lots to see whose arm will get served for lunch. The loser loses a limb only moments before rescue, and soon after the other survivors start getting killed with their arms removed as well. Tired revenge melodrama/horror flick with a bit-o-gore, but mostly just dull talk provided by the familiar TV movie type of cast.

SEVERED TIES
★★ Columbia/TriStar, 1992, R, 94 min.
Dir: Damon Santostefano. Cast: Oliver Reed, Elke Sommer, Billy Morrisette, Denise Wallace, Garrett Morris, Johnny Legend.

Morrisette's experiments in limb replication go awry when his domineering mom (leggy Sommer) and her doctor lover (Reed) try to steal his experimental serum. Billy loses an arm in the resultant melee but grows an entire army of murdering replacements. This tries for the off-the-wall humor of a *Basket Case* or *Re-Animator* but plays mostly like an overextended episode of "Monsters," with only Reed hitting the mark with a nicely deadpan comic performance. Aka *Army.*

SEXORCIST, THE
See: *The Eerie Midnight Horror Show.*

SHADOW OF FEAR
★★ MPI, 1974, NR, 72 min. Dir: Herbert Kenwith.
Cast: Anjanette Comer, Claude Akins, Jason Evers,
Philip Carey, Tom Selleck.

Dan Curtis–produced videotaped TV thriller
with Comer as a beautiful former mental
patient terrorized by a brutal, unseen maniac.
Predictable at every turn, this has only Comer's performance and the chance to see a
young Selleck sans moustache to make it
worth tuning in.

SHADOW PLAY
★★☆ Starmaker, 1986, R, 95 min.
Dir: Susan Shadburne. Cast: Dee Wallace Stone,
Cloris Leachman, Ron Kuhlman, Barry Laws,
Al Strobel, Delia Salvi.

Gossamer-fabricated supernatural thriller
somewhat similar to the later *Ghost.* Wallace
Stone is good as a playwright who visits her
late boyfriend's home and may or may not
find contact with his restless ghost, and Leachman shines as the boyfriend's despondent
mother. The film's emotional content is honest
and on target, though ultimately it drags a bit
and features a mystery subplot that doesn't
work at all.

SHADOWS RUN BLACK
★☆ Vestron, 1981, R, 89 min.
Dir: Howard Heard. Cast: William J. Kulzer,
Elizabeth Trosper, Shea Porter, George J. Engelson,
Dianne Hinkler, Kevin Costner.

And slasher movies don't get much worse
than this disposable dishwater about your
standard-issue woman-hating psycho killer
after coeds whose activities are investigated
by a dedicated cop. Another lame-o attempt at
combining the horror and police thriller genres, it was finally released in '86 by Troma to
take advantage of the likable Costner's subsequent fame (he has a small role as a red herring cowboy).

SHADOWZONE
★★☆ Paramount, 1989, R, 88 min.
Dir: J. S. Cardone. Cast: Louise Fletcher, David
Beecroft, Shawn Weatherley, James Hong,
Lu Leonard, Maureen Flaherty.

A government-backed dream research program discovers that our dreams are actually a
connection to an alternate universe inhabited
by shape-shifting monsters, one of whom
begins murdering the researchers one by one.
An imaginative premise is somewhat hampered by an over-the-top Fletcher, GI Joe doll
hero Beecroft, a comatose heroine who goes
through the entire film nude (there's a nude
guy too, but his head blows up early on), and
a monster who looks like Cronenberg's Fly
dipped in runny Quaker Oats.

SHATTERED SILENCE
★★☆ Platinum, 1971, NR, 88 min.
Dir: Philip Leacock. Cast: Ben Gazzara, Elizabeth
Ashley, Michael Douglas, Karen Pearson, Larry
Reynolds, Marian Waldman, Al Waxman,
Chris Pellett.

Originally known as *When Michael Calls* and
adapted by James Bridges from the John Farris
novel, this features Ashley as a small-town
divorcee haunted by telephone calls from her
supposedly dead young nephew. There's a
good cast and a modicum of suspense in this
Canadian tele-movie, which was originally
broadcast at 73 minutes; this video edition is
taken from the expanded syndication version.

SHE-BEAST, THE
★★☆ Gorgon, 1966, NR, 76 min.
Dir: Michael Reeves. Cast: Barbara Steele,
Ian Ogilvy, John Karlsen, Mel Welles.

Reeves' talent shines through in this first solo
effort about a honeymoon couple in modern
Transylvania. The wife (Steele) falls into a
mountain lake and her life force reactivates a
hideous old witch called Vardella, who goes
on a rampage while desperate husband Ogilvy
tries to restore his lost bride. Starkly photographed and with some audacious, funny
images (such as a bloody sickle tossed by
Vardella across a cast-off hammer), this is
highlighted by Welles' hilarious performance
as a slovenly, peeping Tom innkeeper. Steele,
though, is only in it for about 15 minutes. Aka
La Sorella di Satana: Satan's Sister and *Revenge
of the Blood Beast.*

SHE DEMONS
★☆ Rhino, 1958, NR, 76 min.
Dir: Richard E. Cunha. Cast: Irish McCalla,
Tod Griffin, Victor Sen Young, Rudolph Anders,
Gene Roth, Leni Tana.

Hilarious horror adventure with shipwreck
survivors encountering Nazi mad doc Anders
on an uncharted island where he's busy disfiguring busty native dancing girls in a futile
attempt to restore the beauty of scarred wife
Tana. If Jess Franco had directed episodes of
"Hogan's Heroes" and "Gilligan's Island" and
then edited them together, it might have
looked something like this. Platinum-tressed
McCalla takes the prize as an annoying hero-

ine you'd just love to smack who makes such pronouncements as "Where's my powder blue shortie?" and "You could have at least saved me a pair of toreador pants!" Nufsaid?

SHE FREAK

★☆ Magnum, 1966, NR, 82 min.
Dir: Byron Mabe. Cast: Claire Brennan, Lee Raymond, Lynn Courtney, Bill McKinney, Felix Silla, Ben Moore.

Tawdry *Freaks* rip-off with Brennan as a mercenary waitress who marries a kindly sideshow owner for his money. When her lover kills him, his loyal staff of freaks seek revenge. Tacky and slow, though you *do* get to see "The Addams Family"'s Cousin Itt (Silla) without his hairy suit. Aka *Alley of Nightmares.*

SHERLOCK HOLMES AND THE MASKS OF DEATH

See: *Masks of Death.*

SHERLOCK HOLMES AND THE SPIDER WOMAN

See: *The Spider Woman.*

SHERLOCK HOLMES FACES DEATH

★★★ Key, 1943, NR, 68 min. Dir: Roy William Neill.
Cast: Basil Rathbone, Nigel Bruce, Hillary Brooke, Milburn Stone, Arthur Margetson, Dennis Hoey, Halliwell Hobbes, Gavin Muir.

Solid Holmes mystery-horror with Rathbone investigating several murders at a supposedly cursed estate where the clock strikes 13 and people are manipulated like human chess pieces. There's a good cast and some fine atmosphere in this adaptation of Conan Doyle's "The Musgrave Ritual." Peter Lawford has a bit part.

SHERLOCK HOLMES: MURDER BY DECREE

See: *Murder By Decree.*

SHE'S DRESSED TO KILL

★★☆ USA, 1979, NR, 96 min.
Dir: Gus Trikonis. Cast: Eleanor Parker, Jessica Walter, John Rubinstein, Connie Sellecca, Gretchen Corbett, Joanna Cassidy, Clive Revill, Peter Horton.

Campy TV horror-whodunit similar to *Blood and Black Lace* but without the ambiance. Parker is great as an over-the-hill alcoholic fashion designer whose private showing at her mountaintop mansion is crashed by a mysterious killer who begins offing the models one by one. Not bad at all, with an excellent cast and a fairly unguessable surprise ending. Also shown as *Someone's Killing the World's Greatest Models.*

SHE WAITS

★★☆ Prism, 1972, NR, 73 min.
Dir: Delbert Mann. Cast: Patty Duke, David McCallum, Dorothy McGuire, Lew Ayres, Beulah Bondi, James Callahan.

Widower McCallum brings new bride Duke to the Beverly Hills mansion of bedridden mom McGuire where Patty is promptly possessed by the restless spirit of Dave's witchy first wife. Interesting moods provided by "Dark Shadows" head writer Art Wallace, haunting music, and solid acting uplift this familiar-themed modern-dress TV *Tomb of Ligeia.*

SHE WOLF

See: *Legend of the Wolf Woman.*

SHINING, THE

★★★ Warner, 1980, R, 143 min.
Dir: Stanley Kubrick. Cast: Jack Nicholson, Shelley Duvall, Danny Lloyd, Scatman Crothers, Barry Nelson, Anne Jackson, Joe Turkel, Philip Stone.

There seems to be no middle ground in the response this mammoth adaptation of Stephen King's best book received from the public: people either love it or loathe it. Actually there's something to be said for both camps, though in the end the good points somewhat outweigh the bad. Nicholson gives a now classic out-of-control performance as the crazed caretaker of the massive snowbound Overlook Hotel. The oppressive isolation—coupled with a mental makeup that's pretty shaky to begin with—soon transforms Jack into an ax-wielding madman after wife Duvall and psychic son Lloyd. The pluses include superb photography and set design and a scene-stealing performance from the underused Crothers, while minuses mostly result from overlength and the jettisoning of some of King's creepiest ideas. Not the horror masterpiece it was intended to be, but hardly the flop some have tagged it either. Trimmed from 146 minutes for video, it was hacked down to 119 minutes for foreign play dates.

SHIVERS

See: *They Came From Within.*

SHOCK

★★ Goodtimes, 1946, NR, 70 min. Dir: Alfred L. Werker. Cast: Vincent Price, Lynn Bari, Anabel Shaw, Frank Latimer, Michael Dunne, Reed Hadley.

Price received star billing for the first time in this minor melodrama about a woman (Shaw) who witnesses a murder, goes into shock, and ends up being treated by psychiatrist Price—who also happens to be the killer! A good idea gets medium handling in this sub-Hitchcock chiller, with a typically suave performance from Vinnie.

SHOCK

See: *Beyond the Door 2*.

SHOCKED

See: *Mesmerized*.

SHOCK 'EM DEAD

★☆ Academy, 1991, R, 94 min.
Dir: Mark Freed. Cast: Traci Lords, Stephen Quadros, Troy Donahue, Aldo Ray.

Nerdy pizza boy Quadros sells his soul for fame as a rock star but must kill and suck out the souls of others to keep his new lifestyle. This dumb video shocker makes some bungled attempts at humor but has flat direction and acting and a rock band with a lead singer possessing all the masculinity of Truman Capote.

SHOCKER

★☆ MCA/Universal, 1989, R, 108 min.
Dir: Wes Craven. Cast: Michael Murphy, Peter Berg, Cami Cooper, Mitch Pileggi, Sam Scarber, Ted Raimi.

Berg is a college athlete with an unexplained psychic link to vicious serial killer Pileggi. When the latter kills the former's family and girlfriend and is executed, he returns as a form of energy to possess several people and seek revenge. One of Craven's least interesting efforts, this misguided attempt at creating another *Nightmare on Elm Street* (with Pileggi unsuccessfully set up as the Freddy Krueger substitute) has excellent FX but a mean-spirited storyline and an unsympathetic central performance from Berg. Heather Langenkamp has a bit.

SHOCK TO THE SYSTEM, A

★★★ HBO, 1990, R, 91 min. Dir: Jan Egleson. Cast: Michael Caine, Elizabeth McGovern, Peter Riegert, Swoosie Kurtz, Will Patton, Jenny Wright.

Caine is perfection in this underrated black comedy about a harried New York ad man who turns to murder to dispose of his bitchy wife, elitist boss, and pushy co-worker. A snappy blend of horror, humor, and suspense, this was based on a novel by Andrew Klavan. Favorite exchange: "He was your superior, wasn't he?" "No. He was my boss."

SHOCK TREATMENT

★☆ CBS/Fox, 1981, PG, 94 min. Dir: Jim Sharman.
Cast: Jessica Harper, Cliff De Young, Richard O'Brien, Patricia Quinn, Nell Campbell, Charles Gray.

Lifeless semi-sequel to *The Rocky Horror Picture Show* with Brad and Janet (now played by De Young and Harper) trapped on a game show from hell. One good number ("Little Black Dress") and hard work from Harper, O'Brien, Quinn, and Campbell do not compensate for a pretentious concept and flat presentation. Tim Curry is sorely missed. At the time of this writing, another "official" *Rocky Horror* sequel was in the works.

SHOCK WAVES

★★☆ Starmaker, 1975, PG, 86 min.
Dir: Ken Weiderhorn. Cast: Peter Cushing, John Carradine, Brooke Adams, Luke Halpin, D. J. Sidney, Fred Buch.

Shipwreck survivors from a sunken pleasure craft encounter goggle-wearing albino Nazi zombies who can breath under water and are under the control of mad scientist Cushing. This taut, underrated effort is easily the best treatment of the familiar Nazi zombie theme, with creepy atmosphere and a good early performance from Adams. Aka *Death Corps* and *Almost Human*.

SHOUT, THE

★★☆ RCA/Columbia, 1978, R, 87 min.
Dir: Jerzy Skolimowski. Cast: Alan Bates, Susannah York, John Hurt, Robert Stephens, Tim Curry.

Obscure chiller with Bates as a tramp who has the ability to kill by shouting and becomes involved with composer Hurt and his unsatisfied wife York. Oddball British flick with good acting but a premise that's hard to get a handle on.

SHRIEKING, THE

★★ Prism, 1973, PG, 92 min. Dir: Leo Garen.
Cast: Keith Carradine, Tina Herazo [Cristina Raines], Hilary Thompson, Robert Walker, Jr., Gary Busey, Dan Haggerty, Scott Glenn, John Carradine.

Originally known as *Hex*, this is a really strange period piece with an early, post-WWI biker gang running afoul of witchcraft-practicing sisters in the Nebraska wilderness. A watchably weird but oh-so-strange artifact from an era of filmmaking as different from today as WWI was to the hippies.

SHRIEK OF THE MUTILATED

★☆ Prism, 1973, PG, 85 min. Dir: Mike Findlay.
Cast: Alan Brock, Jennifer Stock, Michael Harris, Tawn Ellis, Darcy Brown, Jack Nubeck.

The phony hunt for a phony "yeti" sparks the action of this bleakly photographed upstate New York quickie. Actually, the four students who join a college professor in search of the elusive monster are being set up by a local cannibal cult. Too nihilistic to be much fun in the usual bad-funny tradition, though there *is* a funny scene where a bickering couple kill each other with an electric knife and toaster.

SHRINE OF LORNA LOVE, THE
See: *Death at Love House.*

SILENCE OF THE LAMBS, THE
★★★☆ Orion, 1991, R, 118 min.
Dir: Jonathan Demme. Cast: Jodie Foster, Anthony Hopkins, Scott Glenn, Ted Levine, Anthony Heald, Diane Baker, Brooke Smith, Charles Napier, Kasi Lemmons, Tracey Walter.

From its misleading opening (a young woman desperately racing through a misty forest turns out to be FBI trainee Foster on an obstacle course) to its two-events-happening-at-once climax, this suspenseful shocker has quickly and deservedly become a modern classic—and the first horror movie ever to cop a best-picture Oscar, with statuettes also going to Foster and an unforgettable Hopkins. Jodie is terrific as the young FBI agent who interviews imprisoned psycho-killer Dr. Hannibal "The Cannibal" Lechter (Hopkins) in an attempt to get a handle on catching transsexual serial killer "Buffalo Bill" (Levine). As tightly wound as a spring, this grabs you from frame one and never lets go with an unshakably bleak mood. Gruesome in spots but not overly gory, with Hopkins establishing himself as the sort of guy who'd give Freddy Krueger nightmares. Based on the novel by Thomas Harris, which was a sequel to *Red Dragon,* which itself was filmed as the non-horror police thriller *Manhunter.*

SILENT MADNESS
★★ Media, 1984, R, 92 min.
Dir: Simon Nuchtern. Cast: Belinda J. Montgomery, Viveca Lindfors, Sydney Lassick, Solly Marx, David Greenan, Elizabeth Kaitan.

Montgomery is earnest as a young psychiatrist after psycho killer Marx who was wrongly released from the asylum and is back at the sorority house where he committed his original crimes. This formula slasher was released theatrically in 3-D and that remains its main distinction. B.J., Viveca, and Sydney try to breathe some life into this but are mostly done in by mechanical writing and direction.

SILENT NIGHT, BLOODY NIGHT
★★☆ Paragon, 1972, R, 83 min.
Dir: Theodore Gershuny. Cast: Patrick O'Neal, Mary Woronov, James Patterson, John Carradine, Astrid Heeren, Walter Abel, Candy Darling, Ondine.

This interesting, low-budget, pre-*Halloween* holiday maniac movie has a disfigured killer escaping the asylum on Christmas Eve and beginning a series of small-town ax murders centered around an old mansion being sold by realtor O'Neal. Imaginatively done despite budgetary limitations, with a couple of gory killings, a haunting sepia-toned flashback featuring Andy Warhol regulars Darling and Ondine, and good turns from Woronov, Carradine, and O'Neal in the Janet Leigh role. Filmed as *Zora* and also released as *The Night of the Dark Full Moon* and *Death House.*

SILENT NIGHT, DEADLY NIGHT
★ IVE, 1984, R, 84 min.
Dir: Charles E. Sellier. Cast: Lilyan Chauvan, Gilmer McCormick, Robert Brian Wilson, Toni Nero, Britt Leach, Linnea Quigley.

Controversial Christmas slasher protested by parent groups outraged by its presentation of a killer dressed as Santa (hardly a new idea to anyone who ever saw *Tales From the Crypt* a decade earlier). Weak acting and outrageous psychology highlight this uninspired hooey in which Wilson is a teenager raised in an orphanage by stern Mother Superior Chauvan after his parents are murdered by a guy in a Claus costume. Come Christmas our hero gets a job in a toy store and, sure enough, is asked to don a Santa suit. Guess what happens? Linnea brightens things briefly in a gratuitous topless cameo, but it's mainly the pits. Expanded for video from the 79-minute theatrical version (which doesn't help), this may be the worst horror film ever to inspire an entire series of follow-ups.

SILENT NIGHT, DEADLY NIGHT PART 2
☆ IVE, 1987, R, 88 min. Dir: Lee Harry.
Cast: Eric Freeman, James L. Newman, Elizabeth Kaitan, Jean Miller, Nadya Wynd, Joanne White.

The second and worst of the "series" features a smirking Freeman as the brother of the original Santa Claus killer who goes on a pointless murder spree of his own. Half the movie seems to be flashbacks to part one, and the rest an annoying pseudo-comedy with a mean-spiritedness that makes viewing a painful experience indeed. Biggest mystery: Why is the old Mother Superior now disfigured and what the hell happened to her accent?

SILENT NIGHT, DEADLY NIGHT 3: BETTER WATCH OUT!
★☆ IVE, 1989, R, 89 min. Dir: Monte Hellman.
Cast: Robert Culp, Richard Beymer, Bill Moseley, Samantha Scully, Eric Da Re, Laura Herring.

It seems almost surreal to see names like Hellman and Culp associated with this why-bother third installment of the worst horror series of the '80s, but here they are anyway. When the comatose killer from part 2 (now played by Moseley) is revived by experiments in psychic phenomena, he seeks out the blind psychic (Scully) whose mind is linked with his. Played for intentional laughs (but far more subtly than its immediate predecessor), this has a couple of chuckles (the funniest scene has Moseley—clad in a hospital gown and with his damaged brain encased in a clear plastic skullcap—hitching a ride from some boob who comments: "Hair transplant, huh?") and above-average acting to relieve the tedium, but it still isn't all that good.

SILENT NIGHT, DEADLY NIGHT 4: INITIATION

★★ LIVE, 1990, R, 85 min. Dir: Brian Yuzna. Cast: Maude Adams, Neith Hunter, Tommy Hinkley, Allyce Beasley, Clint Howard, Reggie Bannister.

Another one of those in-name-only sequels, this has reporter Hunter stumbling upon an L.A. cult of feminist lesbians (who wrote this thing, Jesse Helms?) who worship the biblical Adam's legendary first wife Lilith. The Christmas setting is negligible at best (the only killer Claus this time is on a TV set), with elements from the *The Kiss, Night Angel,* and *Prince of Darkness* tossed around and some really awesome Screaming Mad George FX. Probably the best of an admittedly none-too-hot series.

SILENT NIGHT, DEADLY NIGHT 5: THE TOY MAKER

★★ LIVE, 1991, R, 90 min. Dir: Martin Kitrosser. Cast: Mickey Rooney, Jane Higginson, Tracy Fraim, Brian Bremer, William Thorne, Neith Hunter.

This time we get a mad toy manufacturer called Joe Petto (get it?) played by Rooney. Joe makes evil, living playthings that murder their owners in an uneasy blending of *Halloween III* and *Puppetmaster.* Some good FX and Rooney is amusing, but this is too derivative and unsure of itself to really work as either a straight chiller or a spoof of same. First-time director Kitrosser scripted a couple of the *Friday the 13th* films, while the only connection to part 4 is the reappearance of the Hunter character in a small role.

SILENT NIGHT, EVIL NIGHT

See: *Black Christmas.*

SILENT SCREAM

★★☆ Video Treasures, 1980, R, 87 min. Dir: Denny Harris. Cast: Rebecca Balding, Cameron

Mitchell, Barbara Steele, Yvonne De Carlo, Avery Schreiber, Steve Doubet, Juli Andelman, Brad Reardon.

Finding off-campus housing is more than just the usual hassle for coed Balding, who boards in an old seaside mansion with a murderous thing-in-the-attic: lobotomized ex-teen queen Steele, who has a penchant for stabbing those who remind her of her own tragic youth—like Rebecca and her friends. One of the first post-*Halloween* slashers and better than most, with good, cobwebby settings, believable characters, and Steele at her best as the silent, sad-eyed knifer who likes to listen endlessly to the same melancholy '50s love song while staring into a mirror whose glass has been replaced with a photograph of her younger self.

SILENT SCREAM, THE

★★☆ Thrillervideo, 1980, NR, 50 min. Dir: Alan Gibson. Cast: Peter Cushing, Brian Cox, Elaine Donnally, Anthony Carrick.

Cushing is excellent in this better-than-usual "Hammer House of Horror" segment about a pet shop owner with a private zoo in his basement where the wild animals obey his every command. An interesting idea fairly well handled, though a longer running time might have helped flesh out the premise even more.

SILVER BULLET

★★ Paramount, 1985, R, 95 min. Dir: Daniel Attias. Cast: Gary Busey, Corey Haim, Megan Follows, Everett McGill, Robin Groves, Terry O'Quinn.

Minor-league Stephen King flick (from his novella *Cycle of the Werewolf*) with Haim as a crippled teen in a wheelchair who discovers that the full-moon killer plaguing his small southern town is—gasp!—a werewolf. Totally dysfunctional as a mystery, since the werewolf's human identity is obvious, this has a razor-sharp first 30 minutes, then settles down into routine catch-the-monster plotting with makeup FX that make the werewolf look like a hatless Smokey the Bear! Good performances from Busey (as Haim's drunken uncle), Follows (as an older sister far more complex and interesting than the young hero), and McGill (as the town minister with a hairy secret your three-year-old brother could guess).

SIMON, KING OF THE WITCHES

★☆ Unicorn, 1971, R, 89 min. Dir: Bruce Kessler. Cast: Andrew Prine, Brenda Scott, George Paulsin, Norman Burton, Gerald York, Ultra Violet.

Laughably outdated mod horror with Prine as a hippie warlock who lives in an L.A. storm drain and puts the curse of never-ending rain on the city when girlfriend Scott is killed by a drug overdose engineered by her corrupt politician dad. Not even as much fun as it sounds, though Prine, who was then married to Scott in real life, gives another of his patented nut-case performances in the title role. Originally double-billed with *Werewolves on Wheels*.

SINGLE WHITE FEMALE
★★☆ Columbia/TriStar, 1992, R, 107 min.
Dir: Barbet Schroeder. Cast: Bridget Fonda, Jennifer Jason Leigh, Steven Weber, Peter Friedman, Stephen Tobolowsky, Kenneth Tobey.

A pair of terrific performances from Fonda and Leigh drive this otherwise routine chiller derived from John Lutz's far superior novel *SWF Seeks Same*. Bridget needs a roommate and Jen comes a-callin'; soon she's taking over Brid's life and even impersonating her. After that it isn't long before the sharp objects (including a high heel in one inspired touch) start a-flashin'. Luciano Tovoli's gorgeous photography often gives this the look of an Argento film, but with most of the book's more intriguing aspects thrown out, the suspense is undermined in favor of the usual cheap psycho clichés.

SINISTER INVASION
See: *Alien Terror*.

SINS OF DORIAN GRAY, THE
★★ Playhouse, 1983, PG, 95 min.
Dir: Tony Maylam. Cast: Belinda Bauer, Anthony Perkins, Joseph Bottoms, Olga Karlotos, Michael Ironside, Caroline Yaeger.

This distaff updating of *The Picture of Dorian Gray* plays more like Harold Robbins than Oscar Wilde. Dorian (Bauer) is now an amoral young model and the portrait is a Hollywood screen test that ages and corrupts as she dallies for decades all over New York. Bauer comes on like a poor man's Joan Collins, but Perkins shows the proper elan as her epigramspouting mentor. Made for theatrical release but only shown on television.

SISTERS
★★★ Warner, 1973, R, 92 min.
Dir: Brian De Palma. Cast: Margot Kidder, Jennifer Salt, Charles Durning, William Finley, Lislie Wilson, Bernard Hughes, Mary Davenport, Dolph Sweet.

De Palma's first venture into *Psycho*land, this enjoyable shocker mixes elements from that classic with ideas from *Rear Window* and *Spellbound*. A militant Staten Island reporter (Salt) witnesses a brutal knifing in the apartment next door, seemingly committed by the deranged ex-Siamese twin of French-Canadian fashion model Kidder. When the police can find no evidence of the crime, Salt decides to investigate the murder herself. Although filled with wild inconsistencies and lurid excesses, this film is acted and directed with such style and verve that it hardly matters. Bernard Herrmann's chilling electronic score adds immeasurably to its success. British title: *Blood Sisters*.

SISTER, SISTER
★★☆ Starmaker, 1987, R, 89 min.
Dir: Bill Conden, Cast: Jennifer Jason Leigh, Eric Stoltz, Judith Ivey, Dennis Lipscomb, Benjamin Mouton, Anne Pitoniak.

Honeydewed horror set in the swampy South (à la *Hush . . . Hush, Sweet Charlotte*, an obvious inspiration) about repressed sisters Leigh and Ivey running an antebellum bread-and-breakfast in a mansion filled with dark secrets bordering a bayou full of corpses. Excellent acting, lyrically golden cinematography, and an elegant score give it a lush look, but a silly surprise ending, taking a sudden left-hand turn from psychological suspense into the supernatural, almost throws the whole movie out of whack.

SISTERS OF DEATH
★ Interglobal, 1973, PG, 88 min.
Dir: Joseph A. Mazzuca. Cast: Claudia Jennings, Arthur Franz, Paul Carr, Cheri Howell, Sherry Boucher, Sherry Alberoni.

Cheapo thriller about five former sorority sisters lured to a bogus reunion at a desert castle by the vengeful father of the dead victim of an initiation stunt, who kills them in retaliation. Notable, if at all, for being late exploitation queen Jennings' only horror film and for B-movie regular Franz's startling resemblance to Brother Theodore here. Otherwise, this is just a bad way to waste 88 minutes.

SISTERS OF SATAN
★★☆ Academy, 1975, R, 90 min.
Dir: Juan Lopez Moctezuma. Cast: Tina Romero, Susana Kamini, Claudio Brook, David Silva.

Surprisingly good Mexican chiller from the post-*Exorcist* era with Romero as a carnal witch who corrupts virginal Kamini; the latter is saved from eternal damnation by an exorcism performed by priest Silva. Stylish-looking and often quite inventive, this rises above the pack when compared to most other south-of-the-border shockers. Original title: *Alucarda* and aka *Mark of the Devil Part 3*.

SIX BLACK NOTES
See: *The Psychic*.

SIX WOMEN FOR THE MURDERER
See: *Blood and Black Lace*.

SKEETER
★★ New Line, 1993, R, 95 min.
Dir: Clark Brandon. Cast: Tracy Griffith, Jim Youngs, Charles Napier, Michael J. Pollard.

A straight-faced throwback to a '50s big-bug epic about mutant mosquitoes terrorizing the folk of a small desert community. Nothing special, but fun if you catch it on a good day.

SKULL, THE
★★★ Paramount/Gateway, 1965, NR, 83 min.
Dir: Freddie Francis. Cast: Peter Cushing, Christopher Lee, Patrick Wymark, Jill Bennett, Michael Gough, Nigel Green, Patrick Magee, George Coulouris.

Solid Amicus Films adaptation of Robert Bloch's story "The Skull of the Marquis de Sade," with Cushing as a collector of occult artifacts who falls under the murderous spell of de Sade's possessed skull. An exceptional cast, eerie photography, and imaginative direction make this a minor gem of '60s British horror.

SLAUGHTER
★★☆ 21st Genesis, 1976, R, 80 min.
Dir: Burt Brinkerhoff. Cast: David McCallum, Sandra McCabe, George Wyner, Eric Server, Sterling Swanson, Linda Gray.

Released to theatres as *Dogs,* this low-budget *Jaws* by way of *The Birds* spin-off is ambitious if fatally flawed. When a California college town is attacked by all manner of dogs gone wild, professor McCallum begins an investigation that eventually goes nowhere, with only he and girlfriend McCabe escaping the town with their lives. A nice touch is that all breeds of dog turn vicious, not just the obvious ones, though indifferent production values and often clumsy direction soon take their toll. Future "Dallas" star Gray gets it in a funny *Psycho* parody in which she's savaged in her shower.

SLAUGHTER HIGH
★☆ Vestron, 1985, UR, 89 min.
Dirs: George Dugdale, Mark Ezra, Peter Litten.
Cast: Caroline Munro, Simon Scuddamore, Carmine Iannoccone, Donna Yeager, Gary Martin, Kelly Baker.

Here's an original idea: A former class nerd, both physically and emotionally scarred by a cruel April Fool's Day joke gone wrong, lures

Peter Cushing eyes The Skull *(1965).*

his one-time tormentors to a bogus high school reunion where he dons a harlequin costume and begins stalking and killing them. Filmed as *April Fool's Day* (with the title changed to avoid confusion with the Paramount movie of the same name), this is nothing but cut-and-dried slasher clichés for those who still care, with victims done in by stabbing, crushing, drowning, electrocution, and an acid bath, Munro, cast against type as a bitch, leads a cast of the oldest high school kids in the history of the movies. Also out in a cut R version.

SLAUGHTER HOTEL
★☆ MPI, 1971, R, 89 min. Dir: Fernando Di Leo.
Cast: Klaus Kinski, Margaret Lee, Rosalba Neri, Monica Strebel, John Karlsen, Jamie Garrett.

There's more sex than slaughter in this cheesy Spanish-Italian slasher about a masked maniac preying on the female patients at a private mental clinic situated in an old castle. The victims, most of them nude at the time, are scythed, strangled, stabbed, and even shot through the eye with a crossbow bolt. Also on hand is Klaus as a red herring psychiatrist who eventually emerges as the hero and protects Lee from the killer, who dies in one of the sleaziest scenes on record. U.S. distributor Hallmark proudly trumpeted this as "The Hideous Slaughter of Eight Innocent Nurses!" to cash in on its incidental resemblance to the infamous Richard Speck killings. Original title: *La Bestia Uccide a Sangue Fredda: The Cold-Blooded Beast* and also out as *Asylum Erotica.*

SLAUGHTERHOUSE
★★☆ Charter, 1987, R, 88 min. Dir: Rick Roessler. Cast: Sherry Bendorf, Don Barrett, William Houck, Joe Barton, Jane Higginson, Eric Schwartz.

Curvacious Bendorf decides to make a horror video at an old slaughterhouse, not realizing that it's the hideout of mountainous pig-lover Buddy (Barton), who lives with his demented dad (Barrett) and goes on a Leatherface-like rampage. This *Texas Chainsaw* rip-off is much better than you'd think, with likable characters and clever direction, though it climaxes with another of those annoying freeze-frame open endings. Try *not* to flinch during the opening credits montage.

SLAUGHTERHOUSE ROCK
★★ SVS, 1987, R, 85 min. Dir: Dimitri Logothetis. Cast: Toni Basil, Nicholas Celozzi, Tom Reilly, Donna Denton, Tamara Hyler, Hope Marie Carlton.

OK jailhouse shocker about a group of college students drawn to Alcatraz Island by the ghost of murdered rock star Basil, where Reilly is possessed by the spirit of a cannibalistic prison governor. Dumb-dumb characters and some glaring plot inconsistencies notwithstanding, this offers a couple of good makeup FX and stylish direction.

SLAUGHTER OF THE VAMPIRES
★★ Sinister Cinema, 1962, NR, 72 min. Dir: Roberto Mauri. Cast: Walter Brandi, Dieter Eppler, Graziella Granata, Alfredo Rizzo.

Newlyweds on their honeymoon at a Viennese castle encounter a Dracula-like vampire (Eppler, looking like Grandpa Munster) who makes the bride his own. A corny Italian vampire pic with ridiculously schmaltzy music and a hokily romantic vampire who wants to take the heroine away to "a world of color and sounds you couldn't even begin to imagine." It's like that. Originally released in the U.S. as *Curse of the Blood Ghouls;* Italian version runs 84 min.

SLAVE OF THE CANNIBAL GOD
★☆ Video City, 1978, R, 96 min. Dir: Sergio Martino. Cast: Ursula Andress, Stacy Keach, Claudio Cassinelli, Antonio Marsina.

Ursula, then in her forties, looks great in this otherwise time-wasting early Italian cannibal effort. Keach leads an expedition through the jungles of New Guinea searching for Andress' missing husband; everybody bites it except Ursula, who's painted white by the natives, discovers hubby to be a moldering corpse worshiped as a god, and just barely escapes. Apart from its upscale leads and unacknowledged influence on John Derek's (Andress' ex) awful remake of *Tarzan, the Ape Man,* this hasn't much to offer.

SLAYER, THE
★★ Continental, 1981, R, 80 min. Dir: J. S. Cardone. Cast: Sarah Kendall, Frederick Flynn, Carol Kottenbrook, Alan McRae, Michael Holmes, Carl Kraines.

A surrealist artist and her husband, brother, and sister-in-law take an off-season vacation cottage on Tybee Island off the Georgia coast where they're stalked by a hideous monster that turns out to be a product of the heroine's subconscious fears. An interesting idea suffers from routine handling and predictable slasher movie structuring, though there are some effective passages and creepy creature design by Robert Short.

SLEEPAWAY CAMP
★★ Video Treasures, 1983, R, 84 min. Dir: Robert Hiltzik. Cast: Mike Kellin, Felissa Rose, Jonathan Tierston, Christopher Collet, Karen Fields, Katherine Kamhi, Paul De Angelo, Susan Glazer.

Gritty low-budget *Friday the 13th* clone about a repressed young teen (Rose) raised as a girl (though actually a boy) who puts the knife to all those who give him/her a tough time at summer camp. This demented variation on an overly familiar theme is given slight distinction by Kellin as the camp's harried owner, some good Ed French makeups, and a truly shocking final shot. Retitled *Nightmare Vacation* in England and followed by two direct-to-video sequels.

SLEEPAWAY CAMP 2: UNHAPPY CAMPERS
★★ Nelson, 1988, R, 80 min. Dir: Michael A. Simpson. Cast: Pamela Springsteen, Renée Estevez, Brian Patrick Clarke, Walter Gotell, Tony Higgins, Susan Marie Snyder.

The sisters of Bruce Springsteen and Emilio Estevez duke it out in this black comedy sequel to the '83 *Friday the 13th* wannabe. Springsteen is the now older psycho from the first movie who gets a sex-change operation and takes a job as a summer camp counselor at a resort for obnoxious rich kids where the usual array of druggy, foul-mouthed, sex-starved campers become easy fodder for her knife, chainsaw, guitar string, and battery acid. Probably the best of the *Sleepaways* (which ain't sayin' much), this film has an interesting cast and gory deaths—although its attitude of praising its "moral" maniac while condemning her looser-living, mostly female victims to ignominious fates is faintly offensive.

SLEEPAWAY CAMP 3: TEENAGE WASTELAND

★☆ Nelson, 1989, R, 79 min.
Dir: Michael A. Simpson. Cast: Pamela Springsteen, Tracy Griffith, Michael J. Pollard, Mark Oliver, Kim Wall, Jill Terashita.

It's back to the woods for Angela (Springsteen again), who kills and replaces a girl going to a camp at which inner-city and suburban kids interact—and get butchered. Even more of a comedy than part 2 (half the characters are named for the casts of "The Brady Bunch" and *West Side Story*!) but not nearly as funny as it wants to be. The murder scenes have clearly been trimmed, but the cast isn't bad (though Pollard is wasted as an early victim). And we've got to do something about these inconclusive, open endings.

SLEEPING CAR, THE

★★ Vidmark, 1990, R, 87 min.
Dir: Douglas Curtis. Cast: David Naughton, Kevin McCarthy, Judie Aronson, Jeff Conaway, Dani Minnick, Ernestine Mercer.

A movie about a killer sofa bed doesn't sound too promising, but this direct-to-vid release isn't *that* bad. *American Werewolf* 's Naughton is a thirtyish college student who rents an apartment in an old converted train car haunted by a low-rent Freddy clone called "The Mister" who uses the above-mentioned piece of furniture to off various supporting characters. Most of the victims are impaled on sofa springs until a convenient occultist neighbor (McCarthy) attempts an exorcism. Heavily contrived, but the pun-laden dialogue can be amusing.

SLEEPING WITH THE ENEMY

★★ Fox, 1991, R, 98 min.
Dir: Joseph Ruben. Cast: Julia Roberts, Patrick Bergin, Kevin Anderson, Elizabeth Lawrence, Kyle Secor, Claudette Nevins.

Roberts is an abused wife who fakes her death to escape wealthy, crazed hubby Bergin and starts over in a new town with a new identity and hairdo. Just as she starts getting close to nice guy neighbor Anderson, guess who shows up? One hundred percent predictable, this thriller gets by on Roberts' considerable charm alone.

SLEEPWALKERS

★★ Columbia/TriStar, 1992, R, 89 min.
Dir: Mick Garris. Cast: Madchen Amick, Alice Krige, Brian Krause, Glenn Shadix, Ron Perlman, Cindy Pickett, Lyman Ward, Mark Hamill.

Stephen King's first original screenplay since *Creepshow* is the basis for this silly film in which Krige and Krause are an incestuous pair of mother-and-son cat creatures who live off the souls of virgins and choose sweet high school girl Amick as their next victim. It's certainly watchable, but hokey makeup and too many flat one-liners make this poor man's *Cat People* more laughable than scary. Lots of cameos, including King, Clive Barker, and Tobe Hooper. Aka *Stephen King's Sleepwalkers*.

SLIME PEOPLE, THE

★ Rhino, 1963, NR, 76 min.
Dir: Robert Hutton. Cast: Robert Hutton, Les Tremayne, Susan Hart, Robert Burton, Judee Morton, William Boyce.

"This is no joke!" Boyce exclaims early in this ultra-cheap monster mash, but I have my doubts. B-movie fave Hutton directs himself as the pilot hero battling rubberoid slime monsters from the bowels of the earth who've invaded Los Angeles. Too drawn out to be as much fun as it could have been, though there are some laughs provided by an invasion force of about three monsters, Tremayne as a kook in love with a goat, and Hart as a heroine who *always* carries her pocketbook, no matter what the danger. Originally co-billed with *The Crawling Hand*.

SLITHIS

★★ Media, 1978, PG, 86 min.
Dir: Stephen Traxler. Cast: Alan Blanchard, Judy Motulsky, Mello Alexandria, Dennis Lee Falt.

Pleasant enough '50s-type monster movie about a scaly mutant terrorizing the denizens of Venice, California, where his weird appearance is barely noticed, until hunted down by a high school science teacher and a couple of friends. Cheaply done but fun, with a fairly effective monster suit. Aka *Spawn of the Slithis*.

SLIVER

★★ Paramount, 1993, R, 106 min.
Dir: Phillip Noyce. Cast: Sharon Stone, William Baldwin, Tom Berenger, Martin Landau, Polly Walker, Colleen Camp, CCH Pounder, Nina Foch, Keene Curtis, Nicholas Pryor.

This handsome but mangled and sexed-up version of Ira Levin's suspenser presents Stone as the new tenant in Manhattan's "Horror Highrise," where she finds herself torn between sexy but weird peeper Baldwin and rugged but obsessive Berenger. This opens with a spectacular, heart-stopping falling sequence but goes downhill from there, with too many unbelievable characters (wasting an exceptional supporting cast) and absurd plot twists. Things really get stupid during a hasti-ly reshot denouement in which the killer's identity was altered to appease some pinhead-ed preview audience. Mostly for fans of gratu-itous, body-double simulated-sex scenes—although Stone and Baldwin generate absolutely no screen chemistry. Maybe if Billy had made a play for Tom?

SLUGS

★★ Starmaker, 1987, R, 89 min.
Dir: Juan Piquer Simon. Cast: Michael Garfield, Kim Terry, Philip Machale, Concha Cuetos, Alicia Moro, Santiago Alvarez, Frank Brana, Patty Sheppard.

One of the ickiest, slimiest monster movies since *Squirm* has a strain of mutant, flesh-eat-ing slugs terrorizing an autumnal upstate New York town. Very graphic makeup work (especially a guy's eye bursting out to the accompaniment of a horde of baby slugs) will please gorehounds, but the acting and post-synched dialogue of this U.S.-Spanish flick are hopeless and the musical score (apart from a good title theme) is about as grating as the background music of a bad television com-mercial. More professional-looking than Simon's earlier *Pieces*, but, unfortunately, this adaptation of a novel by Shaun Hutson isn't nearly as funny.

SLUMBER PARTY MASSACRE

★★☆ Embassy, 1983, R, 76 min.
Dir: Amy Jones. Cast: Michele Michaels, Robin Stille, Michael Villela, Jennifer Meyers, Debra Deliso, Andree Honore, Pamela Roylance, Brinke Stevens.

Yet another tacky *Halloween* clone with busty babes menaced by a wild-eyed psycho? Well, yes and no. All the expected clichés are pre-sent (slumber-partying high school girls must contend with crashing boyfriends, practical jokes, and a drill-toting mental hospital escapee), but a humorous approach on the part of director Jones and feminist scripter Rita Mae Brown gives it a sense of fun usually lacking in similar efforts. Well acted by some very likable gals and also mucho gore; this peaks during a hilarious pizza delivery scene. Followed by two sequels.

SLUMBER PARTY MASSACRE II

★★ Nelson, 1987, R, 75 min.
Dir: Deborah Brock. Cast: Crystal Bernard, Kimberly McArthur, Juliette Cummins, Patrick Lowe, Heidi Kozak, Atanas Hitch, Joel Hoffman, Cynthia Eilbacher.

Slick but silly follow-up with plucky Bernard as the now grown younger sis of the girl who offed the driller killer of part one. Tormented by weird dreams involving drill-edged guitar-playing Hitch, Bernard and friends find their all-girl rock band terrorized by the maniac, who's somehow entered into the real world and crashed their slumber party. Overly deriv-ative of the *Nightmare on Elm Street* series and sporting an ending that makes absolutely no sense at all, this has some really bizarre touch-es (like a girl's face turning into a huge exploding zit) and obvious in-jokes (characters have last names like Bates, Krueger, and Voorhees) to make it watchable. Shooting title: *Don't Let Go.*

SLUMBER PARTY MASSACRE III

★☆ New Horizons, 1990, UR, 80 min.
Dir: Sally Mattison. Cast: Keely Christian, Brittain Frye, Hope Marie Carlton, M. K. Harris, David Greenlee, Maria Ford.

More drillin' and more killin' in another sequel nobody asked for. The feminist tradi-tion continues with another woman taking the director's chair, but this poorly slapped-together T&A slasher (with unrated FX) is even cheaper-looking than the original.

SNAKE PIT, THE

See: *The Torture Chamber of Dr. Sadism.*

SNAKE PIT AND THE PENDULUM, THE

See: *The Torture Chamber of Dr. Sadism.*

SNAKE WOMAN, THE

★★ Cinemacabre, 1961, NR, 66 min.
Dir: Sidney J. Furie. Cast: John McCarthy, Susan Travers, Geoffrey Danton, Arnold Marie, Elsie Wagstaff, Frances Bennett.

Undistinguished Brit chiller about a herpetolo-gist who injects his mad pregnant wife with snake venom. The wife then dies giving birth to a cold-blooded baby who grows into the seductive Travers, who haunts the moors and kills in the form of a cobra. Some eerie moments but too talky, lacking the style of *The Reptile* or the campiness of *Cult of the Cobra* to put it over. First released on the bottom half of a double bill with Furie's *Dr. Blood's Coffin.*

SNAPSHOT

See: *The Day After Halloween.*

SNOWBEAST
★★ Goodtimes, 1977, NR, 96 min.
Dir: Herb Wallerstein. Cast: Bo Svenson,
Yvette Mimieux, Robert Logan, Clint Walker,
Sylvia Sidney, Annie McEnroe.

Jaws and *Grizzly* would seem to have been the
inspiration behind this mediocre TV movie. A
large and only barely glimpsed Abominable
Snowman type monster terrorizes a Colorado
ski resort, tearing apart various hot doggers
and snowbunnies until heroes Svenson,
Mimieux, Logan, and Walker decide to hunt it
down. Lots of lurching POV shots in place of
an on-camera monster, a good cast doing
some series slumming, and plenty of hokey
touches highlight this slight tale.

SNOW CREATURE, THE
★☆ Goodtimes, 1954, NR, 70 min. Dir: W. Lee
Wilder. Cast: Paul Langton, Leslie Denison, Teru
Shimada, Rollin Moriyana, Darlene Fields, Bill Phipps.

The first and probably worst of a string of '50s
Abominable Snowman movies, with one of
the creatures captured and brought to L.A. for
the inevitable rampage. *King Kong*, *Them*, and
The Werewolf of London were obvious inspirations, but apart from an effective handling of
its title monster (always obscured by snow,
shadows, or misty glass), this clunkily acted
and slowly paced pic is a real snooze.

SOCIETY
★★☆ Republic, 1989, R, 94 min.
Dir: Brian Yuzna. Cast: Billy Warlock, Devin
Devasquez, Evan Richards, Charles Lucia,
Connie Danese, Heidi Kozak.

Deadpan black comedy about a Beverly Hills
teen (Warlock) who discovers that his family
and other members of the elite upper crust are
actually mutant cannibals who literally feed
off the lower classes. Although this makes the
dramatic blunder of casting hunk Warlock as
the alienated outsider hero (dumpy second
lead Richards would have been a much better
choice), this look into the lifestyles of the rich
and mutated has moments of excellence inter-
spersed with much narrative confusion and
flat performances. It saves most of its very
weird Screaming Mad George FX for its icky,
squishy climax.

SO EVIL, MY SISTER
See: *Psycho Sisters*.

SOLE SURVIVOR
★★ Vestron, 1982, R, 85 min.
Dir: Thom Eberhardt. Cast: Anita Skinner, Kurt
Johnson, Caren Larkey, Brinke Stevens.

Skinner is the only survivor of a jet-liner
crash and begins to be haunted by the non-
survivors, who try to draw her over to the
other side. This updated rip-off of *Carnival of
Souls* is interesting (based as it is on the supposedly true phenomenon that all sole survivors of disasters die within 24 months of
the catastrophe) and has a good performance
from Skinner but is let down by low-budget
handling.

SOMEONE'S KILLING THE WORLD'S GREATEST MODELS
See: *She's Dressed to Kill*.

SOMETHING IS OUT THERE
See: *Day of the Animals*.

SOMETHING IS OUT THERE
See: *The Dark Side of the Moon*.

SOMETHING WAITS IN THE DARK
See: *Screamers*.

SOMETHING WEIRD
★★ Sinister Cinema, 1967, NR, 83 min.
Dir: Herschell Gordon Lewis. Cast: Tony McCabe,
Elizabeth Lee, William Brooker, Ted Heil.

You can't argue with a title like that. McCabe
is a workman whose face is burned by high-
tension wires. Lee is an ugly witch who
promises to restore his face for love. McCabe
then becomes a handsome stage illusionist
with unexplained psychic powers who abandons Lee for phony psychic Brooker. Lee seeks
revenge. Brooker is accidentally disfigured.
Lee promises to restore his face for love. Not
as gory as grue guru Lewis' other horror films,
and certainly far too talky, but not without its
interesting elements. Aka *The Eerie World of
Dr. Jordan*.

SOMETHING WICKED THIS WAY COMES
★★☆ Disney, 1983, PG, 95 min.
Dir: Jack Clayton. Cast: Jason Robards, Jonathon
Pryce, Diane Ladd, Pam Grier, Royal Dano, Vidal
Peterson, Shawn Carson, James Stacy, Mary Grace
Canfield, voice of Arthur Hill.

Uneven adaptation (by the author) of Ray
Bradbury's fantasy about two small boys who
try to stop the invasion of their small Illinois
town by a mysterious carnival headed by a
satanic figure (Pryce) who offers the towns-
people their greatest wish—for the price of
their souls. Very glossy and big-budget, but
Disney's attempt to preserve its family image
at the expense of the horror content robs this
of all tension and suspense. Strong casting and
FX but overall disappointing.

SOMETIMES THEY COME BACK

★★ Vidmark, 1991, NR, 92 min.
Dir: Tom McLoughlin. Cast: Tim Matheson, Brooke Adams, William Sanderson, Robert Rusler.

McLoughlin (*Friday the 13th VI*) helmed this okay TV adaptation of a Stephen King story about a middle-aged schoolteacher (Matheson) haunted by the ghosts of black-leather-jacketed bullies who long ago murdered his brother. Watchable, but the ever-sexy Adams is wasted as Tim's wife. This was co-producer Milton Subotsky's last film. Aka *Stephen King's Sometimes They Come Back*.

SONNY BOY

★★ Media, 1987, R, 98 min.
Dir: Robert Martin Carroll. Cast: David Carradine, Paul L. Smith, Brad Dourif, Conrad Janis, Sydney Lassick, Alexandra Powers, Michael Griffin, Savina Gersak.

One of the weirdest movies ever made, this tells of a band of psychotic criminals (led by Smith and a female-attired Carradine as "Pa" and "Ma"!!!) who kidnap a baby boy as a surrogate son, cut out his tongue, and keep him in a cage. When "Sonny Boy" (Griffin) grows up, discredited doctor Janis sews a monkey tongue into his mouth so that he can narrate the story while falling for Powers. With its sick, sick storyline and killer cast, this should have been great, but it never really takes off.

SON OF BLOB

★★ Video Gems, 1972, PG, 87 min.
Dir: Larry Hagman. Cast: Robert Walker, Jr., Gwynne Gilford, Carol Lynley, Burgess Meredith, Godfrey Cambridge, Shelley Berman, Dick Van Patten, Marlene Clark, Gerrit Graham, Cindy Williams.

All-star tongue-in-cheek follow-up to the original *Blob*. Cambridge is an Alaskan pipeline worker who brings back a piece of the frozen Blob; it quickly thaws out and goes on an all new rampage. A lot of famous faces pop up briefly to become Blob food; this film's flower children heroes are just as dated now as the original's hipsters. Stupid but fun. Also released as *Beware! The Blob* and reissued in 1980 as "The film J.R. shot!" (Hagman also has a cameo).

SON OF DRACULA

★★★ MCA/Universal, 1943, NR, 80 min.
Dir: Robert Siodmak. Cast: Lon Chaney, Jr., Louise Allbritton, Robert Paige, Evelyn Ankers, Frank Craven, J. Edward Bromberg.

One of Universal's best '40s B horrors, this tells of one Count Anthony Alucard (Chaney), a Hungarian nobleman visiting the southern plantation of Dark Oaks. The Count marries the plantation's gloomy mistress (the excellent Allbritton) and turns out to be the son of a certain Transylvanian vampire. An offbeat and surprisingly downbeat vampire tale, this is highlighted by a sullen atmosphere and imaginative special effects. Despite what you may have read elsewhere, the miscast Chaney is indeed playing the *son* of Dracula, *not* the Count himself, as the dialogue and title both clearly indicate.

SON OF FRANKENSTEIN

★★★ MCA/Universal, 1939, NR, 99 min.
Dir: Rowland V. Lee. Cast: Boris Karloff, Basil Rathbone, Bela Lugosi, Lionel Atwill, Josephine Hutchinson, Donnie Dunagan.

Karloff's third and final performance as the monster is featured in this most elaborate of the Universal series. Rathbone hams it up as the son of Henry Frankenstein, who arrives at the family estate to claim his legacy and discovers the monster still living in the blasted laboratory in the care of the broken-necked shepherd Ygor (Lugosi). Impressive settings (designed for color, though the film was ultimately shot in B&W) and a grand score by Frank Skinner, but it's all stolen by Bela as the charmingly sinister Ygor and Atwill as the wooden-armed police inspector.

SON OF GODZILLA

★★ Interglobal, 1967, NR, 84 min.
Dir: Jun Fukuda. Cast: Tadao Takashima, Akira Kubo, Beverly Maeda, Akihiko Hirata, Yoshio Tsuchiya, Kenji Sahara.

The silliest and most juvenile of the '60s Godzilla movies involves scientists conducting weather-control experiments on an island where the Big G arrives to protect his newly hatched son from gigantic preying mantises and a huge spider called Spiga. Originally titled *Gojira no Musuko: Godzilla and Son*, this is occasionally amusing (especially in son Minya's resemblance to ET) but has some of the weakest special effects of the series.

SON OF KONG

★★☆ Turner, 1933, NR, 70 min.
Dir: Ernest B. Schoedsack. Cast: Robert Armstrong, Helen Mack, Frank Reicher, John Marston, Victor Wong, Noble Johnson.

Escaping his creditors, Kong capturer Armstrong returns to Skull Island in search of treasure but instead encounters the 12-foot albino son of Kong. This serio-comic sequel appeared a mere nine months after the original and, though no classic, has good animation (saved

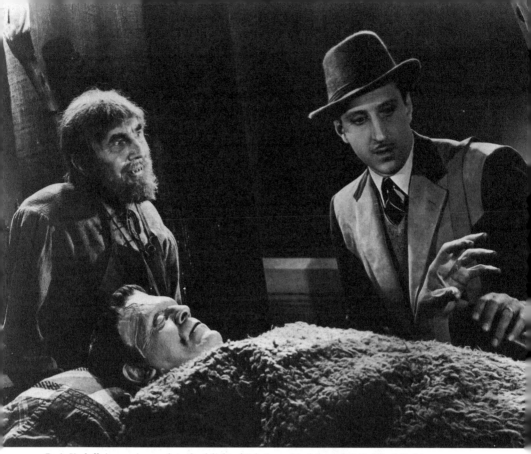

Boris Karloff rises again, much to the delight of Bela Lugosi and the disbelief of Basil Rathbone, in Son of Frankenstein *(1939).*

for the last half hour) and emotional Max Steiner music as its highlights.

SORORITY BABES IN THE SLIMEBALL BOWL-A-RAMA

★★ Urban Classics, 1988, R, 79 min. Dir: David De Coteau. Cast: Linnea Quigley, Andras Jones, Robin Rochelle, Hal Havins, Brinke Stevens, Michelle Bauer.

Two sorority hopefuls, a trio of nerdy nincompoops, and punk babe Linnea run afoul of a mischievous imp unleashed from his bowling trophy prison in an after-hours mall. This minor exploitation item is outfitted with all the usual nudity and (comic) gore. The acting isn't bad, and the film looks pretty good considering its meager $200,000 price tag, making it a slight improvement on the same team's *Creepozoids*. Originally titled *The Imp*.

SORORITY HOUSE MASSACRE

★★ Warner, 1986, R, 74 min. Dir: Carol Frank. Cast: Angela O'Neill, Wendy Martel, Pamela Ross, Nicole Rio, John C. Russell, Gillian Frank.

Halloween clone #240: A psycho escapes from a mental hospital and returns to the sorority house where he first flipped to begin murdering anew. Lots of heavy-breathing POV work, oversexed characters, and predictable twists; only Frank's sometimes stylish direction and O'Neill's appealing heroine make it worth a single watch for slasher completists.

SORORITY HOUSE MASSACRE II

★☆ New Horizons, 1991, R, 77 min. Dir: Arch Stanton [Jim Wynorski]. Cast: Melissa Moore, Robyn Harris, Stacia Zhivago, Dana Bentley.

Originally called *Nightie Nightmare* (hoo boy!), this has nothing to do with the first *SHM* and actually includes flashback sequences from *Slumber Party Massacre* instead! A bunch of underdressed and undertalented pretty young actresses turn an old house into their new sorority digs and are killed off when one of their number is possessed by a dead mass murderer. Virtually the same story (with the almost identical cast) was told the year before in Wynorski's much better *Hard to Die;* only fans of gratuitous shower scenes will have anything to grab onto here.

SORRY, WRONG NUMBER
★★★ Paramount, 1948, NR, 89 min.
Dir: Anatole Litvak. Cast: Barbara Stanwyck, Burt Lancaster, Ann Richards, Wendell Corey, Harold Vermilyea, Ed Begley, Leif Erickson, William Conrad.

Classic suspenser with Stanwyck in an Oscar-nominated role as a bedridden hypochondriac who overhears a telephone plot by her husband to have her murdered. This adaptation of a taut Lucille Fletcher radio play is padded with too many flashbacks but is well acted and builds to a genuinely scary climax. Remade for TV.

SORRY, WRONG NUMBER
★☆ Paramount, 1989, PG, 96 min.
Dir: Tony Wharmby. Cast: Loni Anderson, Hal Holbrook, Patrick Macnee, Carl Weintraub.

Contrived cable TV remake with Loni as a buxom invalid who overhears a murder plot on the phone and discovers too late it is meant for her. Little of this glossy updating works, including the dumb drug-dealing subplot added to the slight original story for padding.

SOUL OF A MONSTER
★★ Sinister Cinema, 1944, NR, 61 min.
Dir: Will Jason. Cast: George Macready, Rose Hobart, Jim Bannon, Jeanne Bates, Erik Rolf.

Hobart is good as a devil disciple who saves the life of humanitarian doctor Macready and then tries to corrupt him. Otherwise, this cheapie Columbia Val Lewton rip-off is pretty dull, with lots of talk about good and evil, lots of talk about love and hate, lots of talk about life and death—in short, lots of talk. One good scene involving the sudden appearance of an el train was clearly inspired by the bus sequence in *Cat People*.

SOULTAKER
★★☆ AIP, 1990, R, 94 min. Dir: Michael Rissi.
Cast: Vivian Schilling, Joe Estevez, Robert Z'Dar, Gregg Thomsen, David Shark, Jane Reiner.

This imaginative but not wholly successful low-budgeter (scripted by lead actress Schilling) is about teens killed in a car crash whose disembodied souls must re-enter their bodies so that they can return to life before the title character (Estevez, Martin Sheen's brother) can whisk them off to eternity. Except for the talented Schilling, the acting isn't especially good and the pace lags some in the middle, but this updated variation on *Carnival of Souls* has a lot to recommend it.

SPACE MISSION TO THE LOST PLANET
See: *Horror of the Blood Monsters*.

SPACE VAMPIRES
See: *Lifeforce*.

SPACE ZOMBIES
See: *The Astro Zombies*.

SPASMS
★★ HBO, 1982, R, 89 min.
Dir: William Fruet. Cast: Peter Fonda, Oliver Reed, Kerrie Keane, Al Waxman, Miguel Fernandes, Marilyn Lightstone.

Sweaty millionaire big game hunter Reed has an unexplained psychic link to the huge African serpent-god that killed his brother. When the creature is brought to a Canadian college town and escapes, Ollie is determined to hunt it down. Shot as *Death Bite*, this has impressive Dick Smith snake-bite makeup but a rather phony-looking monster and lots of heavy-duty hamming from Reed.

SPAWNING, THE
See: *Piranha II: The Spawning*.

SPAWN OF THE SLITHIS
See: *Slithis*.

SPECTRE, THE
See: *The Ghost*.

SPECTRE OF DR. HICHCOCK, THE
See: *The Ghost*.

SPECTRE OF EDGAR ALLAN POE, THE
★★ Unicorn, 1973, PG, 89 min.
Dir: Mohy Quandour. Cast: Robert Walker, Jr., Cesar Romero, Tom Drake, Carol Ohmart, Mary Grover, Marsha Mae Jones.

Entertainingly sleazy, totally fictionalized Poe bio telling of the author's relationship with his beloved Lenore and how her premature burial and resultant madness led them to a country asylum replete with snake pit, torture chamber, and ax murders. Walker has the proper look for his role but is otherwise unconvincing; the veteran supporting cast are better served. The '60s-style theme song, "Lenore," is a dopey highlight.

SPECTRES
★★ Imperial, 1987, R, 93 min.
Dir: Marcello Avallone. Cast: Donald Pleasence, John Pepper, Katrine Michelsen, Massimo De Rossi, Lavinia Grizi, Matteo Gazzolo.

Archeological digging amongst the ruins of Rome uncovers a catacomb-laced tomb containing a strange sarcophagus that, when opened, unleashes a horned demon that rips its way through most of the cast. Sharp-looking but slow, with unsympathetic characters and all the gore saved for the last 20 minutes, when a face is pulled off, a heart torn out, and a head crushed against a wall. The pulled-through-the-bed bit was snagged from the first *Nightmare on Elm Street*.

SPELL, THE

★★ Goodtimes, 1977, NR, 84 min. Dir: Lee Phillips. Cast: Lee Grant, Susan Myers, James Olson, Helen Hunt, Lelia Goldoni, Jack Colvin.

Well-acted but dull TV *Carrie* clone, broadcast only three months after the premiere of the De Palma film, with Myers as an overweight teen who uses witchcraft to get back at her tormenting peers. Grant, always a class act, adds some substance to this as the girl's mom and Myers is good too, but the only well-done sequence is one in which a woman suddenly dies of internal spontaneous combustion. First shown at 74 minutes, the video print is of the expanded TV syndication version.

SPELLBINDER

★★ CBS/Fox, 1988, R, 99 min. Dir: Janet Greek. Cast: Timothy Daly, Kelly Preston, Rick Rossovich, Audra Lindley, Anthony Crivello, Diana Bellamy.

In this slow-moving big-budget witchcraft thriller, a lonely young lawyer (Daly) rescues a beautiful girl from a mugger, falls in love with her, and discovers that she belongs to a satanic coven and has been chosen for an upcoming sacrifice—and that he should have seen *The Wicker Man*. Preston is gorgeous and there are a few flashes of visual imagination, but this sub-*Rosemary's Baby* is sunk mostly by Daly's unbelievably dumb hero who, basically, gets just what's coming to him. Shooting title: *Witching Hour*.

SPELLCASTER

★☆ RCA/Columbia, 1987, R, 83 min. Dir: Rafal Zielinski. Cast: Adam Ant, Gail O'Grady, Richard Blade, Traci Lin, Bunty Bailey, Bill Butler.

A group of young dunderheads, lured to an Italian castle for a million-dollar treasure hunt, are knocked off by satanic Ant—in a five-minute cameo. Never released theatrically, this mostly rotten Empire Pics flick has unsympathetic characters and rubbery make-up FX. It's a perfect example of why the studio folded in the first place.

SPHINX, THE

★★ Sinister Cinema, 1933, NR, 64 min. Dir: Phil Rosen. Cast: Lionel Atwill, Sheila Terry, Theodore Newton, Paul Hurst, Luis Alberni, Robert Ellis.

Atwill shines, as always, in this forgotten early '30s chiller. A series of murders, seemingly committed by kindly Jerome Breen (Atwill), rock New York and a pretty reporter investigates, eventually uncovering the killer's identity and Breen's dark secret. Not without interest; remade as *The Phantom Killer*.

SPHINX

★☆ Warner, 1981, PG, 117 min. Dir: Franklin J. Schaffner. Cast: Lesley-Anne Down, Frank Langella, Maurice Ronet, John Gielgud, Martin Benson, John Rhys-Davies.

A meticulously crafted but utterly dumb adaptation of the Robin Cook novel with Down (in a bad punk do) as a young Egyptologist whose life isn't worth a plugged piaster when she discovers a treasure-laden burial chamber beneath King Tut's tomb. Mummified acting and direction; lots of scenes of Lesley-Anne wandering around old catacombs where she's attacked by bats and rats and a lot of mummies fall on her. As one critic aptly put it: "*Sphinx* stinks!"

SPIDER, THE

See: *Earth vs. The Spider.*

SPIDER BABY

★★★ Admit One, 1964, NR, 80 min. Dir: Jack Hill. Cast: Lon Chaney, Jr., Carol Ohmart, Quinn Redeker, Mary Mitchell, Beverly Washburn, Jill Banner, Sid Haig, Mantan Moreland.

There are good bad movies and there are bad bad movies and then there's this: a bad movie so bizarre, so fascinating, that it's in a class by itself. Lovable ol' Lon is the fatherly chauffeur of the wacky Merrye clan: a group of in-bred weirdos suffering from some phony hereditary disease who degenerate as they grow older, eventually becoming murderous cannibals—one Merrye sister even imagines herself a human spider and kills in arachnid fashion. Not as technically inept as *Plan Nine From Outer Space* or as boring as *House of the Black Death* but definitely of the same poverty-ridden school, with volumes of purple dialogue and ludicrous situations—Lon even sings the rockin' theme song! Not to be missed and also known as *Spider Baby or the Maddest Story Ever Told, Cannibal Orgy or the Maddest Story Ever Told,* and *The Liver Eaters.*

SPIDER BABY OR THE MADDEST STORY EVER TOLD

See: *Spider Baby.*

SPIDER WOMAN, THE

★★★ Key, 1944, NR, 62 min.

Dir: Roy William Neill. Cast: Basil Rathbone, Nigel Bruce, Gale Sondergaard, Dennis Hoey, Vernon Downing, Alec Craig.

A series of deaths sweeping London, called "Pajama Suicides" by the press, are investigated by Sherlock Holmes, who discovers them to be murders committed by Sondergaard, who drives her victims to self-destruction through the bite of a deadly spider. Delightful cat-and-mouse exchanges between Rathbone and Sondergaard and a great World War II propaganda ending in a shooting gallery highlight this fun mystery-chiller. Aka *Sherlock Holmes and the Spider Woman* and followed by *The Spider Woman Strikes Back!*

SPIRAL STAIRCASE, THE
★★★★ Fox, 1946, NR, 83 min. Dir: Robert Siodmak. Cast: Dorothy McGuire, George Brent, Ethel Barrymore, Kent Smith, Rhonda Fleming, Elsa Lanchester, Gordon Oliver, Sara Allgood.

Classic suspenser about a mute turn-of-the-century housemaid (the excellent McGuire) stalked by a maniac with a penchant for killing women with physical imperfections. Still genuinely chilling, this has a surprisingly modern look—electronic score, killer's POV stalking scenes, close-ups of black-gloved hands and a madly staring eye—that has influenced everyone from Hitchcock to Argento. Based on the novel *Some Must Watch* by Ethel Lina White and remade in 1975.

SPIRAL STAIRCASE, THE
★★☆ Warner, 1975, PG, 89 min.
Dir: Peter Collinson. Cast: Jacqueline Bisset,

Jacqueline Bisset is terrorized in The Spiral Staircase *(1975).*

Christopher Plummer, John Philip Law, Gayle Hunnicutt, Mildred Dunnock, Elaine Stritch, Sam Wanamaker, John Ronane.

Updated retread of the classic suspense tale with the beautiful Bisset as a mute girl terrorized by a handicap-hating psycho killer in her grandmother's storm-lashed mansion. Never released to U.S. theatres, this British flick has a good cast but is too mechanically put together to provide many chills or surprises.

SPIRITS
★★ Vidmark, 1991, R, 94 min.
Dir: Fred Olen Ray. Cast: Erik Estrada, Brinke Stevens, Oliver Darrow, Carol Lynley, Robert Quarry, Michelle Bauer.

If you can buy the premise of Mr. "CHIPS" himself as a troubled priest, you might enjoy this cut-rate Ray take on *The Legend of Hell House*. The psychic investigation of a reputedly haunted house leads to the possession of curvaceous Stevens. Carol is a friendly nun, Quarry an occult expert, and Michelle a seductive succubus. You've seen worse, especially from Fred.

ELSA LANCHESTER
(1902–1985)

Born Elizabeth Sullivan, Elsa studied dance with the legendary Isadora Duncan and later married the great Charles Laughton, remaining faithfully by him (despite his less-than-secret double life of homosexuality) until his death in '62. Despite four decades of film work, Lanchester will always be best remembered for her five-minute part in the title role of *Bride of Frankenstein,* an unforgettable vision of Nefertiti hair, bridal shroud, and miles of gray gauze, shrieking in horror at the first sight of her groom-to-be.

Bride of Frankenstein ('35), *Ladies in Retirement* ('41), *The Spiral Staircase* ('46), *Willard* ('71), *Terror in the Wax Museum* ('73), *Arnold* ('73).

SPLATTER UNIVERSITY
☆ Vestron, 1984, UR, 79 min.
Dir: Richard W. Haines. Cast: Francine Forbes,
Dick Biel, Cathy Lacommare, Ric Randig.

Humorless gore fest with Forbes as the new
teacher at a college being terrorized by your
usual brutal maniac after brainless coeds. No
mystery, no suspense, no talent, no sense, no
dice. Also out in a drier R version.

SPLIT, THE
See: *The Manster.*

SPLIT SECOND
★★ HBO, 1992, R, 90 min.
Dirs: Tony Maylam and Ian Sharp. Cast: Rutger
Hauer, Kim Cattrall, Neil Duncan, Michael J. Pollard,
Alun Armstrong, Pete Postlethwaite.

In this muddled sci-fi/horror flick Hauer is a
cop in rainy, near-future London who's on the
trail of a heart-ripping serial killer who turns
out to be an *Alien*-esque demon from hell in
cool shades. There's a certain amount of
atmosphere and Hauer is good, as always, but
this dank shocker makes little sense—especially the title.

SPONTANEOUS COMBUSTION
★☆ Media, 1990, R, 97 min. Dir: Tobe Hooper.
Cast: Brad Dourif, Cynthia Bain, Melinda Dillon,
Jon Cypher, William Prince, Dey Young.

Dourif has the ability to burn things with the
power of his mind in this second-rate
Firestarter rip-off. An interesting cast and some
potentially effective ideas are rendered useless
in what may be the most disappointing in a
string of cinematic disappointments from
Texas Chainsaw auteur Hooper.

SPOOK BUSTERS
★★ Warner, 1946, NR, 68 min. Dir: William
Beaudine. Cast: Leo Gorcey, Huntz Hall,
Bobby Jordan, Gabriel Dell, Tanis Chandler,
Douglass Dumbrille.

Routine Bowery Boys horror comedy with
Dumbrille as a mad scientist who wants to
transplant Sach's (Hall) brain into his pet
gorilla. Why? Does he want a stupid gorilla?
With corny old-house gags and situations, this
is strictly for fans of the series.

SPOOKIES
★★ SVS, 1985, R, 85 min.
Dirs: Eugenie Joseph, Thomas Doran, Brendan
Faulkner. Cast: Felix Ward, Maria Pechukes, Alec
Remser, Dan Scott, Lisa Friede, Nick Gionta.

A group of idiots looking for a place to party

stumble into an old house where an ancient
sorcerer hopes to use their life essence to
revive his comatose, unwilling bride. A female
partier is promptly possessed and then begins
stalking and offing her friends. This ambitious
but dumb New York cheapo has everything
from zombies to an oriental spider lady to a
cellar full of wind-breaking "muck men"; too
bad it doesn't have a story, good acting, or
professional direction. Mostly for fans of
excessive makeup FX. Original title: *Twisted
Souls.*

SPOOKS RUN WILD
★★ Goodtimes, 1941, NR, 69 min.
Dir: Phil Rosen. Cast: Bela Lugosi, Leo Gorcey,
Huntz Hall, Bobby Jordan, Dave O'Brien, Dorothy
Short, Dennis Moore, Angelo Rossitto.

Despite the unbeatable combo of Bela, Gorcey,
Hall, and little Angie, this remains an uninspired East Side Kids/Bowery Boys horror
comedy with our heroes encountering a Dracula-like magician in a creepy old house. An
odd plot twist seems to suggest that Lugosi is
a sex maniac with a taste for teen boys! British
title: *Ghosts in the Night.*

SPOOKY MOVIE SHOW, THE
See: *The Mask.*

SQUIRM
★★★ Vestron, 1976, R, 92 min. Dir: Jeff Lieberman.
Cast: Don Scardino, Patricia Pearcy, R. A. Dow,
Jean Sullivan, Fran Higgins, Peter MacLean.

The first of Lieberman's exceptional low-budgeters, this is also one of the scariest nature-
runs-amok movies ever. Following a heavy
thunderstorm, downed powerlines discharge
enough electricity into the soggy ground
around the tiny town of Fly Creek, Georgia, to
turn the local bloodworm population into a
seething mass of flesh-eating terror. Likable
leads and creepy Rick Baker worms-under-
the-skin makeup help make this an unherald-
ed winner.

STAB
See: *Still of the Night.*

STAGE FRIGHT
★☆ Media, 1982, R, 77 min.
Dir: John Lamond. Cast: Jenny Neumann,
Gary Sweet, Nina Landis, Max Phipps.

In this transparent Aussie slasher, a pretty
actress (Neumann) is unhinged by her mother's death and brutally begins slicing up her
fellow cast members in a play called "Comedy
of Death" with a shard of broken glass. A few

shocking, gory moments but mostly dross. Aka *Nightmares*.

STAGEFRIGHT
★★★☆ Imperial, 1987, UR, 90 min.
Dir: Michel Sovai. Cast: David Brandon, Barbara Cupisti, John Morghen, Martin Philips, Lori Parrel, Mary Sellars.

Dario Argento protégé Sovai directs this often-stunning, though familiarly plotted (script by a pseudonymous Joe D'Mato!) slasher thriller for maximum effect. A crazed killer escapes from a mental hospital and crashes the all-night rehearsal for a horror/musical play and begins eliminating the cast and crew in grisly ways. Also known as *Deleria, Aquarius,* and *Bloody Bird,* this is tension packed (check out the scene where the heroine tries to retrieve the key to her escape from under the killer's feet) and gory to the max and proves that there's still plenty of life in the generally thought dead slasher movie subgenre.

STANLEY
★★ VidAmerica, 1972, PG, 106 min.
Dir: William Grefé. Cast: Chris Robinson, Alex Rocco, Susan Carroll, Steve Alaimo, Mark Harris, Marcie Knight.

Maybe Florida-based director Grefé's most professional-looking movie, this is a well-acted but dull variation (with snakes) of *Willard.* "General Hospital" star Robinson is a Seminole Indian 'Nam vet with a shack full of pet snakes who uses said reptiles to take revenge on smarmy local clothing manufacturer Rocco (hilarious as usual) who specializes in snakeskin apparel. Too long and obvious, but with its share of moments, including Knight as an exotic dancer who bites the heads off snakes.

STARLIGHT SLAUGHTER
See: *Eaten Alive.*

STEPFATHER, THE
★★★ Embassy, 1987, R, 89 min.
Dir: Joseph Ruben. Cast: Terry O'Quinn, Shelley Hack, Jill Schoelen, Stephen Shellen, Charles Lanyer, Jeff Schultz.

Super suspense chiller in which a psycho (O'Quinn) keeps changing his name and appearance and marrying widows with children in an attempt to create the "perfect" family but always ends up hacking them to death when they fail to live up to his ideal of the American dream. Based on a true case, this features outstanding performances from O'Quinn (as a sort-of psychotic sitcom dad)

JILL SCHOELEN
(1970–)
The inheritor of Jamie Lee Curtis' scream queen crown, plucky Jill first caught our attention as the terrorized teen daughter of *The Stepfather.* The pretty brunette always brings a cheery spark to her imperiled heroine spots.

Chiller ('85), *The Stepfather* ('87), *Curse II: The Bite* ('89), *The Phantom of the Opera* ('89), *Cutting Class* ('89), *Popcorn* ('91), *When a Stranger Calls Back* ('93).

---

and Schoelen (as his latest stepdaughter, who catches on to his activities). Scary without being overly gory, this falls down only at the end with yet another stereotypical undying psycho-killer climax. Followed by *Stepfather II: Make Room for Daddy* and *Stepfather III: Father's Day.*

STEPFATHER II: MAKE ROOM FOR DADDY
★★☆ HBO, 1989, R, 86 min.
Dir: Jeff Burr. Cast: Terry O'Quinn, Meg Foster, Caroline Williams, Jonathan Brandis, Mitchell Laurance, Henry Brown.

Everyone's favorite bad dad (O'Quinn) is back in this surprisingly taut follow-up tracing our all-American psycho's escape from an asylum and his wooing of pretty suburban divorcee Foster. If you can swallow the premise that O'Quinn was somehow able to survive the multiple stab and bullet wounds inflicted on him at the end of part I, then there's much to enjoy here; this sequel resists the temptation to merely remake its original by taking a different, prequel-like approach showing how the stepfather chooses and entraps his victims-to-be. Williams steals it as Foster's best friend; hang tough through a slack final third for the hilarious wedding finale.

STEPFATHER III: FATHER'S DAY
★★ HBO, 1992, R, 109 min.
Dir: Guy Magar. Cast: Robert Wightman, Priscilla Barnes, Season Hubley, David Tom, John Ingle, Stephen Mendel.

After some plastic surgery—which conveniently allows the part to be played by a new actor—our deadly daddy (Wightman) woos and weds a suburban divorcee (Barnes) whose wheelchair-bound computer hacker son (Tom) soon catches on to his murderous activities. This is inferior to parts I and II and runs too long. Terry O'Quinn is sorely missed, but

Barnes and Hubley (the latter turning up late as the stepfather's next intended target) are excellent, and there's a bravura tree-shredder finale.

STEPHEN KING'S CAT'S EYE
See: *Cat's Eye.*

STEPHEN KING'S IT
See: *It.*

STEPHEN KING'S SILVER BULLET
See: *Silver Bullet.*

STILL OF THE NIGHT
★★☆ MGM/UA, 1982, R, 90 min. Dir: Robert Benton. Cast: Roy Scheider, Meryl Streep, Jessica Tandy, Josef Sommer, Sara Botsford, Joe Grifasi.

Handsome but sleepy psycho-shocker in the Brian De Palma tradition. Sadly, Benton is no Brian, and this tale of psychiatrist Scheider falling in love with possibly homicidal Streep lacks the usual flamboyance De Palma brings to such Hitchcockian material. Well made and elegantly scored by John Kander, but not very suspenseful; the arbitrary twist ending is the result of heavy pre-release restructuring. Shooting title: *Stab.*

STOLEN FACE
★★ Sinister Cinema, 1952, NR, 72 min. Dir: Terence Fisher. Cast: Paul Henreid, Lizabeth Scott, Andre Morell, Mary Mackenzie.

Early Hammer suspense-horror with Henreid as a plastic surgeon who loses Scott to another man and plans to recreate her by making over the scarred face of psycho Mackenzie. What do you think happens? Good acting and direction in this not very plausible chiller.

STRAIGHT ON TILL MORNING
★★ Thorn/EMI, 1972, R, 96 min. Dir: Peter Collinson. Cast: Rita Tushingham, Shane Briant, Tom Bell, Annie Ross, Clare Kelly, Katya Wyeth.

Tushingham is excellent in this predictable, drab thriller about a plain Jane who discovers that her handsome dream man is really a psychotic killer who hates women. Aka *Till Dawn Do Us Part* and *Dressed for Death.*

STRAIT-JACKET
★★★ RCA/Columbia, 1964, NR, 92 min. Dir: William Castle. Cast: Joan Crawford, Diane Baker, Leif Erickson, George Kennedy, Rochelle Hudson, Howard St. John, John Anthony Hayes, Edith Atwater.

Crawford is peerless as a jittery ex-mental patient who decapitated her unfaithful husband and his lover years ago and is now suspected in a new series of axings around a California farm. Castle's contribution to the post–*Baby Jane* menopausal-maniac cycle, this has a tight Robert Bloch script (somewhat anticipating the structure of the non-Bloch *Psycho II* movie) and strong acting from Crawford, Kennedy (as a creepy handyman who gets it in the neck), and Baker (in her best-ever role as Joan's "helpful" daughter). Lee Majors makes his screen debut as Crawford's headless hubby.

STRANGE ADVENTURE OF DAVID GRAY, THE
See: *Vampyr.*

STRANGE BEHAVIOR
★★☆ RCA/Columbia, 1981, R, 99 min. Dir: Michael Laughlin. Cast: Michael Murphy, Louise Fletcher, Fiona Lewis, Dan Shor, Dey Young, Scott Brady, Marc McClure, Arthur Dignam, Charles Lane, Elizabeth Chesire.

Oddball touches of humor highlight this New Zealand-shot but U.S.-set slasher. A series of gruesome, seemingly senseless murders sweeping a small midwestern town turn out to be the work of local teens transformed by the brain experiments of sultry Lewis (who has rarely had a better showcase for her pouty charms). Full of weird moments and surprising bits of casting, this hits its creative stride at a costume party where everyone bops to Lou Christie's great "Lightnin' Strikes" while dressed as a '60s TV sitcom character and a killer arrives sporting a Tor Johnson mask. Aka *Dead Kids.*

STRANGE CASE OF DR. JEKYLL AND MR. HYDE, THE
★★★ MPI, 1968, NR, 128 min. Dir: Charles Jarrott. Cast: Jack Palance, Billie Whitelaw, Denholm Elliott, Oscar Homolka, Leo Genn, Torin Thatcher.

Dan Curtis produced this excellent Canadian TV version of the oft-filmed tale. Palance (replacing Jason Robards) is remarkably good as both the timid doc and his leering, bestial alter-ego who, thanks to the makeup wizardry of Dick Smith, is less a monster here and more a satyr-like personification of lust and perversion.

STRANGE CASE OF DR. JEKYLL AND MR. HYDE, THE
★★ Cannon, 1989, NR, 52 min. Dir: Michael Lindsay-Hogg. Cast: Anthony Andrews, Laura Dern, Rue McClanahan, Nicholas Guest.

Bland, umpteenth redo of the classic schizo-scare tale. Andrews is earnest as the dull doc turned by his potion into a slick-haired, womanizing creep, but Dern (complete with Kate Hepburn accent) is out of her element in these stodgy period surroundings. Another of Shelley Duvall's "Nightmare Classics" entries, the original story may be a classic but this presentation will produce few nightmares.

STRANGER IN OUR HOUSE
See: *Summer of Fear*.

STRANGER IN THE HOUSE
See: *Black Christmas*.

STRANGER IS WATCHING, A
★★☆ MGM/UA, 1982, R, 92 min.
Dir: Sean S. Cunningham. Cast: Kate Mulgrew, Rip Torn, James Naughton, Barbara Baxley, Stephen Joyce, Shawn Von Schreiber.

Two years after killing a suburban housewife, savage psycho Torn returns to the scene of the crime to kidnap her daughter and husband's new girlfriend (Mulgrew), secreting them in the bowels of New York's Grand Central Station. Efficient adaptation of the Mary Higgins Clark suspense novel with slasher movie trimmings, this has first-rate acting from Torn and Mulgrew but often is needlessly sadistic.

STRANGER ON THE THIRD FLOOR
★★★ Turner, 1940, NR, 63 min. Dir: Boris Ingster. Cast: Peter Lorre, Margaret Tallichet, John McGuire, Elisha Cook, Charles Halton, Ethel Griffies.

An excellent B-movie, and one of Hollywood's first psycho-thrillers, casts McGuire as a reporter wrongly jailed for the murder of his landlord. When girlfriend Tallichet begins an investigation, she discovers the true killer to be ex-mental patient Lorre who prefers the company of dogs to people and refuses to go "back there." Full of striking camerawork and moody settings, this RKO picture is worth seeking out.

STRANGERS IN TOWN
See: *Eye of the Demon*.

STRANGER WITHIN, THE
★★ USA, 1974, NR, 74 min. Dir: Lee Philips. Cast: Barbara Eden, George Grizzard, Joyce Van Patten, David Doyle, Nehemiah Persoff.

TV's favorite genie Eden stars in this routine TV movie in which scripter Richard Matheson mixed *Rosemary's Baby* and *The Exorcist* with a science fiction slant. A woman whose husband has had a vasectomy becomes mysteriously pregnant and gives birth in record time while talking in strange languages and developing a taste for strong coffee, spicy food, and very cold temperatures. Pretty missable, apart from an eerie final scene of a nightgown-clad Barbara and several other women carrying their babies through a sun-dappled forest to meet their alien "husbands."

STRANGE WORLD OF PLANET X, THE
See: *Cosmic Monsters*.

STRANGLER, THE
★★★ Fox, 1964, NR, 89 min. Dir: Bert Topper. Cast: Victor Buono, Diane Sayer, Davey Davison, David McLean, Ellen Corby, Jeanne Bates.

Buono is ideally cast as an obese mama's boy obsessed with strangling nurses who remind him of the Florence Nightingales tending to his nagging, bedridden mom (Corby). Inspired equally by both *Psycho* and the real life Boston Strangler case, this suffers from an abrupt ending (leaving unclear the final fate of spunky, likable heroine Davison) but is worth seeing for Vic's intense acting in one of his few starring roles.

STRANGLER OF BLACKMOOR CASTLE, THE
★★★ Sinister, 1963, NR, 89 min.
Dir: Harald Reindl. Cast: Karin Dor, Ingmar Zeisberg, Dieter Eppler, Hans Neilsen.

A hooded knife murderer stalks the dank corridors of an English lord's castle in this eerie Edgar Wallace adaptation. Noteworthy for its (unacknowledged) influence on the Italian giallo genre, with its masked maniac chopping off heads, flashing knives, and threatening to pierce the eyes of beautiful Dor with a pair of diamond drills, this German thriller is definitely worth seeing.

STRANGLER OF THE SWAMP
★★☆ SVS, 1946, NR, 55 min.
Dir: Frank Wisbar. Cast: Rosemary La Planche, Robert Barrat, Blake Edwards, Charles Middleton, Effie Parnell, Nolan Leary.

Generally regarded as PRC's best horror film, this dated but interesting mood piece has nice moments of atmosphere and a few genuine chills. Middleton (formerly Ming the Merciless in the "Flash Gordon" series) is the gaunt ghost of a ferryman hanged for a murder he didn't commit who haunts those who executed him to their swampy deaths. Middleton is an effectively creepy presence and Wisbar uses his studio-bound swamp set to good effect, but much of the acting and dialogue are hopelessly stiff and stilted. The same story was previously filmed by Wisbar in Germany in 1930 as *Ferryman Maria*.

STRANGLER OF VIENNA, THE
See: *The Mad Butcher.*

STRANGLER'S MORGUE
See: *The Crimes of Stephen Hawke.*

STRAYS
★ MCA/Universal, 1992, R, 83 min. Dir: John McPherson. Cast: Kathleen Quinlan, Timothy Busfield, Claudia Christian, Heather and Jessica Lilley.

This awful made-for-cable rip-off of the superior '60s flick *Eye of the Cat* has Quinlan and Busfield moving into an old house haunted by killer kitty cats. Sexy Christian is wasted in this hooey scripted by one-time "Hardy Boy" Shaun Cassidy! Where's Parker Stevenson when you really need him?

STREET TRASH
★★★ Lightning, 1987, UR, 91 min. Dir: Roy Frumkes. Cast: Mike Lackey, Bill Chepil, Jane Arakawa, Vic Noto, Nicole Potter, R. L. Ryan, Tony Darrow, James Lorinz.

If you want a rude, crude, tasteless movie about rude, crude, tasteless people—this one's for you. A batch of foul-looking hooch called Tenafly Viper is causing derelicts to melt into colorful pools of slime, while a cop with a bad case of Clint Eastwood-itis, a couple of likable nitwits, and a junkyard kingpin battle a small-time Mafioso. As black a black comedy as you're ever gonna find, this is filled with virtuoso camerawork, good characters, hilarious dialogue, and lots of ultra gore. Ever see a bunch of guys play "keep away" with a severed penis? You'll see all that and more. And be sure to hang around for the riotous end credits theme.

STRIPPED TO KILL
★★☆ MGM/UA, 1987, R, 86 min. Dir: Katt Shea Ruben. Cast: Kay Lenz, Greg Evigan, Norman Fell, Tracy Crowder, Athena Worthey, Pia Kamakahi.

Lady cop Lenz goes undercover as a stripper to catch the slasher who is out to eliminate all of L.A.'s exotic female dancers. There's more stripping than slashing, but good direction and the always appealing Lenz make this a most watchable exploitation thriller.

STRIPPED TO KILL II
★★ MGM/UA, 1989, R, 83 min. Dir: Katt Shea Ruben. Cast: Maria Ford, Eb Lottimer, Karen Mayo Chandler, Marjean Holden, Birke Tan, Debra Lamb.

Luscious Ford is a stripper with ESP who dreams that her fellow dancers are being brutally slaughtered—just as they're being killed in real life. More g-strings and terror; the hor-

ror elements (borrowed from *Eyes of Laura Mars*) are more center stage, but this is still not much more than the usual T&A stuff.

STUDENT BODIES
★☆ Paramount, 1981, R, 86 min. Dir: Mickey Rose. Cast: Kristin Riter, Matthew Goldsby, Richard Brando, Joe Flood, Mimi Weddell, Joe Talarowski.

The laughs are few and far between in this witless slasher spoof. An unseen maniac who uses such diverse items as paper clips, plastic trash bags, and an eggplant ("Oh, God! Not an eggplant!") as weapons terrorizes a high school populated by the least-funny group of characters since the last *Cannonball Run* movie, while our plucky young heroine (Riter) tries to unmask him. Sloppy and amateurish; besides, the films this tries to parody are often a lot funnier without ever meaning to be.

STUDY IN TERROR, A
★★★ RCA/Columbia, 1966, NR, 95 min. Dir: James Hill. Cast: John Neville, Donald Houston, Anthony Quayle, John Fraser, Robert Morley, Judi Dench, Barbara Windsor, Adrienne Corri, Frank Finlay, Georgia Brown.

Sherlock Holmes (Neville) investigates the Jack the Ripper murders in this sharp, gory, and atmospheric original Holmes adventure. Solid acting, writing, and direction give this undeservedly neglected mystery-horror film an edge over most other post–Basil Rathbone Sherlock flicks. Shooting title: *Fog;* more-or-less remade as *Murder By Decree.*

STUFF, THE
★★☆ New World, 1985, R, 86 min. Dir: Larry Cohen. Cast: Michael Moriarty, Andre Marcovicci, Garrett Morris, Paul Sorvino, Danny Aiello, Patrick O'Neal, Scott Bloom, Alexander Scourby.

It's the most popular dessert food in America. It's low in calories, delicious tasting, and habit forming. It also takes you over body and mind, rotting you from the inside out and turning you into a hyperactive zombie. A kind of Ben and Jerry's version of *The Blob,* this horror-comedy features good performances from Moriarty as a dumb-smart industrial spy and Sorvino as a right-wing survivalist who comes off as sort of a combination of Sylvester Stallone and Jonathan Winters; though it doesn't always work, it's never dull.

SUBSPECIES
★★★ Paramount, 1991, R, 87 min. Dir: Ted Nicolaou. Cast: Michael Watson, Laura Tate, Angus Scrimm, Anders Hove, Michelle McBride, Irina Movila.

Pretty coeds Tate and McBride run afoul of a

modern-day Transylvanian vampire cult fronted by *Phantasm* Tall Guy Scrimm. Good direct-to-vid flick with flavorful atmosphere and acting, though the pack of cute-ugly *Gremlins*-like creatures who run rampant throughout seem to have been added as an afterthought. Sequels: *Bloodstone: Subspecies II* and *Bloodlust: Subspecies III*.

SUBSTITUTE, THE
★★ Paramount, 1993, R, 89 min.
Dir: Martin Donovan. Cast: Amanda Donohoe, Dalton James, Natasha Gregson Wagner, Marky Mark, Eugene Glazer, Patricia Gage.

Donohoe excels as the murderous title character in this otherwise formula made-for-cable entry in the psycho-bitch subgenre. Amanda is the sort of sub who sleeps with a handsome high school boy (James) and his dad (Glazer) and then kills to thwart various blackmailers and troublemakers. Donovan (*Apartment Zero*) dresses things up a bit, but it's all too routine to matter much, with Marky Mark's inauspicious acting debut making Vanilla Ice look like Cary Grant. Maybe if he took his clothes off…?

SUMMER OF FEAR
★★☆ Thorn/EMI, 1978, NR, 96 min.
Dir: Wes Craven. Cast: Linda Blair, Lee Purell, Carol Lawrence, Jeremy Slate, Macdonald Carey, Jeff East.

Originally shown as *Stranger in Our House*, this is a serviceable TV adaptation of a teen-oriented occult novel by Lois Duncan. When sultry cousin Purell comes to stay, Blair's mistrust of her is dismissed as petty jealousy until Linda discovers that Lee is a hillbilly witch. After a slow start, Craven builds tension well and Linda is always likable and capable making this an okay tele-chiller.

SUNDOWN: THE VAMPIRE IN RETREAT
★★★ Vestron, 1989, R, 104 min.
Dir: Anthony Hickox. Cast: David Carradine, Morgan Brittany, Jim Metzler, Deborah Foreman, Bruce Campbell, Maxwell Caulfield, Dana Ashbrook, John Ireland, M. Emmet Walsh, Dabbs Greer.

Hickox's follow-up to *Waxwork* is in many ways a better film and easily the best vampire western yet concocted. Metzler, wife Brittany, and their kids arrive in a dusty desert town they discover is inhabited entirely by vampires: nice bloodsuckers led by Carradine (they drink plasma from glasses like cocktails) and the neck-munching old guard led by Ireland. The film is well cast (apart from Metzler, who's awful) and quite funny in spots, with a trio of ZZ Top–inspired bearded vampires and a briefly viewed bat creature similar in design to the one featured in Coppola's *Bram Stoker's Dracula*.

SUPERNATURALS, THE
★★ Embassy, 1985, R, 86 min. Dir: Armand Mastroianni. Cast: Maxwell Caulfield, Talia Balsam, Nichelle Nichols, LeVar Burton, Bobby Di Ciccio, Scott Jacoby, Bradford Bancroft, Margaret Shendal.

A sort of *Southern Comfort of the Living Dead Meets 2,000 Maniacs*, this zombie-thon has northern recruits on Deep South training maneuvers falling victim to a squadron of zombified rebel troops massacred during the Civil War. An interesting cast (including members of the casts of the original "Star Trek" and "Star Trek: The Next Generation") and lots of backlit atmosphere give this a boost, even though not much happens until the final 20 minutes or so.

SUPERSTITION
★☆ Lightning, 1982, UR, 85 min.
Dir: James W. Roberson. Cast: James Houghton, Albert Salmi, Lynn Carlin, Larry Pennell, Jacqueline Hyde, Maylo McCashlin, Heidi Bohay, Billy Jacoby.

Shelved for several years after its completion, this low-budget, gored-up *Amityville* clone is about a troubled minister's family who move into a house suffering from a witch's curse and end up spiked, slashed, sawed, drowned, and even microwaved! Splatter fans should appreciate the squishy, unrated FX, while bad-acting buffs will groove on the hilarious histrionics of a surprisingly high-profile cast that includes Salmi, Hyde, and Pennell (Dash Riprock of "The Beverly Hillbillies").

SURF TERROR
See: *The Beach Girls and the Monster*.

SURVIVOR, THE
★★ Warner, 1980, PG, 93 min.
Dir: David Hemmings. Cast: Robert Powell, Jenny Agutter, Joseph Cotten, Angela Punch-McGregor, Ralph Cotterill, Peter Sumner.

Pilot Powell is the sole survivor of a jumbo jet crash and seeks help from psychic Agutter when ghosts of the passengers begin haunting him. After a powerful opening, this becomes little more than an extended "Twilight Zone" episode with a twist ending right out of *Carnival of Souls*.

SUSPIRIA
★★★★ Magnum, 1977, UR, 98 min.
Dir: Dario Argento. Cast: Jessica Harper, Joan Bennett, Alida Valli, Udo Kier, Stefania Casini, Flavio Bucci, Miguel Bosé, Rudolf Schundler.

DARIO ARGENTO
(1943–)

The Italian maestro of terror, Argento's "shock machine" art horror films are stylish, unpredictable, and impossible to copy thrillers mixing graphic violence, lush production trappings, and virtuoso camerawork with bizarre, seemingly meaningless titles. A major player in European cinema, he has yet to receive the attention in the United States that his unique work demands.

The Bird with the Crystal Plumage ('70), *Cat O'Nine Tails* ('71), *Four Flies on Grey Velvet* ('72), *Deep Red* ('76), *Suspiria* ('77), *Dawn of the Dead* (co-producer, co-screenplay, music, '79), *Inferno* ('80), *Unsane* ('83), *Creepers* ('85), *Demons* (producer, co-screenplay, '86), *Demons 2* (producer, co-screenplay, '87), *Terror at the Opera* ('88), *The Church* (producer, co-screenplay, '89), *Two Evil Eyes* (co-director, '90), *The Devil's Daughter* (producer, co-screenplay, '91), *Trauma* ('93).

Argento's masterpiece tells of the terror that befalls American ballet student Harper when she attends the celebrated Tanz Akademie at Frieberg, Germany. After several murders, a maggot infestation, and rumors of witchcraft, Jessica discovers that the Akademie is the haven of one Elena Marcus, a legendary witch known as the "Black Queen." From its shocking opening double-murder to its fiery finish, this is the Italian horror-art film at its very best, full of lush colors, bizarre set design, and very loud Goblin music. A must-see. Also out in a cut R version; followed by *Inferno*.

SVENGALI
★★★ Sinister Cinema, 1931, NR, 80 min.
Dir: Archie Mayo. Cast: John Barrymore, Marian Marsh, Bramwell Fletcher, Donald Crisp, Lumsden Hare, Luis Alberni.

Barrymore's remarkable performance, both chilling and amusing, helps you get through the dated melodramatics of this early talkie version of George Du Maurier's *Trilby*. As the sinister hypnotist who controls the life and will of the pretty singer Trilby, Barrymore exudes a chuckling, friendly sort of menace that makes his Svengali very human and offers a nice contrast to such stunningly creepy scenes as when he sends out his mind over the rooftops of Paris to take control of a sleeping Marsh.

SVENGALI
★★☆ VCL, 1954, NR, 82 min.
Dir: Noel Langley. Cast: Donald Wolfit, Hildegarde Knef, Terence Morgan, Derek Bond, Paul Rogers, David Kossoff.

Gorgeous color photography distinguishes this otherwise routine remake. Wolfit hams it up, as usual, as a sinister maestro who has an unrequited passion for the lovely Knef and uses his hypnotic power in a futile effort to gain her love. Glossy but a bit heavy-handed.

SWAMP THING
★★☆ Embassy, 1982, PG, 91 min.
Dir: Wes Craven. Cast: Louis Jourdan, Adrienne Barbeau, Ray Wise, David Hess, Nicholas Worth, Dick Durock.

Enjoyable film version of DC Comics' existential monster-hero: a scientist transformed by an experimental serum into the half-man, half-plant Swamp Thing. In his first adventure he battles evil genius Jourdan (in a campy performance) and loves evening-gown-clad Barbeau. Surprisingly lighthearted for a Craven film; the Swamp Thing makeup is pretty good, but other makeup FX are substandard. Followed by *The Return of Swamp Thing* and a short-lived TV series.

SWARM, THE
★☆ Warner, 1978, PG, 116 min.
Dir: Irwin Allen. Cast: Michael Caine, Katharine Ross, Richard Widmark, Henry Fonda, Olivia de Havilland, Fred MacMurray, Ben Johnson, Richard Chamberlain, Lee Grant, José Ferrer, Patty Duke, Bradford Dillman.

The master of disaster himself directs the biggest and funniest of the '70s killer bee movies. An extraordinary roster of stars look silly and get stung in this ludicrous tale of African killer bees descending on Texas. This has lots of second-rate special effects, and its ending is copped from Bert I. Gordon's chintzier but more fun *The Beginning of the End*.

SWEENEY TODD, THE DEMON BARBER OF FLEET STREET
See: *The Demon Barber of Fleet Street*.

SWEET KILL
See: *The Arousers*.

SWEET 16
★★ Vestron, 1982, R, 90 min.
Dir: Jim Sotos. Cast: Bo Hopkins, Susan Strasberg, Patrick Macnee, Don Stroud, Sharon Farrell, Dana Kimmell, Aleisha Shirley, Larry Storch, Michael Pataki, Steve Antin.

Stop me if you've heard this, but teens are being stalked by a mysterious slasher who may or may not be pretty birthday girl Shirley, whose beaus have a bad habit of turning up hacked to death. An exceptional cast for this sort of thing, but everything else is strictly ho-hum, with the last-minute explanation of the killer's motivation anything but convincing. The sub–Barry Manilow theme song has to be heard to be appreciated.

SYNGENOR
★★ Southgate, 1990, R, 98 min.
Dir: George Elanjian, Jr. Cast: Starr Andreeff, Mitchell Laurance, David Gale, Riva Spier, Charles Lucia, Melanie Shatner.

In this sequel of sorts to *Scared to Death,* genetic monstrosities bred as warriors escape and terrorize people at the corporate high-rise where they were created. Slow but well made, with some effective gore and a hilariously manic Wings Hauser–like performance from Gale as the chief baddie.

TALE OF A VAMPIRE
★★☆ Vidmark, 1992, R, 92 min.
Dir: Shimako Sato. Cast: Julian Sands, Suzanna Hamilton, Kenneth Cranham, Marian Diamond.

Sands is a pallid, soft-spoken vampire in London who falls for librarian Hamilton, who reminds him of a lost love; their relationship is complicated by Cranham, the late love's vengeful husband. Slow but well acted, this has beautiful visuals and a genuinely moving love story involving lost people who touch briefly before losing each other forever.

TALES FROM BEYOND THE GRAVE
See: *From Beyond the Grave.*

TALES FROM THE CRYPT
★★★ Starmaker, 1972, PG, 92 min.
Dir: Freddie Francis. Cast: Joan Collins, Peter Cushing, Ralph Richardson, Richard Greene, Ian Hendry, Patrick Magee, Barbara Murray, Nigel Patrick, Roy Dotrice, Robin Phillips.

One of Amicus' best anthologies, this stylish adaptation of the classic EC horror comics is very enjoyable. Five people trapped in an underground chamber with a mysterious monk (Richardson) witness vile deeds from their future—or perhaps their past—involving murder, infidelity, greed, cruelty, and jealousy. The best tales are the first (with Collins great as an icy murderess battling a homicidal Santa on Christmas Eve) and the third (with Cushing as an old man who is driven to suicide and then rises from his grave as a crumbly corpse). Francis' rich, visual direction beautifully captures the look and feel of comic panels come to life. Sequel: *Vault of Horror.*

TALES FROM THE CRYPT
★★☆ HBO, 1989–91, 90 min. per tape.
Dirs: Walter Hill, Robert Zemeckis, Richard Donner, Howard Deutch, Tom Holland, Mary Lambert, and Arnold Schwarzenegger. Cast: Lea Thompson, Demi Moore, Lance Henriksen, Amanda Plummer, Bill Sadler, Mary Ellen Trainor, William Hickey, Larry Drake, Joe Pantoliano, Audra Lindley, Robert Wuhl, Kelly Preston, M. Emmet Walsh, Gerrit Graham, Rick Rossovich, Gustav Vintas.

A clutch of episodes from the so-so HBO series based on the classic EC comic stories. Best segments are "And All Through the

FREDDIE FRANCIS
(1917–)

Academy Award–winning British cinematographer and director Francis lent his strong visual style to any number of Hammer and Amicus horrors in the '60s and '70s. Though his films often lack in the acting and narrative departments, they're always interesting to look at.

The Innocents (photographer, '61), *The Brain* ('62), *The Day of the Triffids* (co-director, '63), *Paranoiac* ('63), *Night Must Fall* (photographer, '64), *Nightmare* ('64), *The Evil of Frankenstein* ('64), *Dr. Terror's House of Horrors* ('65), *Hysteria* ('65), *The Skull* ('65), *The Psychopath* ('66), *The Deadly Bees* ('67), *Torture Garden* ('68), *Dracula Has Risen From the Grave* ('68), *Girly* ('70), *Trog* ('70), *The Vampire Happening* ('71), *Tales From the Crypt* ('72), *The Creeping Flesh* ('73), *Tales That Witness Madness* ('73), *Craze* ('74), *Son of Dracula* ('74), *The Ghoul* ('75), *Legend of the Werewolf* ('75), *The Elephant Man* (photographer, '80), *The Doctor and the Devils* ('85), *Cape Fear* (photographer, '91).

Santa gets his claws into Joan Collins in Tales From the Crypt *(1972).*

House" with Drake (of "L.A. Law") as a homicidal Kris Kringle, "Dig That Cat, He's Real Gone" with Pantoliano as a carny performer with the nine lives of a cat, and "Only Sin Deep" with Thompson as a hooker who sells her beauty for great wealth. Other episodes are fair to good, the casting is solid, and Kevin Yagher's clever Crypt Keeper puppet holds it all together.

TALES FROM THE CRYPT PART II
See: *Vault of Horror.*

TALES FROM THE DARKSIDE
★★☆ Worldvision, 1984–88, NR, 90 min. per tape. Dirs: Tom Savini, Jodie Foster, Armand Mastroianni, John Harrison, Michael McDowall, Ted Gershuny, others. Cast: Fritz Weaver, Tippi Hedren, Christian Slater, Justine Bateman, Keenan Wynn, Carol Kane, Lisa Bonet, Darren McGavin, Harry Anderson, Jean Marsh, Debbie Harry, Phyllis Diller, E. G. Marshall,

Jessica Harper, Susan Strasberg, William Hickey, Dick Miller, Brinke Stevens.

This syndicated horror anthology series got off to a shaky start but eventually developed into a fun minor hit, with good scripts derived from the work of Robert Bloch, Clive Barker, Stephen King, Harlan Ellison, and others. Among the notable segments are "Levitation," about a magician's illusion gone terribly awry; "The Circus," featuring a three-ring horror show of vampires, werewolves, and monsters; "Beetles," about a buggy Egyptian curse; and most especially, "Inside the Closet," in which a pretty coed shares a room with a creepy little closet creature.

TALES FROM THE DARKSIDE: THE MOVIE
★★☆ Paramount, 1990, R, 94 min. Dir: John Harrison. Cast: Deborah Harry, Christian Slater, Rae Dawn Chong, William Hickey, James Remar,

David Johansen, Robert Klein, Matthew Lawrence, Julianne Moore, Steve Busemi.

Modestly successful theatrical spin-off from the popular series with Harry as a cannibalistic suburban witch told three tales of dread by dinner-to-be Lawrence. A mummy terrorizes a college campus; a hitman is hired to rub out a murderous cat; and an artist has a run-in with a head-ripping gargoyle. Good makeup (supervised by Dick Smith) and a solid cast make this anthology a *big* improvement on the same production team's *Creepshow 2*.

TALES OF TERROR
★★★ Orion, 1962, NR, 88 min.
Dir: Roger Corman. Cast: Vincent Price, Peter Lorre, Basil Rathbone, Debra Paget, Maggie Pierce, Joyce Jameson, David Frankham, Leona Gage.

Well-presented trilogy of Edgar Allan Poe stories. In "Morella," Price is an alcoholic visited by his dying daughter who is possessed by her dead mother; "The Black Cat" sees Price and Lorre as rivals in a hilarious wine-tasting contest that ends when Peter bricks Vincent and unfaithful wife Jameson behind a cellar wall; and "The Case of Mr. Valdemar" offers a superbly evil Rathbone as a hypnotist who keeps subject Price's mind alive even after his body dies and begins to rot away. One of the most enjoyable of Corman's Poe films, with Richard Matheson's tight scripting benefiting from the anthology format, inventive direction, and a strong cast. Sort of remade as *Two Evil Eyes*, with the first story resurfacing as *The Haunting of Morella*.

TALES THAT WITNESS MADNESS
★★☆ Paramount, 1973, R, 90 min.
Dir: Freddie Francis. Cast: Kim Novak, Joan Collins, Donald Pleasence, Suzy Kendall, Jack Hawkins, Georgia Brown, Peter McEnery, Michael Jayston, Donald Houston, Michael Petrovitch.

An Amicus-inspired anthology set in a madhouse à la *Asylum*. Pleasence is a psychiatrist who tells a visitor to his institution (Hawkins in his last role—he was dubbed by Charles Gray) the bizarre case histories of his four most interesting patients. A young boy slaughters his disagreeable parents with an invisible pet tiger; an antique bicycle takes its rider on a trip into the past; a human-shaped tree develops a passion for its gardener; and a woman's teenage daughter falls victim to a cult of cannibalistic devil worshippers. Scripted by scream queen Jennifer Jayne under a pseudonym, this has a good cast and stylish direction to make the uneven material worthwhile; the first and third episodes are the best.

TANYA'S ISLAND
★★ Simitar, 1980, R, 82 min. Dir: Alfred Sole.
Cast: D. D. Winters [Vanity], Richard Sargent, Mariette Levesque, Don McCleod.

This beautifully photographed but sniggering sex-horror-fantasy is the ultimate variation on the *King Kong* theme. Winters (in her pre-Prince, pre-Vanity days) is a beautiful model living on a tropical island who fantasizes about having sex with a human-like ape, much to the homicidal jealousy of boyfriend Sargent. Winters' stunning good looks and the excellent Rick Baker–Rob Bottin ape costume make watchable an otherwise rather embarrassing effort.

TARANTULA
★★★ MCA/Universal, 1955, NR, 80 min.
Dir: Jack Arnold. Cast: John Agar, Mara Corday, Leo G. Carroll, Nestor Paiva, Ross Elliott, Raymond Bailey, Edwin Parker, Clint Eastwood.

In this crackerjack big-bug movie, Carroll is experimenting with enlarging animals to increase the world's food supply and accidentally unleashes a gigantic spider on a small Arizona community. One of Arnold's quintessential '50s shockers, this has excellent acting, writing, and special effects by Clifford Stine. Best scene: the giant tarantula peeking in a window at *Playboy* centerfold Corday as she prepares for bed.

TARANTULAS: THE DEADLY CARGO
★☆ Star Classics, 1977, NR, 98 min.
Dir: Stuart Hagmann. Cast: Claude Akins, Pat Hingle, Charles Frank, Deborah Winters, Bert Remsen, Howard Hesseman, Tom Atkins, Charles Siebert.

Another unimaginative made-for-TV *Jaws* copy with spiders instead of sharks, ants, or bees. A cargo plane bringing coffee beans and, unknowingly, tarantulas from Central America crashes in southern California, unleashing the creepy-crawlers to munch on farmworkers, cute little kids, and adulterers in a quaint little town. A good TV movie cast is wasted in this lifeless flick, which bears more than a passing resemblance to the later *Arachnophobia*.

TARGETS
★★★☆ Paramount, 1968, PG, 90 min.
Dir: Peter Bogdanovich. Cast: Boris Karloff, Tim O'Kelly, Nancy Hsueh, James Brown, Sandy Baron, Arthur Peterson, Mary Jackson, Tanya Morgan, Monty Landis, Peter Bogdanovich.

Karloff's valedictorial performance is featured in this near-brilliant blending of old and new horror. While aging horror star Byron Orlak

(Karloff) mourns the passing of the kind of screen horror they just don't make anymore, a very real monster, handsome young Bobby Thompson (O'Kelly) takes a high-powered rifle and begins a murder spree that climaxes at the very drive-in where Orlak's last movie is premiering. Karloff's performance is both heartbreaking and humorous, an unforgettable actor in an Oscar-caliber performance, while Bogdanovich has probably never made a better film than this, his first. Look for Mike Farrell (of "M*A*S*H") as a phone booth victim and clips from *The Terror*.

TASTE OF FEAR, A
See: *Scream of Fear*.

TASTE THE BLOOD OF DRACULA
★★★ Warner, 1970, PG, 91 min.
Dir: Peter Sasdy. Cast: Christopher Lee, Linda Hayden, Anthony Corlan, Geoffrey Keen, Peter Sallis, John Carson, Gwen Watford, Ralph Bates, Isla Blair, Michael Ripper.

In Victorian London three dissolute pillars of the community take part in a black magic ceremony to revive Count Dracula. When the men kill the Count's disciple (Bates), the vampire (Lee) seeks revenge by preying on their mawkish teen children. Good direction and an unusually strong subplot (involving moral hypocrisy and the sexual suppression of the young) make this a better than usual Hammer series entry, though the main plot makes little sense because Bates *had* to die to resurrect Dracula in the first place—so why bother with revenge?

TATTOO
★★ CBS/Fox, 1981, R, 103 min.
Dir: Bob Brooks. Cast: Bruce Dern, Maud Adams, John Getz, Leonard Frey, Rikke Borge, Peter Iacangelo.

Here's Dern the way you like him, as twitchy tattoo artist Karl Kinsky in a horny variation on *The Collector*. He is hired to apply some temporary tattoos on fashion model Adams, falls in love with her, and spirits her away to a remote beach house where he turns her into a living canvas for his greatest work. There's some impressive photography and good acting, but this pretentious erotic horror show is more unintentionally funny than anything else.

TEENAGE EXORCIST
★☆ AIP, 1991, R, 89 min.
Dir: Grant Austin Waldman. Cast: Brinke Stevens, Eddie Deezen, Robert Quarry, Michael Berryman, Jay Richardson.

Clunky horror comedy probably inspired by the non-success of Linda Blair's *Repossessed*. Stevens moves into a haunted house and ends up possessed; Deezen is the overaged pizza boy who attempts an exorcism. The cast is certainly game (especially Quarry, who's really very funny as an Irish priest), but they really shouldn't have bothered and neither should you.

TEENAGE FRANKENSTEIN
★★☆ RCA/Columbia, 1957, NR, 72 min.
Dir: Herbert L. Strock. Cast: Whit Bissell, Phyllis Coates, Gary Conway, Robert Burton.

Better known as *I Was a Teenage Frankenstein*, this American International trash classic features the very American Bissell as a British descendant of Baron Frankenstein living in L.A. He creates a putty-faced but beautifully built teen monster (Conway of "Land of the Giants" and *Playgirl* fame) from the bodies of several drag race casualties but doesn't count on the kid's need to cruise the hood for pretty girls. This fun Herman Cohen schlockfest is compromised by being released to video in an edited version (which *does*, however, restore the pale color climax) but is still essential.

TEENAGE MONSTER
See: *Meteor Monster*.

TEENAGE PSYCHO MEETS BLOODY MARY
See: *The Incredibly Strange Creatures Who Stopped Living and Became Mixed-Up Zombies*.

TEENAGE ZOMBIES
★ Sinister Cinema, 1958, NR, 73 min.
Dir: Jerry Warren. Cast: Katherine Victor, Don Sullivan, Steve Conte, Bri Murphy, Paul Pepper, Mitzie Albertson.

Mind-numbing junk involving three teen couples stranded on a remote island where they disrupt evil scientist Victor's plan to contaminate the world's water supply with her zombie-making pellets. Victor has the proper silky presence, but she's undercut by amateurish support and all the usual Warren ham-handedness. Unreleased until 1960, a bit late for the teen monster craze; remade as *Frankenstein Island*.

TEEN WITCH
★★ Media, 1989, PG-13, 1989, 96 min.
Dir: Dorian Walker. Cast: Robin Lively, Dan Gauthier, Zelda Rubinstein, Caren Kaye, Dick Sargent, Shelley Berman, Joshua Miller, Lisa Fuller.

Routine teen horror comedy (à la *Once Bitten*, *The Invisible Kid*, *My Best Friend Is a Vampire*, ad nauseum) with Lively as a girl who discovers that she's a descendant of Salem witches and uses her newfound powers to snare hunky golden boy Gauthier. A good cast does what it can in this mild fare for the "Babysitters Club" set.

TEEN WOLF

★★ Paramount, 1985, PG, 91 min.
Dir: Rod Daniel. Cast: Michael J. Fox, James Hampton, Susan Ursitti, Scott Paulin, Lorie Griffin, Jerry Levine.

Sort of an '80s I Was a Teenage Werewolf played for laughs, with Fox likable as the high school nobody who discovers that a hereditary lycanthropic curse is the easy route to becoming BMOC. Silly and slight, though sincere acting from Fox and Hampton (as his hirsute dad) make this a pleasant diversion. Followed by a cartoon series and Teen Wolf, Too.

TEEN WOLF, TOO

★☆ Paramount, 1987, PG, 95 min.
Dir: Christopher Leitch. Cast: Jason Bateman, John Astin, Kim Darby, Paul Sand, James Hampton, Estee Chandler.

Dopey sequel with Bateman (playing the cousin of the Michael J. Fox character from the first film) finding all the usual college freshman problems complicated by his penchant for turning into a werewolf. This horror comedy has no horror to speak of and precious little comedy; its non-success has spared us a Teen Wolf III, undoubtedly to have starred Kirk Cameron as yet another hairy relative of Fox's.

TELL-TALE HEART, THE

★★ Sinister Cinema, 1960, NR, 81 min.
Dir: Ernest Morris. Cast: Laurence Payne, Adrienne Corri, Dermot Walsh, Selma Vaz Diaz, John Scott, John Martin.

Cheapjack adaptation of Poe's classic tale, obviously made to cash in on the success of the same year's House of Usher. Edgar Allan Poe (Payne) dreams that he's a lame young man who falls in love with a pretty new neighbor (Corri) and murders his best friend (Walsh), whom she prefers. Driven to madness and destruction by the imagined beating of his victim's heart, Poe awakens from the dream to find the same events beginning in real life. This British film suffers from poor photography and a dull script that it tries to beef up via some gore and mild titillation. Aka Panic, Horror Man, and The Hidden Room of 1,000 Horrors.

TEMP, THE

★★ Paramount, 1993, R, 98 min. Dir: Tom Holland.
Cast: Timothy Hutton, Lara Flynn Boyle, Faye Dunaway, Steven Weber, Dwight Schultz, Oliver Platt, Colleen Flynn, Maura Tierney.

Sort of a Hand That Types the Memo psycho thriller with Boyle as the perfect temporary secretary for cookie company exec Hutton, who comes to suspect that she may be responsible for a series of deaths sweeping the corporation. The cast is excellent, but this is weakly structured and suffers from obvious studio cutting (the ending is especially anticlimactic), making it the weakest offering yet from Fright Night helmer Holland.

TEMPTER, THE

★★☆ Embassy, 1974, R, 94 min.
Dir: Alberto de Martino. Cast: Carla Gravina, Mel Ferrer, Arthur Kennedy, Alida Valli, George Coulouris, Anita Strindberg.

Sexually graphic Italiano Exorcist clone (filmed as L'Anticristo: The Antichrist) with Gravina as a wheelchair-bound girl possessed by the spirit of an executed witch ancestress. Carla curses, floats, vomits bile, seduces her father and brother, has sex with a goat, and develops facial lesions even Oxy Ten couldn't help. Good set design and effects work, but the photography is often out of focus and much of the supposedly shocking dialogue ("You stinking pot of shit!") laughably absurd.

TENANT, THE

★★★ Paramount, 1976, R, 124 min.
Dir: Roman Polanski. Cast: Roman Polanski, Isabelle Adjani, Shelley Winters, Melvyn Douglas, Jo Van Fleet, Lila Kedrova, Claude Dauphin, Bernard Fresson.

Polanski directs and stars in this semi-remake of his classic Repulsion. A timid Polish clerk (Polanski) living in Paris moves into the apartment of a suicide victim. When strange things begin to happen (faces staring at him from across the courtyard; personal objects of his predecessor appearing about the flat; neighbors making veiled threats), it would seem that he has become the victim of some bizarre conspiracy. Or has the dead girl returned to possess him and drive him into a reenactment of her sucide? Or maybe, just maybe, it's all in his mind. Beautiful images and an odd international cast (with Winters and Douglas in top form) make this an interesting, if not entirely successful, psychological chiller.

TENEBRAE

See: Unsane.

TEN LITTLE INDIANS

★★ Charter, 1975, PG, 99 min.
Dir: Peter Collinson. Cast: Oliver Reed, Elke Sommer, Richard Attenborough, Stephane Audran, Charles Aznavour, Herbert Lom, Gert Frobe, Maria Rohm.

An almost scene-for-scene remake of the unavailable-on-video 1966 version (both produced by Harry Alan Towers) with the setting changed to a deserted Iranian hotel and another befuddled international cast. It has the usual murders, suspects, and "surprise" ending, with inept direction from Collinson (half the movie seems shot from Hervé Villechaize's eye view) and Orson Welles as the voice of "Mr. Owen." The scene where Rohm is unexpectedly garroted provides this single shock. Remade again in 1989; British title: *And Then There Were None*.

TEN LITTLE INDIANS

★☆ Cannon, 1989, PG, 98 min.
Dir: Alan Birkinshaw. Cast: Donald Pleasence, Brenda Vaccaro, Frank Stallone, Sarah Maur Thorp, Herbert Lom, Moira Lister, Warren Berlinger, Paul L. Smith.

Another bad Harry Alan Towers remake of the Agatha Christie classic with another new setting (an African safari in the '30s) and a bored-looking cast just going through the motions. Even outfitting the story with some post–*Friday the 13th* slasher movie touches fails to bring it much excitement.

TENTACLES

★ Embassy, 1976, PG, 90 min.
Dir: Oliver Hellman [Ovidio Assonitis]. Cast: John Huston, Shelley Winters, Henry Fonda, Bo Hopkins, Claude Akins, Delia Boccardo, Cesare Danova, Sherry Buchanan.

Awful *Jaws* rip-off filmed by Italians in California, where a huge octopus munches on bathers, boatists, and skin divers, ultimately endangering the local sailing regatta. The stars phone in their performances (literally, in the case of Fonda), and the special effects look like they were filmed in someone's swimming pool. Shelley looks more formidable than the octo and, in fact, this would probably have been more frightening had *she* played the monster.

TERMINAL CHOICE

★★ Vestron, 1982, R, 98 min.
Dir: Sheldon Larry. Cast: Joe Spano, Diane Venora, David McCallum, Ellen Barkin, Robert Joy, Nicholas Campbell.

Well-crafted but mediocre *Coma*-type thriller about a Canadian hospital where patients are being killed by a mad doctor aided by the institution's computer system. This has a good cast (though "Hill Street Blues" regular Spano is annoying as the diminutive hero) and some suspense, but tighter editing might have made the plotting a bit more coherent. Aka *Trauma* and *Death Bed* and not released until 1984.

TERRIFIED

★★ Sinister Cinema, 1962, NR, 66 min.
Dir: Lew Landers. Cast: Rod Lauren, Tracy Olsen, Steve Drexel, Stephen Roberts, Denver Pyle.

Minor *Psycho* rip about a hooded fiend after several young people in a spooky ghost town where he buries his victims alive in wet cement. Not released until '64, this doesn't offer much, though any film this cheesy that's pretentious enough to list the leading lady's "coiffures" amongst the credits gets an extra point for chutzpah.

TERROR, THE

★★☆ Goodtimes, 1963, NR, 79 min.
Dir: Roger Corman. Cast: Boris Karloff, Jack Nicholson, Sandra Knight, Dick Miller, Dorothy Neumann, Jonathan Haze.

Remembered by Nicholson as the only movie he ever made without a plot (a debatable point), this infamous quickie was improvised to make use of the castle set from *The Raven* and two days owed on Karloff's contract, with the rest of the film finished on weekends with everyone from Francis Ford Coppola to Monte Hellman contributing to the shooting. Jack is profoundly miscast as a young Napoleonic soldier lost on the Baltic coast who falls in love with the apparent ghost of a beautiful baroness (Knight, at the time Mrs. Nicholson) and gets caught up in a plot against her aged husband (Karloff). Despite almost total confusion, a few of the scenes have a nice spooky quality to them, and the ending is a shocker.

TERROR

See: *Castle of Blood*.

TERROR

★★☆ United, 1978, R, 86 min.
Dir: Norman J. Warren. Cast: John Nolan, Carolyn Courage, James Aubrey, Sarah Keller, Tricia Walsh, Glynis Barber.

A Brit horror film director (Nolan) makes a Hammer-type period gothic about a witch who once cursed his family; soon after, various friends and associates begin dying in grisly ways. Marginally engrossing, this has an interesting depiction of the day-to-day workings of a low-budget movie studio and some especially gory killings: a girl is pinned to a tree with a knife; a guy is impaled on a spiked fence; and Nolan's male lover/assistant is nearly beheaded by an Argento-esque pane of glass. Originally co-billed with *Dracula's Dog*.

TERROR AT LONDON BRIDGE
★★ Fries, 1985, NR, 96 min.
Dir: E. W. Swackhamer. Cast: David Hasselhoff, Stepfanie Kramer, Adrienne Barbeau, Clu Gulager, Randolph Mantooth, Lane Smith, Lindsay Bloom, Ken Swofford, Rose Marie, Paul Rossilli.

The spirit of Jack the Ripper, trapped in a stone of London Bridge now located in Arizona, is unleashed by a drop of blood to commit a series of slashings investigated by hunky, perennially shirtless detective Hasselhoff. A good supporting cast and some effective scenes (Barbeau's body floating downriver à la *Frenzy*; *House of Wax*–type stalking scenes) help along this routine, *Night Stalker*–like TV film. Aka *Bridge Across Time* and *Arizona Ripper*.

TERROR AT RED WOLF INN
★★☆ Academy, 1972, R, 79 min.
Dir: Bud Townsend. Cast: Linda Gillin, John Neilson, Arthur Space, Mary Jackson, Margaret Avery, Janet Wood.

Quirky horror–black comedy about a family of amiable cannibals who lure young girls to their exclusive country inn to unknowingly be served up as the blue plate special. This entertaining minor flick is helped along by its talented cast, including personable heroine Gillin and familiar vets Space and Jackson. Also released as *Terror House* and *The Folks at Red Wolf Inn*.

TERROR AT THE OPERA
★★★☆ Southgate, 1988, UR, 107 min.
Dir: Dario Argento. Cast: Cristina Marsillach, Ian Charleson, Urbano Barberini, Daria Nicolodi, William McNamara, Coralina Cataldi Tassoni, Francesa Cassola, Antonella Vitalé.

Soprano hopeful Betty (Marsillach) is promoted to star of a controversial televised version of Verdi's *Macbeth* when the diva literally breaks a leg. Soon after her triumphant debut, however, she is hounded by a hooded admirer who begins a series of murders in gory tribute, forcing our heroine to watch by tying her down and pinning her eyes open. Argento's first major flop in his home country, never released to U.S. theatres, this pulse-pounding near-masterpiece (redundantly retitled from the more pithy *Opera*) is full of amazing bits of cinematic wizardry, suspenseful situations, and inventive variations on Dario's tried-and-

true grabbag of bizarre images and stylish excesses. A virtual summation of Argento's underappreciated career, this is a must for Dario buffs and pulsating brain tissue fans everywhere. Also out in an R version.

TERROR CASTLE
See: *The Virgin of Nuremberg*.

TERROR CHAMBER, THE
See: *The Torture Zone*.

TERROR CIRCUS
★ Sinister Cinema, 1973, R, 86 min.
Dir: Alan Rudolph. Cast: Andrew Prine, Maneela Thiess, Gyl Roland, Sherry Alberoni.

Bargain basement buffoonery with the everwacky Prine as a madman who imprisons women he tortures and humiliates in his private "circus" while his mutant dad (suffering from radiation poisoning) runs amok. It's hard to imagine the director of *this* going on to anything else, but Rudolph managed to survive this debacle and become a Robert Altman protégé, eventually directing cult classics like *Welcome to L.A.* and *Remember My Name*. Aka *Barn of the Naked Dead* and *Nightmare Circus*.

TERROR CREATURES FROM THE GRAVE
★★☆ Sinister Cinema, 1965, NR, 83 min.
Dir: Ralph Zucker. Cast: Barbara Steele, Walter Brandi, Marilyn Mitchell, Riccardo Garrone, Alfredo Rizzo, Alan Collins.

In this moody, offbeat Steele vehicle, a paralyzed scientist is murdered by his perfidious wife (guess who?) and associates, and his spirit calls on the zombified forms of black plague victims to rise up and avenge him. The film has appropriately dank B&W photography, a haunting theme song ("Pure water will save you . . ."), and La Steele in her usual fine form. Original Italian title: *Cinque Tombe per un Medium: Five Graves for a Medium*. Released in England as *Coffin of Terror* and aka *Tombs of Horror* and *Cemetery of the Living Dead*.

TERROR EYES
See: *Night School*.

TERROR FACTOR, THE
See: *Scared to Death* (1980).

TERROR FROM THE YEAR 5,000
★★ Sinister Cinema, 1958, NR, 70 min.
Dir: Robert J. Gurney. Cast: Ward Costello, Joyce Holden, Frederic Downs, John Stratton, Fred Herrick, Salome Jens.

Scientists experimenting with a time machine

in a lonely old house bring a hideously disfigured woman back from a post-apocalyptic future, and she escapes from the lab and goes on a murder spree. This moody, minor '50s sci-fi/horror has a good performance by Jens and some offbeat touches (like the terror hypnotizing victims with her glittery fingernails) to offset the usual low-budget drawbacks. British title: *Cage of Doom*.

TERROR HOUSE
See: *Terror at Red Wolf Inn*.

TERROR IN SPACE
See: *Planet of the Vampires*.

TERROR IN THE HAUNTED HOUSE
★★ Rhino, 1958, NR, 76 min.
Dir: Harold Daniels. Cast: Cathy O'Donnell, Gerald Mohr, William Ching, John Qualen, Barry Bernard.

O'Donnell is a new bride taken by groom Mohr to a Florida estate that, coincidentally, has been invading her nightmares for years and was once the setting for several brutal ax murders. This slow, talky thriller is best known for its use of subliminal shock devices (Rhino's print substitutes new, animated inserts for the original subliminal cuts) but with or without them is still pretty dull, apart from a somewhat exciting final five minutes. Original title: *My World Dies Screaming*.

TERROR IN THE MIDNIGHT SUN
See: *Invasion of the Animal People*.

TERROR IN THE SWAMP
★★☆ Video Treasures, 1976, PG, 95 min.
Dir: Joy Houck, Jr. Cast: Jack Elam, Dub Taylor, Dennis Fimple, John David Carson, Bill Thurman, Catherine McCleannan.

A couple of knuckleheaded University of Chicago anthropology students search the Louisiana bayous for a legendary Bigfoot-like creature, which they eventually come face to hairy face with. There's a likable cast and a nice tongue-in-cheek attitude in this pleasant drive-in monster pic, which was originally released as *Creature From Black Lake*.

TERROR IN THE WAX MUSEUM
★★ Vestron, 1973, PG, 88 min.
Dir: Georg Fenady. Cast; Ray Milland, Broderick Crawford, Elsa Lanchester, Maurice Evans, John Carradine, Shani Wallis, Louis Hayward, Patric Knowles, Nicole Shelby, Mark W. Edwards.

Well-cast but routine low-budget mystery unconvincingly set in a turn-of-the-century London wax museum being terrorized by a killer who may or may not be the figure of Jack the Ripper come to life. Surprisingly bloodless and old-fashioned for its time, this features Lanchester hamming it up as a greedy biddy who's a constant thorn in the side of museum curator Milland.

TERROR IN THE WOODS
See: *The Forest*.

TERROR IN TOYLAND
See: *Christmas Evil*.

TERROR IS A MAN
★★☆ Sinister Cinema, 1959, NR, 89 min.
Dir: Gerardo de Leon. Cast: Francis Lederer, Greta Thyssen, Richard Derr, Oscar Keese, Lilia Duran, Florey Carlos.

The first and best Filipino horror film, this grim variation on *The Island of Dr. Moreau* is better than you'd imagine. Lederer is Dr. Girard, whose island-bound experiments in advanced evolution have transformed a leopard into a pain-seared, bandage-swathed "man." Dank photography and good acting beef up this talky flick, which finally bursts into action in the last half hour. A mildly gory operation scene is accompanied by a telephone-sounding warning-bell gimmick. Aka *Blood Creature*.

TERROR OF DR. HITCHCOCK, THE
See: *The Horrible Dr. Hitchcock*.

TERROR OF FRANKENSTEIN
★★ Vestron, 1975, PG, 91 min.
Dir: Calvin Floyd. Cast: Per Oscarsson, Leon Vitali, Nicholas Clay, Stacey Dorning.

If you can stay awake, you'll discover that this Swedish-Irish version of Mary Shelley's classic is the closest to its source filmed to date. Oscarsson is good as the ghoulish but sympathetic monster who's driven to murder by his all-consuming loneliness, but being true to the novel doesn't necessarily make for a good movie, as this slow, unimaginative film clearly demonstrates. Aka *Victor Frankenstein*.

TERROR OF GODZILLA
See: *Terror of Mechagodzilla*.

TERROR OF MECHAGODZILLA
★★ Paramount, 1976, PG, 80 min.
Dir: Inoshiro Honda. Cast: Katsuhiko Sasaki, Tomoko Ai, Akihiko Hirata, Tado Nakamura.

A resurrected Mechagodzilla and a huge sea monster called Titanosaurus battle our scaly hero in this so-so (and surprisingly downbeat) entry in the endless series. Unfortunately, Paramount's tape is of the badly edited TV print. Original title: *Mechagoira no Gyakusyu: Revenge of Mechagodzilla* and aka *Terror of Godzilla* and *Monsters from a Prehistoric Planet.*

TERROR OF SHEBA, THE
See: *Persecution.*

TERROR OF THE DOLL
See: *Trilogy of Terror.*

TERROR ON TOUR
☆ Media, 1980, R, 88 min. Dir: Don Edmonds. Cast: Rick Styles, Chip Greeman, Rich Pemberton, Lisa Rodriguez.

Totally worthless slasher about a maniac who dresses up like one of the Clowns, a glitter-rock band, and kills prostitutes. The clowns who made this cheapskate chiller bring it neither style nor energy, making it a complete waste of time and videotape.

TERROR OUT OF THE SKY
★☆ Star Classics, 1978, NR, 96 min. Dir: Lee H. Katzin. Cast: Efrem Zimbalist, Jr., Tovah Feldshuh, Dan Haggerty, Lonny Chapman, Ike Eisenmann, Steve Franken.

They really botched this sequel to the above-average TV film *The Savage Bees*, as this lacks almost everything that made the first one so great. The bees are back but are given a backseat to the (who cares?) love triangle between Feldshuh (playing Gretchen Corbett's old character), older Zimbalist, and beefy Haggerty. Original title: *Revenge of the Savage Bees.*

TERROR STRIKES!, THE
See: *War of the Colossal Beast.*

TERROR TRAIN
★★★ Key, 1980, R, 97 min. Dir. Roger Spottiswoode. Cast: Jamie Lee Curtis, Ben Johnson, Hart Bochner, David Copperfield, Derek MacKinnon, Sandee Currie, Timothy Webber, D. D. Winters [Vanity].

John Alcott photographed this lush-looking slasher with Jamie once again on the run from a masked killer—in this case the emotionally scarred victim of a cruel hazing stunt out to get the hazers during a costume party on a speeding excursion train. Fine work from JLC and Johnson as the sympathetic conductor and one thing's for sure: you'll *never* guess who the killer's disguised as!

TERROR UNDER THE HOUSE
★★ Bargain, 1971, PG, 89 min. Dir: Sidney Hayers.

Cast: Joan Collins, James Booth, Ray Barrett, Sinead Cusack, Tom Marshall, Kenneth Griffith.

British suspense film about a family who imprison and plan to murder the man they hold responsible for the rape-murder of their young daughter. Starts off well but then becomes increasingly shrill and strident, though the twist ending packs a punch. Aka *Revenge, Inn of the Frightened People,* and *Behind the Cellar Door.*

TERRORVISION
★★ Lightning, 1986, R, 82 min. Dir: Ted Nicolaou. Cast: Gerrit Graham, Mary Woronov, Diane Franklin, Chad Allen, Bert Remsen, Alejandro Rey, Jonathan Gries, Jennifer Richards.

The new satellite dish hooked up by dopey do-it-yourselfer Stanley Putterman (Graham) sucks a hungry space monster into his TV set that makes quick work of the swingin' Putterman clan. Though one of Empire Pictures' more standable horror-comedies (often resembling a cross between "Married with Children" and "The Outer Limits"), this wastes both Graham and Woronov, getting most of its laughs from veteran Remsen and busty Richards as a foul-mouthed TV horror hostess called Medusa.

TERROR WITHIN, THE
★★ MGM/UA, 1989, R, 88 min. Dir: Thierry Notz. Cast. George Kennedy, Andrew Stevens, Star Andreeff, Terri Treas.

Routine low-rent *Alien* set in a futuristic underground desert complex where scientists

---

JAMIE LEE CURTIS
(1958–)

Daughter of Janet Leigh and Tony Curtis, the coltish JLC made a considerable impact in her 1978 debut feature, *Halloween,* and quickly came to personify the modern scream queen: strong, beautiful, and resourceful—a survivor. After several further forays into the genre, however, Jamie graduated to bigger, though not usually better, things, recently making a mini-comeback with a couple of big-budget shockers more than a little reminiscent of her earlier horror work.

Halloween ('78), *The Fog* ('80), *Prom Night* ('80), *Terror Train* ('80), *Road Games* ('81), *Halloween II* ('81), *Coming Soon* ('83), *Blue Steel* ('90), *Mother's Boys* ('93).

are terrorized by a monster violently born from a hapless woman raped by a mutant. Sort of like a slicker version of *Creepozoids*, with okay acting but substandard FX. Followed by a sequel.

TERROR WITHIN II, THE

★☆ Vestron, 1991, R, 85 min.
Dir: Andrew Stevens. Cast: Andrew Stevens, Stella Stevens, R. Lee Ermey, Chick Vennera, Burton "Bubba" Gilliam, Clare Hoak.

This needless sequel/remake has Andy battling gooey mutants while trying to find the cure for a plague decimating the world's population. It's a dumb hashing-together of ingredients from *Alien, The Blob, It's Alive!,* and *Mad Max: Beyond Thunderdome,* with especially silly mutant makeup. The writer/director is clearly a big fan of the star.

TEXAS CHAINSAW MASSACRE, THE

★★★★ MPI, 1974, R, 83 min.
Dir: Tobe Hooper. Cast: Marilyn Burns, Gunnar Hansen, Edwin Neal, Allen Danziger, Teri McGinn, Paul A. Partain, Jim Siedow, William Vail.

A quintet of teens visiting a deserted old house in the Texas wilderness fall victim to a family of sadistic, inhuman cannibals. Despite its infamy, this white-knuckle shocker isn't as graphically violent as it's reputed to be but relies instead on sound, editing, and breakneck pacing to create its unforgettable horror and suspense. After a slow start, it begins to

---

TOBE HOOPER
(1946–)

The Texas kid who startled the world with maybe the greatest exploitation title of all time, *The Texas Chainsaw Massacre,* Hooper has shown a real talent for exploring the darker side of the human condition. Unfortunately, following his biggest hit, the Spielberg-influenced *Poltergeist,* he seems to have lost his edge through a series of increasingly colorless and disappointing big-budget studio efforts.

The Texas Chainsaw Massacre ('74), *Eaten Alive* ('76), *Salem's Lot* ('79), *The Funhouse* ('81), *Poltergeist* ('82), *Lifeforce* ('85), *Invaders From Mars* ('86), *The Texas Chainsaw Massacre Part 2* ('86), *Spontaneous Combustion* ('90), *I'm Dangerous Tonight* ('90), *Body Bags* (co-director, '93), *Night Terrors* ('93).

---

masterfully tighten the screws and never lets up until the final frame; this baby can cause you to break out in a sweat even when seen in the dead of winter. Definitely Hooper's finest hour, and it's narrated by John ("Night Court") Larroquette! Followed by *The Texas Chainsaw Massacre Part 2, Leatherface: The Texas Chainsaw Massacre III,* and *Return of the Texas Chainsaw Massacre.*

TEXAS CHAINSAW MASSACRE PART 2, THE

★★ Video Treasures, 1986, UR, 100 min.
Dir: Tobe Hooper. Cast: Dennis Hopper, Caroline Williams, Bill Moseley, Jim Siedow, Bill Johnson, Lou Perry.

This overlong, underwritten sequel features Hopper in a zesty performance as a retired Texas Ranger after the chainsaw family (who murdered his nephew and drove his niece mad), who are now relocated under a dilapidated old Wild West amusement park. Far bloodier than the original, with gory but routine Tom Savini makeup FX, this has some nice black comic touches (like the chainsawers becoming popular Houston caterers) but completely lacks the pacing and grisly atmosphere of its classic predecessor.

THAT COLD DAY IN THE PARK

★☆ Republic, 1969, R, 112 min.
Dir: Robert Altman. Cast: Sandy Dennis, Michael Burns, Luana Anders, Michael Murphy, Susanne Benton, John Garfield, Jr.

One of Altman's earliest and worst films is this demented role-reversal remake of *The Collector.* A repressed spinster (Dennis) takes in a bedraggled younger man (Burns) she falls obsessively in love with, imprisoning him and finally turning to murder in order to keep him. This is more funny than anything else, with Sandy a hoot as the deranged heroine and Burns annoyingly smug as the (often nude) object of her twisted desire.

THEATRE OF BLOOD

★★★★ MGM//UA, 1973, R, 104 min.
Dir: Douglas Hickox. Cast: Vincent Price, Diana Rigg, Ian Hendry, Robert Morley, Coral Browne, Harry Andrews, Jack Hawkins, Milo O'Shea, Diana Dors, Michael Hordern, Dennis Price, Madeline Smith.

This tailor-made vehicle is the hilarious pinnacle of Price's horror film career. As Edward Lionheart, Price has the sort of role actors dream of: a mad, incredibly egotistical Shakespearean actor who avenges himself on the critics who denied him a coveted award by murdering them in various manners inspired by the Bard's works—stabbing, burning,

Vincent Price cradles a dying Diana Rigg in
Theatre of Blood *(1973).*

beheading, impaling, and dismembering his
victims in grisly fashion. Energetic performing
from Price, Rigg (both of them in a variety of
disguises), Morley, Andrews, Dors, and others
combine with Anthony Greville-Bell's witty
script, Michael J. Lewis' lovely score, and
Hickox's smooth direction to create a high-
class shocker of unusual depth and intelligence.

THEATRE OF DEATH

★★★ United, 1967, PG, 88 min. Dir: Samuel Gallu.
Cast: Christopher Lee, Lelia Goldoni, Jenny Till,
Julian Glover, Evelyn Laye, Ivor Dean.

An undeservedly neglected mystery-horror
with Lee great in a good, through small, role
as the bitchy head of a Parisian grand guignol
theatre troupe. When a series of vampire-like
murders begin, police doctor Glover suspects
a member of Lee's company—perhaps even
the director himself. This British film suffers
from obviously fake, studio-bound settings
but has a solid script, good cast, and attractive
Gil Taylor photography as compensation.
Good Lee line, commenting on an actor's performance: "That was about as frightening as

VINCENT PRICE
(1911–1993)

The modern master of movie menace
was born in St. Louis, Missouri, and
made his Broadway debut in *Victoria
Regina* opposite Helen Hayes. A contract
with Universal Pictures placed him in a
couple of horror features, but it wasn't
until the success of the 1953 3-D smash
House of Wax that Price was given a
plum horror part. He thereafter solidi-
fied his terror king reputation with
appearances in several delightfully crass
William Castle chillers and the inexpensive but lush-looking Edgar Allan Poe
adaptations of Roger Corman. Velvet-
voiced Vinnie was also a world-
renowned art expert, author, and
gourmet. Once referred to as the "King
of the Hamsters," Price was actually a
much better and more versatile actor
(especially in comedy) than he was ever
given credit for by most mainstream
film critics.

Tower of London ('39), *The Invisible Man
Returns* ('40), *The House of Seven Gables*
('40), *Shock* ('46), *Abbott and Costello Meet
Frankenstein* (voice only, '48), *House of
Wax* ('53), *The Mad Magician* ('54), *The
Fly* ('58), *House on Haunted Hill* ('58), *The
Bat* ('59), *Return of the Fly* ('59), *The Tin-
gler* ('59), *House of Usher* ('60), *The Pit and
the Pendulum* ('61), *Tales of Terror* ('62),
Tower of London ('62), *The Raven* ('63),
Diary of a Madman ('63), *Twice-Told Tales*
('63), *The Haunted Palace* ('64), *The Come-
dy of Terrors* ('64), *The Last Man on Earth*
('64), *The Masque of the Red Death* ('64),
Tomb of Ligeia ('65), *Dr. Goldfoot and the
Bikini Machine* ('65), *War-Gods of the Deep*
('65), *Dr. Goldfoot and the Girl Bombs* ('66),
House of 1,000 Dolls ('67), *The Conqueror
Worm* ('68), *Spirits of the Dead* (narrator,
'69), *The Oblong Box* ('69), *Scream and
Scream Again* ('70), *Cry of the Banshee*
('70), *The Abominable Dr. Phibes* ('71), *An
Evening with Edgar Allan Poe* ('72), *Dr.
Phibes Rises Again!* ('72), *Theatre of Blood*
('73), *Madhouse* ('74), *The Devil's Triangle*
(narrator, '74), *The Monster Club* ('81),
House of the Long Shadows ('83), *Bloodbath
at the House of Death* ('84), *Once Upon a
Midnight Scary* ('85), *Escapes* ('86), *The
Offspring* ('87), *Dead Heat* ('88), *Edward
Scissorhands* ('90).

an old woman spearing a cocktail cherry!" Aka *Blood Fiend* and *Female Fiend*.

THEM!

★★★★ Warner, 1954, NR, 92 min.
Dir: Gordon Douglas. Cast: James Whitmore, Edmund Gwenn, Joan Weldon, James Arness, Onslow Stevens, Sean McClory, Chris Drake, Sandy Descher.

Mysterious disappearances and bizarre destruction in the New Mexico desert turn out to be the work of a colony of radiation-enlarged ants. Moody and suspenseful, this was the first and best of the '50s big-bug thrillers, with a taut script, top acting, and excellent full-scale monster mock-ups. Look for Fess Parker, Dub Taylor, Richard Deacon, and Leonard Nimoy in small roles.

THERE'S NOTHING OUT THERE

★★☆ Prism, 1990, R, 90 min.
Dir: Rolfe Kanefsky. Cast: Craig Peck, Wendy Bednarz, Mark Coliver, Bonnie Bowers.

This entertaining semi-amateur semi-spoof has a group of college kids on spring break being eaten by a slimy green (and only briefly seen) monster while staying at a cabin in the woods. A nice touch is making the reluctant hero (Peck) a horror film buff who starts to figure out what's going on but is never believed. A not so nice touch is the way this exploits the bodies of its (admittedly attractive) female cast members, most all of whom have gratuitous nude or topless scenes.

THEY CAME FROM WITHIN

★★★ Vestron, 1975, R, 87 min. Dir: David Cronenberg. Cast: Paul Hampton, Joe Silver, Lynn Lowry, Barbara Steele, Allan Migicovsky, Susan Petrie.

Cronenberg's first feature is like a venereal disease remake of *Night of the Living Dead*. A scientifically created parasite, designed to replace diseased body parts but developing instead into a sex-and-violence craving monster, runs rampant through a Canadian apartment complex, transforming its residents into sex-crazed zombies. Tasteless in a good-humored sort of way, this has impressive low-budget Joe Blasco makeup effects and some good shocks, like the phallic parasite attacking scream queen Steele in her bathtub or bursting from Migicovsky's stomach. Originally titled *Shivers*; British title: *The Parasite Murders*.

THEY LIVE!

★★ MCA/Universal, 1988, R, 95 min.
Dir: John Carpenter. Cast: Roddy Piper, Meg Foster, Keith David, Raymond St. Jacques, George "Buck" Flower, Peter Jason.

Carpenter's politically tinged reworking of *Invasion of the Body Snatchers* has pro wrestler Piper as an out-of-work construction worker who discovers that our planet is really run by ghoulish aliens in human form. An interesting, funny idea gets medium handling in this sci-fi/horror outing, which is marred mostly by too much macho posturing and too many dumb plot twists (like Piper surviving a fall through a plate glass window and down a rocky hillside with nary a scratch).

THEY SAVED HITLER'S BRAIN!

★ United, 1963, NR, 74 min.
Dir: David Bradley. Cast: Walter Stocker, Audrey Clarie, Carlos Rivas, John Holland, Dani Lynn, Marshall Reed, Nestor Raiva, Bill Freed.

Hilariously awful trash classic involving Nazis, spies, nerve gas, kidnapping, killings, and the living, decapitated head of you-know-who, referred to here as Mr. H. Filmed initially in the late '50s or early '60s, this has a new opening shot several years later that has nothing to do with the rest of the movie! Hitler's head hasn't much to do—it does burn well, however—but there *is* some nice photography from film noir veteran Stanley Cortez. Originally titled *Madmen of Mandoras* and aka *The Amazing Mr. H* and *The Return of Mr. H*.

THING, THE

★★★★ Turner, 1951, NR, 80 min. Dir: Christian Nyby. Cast: Kenneth Tobey, Margaret Sheridan, Robert Cornthwaite, Douglas Spencer, Dewey Martin, James Young, John Dierkes, James Arness.

Howard Hawks produced this classic '50s monster movie in which scientists and the military debate the fate of an alien found frozen in a block of ice near a crashed spaceship at the North Pole. The alien (Arness) has its own ideas, however, as it thaws out and goes on a murderous rampage. A brilliant mixture of sci-fi and traditional horror film elements (the monster looks like the Frankenstein monster and drinks blood like Dracula), this has a terrific no-star cast, sharp dialogue, some real scares, and an eerie Dimitri Tiomkin score. Based on the story "Who Goes There?" by John Campbell and aka *The Thing From Another World*.

THING, THE

★★★ MCA/Universal, 1982, R, 108 min.
Dir: John Carpenter. Cast: Kurt Russell, Wilford Brimley, Richard Dysart, Donald Moffat, Keith David, David Clennon, Richard Masur, T. K. Carter.

This misunderstood, ultra-violent remake is closer to the original Campbell story and just may be the goriest major studio film *ever*. At an Antarctic research station, a long-dormant alien monstrosity takes over the bodies of a number of men as it goes on a destructive rampage. Although beautifully photographed and sprinkled with clever homages to the first film version, this is unfortunately burdened with dull, uninvolving characters. Nonetheless well worth seeing for Rob Bottin's astounding FX work.

THING FROM ANOTHER WORLD, THE
See: *The Thing*.

THIRST
★★★ Media, 1979, R, 98 min.
Dir: Rod Hardy. Cast: Chantal Contouri, David Hemmings, Rod Mullinar, Henry Silva, Shirley Cameron, Max Phipps.

Contouri is a beautiful young woman chosen as the new member of a modern-day vampire cult because she is a descendant of the infamous Countess Elizabeth Bathoray. At the vampires' private "clinic" Chantal discovers that young people are being bred like cattle for their blood. This interesting, well-directed Aussie thriller has an appealing heroine and mixes *Repulsion*-type psychological thrills with more traditional vampire pic elements to good effect.

THIRSTY DEAD, THE
★ Interglobal, 1974, PG, 88 min.
Dir: Terry Becker. Cast: Jennifer Billingsley, John Considine, Judith McConnell, Tani Guthrie.

A real snooze about kidnapped bimbos abducted from Manila and taken to the jungle lair of a cult of ageless weirdos in mini-skirts who remain young thanks to a secret potion derived from the blood of young women. Not even good for unintentional laughs, this tacky '50s-type chiller (complete with '70s gore) has awful acting, phony-looking sets, and was directed by the guy who played Chief Sharkey on the old "Voyage to the Bottom of the Sea" TV show.

13 GHOSTS
★★☆ 1960, Goodtimes, NR, 82 min.
Dir: William Castle. Cast: Charles Herbert, Jo Morrow, Martin Milner, Donald Woods, Rosemary De Camp, Margaret Hamilton.

Fun Castle thriller about an "average American family" (with a busty teen daughter named Medea!) who inherit an old mansion complete with a dozen spooks and a special "ghost viewer" with which to see them. Vastly entertaining, if a bit silly, this has the Wicked Witch of the West herself as a dour housekeeper and one good *House on Haunted Hill*–like shock. Originally it was released at 85 minutes with a prologue in which Castle explains the function of the "ghost viewer"—used for the Illusion-O theatrical release gimmick—which allowed viewers to either see or block out the spirits depending on which colored lens they looked through. In the video print the ghosts all appear a bit vague and washed out.

THIRTEENTH GUEST, THE
★★☆ Turner, 1932, NR, 69 min.
Dir: Albert Ray. Cast: Ginger Rogers, Lyle Talbot, J. Farrell McDonald, Paul Hurst, Eddie Phillips, Frances Rich.

Good, old-fashioned thunderstorm mystery with Rogers in her first starring role. Thirteen years after a dinner party at which the host dropped dead, the survivors are gathered at the victim's decaying mansion where a hooded figure begins bumping them off. In a clever twist, Ginger is done in early on, only to reemerge later in another identity. Nice cobwebby atmosphere plus a dose of hokey comic relief. Remade as *Mystery of the Thirteenth Guest*.

THIRTEENTH REUNION, THE
★★ Thrillervideo, 1980, NR, 50 min.
Dir: Peter Sasdy. Cast: Julia Foster, Dinah Sheridan, Warren Clarke, Norman Bird.

Chunky reporter Foster does an investigation on a popular slimming clinic and uncovers a nest of cannibals. Okay "Hammer House of Horror" episode with an interesting premise and pleasantly offbeat heroine but suffers from dull handling and a disappointing ending.

1,000 CRIES HAS THE NIGHT
See: *Pieces*.

THOU SHALT NOT KILL...EXCEPT
★★ Prism, 1987, UR, 94 min.
Dir: Josh Becker. Cast: Brian Schulz, John Manfredi, Robert Rickman, Tim Quill, Cheryl Hanson, Sam Raimi.

Vietnam vets battle a bloodythristy Manson-like cult in this grim, sometimes funny splatter horror-actioner. Slow to go but with a funny performance from *Evil Dead* director Raimi as the head cultist, some interesting direction, and lots of climactic bloodshed.

THREE FACES OF FEAR, THE
See: *Black Sabbath*.

THREE ON A MEATHOOK
★ Regal, 1972, R, 77 min. Dir: William Girdler.
Cast: Charles Kissinger, James Pickett, Sherry Steiner, Madelyn Buzzard, Marsha Tarbis, Carolyn Thompson.

Cheap *Psycho* rip-off about a young farmer who's convinced by his father that he is responsible for the gory murders of young women committed on their farm. The Hitchcock homages come thick and fast, but Girdler is no Hitch or even a William Castle, and the film quickly succumbs to its poor acting, hokey music, and cheesy gore effects. And talk about your surprise endings. . . .

THRILLED TO DEATH
See: *Night Warning.*

TICKS
See: *Infested.*

TILL DAWN DO US PART
See: *Straight on Till Morning.*

TILL DEATH DO US PART
See: *Buried Alive* (1988).

TIME AFTER TIME
★★★ Warner, 1979, PG, 112 min.
Dir: Nicholas Meyer. Cast: Malcolm McDowall, David Warner, Mary Steenburgen, Charles Cioffi, Kent Williams, Patti D'Arbanville.

In Victorian times writer-inventor H. G. Wells (McDowall) manufactures a time machine used by Jack the Ripper (Warner) to escape to 1970s San Francisco. Wells follows him and discovers, while falling in love with bank officer Steenburgen, that the modern world is far from the utopia he had envisioned. A whimsical blend of horror, sci-fi, comedy, romance, and social commentary, this has excellent acting (particularly Steenburgen in her starmaking performance) and a beautiful score by Miklos Rozsa.

TIME WALKER
★☆ Charter, 1983, PG, 85 min.
Dir: Tom Kennedy. Cast: Ben Murphy, Nina Axelrod, Kevin Brophy, James Karen, Shari Belafonte-Harper, Antoinette Bower, Darwin Jostin, Austin Stoker, Sam Chew, Jr., Greta Blackburn.

A strange mummy found beneath King Tut's tomb is taken to a California university where x-ray treatments revive it and it takes off after five crystals stolen from its sarcophagus. A silly combination of genres (the mummy turns out to be an ancient alien stranded on earth for 3,000 years), this has a good exploitation cast that mostly just goes through the motions.

There's one nice image of the mummy staring sadly up at the star-studded night sky, but otherwise it's a waste.

TINTOREA
★ Media, 1977, R, 91 min.
Dir: Rene Cardona, Jr. Cast: Susan George, Hugo Stiglitz, Fiona Lewis, Jennifer Ashley, Priscilla Barnes, Andres Garcia.

Awful U.S.-British-Spanish-Mexican *Jaws* rip-off with Stiglitz as a fisherman more interested in bedding the cast's assorted beauties than hunting down the film's rampaging great white. Lots of gore and gratuitous nudity in an otherwise dull exploiter. Aka *Tintorea: Bloody Waters.*

TINTOREA: BLOODY WATERS
See: *Tintorea.*

TITAN FIND
See: *Creature.*

TO ALL A GOODNIGHT
★★ Media, 1980, R, 83 min.
Dir: David Hess. Cast: Jennifer Runyon, Forrest Swanson, Judith Bridges, Linda Gentile, Katherine Herrington, Sam Shamshak.

Coeds at the exclusive Calvin Finishing School are finished by a Santa-suited psycho out to avenge the accidental death of a hazing victim. This unimaginative but presentable Christmas carnage was directed by the lead loony in *The Last House on the Left* and scripted by *Incredible Melting Man* star Alex Rebar.

TO DIE FOR
★★☆ Academy, 1989, R, 92 min.
Dir: Deren Sarafian. Cast: Brendan Hughes, Sydney Walsh, Steve Bond, Amanda Wyss, Scott Jacoby, Duane Jones.

A reincarnated Dracula (Hughes) moves to Los Angeles and falls in love with pretty Walsh while turning best friend Wyss into a vampire and battling long-ago victim Bond. A not-bad updating of the old Count Yorga concept, this is marred somewhat by dumb comic bits but has good acting and some clever direction. Jones is wasted in his last role as a real estate broker. Followed by a sequel.

TO DIE FOR 2: SON OF DARKNESS
★★ Vidmark, 1991, R, 98 min.
Dir: David F. Price. Cast: Michael Praed, Rosalind Allen, Steve Bond, Amanda Wyss, Scott Jacoby, Remy O'Neill.

Adequate follow-up with Allen as the young woman who unknowingly adopts the son of

Dracula (the result of the affair between the Count and the heroine of part one) and ends up fighting Drac (now played by Praed) and his nemesis Bond for the kid's soul. Gorier and less "relationship"-oriented than the first movie but also less satisfying; mostly for completists and Praed groupies. Aka *Son of Darkness: To Die For II.*

TO KILL A CLOWN

★★ Media, 1972, R, 104 min.
Dir: George Bloomfield. Cast: Alan Alda, Blythe Danner, Heath Lamberts, Eric Clavering.

Alda and Danner are good in this otherwise weird, unsatisfying chiller about an unhappily married couple trapped on a secluded island with a crippled and crazed 'Nam vet (a cast-against-type Hawkeye). Typical early '70s clichés.

TO LOVE A VAMPIRE

See: *Lust for a Vampire.*

TOMB, THE

★★☆ TWE, 1985, R, 83 min. Dir: Fred Olen Ray. Cast: Cameron Mitchell, John Carradine, Sybil Danning, Michelle Bauer, Susan Stokey, David Pearson, Richard Alan Hench, Kitten Navidad.

Probably Ray's most entertaining potboiler, this features veteran B-babe Bauer in her best role as an ancient Egyptian vampire-sorceress. Accidentally unleashed from her tomb by treasure hunter Pearson, she travels to L.A. to retrieve the artifacts stolen from her. Lots of fun, with hilarious dialogue and the usual unsubtle in-jokes. The top-billed star trio, however, haven't much to do.

TOMB OF LIGEIA

★★★☆ HBO, 1965, NR, 81 min.
Dir: Roger Corman. Cast: Vincent Price, Elizabeth Shepherd, John Westbrook, Derek Francis, Oliver Johnston, Richard Vernon.

Corman's last Poe film is one of his best. Headstrong Lady Rowena (Shepherd) falls in love with reclusive neighbor Verdon Fell (Price), not counting on the sinister influence of his first wife Ligeia (Shepherd as well) reaching out from the grave to destroy his second marriage. Price (in a role written with Richard Chamberlain in mind) is too old for his part but still manages to contribute one of his best, most understated performances, and Shepherd is excellent. Filmed on actual English locations, this eschews the usual studio-bound atmospherics of the other Poe movies to good effect, though its fiery finale is a tad too familiar-looking, replete with the usual

stock shots of falling timbers from *The Fall of the House of Usher.*

TOMB OF THE LIVING DEAD

See: *The Mad Doctor of Blood Island.*

TOMB OF TORTURE

★★ Modern Sound, 1963, NR, 87 min.
Dir: Anthony Kristye [Antonio Boccacci].
Cast: Annie Albert, Thony Makey, Mark Marian, Elizabeth Queen, William Gray.

Lovely Anna (Albert) is haunted by a series of strange nightmares involving a dead lookalike Countess. Is she possessed? Routine continental period piece with all the usual accoutrements, though the slovenly, disfigured, hunchbacked butler is a pretty memorable character. Original title: *Metempsycose: Metempsychosis.*

TOMBS OF HORROR

See: *Terror Creatures From the Grave.*

TOMBS OF THE BLIND DEAD

★★☆ Paragon, 1971, R, 85 min.
Dir: Amando de Ossorio. Cast: Lone Fleming, Cesar Bruner, Helen Harp, Joseph Thelman, Maria Sylva, Rufing Ingelis.

The first of four Spanish flicks shot by de Ossorio concerning the Knights Templar: witchcraft-practicing monks who were executed centuries ago and now rise from their mass grave as blood-drinking ghouls on horseback. Being blind (their eyes have been eaten out by crows), they find their victims through sound. The Templars make for a very unique screen monster and there is some eerie atmosphere, but far too much time is taken up by the usual assortment of uninteresting victims and sex scenes. Originally *La Noche del Terror Ciego: Night of Blind Terror* and aka *Night of the Blind Dead.* Sequels: *Return of the Evil Dead, Horror of the Zombies,* and *Night of the Death Cult.*

TOMMYKNOCKERS, THE

★★ Vidmark, 1993, NR, 125 min. Dir: John Power.
Cast: Jimmy Smits, Marg Helgenberger, Joanna Cassidy, E. G. Marshall, Traci Lords, Robert Carradine, Cliff De Young, Allyce Beasley.

This hacked-down (from 192 minutes) video version of the two-part Stephen King TV movie isn't as boring but loses a lot in the way of characterization. Helgenberger discovers a strange green light coming from a long-buried alien flying saucer containing the mummified forms of evil extraterrestrials seeking a return to life. Shot in New Zealand, this has a solid cast (Smits and Cassidy are the best), but the

RICHARD CARLSON
(1912–1977)

A popular horror and sci-fi leading man of the '50s, Carlson started out as a typically bland '40s juvenile lead before maturing into the strong and thoughtful battler of monsters he was to become a decade later. Although bouts with alcoholism sometimes blighted his career, he had real talent and could always be called upon to give a totally committed performance in even the most ludicrous of circumstances.

The Ghost Breakers ('40), *Hold That Ghost* ('41), *The Amazing Mr. X* ('48), *It Came From Outer Space* ('53), *Creature From the Black Lagoon* ('54), *The Maze* ('54), *Tormented* ('60), *The Power* ('68), *The Valley of Gwangi* ('69).

plot is little more than a second-rate rip of *Invasion of the Body Snatchers* and *Five Million Years to Earth*. At least they didn't compromise the original story's downbeat ending. And how about former underage porn queen Lords' casting in a major network tele-movie!

TOOLBOX MURDERS, THE
★ United, 1978, R, 93 min.
Dir: Dennis Donnelly. Cast: Cameron Mitchell, Pamelyn Ferdyn, Wesley Eure, Aneta Corsaut, Nicolas Beauvy, Kelly Nichols.

Infamous hardware horror in which Mitchell is a ski-masked psycho drilling, hammering, and nail-gunning the women of an L.A. apartment block. It's vulgar and embarrassing, with porn star Nichols featured in one endless scene where she masturbates in the bathtub before Mitch (literally) nails her and a legendary moment when he croons "Motherless Child" while sucking on a lollypop!

TOO SCARED TO SCREAM
★★ Vestron, 1982, R, 104 min. Dir: Tony Lo Bianco.
Cast: Mike Connors, Anne Archer, Ian McShane, Carrie Nye, Maureen O'Sullivan, Murray Hamilton, Leon Issac Kennedy, John Heard.

Actor Lo Bianco directed this routine stalker filmed as *The Doorman*. Police detective Connors (an old hand at this sort of thing) and partner Archer investigate a series of brutal murders in a Manhattan high-rise with mother-dominated doorman McShane as the main suspect. Basically just a gorier than usual TV movie.

TORMENT
★★ Nelson, 1985, R, 85 min.
Dirs: Samson Aslanian, John Hopkins. Cast: Taylor Gilbert, William Witt, Eve Brenner, Warren Lincoln.

Just one more stalk-and-slash opus with Frisco cop Witt after another woman-killing maniac who ends up menacing his girlfriend Gilbert and invalid mom Brenner. Well made on a budget but all too familiar; sometimes admired.

TORMENTED
★★☆ Sinister Cinema, 1960, NR, 75 min.
Dir: Bert I. Gordon. Cast: Richard Carlson, Juli Redings, Susan Gordon, Lugene Sanders, Joe Turkel, Gene Roth.

Pianist Carlson allows mistress Redings to fall from a lighthouse tower to her death so that he can marry wealthy fiancee Sanders. The happy couple soon find their marital bliss disrupted, however, by a vengeful ghost who haunts them in the form of a disembodied head, hand, or clump of seaweed. Carlson and Redings are good in this more "adult" than usual Gordon flick, which mixes creepy atmosphere with blatant special effects.

TORMENTED, THE
See: *The Eerie Midnight Horror Show.*

TORSO
★★☆ Prism, 1974, R, 89 min.
Dir: Sergio Martino. Cast: Suzy Kendall, John Richardson, Tina Aumont, Luc Merenda, Roberto Bisacco, Angela Covello.

Typical Italian stalker with Kendall and her coed friends terrorized at a remote villa by a hooded maniac with a hacksaw and body-dismembering fetish. The film is well photographed and features some very beautiful starlets, but the blunt editing in the U.S. version softens its originally super-high violence quota. Original title: *I Copri Presentano Tracce di Violenza Carnale: The Bodies Show Signs of Carnal Violence.*

TORTURE CHAMBER OF BARON BLOOD, THE
See: *Baron Blood.*

TORTURE CHAMBER OF DR. SADISM, THE
★★★ Magnum, 1967, PG, 75 min.
Dir: Harold Reindl. Cast: Christopher Lee, Lex Barker, Karin Dor, Karl Lange, Christiane Rucker, Vladimir Medar.

Count Regula (Lee) is drawn-and-quartered for his satanic activities and 35 years later returns from the dead to exact his revenge on the children of his executioners. Dor is lowered into a snake pit while Barker is strapped beneath a razor-sharp pendulum. This loose—to state the obvious—version of Poe's "The Pit and the Pendulum" has attention-grabbing atmosphere—a forest filled with twisted, hanging corpses; dungeon walls made of human skulls—and a great performance from Lee, making it one of his best Euro-horrors. Aka *Die Schlangengrube und das Pendel: The Snake Pit and the Pendulum, The Snake Pit, Blood Demon,* and *Castle of the Walking Dead.* Beware of edited prints.

TORTURE DUNGEON
☆ Midnight, 1970, R, 80 min.
Dir: Andy Milligan. Cast: Jeremy Brooks, Susan Cassidy, Patricia Dillon, Donna Whitfield, Haal Borske, Maggie Rogen.

Milligan's tacky variation on *Tower of London* has Brooks as a loony Duke of Norwich who slashes and hacks his way to the throne of England. Hilariously bad acting and period anachronisms abound. Originally co-billed with *Bloodthirsty Butchers.*

TORTURE GARDEN
★★★ RCA/Columbia, 1967, NR, 92 min.
Dir: Freddie Francis. Cast: Jack Palance, Burgess Meredith, Beverly Adams, Peter Cushing, Maurice Denham, Barbara Ewing, Michael Bryant, John Standing, Robert Hutton, Michael Ripper.

Entertaining anthology with Meredith as the rascally Dr. Diabolo who gives four patrons to his carnival inner sanctum a glimpse into their future. A murderer falls under the spell of a cat that eats human heads; a young actress discovers that the top Hollywood stars are actually robots in human form; a girl finds her romance with a famous pianist thwarted by his jealous piano; and a collector of Edgar Allan Poe memorabilia raises the author from the dead. Solid Robert Bloch script derived from some of his "Weird Tales" stories and slick direction from Francis make this a fun omnibus. Released theatrically on a double bill with *Berserk!*

TORTURE ZONE, THE
★☆ MPI, 1968, PG, 87 min.
Dirs: Juan Ibanez, Jack Hill. Cast: Boris Karloff, Julissa Santanon, Yerye Beirut, Carlos East, Isela Vega, Eva Muller.

Originally titled *El Camara del Terror: The Terror Chamber* and shown on TV as *The Fear Chamber,* this is one of Karloff's more enjoyable Mexican cheapies—but that still ain't sayin' much. Boris is a bedridden scientist whose assistants experiment with a "living"

rock that lives on human adrenaline procured from women boarders terrorized in a private torture chamber. Utterly dumb and overcomplicated but with a hilarious turn from Mexican horror vet Beirut as a lab toadie who wants to be "Kink of the Vorld!"

TO SLEEP WITH A VAMPIRE
★★ New Horizons, 1992, R, 76 min.
Dir: Adam Friedman. Cast: Scott Valentine, Charlie Spradling, Richard Zobel, Ingrid Vold, Stephanie Hardy.

A well-directed but highly unnecessary remake of *Dance of the Damned* in which Valentine now plays the vampire, talking of life, love, and death with despondent stripper Spradling (who's quite good). An arty but empty "erotic chiller," this almost overcomes Valentine's miscasting and the familiarity of its setup through the sheer inventiveness of its director—but not quite.

TO THE DEVIL . . . A DAUGHTER
★★☆ New Star, 1976, R, 88 min.
Dir: Peter Sykes. Cast: Richard Widmark, Christopher Lee, Nastassja Kinski, Honor Blackman, Denholm Elliott, Anthony Valentine.

Hammer Films' only post-*Exorcist* theatrically released horror film was this muddled but interesting adaptation of Dennis Wheatley's novel about a renegade priest (Lee) attempting to unite a young novitiate (Kinski) with the spawn of the demon Asteroth. Widmark is an author of occult novels (like *The Devil Walks Among Us*) recruited by the girl's distraught dad (Elliott) to help save her. Poor editing and cheesy effects (like a bloody little hand puppet to represent the demon baby) keep this from being anything more than a mild success.

TOUCH OF MELISSA, THE
See: *The Touch of Satan.*

TOUCH OF SATAN, THE
★★☆ King of Video, 1971, PG, 87 min.
Dir: Don Henderson. Cast: Michael Berry, Emby Mellay, Lee Amber, Yvonne Winslow, Jeanne Gerson, Lew Lorn.

Well-done cheapie about a young wanderer who falls in love with a farmgirl whose wizened great grandmother is committing a series of sickle murders. A twist at the end reveals that our heroine is actually the *older sister* of the murdering crone who's managed to retain her youth and beauty through a pact with the devil. Good acting, makeup, and camerawork in this likable rural shocker. Aka *The Touch of Melissa* and *Night of the Demon.*

TOURIST TRAP
★★☆ Paramount, 1979, PG, 85 min.
Dir: David Schmoeller. Cast: Chuck Connors,
Jocelyn Jones, Jon Van Ness, Tanya Roberts, Robin
Sherwood, Keith McDermott.

Weird, haunting variation on *Carrie* and *The
Texas Chainsaw Massacre* with Connors as a
lonely madman who runs a backwoods tourist
trap museum where he brings the dummies to
life with his telekinetic ability. This is almost
totally senseless and confusing, but it has an
air of almost surreal beauty in some of its
scenes and is graced by one of Pino Donaggio's loveliest scores. Aka *Nightmare of Terror.*

TOWER OF EVIL
★★☆ Gorgon, 1972, R, 90 min.
Dir: Jim O'Connolly. Cast: Bryant Halliday, Jill
Haworth, Mark Edwards, Anna Palk, Jack Watson,
Derek Fowlds, Dennis Price, George Coulouris.

A gory, ahead-of-its-time slash flick with a
series of brutal murders committed on a misty
island off the coast of England. Complete with
nude sex scenes; bloody, imaginative murders;
a disfigured, Jason-like killer; and a twist ending, this could have been the *Friday the 13th* of
its day if it hadn't been released in the U.S. in
a drastically cut 85-minute version called *Horror on Snape Island.* Good line: "Don't you
want to come and protect me from things that
go bang in the night?" Reissued as *Beyond
the Fog.*

TOWER OF LONDON
★★★ MCA/Universal, 1939, NR, 92 min.
Dir: Rowland V. Lee. Cast: Basil Rathbone,
Boris Karloff, Vincent Price, Nan Grey, John Sutton,
Barbara O'Neal, Ian Hunter, Leo G. Carroll,
Rose Hobart, Miles Mander.

This elaborate (for Universal) period chiller is
like Shakespeare's *Richard III* without the pre-
tentions and with an accent on the violence
and horror. Rathbone is the power-mad crook-
back and Karloff his dedicated, club-footed
chief torturer, while Price makes his horror
debut as the ill-fated Duke of Clarence,
drowned in a wine vat. In the Roger Corman
remake, Price was promoted to the role of
Richard, and though not as good a film, it at
least has more horrific highlights. The cast is
outstanding.

TOWER OF LONDON
★★ MGM/UA, 1962, NR, 77 min.
Dir: Roger Corman. Cast: Vincent Price, Michael Pate,
Joan Freeman, Robert Brown, Bruce Gordon, Joan
Camden, Charles Macaulay, Sandra Knight.

Price camps it up as Richard III in this cardboard remake of the 1939 original. The crook-
back tortures and murders his way to the
throne as Knight is stretched on the rack;
Macauley drowned in a vat of wine; and Gordon fed to the rats. This is far less exciting
than it sounds, however, lacking the atmosphere and scope of the Poe films Corman was
making for AIP at the same time.

TOWER OF TERROR
See: *Assault.*

TOWN THAT DREADED SUNDOWN, THE
★★☆ Warner, 1976, R, 90 min.
Dir: Charles B. Pierce. Cast: Ben Johnson,
Andrew Prine, Dawn Wells, Jimmy Clem,
Cindy Butler, Charles B. Pierce.

Fairly taut thriller based on a true story about
a hooded psychopath terrorizing a small
Texarkana town in the late 1940s. There are
some scary scenes, as well as good acting from
Johnson as an investigating Texas Ranger and
Wells (Mary Ann on "Gilligan's Island") as a
near victim.

TOXIC AVENGER, THE
★★★ Vestron, 1985, UR, 82 min.
Dirs: Michael Herz, Samuel Weil. Cast: Mitchell
Cohen, Andree Maranda, Mark Torgl, Gary
Schneider, Cindy Manion, Jennifer Baptist.

Hilarious gore-romp about Melvin, the schlep-
py nerd mop boy at a New Jersey health club
who is transformed by a drum of toxic waste
into the hideous but kind-hearted mutant
the Toxic Avenger. Very gross but also very
funny; nothing is sacred here as old ladies are
beaten up, seeing eye dogs shot, and little kids
squashed by cars. Way over the top but with
an odd, endearing little charm all its own—
for those who can appreciate it. Followed by
two sequels, this may be the only gore flick
ever to inspire a TV cartoon series: "Toxic
Crusaders!"

TOXIC AVENGER PART II, THE
★★ Warner, 1988, R, 95 min.
Dirs: Lloyd Kaufman, Michael Herz. Cast: Ron Fazio,
John Altamura, Phoebe Legere, Rikiya Yasouka,
Tsutomu Sekine, Mayako Katsuragi.

After hometown Tromaville has been
destroyed by an evil corporation, Toxie travels
to Japan to find his long lost dad. This silly
sequel tries less to gross you out than the original, substituting slapstick sequences that
mostly don't work and lots of juvenile humor.
Has its funny passages, though, especially
near the beginning.

TOXIC AVENGER PART III: THE LAST TEMPTATION OF TOXIE, THE

★☆ Warner, 1989, R, 86 min.
Dirs: Lloyd Kaufman, Michael Herz.
Cast: Ron Fazio, John Altamura, Phoebe Legere, Lisa Gaye, Jessica Dublin, Rick Collins.

Toxie's out of work and tempted to turn bad in this dopey continuation of the series. Sometimes funny almost in spite of itself but mostly a chore.

TOXIC ZOMBIES

★☆ Raedon, 1980, R, 85 min. Dir: Charles McCrann.
Cast: Charles Austin, Beverly Shapiro, Dennis Helfend, Judy Brown, Paul Haskin, John Amplas.

Released theatrically as *Bloodeaters,* this Pennsylvania-shot *Night of the Living Dead* spin-off concerns government-poisoned marijuana transforming its hippie farmers into bloodlusting zombies. Bloody but tedious, with a *very* slow pace and awful acting, apart from teen heroine Brown and a miscast Amplas as the world's first high school-aged FBI agent.

TRACK OF THE MOONBEAST

★ Prism, 1973, PG, 84 min.
Dir: Dick Ashe. Cast: Chase Cordell, Donna Leigh Drake, Gregorio Sala, Patrick Wright, Francine Kessler, Joe Blasco.

Cheapo monster movie with good makeup. A young scientist is hit by a meteor fragment and soon begins mutating into a scaly creature. Awful acting but there's an effective critter designed and played by Blasco, with the hands manufactured by Rick Baker.

TRACK OF THE VAMPIRE

★★☆ Sinister Cinema, 1966, NR, 75 min.
Dirs: Jack Hill and Stephanie Rothman. Cast: William Campbell, Marissa Mathes, Lori Saunders, Sandra Knight, Sid Haig, Jonathan Haze.

The production history of this film is actually a lot more interesting than the movie itself. Originally a Yugo suspense film called *Operation Titian,* it was recut by Hill and new sequences were added to make it the chiller *Blood Bath.* Then Rothman added a few more scenes and the vampire angle for this final incarnation. The plot, such as it is, features the always interesting Campbell as a Venice, California, artist who is possessed by the spirit of a vampire ancestor and murders his models, turning them into works of art. Choppy and confusing, but with a good cast and some really eerie moments.

TRANSIT

See: *The First Power.*

TRANSMUTATIONS

★★ Vestron, 1985, R, 103 min.
Dir: George Pavlou. Cast: Denholm Elliott, Steven Berkoff, Nicola Cowper, Larry Lamb, Miranda Richardson, Ingrid Pitt.

Stylish but unsatisfying mixture of fantasy, horror, and crime melodrama scripted by Clive Barker. A violent gangster (Berkoff) becomes obsessed with recovering his lost mistress (Cowper) who's been kidnapped by mutants living in a labyrinth of tunnels beneath London. Interesting directorial touches and a good cast do what they can to salvage this confusing film, which somewhat predates elements better explored by Barker in *Nightbreed.* Original British title: *Underworld.*

TRANSYLVANIA 6-5000

★☆ New World, 1985, PG, 90 min.
Dir: Rudy De Luca. Cast: Jeff Goldblum, Ed Begley, Jr., Geena Davis, Joseph Bologna, Carol Kane, Jeffrey Jones, Michael Richards, John Byner, Teresa Ganzel, Norman Fell.

Goldblum and Begley make a potentially good team and there's a terrific supporting cast but this typically '80s *Abbott and Costello Meet Frankenstein* tribute isn't even as funny as *The Bowery Boys Meet the Monsters.* Jeff and Ed are tabloid reporters in Transylvania who find that they don't have to make up stories about monsters and vampires when they encounter mad doc Bologna and his monstrous entourage. Only Davis (as a sex-starved vampiress), Jones (as a tourist-trapping innkeeper out to turn a fast buck), and Richards (as a goofy manservant) bring any spark to the proceedings. The *trailer* was funnier!

TRANSYLVANIA TWIST

★★☆ MGM/UA, 1989, PG, 82 min.
Dir: Jim Wynorski. Cast: Robert Vaughn, Teri Copley, Steve Altman, Angus Scrimm, Howard Morris, Jay Robinson, Steve Franken, Ace Mask, Monique Gabrielle, Brinke Stevens.

Wynorski's best film to date, in fact his *only* good film to date, is a funny Abbott and Costello/*Fearless Vampire Killers*–type spoof with Copley as a rock singer who travels to Transylvania to collect an inheritance and encounters vampire uncle Vaughn, glowering butler Scrimm, and stock footage of Boris Karloff. Altman's so-called comic relief—comic relief in a comedy?—is fairly annoying, but the rest of the cast is in fine form, there's an amusing rock video parody, and cameos by Jason, Freddy, Leatherface, Pinhead, the cucumber creature from *It Conquered the World,* and Forry Ackerman.

TRAPPED

★★ MCA/Universal, 1989, NR, 96 min.
Dir: Fred Walton. Cast: Kathleen Quinlan,
Bruce Abbott, Ben Loggins, Katy Boyer.

A feminist *Die Hard* with horror movie overtones as Quinlan is stalked through an L.A.
high-rise after dark by psycho Loggins.
Mechanical made-for-TV suspense film with
marked similarities to the Brian Clemens Brit
tele-flick *I'm the Girl He Wants to Kill.*

TRAUMA

★★ Sinister Cinema, 1962, NR, 93 min.
Dir: Robert Malcolm Young. Cast: John Conte,
Lynn Bari, Lorrie Richards, David Garner,
Warren Kemmerling.

A wealthy young girl (Richards) marries her
former guardian and returns to the spooky old
family mansion where she is assaulted by
memories of her aunt's murder. A well-acted
but too-familiar sub-*Psycho* '60s shocker.

TRAUMA

★★☆ WorldVision, 1993, UR, 106 min.
Dir: Dario Argento. Cast: Asia Argento, Christopher
Rydell, Piper Laurie, Frederic Forrest, Brad Dourif,
James Russo, Laura Johnson, Hope Alexander-Willis.

Argento's latest in many ways disappoints
but, as always with the maestro, is not completely unworthy. Set and filmed in Min-
neapolis, this has Dario's daughter, Asia, as an
anorexic teen who witnesses the brutal decapitations of her parents by a mysterious psycho
known as the Headhunter. Will the plucky
Ms. Argento remember a vital clue to the
killer's identity before he adds her to his list of
victims? In this reworking of several major
themes from his classic *Deep Red,* Argento
adds several new bravura set-pieces to his
already burgeoning résumé. The eclectic cast
is in good form, but the film is done damage
by a script (co-authored by Argento and
T.E.D. Klein) that looks suspiciously like it
was made up as they went along. Also available in a cut R version.

TREMORS

★★☆ MCA/Universal, 1990, PG-13, 96 min.
Dir: Ron Underwood. Cast: Kevin Bacon, Fred Ward,
Finn Carter, Michael Gross, Reba McEntire, Bobby
Jacoby, Charlotte Stewart, Victor Wong.

Very entertaining tribute to '50s monster
flicks, *Them!* and *Tarantula* in particular, about
a tiny desert community menaced by huge
worms. Modest special effects but good acting
(especially Gross and country singer McEntire
as married survivalists) and pleasant humor
make this a nice surprise.

TRICK OR TREAT

★★ Lorimar, 1986, R, 97 min. Dir: Charles Martin
Smith. Cast: Marc Price, Lisa Orgolini, Tony Fields,
Gene Simmons, Ozzy Osbourne, Elaine Joyce.

Silly heavy metal horror about a teen head-
banger (Price) who brings his dead idol back
from the grave by playing his last album back-
wards. Trouble begins when the singer
(Fields) turns out to be a horrible hellspawn
out to corrupt our innocent hero. Good FX but
otherwise terribly flat and reactionary, with
far too many *Nightmare on Elm Street*–like elements. Actor-director Smith has a cameo as
the high school principal.

TRICK OR TREATS

★☆ Vestron, 1982, R, 91 min.
Dir: Gary Graver. Cast: Jackelyn Giroux,
David Carradine, Carrie Snodgress, Peter Jason,
Steve Railsback, Chris Graver, Jillian Kesner,
Paul Bartel.

About the four thousandth *Halloween* rip-off
and one of the worst and most blatant. On
Halloween night a kook (Jason) escapes from
the asylum disguised as a nurse, à la *Dressed to
Kill*, in order to avenge himself on his ex-wife
and her husband. When he gets home, though,
he finds them out and his obnoxious,
prankster son in the care of a pretty babysitter
(Giroux). Tries to be funny but isn't, with
grainy photography and wasted appearances
by Carradine, Snodgress, and Railsback.

KAREN BLACK
(1942–)

The lovely lass with the slightly crossed
eyes and sexy, devil-may-care demeanor,
Karen has embraced the genre (after playing opposite everyone from Jack Nicholson to Charlton Heston) as a career-
enhancing rather than career-saving
move and done quite well for herself.
Can we *ever* forget her hellacious battle
with the tiny devil doll in *Trilogy of
Terror?*

The Pyx ('73), *Trilogy of Terror* ('75), *Burnt
Offerings* ('76), *The Strange Possession of
Mrs. Oliver* ('77), *Invaders from Mars* ('86),
Eternal Evil ('86), *It's Alive III: Island of the
Alive* ('86), *The Invisible Kid* ('87), *Out of
the Dark* ('89), *Night Angel* ('89), *Overex-
posed* ('90), *Dead Girls Don't Dance* ('90),
Auntie Lee's Meat Pies ('91), *Mirror, Mirror*
('91), *The Haunting Fear* ('91), *Evil Spirits*
('91), *Children of the Night* ('92).

TRILOGY OF TERROR
★★★ MPI, 1975, NR, 72 min.
Dir: Dan Curtis. Cast: Karen Black, Robert Burton, John Karlen, George Gaynes, James Storm, Kathryn Reynolds, Gregory Harrison, Tracy Curtis.

Black is terrific in this trio of Richard Matheson tales. The first two are fairly routine: "Julie," about a college teacher who turns out to be a man-killing succubus, and "Millicent and Therese," a predictable tale of voodoo and split personalities. The final tale, "Amelia," is another matter entirely. Detailing a young woman's battle with a bloodthirsty Zuni fetish doll imbued with the life force of a native hunter, it is 20 minutes of pure gold, a masterful piece of horror filmmaking with simple but wholly convincing effects and a marvelous solo turn by Black as the besieged victim. One of Curtis' best efforts, the final segment is also available from MPI as a short retitled *Terror of the Doll*.

TROLL
★☆ Vestron, 1986, PG-13, 83 min. Dir: John Carl Buechler. Cast: Michael Moriarty, Shelley Hack, Noah Hathaway, Jennifer Beck, June Lockhart, Sonny Bono, Garry Sandy, Julia Louis-Dreyfus.

A San Francisco apartment building is terrorized by a troll who takes on the form of a little girl (Beck) while transforming residents into various supernatural creatures. Another forgettable *Gremlins* Empire Pictures knock-off, this has a typically manic Moriarty and rubbery makeup FX. Mainly for those who've just *gotta* see Bono turned into a five-foot avocado.

TROLL 2
☆ Columbia/TriStar, 1990, PG-13, 94 min. Dir: Drake Floyd [Aristide Massacessi]. Cast: Michael Stephenson, Connie McFarland, George Hardy, Margo Prey.

This bogus Italian-made "sequel" is one of the worst. Stephenson is a kid who is in contact with his granddad's ghost whose family is menaced by a witch and her troll minions. Crammed with cheesy makeup FX, a nonexistent plot, and some of the most awful acting in screen history, this has to be seen to be believed—but please don't.

TROLLENBERG TERROR, THE
See: *The Crawling Eye*.

TURN OF THE SCREW, THE
★★☆ Thrillervideo, 1974, NR, 128 min. Dir: Dan Curtis. Cast: Lynn Redgrave, Megs Jenkins, Jasper Jacob, Eve Griffith, James Laurenson, Kathryn Leigh Scott.

A surprisingly deft and subtle videotaped adaptation of the Henry James classic, scripted by William F. Nolan. Redgrave excels as the repressed governess who comes to fear that her young charges are possessed by a pair of malevolent ghosts—though this "possession" may only be the product of an overactive imagination. Despite an indifferent technical quality, there's a nice gothic flavor enhanced by good location work and fine performances, including Jenkins in a re-creation of her earthy Mrs. Gorse role from Jack Clayton's *The Innocents*.

TURN OF THE SCREW, THE
★★☆ Cannon, 1989, NR, 55 min. Dir: Graeme Clifford. Cast: Amy Irving, David Hemmings, Balthazar Getty, Micole Mercurio.

Probably the best entry in Shelley Duvall's "Nightmare Classics" cable series, this well-directed version of the James story well-casts Irving as the governess who battles ghosts for the souls of the two children in her care. Less psychologically slanted than earlier treatments, with nice atmosphere and solid performing.

TURN OF THE SCREW, THE
★★ LIVE, 1992, R, 95 min. Dir: Rusty Lemorande. Cast: Patsy Kensit, Julian Sands, Stephane Audran, Marianne Faithfull, Joseph England, Clare Szekores.

Reset, for no apparent reason, in the 1960s, this well-produced but uninspired French-British remake has good work from Kensit as the governess who comes to suspect that her young charges are possessed. But it is relentlessly predictable and drawn out. The 1961 film *The Innocents* remains the definitive version.

TWICE DEAD
★★ Nelson, 1988, R, 87 min. Dir: Bert Dragin. Cast: Tom Breznahan, Jill Whitlow, Jonathan Chapin, Sam Melville, Brooke Bundey, Todd Bridges, Christopher Burgard, Joleen Lutz.

An impoverished family move into an old mansion they've inherited where the teenage kids have their hands full fighting off both a violent street gang and the vengeful ghost of a suicidal ham actor. The offbeat setting (a crime-infested urban neighborhood instead of a sinister rocky sea coast or dark forest) and the heroes' side interest (they're amateur makeup enthusiasts) are the only notable contributions of this well-cast but routine video time-waster.

TWICE-TOLD TALES
★★☆ MGM/UA, 1963, NR, 119 min.
Dir: Sidney Salkow. Cast: Vincent Price, Sebastian Cabot, Mari Blanchard, Brett Halsey, Joyce Taylor, Beverly Garland, Richard Denning, Abraham Sofaer.

Nathaniel Hawthorne stories get the *Tales of Terror* treatment in this trilogy. In "Dr. Heidegger's Experiment" a mysterious serum restores youth to two old men and brings a dead girl back to life; "Rappaccini's Daughter" tells of a doctor whose daughter's steady diet of poison has given her a touch of death; and a condensed "The House of Seven Gables" deals with treasure hunting and ghosts in an old mansion. Florid acting (especially from Price in three roles) and bright colors, but hurt by over-length and some cheapie special effects.

TWILIGHT PEOPLE, THE
★☆ United, 1971, R, 84 min. Dir: Eddie Romero. Cast: John Ashley, Pat Woodell, Pam Grier, Charles Macauley, Jan Merlin, Eddie Garcia.

Another Filipino Ashley vehicle, this one borrows its plot from both *The Island of Dr. Moreau* and *The Most Dangerous Game.* Shipwreck survivor John is stranded on an island with a mad doctor busily turning animals into quasi-humans *and* an evil ex-Nazi who hunts them as prey. Will animal/human rights activist Ashley lead the hum-animals in revolt? Dumb but with enough bizarre little touches—like Grier as a sexy panther girl—to make it worth a look for Filipino horror fanatics. Aka *Island of the Twilight People* and *Beasts.*

TWILIGHT ZONE, THE
★★★☆ CBS/Fox, 1959–64, NR, 50 min. per tape. Dirs: Douglas Heyes, John Brahm, Jack Smight, Richard Donner, Ida Lupino, Lamont Johnson, others. Cast: Burgess Meredith, William Shatner, Anne Francis, Agnes Moorehead, Cliff Robertson, Robert Redford, Inger Stevens, Jack Klugman, Art Carney, Vera Miles, Kevin McCarthy, Telly Savalas, Billy Mumy, Hazel Court, Claude Akins, Donna Douglas.

Rod Serling's classic TV series mixing horror, fantasy, science fiction, and allegory is slowly but surely being released by CBS/Fox in two-episodes-per-tape packages. Favorite segments include "Long Live Walter Jameson" with McCarthy as an ageless college prof; "It's a *Good* Life" with Mumy as an omnipotent little brat; "Living Doll" with Savalas vs. a killer plaything; "Eye of the Beholder" with Douglas as a beauty shunned in a world of ugliness; "The Dummy" with Robertson as an obsessed ventriloquist; and "The After Hours" with Francis menaced by living mannequins in a shadowy department store. An updated '80s

version of show—mixing remakes of old episodes with new, original segments—had its moments but was mostly a bust.

TWILIGHT ZONE—THE MOVIE
★★☆ Warner, 1983, PG, 101 min.
Dirs: John Landis, Steven Spielberg, Joe Dante, George Miller. Cast: Dan Aykroyd, Albert Brooks, Scatman Crothers, John Lithgow, Vic Morrow, Kathleen Quinlan, Jeremy Licht, Kevin McCarthy, Abbe Lane, Donna Dixon, Dick Miller, voice of Burgess Meredith.

Uneven homage to the series never finds the proper mix of humor, horror, and wonder that the original so deftly balanced. Aykroyd and Brooks are funny in the pre-credits sequence (which ends with the movie's one good jolt), but Landis' segment, about a time-traveling bigot, is heavy-handed and obvious, and Spielberg's, with oldsters recapturing lost youth, so treacly you might want to get any diabetics in your family out of the room while watching. Things pick up, though, with Dante's funny-scary episode about a kid who holds people prisoner as a surrogate family in a cartoon world, and peak with Miller's remake of the classic episode about a nervous airline passenger (a terrific Lithgow) who sees a gremlin attacking the wing of the plane. A mixed bag of misplaced tribute that will probably remain best known for the cause célèbre resulting from the accidental, on-camera deaths of Morrow and two child actors and director Landis' subsequent trial and acquittal. Good score by Jerry Goldsmith.

TWINKLE, TWINKLE, KILLER KANE
See: *The Ninth Configuration.*

TWINSANITY
★★ Embassy, 1970, R, 91 min. Dir: Alan Gibson. Cast: Judy Geeson, Martin Potter, Alexis Kanner, Michael Redgrave, Freddie Jones, Peter Jeffrey.

Originally released as *Goodbye Gemini,* this minor British suspense flick features Geeson and Potter as near-incestuous twins who get mixed up with blackmail, madness, and murder in the oh-so-mod London of 1970. Good performances redeem this trite horror-mystery.

TWINS OF DRACULA
See: *Twins of Evil.*

TWINS OF EVIL
★★★ VidAmerica, 1971, R, 85 min. Dir: John Hough. Cast: Peter Cushing, Madeleine Collinson, Mary Collinson, Dennis Price, Damien Thomas, David Warbeck, Isobel Black, Kathleen Byron.

The third and final entry in Hammer's "Karn-stein" trilogy is one of the company's most entertaining '70s films. Cushing is a steely witch hunter whose gorgeous twin nieces (the Collinsons, *Playboy*'s first twin playmates) become involved with a descendant of vam-piress Mircalla Karnstein. Lush production, strong direction, and a spirited cast (Thomas is outstanding as the flamboyant Count Karn-stein) help make this a must for Hammer enthusiasts. This video print is taken from the original Brit theatrical version and contains additional gore and nudity trimmed from the U.S. release prints. Aka *Vampire Virgins* and *Twins of Dracula*.

TWISTED
★★ Hemdale, 1986, R, 82 min. Dir: Adam Holender. Cast: Christian Slater, Lois Smith, Tandy Cronyn, Brooke Tracy, Dina Merrill, Dan Ziskie.

Heartthrob Slater had an early role as a psy-chotic teen out to get his little sister's babysit-ter in this unimaginative potboiler. Chris and Lois are good, but it's not hard to see why this very-low-budget stalker was shelved until '92.

TWISTED BRAIN, THE
★☆ United, 1973, PG, 85 min. Dir: Larry N. Stouffer. Cast: Pat Cardi, Rosie Holotik, Austin Stoker, John Niland, Joy Hash.

Released to theatres as *Horror High,* this grainy *Carrie* predecessor has a good performance from Cardi as a brainy nerd who transforms into a monster to bump off his enemies, thanks to a chemical compound of his own creation. Otherwise, though, this is just anoth-er drive-in clunker with lots of bad polyester fashions and overdark photography.

TWISTED SOULS
See: *Spookies.*

TWITCH OF THE DEATH NERVE
See: *Bay of Blood.*

TWO EVIL EYES
★★☆ Media, 1990, R, 121 min. Dirs: George A. Romero and Dario Argento. Cast: Adrienne Barbeau, Harvey Keitel, Madeline Potter, Ramy Zada, John Amos, E. G. Marshall, Sally Kirkland, Martin Balsam, Kim Hunter, Tom Atkins, Bingo O'Malley, Tom Savini.

This two-part tribute to Poe from two top horror directors is disappointing but has its moments. Romero's "The Facts in the Case of Mr. Valdemar" is a tired let's-kill-him-for-his-money-but-he-comes-back-from-the-dead-for-revenge affair sparked only by a strong performance from Barbeau and some good

set design. Argento's "The Black Cat," on the other hand, is a fairly effective tribute to Poe in general, with powerhouse acting from Keitel as a crime photographer obsessed with images of violent death and a cat he feels is out to kill him. Worth seeing for this second segment alone.

TWO FACES OF EVIL, THE
★★ Thrillervideo, 1980, NR, 50 min. Dir: Alan Gibson. Cast: Anna Caulder-Marshall, Gary Raymond, Paul Hawkins, Jenny Laird.

An interestingly directed but strange and con-fusing "Hammer House of Horror" segment about a vacationing family who get involved in a vague supernatural plot to replace them with deadly doppelgangers. Maybe the weird-est entry in this short-lived TV series.

TWO LOST WORLDS
★☆ SVS, 1950, NR, 62 min. Dir: Norman Dawn. Cast: James Arness, Laura Elliott, Bill Kennedy, Gloria Petroff, Tom Hubbard, Jane Harlan.

This one barely qualifies as a horror movie, as it spends two-thirds of its brief running time rehashing old historical romance and pirate movie clichés before settling down on its stock footage–infested prehistoric island. Arness is the stalwart hero who rescues girlfriend Elliott from footage from *One Million B.C.* Big Jim has

---

HERSCHELL GORDON LEWIS
(1926–)

The guru of gore started out as a college English prof(!!!) before producing several soft-core "nudies" in the early '60s. He struck gold when he directed the leg-endary *Blood Feast,* a neoclassical mixture of stage blood, animal entrails, and some of the worst acting in history, and never looked back. His films are surprisingly slick-looking, considering their budgets, and can mostly all be enjoyed as unin-tended and sometimes *intended* comedies. Since retiring from films in the early '70s, H. G. has run a successful Chicago ad agency and hopes someday to make *Blood Feast II!*

Blood Feast ('63), *Two Thousand Maniacs!* ('64), *Color Me Blood Red* ('65), *Monster a Go-Go* (co-director, '65), *Something Weird* ('66), *The Gruesome Twosome* ('67), *A Taste of Blood* ('67), *She-Devils on Wheels* ('68), *The Wizard of Gore* ('70), *The Gore-Gore Girls* ('72).

---

always, reportedly, been embarrassed by his participation in *The Thing,* but this is the movie he should *really* be ashamed of.

TWO THOUSAND MANIACS!
★★★ Sleaziest, 1964, NR, 87 min. Dir: Herschell Gordon Lewis. Cast: Connie Mason, Thomas Wood, Jeffrey Allen, Ben Moore, Shelby Livingston, Gary Bakeman, Jerome Eden, Mark Douglas.

Oh, the South is gonna rise again! The *best* of the H. G. Lewis gore series, this one has some story to speak of, a sort of *Bloody Brigadoon,* plus good locations and a refreshing, *intentional* sense of humor. Three Northern couples are waylaid to a small Georgia community inhabited by the bloodthirsty ghosts of Civil War massacre victims who ax, crush, flay, and draw-and-quarter them in revenge. A delightfully broad performance from Allen as the town mayor and the good-natured grossness of an old Warner Brothers cartoon make this the closest Lewis ever came to making a professional, breakthrough feature. Some of the supporting performances, though, have all the effect of fingernails scraping on a blackboard.

UNBORN, THE
★★★ RCA/Columbia, 1991, R, 83 min. Dir: Rodman Flender. Cast: Brooke Adams, Jeff Hayenga, James Karen, K. Callan, Jane Cameron.

Adams experiences the creepiest pregnancy since Mia Farrow moved into the Dakota in this potent updating of the *It's Alive* theme. Brooke and her hubby can't conceive, so she goes to evil fertility specialist Karen whose secret agenda involves the creation of a master race of super-intelligent infants. Starts slowly but eventually builds to some really unexpected twists and turns, and both Adams and a cast-against-type Karen are excellent. An impressive debut for Flender.

UNBORN II, THE
★★☆ New Horizons, 1993, R, 82 min. Dir: Rick Jacobson. Cast: Michele Greene, Scott Valentine, Robin Curtis, Brittney Powell, Carol Ita White, Leonard O. Turner.

Greene, in the role originated by Brooke Adams, tries to raise her ugly mutant baby in a quiet suburban neighborhood, but the little brat just can't seem to stay out of trouble. And then there's Curtis as a gun-totin' mom of another superbaby out to wipe them all off the face of the planet. This more tongue-in-cheek sequel owes a lot to Larry Cohen's *It Lives Again* and does a fairly good job of balancing gripping scenes of Curtis murderously stalking playgrounds and maternity wards against such silliness as Greene punching out her pug-ugly rubber offspring in a ridiculously out-of-control climax.

UNCANNY, THE
★★☆ Prism, 1977, PG, 87 min. Dir: Denis Heroux. Cast: Peter Cushing, Samantha Eggar, Ray Milland, Donald Pleasence, Susan Penhaligon, John Vernon, Joan Greenwood, Alexandra Stewart, Simon Williams, Chloe Franks.

Middling anthology with Cushing as an author who illustrates his theory of a feline conspiracy against mankind to a skeptical Milland with a trio of tales. Young lovers after an old lady's fortune fail to reckon with her vengeful pets; a little girl is taught black magic by a witch's familiar; and a 1930s horror actor and his mistress are driven to their deaths by his murdered wife's devoted kitty. This is sluggish but well cast, with Eggar and Pleasence an especial delight in the spoofy final segment.

UNCLE WAS A VAMPIRE
★★☆ Sinister Cinema, 1959, NR, 83 min. Dir: Stefano Steno. Cast: Christopher Lee, Renato Rascel, Sylva Koscina, Kai Fisher, Susanna Loret, Antie Geerk.

A vampire nobleman (Lee) visits his nephew at the family estate, only to discover the place converted to a hotel and the entitled nephew (Rascel) working as a bellhop. Outraged, the uncle puts the bite on poor Renato, who unexpectedly becomes the most popular man at the resort. Pleasant spoof with good work from Lee and the impish Rascel. Theme song: "Dracula Cha-Cha-Cha." Aka *Tempe Duri per I Vampiri: Hard Times for Vampires* and *Hard Times for Dracula.*

UNDERSTUDY: GRAVEYARD SHIFT II, THE
★☆ Virgin Vision, 1988, R, 88 min. Dir: Gerard Ciccoritti. Cast: Silvio Oliviero, Wendy Gazelle, Mark Soper, Ilse Von Glatz, Tim Kelleher, Leslie Kelly.

Dull sequel to the popular, and better, direct-to-vid *Graveyard Shift* with that film's bloodsucker (Oliviero) in Hollywood, where he romances B horror queen Gazelle and lands a part in a cheapo vamp flick called *Blood Lover*. Apart from the inventive use of a pool cue as decapitation device, this self-consciously glitzy follow-up hasn't much to offer.

UNDERTAKER AND HIS PALS, THE

★ Flamingo, 1967, NR, 60 min. Dir: David C. Graham. Cast: Warene Ott, Robert Lowery, Rad Fulton, Ray Dannis, Marty Feldman, Rick Cooper.

An undertaker who runs the cut-rate Shady Rest Funeral Parlor has a deal with a pair of murderous diner owners who kill and mutilate various people (mostly women) with the UT burying the victims and leftovers served at the diner—a popular hangout for the cast of *Alive*, I'm sure. Poor gore-comedy rip-off of splatter guru Herschell Gordon Lewis' horror films shot on a microscopic budget; this tries really hard to be funny but rarely is, and it's marred by static photography and choppy editing. The first few minutes are in B&W, with the film switching to color during the first murder—does that make this the splatter *Wizard of Oz*?

UNDERWORLD

See: *Transmutations*.

UNDYING MONSTER, THE

★★★ Sinister Cinema, 1942, NR, 60 min. Dir: John Brahm. Cast: James Ellison, Heather Angel, John Howard, Bramwell Fletcher, Aubrey Mather, Heather Thatcher.

Twentieth Century-Fox combined elements of both the Universal and Val Lewton horror techniques for this model B movie adapted from a much duller novel by Jessie Douglas Kerruish. A series of brutal murders committed in an English village is traced to a member of the local gentry suffering a hereditary werewolf curse. This impressive B&W flick is sharply photographed and just brimming with mood and suspense—and has a monster not clearly shown until the final few minutes.

UNEARTHLY, THE

★★☆ Rhino, 1957, NR, 70 min. Dir: Brooke L. Peters [Boris Petroff]. Cast: John Carradine, Allison Hayes, Myron Healey, Tor Johnson, Sally Todd, Arthur Batanides.

Campy low-budget rip of *The Black Sleep* with mad doc Carradine experimenting with a new gland he's created (it looks like a piece of bacon) that he hopes will give his subjects (unsuspecting patients at his Georgia private rest home) immortality. What he ends up with is a cellar full of undying mutant monsters.

Good Harry Thomas makeup and a notably bent cast make this well worth a look-see.

UNHINGED

★ Lighthouse, 1982, UR, 78 min. Dir: Don Gronquist. Cast: Laurel Munson, J. E. Penner, Sara Ansley, Virginia Settle.

Schlocky slasher about a trio of teen girls on their way to a rock concert who end up stranded at the remote mansion of a batty old lady whose repressed transsexual daughter-son begins killing them off. A bungled non-thriller, this contains ham-fisted references to Hitchcock, De Palma, and Craven and displays a cruel misogynistic streak. Also available in edited R-rated form.

UNHOLY, THE

★★ Vestron, 1988, R, 100 min. Dir: Camilo Vila. Cast: Ben Cross, Hal Holbrook, Ned Beatty, Jill Carroll, William Russ, Trevor Howard, Claudia Robinson, Nicole Fortier.

Laughably overblown *Exorcist*-type supernatural shocker in which Cross is a sincere young priest who miraculously survives a fall from a tall building and is then assigned the position of parish priest to a New Orleans church haunted by a demon known as "Desiderius." Co-scripted by Philip Yordan, this has moments of interest and a fine cast, but both are mostly lost amid a torrent of gory FX and a she-demon (Fortier) who looks like a *Penthouse* centerfold wearing one of Cher's old nighties.

UNINVITED, THE

★★★★ MCA/Universal, 1944, NR, 98 min. Dir: Lewis Allen. Cast: Ray Milland, Ruth Hussey, Gail Russell, Donald Crisp, Cornelia Otis Skinner, Alan Napier.

Classic haunted house movie based on the novel *Uneasy Freehold* by Dorothy MacArdle. A brother and sister (Milland and Hussey) rent an old mansion on the Cornish coast of England they discover to be inhabited by a pair of female spirits, one good and one evil—but which is which? Good acting, photography, and set design; the memorable Victor Young score includes the famous ballad "Stella By Starlight."

UNINVITED

★☆ New Star, 1988, PG-13, 90 min. Dir: Greydon Clark. Cast: George Kennedy, Alex Cord, Clu Gulager, Toni Hudson, Eric Larson, Clare Carey.

This one almost defies description. Clark, the guy who brought us satanic pom-pom girls

Ray Milland and Ruth Hussey ain't afraid of no ghosts in The Uninvited *(1944).*

and killer pizzas from outer space, strikes back with another first: a radioactive pussycat with a murderous mutant rat living in its stomach! I swear! Said kitty escapes from some experimental lab or another and stows away on mobster Cord's yacht, where it terrorizes hambones Cord, Kennedy, and Gulager (the latter sporting a hilarious set of ill-fitting dentures) as well as a couple of good lookin' bikini babes. This has some of the worst acting, most overdone bladder makeup FX, and the phoniest ship miniature you've ever seen—in short, it's a movie trash collector's delight.

UNLAWFUL ENTRY

★★☆ Fox, 1992, R, 111 min.
Dir: Jonathan Kaplan. Cast: Kurt Russell, Ray Liotta, Madeline Stowe, Roger E. Mosley, Ken Lerner, Deborah Offner, Carmen Argenziano, Dick Miller.

A riveting performance by Liotta distinguishes this by-the-book entry in the early '90s spate of mainstream psycho movies. Ray plays a handsome, earnest young cop who befriends Russell and Stowe after a break-in at their house but soon begins to show dangerously obsessive tendencies. A strange twist in the early going seems to suggest that Ray has a thing for *Kurt* rather than Maddie, but things soon settle into a more routine groove, with a reality quotient no greater than *Psycho Cop*'s but some good moments just the same.

UNNAMABLE, THE

★★☆ Starmaker, 1988, R, 87 min.
Dir: Jean-Paul Ouellette. Cast: Charles King, Mark Kinsey Stephenson, Alexandra Durrell, Laura Albert, Eben Ham, Blane Wheatley.

College kids spend the night in an old cemetery-side house where they fall victim to a cloven-hooved she-demon living in the attic. Good gore and a restrained handling of the titular creature, but cloddish characters and a lame ending keep this minor H. P. Lovecraft adaptation out of the same league as Stuart Gordon's *Re-Animator* and *From Beyond*.

UNNAMABLE II: THE STATEMENT OF RANDOLPH CARTER, THE
★★ Prism, 1992, R, 104 min.
Dir: Jean-Paul Ouellette. Cast: Mark Kinsey Stephenson, Charles Klausmeyer, Maria Ford, John Rhys-Davies, David Warner, Peter Breck, August West, Alexandra Durrell.

This mediocre sequel starts well but soon loses its way and runs way too long. The unnamable returns and mutates into both a beautiful young lady (Ford, who goes through almost the entire film sans clothing) and an even nastier form of itself. The usual bozo college types keep the body count up, while heroes Stephenson and Klausmeyer (aping Jeffrey Combs and Bruce Abbott in the *Re-Animator* movies) try to stop the monster's rampage. Slickly made but frustratingly uneven. Aka *The Unnamable Returns*.

UNNAMABLE RETURNS, THE
See: *The Unnamable II: The Statement of Randolph Carter*.

UNNATURAL
★★ Sinister Cinema, 1952, NR, 90 min.
Dir: Arthur-Maria Rabenalt. Cast: Hildegarde Knef, Erich von Stroheim, Karl Boehm, Trude Hesterberg.

Originally titled *Alraune*, this is an interestingly cast but hokey and ponderous melodrama with von Stroheim as a doctor who creates a woman (Knef) through artificial insemination using the sperm of a killer. It comes as no surprise then when Hildegarde proves to be an immoral seductress and murderess. This German production is mainly for fans of von Stroheim's patented form of overacting.

UNSANE
★★★ Fox Hills, 1982, R, 91 min.
Dir: Dario Argento. Cast: Anthony Franciosa, John Saxon, Daria Nicolodi, John Steiner, Giuliano Gemma, Veronica Lario, Christian Borromeo, Mirella D'Angelo.

Argento's *Tenebrae* makes it to video with a new title and minus about 10 minutes of its more explicit violence (robbing it of an extra 1/2 star) but even with these cuts remains one of his tightest, most watchable films. Thriller writer Franciosa is in Rome on a book tour when a crazed killer begins using his latest novel as inspiration for a series of razor and ax slayings. Graced with Luciano Tovoli's hypnotic, neon-colored camerawork (though about half the famous Louma crane "prowling over the house" shot has been trimmed), a jazzy score, and better-than-average performances, this is one of the Italian maestro's most enjoyable efforts.

UNSEEN, THE
★★☆ VidAmerica, 1981, R, 89 min.
Dir: Peter Foleg. Cast: Barbara Bach, Sydney Lassick, Lelia Goldoni, Stephen Furst, Doug Barr, Karen Lamm.

Minor but suspenseful psychological thriller with the beauteous Bach as a TV reporter spending the night in a creepy old house also inhabited by the cellar-dwelling offspring (Furst) born of the incestuous relationship between the house's jovial owner (Lassick) and his sad-eyed sister (Goldoni). Considering the exploitable subject matter, this is surprisingly restrained, with convincing performances from Lassick and Goldoni and subtle Craig Reardon monster makeup.

UP FROM THE DEPTHS
★ Vestron, 1979, R, 75 min. Dir: Charles B. Griffith. Cast: Sam Bottoms, Susanna Reed, Virgil Frye, Kedric Wolfe, Denise Hayes, Charles Howerton.

Rock-bottom Filipino *Jaws* imitation with a huge prehistoric plastic fish munching on vacationers staying at an exclusive Hawaiian resort. When the frantic resort owners hold a contest to catch the monster, further carnage erupts. A disappointing comedown for former Roger Corman associate Griffith, this is supposed to be a comedy. I think. Remade as *Demon of Paradise*.

VAGRANT, THE
★★ MGM/UA, 1992, R, 91 min.
Dir: Chris Walas. Cast: Bill Paxton, Michael Ironside, Marshall Bell, Mitzi Kapture, Colleen Camp, Marc McClure, Stuart Pankin, Patrika Darbo.

A good cast—especially Paxton—struggles with this uneven horror-comedy about a self-absorbed yup (Bill) who thinks that the bum living in a vacant lot across the street wants to kill him and take over his house. Marginally horrific character study that falls flat too much of the time for its own good.

VALLEY OF GWANGI, THE

★★★ Warner, 1969, G, 95 min.
Dir: Jim O'Connolly. Cast: James Franciscus,
Gila Golan, Richard Carlson, Laurence Naismith,
Freda Jackson, Curtis Arden.

An unjustly overlooked Ray Harryhausen
cowboys vs. dinosaurs animation epic set in
Mexico but shot in Spain. Franciscus and
friends discover a lost valley inhabited by prehistoric creatures and bring a 12-foot allo-
saurus called Gwangi back to display in a
Wild West show. Naturally, Gwangi escapes
and goes on a rampage, which climaxes in a
blazing cathedral. One of Ray's best, with a
good cast having fun with their stereotypical
characters and a genuinely rousing ending.

VAMP

★★☆ Starmaker, 1986, R, 94 min.
Dir: Richard Wenk. Cast: Grace Jones, Chris
Makepeace, Dedee Pfeiffer, Robert Rusler,
Sandy Baron, Gedde Watanabe.

A trio of college freshmen check out a seedy
night club looking for a stripper to entertain at
a frat party and fall prey to a pack of vampires
led by Katrina (Jones). This likable combination of *Fright Night* and *After Hours* features a
personable cast and a healthy appreciation of
the Hammer vampire classics but bogs down a
bit in the middle before wrapping things up
with a bang.

VAMPIRE

See: *Vampyr.*

VAMPIRE, THE

See: *The Devil's Commandment.*

VAMPIRE, THE

★★★ Sinister Cinema, 1957, NR, 84 min.
Dir: Fernando Mendez. Cast: German Robles,
Ariadna Welter, Abel Salazar, Carmen Montejo,
José Luis Simenez, Mercedes Solar.

The first and best of the myriad Mexican horror movies imported north of the Rio Grande
in the '50s and '60s by K. Gordon Murray.
Robles is the tusked and tuxedoed Count
Lavud, alias Mr. Duval, who puts the bite on
the women of a misty hacienda called the
Sycamores. The usual cheesy dubbing hurts,
but there's also lots of cobwebs and smoke,
clever directorial touches, and pleasant comic
relief. This is notable also as one of the first
horror films to show a vampire with fangs.
Sequel: *The Vampire's Coffin.*

VAMPIRE AT MIDNIGHT

★☆ Key, 1987, R, 89 min. Dir: Gregory McClatchy.

Cast: Jason Williams, Gustav Vintas, Lesley Milne,
Esther Alise, Jeanie Moore, Robert Random.

Imagine, if you will, a cross between *Count
Yorga, Vampire* and *Dirty Harry.* Then again,
don't, as this dull vanity piece (co-produced
and co-written by *Flesh Gordon* star Williams)
is a real bore. An L.A. cop (Williams) hunts a
creepy pop psychologist (Vintas) who may be
a murderous vampire—but probably isn't.
This *might* have worked with Clint Eastwood
and Christopher Lee in the leads, but with
these two guys—forget it!

VAMPIRE BAT, THE

★★☆ Goodtimes, 1933, NR, 62 min.
Dir: Frank Strayer. Cast: Lionel Atwill, Fay Wray,
Melvyn Douglas, Dwight Frye, Maude Eburne,
Robert Fraser.

Hokey but fun '30s low-budgeter obviously
patterned after both *Dracula* and *Frankenstein.*
Atwill is typically terrific in one of his
archtypical mad doctor roles as a scientist who
sends his hypnotized butler out to commit a
series of vampire-like murders to gather the
blood needed to keep Lionel's experimental
new life form (a blob of matter in a fish tank)
alive. No classic but enjoyable, with Frye, as a
bat-loving loony, and Wray, as the imperiled
heroine with the nerve to question Atwill's
sanity, both in top form.

VAMPIRE BEAST CRAVES BLOOD, THE

See: *The Blood Beast Terror.*

VAMPIRE HAPPENING, THE

★☆ United, 1971, NR, 97 min.
Dir: Freddie Francis. Cast: Pia Dagermark, Ferdy
Mayne, Thomas Hunter, Ingrid van Bergen.

Pathetic horror comedy starring Dagermark of
Elvira Madigan fame as a girl possessed by a
lookalike vampire ancestress. Veteran Hammer director Francis and the always amusing
Mayne (in a cameo as Dracula) do what they
can to enliven this German sausage-stuffer.

VAMPIRE HOOKERS

★ Magnum, 1979, R, 79 min. Dir: Cirio H. Santiage.
Cast: John Carradine, Bruce Fairbairn, Trey Wilson,
Karen Stride, Lenka Novak, Katie Dolan.

Stupid, leering comedy with Carradine as a
Shakespeare-spouting old vampire living with
a trio of luscious, negligeed ladies who lure
sailors to their cemetery hideout for a quick
bite. Even at only 79 minutes, this Filipino
cheapie seems *long*—with one endless slow-
motion soft-core sex scene and an awful ending—and was apparently edited by someone
with a very poor memory.

VAMPIRE LOVERS, THE
★★★ Orion, 1970, R, 90 min.
Dir: Roy Ward Baker. Cast: Ingrid Pitt, Peter Cushing, Dawn Addams, Kate O'Mara, George Cole, Douglas Wilmer, Pippa Steel, Madeline Smith, Jon Finch, Ferdy Mayne.

Sensuous Hammer film scripted from J. Sheridan Le Fanu's *Carmilla* about a lesbian vampire (Pitt) preying upon the beautiful teen daughters of several 19th-century Styrian noblemen. An attractive production of rich colors and design, it contains (now mild) nudity and eroticism that was considered a daring ploy by Hammer back in 1970. Pitt and Cushing (in a small role) are excellent. Sequels: *Lust for a Vampire* and *Twins of Evil*.

VAMPIRE MEN OF THE LOST PLANET
See: *Horror of the Blood Monsters.*

VAMPIRE OVER LONDON
See: *My Son, The Vampire.*

VAMPIRE PLAYGIRLS
See: *The Devil's Nightmare.*

VAMPIRE PLAYGIRLS
See: *Dracula's Great Love.*

VAMPIRE'S COFFIN, THE
★★☆ Sinister Cinema, 1957, NR, 86 min.
Dir: Fernando Mendez. Cast: German Robles, Ariadna Welter, Abel Salazar, Yerye Beirute, Carlos Ancira, Alicia Montoya.

In this so-so sequel to *The Vampire,* Count Lavud (Robles) is revived when the stake is

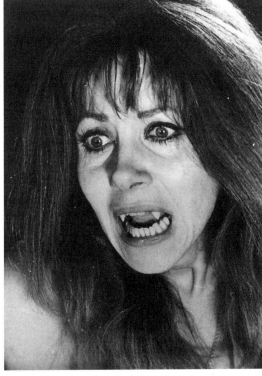

Ingrid Pitt goes out for a bite in The Vampire Lovers *(1970).*

removed from his chest and heads for Mexico City, where he once again begins stalking the lovely Welter. Some good atmosphere in a shadowy wax museum and an exciting ending, but mostly just a lot of running around.

VAMPIRE'S KISS
★★ HBO, 1988, R, 96 min.
Dir: Robert Bierman. Cast: Nicholas Cage, Jennnifer Beals, Maria Conchita Alonso, Elizabeth Ashley, Kasi Lemmons, Bob Lujan.

A lonely New York literary agent (Cage) begins turning into a vampire—or has a nervous breakdown—after a one-night stand with an alluring femme fatale (Beals). This uneven black comedy has some excellent, telling moments as it examines the hollowness of a life spent pursuing money and career above all else, but it can't find a consistent point of view and Cage's erratic, off-putting performance grates too much.

VAMPIRES OF PRAGUE
See: *Mark of the Vampire.*

INGRID PITT
(1944–)

Born in Poland as Ingoushka Petrov, Ingrid did stage work in both Germany and Spain before landing her first film role in the Spanish horror flick *The Sound of Horror* in 1965. After attracting attention in a supporting role in the terrific WWII actioner *Where Eagles Dare* four years later, Pitt was signed by Britain's Hammer Films, where she all too briefly became one of their most popular femmes fatales.

The Sound of Horror ('65), *The Omegans* ('68), *The Vampire Lovers* ('70), *Countess Dracula* ('71), *The House That Dripped Blood* ('71), *The Wicker Man* ('73), *Transmutations* ('86).

VAMPIRE WOMAN
See: *Crypt of the Living Dead.*

VAMPYR
★★★☆ Kino, 1932, NR, 65 min.
Dir: Carl Theodore Dreyer. Cast: Julian West,
Sybille Schmitz, Rena Mandel, Maurice Schultz,
Henrietta Gerard, Jan Hieronimko.

This French-German adaptation of Le Fanu's
Carmilla remains one of the minor masterpieces of '30s horror. A young traveler (West)
is pressed into service by a strange old man to
save a pair of beautiful sisters from an old hag
(Gerard) who turns out to be a vampire.
Rough going but worth seeing for its atmosphere (a piece of gauze was placed before the
camera lens to impart a grainy, dreamlike tex-
ture to the photography) and an oft-imitated
sequence where the hero imagines himself
buried alive. Aka *Vampire, Castle of Doom,* and
The Strange Adventure of David Gray.

VAMPYRES
★★ Magnum, 1974, UR, 86 min.
Dir: Joseph [José] Larraz. Cast: Marianne Morris,
Anulka, Murray Brown, Brian Deacon, Sally Faulkner,
Michael Byrne.

Silly soft-core sex-horror about a pair of murdered lesbians (Morris and Anulka) who
haunt an old English estate, seducing various
passersby of both sexes in order to suck their
blood—among other things. Beautiful autumnal settings and photogenic leads, but the
characters are dull and the gore scenes get to
be a bit much—the girls have no fangs and so
must slash and *lick* their victims to death! This
British flick was originally released in the U.S.
with an X rating and is available on tape in
both unrated and R versions. Aka *Vampyres,
Daughters of Dracula.*

VAMPYRES, DAUGHTERS OF DRACULA
See: *Vampyres.*

VANISHING, THE
★★★ Fox/Lorber, 1988, R, 107 min.
Dir: George Sluizer. Cast: Bernard-Pierre Donnadieu,
Gene Bervoets, Johnanna Ter Steege, Gwen Eckhaus.

This arty Dutch psychological thriller became
a surprise hit on the art house circuit. When
his new bride disappears on their honeymoon,
a man (Bervoets) spends years obsessively trying to find her—with very disturbing results.
This keeps you guessing throughout and is
well directed by Sluizer. The chillingly
ambiguous twist ending will stay with you for
days—and is far more satisfying than the new,
upbeat ending contrived for the remake.

VANISHING, THE
★★ Fox, 1993, R, 109 min.
Dir: George Sluizer. Cast: Jeff Bridges,
Kiefer Sutherland, Nancy Travis, Sandra Bullock,
Park Overall, Lisa Eichhorn, Maggie Linderman,
George Hearn.

The director of the superior original helms this
very "Hollywoodized" remake in which
Bridges is the madman who kidnaps vacation-
er Bullock, and Sutherland is her grief-stricken
boyfriend who spends years trying to find out
what happened to her. This beefs up the role
of secondary heroine Travis and supplies a
totally unjustified happy ending—unlike the
Dutch version's chillingly effective downbeat
one—but is sufficiently well made to stand on
its own as an okay thriller with an especially
daring performance from Bridges.

VANISHING BODY, THE
See: *The Black Cat.*

VARAN THE UNBELIEVABLE
★☆ United, 1958, NR, 70 min.
Dirs: Inoshiro Honda, Jerry A. Baerwitz.
Cast: Myron Healey, Ysuruko Kobayashi,
Clifford Kawada, Derick Simatsu, Kozo Nomura,
Ayami Sonoda.

First released in the States in '62 with new
scenes added featuring the stalwart Healey,
this mostly incomprehensible Toho monster
pic (originally *Daikaiju Baran: The Monster
Baran*) has yet another huge monster, this one
risen from a mountain lake, rampaging
through Japan. The American scenes splice in
badly with the original material, and the
effects are something less than special. It's
unbelievable, all right.

VAULT OF HORROR
★★☆ Nostalgia Merchant, 1973, R, 86 min.
Dir: Roy Ward Baker, Cast: Glynis Johns, Daniel
Massey, Terry-Thomas, Tom Baker, Anna Massey,
Curt Jurgens, Michael Craig, Dawn Addams,
Denholm Elliott, Edward Judd.

Okay follow-up to Amicus' popular *Tales From
the Crypt* anthology presents five more EC
comics stories, bridged this time by a group of
men telling each other of their recurring nightmares. The first and the last are the best of the
bunch: a murderer becomes the main course at
a vampire restaurant, and an artist uses
voodoo to avenge himself on his enemies. A
great cast, but the attempt made to mix the
horror with dry wit really doesn't come off.
Originally released with an unfair R rating, it
would easily get a PG-13 today and was reissued as *Tales From the Crypt Part II.*

VEIL, THE
See: *Haunts.*

VELVET HOUSE
See: *Crucible of Horror.*

VELVET VAMPIRE, THE
★★ Embassy, 1971, R, 80 min.
Dir: Stephanie Rothman. Cast: Celeste Yarnall, Michael Blodgett, Sherry Miles, Gene Shane.

Typical early '70s sex-vampire movie enhanced by some interesting direction and good photography. Beautiful bloodsucker Yarnall lures a dopey young couple she mets at a chi-chi L.A. art gallery to her Mojave desert home where she preys upon their blood and sexual appetites. Aggressively bad performing and an obvious *Count Yorga* twist ending weigh it down. British title: *The Waking Hour.*

VENGEANCE
See: *The Brain* (1962).

VENGEANCE OF THE MUMMY
See: *The Mummy's Revenge.*

VENGEANCE OF THE ZOMBIES
★★☆ All Seasons, 1972, R, 87 min.
Dir: Leon Klimovsky. Cast: Paul Naschy, Rommy, Mirta Miller, Vic Winner, Maria Kosti, Luis Ciges.

In this enjoyably gross *Night of the Living Dead* variant set in England, Naschy has three roles: the Hindu mystic Krishna; his evil, disfigured, zombie-making brother; and the devil in a dream sequence in which young women are killed and brought back as murderous walking corpses. There are scenes inspired by *House of Wax* and *Twitch of the Death Nerve* plus a hilariously out-of-place theme song. Original Spanish title: *La Rebellion de las Muertas: Rebellion of the Dead* and aka *Walk of the Dead.*

VENGEANCE: THE DEMON
See: *Pumpkinhead.*

VENOM
See: *The Legend of Spider Forest.*

VENOM
★★☆ Vestron, 1982, R, 93 min.
Dir: Piers Haggard. Cast: Klaus Kinski, Oliver Reed, Nicol Williamson, Sarah Miles, Sterling Hayden, Susan George, Cornelia Sharpe, Michael Gough.

An entertaining, if unintentionally hilarious, *Jaws*-influenced thriller about a kidnapping complicated by a deadly black mamba snake that traps both the kidnappers and their hostages in a London townhouse. Originally

Anna Massey is all smiles in Vault of Horror *(1973).*

to be directed by Tobe Hooper, this is slick but very silly; the cast seem to be having a bad-acting contest, with Gough swiping it as a snake expert apparently afraid of snakes—when the mamba attacks, he's the first one to get the hell outta there!

VENUS IN FURS
★★☆ Republic, 1969, X, 86 min. Dir: Jess [Jesus] Franco. Cast: James Darren, Barbara McNear, Maria Rohm, Klaus Kinski, Dennis Price, Margaret Lee.

This weird erotic horror-mystery just may be Señor Franco's best feature. Darren is a jazz trumpeter obsessed with Venus (Rohm), a beautiful brunette who bears an uncanny resemblance to Wanda, a girl gang-raped and murdered by a trio of jet-setters who are themselves being bumped off, one by one. Could it be that Venus is really Wanda, back from the grave? Set in Istanbul and Rio, this has lush color, a surprisingly upscale cast, a plot that makes little sense, and a truly shocking double-twist ending. And don't let the X rating put you off, as this is no more explicit that your average R. Also released as *Paroxismus.*

JESUS [JESS] FRANCO
(1930–)

Probably the world's most prolific director, the Madrid-born Franco once worked with none other than Orson Welles on several unrealized projects before becoming the premier purveyor of Euro-sleaze trash horror films. The king of the zoom lens, he's somehow managed to cajole all manner of heretofore legit actors into appearing in all manner of perverse pieces of shock celluloid. Ya gotta admire the guy.

The Awful Dr. Orlof ('62), *Dr. Orloff's Monster* ('64), *The Diabolical Dr. Z* ('65), *Attack of the Robots* ('66), *Kiss Me, Monster* ('67), *Succubus* ('67), *Justine* ('68), *The Blood of Fu Manchu* ('68), *The Castle of Fu Manchu* ('68), *Venus in Furs* ('69), *Eugenie, the Story of Her Journey Into Perversion* ('69), *Count Dracula* ('70), *Mrs. Hyde* ('70), *Night of the Blood Monster* ('70), *A Virgin Among the Living Dead* ('71), *Lesbian Vampires* ('71), *The Demons* ('72), *The Screaming Dead* ('72), *The Erotic Rites of Frankenstein* ('72), *Erotikill* ('73), *Jack the Ripper* ('76), *Demoniac* ('79), *Man Hunter* ('80), *Bloody Moon* ('81), *Oasis of the Zombies* ('82), *Revenge in the House of Usher* ('83), *Treasure of the White Goddess* ('84), *Faceless* ('88).

VERTIGO
★★★★ MCA/Universal, 1958, PG, 128 min.
Dir: Alfred Hitchcock. Cast: James Stewart, Kim Novak, Barbara Bel Geddes, Tom Helmore, Henry Jones, Raymond Bailey.

Stewart is an acrophobic Frisco ex-cop hired by college buddy Helmore to trail the latter's wife (Novak) who claims to be possessed by the ghost of her suicidal great-grandmother. When Novak "dies" in a leap from a mission tower, a grieving Stewart, who has fallen in love with his quarry, tries to recreate her in another girl, with surprising and tragic results. Though only bordering on the horror genre, this masterpiece creates for itself an atmosphere of the supernatural far more convincing than those devised for other, more standard occult fare, thanks to Hitchcock's dream-like direction and Bernard Herrmann's haunting score. Excellent acting from Stewart and Novak; partly remade as *Obsession*.

VICTIM, THE
See: *Out of Contention*.

VICTOR FRANKENSTEIN
See: *Terror of Frankenstein*.

VIDEO DEAD, THE
★★ Embassy, 1987, R, 90 min.
Dir: Robert Scott. Cast: Roxanna Augesen, Rocky Duvall, Michael St. Michaels, Jennifer Miro, Vickie Bastel, Sam David McCelland.

Teen sister and brother Augesen and Duvall battle a squad of zombies released from a haunted TV set that always plays the same cheap horror film—even when unplugged! This vid pic is slow and stupid in spots but has likable characters and takes several genuinely surprising turns of plot—for what plot there is. You could do worse.

VIDEODROME
★★★☆ MCA/Universal, 1982, R, 88 min.
Dir: David Cronenberg. Cast: James Woods, Deborah Harry, Sonja Smits, Peter Dvorsky, Les Carlson, Jack Creley.

Cronenberg's most wacked-out and challenging pre–*Naked Lunch* film has a powerhouse performance from Woods as the maverick program director of a cable TV station who discovers the existence of "Videodrome": a gory sado-sexual torture-horror show. Although it at first appears that "Videodrome" is coming from some unknown foreign country, it eventually transpires that the show can cause deadly brain tumors in the viewer and has been concocted by some right-wing types out to eliminate the sort of human "scum" who would watch it in the first place. Confident supporting performances capture every little shade and nuance of their characters. Tight, imaginative writing and direction from Cronenberg and some awesome Rick Baker make-up FX underscore one of the Canadian horror maestro's best.

VILLAGE OF THE DAMNED
★★★☆ MGM/UA, 1960, NR, 77 min.
Dir: Wolf Rilla. Cast: George Sanders, Barbara Shelley, Michael Gwynn, Laurence Naismith, Martin Stephens, John Phillips.

Impressively understated version of John Wyndham's novel *The Midwich Cuckoos*. Most of the women of a small English village turn up pregnant after everyone is inexplicably rendered unconscious for 12 hours, and nine months later they give birth to strangely similar blonde babies with supernormal mental abilities. Crisp and chilling, with solid acting from a great British ensemble cast and sharp monochrome photography. Sequel: *Children of the Dammed*.

VILLAGE OF THE GIANTS

★☆ Embassy, 1965, NR, 82 min. Dir: Bert I. Gordon. Cast: Tommy Kirk, Beau Bridges, Ronny Howard, Charla Doherty, Johnny Crawford, Tim Rooney, Tisha Sterling, Joy Harmon, Toni Basil, Joe Turkel.

A little boy called Genius (Howard) invents some gunk that transforms ducks into colossal slam-dancers and a gang of bratty teens into town-tearing terrors. As you can tell, this is Bert's first version of H. G. Wells' *The Food of the Gods*, rewritten for the "American Bandstand" set. There are lots of laughable effects and campy dialogue, but this is an opus I'd bet its better-known stars would like to forget. Remade by Gordon as *Food of the Gods*.

VINDICATOR, THE

★★☆ CBS/Fox, 1986, R, 88 min. Dir: Jean-Claude Lord. Cast: Teri Austin, Richard Cox, Pam Grier, Maury Chaykin, David MacIlwraith.

Not bad mix of sci-fi and horror with Cox as a scientist slain by rival MacIlwraith. His brain is then placed in the head of the indestructible robot he has created, which then goes on the inevitable rampage. There's good acting, plus an imaginative, *Terminator*-like robot suit designed by Stan Winston, in this Canadian updating of *The Colossus of New York*. Original title: *Frankenstein '88*.

VINEYARD, THE

★☆ Starmaker, 1989, R, 95 min. Dirs: William Rice, James Hong. Cast: James Hong, Karen Witter, Cheryl Lawson, Mike Wong.

A bad hydrid of the mad doctor and stalker subgenres in which Wong is an evil scientist/winemarker/film producer who lures the usual carload of dunderheads to his estate for the blood he needs to stay immortal. Has a couple of nice, gruesome moments but mainly just dies on the vine.

VIRGIN AMONG THE LIVING DEAD, A

★ Edde Entertainment, 1971, R, 95 min. Dir: Jess [Jesus] Franco. Cast: Christina von Blanc, Britt Nichols, Howard Vernon, Paul Muller, Ann Libert, Rose Kiekens.

Laughably awful Franco fest about a pretty but dumb heiress (von Blanc) who travels to the Honduran mansion of her late father to collect an inheritance and comes up against various zombie relatives, retard manservants, and lesbian nymphets. Horrible dubbing does make for some fun (particularly during an uproarious reading-of-the-will scene), and there are the usual sick-weird touches (like a girl doing her toenails during a funeral) to help make this watchable junk—but it's still

junk. Aka *Among the Living Dead; Christina, Princess of Eroticism;* and *Zombie 4*.

VIRGIN OF NUREMBERG, THE

★★☆ Panther, 1963, NR, 83 min. Dir: Anthony Dawson [Antonio Margheriti]. Cast: Christopher Lee, Rossana Podesta, Georges Riviere, Jim Nolan, Anny Delli Uberti, Mirko Valentin.

Originally released in the U.S. as *Horror Castle*, this gleefully gruesome German-Italian flick stars Podesta as a bride who encounters a hooded, sadistic psycho-killer known as "The Punisher" haunting her husband's Rhine castle. Lee is badly dubbed in a secondary role as the castle's disfigured majordomo, and there's an annoying, tinny theme, but a memorably twisted villain and some very gross scenes (including an unforgettable sequence where a rat cage is placed over a girl's face as her nose is eaten off) make this an above-average '60s Euro-shocker. Aka *Castle of Terror* and *Terror Castle*.

VIRGINS AND THE VAMPIRE, THE

See: *Dungeon of Terror*.

VIRGINS FOR THE HANGMAN

See: *The Bloody Pit of Horror*.

VIRGIN WITCH, THE

★☆ Prism, 1970, R, 85 min. Dir: Ray Austin. Cast: Ann Michelle, Vicky Michelle, Keith Buckley, Patricia Haines, Neil Hallett.

There are lots of good-lookin' chicks but few chills in this Brit clinker about a pair of gorgeous sisters who get mixed up with modeling and witchcraft in mod London. Dull and exploitive, with sexist, reactionary views of women, lesbians, witches, you name it. Aka *Lesbian Twins*.

VISIONS OF EVIL

★★ Prism Entertainment, 1973, PG, 90 min. Dir: Harry Thomason. Cast: Lori Saunders, Dean Jagger, Bob Ginnaven, Seymour Treitman.

Originally called *So Sad About Gloria*, this very minor lady-in-distress thriller features Saunders (of TV's "Petticoat Junction") as an heiress terrorized in her Georgia mansion by a menacing ax man in a Tor Johnson mask. An early effort from "Designing Women" co-creator Thomason, this has a great-funny shock-twist ending but not much else.

VISITING HOURS

★★☆ CBS/Fox, 1981, R, 105 min. Dir: Jean-Claude Lord. Cast: Lee Grant, William Shatner, Linda Purl, Michael Ironside, Lenore Zann, Harvey Atkin.

Harrowing, above-average, bedpans-of-terror slasher with Grant as a feminist newscaster stabbed in her home by misogynic maniac Ironside. Lee survives and is sent to the local hospital where Mike follows to continue his chauvinistic reign of terror. All the usual clichés are present and accounted for, but a strong cast and direction make this worth seeing. Filmed as *The Fright*.

VISITOR, THE
★ Vidmark, 1978, R, 90 min.
Dir: Michael J. Paradise [Guilio Paradisi].
Cast: John Huston, Shelley Winters, Glenn Ford, Mel Ferrer, Joanne Nail, Lance Henriksen, Sam Peckinpah, Paige Conner.

Atrocious mishmash of scenes and ideas from just about every popular horror and sci-fi flick of the '70s. Huston is the title character, a visitor from space—or maybe an emissary from God—who's after young Conner, an obnoxious demonic brat who's using her supernatural powers to off the supporting cast. Scenes are generously pinched from *The Exorcist, Exorcist II, The Omen, Omen II,* even *Close Encounters of the Third Kind!* Funniest scene: Shelley finally decides she's had enough and begins slapping little Paige around. Ford is wasted.

VISITOR FROM THE GRAVE, A
★★☆ Thrillervideo, 1980, NR, 50 min.
Dir: Peter Sasdy. Cast: Kathryn Leigh Scott, Simon MacCorkindale, Gareth Thomas, Mia Nadasi.

Scott (Maggie Evans on "Dark Shadows") kills an intruder in her country cottage by blasting his face off with a shotgun. Husband Mac-Corkindale buries the dead body in the woods (for fear former mental patient Kath will be put back in the funny farm permanently), but soon the gory corpse begins stalking our terrified heroine. Or does it? Solid "Hammer House of Horror" episode with a rather predictable plot, ultimately redeemed by good acting and decent direction.

VISITORS, THE
★☆ Vidmark, 1989, R, 102 min.
Dir: Joakim Ersgard. Cast: Keith Berkeley, Lena Endre, John Force, Joanna Berg, John Olson, Brent Landiss.

Awkward Swedish haunted-house flick about an estranged family moving into an old mansion that comes complete with a murderous demonic entity living in the attic at no extra charge. Not without its atmosphere and mood, but a crippling pace and a bad dubbing job make it a strain to endure.

VOODOO BLOODBATH
See: *I Eat Your Skin.*

VOODOO DAWN
★☆ Columbia/TriStar, 1989, R, 83 min.
Dir: Steven Fierberg. Cast: Raymond St. Jacques, Theresa Merritt, Tony Todd, Gina Gershon, Kirk Baily, J. Grant Albrecht.

In this tepid version of John Russo's novel about voodoo and zombie-making amongst migrant farm workers, savage high priest Todd turns city boy Albrecht into one of the walking dead. Fine actors like St. Jacques and Merritt are wasted, while Todd gives a robust performance in a small role. There's a great zombie melt-down scene near the end—but absolutely nothing else.

VOODOO WOMAN
★★ RCA/Columbia, 1957, NR, 77 min.
Dir: Edward L. Cahn. Cast: Marla English, Tom Conway, Mike "Touch" Connors, Lance Fuller, Mary Ellen Kay, Paul Dubov.

Silly AIP cheapie with Conway, in a goofy hat, as a scientist experimenting with jungle voodoo who turns bad and beautiful English into a murderous monster—a revamped *She Creature* suit in a sack dress. More talk than action but with a good cast and a smattering of laughs. Remade as *Curse of the Swamp Creature.*

VOYAGE
★★ Fox, 1993, R, 86 min.
Dir: John MacKenzie. Cast: Rutger Hauer, Karen Allen, Eric Roberts, Connie Nelson.

Another *Dead Calm*–inspired horror-on-the-high-seas TV item with two couples taking a boat trip and somebody beginning to terrorize somebody else in a very predictable fashion. The cast is good, but this unadventurous voyage really isn't worth the trip.

VULTURE, THE
★☆ IVE, 1967, NR, 92 min. Dir: Lawrence Huntingdon. Cast: Broderick Crawford, Akim Tamiroff, Robert Hutton, Diane Clare, Patrick Holt, Annette Carrell.

Ridiculous rip-off of *The Fly* about an old scientist (Tamiroff) whose experiments in teleportation combine his atoms with those of the title bird, the familiar of a legendary sorcerer. Silly performances (Crawford takes the cake as an *English* squire!) and a monster glimpsed mostly as a pair of big chicken feet dominate this cheap yock fest originally co-billed with *The Deadly Bees*—I'll leave the bad birds-and-the-bees jokes to you.

W

★★ Embassy, 1974, PG, 95 min.
Dir: Richard Quine. Cast: Twiggy, Dirk Benedict,
Michael Witney, John Vernon, Eugene Roche,
Alfred Ryder.

Contrived suspenser with Benedict menacing
former wife Twiggy and husband Witney after
his release from prison where he served a
term for supposedly killing her! A good cast
struggles against inadequate material and
direction. Also released as *I Want Her Dead*.

WACKO

★☆ Vestron, 1981, R, 84 min.
Dir: Greydon Clark. Cast: Joe Don Baker,
Stella Stevens, George Kennedy, Julia Duffy,
Scott McGinnis, Elizabeth Daily, Andrew Dice Clay,
Jeff Altman.

A crazed killer wearing a pumpkin on his
head murders students at Hitchcock High
with a lawnmower while sheriff Baker (paro-
dying his *Walking Tall* performance) tries to
guess whodunit. Baker, Stevens, Kennedy, and
Duffy (doing her "Newhart" bit for the first
time) are wasted in a transparent horror-comedy for those who find the *Porky's* movies the
height of sophisticated jocularity.

WAIT UNTIL DARK

★★★☆ Warner, 1967, NR, 108 min.
Dir: Terence Young. Cast: Audrey Hepburn, Alan
Arkin, Richard Crenna, Efrem Zimbalist, Jr., Jack
Weston, Julie Herrod, Samantha Jones, Frank O'Brien.

Scary adaptation of the Frederick Knott play
with Hepburn as a blind housewife manipulated and then terrorized by psychotic thug
Arkin, who's after a heroin-filled doll secreted
somewhere in her NYC apartment. Hepburn's
gossamer vulnerability and Arkin's oily villainy highlight this shocker whose ending—
like that of *Carrie* a decade later—has been
copied dozens of times since.

WAKING HOUR, THE

See: *The Velvet Vampire*.

WALK OF THE DEAD

See: *Vengeance of the Zombies*.

WALPURGIS NIGHT

See: *The Werewolf vs. The Vampire Woman*.

WANT A RIDE, LITTLE GIRL?

See: *Impulse* (1974).

WARD 13

See: *Hospital Massacre*.

WARLOCK

★★★ Vidmark, 1988, R, 102 min. Dir: Steve Miner.
Cast: Julian Sands, Lori Singer, Richard E. Grant,
Mary Woronov, Richard Kuss, Allan Miller.

Sands is great in this fairly involving thriller
about a condemned warlock who time-travels
to contemporary L.A. to find an ancient supernatural bible while being pursued by witch
hunter Grant. Singer is annoying as a young
waitress who gets caught up in their battle
and there's needless *Terminator-Highlander* elements tossed into the plot, but overall this
long-shelved (not released until '91) flick is
well worth a look.

WARLOCK: THE ARMAGEDDON

★★☆ Vidmark, 1993, R, 98 min.
Dir: Anthony Hickox. Cast: Julian Sands,
Paula Marshall, Chris Young, Joanna Pacula,
R. G. Armstrong, Charles Hallahan, Ferdy Mayne,
Zach Galligan.

The warlock (Sands) is reborn to collect a set
of runestones needed to bring satan back to
earth. When this slick sequel concentrates on
the warlock's bloody exploits, it really hums.
Unfortunately, too much time is wasted on the
cutesy-poo romance between supernaturally
powered high schoolers Marshall and Young,
this imbalance often making the film look like
a later Hammer Dracula sequel. The special
effects run the gamut from imaginative to
amateurish. Best scene: Sands turning a victim
into a piece of modern art.

WARLOCK MOON

★★ Unicorn, 1973, R, 85 min.
Dir: William Herbert. Cast: Laurie Walters,
Joe Spano, Edna Macafee, Charles Raino,
Ray Goman, Steve Solinsky.

Minor low-budget cannibal chiller about a girl
(Walters) sought by flesh-devouring cultists
operating out of a health spa. Tries for black
comedy but rarely succeeds. I wonder if former "Hill Streets Blues" regular Spano lists
this baby on his résumé.

WARNING SIGN

★★ CBS/Fox, 1985, R, 99 min. Dir. Hal Barwood.
Cast: Sam Waterston, Kathleen Quinlan, Yaphet

Dean Parkin in a reflective mood in War of the Colossal Beast *(1958).*

Kotto, Jeffrey DeMunn, Richard Dysart, G. W. Bailey, Scott Paulin, Rick Rossovich.

The China Syndrome meets *Dawn of the Dead* in this sleek big-studio thriller inspired by cheap Italian flicks like *Night of the Zombies.* Quinlan is the security chief at a genetic research lab where experiments get out of hand and most of the scientists are transformed into murderous zombies. Fairly tense for its first third, this soon degenerates into the usual clichés, defeating even talents like Quinlan, Waterston, and DeMunn. Shooting title: *Biohazard.*

WAR OF THE COLOSSAL BEAST

★★☆ Columbia/TriStar, 1958, NR, 68 min.
Dir: Bert I. Gordon. Cast: Sally Fraser, Roger Pace, Russ Bender, Dean Parkin, Rico Alaniz, George Becwar.

The colossal man (now horribly disfigured and played by Parkin) is discovered alive in Mexico and taken to Los Angeles where he escapes and runs amok. A fairly well-done sequel to *The Amazing Colossal Man,* this lacks that film's emotional involvement but has better special effects and grisly makeup. The ending is in color. Aka *Revenge of the Colossal Man* and *The Terror Strikes!*

WAR OF THE GARGANTUAS

★★☆ Paramount/Gateway, 1967, G, 93 min.
Dir: Inoshiro Honda. Cast: Russ Tamblyn, Kumi Mizuno, Kenji Sahara, Kipp Hamilton.

Originally conceived as a sequel to *Frankenstein Conquers the World* (1965) but altered in the editing after it was realized that the monsters looked more like King Kongs than Frankensteins, this is a stupid but totally likable Toho monster rally. Tamblyn is laughably earnest as a young scientist trying to save his friendly brown gargantua, who is being blamed for all the death and destruction caused by his vicious green twin. The FX are surprisingly elaborate for a later-60's Japanese giants flick, but the real attraction is some great unintentional comedy supplied by such scenes as the evil gargantua grabbing a woman at the Tokyo airport, swallowing her whole, and then spitting out her dress, and a nightclub scene where "guest star" Hamilton sings a wonderfully dreadful song called "The Words Get Stuck in My Throat," does the twist, and gets carried away. Aka *Sanda tai Gailah: Sanda vs. Gailah.*

WAR OF THE MONSTERS

See: *Gamera vs. Barugon.*

WASP WOMAN, THE

★★☆ Rhino, 1959, NR, 72 min.
Dir: Roger Corman. Cast: Susan Cabot, Anthony Eisley, Barboura Morris, Frank Gerstle, Michael Mark, Bruno Ve Sota.

Enjoyable early Corman about an aging cosmetics firm owner (the excellent Cabot) who takes a youth serum derived from wasp enzymes, regains her lost beauty, but also periodically transforms into a murderous insectoid thing. Silly but compelling, this has a real air of credibility in the scenes showing the day-to-day workings of Cabot's company. Corman has a cameo as a doctor. Originally double-billed with *The Beast of Haunted Cave.*

WATCHER IN THE WOODS, THE

★★☆ Disney, 1980, PG, 83 min.
Dirs: John Hough, Vincent McEvetty. Cast: Bette Davis, David McCallum, Carroll Baker, Lynn-Holly Johnson, Kyle Richards, Ian Bannen.

Fair haunted house chiller made during a time when Disney was desperately trying to change its image. A nice American family move into a scheduled English mansion that may or may not be haunted by the ghost of its landlady's (Davis) daughter. Atmospheric but confused, it was heavily reedited before release with some science fictional elements at the climax removed and a new ending, shot by McEvetty, substituted.

WATCHERS
★☆ IVE, 1988, R, 92 min. Dir: Jon Hess. Cast: Corey Haim, Michael Ironside, Barbara Williams, Lala, Duncan Fraser, Blu Mankuma.

Haim befriends a dog with the ability to communicate with humans that turns out to be part of a government experiment and is psychically linked with the violent monster hunting it. Stupid adaptation of the Dean R. Koontz novel, this was refashioned as a vehicle for teen twit Haim. Only Ironside's typically harrowing acting saves this mess, which features one of the worst monster designs in years.

WATCHERS II
★★ IVE, 1990, R, 97 min. Dir: Thierry Notz. Cast: Marc Singer, Tracy Scoggins, Jonathan Farwell, Irene Miracle, Mary Woronov, Tom Poster.

Basically just a remake of part one with a higher body count, this features another genius pooch and yet another mutant monster (who bears an unfortunate resemblance to the catfish creature from *Blood Waters of Dr. Z*) who get mixed up with army guy Singer and researcher Scoggins. Better than the first film but basically just business as usual; Woronov is wasted.

WATCH ME WHEN I KILL
★☆ HBO, 1981, R, 94 min. Dir: Anthony [Antonio] Bido. Cast: Richard Stewart, Sylvia Kramer, Umberto Raho.

Imitative Italian giallo about a dancer and her boyfriend who get involved with a slasher terrorizing Rome. Nothing you haven't seen a thousand times before or since, though the scene where a woman's face is boiled in a pot of stew is a lip-smacking first. Herman Cohen was executive producer.

WATTS MONSTER, THE
See: *Dr. Black, Mr. Hyde.*

WAXWORK
★★☆ Vestron, 1988, UR, 97 min. Dir: Anthony Hickox. Cast: Zach Galligan, Deborah Foreman, Michelle Johnson, David Warner, Patrick Macnee, Dana Ashbrook, Miles O'Keeffe, John Rhys-Davies.

Four yuppie college students attend the midnight opening of a mysterious wax museum where their combined life force is used to reanimate the evil characters (Dracula, Frankenstein, a werewolf, etc.) represented in each tableaux. A basically interesting premise is somewhat sabotaged by uneven direction and unsympathetic lead characters, though good work from a sarcastic Warner and spritely Macnee and clever homages to *Dracula, The Mummy,* and *Night of the Living Dead* keep it afloat. Also out in a cut R version.

WAXWORK II: LOST IN TIME
★★ LIVE, 1991, R, 104 min. Dir: Anthony Hickox. Cast: Zach Galligan, Monika Schnarre, Alexander Godunov, David Carradine, Bruce Campbell, John Ireland, Martin Kemp, Marina Sirtis, Maxwell Caulfield, Juliet Mills, Sophie Ward, Patrick Macnee.

Homage-happy follow-up with Galligan and Schnarre (replacing Deborah Foreman) timetripping and fighting monsters from medieval times right through to the 21st century. It's pointlessly titled (since there's no waxworks at all this time 'round) but there are on-target tributes to *The Haunting, Andy Warhol's Frankenstein, Aliens, Dawn of the Dead,* and Corman's *The Raven* and lots of guest stars. This was Ireland's last film; look for Drew Barrymore in the *Nosferatu* sequence. Aka *Lost in Time.*

WEB OF THE SPIDER
★★ Sinister Cinema, 1970, PG, 94 min. Dir: Anthony Dawson [Antonio Margheriti]. Cast: Anthony Franciosa, Michele Mercier, Klaus Kinski, Marisa Mell, Peter Carsten, Silvano Tranquilli.

Margheriti's full-color remake of his own *Castle of Blood* retells the tale of a reporter (Franciosa) who spends the night in a haunted castle as part of a wager with Edgar Allan Poe (Kinski). Has some of the atmosphere of Roger Corman's early Poe films, with richly colored lighting and lots of cobwebs and fog, but Barbara Steele is sorely missed. Kinski is very restrained too—for *him* it's restrained! Aka *Nella Stretta Morsa del Ragno: In the Grip of the Spider* and *And Comes the Dawn . . . But Colored Red.*

WELCOME TO ARROW BEACH
★★ Magnetic, 1973, R, 99 min. Dir: Laurence Harvey. Cast: Laurence Harvey, Joanna Pettet, Stuart Whitman, John Ireland, Meg Foster, Gloria LeRoy, Altovise Davis, Jesse Vint.

Harvey directed himself in his last film, an extremely odd shocker about a Korean war vet who lives with his sister in a remote beach house and occasionally snacks on a passing hitchhiker or beachcomber—having developed a taste for human flesh after being forced to eat a buddy while stranded behind enemy lines. A sleazy subject is given surprisingly upscale casting and production dress, though distributor Warner Brothers barely released this, probably out of embarrassment. Foster is especially good as a near victim, as is LeRoy as a sadly sympathetic overaged cheesecake model. Also out in a cut version called *Tender Flesh*.

WELCOME TO SPRING BREAK

★★ IVE, 1988, R, 90 min. Dir: Harry Kirkpatrick [Umberto Lenzi]. Cast: Nicholas De Toth, Sarah Buxton, John Saxon, Michael Parks, Lance Le Gault, Rawley Valverde.

A black-helmeted psycho (who may or may not be a recently executed gang leader back from the grave) terrorizes college brats during Florida spring break in this stalker updating of *Where the Boys Are*. Slickly done with a solid cast, but the killer's mystery identity is obvious, the synth score is mainly leftover riffs from *Creepers*, and far too much time is frittered away on juvenile *Porky's*-style comedy.

WEREWOLF AND THE YETI, THE

See: *Night of the Howling Beast*.

WEREWOLF AT MIDNIGHT

See: *The Werewolf of Washington*.

WEREWOLF IN A GIRL'S DORMITORY

★★ Sinister Cinema, 1961, NR, 83 min. Dir: Richard Benson [Paolo Heusch]. Cast: Barbara Lass, Carl Schell, Curt Lowens, Maurice Marsac, Maureen O'Connor, Alan Collins.

A great title masks a fairly ordinary '60s B horror. Murders at a continental school for wayward girls turn out to have been committed by the werewolf headmaster (Lowens). The makeup is little more than plastic fangs and five o'clock shadow, but this Italian-Austrian co-production has a few good scenes plus the notable theme song "The Ghoul in School." Aka *Lycanthropus, Death in the Full Moon,* and *I Married a Werewolf*.

WEREWOLF OF LONDON, THE

★★☆ MCA/Universal, 1935, NR, 75 min. Dir: Stuart Walker. Cast: Henry Hull, Warner Oland, Valerie Hobson, Spring Byington, Lester Matthews, Lawrence Grant, Ethel Griffies, Zeffie Tilbury.

This forgotten first werewolf film from Universal Pictures is dated but not unworthy. Hull (who clearly did not relish this role) is a Brit botanist bitten by werewolf Oland in Tibet. Come the next full moon, only the petals of the rare flower *Maripasia lumina lupina* can save Hull from a wolfish transformation. Originally intended as a vehicle for Karloff and Lugosi, this is too derivative of

Mamoulian's *Dr. Jekyll and Mr. Hyde* and the Jack Pierce makeup is minimal, but Oland is excellent and Byington provides a few unobtrusive laughs.

WEREWOLF OF WASHINGTON, THE

★★ Monterey, 1973, PG, 90 min. Dir: Milton Moses Ginsberg. Cast: Dean Stockwell, Biff Maguire, Clifton James, Michael Dunn, Jane House, Beeson Carroll, Jacqueline Brookes, Thayer David.

A Watergate horror-comedy doesn't sound too hot, but this '70s curio isn't *that* bad. Stockwell is marvelously deadpan as a presidential press secretary bitten in Budapest by a werewolf. Back in D.C., a series of full moon murders put the prez (Maguire) in hot water. Dated and heavy-handed, this has a werewolf that looks like he just strolled off the set of *The Shaggy Dog,* but the cast is great and there are a few chuckles. Aka *Werewolf at Midnight*.

WEREWOLF'S SHADOW, THE

See: *The Werewolf vs. The Vampire Woman*.

WEREWOLF VS. THE VAMPIRE WOMAN, THE

★★★ Sinister Cinema, 1970, R, 86 min. Dir: Leon Klimovsky. Cast: Paul Naschy, Patty Sheppard, Gaby Fuchs, Barbara Capell, Andres Resino, Julio Pena.

Naschy's best film, this really is the one that put him on the Euro-horror map. Waldemar the werewolf is revived when doctors foolishly remove the silver bullets from his heart during an autopsy. Later he attempts to save a pair of curvaceous coeds from the resurrected vampiress Countess Wandesa de Nadasdy (Sheppard). Fast, furious, and fun, this is el Hombre Lobo at his best. Aka *La Noche de Walpurgis: Walpurgis Night, The Werewolf's Shadow,* and *Blood Moon;* remade as *The Craving*.

WEREWOLVES ON WHEELS

★ Unicorn, 1971, R, 86 min. Dir: Michel Levesque. Cast: Stephen Oliver, D. J. [Donna] Anderson, Severn Darden, Billy Gray, Duece Barry, Gray Johnson.

What might seem like an unbeatable combination for a really great drive-in flick, a monster-biker movie, goes down the tubes with this dull, badly directed mess. A tough motorcycle gang encounter a bunch of devil-worshipping monks in the desert, and after a lot of bad acting and worse dialogue two of the bikers are turned into werewolves who rampage for maybe five minutes before getting killed. Seems to go on forever.

PAUL NASCHY
(1936–)

The Spanish king of horror was born Jacinto Molina (his usual screenwriting name) and was a circus performer and weight lifter before embarking on a career in films in the late '60s with his first big hit, *Mark of the Wolf Man*. The first instance in which Naschy played his best-known character, werewolf Waldemar Daninsky, the film was shot in widescreen *and* 3-D but was shown flat and severely edited when it turned up on U.S. shores as the misleadingly retitled *Frankenstein's Bloody Terror*. An enthusiastic, if undisciplined, player, lately Paul has taken to directing as well as writing and starring in his gory, entertaining flicks.

Frankenstein's Bloody Terror ('68), *Nights of the Wolf Man* ('69), *Assignment Terror* ('70), *The Werewolf vs. the Vampire Woman* ('70), *Fury of the Wolf Man* ('71), *Jack the Ripper* ('71), *Dr. Jekyll and the Wolf Man* ('71), *The Hunchback of the Morgue* ('72), *Dracula's Great Love* ('72), *Beyond the Living Dead* ('72), *Horror Rises From the Tomb* ('72), *Vengeance of the Zombies* ('72), *Curse of the Devil* ('73), *The Mummy's Revenge* ('73), *House of Psychotic Women* ('73), *Night of All Horrors* ('73), *Exorcism* ('74), *Crimson* ('74), *The Devil's Possessed* ('74), *The People Who Own the Dark* ('75), *Night of the Howling Beast* ('75), *Inquisition* ('76), *Human Beasts* ('80), *The Craving* ('80), *Mystery of Monster Island* ('81), *Panic Beats* ('83), *The Beast and the Magic Sword* ('83), *Howl of the Devil* ('87).

WHAT A CARVE UP!
★★ Sinister Cinema, 1961, NR, 87 min.
Dir: Pat Jackson. Cast: Sidney James, Kenneth Connor, Shirley Eaton, Dennis Price, Donald Pleasence, Michael Gough, Valerie Taylor, Michael Gwynn.

This silly spoof of the horror genre, often looking like a lost "Carry On" film, is, believe it or not, a remake of Karloff's *The Ghoul*! An unsuspecting horror story writer joins a friend at a family reunion at a mist-enshrouded mansion where a will is read, a club-footed butler (Gough) lurks, a hooded fiend strikes, and murders occur. A good cast and a few laughs. Original U.S. release title: *No Place Like Homicide*.

WHATEVER HAPPENED TO AUNT ALICE?
★★★ CBS/Fox, 1969, PG, 100 min.
Dir: Lee H. Katzin. Cast: Geraldine Page, Ruth Gordon, Rosemary Forsyth, Robert Fuller, Mildred Dunnock, Joan Huntington, Peter Brandon, Michael Barbera.

Page and Gordon are terrific in this farfetched but very entertaining gothic barn burner. While investigating the disappearance of an old friend, Aunt Alice (Ruth) stumbles upon the diabolical doings of Mrs. Marrable (Page), who has been hiring and then killing a succession of elderly housekeepers for their savings. Excellent photography, offbeat desert locations, and a great cast underscore this Robert Aldrich–produced *Baby Jane* spin-off, which is based on the novel *The Forbidden Garden* by Ursula Curtiss.

WHAT EVER HAPPENED TO BABY JANE?
★★★★ Warner, 1962, NR, 134 min.
Dir: Robert Aldrich. Cast: Bette Davis, Joan Crawford, Victor Buono, Anna Lee, Marjorie Bennett, Maidie Norman, Barbara [B. D.] Merrill, Robert Cornthwaite.

Well, she becomes a sadistic old crone who torments her crippled sister in this classic black comic camp shocker based on the novel by Henry Farrell. Davis is superb in the trendsetting role of the blowsy, boozy former child star, whether croaking "I've Written a Letter to Daddy" or socking it to former movie star sister Blanche (Crawford): "Butcha are, Blanche; ya are in that chair!" Crawford is no slouch either, as her face glows with happiness while watching one of her old movies on TV, and the ladies are perfectly matched with Buono (in his film debut) as the mountainous mama's boy/pianist who tries to help Bette in a foredoomed comeback attempt. Its blockbuster success leading to a whole slew of "Crazy Mama" flicks featuring Bette, Joan, Shelley Winters, Agnes Moorehead, Olivia de Havilland, and others; forget that awful TV remake with the Redgrave sisters and settle only for the untoppable original.

WHAT'S THE MATTER WITH HELEN?
★★★☆ MGM/UA, 1971, PG, 97 min.
Dir: Curtis Harrington. Cast: Debbie Reynolds, Shelley Winters, Dennis Weaver, Agnes Moorehead, Michael MacLarimour, Yvette Vickers, Helene Winston, Logan Ramsey.

One of Harrington's best, this Henry Farrell–scripted *Baby Jane* offshoot features Reynolds and Winters as the widowed mothers of a pair of teen murderers (and possible gay lovers) who move to 1930s tinseltown to open a school for Shirley Temple wannabes.

"What, no Pepsi?" Joan Crawford in Whatever Happened to Baby Jane? *(1962).*

Debbie embraces this new life, but Shelley's religious fanaticism and repressed lesbianism soon take their bloody toll. Harrington beautifully captures the kitchy glamour of '30s Hollywood and there are memorable turns from Reynolds, Winters, and MacLarimour as a pompous elocution instructor. Look for Harry Dean Stanton as a lawyer in the opening scene and for Robbi Morgan, the little girl imitating Mae West, who grew up to get her throat graphically slashed as the hitchhiker-victim in the original *Friday the 13th*.

WHAT THE PEEPER SAW

★☆ Embassy, 1971, R, 89 min. Dir: James Kelly. Cast: Mark Lester, Britt Ekland, Hardy Kruger, Lilli Palmer, Harry Andrews, Conchita Montez.

Sicko updating of *The Bad Seed* with Lester as an evil brat who murdered his mother and is now plotting the death of sexy stepmom Ekland. Mark's a long way from *Oliver!* in this ugly little number, which is barely salvaged by its strong cast. Aka *Night Child* and *Night Hair Child*.

WHAT WAITS BELOW

★☆ Vestron, 1983, PG, 82 min.
Dir: Don Sharp. Cast: Robert Powell, Lisa Blount, Timothy Bottoms, Richard Johnson, Anne Heywood, Liam Sullivan.

Explorers and government workers building an underground military complex meet snake-like monsters and a tribe of albino mutants in this dull updating of *The Mole People*. An interesting cast and talented director are wasted on trite, juvenile material. Shooting title: *Secret of the Phantom Caverns*.

WHEELS OF TERROR

★★☆ Paramount, 1990, PG-13, 96 min.
Dir: Christopher Cain. Cast: Joanna Cassidy, Marcie Leeds, Carlos Cervantes, Arlen Dean Snyder.

Surprisingly potent variation on *Duel* and *The Car* with the always great Cassidy as a bus-driving mom out to save daughter Leeds from a sinister black sedan that has been kidnapping, raping, and murdering little girls. Contrived but with some good suspense, this cable chiller is well done in its own modest way.

WHEN A STRANGER CALLS
★★☆ RCA/Columbia, 1979, R, 97 min.
Dir: Fred Walton. Cast: Carol Kane, Charles Durning, Colleen Dewhurst, Tony Beckley, Rachel Roberts, Ron O'Neal, Carmen Argenziano, Rutanya Alda.

A stunning first 15 minutes and a suspenseful wrap-up are the best things about this *Halloween* imitation. Kane is unnervingly vulnerable as a teenaged babysitter who gets threatening phone calls from a maniac who then kills the kids she's watching and is nabbed by the cops. Years later the killer (Beckley) is released from an asylum and goes after Carol once again, who has since married and has kids of her own. Strikingly photographed and very well acted, but a dull mid-section (detailing Beckley's pursuit of middle-aged barfly Dewhurst) and a foredoomed attempt to make the maniac into a sympathetic character mar an otherwise taut tale. Based on a short directed by Walton called *The Sitter*.

WHEN A STRANGER CALLS BACK
★★ MCA/Universal, 1993, R, 95 min.
Dir: Fred Walton. Cast: Carol Kane, Charles Durning, Jill Schoeleon, Karen Austin, Gene Lythgow.

Now working to help the victims of stalkers, the original's heroine (Kane) tries to save a babysitting college coed (Schoeleon) from the attentions of a psycho mime—really! This made-for-cable sequel starts out great (not unlike the first film) but then drowns in a sea of melodrama before its contrived but scary ending.

WHEN DINOSAURS RULED THE EARTH
★★★ Warner, 1970, PG, 96 min.
Dir: Val Guest. Cast: Victoria Vetri, Robin Hawdon, Patrick Allen, Drewe Henley, Sean Caffrey, Imogen Hassall.

Good follow-up to Hammer's *One Million Years B.C.* (not yet available on video) with *Playboy* playmate Vetri as the cave gal who's near-sacrificed by her tribe, befriended by a dinosaur mother and child, and falls in love with amiable cave guy Hawdon. Goofy fun with terrific Jim Danforth FX. It was originally 100 minutes, but a nude scene in a cave was cut to get a PG rating. Sequel *Creatures the World Forgot*.

WHEN MICHAEL CALLS
See: *Shattered Silence.*

WHEN THE SCREAMING STOPS!
★★ Avid, 1973, R, 84 min.
Dir: Amando de Ossorio. Cast: Tony Kendall, Helga Line, Silvia Tortosa, Loretta Tovar.

Silly Spanish sea monster thriller from the director of the "Blind Dead" series. Line is a beauty living in a treasure-strewn Rhine cave who is actually the legendary Lorelei, a siren with the ability to transform into a scaly monster who rips out and then devours the hearts of young women. This has the usual tits and gore of an early '70s continental cheapo, plus the gimmick of a flashing red light preceding the fairly mild slaughter scenes. Favorite line: "Let's get out of here; this place is hard on my nerves!" Original title: *Las Garras de Lorelei: The Lorelei's Grasp.*

WHERE ARE THE CHILDREN?
★★ RCA/Columbia, 1986, R, 97 min.
Dir: Bruce Malmuth. Cast: Jill Clayburgh, Frederic Forrest, Max Gail, Barnard Hughes, Elizabeth Wilson, Clifton James, Harley Cross, Elizabeth Harnois.

Clayburgh, during her mostly inactive post-feminist period, stars in this routine version of the Mary Higgins Clark novel. When her kids are kidnapped by a crazed psycho (Forrest), Jill falls under suspicion because the same thing happened years before to the children of her first marriage—when things ended in murder. Originally this was a Brian de Palma project; at least he could have brought a bit of pizzazz to this well-photographed but dull opus. Could almost be a TV movie of the week.

WHISPERS
★★ Vidmark, 1989, R, 90 min.
Dir: Douglas Jackson. Cast: Victoria Tennant, Chris Sarandon, Jean LeClerc, Peter MacNeill, Linda Sorenson, Jackie Burroughs.

An annoyingly ordinary adaptation of a good book by Dean R. Koontz in which a woman (Tennant) kills an attacker in her apartment who seemingly returns from the grave to continue to stalk her. Blandly acted, written, and directed, this potboiler makes even incestuous, homosexual necrophilia seem dull. Aka *Dean R. Koontz's Whispers.*

WHISPERS IN THE DARK
★★☆ Paramount, 1992, R, 101 min.
Dir: Christopher Crowe. Cast: Annabella Sciorra, Jamey Sheridan, Anthony La Paglia, Alan Alda, Jill Clayburgh, Deborah Unger, John Leguzama, Jacqueline Brookes.

Bela Lugosi is the voodoo master of White Zombie *(1932).*

Soon after psychiatrist Sciorra becomes obsessed with sado-sexual patient Unger, the latter turns up brutally murdered. Seems both women were unknowingly dating the same guy (Sheridan)—but is he the killer? This veers unevenly from horror to psycho-drama and back again, but when it *does* work it works quite well—if you can overlook some glaring story holes. The tense climax owes more than a tad to the ending of the original *Friday the 13th.*

WHITE BUFFALO, THE

★★ MGM/UA, 1977, PG, 97 min.
Dir: J. Lee Thompson. Cast: Charles Bronson, Kim Novak, Jack Warden, Will Sampson, Clint Walker, Stuart Whitman, Slim Pickens, John Carradine.

Odd, allegorical horror-western about the last days of Wild Bill Hickok (Bronson) who's tormented by dreams of a huge white buffalo—a monster that turns out to be only too real. Bronson gives one of his best performances as the tired gunslinger and there's some effective atmosphere, but this strange, ambitious film fails by trying to be too many things for too many audiences. Aka *Hunt to Kill.*

WHITE OF THE EYE

★★☆ Paramount, 1987, R, 111 min.
Dir: Donald Cammell. Cast: David Keith, Cathy Moriarty, Art Evans, Alberta Watson, Alan Rosenberg, Danielle Smith.

This halfway successful stalker has rich ambiance, sleek, Argento-esque direction, and good performances but suffers from a frustrating plot. Affluent Arizona housewives are being murdered by an especially vicious slasher, and suspicion falls on trendy audio equipment installer Keith. Though wife Moriarty wants to believe in her loving husband, she soon has her doubts. Overlong and with a really dumb ending ("Do you want me to shoot you?") but not without its rewards.

WHITE ZOMBIE

★★★ Sinister Cinema, 1932, NR, 67 min.
Dir: Victor Halperin. Cast: Bela Lugosi, Madge Bellamy, John Harron, Robert Fraser, Joseph Cawthorn, Brandon Hurst.

This entertaining antique boasts one of Lugosi's best performances. Bela is Murder Legendre, voodoo master of Haiti, who puts the whammy on bride-to-be Bellamy at the behest of jealous Fraser. Lugosi spirits the zombified young lady away to his cliff-top castle where he makes plans to dispose of Fraser in order to keep Madge for himself. Stilted supporting performances and dialogue, but some beautiful fairy tale imagery and Bela's towering presence make this the best independently made horror film of the 1930s. Sequel: *Revolt of the Zombies*.

WHO ARE YOU?

See: *Beyond the Door*.

WHOEVER SLEW AUNTIE ROO?

See: *Who Slew Auntie Roo?*

WHO SLEW AUNTIE ROO?

★★☆ Vestron, 1971, PG, 89 min. Dir: Curtis Harrington. Cast: Shelley Winters, Mark Lester, Ralph Richardson, Lionel Jeffries, Hugh Griffith, Judy Cornwell, Michael Gothard, Chloe Franks.

Another entry in the post-menopausal psychosis genre for the indefatigable Shelley. This time she's Aunt Roo, a kind but crazy ex-vaudevillian living in post-WWI England who gives an annual Christmas party for the local orphans and comes to believe that Franks is the reincarnation of her own dead daughter. Lester is the girl's brother who imagines that Winters is the witch from "Hansel and Gretel" and sets out to rescue his sister from her. Handsome photography and set design and La Winters at her best—her apple-eating scene is a show stopper—make this a must for "Crazy Mama" fans. Aka *The Gingerbread House* and *Whoever Slew Auntie Roo?*

WICKED, THE

★★ Hemdale, 1987, R, 87 min. Dir: Colin Eggleston. Cast: Brett Cumo, Richard Morgan, Angela Kennedy, John Doyle.

This tired Aussie vampire film (with comic overtones) is about a group of young idiots who make the mistake of spending the night in the creepy home of vampire Sir Alfred Terminus and his undead family. It's for vampire fanatics only. Aka *Outback Vampires*.

WICKED STEPMOTHER, THE

★ MGM/UA, 1989, PG-13, 93 min. Dir: Larry Cohen. Cast: Bette Davis, Barbara Carrera, Colleen Camp, David Rasche, Tom Bosley, Lionel Stander, Richard Moll, Evelyn Keyes, Laurene Landon, James Dixton.

The curse of the awful last picture strikes again as Davis makes her big-screen farewell in this lousy horror-comedy she walked out on after only a few days of shooting. Cohen salvaged the pic by rewriting the script with Carrera (as Bette's daughter) substituting for Mother Goddam in the new footage. He shouldn't have bothered. In any case this less-than-humorous tale of withered witch Davis' attempt to take over wealthy Stander's Beverly Hills family is for masochistic movie buffs alone. The unexpected Joan Crawford cameo provides the sole chuckle.

WICKER MAN, THE

★★★☆ Magnum, 1973, R, 95 min. Dir: Robin Hardy. Cast: Christopher Lee, Edward Woodward, Britt Ekland, Diane Cilento, Ingrid Pitt, Lindsey Kemp.

Woodward is a perplexed Scottish cop searching for a missing young girl on remote Summerisle Island who comes to fear that she is being prepared as a virgin sacrifice by the pagan islanders who worship the gods of nature. This much-lauded Brit flick has zesty performances and a well-written script by Anthony Shafer but was badly cut and then shelved by original distributor Warner Brothers, making its video release all the more valuable. With a memorable nude dancing scene from Ekland, a genuinely shocking (and rather funny) twist ending, and Lee in his best role as the sinisterly jovial Lord Summerisk.

WILD BEASTS

★★ Lightning, 1983, R, 91 min. Dir: Franco E. Prosperi. Cast: Lorraine de Selle, John Aldrich, Ugo Bologna, Louisa Lloyd.

When their water supply becomes contaminated with PCP(???), the animals of a Berlin zoo go wild, escape their cages, and begin killing all manner of passersby. This decent-looking but unintentionally funny Italiano flick has a couple of super-gore scenes—a necking couple chewed up by rats; a girl's head crushed by an elephant—but is too drawn out and preposterous to build much tension. The rampaging polar bear at the climax looks mostly like he's just trying to find a good spot to take a nap.

WILLARD

★★☆ Prism, 1971, PG, 91 min. Dir: Daniel Mann. Cast: Bruce Davison, Ernest Borginine, Elsa Lanchester, Sondra Locke, Jody Gilbert, Joan Shawlee.

Popular in its day, this adaptation of Stephen Gilbert's *Ratman's Notebooks* is rather too ordinary to attain true classic status. Davison is good as the title character, a mother-dominated, boss-abused nebbish who befriends a pack of rats living in his basement and eventually trains them to dispose of his enemies. Scenes of swarming rats attacking Borgnine (who's hilarious as Willard's gruff employer) or Davison are still potent, but overall this lacks focus and drive. Followed by *Ben*.

WILLIES, THE

★★ Prism, 1990, PG-13, 91 min.
Dir: Brian Peck. Cast: Sean Astin, James Karen, Kathleen Freeman, Clu Gulager, Jeremy Miller, Suzanne Goddard, Dana Ashbrook, Kimmy Robertson.

While camping out, kids spin weird tales involving a monster in the men's room and a fat kid (who looks like a prepubescent Ralph Kramden) who pulls the wings off flies and gets an appropriate comeuppance. Slightly amusing, but too broad and kiddiefied to be of much interest.

WIND, THE

★☆ Vestron, 1987, R, 92 min. Dir: Nico Mastorakis.
Cast: Meg Foster, Wings Hauser, Steve Railsback, David McCallum, Robert Morley.

Beautiful, blue-eyed Foster plays a mystery authoress menaced by crazed handyman Hauser one windy night at a remote Greek vacation cottage. Dull suspenser wasting a good cast, though any film with Wings as a wacko can't be all bad. Needless to say, *The Wind* blows.

WINGED SERPENT, THE

See: *Q*.

WITCHBOARD

★★ Magnum, 1987, R, 98 min.
Dir: Kevin S. Tenney. Cast: Tawny Kitaen, Todd Allen, Stephen Nichols, Kathleen Wilhoite, Burke Byrnes, Rose Marie.

Mediocre supernatural thriller that became an unexpected box-office hit. Gorgeous Kitaen tries to contact a spirit using a ouija board and ends up possessed by the evil ghost of an ax-wielding black magician. Far too much time is spent on everyday details in the lives of stupid characters you care nothing for, but some imaginative touches and Wilhoite's spirited turn as a kooky psychic are slight compensation.

WITCHBOARD 2: THE DEVIL'S DOORWAY

★★☆ Republic, 1993, R, 98 min.
Dir: Kevin S. Tenney. Cast: Ami Dolenz, Timothy Gibbs, John Gatins, Laraine Newman, Marvin Kaplan, Julie Michaels.

This sequel is better than part one but still awfully silly. Dolenz is a pretty artist who becomes possessed by the vengeful spirit of murder victim Michaels after she finds a

CHRISTOPHER LEE
(1922–)

This tall, dignified, rather pompous-looking Brit actor was the perfect choice for a more modern version of Count Dracula when he starred in Hammer Films' remake of the story, *Horror of Dracula*, back in '58. Quickly becoming one of the most popular actors in the world, Lee was seen in a variety of terror roles over the next 15 years, often teamed with fellow superstar and real-life good friend Peter Cushing. Never really happy with most of his horror films, he was constantly being disappointed at Hammer's increasingly unimaginative handling of the Dracula character. Chris more or less abandoned the genre in '74, though he's made the odd contribution to it since in mostly bad to mediocre films.

Alias John Preston ('56), *The Curse of Frankenstein* ('57), *Horror of Dracula* ('58), *Corridors of Blood* ('58), *The Hound of the Baskervilles* ('59), *The Mummy* ('59), *Uncle Was a Vampire* ('59), *The Man Who Could Cheat Death* ('59), *Horror Hotel* ('60), *The Two Faces of Dr. Jekyll* ('60), *Scream of Fear* ('61), *The Hands of Orlac* ('61), *Terror of the Tongs* ('61), *Hercules in the Haunted World* ('61), *Sherlock Holmes and the Deadly Necklace* ('63), *Terror in the Crypt* ('63), *What!* ('63), *Horror Castle* ('63), *Castle of the Living Dead* ('64), *The Gorgon* ('64), *Dr. Terror's House of Horrors* ('65), *She* ('65), *The Face of Fu Manchu* ('65), *Dracula, Prince of Darkness* ('66), *Rasputin, the Mad Monk* ('66), *Ten Little Indians* (voice only, '66), *The Brides of Fu Manchu* ('66), *Theatre of Death* ('67), *Circus of Fear* ('67), *The Torture Chamber of Dr. Sadism* ('67), *The Vengeance of Fu Manchu* ('67), *The Devil's Bride* ('68), *The Blood of Fu Manchu* ('68), *The Crimson Cult* ('68), *Dracula Has Risen From the Grave* ('68), *The Castle of Fu Manchu* ('68), *The Oblong Box* ('69), *Eugenie, the Story of Her Journey Into Perversion* ('69), *Scream and Scream Again* ('70), *Taste the Blood of Dracula* ('70), *Count Dracula* ('70), *Night of the Blood Monster* ('70), *Scars of Dracula* ('71), *The House That Dripped Blood* ('71), *I, Monster* ('71), *Poor Devil* ('72), *Horror Express* ('72), *Dracula A.D. 1972* ('72), *Nothing But the Night* ('72), *The Creeping Flesh* ('73), *Raw Meat* ('73), *The Satanic Rites of Dracula* ('73), *Dark Places* ('73), *The Wicker Man* ('73), *To the Devil, a Daughter* ('76), *Meatcleaver Massacre* (narrator, '77), *House of the Long Shadows* ('83), *The Howling II* ('85), *Murder Story* ('89), *Gremlins 2: The New Batch* ('90), *Curse III: Blood Sacrifice* ('91), *The Funny Man* ('93).

haunted ouija board in her new loft apartment. Certainly contrived, with an annoying hero in Gibbs, but the photography and FX are highly imaginative and Kaplan has an amusing cameo as a Jewish occult expert. Aka *Witchboard 2: The Return*.

WITCHBOARD 2: THE RETURN
See: *Witchboard 2: The Devil's Doorway*.

WITCHCRAFT
★★ Academy, 1988, R, 90 min. Dir: Robert Spera. Cast: Anat Topol-Barzilai, Gary Sloan, Mary Shelley, Deborah Scott.

Like *Witchboard*, this makes a foredoomed attempt at respectability by concentrating on character development but is done in by a dull, unbelievable screenplay. Topol-Barzilai is a young mother who discovers that her husband and his mother (actually his other wife!) are satanists who want her newborn for some unknown reason or another. With better acting than you might expect but all the usual low-budget restrictions. Followed by several sequels.

WITCHCRAFT
See: *Witchery*.

WITCHCRAFT II: THE TEMPTRESS
★☆ Academy, 1989, R, 88 min. Dir: Mark Woods. Cast: Charles Solomon, Mia Ruiz, Delia Sheppard.

Solomon is the baby from part one now grown into a troubled teen pursued by big-breasted witch Ruiz who wants him to sire her anti-Christ offspring. Good for a few laughs but that's about it. The approach to eroticism bespeaks the *Hustler* magazine school of sexiness.

WITCHCRAFT III: THE KISS OF DEATH
★★ Academy, 1990, R, 85 min. Dir: R. L. Tillman. Cast: Charles Solomon, Lisa Toothman, William L. Baker, Leanne Hall, Dominic Luciano.

Solomon is back again, this time battling psychic vampire Luciano for pretty girlfriend Toothman. Probably the best of the series—small praise that—this has a good performance from Luciano and some clever scriptural touches.

Christopher Lee leads the celebrants in The Wicker Man *(1973).*

WITCHCRAFT IV: VIRGIN HEART
★★ Academy, 1992, R, 92 min.
Dir: James Meredino. Cast: Charles Solomon, Julie Strain, Clive Pearson, Barbara Dow.

Solomon returns as good warlock/lawyer Will, who continues his battle against evil aided by a beautiful stripper played by *Penthouse* model Strain. Low-octane erotic horror for fans of this inexplicably popular direct-to-video series.

WITCHCRAFT V: DANCE WITH THE DEVIL
★☆ Academy, 1993, R, 94 min.
Dir: Talun Hsu. Cast: Marklen Kennedy, Carolyn Taye-Loren, David Huffman, Nicole Sassaman.

Kennedy takes over the hero role in this fifth entry in which he battles evil warlock Huffman (looking like Michael Bolton's bad brother). This has so much femme nudity and simulated sex, it looks more like a soft-porn flick than a horror movie. Followed by *Witchcraft VI.*

WITCHERY
★★☆ Vidmark, 1989, UR, 95 min.
Dir: Martin Newlin [Fabrizio Laurenti].
Cast: Linda Blair, David Hasselhoff, Catherine Hickland, Annie Ross, Hildegard Knef, Leslie Cumming.

People trapped in a deserted hotel on an island off the New England coast are brutally killed thanks to the curse of witch Knef. A good cast (Linda especially) and some imaginative direction distinguish this routinely structured body count flick. Unrated, this contains some fairly graphic violence—like Ross' lips sewn together before she's stuffed up a chimney and roasted alive—cut from the cable TV version. Aka *Witchcraft* and *Ghosthouse 2.*

WITCHES' BREW
★★☆ HBO, 1979, PG, 93 min.
Dirs: Richard Shore, Herbert L. Strock.
Cast: Richard Benjamin, Teri Garr, Lana Turner, Kathryn Leigh Scott, Kelly Jean Peters, Jordan Charney.

Pleasant comic retelling of *Burn, Witch, Burn* (not yet on video) with Benjamin as a flustered college prof who discovers that wife Garr is furthering his career through amateur witchcraft and that powerful "professional" witch Turner is planning on reincarnating herself in Garr's younger body. Marked by its rocky production history, this has a slow beginning but then starts to get good, with fine work from Dick, Teri, and Lana and a clever Dave Allen animated demon creature. Aka *Which Witch Is Which?* and *It's u Charmed Life.*

WITCHES OF EASTWICK, THE
★★☆ Warner, 1987, R, 118 min.
Dir: George Miller. Cast: Jack Nicholson, Cher, Susan Sarandon, Michelle Pfeiffer, Veronica Cartwright, Richard Jenkins, Keith Joachim, Carel Struycken.

Lightweight adaptation of John Updike's allegorical novel about three lovely New England ladies who dabble in witchcraft and conjure up the living devil (in the form of a perfectly cast Nicholson) to fulfill their dull lives. Jack is a treat and the women are all beautiful, but the jarring changes in tone (from comedy to drama to romance to horror) give this film a schizy, confused feel, particularly in the final, FX-filled half hour.

WITCHES TORTURED TILL THEY BLEED
See: *Mark of the Devil.*

WITCHES TORTURED TILL THEY DIE
See: *Mark of the Devil Part II.*

WITCHFINDER GENERAL
See: *The Conqueror Worm.*

WITCHFIRE
★☆ Lightning, 1985, R, 92 min.
Dir: Vincent J. Primitera. Cast: Shelley Winters, Frances De Sapio, Corrine Chateau, Gary Swanson.

Unintentionally uproarious suspense flick in which Winters is a mental hospital escapee who imagines herself a witch. Aided by fellow inmates De Sapio and Chateau, she kidnaps hunter Swanson who she believes is her late psychiatrist risen from the dead. Talky and slack, but Shelley ("I may be insane but I'm not stupid!") tries to give it a much-needed lift.

WITCHING, THE
★★☆ Video Treasures, 1972, R, 80 min.
Dir: Bert I. Gordon. Cast: Orson Welles, Pamela Franklin, Michael Ontkean, Lee Purcell, Harvey Jason, Lisa James.

Mr. B.I.G.'s version of *Rosemary's Baby*—released to theaters as *Necromancy*—with Franklin and Ontkean as a young couple who run afoul of Welles (in a false nose and beard) and his hippie witchcraft cult who want to raise Orson's son from the grave. Not exactly great filmmaking but modestly entertaining, with typically fine work from Pam. Some nude coven scenes cut from the original to get a PG rating have been restored to this video print, but the original *Dead of Night*–inspired twist ending has been cut. Aka *The Toy Factory* and *A Life for a Life.*

WITCHING TIME

★★☆ Thrillervideo, 1980, NR, 50 min.
Dir: Don Leaver. Cast: Jon Finch, Patricia Quinn,
Prunella Gee, Ian McCulloch.

Witch Quinn escapes her 16th-century execution by transporting herself into the present,
where she puts her spell on composer Finch.
My favorite "Hammer House of Horror"
episode, this has outstanding work from Finch
and Quinn, though it's marred by blunt edits
removing the ample nudity for U.S. TV.

WITCHMAKER, THE

★★☆ Interglobal, 1969, R, 99 min.
Dir: William O. Brown. Cast: Anthony Eisley, Thorndis
Brandt, John Lodge, Alvy Moore, Shelby Grant,
Robyn Millan, Warene Ott, Larry Vincent.

Enjoyable cheapo about a series of grisly
Louisiana swamp murders traced to a warlock
(Lodge) who is gathering blood to restore the
beauty of a 200-year-old witch. Enthusiastic
performances and an unexpected ending make
the difference. Aka *The Legend of Witch Hollow.*

WITCH'S MIRROR, THE

★★★ Sinister Cinema, 1960, NR, 75 min.
Dir: Chano Ureta. Cast: Rosita Arenas, Armando
Calbo, Isabella Corona, Dina De Marco, Carlos Nitro,
Alfredo R. Barron.

Above-average Mexican horror opus about a
witch murdered by her unfaithful husband
whose second wife is disfigured by the first's
vengeful ghost. The husband, who's also a
surgeon, then turns to radical face transplants
to restore her lost looks. Offbeat touches borrowed from *Rebecca, Diabolique, The Horror
Chamber of Dr. Faustus,* and others plus atmospheric direction transcend the usual bad dubbing and clichés.

WITCHTRAP

★★ Magnum, 1989, R, 90 min. Dir: Kevin S. Tenney.
Cast: James W. Quinn, Kathleen Bailey, Linnea
Quigley, Judy Tatum, Ron Zapple, Hal Havins.

In this low-rent *Legend of Hell House,* a millionaire hires a group of psychic researchers to
investigate the supposedly haunted house he's
just bought, with murderous results. Certainly
watchable (thanks mainly to Linnea) but done
irreparable harm by hero Quinn, who seems
to fancy himself a poor man's Bill Murray and
keeps making an ass of himself with a constant stream of unfunny quips.

WITHOUT WARNING

★☆ HBO, 1980, R, 89 min.
Dir: Greydon Clark. Cast: Jack Palance, Martin
Landau, Cameron Mitchell, Neville Brand, Tarah
Nutter, Christopher S. Nelson, Sue Ane Langdon,
Ralph Meeker, Larry Storch, Kevin Peter Hall.

A bald-domed alien (Hall, looking like an
"Outer Limits" reject) hunts humans in the
backwoods by flinging hairy flying pizzas at
them that suck out all their victims' blood in
slurpy detail. This is notable only for the
record number of washed-up character actors
who appear as rednecks, with Palance obviously finding it hard to keep a straight face
and Landau outdoing himself as a loony 'Nam
vet even Rambo would waste. Also released as
It Came Without Warning.

WIZARD OF GORE, THE

★★ Sleaziest, 1970, R, 96 min.
Dir: Herschell Gordon Lewis. Cast: Ray Sager,
Judy Cler, Wayne Ratay, Phil Laurenson,
Jim Rau, John Elliot.

Typically outrageous H. G. gore romp along
ludicrously metaphysical lines and a must for
Lewis lovers. Sager is awful but quite funny as
Montag the Magnificent, whose stage act con-
sists exclusively of the multilation of pretty
young women via swords, saws, spikes, and a
punch press. It all seems an amazing illusion
until the volunteers turn up later dead in similar circumstances. Will dippy talk show hostess Cler and her dense reporter boyfriend
Ratay discover the connection? I doubt it. Acting and technical credits are all bottom-of-the-
barrel but there's some fun to be had for the
initiated and an existential ending not to be
believed.

WOLF

★★☆ Columbia/TriStar, 1994, R,
125 min. Dir: Mike Nichols. Cast: Jack Nicholson,
Michelle Pfeiffer, Christopher Plummer,
James Spader, Kate Nelligan.

This upscale werewolf movie looks, in both
dramatic approach and makeup FX, like a '90s
Werewolf in London. Nicholson is great as a
middle-aged Manhattan book editor whose
life takes a surprising turn for the better when
he's bitten one snowy night by a werewolf; the
emerging animal instincts cause him to grow
increasingly more aggressive both professionally and romantically. Ambitious but uneven,
this doesn't always work (particularly in the
ill-defined relationship between Nicholson
and boss' daughter Pfeiffer and the indifferent
ending), but with Jack in control it's never a
dull ride.

WOLFEN

★★★ Warner, 1981, R, 115 min.
Dir: Michael Wadleigh. Cast: Albert Finney, Diane

Lon Chaney, Jr., gets an armful of Evelyn Ankers in The Wolf Man *(1941).*

Venora, Gregory Hines, Edward James Olmos, Tom Noonan, Dick O'Neill.

Based on Whitley Strieber's novel, this is an interesting variation on the usual werewolf theme and Wadleigh's first film since *Woodstock*. Finney is a New York detective investigating a string of brutal murders that may be the work of environmental terrorists or even native American werewolves but are actually being committed by the wolfen: a breed of large, super-intelligent wolves that live secretly in the inner cities and feed on the derelict and homeless and are now killing in order to protect their soon-to-be renovated home turf of the South Bronx. Good acting (especially from Hines in his screen debut as a jivey coroner), imaginative photography, and well-done gore (including a supremely realistic decapitation) make this sometimes slow, overlong "Thinking Man's" monster movie worth watching.

WOLF MAN, THE

★★★☆ MCA/Universal, 1941, NR, 70 min.
Dir: George Waggner. Cast: Lon Chaney, Jr., Evelyn Ankers, Claude Rains, Ralph Bellamy, Bela Lugosi, Maria Ouspenskaya, Patric Knowles, Warren William, Fay Helm, Forrester Harvey.

Classic cinematic lycanthropy with Chaney as tragic Larry Talbot, the unlikely heir to a Welsh estate who is bitten one foggy night by gypsy werewolf Lugosi. Soon after, he begins turning into a hirsute monster destined to kill anyone in whose palm he spies the dreaded sign of the pentagram. One of the all-time great monster movies, this has atmospheric direction, an intelligent script by Curt Siodmak, a moody score by Charles Previn and Hans J. Salter, great Jack Pierce makeup, and a powerful cast, including Ouspenskaya in her definitive gypsy role. Followed by four sequels, beginning with *Frankenstein Meets the Wolf Man*.

LON CHANEY, JR.
(1906–1973)

Born Creighton Chaney, Lon Jr. did stunt work and bits during the '30s until he was successfully cast in the stage and screen productions of John Steinbeck's *Of Mice and Men* as the child-like Lenny. His success as Larry Talbot, the doomed lycanthrope of *The Wolf Man,* made him Universal's number-one horror star of the '40s. When the bottom dropped out of the horror market, he became a successful '50s character actor, although his later years saw him mostly in zero-budget drek unworthy of his talents.

One Million B.C. ('40), *Man-Made Monster* ('41), *The Wolf Man* ('41), *The Ghost of Frankenstein* ('42), *The Mummy's Tomb* ('42), *Frankenstein meets the Wolf Man* ('43), *Son of Dracula* ('43), *Calling Dr. Death* ('43), *Ghost Catchers* ('44), *Weird Woman* ('44), *The Mummy's Ghost* ('44), *Dead Man's Eyes* ('44), *House of Frankenstein* ('44), *The Mummy's Curse* ('44), *The Frozen Ghost* ('45), *Strange Confession* ('45), *House of Dracula* ('45), *Pillow of Death* ('46), *Abbott and Costello Meet Frankenstein* ('48), *Bride of the Gorilla* ('51), *The Black Castle* ('52), *The Indestructible Man* ('56), *The Black Sleep* ('56), *The Cyclops* ('57), *The Alligator People* ('59), *Face of the Screaming Werewolf* ('59), *The Devil's Messenger* ('59), *The Haunted Palace* ('64), *Witchcraft* ('64), *Spider Baby* ('64), *House of the Black Death* ('65), *Dr. Terror's Gallery of Horrors* ('67), *Hillbillies in a Haunted House* ('67), *Dracula vs. Frankenstein* ('71).

WOLFMAN
★ HBO, 1979, R, 101 min. Dir: Worth Keeter, Cast: Earl Owensby, Kristine Reynolds, Julian Morton, Ed L. Grady.

Terrible regional monster flick produced by and starring southern movie kingpin Owensby as a British heir in 1910 who's cursed with lycanthropy. This grade-Z 1940s-type tripe isn't even up to the worst of Paul Naschy's Spanish werewolf flicks.

WOLF WOMAN, THE
See: *Legend of the Wolf Woman.*

WOMAN EATER, THE
★☆ Sinister Cinema, 1957, NR, 70 min.
Dir: Charles Saunders. Cast: George Coulouris,

Vera Day, Joy Webster, Peter Wayn, Jimmy Vaughn, Marpessa Dawn.

Okay, stop sniggering! This tacky, Monogram-like mad doctor flick actually concerns a Brit botanist (Coulouris) who brings home a weird tropical tree that has a taste for female flesh and sap that can raise the dead. The saps who made this English trifle may have been deadly serious but this plays best as a comedy, with plenty of Coulouris hamming and a monster tree about as scary as your average weeping willow. British title: *Womaneater.*

WOMANEATER
See *The Woman Eater.*

WOMAN HUNT, THE
★☆ Charter, 1972, R, 81 min.
Dir: Eddie Romero. Cast: John Ashley, Laurie Rose, Sid Haig, Lisa Todd, Eddie Garcia, Pat Woodell.

Haig hunts honies in the wilds of the Philippines in this feminist-sexist updating of *The Most Dangerous Game.* Ashley is the hero, as usual, and "Hee-Haw" tootsie Todd is a black-clad lesbian in this dumbbell horror-adventure.

WOMAN IN GREEN, THE
★★☆ Key, 1945, NR, 68 min.
Dir: Roy William Neill. Cast: Basil Rathbone, Nigel Bruce, Hillary Brooke, Henry Daniell, Paul Cavanagh, Matthew Boulton, Eve Amber, Mary Gordon.

Sherlock Holmes (Rathbone) investigates a series of Ripper-type killings in which all the victims are young women whose right forefingers are hacked off. The eventual culprit turns out to be Professor Moriarty (Daniell), who's using the murders and hypnosis as part of a blackmail plot. Good work from Rathbone, Daniell, and Brooke (as a sultry femme fetale) and some imaginative direction bolster this (very) loose adaptation of Conan Doyle's "The Adventure of the Empty House."

WOMAN OBSESSED, A
★★ Academy, 1989, R, 104 min.
Dir: Chuck Vincent. Cast: Ruth Raymond, Gregory Patrick, Linda Blair, Troy Donahue, Carolyn Van Bellinghen, Christina Veronica.

Aka *Bad Blood,* this *Misery*-type low-budget thriller stars Raymond as a wealthy mad-woman who is reunited with her grown son (Patrick, in a very annoying performance), who was taken away from her years before. She imprisons him in her Long Island mansion and kills anyone who tries to stop her. Minor fare from former porno director Vincent. Blair is wasted but Raymond is good and there's a great scene where she plays "This Little Piggy" with a captive Patrick's toes.

WOMAN WHO CAME BACK, THE
★★☆ SVS, 1945, NR, 68 min.
Dir: Walter Colmes. Cast: Nancy Kelly, John Loder, Otto Kruger, Ruth Ford, Jeanne Gail, Harry Tyler.

A Republic Pictures imitation of a Val Lewton thriller with Kelly as a young New England woman obsessed with the idea that she is possessed by the spirit of a vengeful local witch. Well directed and edited, this has good acting from Kelly and Kruger, but the plot has more than its share of holes and there's an especially ridiculous, cop-out ending.

WORLD OF THE VAMPIRES, THE
★★☆ Sinister Cinema, 1960, NR, 75 min.
Dir: Alfonso Corona Blake. Cast: Guillermo Muray, Erna Martha Bauman, Silvia Fournier, Maricio Garces, Rafael Del Rio.

Somewhat better than the usual run-of-the-coffin Mexican vampire movie, this tells of the revenge one Count Subotey (Muray) extracts against the Colman family, whose ancestors once tried to destroy the Count several centuries before. Silly and pleasant, with such unlikely atmosphere as a huge pipe organ in a cave used to serenade Subotey's bat-faced minions, a vampire bat with a woman's face, and a convenient pit lined with pointed wooden stakes the Count trips into at fade-out time.

WORM EATERS, THE
☆ WesternWorld, 1977, R, 94 min.
Dir: Herb Robins. Cast: Herb Robins, Lindsay Armstrong Black, Joseph Sacket, Muriel Cooper.

Ted V. Mikels (yipe!) produced this unwatchable, nearly plotless putridity about a demented worm farmer (director Robins) who eats his crop regularly and comes to believe that he is a "worm man" who somehow passes this dumb predilection on to those he has the unaccountable urge to bite. This baby bites all right, with awful acting from a cast who were seemingly hired solely for their willingness to put live worms in their mouths. Does Equity know about this?

WRAITH, THE
★★ Vestron, 1986, PG-13, 92 min.
Dir: Mike Marvin. Cast: Charlie Sheen, Nick Cassavetes, Randy Quaid, Sherilyn Fenn, Griffin O'Neal, Clint Howard.

Silly combination of supernational thriller and teen car crash movie with Sheen (just before *Platoon* made him a star) as a ghostly do-gooder in a fancy, hopped-up black Dodge Turbo Interceptor who battles a gang of scuzzy, desert-based car thieves and killers headed by Cassavetes. Flashy opticals and photography and a good relatives-of-the-rich-and-famous cast help make up for a confusing story and paper-thin characters.

WRESTLING WOMEN VS. THE AZTEC MUMMY, THE
★★☆ Sinister Cinema, 1964, NR, 77 min.
Dir: Rene Cardona. Cast: Lorena Velazquez, Elizabeth Campbell, Armando Silvestre, Maria Eugenia San Martin, Chucho Salinas, Ramon Bugarini.

One of the greatest titles of all time and one of the most enjoyable Mexican horrors. Lady wrestlers Velazquez and Campbell battle both a low-budget Fu Manchu bad guy and the dreaded Aztec mummy who, since his last film appearance, has somehow developed the ability to transform his bandaged self into a spider and vampire bat. Hilariously fun trash originally titled *Las Luchadoras contra la Momia: The Wrestling Women vs. the Mummy* and also available in a shortened *musical* version from Rhino video called *Rock 'n' Roll Wrestling Women vs. the Aztec Mummy.*

WRESTLING WOMEN VS. THE MUMMY, THE
See: *The Wrestling Women vs. the Aztec Mummy.*

X FROM OUTER SPACE, THE
★ Orion, 1967, NR, 89 min. Dir: Kazui Nihonmastsu. Cast: Peggy Neal, Eiji Okada, Shinichi Yanagisawa, Itoko Harada, Franz Gruber.

Gilala, a gigantic rubber chicken monster created from a single alien cell brought to earth attached to an orbiting spacecraft, terrorizes Japan in this especially silly sub-*Godzilla* monster flick. Tacky special effects and poor dubbing aplenty for fans of this particular genre. Original title: *Uchu Daikaiju Guilala: The Monster Gilala.*

X-RAY
See: *Hospital Massacre.*

X—THE MAN WITH X-RAY EYES
★★★ Orion, 1963, NR, 79 min. Dir: Roger Corman. Cast: Ray Milland, Diana van der Vlis, Harold J.

RAY MILLAND
(1905–1988)

A British leading man in Hollywood who started in low-budgeters but eventually became a major star of the '40s, Milland won an Oscar for his performance in 1945's *The Lost Weekend*. Like many of his female contemporaries, he turned to horror in the '60s and '70s, playing both heroes and villains with equal aplomb.

The Uninvited ('44), *Alias Nick Beal* ('49), *The Premature Burial* ('62), *X—The Man With X-Ray Eyes* ('63), *Daughter of the Mind* ('69), *Black Noon* ('71), *Frogs* ('72), *The Thing With Two Heads* ('72), *Terror in the Wax Museum* ('73), *Night of the Laughing Dead* ('73), *The Dead Don't Die* ('75), *Look What's Happened to Rosemary's Baby* ('76), *The Uncanny* ('77), *Cruise Into Terror* ('78), *The Darker Side of Terror* ('79), *The Attic* ('80), *Sherlock Holmes and the Masks of Death* ('84), *The Sea Serpent* ('86).

Stone, Don Rickles, John Hoyt, John Dierkes, Morris Ankrum, Dick Miller, Jonathan Haze, Barboura Morris.

Milland (as good here as in *The Lost Weekend*) is Dr. James Xavier, a surgeon who develops special eye drops to improve his vision. Eventually he begins seeing through clothes, skin, buildings, and finally all the way to the end of the universe, where a vision of God causes him to rip his eyes out. A surprisingly sober film for Corman from this period (his Poe films were becoming increasingly spoofy), this features a strong dramatic turn from Rickles as a greedy carny barker who briefly exploits Milland. And remember: "If thine eye offend thee. . . ." Aka *The Man with the X-Ray Eyes*.

XTRO
★★ HBO, 1982, R, 81 min.
Dir: Harry Bromley Davenport. Cast: Bernice Stegers, Philip Sayer, Danny Brainin, Simon Nash, Maryam D'Abo, David Cardy.

Sayer is abducted by aliens who mutate him into a crab-walking creature that returns to earth several years later and rapes a beautiful blonde. Said blonde then immediately balloons up and gives birth to the hero in his original form—huh?—who then returns to his estranged wife (Stegers) to fight her for custody of their young son while slowly changing back into his extraterrestrial alter-ego. This *very* strange mix of *Alien, Close Encounters of the Third Kind,* and *Kramer vs. Kramer*(!!!) earns a point or two for sheer nerve if nothing else, but terminal dumbness makes it less than compulsive viewing buoyed by a couple of way-out-there makeup FX scenes. Followed by an only-the-name's-the-same sequel.

XTRO II: THE SECOND ENCOUNTER
★★ New Line, 1991, R, 89 min.
Dir: Harry Bromley Davenport. Cast: Jan-Michael Vincent, Paul Koslo, Tara Buckman, Jano Frandsen, Nicholas Lea, Rachel Hayward.

Although they share the same director, this has nothing to do with the original *Xtro* and is actually a semi-remake of the much better *Shadowzone*. Experiments in finding an "alternate universe" unleash a murderous monster that bumps off a bunch of annoying characters who argue a lot in a vast underground scientific complex. Although well made, this rehashes all the same old science vs. the military bits that have been around since the original *Thing* (you can easily tell whose side the filmmakers are on since the scientists are all pasty and neurotic and the soldiers look like Chippendale dancers), is lacking in suspense and originality, and has dumb-dumb "macho" dialogue to spare.

YOG, MONSTER FROM SPACE
★★ Orion, 1970, G, 84 min.
Dir: Inoshiro Honda. Cast: Akira Kubo, Atsuko Takahashi, Yoshio Tsuchiya, Kenji Sahara, Noritake Saito, Yukiko Kobayashi.

An alien life force is brought to earth by a downed satellite and possesses various creatures—a squid, a crab, and a turtle—on a Pacific atoll, turning them into huge, destructive monsters. Some eerie scenes and effects (the alien's power is disrupted by the screeching of bats that flutter about the heads of the possessed monsters) and a slightly different than usual storyline distinguish this okay Toho monster movie. Japanese title: *Nankai no Daikaiju: Monster Amoeba From Space;* aka *Space Amoeba*.

YONGARY, MONSTER FROM THE DEEP
★☆ Orion, 1967, NR, 79 min. Dir: Kiduck Kim. Cast: Yungil Oh, Chungin Nam, Soonjai Lee, Moon Kang.

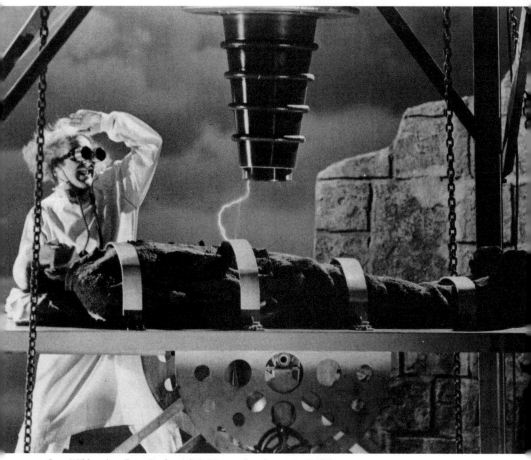

Gene Wilder gives Peter Boyle a jolt in Young Frankenstein *(1974).*

A Korean imitation of a Japanese monster movie about a gigantic gasoline-drinking, disco-dancing horned beastie unleashed by a Chinese earthquake and heading for Korea. The usual nonsense punctuated by plenty of laughs. Original title: *Dai Koesu Yongkari: The Monster Yongkari.*

YOU BETTER WATCH OUT!

See: *Christmas Evil.*

YOU'LL FIND OUT

★★ Budget, 1940, NR, 97 min.
Dir: David Butler. Cast: Boris Karloff, Bela Lugosi, Peter Lorre, Kay Kyser, Dennis O'Keefe, Helen Parrish, Ginny Simms, Ish Kabibble.

Anyone expecting much from this momentous teaming of Boris, Bela, and Peter will be extremely disappointed, as this routine old-dark-house comedy is mostly a vehicle for Big Band leader Kyser and his crew. Parrish is a pretty young heiress marked for death by the horror boys; Kyser and O'Keefe come to the rescue. Snore. Lots of forgettable '40s "swing" music. How about a remake in which Jason, Freddy, and Michael Myers meet Marky Mark? Aka *Here Come the Boogie Men.*

YOUNG DRACULA

See: *Andy Warhol's Dracula.*

YOUNG FRANKENSTEIN

★★★☆ Fox, 1974, PG, 105 min.
Dir: Mel Brooks. Cast: Gene Wilder, Peter Boyle, Madeline Kahn, Marty Feldman, Cloris Leachman, Teri Garr, Kenneth Mars, Gene Hackman.

Brooks' best film is this hilarious spoof of classic horror flicks shot in glorious black-and-white. Dr. Frederick Frankenstein (Wilder) is so embarrassed by his infamous grandfather's activities that he goes around mispronouncing the family name until he inherits the ancestral Transylvanian castle where Granddad's diary ("How I Did It!") fires him with the impetus to create a monster of his own. On-target performances from Wilder, Boyle as the monster, Feldman as a hunchback with a movable hunch, Kahn as the fiancée who quite literally becomes the bride of Frankenstein, and Mars as a police inspector with a wooden arm, eyepatch, and monocle (over the eyepatch!), plus Brooks' knowing script (co-authored with Wilder) and direction (even reusing some of the original *Frankenstein* lab equipment) make this one of the most delightful horror comedies ever. "Ah, sweet mystery of life, at last I've found you. . . ."

YOUNG HANNAH, QUEEN OF THE VAMPIRES
See: *Crypt of the Living Dead.*

YOUNG MAN, I THINK YOU'RE DYING!
See: *The Beast in the Cellar.*

YOUNG, THE EVIL, AND THE SAVAGE, THE
See: *Schoolgirl Killer.*

ZAAT
See: *Attack of the Swamp Creature.*

ZAPPED!
★☆ Nelson, 1982, R, 96 min.
Dir: Robert J. Rosenthal. Cast: Scott Baio, Willie Aames, Heather Thomas, Scatman Crothers, Felice Schacter, Robert Mandan, Sue Ane Langdon, Greg Bradford.

Awkward, mostly unfunny spoof of *Carrie* with Baio as a high school kid who accidentally acquires telekinetic powers he spends most of the film using to get girls to pop their tops. There's a good supporting cast but this probably plays better if your IQ is several numbers lower than the film's running time.

ZAPPED AGAIN!
★ Nelson, 1989, R, 93 min. Dir: Doug Campbell. Cast. Todd Eric Andrews, Kelli Williams, Reed Rudy, Linda Blair, Karen Black, Lyle Alzado.

The world needs a sequel to *Zapped!* like it

needs a sequel to *Hudson Hawk,* but here it is anyway. Another nerdy teen (Andrews) develops telekinesis and more babes are disrobed and jerky jocks humiliated. Blair and Black are seriously wasted, while Andrews makes Scott Baio look like Marlon Brando in his prime.

ZERO BOYS, THE
★★ Vestron, 1986, R, 89 min.
Dir: Nico Mastorakis. Cast: Dan Hirsch, Kelli Maroney, Tom Shell, Jared Moses, Crystal Carson, John Michaels.

Macho survivalists and their girlfriends go for a weekend of camping and encounter a creepy old house in the backwoods inhabited by a demented killer. Passable mix of *Deliverance* and any one of a dozen or more slashers (*The Final Terror* comes immediately to mind) from Mastorakis, Greece's answer to Fred Olen Ray.

ZOLTAN, HOUND OF DRACULA
See: *Dracula's Dog.*

ZOMBIE
See: *Dawn of the Dead.*

ZOMBIE
★★★ Magnum, 1980, UR, 91 min. Dir: Lucio Fulci. Cast: Tisa Farrow, Ian McCulloch, Richard Johnson, Olgar Karlatos, Al Cliver, Auretta Gay.

The most popular of Italian gore author Fulci's barf-bag epics, this *Dawn of the Dead* cash-in (originally titled *Zombie 2* so as to appear to be

---

LUCIO FULCI
(1916–)

This jack-of-all-trades Italian director finally came into his own after a long and eventful exploitation career with a series of graphic, anything-goes gore flicks in the late '70s and early '80s. Although often derivative of Argento, Romero, and others, the grand old man of Neopolitan grue can be a stylist when he wants to be, and several of his horrors have a real raw, disturbing power to them.

Don't Torture the Duckling ('72), *Schizoid* ('73), *The Psychic* ('78), *Zombie* ('80), *The Gates of Hell* ('81), *The Black Cat* ('81), *Seven Doors of Death* ('81), *The House by the Cemetery* ('81), *The New York Ripper* ('82), *Eye of the Evil Dead* ('83), *Aenigma* ('87), *Zombie 3* ('88), *Voices From Beyond* ('89), *Cat in the Brain* ('90).

a sequel to *Dawn,* which was released in Europe as *Zombie*) just may be the ultimate Neapolitan living dead gross-out of them all. Farrow (Mia's kid sister) and McCulloch travel to the Bahamas in search of her missing father and end up on an island overrun with voodoo-spawned zombies being experimented on by doctor Johnson. With mounds o' maggots, ruptured arteries spewing like out-of-control firehoses, and one unforgettable shot of Karlatos' bulging eye pierced by an enormous shard of wood, this is definitely not recommended to those who found *Free Willy* to be their particular cup of tea. British title: *Zombie Flesh Eaters.*

ZOMBIE 2
See: *Zombie.*

ZOMBIE 3
See: *Burial Ground.*

ZOMBIE 4
See: *A Virgin Among the Living Dead.*

ZOMBIE CREEPING FLESH
See: *Night of the Zombies* (1981).

ZOMBIE FLESH EATERS
See: *Zombie.*

ZOMBIE HIGH
★☆ Cinema Group, 1987, R, 91 min. Dir: Ron Link. Cast: Virginia Madsen, Richard Cox, Kay Kuter, James Wilder, Sherilyn Fenn, Paul Feig.

An interesting idea—a school where our yuppie future leaders are created by evil instructors who alter their brain patterns and stay youthful by shooting up with the kids' cerebral fluid—gets bungled by bad handling here. Madsen is gorgeous but not even she, not to mention Fenn, and a fairly lively ending are enough to keep you watching. Aka *The School That Ate My Brain.*

ZOMBIE ISLAND MASSACRE
★ Media, 1984, R, 88 min. Dir: John N. Carter. Cast: Rita Jenrette, David Broadnax, Tom Cantrell, Diane Clayre Holub, Ian McMillan, Debbie Ewing.

Although this sounds like another Italian living dead–gore epic, it's actually a pretty tame and boring voodoo-stalker-whodunit with Washington wife–*Playboy* slut Rita as a bleating babe with big breasts who takes an endless shower to a reggae beat in the first five minutes and emerges as the virtual sole survivor of this Troma-released tomfoolery. The sort of movie that takes forever to get going and once

it does makes you realize that it was hardly worth the trip.

ZOMBIE LAKE
☆ Wizard, 1980, R, 91 min. Dir: J. A. Laser [Jean Rollin]. Cast: Howard Vernon, Pierre Escourrou, Anouchka, Robert Foster, Nadine Pascal, Gilda Arancio.

Originally to be directed by Jess Franco, this lousy Spanish-French drek was probably filmed the week *Shock Waves* opened in Europe. A troop of Nazi soldiers are killed by Swiss villagers and dumped into a mountain lake; a dozen years later they rise up as zombies to munch on bathing beauties, a girls basketball team, and various locals until lured to their doom in a burning windmill by the young daughter of one of their number. Lots of plot padding and maybe the worst dubbing job you've ever seen. Original title: *El Lago de los Muertos Vivientes: Lake of the Living Dead.*

ZOMBIE NIGHTMARE
★ Starmaker, 1987, R, 84 min. Dir: Jack Bravman. Cast: Adam West, Jon Mikl Thor, Tia Carrere, Linda Singer, Frank Dietz, Manuska Rigaud.

I can see it now: an overexcited producer comes up with this sure-fire title (shades of both Romero and Craven—what a concept!) and then gets his son-in-law to knock out a script about a musclebound bonehead (Thor) who's run down by a carload of overaged high school punks. His distraught mom then turns to the neighborhood voodoo priestess (Rigaud, who looks like Tina Turner but sounds like Acquanetta) to raise him up as a vengeful zombie. West is also on hand as a detective to remind you why he wasn't in the *Batman* remake, and there's the usual out-of-the-blue shock-twist ending to wake you up—though you might do better catching up on your sleep.

ZOMBIES
See: *I Eat Your Skin.*

ZOMBIES
See: *Dawn of the Dead.*

ZOMBIES OF MORA TAU
★★☆ RCA/Columbia, 1957, NR, 70 min. Dir: Edward L. Cahn. Cast: Allison Hayes, Gregg Palmer, Joel Ashley, Autumn Russell, Morris Ankrum, Majorie Eaton.

Sam Katzman–produced '50s schlock horror about an expedition to recover a cache of diamonds from a sunken ship off the African coast guarded by the living dead. Although

LARRY BUCHANAN
(1923–)

The Texan master of movie mediocrity, Larry is best known for his mind-numbing mid-1960s remakes of several old American International horror flicks. Sold directly to TV, these minimalistic masterpieces have been a stounding late-night TV viewers for nearly three decades now and prove, if nothing else, that *anyone* can make a movie if they really want to.

The Naked Witch ('61), *Mars Needs Women* ('64), *The Eye Creatures* ('65), *Curse of the Swamp Creature* ('66), *Zontar, the Thing From Venus* ('66), *Creature of Destruction* ('67), *In the Year 2889* ('67), *"It's Alive!"* ('68), *The Loch Ness Horror* ('78).

marred by phony underwater FX and sound effects that sound like Three Stooges leftovers (they probably were), this is worth watching for some creepy graveyard scenes and the always welcome presence of Hayes as the expedition leader's slutty wife. British title: *The Dead That Walk.*

ZOMBIES ON BROADWAY
★★ Turner, 1945, NR, 68 min.
Dir: Gordon Douglas. Cast: Wally Brown, Alan Carney, Bela Lugosi, Anne Jeffreys, Sheldon Leonard, Ian Wolfe, Darby Jones, Sir Lancelot.

Brown and Carney, RKO's budget answer to Abbott and Costello, star in this mild spoof about a pair of bumbling publicists looking for a genuine zombie for a nightclub act who run into jungle mad scientist Lugosi. Bela is better served here than in most of his '40s cheapies, and director Douglas (*Them!*) manages to give this the atmosphere of an unofficial sequel to *I Walked With a Zombie* (even to reusing zombie performer Jones and calypso singer Sir Lancelot), but Brown and Carney's comic antics are mostly an acquired taste not worth acquiring. Retitled *Loonies on Broadway* in England.

ZONTAR, THE THING FROM VENUS
☆ Sinister Cinema, 1966, NR, 80 min.
Dir: Larry Buchanan. Cast: John Agar, Anthony Houston, Susan Bjurman, Pat Delaney, Neil Fletcher, Warren Hammack.

Every once in a while a schlock horror movie builds for itself a reputation it would be hard-pressed to live up to. Such is the case with this twenty-buck remake of Corman's *It Conquered the World*. Though just brimming with stilted acting, screwy dialogue ("No wonder you live in a cave, you're ugly!"), and cheapo FX (the monster is negatived to death) to spare, this lacks the inherent charm of a *Plan Nine from Outer Space* to make it compelling viewing. Frankly, it's pretty slow and drawn out and hardly stands as Buchanan's finest/worst hour and twenty minutes.

Edited by Selma Friedman and Virginia Croft
Senior Editor: Paul Lukas
Book and cover design: Bob Fillie, Graphiti Graphics
Production Manager: Ellen Greene